The Intellectuals
and the Powers

Selected Papers of Edward Shils, I

Edward Shils

The Intellectuals
and the Powers
and Other Essays

The University of Chicago Press

Chicago and London

The University of Chicago Press, Chicago 60637
The University of Chicago Press, Ltd., London
© 1972 by The University of Chicago
All rights reserved. Published 1972
Printed in the United States of America
International Standard Book Number: 0-226-75315-8
Library of Congress Catalog Card Number: 79-178196

Contents

Contents

Introduction

I

In my youth I was an avid reader of Flaubert, Baudelaire, T. S. Eliot, and Turgenev; Sorel, Taine, and Renan. I also read Sombart's *Der proletarische Sozialismus: "Marxismus"* and a little book by Kurt Geyer, *Der Radikalismus, in der deutschen Arbeiterbewegung* (1923) now long forgotten, Roberto Michels *Political Parties* and Henry de Man's *The Psychology of Socialism* as well as a vast amount of nineteenth-century political and belletristic literature. These writers made me ask the question; Why did the writers, historians, philosophers and other intellectuals, some great and all interesting, feel such revulsion for their own societies, for the institutions through which they were ruled and the persons who ruled them? Marx and Engels touched on the problem but they seemed to me to be more interesting for the evidence which their own actions provided rather than for their arguments and analyses. In the 1930s I witnessed with revulsion the rush of the Gadarene intellectuals in the United States and Europe into the arms and snares of their respective communist parties. I saw and did not like the silliness, dishonesty, and self-deception of some of the best-educated and the most cultivated and many of the half-educated intellectuals of several generations. New intellectual organs were created to provide a platform for these twisters; others already established were taken over, and the intellectual air was filled with their uniform voices.

By this time I had also read the writings of Karl Mannheim and Max Weber. *Wissenschaft als Beruf* made a great impression on me. It helped to define a standpoint from which the fellow-traveling and communist intellectuals of the 1930s were to be criticized. The expulsion of the academic Jews from Germany brought me into intimate contact with a number of persons who had been central to or at the edge of some of the characteristic activities of the Weimar Republic. The decade and a half of the Weimar Republic seemed to me to have been a wonderful time; I thought of it as having been begun and conducted for the most part by men of goodwill, unaided at best and most of the time frustrated by Junkers, businessmen, communist and nationalist fanatics, and despised or disregarded by most of the prominent intellectuals of the time. It seemed such a pity to me that the intellectuals should have been responsible for destroying a society which in so many respects conferred such benefits on intellectuals.

The intellectuals of the Weimar Republic, with all their talent and, in some cases, genius, had helped by their active mischief and by their complaisant indifference or approval to ruin what might have been a decent society. Of course, they were not exclusively responsible. Even had they been more sensible, they might not have been able to withstand the ravages of military defeat and national humiliation, inflation and unemployment, the cruel manipulations of the KPD, dominated by the Soviet Communist Party, the brutality of the nationalist sects, the infidelity of the army and the civil service.

During the Second World War, I hoped for a somewhat better time thereafter. I remembered Jules Romains's *Les hommes de bonne volonté* and H. G. Wells's *Open Conspiracy*; I thought of the intellectuals in the role of a saving remnant and as a leaven—Alfred Weber's and Karl Mannheim's idea of the *freischwebende Intelligenz*; I did not think it was likely to occur but I thought that it was desirable.

Immediately after the end of the war, I met Leo Szilard through some old Weimar friends. For a short time we formed a two-member alliance; Szilard conducted and tried to control a vast network of such two-member alliances. He was a wonderful man but he was a conspirator, a benevolent conspirator, more benign and warmhearted than the Webbs, but a conspirator nonetheless. He regarded politicians as instruments, not as collaborators. Through Szilard and other friends, I took part in the movement of the American scientists as they emerged from the secrecy of the Manhattan Project. I had a hand in the formation of the *Bulletin of the Atomic Scientists* and was able to witness a major effort by a group of intellectuals to influence governmental policy, not to block it as to frustrate it or to disparage it but to influence it. The campaigns for international control over the development of atomic energy and for civilian control over its domestic development afforded me many opportunities to observe and reflect on my original question, now much elaborated.

Beginning in 1946, I was a member of the staff of the London School of Economics, where I taught sociology. The London School of Economics, often said to be the most important institution of higher education in Asia and Africa, was at that time, as it had been ever since Sir William Beveridge became its director, the scene of animated discussion, perhaps livelier and more diverse than at any other institution in the world. It had attracted large numbers of students from the Asian parts of the then British Empire, which was in the course of becoming the Commonwealth. In the forties, African students began to attend the School in larger numbers and West Indian students began to come up. Students from the United

States had always constituted a substantial proportion of the graduate students of the School; many of them were attracted by the fame of those two eminent socialists, R. H. Tawney and Harold Laski. (This was before the ascendancy of Karl Popper and Michael Oakeshott. The former came to the School the same year I did; the latter came only in 1950 after the death of Harold Laski, to whose chair he was elected.) Lionel Robbins and Friedrich Hayek were powerful figures in the School, but the strong tone of moderate and conservative antisocialist liberalism which they imparted had not yet entered into the external image of the School.

It was a time when the dissolution of the British Empire was coming into full flood. Jeremy Bentham's titular exhortation "Emancipate your colonies" had finally become a part of policy. I saw large numbers of "colonial students" and had the good fortune to become well acquainted with some of them, a few of whom have since become outstanding scholars, some of whom have disappeared into the civil services and colleges and universities of their countries. Most of them have disappeared altogether; at least they have disappeared from my view, although I hope they are surviving and comfortable in the travail through which their societies are now passing. I used to go to Indian restaurants, then less common in London than they are now, where I would find myself at the same table as young Indians. I would try to imagine what role they would take in the independent societies with which they were so preoccupied. I imagined them as politicians, civil servants, and journalists and I wondered what would become of their high and simple ideals and whether they would be able to overcome the amalgam of oppositional and utopian attitudes which so many of them seemed to have.[1]

Concurrently with my experience of "intellectuals in the new states" in London, I maintained in the other half of my Anglo-American life a very close connection with the atomic scientists' movement in the United States. The University of Chicago provided hospitality for one of the major centers of the movement, and the *Bulletin of the Atomic Scientists* was produced there, and that made my collaboration easy. I saw much of many scientists, some famous like Harold Urey, Eugene Wigner, James Franck, and, of course, Leo Szilard, and others less famous at that time, like Eugene Rabinowitch and John Simpson and still others who have since not become famous at all. They all impressed me with their remarkable sense of

---

1. I might state here that only my two dear pupils S. N. Eisenstadt and Joseph Gross (now Ben-David)—who passed from being Palestinians to being Israelis while they were studying Max Weber, Freud, methods of empirical research, and social and psychological conditions of political democracy in my classes—were free of these two attitudes.

civic responsibility and their goodwill toward mankind. (At the fringes there were the continuators and successors of the fellow travelers of the 1930s, a continuous reminder of the capacity of intellectuals in politics for folly and malevolence.) I attended numerous meetings, long "briefings," went barnstorming and wrote frequently in the *Bulletin* through the campaigns for international control and civilian control and then when the loyalty and security mania began to occupy our minds. The first McCarthyism engaged my intimate attention for nearly a decade until its demise. All these experiences and the studies which accompanied them kept fresh the question which I had put to myself many years earlier. In the early 1950s, I began to teach about intellectuals and I wrote the draft of the book which I had originally planned. I put it aside so that I could learn more about the subject. The manuscript dealt mainly with the politics of literary and academic intellectuals in Europe and America. I had a chapter in it on "intellectuals in societies without sovereignty." It was based on a paper I gave in a seminar of Bert Hoselitz on economic development and cultural change in about 1952. I had been asked to speak about the "sociology of knowledge" but had not felt up to it and spoke about intellectuals in underdeveloped countries instead. It was very thin. I decided I must learn more about it. I decided that I needed a more ordered and intensive body of observations than my casual experiences in London and a random reading of Indian periodicals had afforded. After some uncertainty as to whether I should go to the West Indies or India to do this work, I decided on India. I went to India for an extended period over 1955 and 1956 and returned every year but one until 1967. Over the past decade and a half I have kept in very close touch with Indian (and to some extent Pakistani and Ceylonese) intellectual developments.

In 1953, when I was teaching at the University of Manchester, I came through Professor Michael Polanyi, whom I had met through Leo Szilard, into contact with the Science and Freedom Committee which Polanyi was just forming under the auspices of the Congress for Cultural Freedom. (This body has since been succeeded by the International Association for Cultural Freedom.) Through my association with Szilard I had become interested in the structure of the scientific community. The McCarthyist agitation about "secrets" had intensified my interest in scientists.

My old interest in academic freedom (on which I had conducted an enquiry at the end of the 1930s) was being complemented by an interest in still undelineated problems of science policy. The problems which concerned me went beyond the freedom of scientific research and publication to the criteria of scientific choice, the machinery of decision-making in science policy and the relations between scientists, politicians, and civil servants in the formation of policy, not only about science but about other problems on which science impinged.

I had hoped for some years to have the *Bulletin of the Atomic Scientists* transformed into a journal to deal with science policy in the broad sense in which I conceived it, but the pressure of immediate events was always so great that this project had to be given up. By the beginning of the sixties, however, thanks to the undemanding generosity of Mr. Michael Josselson—then executive secretary of the Congress for Cultural Freedom—and the Ford Foundation, I was enabled to create *Minerva*, a quarterly which deals with intellectual policy in the widest sense, including both scientific research and higher education. I had hoped, and still hope, to deal there with cultural policy in other spheres, but have not yet done so.

In the fifties, the old dissatisfaction of American intellectuals with the state of their culture in society took a new form. It became a critique of "mass culture." This was not a phenomenon with which I had ever had much sympathy. Looking at television and reading comic strips had never appeared to me to be a worthwhile activity for educated persons; I had given up baseball at the age of fifteen or sixteen and had never gone in for crime novels or burlesque shows, but I did find the condescending and bitter abuse by certain intellectuals of those who enjoyed these pastimes rather distasteful. It seemed to me unworthy for disappointed and broken-down Trotskyites and *Edelmarxisten*, mostly of Frankfurt provenience, to take revenge on the working and middle classes for not having measured up to their unrealistic and uninvited expectations. I entered into these discussions.

I had begun my interest in intellectuals with my eye on Germany. I had long had a deep admiration for German universities, which I did not know at first hand, and in the course of years had acquired some knowledge of them. Abraham Flexner's *Universities, English, German, and American* and the glimpses of German university life to be obtained from Marianne Weber's biography of Max Weber, Lujo Brentano's *Aus meinen Leben*, Wilamowitz-Moellendorf's and Friedrich Paulsen's autobiographies as well as the many volumes of *Die Wissenschaft der Gegenwart in Selbstdarstellungen* seduced me into enthusiasm for the German university in its greatest age. My connections with many German academic exiles in the 1930s did not diminish my admiration. It had in fact begun when I first went to the museum of Middle Eastern antiquities at the University of Pennsylvania when I was about ten years old and saw on the descriptions of many of the exhibits that the originals were in Berlin.

The debate about the proper functions of the university, animated by Robert Hutchins at the University of Chicago in the

1930s, heightened my interest, and Max Weber's *Wissenschaft als Beruf* sharpened it. Experience in a number of university systems after the war and the McCarthyite attack on universities made me think beyond the question of academic freedom to the proper organization of intellectual institutions which would enable them best to meet their intellectual and social obligations. My editorship of *Minerva*, which has lain across the two periods of indiscriminate and well-financed expansion of the universities and the savage attacks on universities by students and then by teachers and publicists, has extended the radius of my concern with intellectuals, their work, their institutions, and their relations with society, culture, and the nonintellectual parts of mankind.

II

This is the background out of which the essays in this volume have arisen. The first essays are an attempt to broaden the range of problems ordinarily treated in writings on intellectuals. After having begun with a concentration of attention on the negative or alienated relations of intellectuals with their societies, I tried to put the alienated sector of the intellectual stratum into a more realistic perspective which would reveal the fact that by no means all intellectuals have been in opposition to their societies. In these opening essays I have attempted to go beyond the relations, both positive and negative, of intellectuals to the civil order of their respective societies. I have attempted to deal with intellectual institutions and the institutionalization of intellectual production. I have also dealt in these papers with the secondary traditions of intellectuals, which are the most significant in determining the relations of intellectuals to the civil order. I have, however, not dealt sufficiently with the specifically technical or primary traditions of intellectual production, and this omission runs generally throughout the essays in this volume, but not equally so.

The essays in the second part of this collection deal with intellectuals and advanced countries. Again, for the most part, the emphasis is on the secondary traditions and on the relations of intellectuals to civil order. Most attention is given to intellectuals in Great Britain and the United States, although some attention is paid to intellectuals in other Western European countries.

In this part also are contained the essays in which I deal with the intellectuals in relation to "mass culture." Only one essay deals with "high culture."

The essays in the third part of the volume deal with under-developed countries. These deal not only with the civil relations of intellectuals but also with the problems of the establishment of effective intellectual communities. My writings on India have been reserved for another volume in this series; hence, the essays in this part deal generally in a very broad way with Asian and African intellectuals.

Some of the essays are devoted entirely to intellectual institutions, their establishment and functioning, in underdeveloped countries.

It will be seen that the essays in this volume are fragments of an unfinished mosaic. There are many omissions. The reason for the omissions is that each essay arose in the course of a process of the author's self-education. Practically all of the essays were written after the first draft of the book referred to above. They represent an effort to develop certain points which at that time seemed to me to be obscure and important. Some of them were simultaneously efforts to round out the approach contained in the draft volume as well as being responses to then current situations in the United States, Europe, Asia, and Africa.

I think I can say that, despite the occasional fragmentary character of these essays, they represent the movement toward a more comprehensive and coherent understanding of the nature of intellectual work, of the roles and institutions in which intellectual works are produced, as well as dealing more systematically than has been done hitherto with the relations between intellectuals and their societies.

It will be noticed that the analysis of intellectual institutions in these essays is rather thinly represented, and where it does occur, it is usually with respect to very specific matters, such as university government, academic freedom, etc. The essay on the scientific community is also of a high degree of generality, understandable in view of the fact that it was the first effort to delineate this phenomenon, but, even with this extenuation, its generality remains. Likewise, the phenomenological analysis of the structure or pattern of intellectual traditions was not sufficiently attended to. In all of these matters I think that I have made considerable progress since the papers in this volume were written, and they will be more fully and more adequately dealt with in the book on intellectuals which I am writing. The papers in this book may, indeed, be regarded as explorations preliminary to this larger and more systematic work. Since, however, this will not be available for several years and since many of these essays represent fairly well-rounded and self-contained treatments of the subjects with which they set out to deal, I believe there is sufficient justification for publication in their present form.

Part One

Intellectuals

1 The Intellectuals and the Powers: Some Perspectives for Comparative Analysis

In religion, in art, in all spheres of culture and politics, the mass of mankind in all hitherto known societies have not, except for transitory interludes, been preoccupied with the attainment of an immediate contact with the ultimate principles implicit in their beliefs and standards. The directly gratifying ends of particular actions, the exigencies of situations, considerations of individual and familial advantage, concrete moral maxims, concrete prescriptions and prohibitions, preponderate in the conduct of the majority of persons in most societies, large and small. The systematic coherence and the deeper and more general ground of beliefs and standards only intermittently hold their attention and touch on their passions. Ordinary life in every society is characterized by an unequal intensity of attachment to ultimate values, be they cognitive, moral, or aesthetic, and an unequal intensity of the need for coherence. Ordinary life shuns rigorous definition and consistent adherence to traditional or rational rules, and it has no need for continuous contact with the sacred. Ordinary life is slovenly, full of compromise and improvisation; it goes on in the "here and now."

In every society, however, there are some persons with an unusual sensitivity to the sacred, an uncommon reflectiveness about the nature of their universe and the rules which govern their society. There is in every society a minority of persons who, more than the ordinary run of their fellow men, are inquiring, and desirous of being in frequent communion with symbols which are more general than the immediate concrete situations of everyday life and remote in their reference in both time and space. In this minority, there is a need to externalize this quest in oral and written discourse, in poetic or plastic expression, in historical reminiscence or writing, in ritual performance and acts of worship. This interior need to penetrate beyond the screen of immediate concrete experience marks the existence of the intellectuals in every society.

The Tasks of Intellectuals

The personal need alone does not, however, create the body of intellectuals, nor does it determine its magnitude or its position within the structure of society. In every society, even among those

Previously published in a slightly different form in *Comparative Studies in Society and History*, vol. 1, no. 1 (October 1958), pp. 5-22.

sections of the population without the very pronounced sensitivity to remote symbols which characterizes the intellectuals, there is an intermittent need for contact with the sacred, and this gives rise to a demand for priests and theologians and to institutions or procedures for the education of these in the techniques and meanings of their functions. In every society, among those who cannot create images in the form of stories or pictures or statues or other works or art, there is still a considerable fraction which is receptive and indeed even demanding of the gratification provided by verbal images, colors, and forms. These persons provide the demand for art and literature, even though they themselves cannot create art or literature. Every society has a need for contact with its own past, and in more differentiated societies rulers seek to strengthen their claim to legitimacy by showing the continuity of their regimes with the great personalities of the past. Where this cannot be provided by the powers of individual memory within the kinship group, historical chroniclers and antiquarians are required. Correspondingly, ecclesiastical and proto-ecclesiastical bodies must likewise show the spiritual wealth of their antecedents and their living relevance; this gives rise to hagiography and the activity of the hagiographer. In societies on larger then tribal scale, with complex tasks and traditions, the education—at least of those who are expected to become rulers or the associates, counselors, and aides of rulers—is called for; this requires teachers and a system of educational institutions. In any society which transcends the scale of a kinship group, in which the organs of authority acquire a more or less continuous existence, there is a need for administrators capable of keeping records and issuing rules and decrees. These activities require a certain fairly high level of education, which in turn requires institutions with teaching staffs, whether they be palace schools or privately or state-conducted academies or universities. Members of every society, and above all those who exercise authority in it, need to have at least intermittently some sense of the stability, coherence, and orderliness of their society; they need therefore a body of symbols, such as songs, histories, poems, biographies, constitutions, etc., which diffuse a sense of affinity among the members of the society.

The intellectuals' activities and their situation in society are the products of a compromise and an articulation of the intellectual disposition and the needs of society for those actions which can be performed only by persons who of necessity, by virtue of the actions they perform, are intellectuals. The larger the society and the more complex the tasks its rulers undertake, the greater the need therefore for a body of religious and secular intellectuals.

All these needs would exist even if there were no especially sensitive, inquiring, curious, creative minds in the society. There would be intellectuals in society even if there were no intellectuals by disposition.[1]

The Functions of Intellectuals

The moral and intellectual unity of a society, which in the size of its population and its territory goes beyond what any one man can know from his average firsthand experience and which brings him into contact with persons outside his kinship group, depends on such intellectual institutions as schools, churches, newspapers, and similar structures. Through these, ordinary persons, in childhood, youth, or adulthood, enter into contact, however extensive, with those who are most familiar with the existing body of cultural values. By means of preaching, teaching, and writing, intellectuals infuse into sections of the population which are intellectual neither by inner vocation nor by social role, a perceptiveness and an imagery which they would otherwise lack. By the provision of such techniques as reading and writing and calculation, they enable the laity to enter into a wider universe. The creation of nations out of tribes, in early modern times in Europe and in contemporary Asia and Africa, is the work of intellectuals, just as the formation of the American nation out of diverse ethnic groups is partly the work of teachers, clergymen, and journalists. The legitimation of the reigning authority is naturally a function of many factors, including the tendencies within a population towards submission to and rejection of authority, the effectiveness of the authority in maintaining order, showing strength, and dispensing a semblance of justice. The legitimacy of authority is, however, a function of what its subjects believe about it; beliefs about authority are far from resting entirely on firsthand experience, and much of what is believed beyond first-hand experience is the product of traditions and teachings which are the gradually accumulated and attenuated product of the activities of intellectuals.

Through their provision of models and standards, by the presentation of symbols to be appreciated, intellectuals elicit, guide, and form the expressive dispositions within a society. Not that the expressive life of a society is under the exclusive dominion of its intellectuals. Indeed the situation has never existed—and in fact could never exist—in which the expressive life of a society, its aesthetic tastes, its artistic creation, or the ultimately aesthetic grounds of its ethical judgments fell entirely within the traditions espoused by the intellectuals of the society. Societies vary in the extent to which the

1. The demand for intellectual services can sometimes exceed the supply of qualified persons; it will always exceed the supply of truly creative individuals. More frequently, however, modern societies have experienced an excess of the supply of technically qualified persons over the demand for their services.

expressive actions and orientations are in accordance with what is taught and represented by the dominant intellectuals. With these variations much of the expressive life of a society, even what is most vulgar and tasteless, echoes some of the expressive elements in the central value system represented by the intellectuals.

The first two functions treated above show the intellectuals infusing into the laity attachments to more general symbols and providing for the laity a means of participation in the central value system. Intellectuals are not, however, concerned only to facilitate this wider participation in certain features of the central value system. They are above all concerned with its more intensive cultivation, with the elaboration and development of alternative potentialities. Where creativity and originality are emphatically acknowledged and prized, and where innovation is admitted and accepted, this is perceived as a primary obligation of intellectuals. However, even in systems where individual creativity is not seen as a positive value, the labor of powerful minds and irrepressible individualities working on what has been received from the past, modifies the heritage by systematization and rationalization and adapts it to new tasks and obstacles. In this process of elaboration, divergent potentialities of the system of cultural values are made explicit and conflicting positions are established. Each generation of intellectuals performs this elaborating function for its own and succeeding generations, and particularly for the next succeeding generation.

These specifically intellectual functions are performed not only for the intellectuals of a particular society but for the intellectuals of other societies as well. The intellectuals of different societies are ordered in a vague hierarchy, in which the lower learn from the higher. For Southeast Asia, the Indian intellectuals, in the Middle Ages and early modern times, performed this educative function. The intellectuals of republican and imperial Rome learned from Greek intellectuals. For Japan, for a time, Chinese intellectuals performed this function. In modern times, the British intellectuals, through Oxford, Cambridge, and the London School of Economics, have formed the intellectuals of India, Africa, and for a long time the United States. In the nineteenth century, German academic intellectuals provided a worldwide model, just as in the nineteenth and twentieth centuries French artistic and literary intellectuals have provided models of development for aesthetically sensitive intellectuals all over the civilized world. In the eighteenth century, the intellectuals of the French Enlightenment inspired their confreres in Spain, Italy, Prussia, and Russia. This function is performed for the intellectual community above all. The laity only comes to share in it at several removes and after a lapse of time.

The function of providing a model for intellectual activity, within and among societies, implies the acceptance of a general criterion of superior quality or achievement. The pattern of action of a certain group of intellectuals comes to be regarded as exemplary because it is thought to correspond more closely to certain ideal requirements of truth, beauty, or virtue. Such standards are never the objects of complete consensus, but they are often widely accepted over very extensive areas of the world at any given time.

The process of elaborating and developing further the potentialities inherent in a "system" of cultural values entails also the possibility of "rejection" of the inherited set of values in varying degrees of comprehensiveness. In all societies, even those in which the intellectuals are notable for their conservatism, the diverse paths of creativity, as well as an inevitable tendency toward negativism, impel a partial rejection of the prevailing system of cultural values. The very process of elaboration and development involves a measure of rejection. The range of rejection of the inherited varies greatly; it can never be complete and all-embracing. Even where the rejecting intellectuals allege that they are "nihilistic" with respect to everything that is inherited, complete rejection without physical self-annihilation is impossible.

It is practically given by the nature of the intellectuals' orientation that there should be some tension between the intellectuals and the value orientations embodied in the actual institutions of any society. This applies not only to the orientations of the ordinary members of society, i.e., the laity, but to the value orientations of those exercising authority in the society, since it is on them that the intellectuals' attention is most often focused, they being the custodians of the central institutional system. It is not this particular form of "rejection" or alienation which interests us most at the moment. Rather it is the rejection by intellectuals of the inherited and prevailing values of those intellectuals who are already incorporated in ongoing social institutions. This intra-intellectual alienation or dissensus is a crucial part of the intellectual heritage of any society. Furthermore it supplies the important function of molding and guiding the alternative tendencies which exist in any society. It provides an alternative pattern of integration for their own society, and for other societies the intellectuals of which come under their hegemony (e.g. the Fabian socialists in Britain and the Indian intellectuals, or the French and British constitutional liberals of the early nineteenth century and the intellectuals of many countries in Southeastern Europe, South America, Asia, etc.).

It is not only through the presentation of orientations toward general symbols which reaffirm, continue, modify, or reject the society's traditional inheritance of beliefs and standards that intellectuals leave their mark on society. The intellectuals do not exhaust their function through the establishment of a contact for the laity with the sacred values of their society. They fulfill authoritative, power-exercising functions over concrete actions as well. Intellectuals have played a great historical role on the higher levels of state administration, above all in China, in British and independent India, in the Ottoman Empire, and in modern Europe. Sovereigns have often considered a high standard of education, either humanistic or technical-legal, confirmed by diplomas and examinations, necessary for the satisfactory functioning of the state. The judiciary, too, has often been a domain of the intellectuals. In private economic organizations, the employment of intellectuals in administrative capacities has been uncommon to the point of rarity. Nor have intellectuals ever shown any inclination to become business enterprisers. It is only since the nineteenth century that business firms, first in Germany, then in America, and latterly in other industrialized countries, have taken to the large-scale employment of scientists in research departments and, to a much smaller extent, in executive capacities.

Equal in antiquity to the role of the highly educated in state administration is the role of the intellectual as personal agent, counselor, tutor, or friend to the sovereign. Plato's experience in Syracuse, Aristotle's relations with Alexander, Alcuin's with Charlemagne, Hobbes and Charles II prior to the Restoration, Milton and Cromwell, Lord Keynes and the Treasury, and the "Brains Trust" under President F. D. Roosevelt, represent only a few of numerous instances in ancient and modern states, oriental and occidental, in which intellectuals have been drawn into the entourage of rulers, their advice and aid sought, and their approval valued. Again, there are many states and periods in which this has not been so. The court of Wilhelm II, for example, drew relatively little on the educated classes of the time; important episodes of Chinese history are to be seen as a consequence of the intellectuals' reaction to the ruler's refusal to draw them into his most intimate and influential circle of counselors; American administrative and political history from the time of the Jacksonian revolution until the New Liberalism of Woodrow Wilson, was characterized by the separation of intellectuals from the higher administrative and the legislative branches of government. Intellectuals have emerged occasionally in monarchies at the highest pinnacles of authority, through sheer accident or at least through no deliberate process of selection. Asoka, Marcus Aurelius, Akhnaton, are only a few of the scattered coincidences of sovereignty and the concern with the highest truths. In the last century and a half under conditions of liberal-democratic party politics, Benjamin Disraeli, William Gladstone, F. M. Guizot, Woodrow Wilson, Jawaharlal Nehru, Thomas Masaryk, etc., have provided impressive instances of intellectuals who have been able, by their own efforts and a wide appreciation for their gifts of civil politics enriched by an intensity of intellectual interest and exertion, to play a notable role in the exercise of great political authority. This has not been accidental; liberal and constitutional politics in great modern states and liberal and "progressive" nationalist movements in subject territories have to a large extent been "intellectuals' politics."

Indeed, in modern times, first in the West and then, in the nineteenth and twentieth centuries, at the peripheries of Western civilization and the Orient, the major political vocation of the intellectuals has lain in the enunciation and pursuit of the ideal. Modern liberal and constitutional politics have largely been the creation of intellectuals with bourgeois affinities and sympathies, in societies dominated by landowning and military aristocracies. This has been one major form of the pursuit of the ideal. Another has been the cultivation of ideological politics, i.e., revolutionary politics working outside the circle of constitutional traditions. Prior to the origins of ideological politics (which came into the open with the European Reformation), conspiracies, putsches, and the subversion of the existing regime, although they often involved intellectuals, were not the objects of a particular affinity between intellectuals and revolutionary tendencies. In modern times, however, with the emergence of ideologically dominated political activities as a continuously constitutive part of public life, a genuine affinity has emerged.

Not by any means all intellectuals have been equally attracted by revolutionary politics. Moderates and partisans in civil politics, quiet apolitical concentration on their specialized intellectual preoccupations, cynical antipolitical passivity, and faithful acceptance and service of the existing order, are all to be found in substantial proportions among modern intellectuals, as among intellectuals in antiquity. Nonetheless, the function of modern intellectuals in furnishing the doctrine of revolutionary movements is to be considered as one of their most important accomplishments.

The Structure of the Intellectual Community

The performance of the functions enumerated above is possible only through a complex set of institutional arrangements. The institutional system in which intellectual objects are reproduced or created has varied markedly in history. Its variations have at least in part been affected by the nature of the intellectual tasks, the volume of the intellectual heritage, the material resources necessary and available for intellectual work, the modes of reproduction of intellectual achievements, and the scope of the audience.

The creation of imaginative works of literature and the production of works of analysis and meditation, at least since the end of the age of anonymity, has been a work of the individual creator, working under his own self-imposed discipline. As regards the actual work of creation, he has been free of the control imposed by corporate organization. Within the limits of what has been made available to him by his culture, he has chosen the tradition under which he was to work, the style, the attitude and the form. Considerations of flattering a prince or pleasing a patron or the reading public or a publisher have often entered extraneously—but not more than that—into the central process of creation; the process of creation itself has always been a process of free choice and adaptation. The avoidance of the strictures of the censor or the displeasure of a tyrant have also been only extraneous factors in a process of individual creation. For this reason the creation of literature has never been corporately organized. The literary man has always been a self-propelling entity. After the development of printing and the emergence of a large reading public, it became possible in the most advanced countries of the Western world for a small number of successful authors of both superior and inferior literature to earn substantial sums of money and for many to earn enough to maintain themselves. For this to happen required not only a large public, sufficiently well-educated, and relatively inexpensive means of large-scale mechanical reproduction, but a well-organized system of book and periodical distribution (publishers, booksellers, editors), a means of giving publicity to new publications (reviews, bibliographies, and literate convivial circles), and laws protecting rights to intellectual property (copyright laws). In the Western countries and in Japan, where the book trade is relatively well-organized, where there are many periodicals, and where there is a large reading public, there is room for thousands of freelance intellectuals; in other countries in Asia and Africa, the small size of the literate public and the ineffective machinery of publication and distribution, confines to rather a small figure the number of freelance intellectuals. But they exist there nonetheless and represent a genuine innovation in the cultural and social history of these countries.

Prior to these developments—which emerged only in the eighteenth century in Western Europe and later in other cultures—creative literary intellectuals were forced to depend on different sources of income. The minnesingers and troubadours who sought to sell their songs in return for hospitality, the Chinese philosopher-adventurers of the period of the Warring States who sought to enter the employment of princes as their counselors, poets in Moghul courts, the Brahmin pandits at the courts of the Peshwa, and the European humanists as stipendiaries of the ecclesiastical and secular princely courts at the beginning of the modern age, were approximations of the independent freelance intellectual whose wares were supplied for payment. They were not genuinely freelance since they were paid in pensions or stipends or in kind rather than through the sale of their products by contractual agreement. As intellectual clients rather than as autonomous agents, they constituted a patrimonial approximation to the freelance intellectual. The patronage of princes, great noblemen and courtiers, financiers and merchants, has contributed greatly to the support of the intellectual activities of those who inherited no wealth, at a time and in fields of intellectual activity in which the sale of intellectual products could not find a large and wealthy enough public of purchasers. The creation of sinecures in government for literary men has been one form of patronage which shades off into gainful employment in the career of the civil servant. This latter means of maintenance, which was known in China over several millennia, has found many practitioners in the nineteenth and twentieth centuries in the West, above all in Great Britain. Diplomacy, military service, employment in commerce and even industry, have provided the livelihood of many authors for whom literature has been an avocation. Thus, patronage, sinecures, and government service, together with the most favorable of all, the independent position of the aristocrat, gentry, and rentier-intellectual who lived from inherited wealth, provided almost the sole means of maintenance for those who aspired to do intellectual work. These were appropriate not only to literary creation but to philosophy, science, and scholarship. These were the ways in which the greatest poets and philosophers of antiquity lived—except for the Sophists, who were freelance intellectuals—as well as the great Chinese and Persian poets, the humanist scholars of the European Renaissance, and the leading scientists of early modern times.

Those intellectuals who took as their task the cultivation of the sacred symbols of religious life lived either in monasteries, endowed by wealthy patrons, or by begging for their daily needs and by occasional patronage. Merchants and bankers, tillers of the soil and handicraftsmen, and professional military men produced from their ranks very few intellectuals—the last, more than the first two groups. The secular and sacred officialdom and the legal profession nearly monopolized the capacity to read and write, and they attracted to their ranks—within the limits imposed by the opportunities afforded by the prevailing system of social selection—the intellectually disposed, and provided them with the leisure and facilities to perform intellectual work as a full-time vocation or as an auxiliary activity. The nature of the tasks which these intellectuals assumed, the relative quantitative meagerness of the intellectual heritage, the restricted size of their audience, and the small demand for intellectual services meant that intellectual activities required little corporate organization.

The development of the *modern* university—first in Germany, Holland, and Sweden, then in France, then in Great Britain, later in the United States, Russia and Japan, and more recently in Canada, Australia, India and other Commonwealth countries—has changed the structure of the intellectual community. Science, which was once the work of amateurs—rentiers, civil servants, and noblemen, for the most part—and scholarship, which was almost a monopoly of monks, secular officials, and rentiers, have now come into the almost exclusive jurisdiction of universities. The relationship between teacher and pupil through the laboratory, the research seminar, and the dissertation, has led to a great multiplication of the scientific and scholarly output and strengthened the continuity of intellectual development. In turn, the degree of specialization has been greatly increased as a result of the greater density of scientific and scholarly knowledge and the pursuit of the idol of originality. The independent intellectual, and the intellectual living on the income from the sale of his works and from patronage, still exist, and their creativity and productivity have not obviously diminished. The intellectual, however, who lives from a salary as a member of an institution devoted to the performance of intellectual work—teaching and scientific and scholarly research—has greatly increased in numbers, and his works make up a larger and larger proportion of the total intellectual product of every modern society.

The increased volume and complexity of the heritage of science and scholarship and the demand for continuity as well as the wider insistence on diplomatization, have aggrandized the student body. This stratum of the intellectuals, which in the nineteenth century already had acquired a special position in European public life, in the twentieth century has greatly expanded. In every country where national sensibilities are very tender, and which has been in a state of political, economic, or cultural dependency, the university (and high school) student body has taken on a special role in political life. It has become the bearer of the idea of nationality.

Concomitantly the absorption of intellectuals into executive positions—"staff and line" posts within large corporate organizations concerned not with intellectual matters but with the exercise of authority, the production and sale of material objects, i.e., consumption goods, capital equipment, weapons of war, etc.—has greatly increased. Science, which was a profound toy of amateurs until the nineteenth century, became by the end of that century a vital component of economic life. It has spread from the chemical industry into agriculture, into nearly every branch of industry, and into important sectors of commerce. In the first and second world wars, scientists, and increasingly pure scientists, were drawn into involvement with the armed forces. Scientists have become increasingly involved in research closely connected with agriculture, supported and conducted within institutions controlled by public and private bodies concerned with the improvement of plant and animal strains, with ecology, etc.

The spread of literacy, leisure, and material well-being, and the development of the mechanical means of reproduction and transmission of symbols in sounds and image, have also resulted in the creation of new corporate organizations in which intellectuals are employed. Whereas the creation of cultural objects for consumption by the educated was until nearly the end of the nineteenth century the work, at varying levels of quality, of the freelance intellectual, who sold his work to an enterpriser—a printer-bookseller—or whose work was commissioned by the latter, recent developments bring the intellectual producer of this kind of cultural object within the framework of a corporate organization, e.g. a film studio, a radio or television network.

The trend in the present century, therefore, in all countries of the world, liberal and totalitarian, has been toward an increasing incorporation of intellectuals into organized institutions. This represents a modification of the trend toward an increase in the proportion of institutionally independent intellectuals which had set in with the development of printing, and which in itself constituted—at least in numbers and in the quantity of intellectual products—a new phase in world history.

This diversity and specialization of intellectuals in the twentieth century raises a question concerning the extent to which they form a community, bound together by a sense of mutual affinity, by attachment to a common set of rules and common identifying symbols. They do not form such a community at present. There are, however, numerous subcommunities within the larger intellectual universe which do meet these criteria. The particular fields of the natural sciences and even science as a whole and scholarship as a whole do define actual communities bound together by the acceptance of a common body of standards—and this, even though there are controversy and disagreement within every field. These communities are only partially and very inadequately embodied in the professional and scientific societies. The literary and artistic worlds, too, form such communities with vague and indeterminate boundaries—even more vague and indeterminate than the boundaries of the scholarly and scientific communities.

These communities are not mere figures of speech. Their common standards are continually being applied by each member in his own work and in the institutions which assess and select works and persons for appreciation or condemnation. They operate like a common-law system without formal enactment of their rules but by the repeated and incessant application and clarification of the rules. The editors of learned scientific, scholarly, and literary journals, the readers of publishing houses, the reviewers of scientific, scholarly, and literary works, and the appointments committees which pass judgments on the candidates for posts in universities or scientific research institutes, are the central institutions of these communities. The training of the oncoming generations in colleges and universities in the rules of the respective intellectual communities specifies these rules by example and transmits them by the identification of the research student with his teacher, just as in ancient India the disciple sitting at the feet of his *guru* acquired not only a knowledge of the concrete subject matter but also the rules and the disposition for its interpretation and application. The award of prizes and distinctions such as the Nobel Prize or election to membership in the Royal Society or to a famous continental academy establishes models and affirms the rightness of certain patterns of thought. The most original scientists, the most profound thinkers, the most learned scholars, the greatest writers and artists provide the models, which embody the rules of the community, and teach by the example of their achievement.

The worldwide character of the community formed by mathematicians or physicists or other natural scientists approximates most closely to the ideal of a body, bound together by a universal devotion to a common set of standards derived from a common tradition and acknowledged by all who have passed through the discipline of scientific training. Even here however, specialization and considerations of military security impair the universality of the scientific community. In other fields of intellectual work, boundaries of language, national pride, and religious, political, and ethical beliefs engender reluctance to accept the claims of standards of intellectual communities to universal observance. Technical specialization, the reduction of the general humanistic component in secondary and higher education, and the intensification of the ideological factor in politics all resist the claims of the communities which in the modern world have nonetheless managed, despite enduring cleavages and intermittent crises, to command the allegiance of intellectuals.

Despite all impediments and counterclaims, the intellectual communities remain really effective systems of action. Whatever their distortions, they transmit the traditions of intellectual life and maintain its standards in various special fields and as a whole.

The Traditions of Intellectuals

Intellectual work is sustained by and transmits a complex tradition which persists through changes in the structure of the intellectual class. In these traditions, the most vital ones are the standards and rules in the light of which achievement is striven for and assessed and the substantive beliefs and symbols which constitute the heritage of valid achievement. It is by participation in these traditions of perception, appreciation, and expression, and by affirmation of the importance of performing in the modes accredited by these traditions, that the intellectual is defined. One could almost say that if these traditions did not confront the intellectual as an ineluctable inheritance, they could be created anew in each generation by the passionate disposition of the "natural" intellectual to be in contact, by perception, ratiocination, or expression, with symbols of general scope. They are traditions which are, so to speak, given by the nature of intellectual work. They are the immanent traditions of intellectual performance, the accepted body of rules of procedure, standards of judgment, criteria for the selection of subject matters and problems, modes of presentation, canons for the assessment of excellence, models of previous achievement and prospective emulation. Every field of intellectual performance, more than any other craft or profession possessing a long and acknowledged accumulation of achievements, has such a cultural tradition, always—though at varying rates—being added to and modified. What is called scientific method in each particular field of science or scholarship, and the techniques of literary creation and of work in the plastic and other arts, possess such a tradition, and without that tradition even the greatest and most creative geniuses who seek to discover and create in that domain could not be effective. Colleges and universities, scientific, scholarly, and artistic journals, museums, galleries—in short, the whole system of intellectual institutions—exist to select those who are qualified to work within these traditions and to train them in their appreciation, application, and development. Even the most creative and rapidly developing domains of intellectual performance could disregard them only with very great loss.

These traditions, though they make neither direct nor logically implicit reference to the position of their adherents in relation to the surrounding society and the authorities which rule it, seem from their very structure to entail a measure of tension between themselves and the laity. The very intensity and concentration of commitment to these values which are remote from the executive routines of daily life in family, firm, office, factory, church, and civil service, from the pleasures of the ordinary man and the obligations, compromises, and corruptions of those who exercise commanding authority in church, state, business, and army—entail an at least incipient sense, on each side, of the distance which separates these two trends of value orientation.

Intellectual work arose from religious preoccupations. In the early history of the human race, it tended, in its concern with the ultimate or at least with what lies beyond the immediate concrete experience, to operate with religious symbols. It continues to share with genuine religious experience the fascination with the sacred or the ultimate ground of thought and experience, and the aspiration to enter into intimate contact with it. In secular intellectual work, this involves the search for the truth, for the principles embedded in events and actions, or for the establishment of a relationship between the self and the essential, whether the relationship be cognitive, appreciative, or expressive. Intellectual action of an intense kind contains and continues the deeper religious attitude, the striving for contact with the most decisive and significant symbols and the realities underlying those symbols. It is therefore no stretching of the term to say that science and philosophy, even when they are not religious in a conventional sense, are as concerned with the sacred as religion itself. In consequence of this, in our enumeration of the traditions under which intellectual pursuits are carried on, we should say that the tradition of awesome respect and of serious striving for contact with the sacred is perhaps the first, the most comprehensive, and the most important of all traditions of the intellectuals. In the great religious cultures of Islam, Buddhism, Taoism, and Hinduism, prior to the emergence of a differentiated modern intellectual class, the care of the sacred through the mastery, interpretation, and exposition of sacred writings and the cultivation of the appropriate mental states or qualities were the first interests of the intellectuals. (In China, the development of a class of Confucian intellectual-civil servants produced its own tradition, more civil and aesthetic than religious in the conventional meaning.) In the West too, in antiquity, a substantial section of the philosophical intelligentsia bore this tradition, and, on the higher reaches, even those who cut themselves off from the tribal and territorial religions continued to be impelled by such considerations (Pythagoras, Euclid, Ptolemy, Aristotle, Plato, Socrates, Lucretius, Seneca). In modern times, although attracting a diminishing share of the creative capacities of the oncoming intellectual elite, religious orientations still remain a major preoccupation of a substantial fraction of the educated classes and not less of the most creative minds.

With this striving for contact with the ultimately important comes the self-esteem which always accompanies the performance of important activities. One who makes an effort to understand the traditions of the intellectuals and their relations with the authorities who rule the other sections of society at any given time, must bear in mind the crucial significance of the self-regard which comes from preoccupation and contact with the most vital facts of human and cosmic existence, and the implied attitude of derogation toward those who act in more mundane or more routine capacities.[2]

When intellectuals ceased to be solely bearers of religiosity, the very act of separation, however gradual and unwitting and undeliberate, set up a tension between the intellectuals and the religious authority of their society. Insofar as they were not merely civil servants and counselors to princes—itself an unsettling, tension-generating relationship—there was created a tension between the public authorities and the intellectuals. Ecclesiastical and exemplary religious authority became an object of the distrust of intellectuals, and insofar as the authority of the government of earthly affairs associated itself with the religious powers, it too shared in that skepticism. The attitude is by no means universal, nor need the distrust be aggressive. Confucian civil servants, disdainful toward Taoism or Buddhism, did not become rebels against their sovereigns as long as they themselves were treated respectfully. In the West, where the separation of religious and other intellectual activities has become most pronounced, a more general feeling of distance from authority has been engendered and has become one of the strongest of the traditions of the intellectuals. First in the West, and then in the past half-century in Africa and Asia among intellectuals who have come under the Western traditions, the tradition of distrust of secular and ecclesiastical authority—and in fact of tradition as such—has become the chief secondary tradition of the intellectuals. As such, it is nurtured by many of the subsidiary traditions such as scientism, revolutionism, progressivism, etc., which we shall treat below.

The tension between the intellectuals and the powers—their urge to submit to authority as the bearer of the highest good, whether it be order or progress or some other value, and to resist or condemn authority as a betrayer of the highest values—comes ultimately from the constitutive orientation of the intellectuals toward the sacred.

2. Naturally, this sentiment is not equally shared by all intellectuals. Not all are equally involved in these "vital facts"—and therefore not all have the same feeling of the dignity of their own activities. Intellectuals vary greatly in their sensitivity to their traditions—just as do the laity with respect to their traditions—but even in those who are relatively insensitive, there remains a considerable unwitting assimilation of many elements of these central traditions.

Practically all the more concrete traditions in the light and shadows of which intellectuals have lived express this tension. We shall note, in brief, some of these traditions which, however diverse in their age and origins, have played a great part in forming the relations of the modern intellectuals to authority. They are (a) the tradition of scientism, (b) the romantic tradition, (c) the apocalyptic tradition, (d) the populistic tradition, and (e) the tradition of antiintellectual order.

All of these traditions are in conflict with other traditions of deference toward ecclesiastical and temporal authorities and the expectation of a career in their service. Even in those modern cultures where the traditions of the intellectuals' acceptance of authority are strongest, in modern Britain and modern Germany, they have by no means had the field to themselves. Similarly in modern Asia, where variants of the traditions of devotion to the religiously sacred values and the service of temporal authority have, in ancient as well as modern times, had a powerful hold, anti-authoritarian and anticivil traditions, diffused from the West and nurtured by related traditions derived from Taoism, Buddhism, and Hinduism, have found an eager and widespread reception.

The *tradition of scientism* is the tradition which denies the validity of tradition as such; it insists on the testing of everything which is received and on its rejection if it does not correspond with the "facts of experience." It is the tradition which demands the avoidance of every extraneous impediment to the precise perception of reality, regardless of whether that impediment comes from tradition, from institutional authority, or from internal passion or impulse. It is critical of the arbitrary and the irrational. In its emphasis on the indispensability of firsthand and direct experience, it sets itself in opposition to everything which comes between the mind of the knowing individual and "reality." It is easy to see how social convention and the traditional authority associated with institutions would fall prey to the ravages of this powerfully persuasive and corrosive tradition.

The *romantic tradition* appears at first sight to be in irreconcilable opposition to the tradition of scientism. At certain points, such as the estimation of the value of impulse and passion, there is a real and unbridgeable antagonism. In many important respects, however, they share fundamental features. Romanticism starts with the appreciation of the spontaneous manifestations of the essence of concrete individuality. Hence it values originality, i.e. the unique, that which is produced from the genius of the individual (or the folk), in contrast with the stereotyped and traditional actions of the philistine. Since ratiocination and detachment obstruct spontaneous expression, they are thought to be life-destroying. Institutions which have rules and which prescribe the conduct of the individual members by conventions and commands are likewise viewed as life-destroying. The bourgeois family, mercantile activity, the market, indeed civil society in general, with its curb on enthusiasm and its sober acceptance of obligation, are repugnant to the romantic tradition—all are the enemies of spontaneity and genuineness; they impose a role on the individual and do not permit him to be himself. They kill what is living in the folk. Civil society has no place for the intellectual, who is afflicted with a sense of his moral solitude within it. The affinities of the romantic tradition to the revolutionary criticism of the established order and to the bohemian refusal to have more part in it than is absolutely necessary are obvious. It too is one of the most explosively antiauthoritarian, and even anticivil, powers of modern intellectual life.

The *revolutionary tradition*, which has found so many of its leading recipients and exponents among intellectuals, draws much from scientism and romanticism, but essentially it rests on one much older, namely the *apocalyptic* or millenarian tradition. The belief that the evil world as we know it, so full of temptation and corruption, will come to an end one day and will be replaced by a purer and better world, originates in the apocalyptic outlook of the prophets of the Old Testament. It is promulgated in the Christian idea of the Kingdom of God, which the earlier Christians expected in their own time, and it lingers as a passionately turbulent stream, dammed up and hidden by the efforts of the Church, but recurrently appearing on the surface of history through the teaching and action of heretical sects. It received a powerful impetus from Manichaeanism. In the Donatists, in the Bogomils, in the Albigensians and Waldensians, in the Hussites and Lollards, in the Anabaptists and in the Fifth Monarchy Men, in the belief that the evil world, the world of the Children of Darkness, would be destroyed and supplanted by the world of the Children of Light after a decisive judgement by the Sovereign of the universe, this tradition has lived on. It has come down to our own times in a transmuted form. Although it still exists in its religious form among numerous Christian and quasi-Christian sects in Europe, America, and Africa, its true recipients are the modern revolutionary movements and above all the Marxian movements. Marxian writers of the early part of this century acknowledged the Anabaptists, the Fifth Monarchy Men, the Levellers and the Diggers, as their forerunners, and although the Bolsheviks have been less willing to admit Russian sectarianism as an antecedent, there can be little doubt that the Russian sectarian image of the world and its cataclysmic history made it easier for the Marxian conception of society and its historical destiny to find acceptance in Russia. The disposition to distinguish sharply between good and evil and to refuse to admit the permissibility of any admixture, the insistence that justice be done though the heavens fall, the obstinate refusal to compromise or to tolerate compromise—all the features of doctrinaire politics, or the politics of the ideal, which are so common among the modern intellectuals, must be attributed in some measure at least to this tradition.

Another of the traditions which has everywhere in the world moved intellectuals in the last century and a half is the *populistic tradition*. Populism is a belief in the creativity and in the superior moral worth of the ordinary people, of the uneducated and unintellectual; it perceives their virtue in their actual qualities or in their potentialities. In the simplicity and wisdom of their ways, the populist tradition alleges that it has discerned virtues which are morally superior to those found in the educated and in the higher social classes. Even where, as in Marxism, the actual state of the lower classes is not esteemed, they are alleged to be by destiny fitted to become the salvationary nucleus of their society. Romanticism with its distrust of the rational and calculating elements in bourgeois society, revolutionism with its hatred of the upper classes as the agents of wicked authority, the apocalyptic attitude which sees the last coming first and which alleges that official learning (religious and secular) has falsified the truths which the Last Judgement and the leap into freedom will validate—all these manifest a populistic disposition. German historical and philological scholarship in the nineteenth century—imbued with the romantic hatred of the rational, the economic, the analytic spirit, which it castigated as the source and product of the whole revolutionary, rationalistic trend of Western European culture—discovered in the nameless masses, the folk, the fountain of linguistic and cultural creativity. French socialism went a step further, and Marxism elevated this essentially romantic outlook into a systematic "scientific" theory.

In all countries peripheral to the most creative centers of Western culture at the height of its hegemony over the modern mind, intellectuals were both fascinated and rendered uneasy by the culture of Western Europe. Not only in early nineteenth-century Germany, but in Russia of the fifties, in the twentieth-century middlewestern United States, in Brazil (in the doctrine of "Indianism"), in the resentful and embittered Weimar Republic, in India since the ascendancy of Gandhi and in the emerging intelligentsias of the new countries of Africa, populistic tendencies are massively at work. In all these countries the intellectuals have been educated either in foreign countries or in institutions within their own countries modeled on those at the center of the culture they sought or seek to emulate. In all these countries the intellectuals have developed anxiety about whether they have not allowed themselves to be currupted by excessive permeation with the admired foreign culture. To identify themselves with the people, to praise the culture of the ordinary people as richer, truer, wiser, and more relevant than the foreign culture in which they have themselves been educated, has been a way out of this distress. In most of these cases it is a protest against the "official" culture, the culture of the higher civil servants, of the universities, and of the culture—political, literary, and philosophical—which has come out of them. As such, it has fused easily with the other traditions of hostility to civil institutions and civil authority.

There is another tradition, closely connected with all of these and yet apparently their negation, which merits mention. This is the *antiintellectual tradition of order.* Best known in the West in the form of French positivism (Saint-Simon and Comte), it has its roots in antiquity and in the belief that excessive intellectual analysis and discussion can erode the foundations of order. Plato's attitude toward poets had its parallel in the burning of the books by the former Confucian, Li-Ssu, at the origin of the Ch'in Dynasty; Hobbes's analysis of the role of intellectuals in bringing about the English civil war, Taine's interpretation of the significance of the *philosophes* in bringing on the French Revolution of 1789, and the ideas of Joseph de Maistre, all testify to the ambivalence in the traditional antiauthoritarianism of intellectuals.

In Conclusion

Intellectuals are indispensable to any society, not just to industrial society, and the more complex the society, the more indispensable they are. An effective collaboration between intellectuals and the authorities which govern society is a requirement for order and continuity in public life and for the integration of the wider reaches of the laity into society. Yet, the original impetus to intellectual performance, and the traditions to which it has given rise and which are sustained by the institutions through which intellectual performance is made practicable, generate a tension between intellectuals and the laity, high and low. This tension can never be eliminated, either by a complete consensus between the laity and the intellectuals or by the complete ascendancy of the intellectuals over the laity.

Within these two extreme and impossible alternatives, a wide variety of forms of consensus and dissensus in the relations of the intellectuals and the ruling powers of society have existed. The discovery and the achievement of the optimum balance of civility and intellectual creativity are the tasks of the statesman and the responsible intellectual. The study of these diverse patterns of consensus and dissensus, their institutional and cultural concomitants, and the conditions under which they have emerged and waned are the first items on the agenda of the comparative study of the intellectuals and the powers.

2 Ideology

Ideology is one among the variety of comprehensive patterns of beliefs—cognitive and moral, about man, society, and the universe in relation to man and society—which exist in differentiated societies. These comprehensive patterns of belief comprise outlooks and creeds ("suboutlooks"), movements of thought, and programs, as well as ideologies.

These comprehensive patterns differ from each other in their degree of (a) explicitness and authoritativeness of formulation, (b) internal systemic integration, (c) acknowledged affinity with other contemporaneous patterns, (d) closure, (e) imperativeness of manifestation in conduct, (f) accompanying affect, (g) consensus demanded of exponents, and (h) association with a corporate collective form deliberately intended to realize the pattern of beliefs. Ideologies are characterized by a high degree of explicitness of formulation over a very wide range of the objects with which they deal; for their adherents there is an authoritative and explicit promulgation. They are relatively highly systematized or integrated around one or a few preeminent values (e.g., salvation, equality, or ethnic purity). They are more insistent on their distinctiveness from and unconnectedness with other outlooks or ideologies in their own society; they are more resistant against innovations in their beliefs and deny the existence or the significance of those which do occur. Their acceptance and promulgation have highly affective overtones. Complete subservience to the ideology is demanded of those who accept it, and it is regarded as essential and imperative that their conduct should be completely permeated by it. All adherents of the ideology are urgently expected to be in complete agreement with each other; corporate collective form is regarded as the appropriate mode of organization of adherents to maintain discipline over those already committed and to win over or dominate those not already committed to it.

Outlooks (and creeds) tend to lack one authoritative and explicit promulgation. They are pluralistic in their internal structure, not systematically integrated (creeds or "suboutlooks" have a greater likelihood of systematic integration when they are elaborated by a

Previously published in a slightly different form in the *International Encyclopaedia of the Social Sciences,* David L. Sills, editor. (New York: Macmillan Company and Free Press, 1968), vol. 7, pp. 66-76. Copyright © 1968 by Crowell Collier and Macmillan, Inc.

school of thought). Outlooks are inclusive rather than disjunctive in their relations with other patterns of thought. (Creeds or "subout-looks" are less inclusive, but they too do not form sharp boundaries around themselves.) Outlooks contain within themselves a variety of creeds or "suboutlooks", which differ from each other by divergent emphasis on different elements in the outlook; they are often in conflict with each other on particular issues. The vagueness and diffuseness of outlooks and creeds is paralleled by the unevenness of the pressure for their observance in action. In expression, they are less affective. They are less demanding of consensus among their bearers. Outlooks and creeds, too, have their organizational counter-parts.

Outlooks and creeds are the characteristic patterns of belief in those sections of the society which affirm or accept the existing order of society. One or another of the creeds is characteristically integrated into the central institutional system while the others are not remote from it. Creeds which become alienated from the central institutional system tend to acquire the properties of ideologies, over and above the element of alienation. Ideologies sometimes but do not normally dominate central institutional systems. Ideologies which dominate central institutional systems have a tendency to be transformed in the direction of creeds, and not merely with respect to their relationship to the central institutional system.

A movement of thought is a more or less explicit and systematic intellectual pattern, developed in the course of generally undirected collaboration and division of labor. It is elaborate and compre-hensive. like ideologies, outlooks, and creeds. Insofar as it does not insist on total observance in behavior, a complete consensus among its adherents, and closure vis-a-vis other intellectual constructions, it does not become an ideology.

A program is a specification and narrowing of the focus of interest of an outlook, creed, or movement of thought onto a particular, limited objective. Depending on the pattern from which it originates, its relationship to more general cognitive and moral principles will be more or less elaborate and explicit. Since its major feature is the limited range of its objectives, in practice it is less likely to be immediately ideological in its origin or destination.

Movements of thought and programs tend to be dissensual towards contemporaneous outlooks and creeds and the practices through which these operate institutionally. Ideology differs from them, however, with respect to the intensity of the affect which accompanies its dissent, the completeness of its corporate self-separation, and of its intellectual closure, as well as in the range of its aspiration to encompass in cognition, evaluation, and practice all available objects and events.

Ideologies and those who espouse them allege to speak for a transcendent entity—a stratum, a society, a species, or an ideal value—which is broader than the membership of the corporate entity. Corporate carriers of ideologies, whatever their actual practice, claim to act on behalf of an "ideal," the beneficiaries of which always go beyond the members of the ideological group. The ideal always diverging from the existent, the ideology contends for the realization of a state of affairs which is alleged by its proponents either never to have existed previously or to have existed in the past but no longer to be in existence. (Karl Mannheim [*Ideology and Utopia*] designated the former ideals as utopias, the latter as ideologies. He also included under ideology sets of beliefs which affirm the existing order and which we designate as outlooks and suboutlooks, schools of thought and programs. Neither his terminology nor his classifications are adhered to in this paper.)

Ideology and Central Value Systems

Ideologies contend more strenuously than does the prevailing outlook or the constituent and overlapping creeds for a purer, fuller, or more ideal realization of particular cognitive and moral values than exists in the society in which the ideology obtains. Ideologies are more insistent on continuous contact with sacred symbols and with a fuller manifestation of the sacred in the existent. Whereas the outlooks and creeds connected with the central institutional system demand in their programmatic aspects segmental changes and changes which do not diverge profoundly from what already exists, ideologies impel their proponents to realize the ideal which is contained in the sacred through a "total transformation." They seek this completeness through total conquest or conversion or by total withdrawal from it so that the purer, ideal form of value can be cultivated in isolation from the contaminating influence of the environing society of the moment. Whereas the bearers of each of the several creeds of a prevailing outlook accept some measure of community with other creeds, the exponents of an ideology, being set against other ideologies and particularly against the dominant outlook (and creeds), stress the differences of their ideology vis-a-vis the other outlooks and ideologies within the society, and disavow the identities and affinities.

Nonetheless, every ideology, however great the originality of its creators, arises in the midst of an ongoing culture. However passionate its reaction against that culture, it cannot entirely divest itself of important elements of that culture. Ideologies are responses to insufficient regard for some particular element in the dominant outlooks and are attempts to place that neglected element in a more central position and to bring it into fulfillment. There are, therefore, always marked substantive affinities between the moral and cognitive orientations of any particular ideology and those of the outlooks and creeds which prevail in the environing society and which to greater or lesser degrees affirm or accept the central institutional and value systems.

In their formal structure, both the outlooks and the creeds which affirm or accept the central institutional and value system are constellations of very loosely integrated and ambiguous moral and cognitive propositions and attitudes toward a variety of particular, often quite concrete, objects and situations. In the minds of most of those who share them, they do not form consistent systems each concentrated on one central theme, principle, value, or symbol. An ideology is an intensification and generalization of certain of these propositions and attitudes, a reduced emphasis on others, and their subordination to one, or very few, which is, or are, raised to a position of predominance. An ideology differs therefore from a prevailing outlook and its creeds through *its greater explicitness*, its greater *internal integration* or *systematization*, the *comprehensiveness* of its scope, the *urgency* of its application, and the much higher *intensity of concentration* on certain central propositions or evaluations.

Because of these common structural properties, and despite their affinities with the dominant outlooks and creeds, ideologies, whether "progressive" or "traditionalistic," "revolutionary" or "reactionary," have certain common substantive features as well. They entail an aggressive alienation from the existing society; they recommend the transformation of the lives of their exponents in accordance with specific principles; they insist on consistency and thoroughgoingness in their exponents' application of principles; and they recommend the complete dominion over the societies in which they live or a total, self-protective withdrawal from them. (Even where the exponents of an ideology have been successful in attaining the key positions from which power is exercised in the central institutional system, the alienation of the exponents of the ideology from the outlook of the society and its creeds over which they exercise power still operates.)

Since ideologies are intellectual constructions, they passionately oppose the productions of the cultural institutions of the central institutional system. They claim that these have distorted the truth about "serious" things, and that they do so to maintain a system of injustice in the earthly order.

Ideologies insist on the primary value of the realization of principles in conduct; this is one of the reasons with which they accuse the central value and institutional systems of hypocrisy, the compromise of principles, and corruption by power. Corresponding to this rigorist attitude, ideologies and their exponents, whether out of power or in central positions of power over society, are relentlessly critical of the inconsistencies and shortcomings of conduct with respect to principles of right and justice in sectors of society over which they do not have complete control. Ideologies demand an intense and continuous observance of their imperatives in the conduct of their exponents; ideological groups tend to impose a stringent discipline on their members.

Some parts of these transindividual outlooks are more in the possession of some individuals and less in the possession of others; the latter might have a predilection for elements different from those espoused by the former. An ideology insists on a greater completeness of possession by each of those who are committed to sharing in it; there is less of a division of labor among the bearers of ideologies than there is among the bearers of a prevailing outlook or creed.

Ideological Politics

Ideologies are always concerned with authority, transcendent and earthly, and they cannot therefore avoid being political except by the extreme reaction of complete withdrawal from society. Even in ages which saw no public politics permitted, ideological groups forced themselves into the political arena. Since the seventeenth century, every ideology has had its views on politics; indeed, since the nineteenth century some ideologies have come apparently to have views about nothing but politics.

This appearance of thinking of nothing but politics is not the attitude of the professional politician, who lives for politics to the exclusion of everything else. Ideologies which concentrate on politics do so because for them politics subsumes everything else. The evaluation of authority is the center of the ideological outlook; it is around this evaluation that all other objects and their evaluations are integrated. Everything is political for ideological politics. No sphere has any intrinsic value of its own. There is no privacy, no autonomous spheres or art or religion or economic activity or science. Each, in this view, is to be understood politically. (This is true of Marxism as well, despite the fact that it is reputed to have made everything dependent on economic relationships. The relations of production were property relations, i.e., relationships of authority, supported by the power of the state!)

Ideology, whether nominally religious or antireligious, is concerned with the sacred. Ideology seeks to sacralize existence by bringing every part of it under the dominion of the ultimately right principles. The sacred and the sacrilegious reside in authority, the former in the authority acknowledged by ideology, the latter in that which prevails in the wicked world. Ordinary politics are the kingdom of darkness; ideological politics are the struggle of light against darkness.

Participation in the routine life of the civil political order is alien to the ideological spirit. In fact, there are many adulterations of this ideological purity, and purely ideological politics are marginal and exceptional. The need to build a machine strong enough to acquire power in the state, even by conspiracy and subversion, enforces compromises and concessions to the ongoing political order and to the less than complete ideological orientation of potential and desired supporters. Failure, too, damages the purity of ideological politics. The pressure of competition enforces alliances and the adoption of procedures which are alien to its nature. Nonetheless, ideological politics in splinters of rancorous purity or in attenuation often penetrates some way into civil politics.

Likewise among intellectuals there are many who have inherited an ideological tradition and to whom ideological politics appeal as the only right politics. Even where intellectuals often appear to be convinced of the inefficacy of ideological politics, the categories in which they view the world as it is, its techniques and its heroes, stir and master their imaginations.

The Bearers of Ideology

The disposition toward ideological construction is one of the fundamental properties of the human race, once it reaches a certain stage of intellectual development. It is, however, a disposition which is usually latent. It finds its fullest expression in a charismatic ideologist, a person with an overwhelmingly powerful drive to be in contact with the sacred and to promulgate that contact in comprehensive and coherent terms. The charismatic ideologist cannot, however, construct an ideology in isolation from a collectivity on behalf of which he speaks and with which it must be shared. An ideology-like intellectual construction produced in isolation from a political or religious sect would be no more than a system of religious, moral, social, and political philosophy. It becomes more than a rigorous system of moral, social, and political philosophy based on fundamental propositions about the cosmos and history when it is shared by a community constituted by the acceptance of that outlook.

The characteristic and primal bearer of an ideology is an *ideological primary group* (what Schmalenbach called a *Bund*). The bond which unites the members of the ideological primary group to each other is the attachment to each other as co-sharers of the ideological system of beliefs, the perception of the other as being in possession of or being possessed by the sacredness inherent in the acceptance of the ideology. In the ideological primary group, personal, primordial, and civil qualities are attenuated or suppressed in favor of the quality of "ideological possession." A comrade is a comrade by virtue of his beliefs, which are perceived as his most significant qualities. A fully developed ideological primary group is separated by sharply defined boundaries from the "world," from which it seeks to protect itself or over which it seeks to triumph. Stringent discipline over conduct and belief is a feature of ideological primary groups; intense solidarity and unwavering loyalty are demanded.

In reality, of course, the ideological quality never completely supplants all other qualities, and ideological primary groups are never completely realized. Ideological primary groups are subject therefore to recurrent strains not only because of the inherent strains within the ideology as an intellectual system but also because the other qualities become, in various measures, for many of the members of the group, significant qualities on the bases of which supplementary and often alternative and contradictory attachments are formed. Even the most disciplined ideological primary group is under the strain of divergent beliefs among members as well as the pull of their various attachments to the "world."

Ideologies are often espoused by more loosely integrated circles, particularly when the ideology itself has moved into a condition of disintegration. Ideologies have a self-reproductive power. Echoes and fragments of ideologies go on after their primal bearers have died or dissolved in defeat or disillusionment. They turn into movements borne by schools of thought. Fragments of ideology also become transformed into creeds and outlooks.

The Emergence of Ideologies

An ideology is the product of the need for an intellectually imposed order on the world. The need for an ideology is an intensification of the need for a cognitive and moral map of the universe, which in a less intense and more intermittent form is a fundamental, although unequally distributed, disposition of man.

Ideologies arise in conditions of crisis, in sectors of society to whom the hitherto prevailing outlook has become unacceptable. An ideology arises because there is a strongly felt need for an explanation of important experiences which the prevailing outlook does not explain, because there is a need for the firm guidance of conduct which, similarly, is not provided by the prevailing outlook, and because there is a need, likewise strongly felt, for a fundamental vindication of legitimation of the value and dignity of the persons in question. Mere rejection of the existing society and the prevailing outlook of the elites of that society is not sufficient. For an ideology to exist, there must also be an attendant vision of a positive alternative to the existing pattern of society and its culture and an intellectual capacity to articulate that vision as part of the cosmic order. Ideologies are the creations of charismatic persons with a powerful, expansive, and simplified vision, who also possess high intellectual and imaginative powers. An ideology, by placing at its very center certain cosmically, ethically fundamental propositions, brings to those who accept it the belief that they are in possession and in contact with what is ultimately right and true.

Some personalities are ideological by constitution. They feel continuously a need for a clearly ordered picture of the universe, and of their own place in it. They need clear and unambiguous criteria as to what is right and wrong in every situation. They must be able to explain whatever happens by a clear and readily applicable proposition, itself derived from a central proposition. Other persons become ideological in conditions of private and public crisis, which accentuate the need for meaningful moral and cognitive order. (When the crisis abates, the latter become less ideological.)

An ideology cannot come into existence without the prior existence of a general pattern of moral and cognitive judgments against which it is a reaction and of which it is a variant. It requires, in other words, a cultural tradition from which to deviate, and from which to draw the elements which it intensifies and raises to centrality. An intellectualized religion provides the precondition for the emergence of ideology since the former contains explicit propositions about the nature of the sacred and its cultivation, which is what ideologies are about. The fact that an ideology already exists serves both to form an ideological tradition and to provide a medium in which ideological dispositions can be precipitated by emulation and self-differentiation.

Ideologies and ideological orientations have existed in all high cultures. They have, however, been especially frequent in Western culture. The continuous working of the prophetic tradition of the Old Testament and the salvationary tradition of the mystery religions and of early Christianity have provided a set of cultural dispositions which have been recurrently activated in the course of the Christian era in the West. The secularization of the modern age has not changed this at all. The growth of literacy and of the educated classes and the "intellectualization" of politics have widened receptivity to ideological beliefs. The spread of Western ideas to Asia and Africa has been a spread among many other things of a culture full of ideological potentiality. (On the social origins of the bearers of ideology, little can be said. It was Max Weber's view that they came from the strata of traders and handicraftsmen, and from sections of society which are shaken by a disruption in their conventional mode of life. There is some plausibility in this hypothesis. They also appear to come from educated circles and from ethnic "outsiders," whose prior alienation makes them receptive to ideological beliefs.)

Endogenous and Exogenous Changes in Ideologies

Proponents of ideologies obdurately resist the explicit introduction of revision of their articles of belief. They aspire and pretend to systematic completeness. They do not appear to their proponents to be in need of improvement. Nonetheless, ideologies are never completely consistent or completely adequate to the facts of experience which they claim to interpret and dominate. Even the most systematically elaborated ideology, like all systems of belief, scientific and nonscientific, contains inconsistencies, ambiguities, and gaps. These render likely disputes among the adherents of the ideology who espouse divergent ways of filling the gaps and clarifying the ambiguities, each claiming that his way represents the "correct" interpretation of the unchanged and unchangeable fundamentals. Inconsistencies and ambiguities may be perceived on purely intellectual grounds, and the efforts to repair them may be motivated primarily by a concern for intellectual clarity and harmony. Such efforts are likely to arouse antagonism from the more orthodox exponents of the ideology, i.e., those who adhere to the previously dominant interpretation. In this way, either through the triumph of the innovators or the triumph of the orthodox, the previous formulation of the ideology undergoes a change.

In addition to these more intellectual sources of change in ideologies, endogenous changes occur in consequence of conflicts among the proponents of divergent policies which appear to be equally sanctioned by the ideology. As a result of the triumph of one of the contending groups over the other, new emphases and developments occur within the ideology. These very properties, which are sources of instability in ideologies and in the groups which support them, are also the condition of their further development to confront new situations and of their adaptation and compromise with the intractability of reality as an object of exhaustive cognition and control. It is through such internal changes that ideologies sometimes move back toward the prevailing outlook or contribute, by their reentry, to the modification of the prevailing outlook of the cultural value system.

Ideologies also change because of the pressure of external reality. The "world" does not easily accommodate itself to the requirements of ideologies. The "facts" of life do not fit their categories; those whose existence is among these facts do not yield to the exhortations and offensives of the ideologists. The proponents of ideologies are often defeated in their campaigns for total transformation. Defeat is a shock, a pressing occasion for revision of the ideology to make it fit the "facts" which have imposed themselves. Despite resistance, the ideology is retouched, at first superficially, later more deeply. Fissures among the ideologists, accompany this struggle to cope with the impregnability of the "world."

Another external factor which places a strain on ideology is the diminution of the crisis which gave rise to it and the consequent dissipation of ideological orientation. Those whom crisis had enflamed into an ideological state of mind either withdraw from or loosen their connections with the ideological primary group; if they are influential enough, they modify and adapt it to the demands of life in the environing society, to which they once more become assimilated. Under these conditions, the sharply defined boundaries become eroded. The members cease to define themselves exclusively by their ideological qualities. The specific modifications which the ideology introduced to differentiate it from the predominant outlook in the central institutional and value systems make the ideology less disjunctive, and its distinctive ideological elements fade into a ceremonially asserted formula. Quite frequently, the ideological accentuation returns to the prevailing, more widely shared outlook as an accentuation, as an intensification of those features of the prevailing outlook or creed which had previously been in a blurred and unemphasized state.

Quasi-ideological Phenomena

The potentialities of ideological orientations relatively seldom come to realization. Quite apart from the tenacious hold of the central institutional and value systems on many persons who are simultaneously ideologically disposed, ideological orientations often do not eventuate in fully developed ideologies or ideological primary groups because the ideological needs of those who come under their influence are not sufficiently intense, comprehensive, or persistent. Without a powerful ideological personality, powerful in intelligence and imagination, ideological propensities in the more ordinary human vessels of ideological needs do not attain fulfillment.

Furthermore, once an ideological primary group has fallen into dilapidation, the ideology persists in a somewhat disaggregated form among the late members of the group. In that form, too, it continues to find adherents who, without the discipline of an ideological primary group, select certain congenial elements of the ideology for application and development. They become an ideological tradition, which is available to subsequent ideologists and ideological primary groups.

Sometimes certain of these elements become a *program* of aggressive demands and criticism against the central institutional and value systems. Programs, like ideologies, also emerge from prevailing outlooks and suboutlooks, through "taking seriously" some particular element in the outlook and seeking to bring it to fulfillment within the existing order. A program accepts much of the prevailing institutional and value systems, although it fervently rejects one sector. Thus, a program stands midway between an ideology and a prevailing outlook or suboutlook. It can be reached from either direction (and testifies thereby to the affinities between ideologies and outlooks and creeds).

The programmatic forms of ideological orientation are sometimes concentrated on particular and segmented objects, e.g., the abolition of slavery or the rights of a particular sector of the population such as an ethnic group or a social stratum. They do not expand to the point where they embrace the whole society as the objects of the sought-for transformation. Attachment to the central institutional or value systems might be so strong that it survives an intense but segmental alienation with respect to particular institutional practices or particular beliefs. This is characteristic of certain modern "reform movements." These have focused their attention and efforts on a specific segment of the central institutional system, attacking it with a rigorism which insists on the conformity of conduct with moral principles, and which will neither yield nor compromise. The programs and the movements which are their structural counterparts do not insist on the complete transformation of the whole society but they are uncompromisingly insistent on the attainment of their particular restricted, ideally prescribed end.

Often these movements have, in such instances, been borne by a small circle of persons organized into a quasi-ideological primary group which to some extent draws boundaries around itself and regards itself as disjunctively separated from its enemies, who are not, however, as in more fully developed ideological primary groups, regarded as identical with the totality of the environing society.

A creed differs from an ideology, though it often shades off into one. Because creeds do not tend to take a sharply bounded corporate form and because they have very little orthodoxy compared with ideologies they cannot command the concerted intellectual power of ideologies. Subscription to them tends therefore to be partial, fragmentary, and occasional. Unless a creed is taken in hand by a school of thought it does not undergo systematic elaboration and its scope is not broadened to a point of universal comprehensiveness. Its founder or inspiring genius might have created a coherent system of moral, social, and political philosophy, which in its comprehensiveness, elaborateness, and explicitness might be equivalent to the intellectual core of an ideology, but if he forms neither a school of thought nor an ideological primary group, his influence, however great, will be carried by the winds. Each will take from it what he wants: it will become a pervasive influence but it will lose the unity and the force which it would have needed to be an ideology. If, furthermore, the great thinker is neither far-reachingly alienated from the central value and institutional systems of his society (and thus has no need for disjunction) nor unqualifiedly insistent on the complete realization of his doctrine in the conduct of his followers, there is little chance that an ideology will flow from his intellectual construction. At best, he will generate a creed or a school of thought.

Proto-ideological Phenomena

Another variant of ideological phenomena is to be seen in those collectivities which, although "sodality-like" in structure, such as adolescent gangs and military and paramilitary units, do not have the intellectual patterns which we call ideological. Alienated in outlook from the prevailing outlook associated with the central institutional and value systems, they draw sharply defined boundaries around themselves. They insist on a concentration of loyalty to the group and on stringent discipline to the standards of the group. They have simplistic criteria of partisanship and enmity. They do not, however, develop or espouse a coherent moral and intellectual doctrine. They have no well-developed, principled view of the contemporary society which surrounds them, and, no less important, they have no image of a comprehensive order to replace permanently the order from which they are alienated. The "world" is their enemy with which they are at war, but they have no interest in taking it over and refashioning it in the name of a cosmically significant principle. In this respect they approximate the "withdrawn" ideological primary groups, but unlike these they are aggressively at war with an enemy and they lack an intellectual culture.

The failure of proto-ideological primary groups to develop an ideology might be attributed to the insufficient intellectual endowment of their members and above all to the absence of a charismatic ideological personality, sufficiently educated or sufficiently creative intellectually to provide them with a more complex system of beliefs. They lack sufficient contact with both the central value system and the tradition of ideological orientation. They are "rebels without a cause." (The boys' gang cultures of the great cities of the Western world are typical of these proto-ideological formations, in contrast with the more ideological German youth groups of the last years of the nineteenth century to the coming of World War II.)

The Functions of Ideologies

Ideologies are often accepted by persons who by temperament or by culture are ideologically predisposed. Such persons might be inclined to express their views with aggressive affect, they might feel a strong need to distinguish between comrades and enemies, or they might have been raised in a salvationary, apocalyptic culture. There are, however, persons who are neither but who come under ideological influence fortuitously or through the strain of crisis when they need the support of an ideology. For such persons, ideologies— up to a point and for a limited time—can exert a powerful influence. By making them conceive of themselves as in contact with the ultimate powers of existence, their motivation to act will be greatly reinforced. They will gain courage from perceiving themselves as part of a cosmic scheme; actions which they would not dare to envisage before now will have the legitimacy which proximity to the sacred provides.

Ideologies intend either the disruption of the central institutional and value systems by conflict with them or the denial of their claims by withdrawal from them. They aim in the former case at "total" replacement. They do not succeed in this even where their bearers are successful in the acquisition of power in the larger society. Where an ideological primary group succeeds in overcoming existing elites and comes to rule over the society, it is incapable of completely and enduringly suppressing the previously predominant outlook. It is unsuccessful on a number of grounds, first of all because of the strength of attachments to the central value systems among the population at large and because, in view of this, the resources for their suppression available to the ideological elites are not adequate— too much remains outside the scope of their control or surveillance. Then as time passes, some, although never all, of the previously prevailing outlook reasserts itself. This process is assisted by the fact that the members of the ideological primary group themselves, in the course of time, fall away from their zealous espousal of the ideology. When they fall away, many of them fall back toward one of the cultural outlooks from which the ideology sprang. Partial return occurs also because as the ideological primary group continues in power, the obstacles to the realization of their goals, the multiplicity of alternative paths of action, etc., cause some of the members of the group (especially newly recruited ones) to have recourse to ideas which fall outside the once-adhered-to, ideological system of thought.

Although ideological primary groups, whether or not they succeed in their aspiration to rule, inevitably fail in the fulfillment of their global aspirations, they often leave a profound impact on the "normal" pattern of value orientations which they have sought to overcome and which either persists or reasserts itself. They leave behind adherents who survive despite failure and in the face of restoration. Where routinization occurs, as in the case of an ideological elite which is not expelled from authority, the new routine is never the same as the one which it replaced, however much it diverges from the stringent demands of the ideology in the name of which it was originally established.

Once the ideological orientation comes to be passed on to the next generation by tradition as well as by systematic teaching, it encounters the resistances which are characteristic of intergenerational relationships, and these in their turn introduce modification in the direction of compromise and adaptation to primordial and personal needs as well as to civil exigencies. But there, too, the ideological orientation has not lived in vain. Those who appear to reject it or to have become more indifferent to it live under a tradition which has absorbed at least some of the heightened accents which the ideology has brought to the constellation of elements taken over from the prevailing outlook or suboutlooks.

Where an expansive ideological primary group does not succeed in attaining dominance, if it endures for a substantial period and has impinged on the awareness of the custodians of the central institutional and value system, it precipitates a partial reorientation of the previously dominant outlook, bringing about a new emphasis within the framework of the older outlook. It renews sensibilities, it heightens consciousness of the demands of moral and cognitive orientations which have slipped into a state of partial ineffectiveness. The old order against which it contended is never the same because the old order has adapted itself and assimilated into itself some of the emphases of the ideology.

Truth and Ideology

The question of the relationship between truth and ideology has been raised by the tradition of European thought which culminated in Marxism and in the sociology of knowledge developed by Karl Mannheim. According to this view, ideology was by its nature untruthful since it entailed a "masking" or "veiling" of unavowed and unperceived motives or "interests." These "interests" impelled the deception of antagonists and the transfiguration of narrow sectional ends and interests through their ostensible universalization. They distorted reality to the ideologists as well as to their antagonists. Ideology was a manifestation of a "false consciousness," and, given the position of the ideologists in the historical process and in the development of the spirit, it could not be otherwise.

Viewed from a more dispassionate standpoint, which is less involved in a particular historical metaphysic and less involved in proving everyone else wrong and itself incontestably and cosmically right, the question of the compatibility of scientific or scholarly truth with ideology does not admit of a single univocal answer. Ideologies, like all complex cognitive patterns, contain many propositions, and even though the ideologies strive and claim to possess systematic integration, this is seldom the case. Hence, true propositions can coexist with false ones. Ideologies hostile to the prevailing outlook and the central institutional system of that society have, not infrequently, contained truthful propositions about important particular features of the existing order, or they have pointed to particular variables, which were either not perceived or not acknowledged by scholars and thinkers who took a more affirmative or at least a less alienated attitude towards the existing order. On the other hand, they have no less frequently been in fundamental error about very important aspects of social structure, especially about the working of the central institutional system, about which they have had so many hostile fantasies.

With reference to the cognitive truthfulness of ideologies, it should be pointed out that no great ideology has ever regarded the disciplined pursuit of truth by the procedures and in the mood characteristic of modern science as part of its obligations. The very conception of an autonomous sphere and an autonomous tradition of disciplined intellectual activity is alien to the totalistic demands of the ideological orientation. Ideologies do not accredit the independent cognitive powers and strivings of man. This view is shared by the proposition that ideologies must necessarily be distortions of reality because they are impelled by considerations of prospective advantage or of interest. Like the ideological orientation, the view that asserts the inevitability of false consciousness assumes that cognitive motives and standards play little part in the determination of success or failure in the assessment of reality. It assumes that training in observation and discrimination, discipline in their exercise, rational criticism, and intellectual tradition are of little importance in the formation of propositions about reality. This is obviously incorrect in principle—even though, in reality, evaluative and therewith ideological orientations have often hampered the free exercise of the powers of reason, observation, and judgment. Its incorrectness must be acknowledged as such by those who assert that all knowledge is ideological and truth cannot be discerned because interests and passions interfere—at least if they believe in the truthfulness of their own assertion.

It is, of course, true that the ideological culture—in the sense described earlier—does in fact often interfere with the attainment of truth. To the extent that it does so, it is, however, a result of the closure of the ideological disposition to new evidence and its distrust of all who do not share the same ideological disposition. The chief source of tension between ideology and truth lies, therefore, in the demands of the exponents of ideologies for disciplined adherence on the part of their fellow believers, and their concurrent insistence on the unity of belief and conduct. Both these features of the ideological orientation make for dogmatic inflexibility and unwillingness to allow new experiences to contribute to the growth of truth. This applies particularly to the social sciences, the subject matter of which overlaps so considerably with that of ideology, and which is therefore so often the object of ideological and quasi-ideological judgments. The tension is less pronounced with respect to the natural sciences. There, too, however, since ideologies concern themselves with man's nature and the nature of the universe, and because they insist on the unity of knowledge, they inhibit the growth of understanding. Thus, however great the insight contained in some ideologies, the potentialities for the further development of understanding within the context of the ideology or by the efforts of the ideologists—especially where the proponents succeed in establishing control of the central institutional system, and above all of the central cultural institutional system—are hampered and deformed.

A related question, which has often been discussed, is whether all forms of scientific knowledge in the natural and social sciences are parts of ideologies. In the sense in which ideology has been defined and used in the foregoing analysis, this proposition must be rejected. The great advances in scientific knowledge have been influenced here and there by fragments of ideologies or quasi ideologies, just as they have been influenced by prevailing outlooks and suboutlooks. (The latter by virtue of their inherent pluralism allow more freedom for the uninhibited exercise of the cognitive powers of man.) But science is not and has never been an integral part of an ideological culture. The spirit in which science works is alien to ideology. Marxism is the only great ideology which has had a substantial scientific content, and the social sciences have in certain respects benefited from it. Nonetheless, the modern social sciences have not grown up in the context of ideologies, and their progress has carried with it an erosion of ideology. It is true that the social sciences have formed part of the prevailing outlook or suboutlooks of sectors of the educated classes of various modern societies. They have often been oppositional and critical toward various aspects of the existing social and cultural systems—but they have been so more as parts of some suboutlook rather than as part of an ideology. Strictly understood, they have absorbed and attenuated bits of ideologies but they themselves have not been either ideologies or parts of ideologies. They have not been ideological. Indeed, they have had a solvent effect on ideologies and in a sense are antiideological.

Insofar as the social sciences have been genuinely intellectual undertakings, with their own rules of observation and judgment, open to criticism and revision, they have not been ideological and are in fact antipathetic to ideology. The fact that they have come increasingly to contribute to the prevailing outlook of their respective societies is not and cannot be a judgment concerning their truthfulness.

All this is not intended to deny that scientific activities and outlooks, both in procedure and in substance, are parts of a general culture or in the sense used above, a prevailing outlook. But they are very loosely integrated parts of those cultures or outlooks—just as the various parts of science are not completely integrated among themselves. It is characteristic of prevailing outlooks to be loosely integrated, and no single element predominates exclusively over the others. In a great variety of ways the scientific and nonscientific parts of prevailing outlooks and suboutlooks influence each other, and at the same time each possesses considerable autonomy. It is likely that this relationship will become more intense in the future and that scientific knowledge, although never becoming exclusively dominant, will have an even greater influence on prevailing outlooks and suboutlooks than it has had hitherto. For all these reasons, assertions to the effect that "science is an ideology" or "the social sciences are as ideological as the ideologies they criticize" must be rejected.

The End of Ideology

In the 1950s, with the beginning of the "thaw" in the communist countries and the growing disillusionment about the realization of Marxist ideology in the advanced countries, reference was frequently made to an "end of ideology." The conception was originally intended by those who propounded it to refer to the then obtaining situation. Antagonists of the idea took it, however, to imply that ideologies in the sense used in this article could never again exist. They took it also to mean that ideals, ethical standards, general or comprehensive social views and policies, were no longer either relevant or possible in human society. This was a misunderstanding engendered to some extent by the failure of both proponents and critics of the concept of the "end of ideology" to distinguish between ideology and outlook. A better understanding of the distinction might have obviated much of the contention. It is still worthwhile to attempt to clarify some of the issues raised by the phrase.

In the first place, it is obvious that no society can exist without a cognitive, moral, and expressive culture. Standards of truth, beauty, goodness are inherent in the structure of human action. The culture which is generated from cognitive, moral, and expressive needs and which is transmitted and sustained by tradition is part of the very constitution of society. Thus every society, having a culture, will have a complex set of orientations toward man, society, and the universe in which ethical and metaphysical propositions, aesthetic judgments, and scientific knowledge will be present. These will form the outlooks and suboutlooks of the society. Thus there can never be an "end" of outlooks or suboutlooks. The contention arose from the failure to distinguish these and ideology in the sense here understood.

But the theoretical conception implicit in the idea of "the end of ideology" goes further than this. It asserts not only that the culture referred to is capable of being in a state of loose integration, with much autonomy of its different parts, but that in fact the ongoing cultures of societies of any considerable degree of differentiation are bound most of the time to be in that state, and that they cannot be completely supplanted by ideologies. This same implicit theory regards an ideological state of high integration of the elements of a culture to be a marginal state and a highly unstable one. The ideological state is one which is incapable of enduring extension to an entire society.

The exponents of the "end of ideology" were taking note of (a) the recession of the titanic attempts in Europe to extend the ideologies of fascism and communism to entire societies, and (b) the diminution of the belief among Western intellectuals that such extensions were enduringly possible and desirable.

Moreover, the exponents of the "end of ideology" did not assert or imply that the human race had reached a condition or a stage of development in and after which ideologies could no longer occur. The potentiality for ideology seems to be a permanent part of the human constitution. In conditions of crisis when hitherto prevailing elites fail and are discredited, when the central institutions and culture with which they associate themselves seem unable to find the right course of action, ideological propensities are heightened. The need for a direct contact with the sources or powers of creativity and legitimacy and for a comprehensive organization of life permeated by those powers is an intermittent and occasional need in most human beings and an overwhelming and continued need in a few. The confluence of the aroused need in the former with the presence of the latter generates and intensifies ideological orientations. As long as human societies are afflicted by crises, and as long as man has a need to be in direct contact with the sacred, ideologies will recur. The strongly ideological elements in the tradition contained in the modern Western outlook are almost a guarantee of the persistent potentiality. The idea of the "end of ideology" was only an assertion that the potentiality for ideology need not always be realized, and that the potentiality was receding in the West, in the fifties. It asserted that this was coming to be recognized and that both the facts and their recognition were desirable for the good ordering of society and man's well-being.

3   Ideology and Civility

I

An ideological outlook encircled and invaded public life in the Western countries during the nineteenth century, and in the twentieth century it threatened to achieve universal dominion. The intellectual classes which concerned themselves with politics were particularly affected. The intensity of the attack has varied from country to country. It has been least severe in the United States and Great Britain; in France, Germany, Italy, and Russia, it possessed an overwhelming power. Wherever it became sufficiently strong, it paralyzed the free dialectic of intellectual life, introducing standards irrelevant to discovery and creation, and in politics it inhibited or broke the flexible consensus necessary for a free and spontaneous order. It appeared in a variety of manifestations, each alleging itself to be unique. Italian Fascism, German National Socialism, Russian Bolshevism, French and Italian Communism, the Action Française, the British Union of Fascists—and their fledgling American kinsman, "McCarthyism," which died in infancy—have all, however, been members of the same family. They have all sought to conduct politics on an ideological plane.

What are the articles of faith of ideological politics? First and above all, the assumption that politics should be conducted from the standpoint of a coherent, comprehensive set of beliefs which must override every other consideration. These beliefs attribute supreme significance to one group or class—the nation, the ethnic folk, the proletariat—and the leader and the party as the true representative of these residences of all virtue, and they correspondingly view as the seat and source of all evil a foreign power, an ethnic group like the Jews, or the bourgeois class. Ideological politics have not been merely the politics of a dualistic faith which confines itself to the political sphere. The centrality of this belief has required that it radiate into every sphere of life—that it replace religion, that it provide aesthetic criteria, that it rule over scientific research and philosophic thought, that it regulate sexual and family life.

It has been the belief of those who practice politics ideologically that they alone have the truth about the right ordering of life—of life as a whole, and not just of political life. From this has followed a deep distrust of the traditional institutions—family, church,

Previously published in a slightly different form in *Sewanee Review*, vol. 66, no. 3 (July-September, 1958), pp. 450-80.

economic organizations, and schools—and the institutional system through which politics have been conventionally carried on in modern society. Ideological politics have required, therefore, a distrust of politicians[1] and of the system of parties through which they work. Insofar as ideological politics have been carried on by organizations calling themselves political parties, it has only been because that term has become conventional for organizations actively concerned with politics. It has not signified that their proponents were ready to participate constitutionally in the political system. Extra-constitutionality has been inherent in their conceptions and aspirations, even when their procedures have seemed to lie within the constitution—and by constitution, we mean not just written constitution, laws, and judicial decisions, but the moral presuppositions of these. Ideological politics have taken up a platform outside the "system." In their agitation, ideological politicians have sought to withdraw the loyalty of the population from the "system" and to destroy it, replacing it by a new order. This new order would have none of the evils which make up the existing system; the new order would be fully infused with the ideological belief which alone can provide salvation.

Ideological politics are alienative politics. They are the politics of those who shun the central institutional system of the prevailing society. Ideological politicians feel no affinity with such institutions, and they participate in them for purposes very different from those who have preceded them in the conduct of these institutions.[2]

1. The hostile attitude toward politicians, toward the "parliamentary talking shop," with its unprincipled compromise of interests, and the petty quality of the personnel of civil politics are continuing themes of the ideologist. Hitler said that politicians were "people whose only real principle was unprincipledness, coupled with an insolent and pushing officiousness and shamelessly developed mendacity" (*Mein Kampf* [Munich, 1941], p. 72). "Parliament itself is given up to talk for the special purpose of fooling the 'common people'" (Lenin, "State and Revolution," in *Towards the Seizure of Power,* book 2, *Collected Works,* vol. 221 [New York, 1932], p. 186). At the other pole of intellectual sophistication, Edmund Wilson, during his own ideological phase, once wrote, "Our society has . . . produced in its specialized professional politicians one of the most obnoxious groups which has ever disgraced human history—a group that seems unique in having managed to be corrupt, uncultivated, and incompetent all at once" (*New Republic,* 14 January 1931, reprinted in *The Shores of Light* [London, 1952], p. 529). The antipolitical literature of the ideological intellectual is vast: Hilaire Belloc and G. K. Chesterton, *The Party System* (London, 1911), is representative.

2. Aneurin Bevan, who had within him, together with other gifts, a powerful ideological strain, wrote of the radical's entry into the House of Commons: "Here he is, a tribune of the people, coming to make his voice heard in the seats of power . . . The first thing he should bear in mind is that these were not his ancestors. His ancestors had no part in the past, the accumulated dust of which now muffles his own footfalls. His forefathers were tending sheep or plowing the land, or serving the statesmen whose names he

For the ideological politician, membership in a parliamentary body or the acceptance of office involves only an opportunity to overthrow and destroy the system rather than to work within it and improve it.[3]

Ideological politics are the politics of "friend-foe,"[4] "we-they," "who-whom."[5] Those who are not on the side of the ideological politician are, according to the ideologist, against him.

Thus, moral separatism arises from the sharp, stable, and unbridgeable dualism of ideological politics which makes the most radical and uncompromising distinction between good and evil, left and right, national and unnational, American and un-American. Admixtures are intolerable, and where they exist they are denied as unreal, misleading, or unstable.[6]

Ideological politics have been obsessed with totality. They have been obsessed with futurity. They have believed that sound politics require a doctrine which comprehends every event in the universe, not only in space but in time. To live from year to year and to keep afloat, to solve the problems of the year and of the decade are not enough for ideological politics. Ideological politicians must see their actions in the context of the totality of history. They must see themselves moving toward a culmination of history, either a new epoch, totally new in every important respect, or bringing to a glorious fulfillment a condition which has long been lost from human life. Whether totally without precedent or a renewal of the

---

sees written on the walls around him, and whose portraits look down upon him in the long corridors . . . In him, his people are here for the first time and the history he will make will not be merely an episode in the story he is now reading. It must be wholly different, as different as the social status he now brings with him" (*In Place of Fear* [New York, 1952], p. 6).

3. Cf. Leon Trotsky, *Whither England?* (New York, 1925), pp. 111-12: "We Communists are by no means disposed to advise the . . . proletariat to turn its back on Parliament. . . . The question . . . is not whether it is worthwhile to use the Parliamentary method at all, but . . . is it possible to use Parliament, created by Capitalism, in the interests of its own growth and preservation, as a lever for the overthrow of capitalism."

4. Carl Schmitt, *Der Bergiff des Politischen* (Munich, Leipzig, 1932), pp. 14 ff.

5. Striking evidence of the separatism of ideological politics may be found in N. Leites, *The Study of Bolshevism* (Glencoe, Ill., 1953), pp. 291-309, 384-90, 430-42.

6. Cf. Raymond Aron, *The Opium of the Intellectuals* (New York: Doubleday, 1957), chap. 1, "The Myth of the Left." The deep-rootedness of the mythology of left and right among intellectuals of the Marxist tradition, and its penetration even into allegedly scientific research in sociology and social psychology, are treated in my essay "Authoritarianism 'Left' and 'Right,'" in Richard Christie and Marie Jahoda, *Studies in the "Authoritarian Personality"* (Glencoe, Ill., 1954), pp. 24-49.

long lost, the ultimate stage will be something unique in history.[7]
Everything else is a waiting and a preparation for that remote event.

II

What are the grounds for thinking that the age of ideological politics
is passing? How can we summon the naïveté to think such a thing,
when the world is frozen into a menacing division engendered and
maintained by Bolshevik ideas, when the communist parties of
France and Italy are among the largest in their countries, when in
the Middle East, in Africa, and in Asia passionate nationalist and
ethnic ideologies continuously encroach on rational judgment and
reasonable moral action.

Yet the expectation is not simply frivolously optimistic. The very
heart which has sustained ideological politics among intellectuals
over the past century is gradually losing its strength. Marxism is
decomposing. The mythology of Bolshevik Marxism, the true nature
of which was seen at first only by Bertrand Russell, Waldemar
Gurian, and a handful of European Social Democrats and liberals,
began its own self-deflation in the mid-1930s, at the moment of its
maximum appeal to the world's intellectuals. The Moscow Trials
were the first major step in the breakdown of the communist claim
that in the Soviet Union the ultimate stage of human history, the
true realm of freedom, was being entered upon. The Berlin uprising
of 17 June 1953 was a step further. The realm of harmony through
which mankind would transcend its conflict-ridden history was
unveiled as a phantasm when Russian tanks shot down German
workingmen in the streets of Berlin. According to Marxism, there
could only be harmony between socialist societies bound together
by the solidarity of the proletariat, but the Soviet Union showed no
compunction about suppressing the East German workers by force.
The eagerness with which Hungarian and Polish intellectuals greeted
their prospective emancipation from a compulsory Marxism and the
Russian repression of the Hungarian Revolution of 1956 also
contributed to the demythologizing of Marxism.

Political events alone have not discredited Marxism. Perhaps more

7. The Communist Manifesto declared that in place of a class society with
its classes and class antagonisms there would be a new free society "in which
the free development of each is the condition for the free development of all."
In the first edition, this was regarded by its authors as an entirely unique
condition: "The history of all hitherto existing society" being "the history of
class struggles." In 1888, Engels added a footnote which corrected this view,
saying "all written history" was the history of class conflict. There had been a
prehistorical period of communally owned property which was free of class
conflict. Communism would thus be a renewal on a higher plane of what had
been lost since the beginning of history (Marx and Engels, *Historisch-kritsche
Gesamtausgabe,* part 1, vol. 6 [Moscow, Leningrad, 1933], pp. 525-26, 546).

important is its sheer unresponsiveness to the multiplicity of life itself. People still have a need to believe, but Marxism cannot satisfy it. Its formulae are too simple, and it offers nothing to those who are attempting to establish their intellectual individuality in the face of large-scale organizations and their accompanying professional specialization. The humanitarian element in Marxism—its alleged concern for the poor—can have no appeal when there are still many very poor people in communist countries, and the poor in capitalist countries can now be seen to be much better off than their opposite numbers in communist countries. Marxist utopianism has lost its power of conviction—the world is too tired and even, in this respect, too wise to be aroused by promises of a future which might be spurious and which would not be much different from the present. Journals like *Dissent* in the United States and the *Universities and Left Review* in Great Britain have been valiant and touching efforts to save something of the ideological heritage. But they show how much ideological politics are now on the defensive, and how uncertain they are of the validity of their position. They know that their myth has faded, and that with good grounds, the intellectual spirit of the times is running against them. In every sphere of intellectual life, in economic theory, in history, and in sociology, Marxism has lost its power to attract because it is too simplistic, too threadbare intellectually and morally, and too often just wrong or irrelevant to the problems of the contemporary mind.[8] The emergence of the social sciences as major subjects of university research and teaching—even though they have their serious limitations and even though they sometimes bear a Marxist imprint—constitutes a major factor in the tarnishing of Marxism.

Nationalism too has lost its doctrinal grip on the intellectuals of the West. Its deeper, primordial hold is very strong, but it does not reach into the plane where it could provide for political judgment and action, and even less does it provide a criterion for regulating other spheres of life. In the twentieth century among Western intellectuals doctrinal nationalism has never been long preponderant, although in France among the followers of Maurras and Barrès there has been a persistent and virulent minority. In Germany, it for a time suffocated reason, and in Italy under fascism it found many willing proponents. Now, however, it is dormant. It might even be said that it is at its lowest ebb in Europe and America since the Risorgimento and the movement for the unification of the Reich. The hideous example of National Socialism, the terrible national

8. Even Professor Merleau-Ponty, against whose ingenious efforts to fuse existentialism and early Marxism Professor Aron directed an unsparingly detailed and devastating criticism, lost some of his confidence in Marxism in his last years.

intoxication, and the monstrous deeds committed in the name of the nation have for the time being at least exhausted the ideological passions of the German people—intellectuals and laity. The fatigue and waste of the past world wars and the ominous possibility of an even worse war to come add themselves to all the other elements in the constitution of the intellectual outlook to render nationalistic enthusiasm one of the least attractive of all the available alternatives of the present time.

Moreover, the asperities of the debate between socialism and capitalism seem to be fading. The achievements of the American and Western European economies since the war, together with the political equivocality of centrally planned economies, the failures of economic planning in the Soviet satellite states, the reintroduction of the principles of the market economy into their economies by some of the communist states, and the modest and by no means glamorous achievements of nationalized industries in England and France, have cooled the fires of a century-long dispute between the proponents of socialism and the advocates of capitalism.

The more valid aspirations of the older humanitarian elements which were absorbed into Marxism have been more or less fulfilled in capitalist countries. The socialist and communist countries have neither realized their more grandiose ideals at all nor achieved their more reasonable aspirations any better than the capitalistic countries.

The Negro problem in the United States of course arouses passions, but no doctrines, no principles offer an apparently easy way out. The "woman question" has settled down to being a perennial headache, curable by no enunciation or espousal of clear and unambiguous principles. The ideology of egalitarianism has left the fundamental precipitate of moral egalitarianism from which it originally arose, but as a universally applicable principle it has lost its glamor. It seems almost as if what was sound in the older ideologies has been realized and what was unsound has demonstrated its unsoundness so obviously that enthusiasm sustained by reason can no longer be summoned.

Of course, ideological politics, Marxist, Islamic, Arabic, Hindu, Pan-African, and other, still exist in the new states outside the West in a vehement, irreconcilable form and often with great influence. But many in the West who sympathize with the desires and deplore the excesses are inclined to believe that they too will pass when the new states in which they flourish become more settled and mature. Looking back from the standpoint of a newly achieved moderation, Western intellectuals view the ideological politics of Asia and Africa, and particularly nationalism and tribalism, as a sort of measles which afflicts a people in its childhood but to which adults are practically immune.

There seems to be no alternative ideology for the intellectuals to turn to now, nothing to absorb their intelligence, nothing to inflame their capacity for faith and their aspirations toward perfection. The conservative revival, though genuine, is moderate. People take Burke in their stride. They have become "natural Burkeans" without making a noise about it. The *National Review,* despite its clamor, is isolated and unnoticed, and the effort to create a "conservative ideology" which would stand for more than moderation, reasonableness, and prudence has not been successful.[9]

There seem to be no good grounds for ideological politics. Thus, it appears reasonable to think that the age of ideological politics is gradually coming to its end. The flurries of romantic enthusiasm of the late 1960s do not belie the deeper trend.

III

One of the grounds for believing that the age of ideological politics is ending is its modernity.

Professor Aron has put forward the view that ideological politics originated in the French Revolution.[10] There is much truth to this contention. Ideological politics did indeed come into the forum of public life only at the end of the eighteenth century in an outburst not hitherto experienced by the human race.

The reason for this relatively recent appearance of ideological politics on a grand scale is not far to seek. Until recent centuries politics were not public. In the aristocratic republics and in the ancient city democracies, politics did not engage the attention of the mass of the population. Politics were the concern of rulers and of those who aspired to become rulers. The aspiration was, however, spread over a relatively small section of the population. Tribal, feudal, and dynastic interests, which were uppermost in the political life of societies before modern times, did not nourish the ideological outlook. There was, moreover, no intellectual class as a major factor in politics. Where the educated were taken into the civil service, as in China, in ancient Rome, and in the European Middle Ages, the bureaucratic ethos and personal dependence on the prince, to say nothing of the type of education preparatory for the civil service career, discouraged the emergence of an ideological orientation. The intrigues of court politics did not foster the success of the ideo-

9. Cf. Irving Kristol, "Old Truths and the New Conservatism," *The Yale Review,* Spring, 1958, pp. 365-73.
10. Aron, p. 42. The same view was put forward by Professor D. W. Brogan in his most interesting essay, "Was the French Revolution a Mistake?" *Cambridge Journal,* vol. 1, no. 1 (October 1947), pp. 43-55.

logically minded man. There was no class of independent professional literary men and journalists, free of patrons and of the need to remain on the right side of the authorities.

The violent political struggles of the Greek city-states and of the last decades of the Roman Republic, even where they involved the bitterest class antagonisms, did not become ideological. They were fought on behalf of "interests." The notions of "justice" and of the "good social order" did not enter into them except peripherally.

The ideological orientation toward life existed, of course, as it must exist wherever human society exists. It passed judgment on all things, and so it passed judgment on political things. It censured the existing political order as a realm of iniquity, and counseled and predicted its destruction. This ideological attitude toward politics did not, however, enter the sphere of political activity, because the kinds of persons who espoused it or came under its influence were not admitted into the circles which discussed and decided on succession to political office and on the actions of governments.

As long as politics were not an instrument of justice or of the realization of the right social order and were concerned with the mere maintenance of order, the conservation of the power of dynasties and classes which already had or sought it, there was no room for ideological politics. Those who practiced politics were not susceptible to them, except on rare occasions, and they found no following even where great individual personalities were moved by ideological—above all, religious—considerations.

The invention of printing and the possibility arising therefrom of diffusing arguments to a wider public, the Protestant belief that the Bible and not the priesthood is the vehicle of the sacred, and the slow and gradual rising of the mass of European populations from their torpor—all of these had much to do with the creation of the necessary conditions for ideological politics. The crucial element, however, was the creation of a class of intellectuals no longer dependent exclusively on patronage or inheritance for their livelihood.

The body of intellectuals which came into existence in the sixteenth century was a new phenomenon in world history. It consisted of men whose sensibility, intelligence, and imagination carried them beyond the standards and requirements of everyday life; they were no longer forced to depend on church or state or princely, aristocratic, or mercantile patronage for their existence. Their capacity for loyalty thus liberated, they were endowed with the freedom to attach themselves to symbols beyond those embodied in existing ecclesiastical and governmental institutions. The steady growth in the scale and importance of this stratum of the population in modern European societies is perhaps the decisive factor in the "ideologization" which, on its better side, has been called the "spiritualization of politics." The intellectuals—who before the development of specialized technical training were coterminous with the educated classes—have lived in a permanent tension between earthly power and the ideal, which derives from their nature as intellectuals. They have not, however, created from within themselves the imagery and passion of ideological politics. The numerous traditions which they have developed, e.g., the romantic tradition, the scientistic tradition, the bohemian tradition, important though they have been in disposing intellectuals toward ideological politics, would scarcely have been sufficient to give to such politics their extraordinary attraction and compellingness.

Ideological politics are rooted in an ideological tradition which lives in our midst through invisible radiations coming down from the depths of our Western past. They are sustained by our Judaic-Christian culture, by passions which are part of our souls, and by the nature of human society.

The millenarian tradition which is the oldest source of the ideological outlook is an ever-present potentiality in Christian teaching and experience; it is usually maintained, for most persons, most of the time, in a state of latency. It has a living existence in the life of the Protestant sects and in the records of the saints of every Christian society. Even where religious belief has become attenuated or has evaporated, the millenarian expectations and judgments have persisted in an aromatic tradition which, on occasion, becomes crystallized in a sensitive and receptive person. Religious enthusiasm, as the late Ronald Knox[11] showed with such compassionate understanding and as Professor Cohn,[12] writing from a very different point of view, has corroborated, has never been absent from Western civilization. As early as pre-Exilic times, Jewish prophets foretold the cataclysmic end of time and the world as we know it, a Day of Wrath and a Last Judgment, when sinners, individual and corporate, would be cast down, and a regenerated Israel would populate Palestine and a second Eden.

The expectations of a Last Judgment on a sinful temporal order took a deep root in the early Christian communities. The tradition did not die out as the Church settled down to live on as an institution. Manichaeism, with its basic distinctions between light and darkness and its conception of the universe as a field of irreconcilable struggle between the forces of light and the forces of darkness, found hospitality in the Christian circles where this chiliastic tradition persisted. No church, indeed, no established

11. *Enthusiasm: A Chapter in the History of Religion, with Special Reference to the XVII and XVIII Centuries* (Oxford, 1950).
12. *The Pursuit of the Millennium* (London, 1957).

institution, could survive if its members expected an imminent end of the world and its subsequent replacement by the Kingdom of God. It was to meet this view that Saint Augustine elaborated his conception of the Church itself as the Kingdom of God on earth. But for those with a great sensitivity to the sacred, and disciplined intellect, no living church could ever represent the Kingdom of God. Insofar as it refused to preach the proximate realization of the Kingdom of God, it rendered itself subject to their most anguished and harshest criticism.

Professor Cohn, who was not concerned either to support the Marxist view that millenarian sectarianism was merely the ideology of a class conflict expressed in a religious idiom or to espouse the anti-Marxist view which argues that millenarianism was solely an expression of a hypersensitive and perhaps disordered religiosity, was at his best when he showed how it fused with the animosities of class, of ethnic hatreds, and of fantasies of national glory. The hatred-filled fantasies of princes, lords, wealthy merchants, the pope, Jews, Turks, Italians, Saracens were amalgamated with the frightful images of Satan and the Antichrist. In its meandering and tragic history, full of misery, persecution, and violence, rabid and deluded yearnings, false messiahs, deranged visions, hostility, and pitched battles, a single complex theme runs unbrokenly. This is the central theme of the ideological orientation toward existence.

The ideological outlook is preoccupied with the evil of the world as it exists; it believes in the immiscibility of good and evil. It distinguishes sharply between the children of light and the children of darkness. It believes that no earthly action can ameliorate or attenuate evil. It exhibits a violent hatred of the existing cosmic order, and especially of its earthly beneficiaries, governmental, economic, and ecclesiastical authorities, indeed, of authorities of any kind. It regards authority as an agent of evil and as a compromise with evil.

The mass of mankind lives in constant temptation and seduction by evil; the petty concerns of daily work and commerce, attachment to family, loyalty to friends, and the quest of private advantage are all inextricably involved with evil. Those who take upon themselves to rule the world as it is, are either corrupt in their very nature to begin with, or become so through their contact with authority, which is diabolical by nature.

The ideological outlook expressed by millenarianism asserts, however, that the reign of evil on the earth is of finite duration. There will come a moment when time and history as we know them shall come to an end. The present period of history will be undone by a cosmic act of judgment which will do justice to the wronged and virtuous by elevating them to eternal bliss, and equal justice to the powerful and wicked by degrading and destroying them for all time to come. The order which will be ushered in by the cosmic last judgment will be a new realm of perfect harmony and peace, in which all men will live in accordance with the ultimate criteria of justice and mutual love. No conflict will mar their existence; there will be no scarcity to degrade and cramp them.

To usher in this glorious epoch requires heroism on the part of the small number of consecrated persons who live strictly in accordance with the dictates of the highest judgment. Heroism is required, above all, to give witness to the truth of the standards which ultimately will come to prevail and to help to inaugurate this totally new phase of existence.

Despite its extraordinary persistence, the millenarian tradition has been no ordinary tradition transmitted by the elders of a society to their next generation. Its reception is not the ordinary reception of tradition as something given, but a search and a yearning. There is no evidence of continuity of the movement of this tradition from person to person, and it is not commonly taught in any society. It is a phenomenon of the sinks and corners of society, and it creates groups which, in a state of inflammation, are remarkably short-lived as compared with the long history of the churches. The tradition, however, has a long and continuous history.[13] From the Near Eastern seedbed of enthusiastic religiosity, millenarian Christian sectarianism spread into Southeastern Europe and North Africa, from Bulgaria into Northern Italy, from Northern Italy into Southern France, from Southern France into the Low Countries, from the Low Countries into Germany and Central Europe and then into England. Yet the mechanism of its transmission remains a mystery. There is some evidence of personal links of the founders and spreaders of particular variants of millenarianism, but this does not explain why the soil was so fertile for their labors.

Similarly, although the inner affinities of millenarianism and modern revolutionary politics are now perfectly obvious,[14] the lines of filiation are more difficult to trace. The German Marxists' discovery of their own ancestry in the Anabaptists of Munster, in the

13. Cf. LeRoy Edwin Froom, *The Prophetic Faith of Our Fathers. The Historical Development of Prophetic Interpretation* (Washington, D.C.: Review and Herald, 1948), vols. 1-4; Steven Runciman, *The Medieval Manichee: A Study of the Christian Dualist Heresy* (Cambridge, 1947); Dmitri Obolensky, *The Bogomils: A Study in Balkan Neo-Manichaeism* (Cambridge, 1948); Knox, *Enthusiasm.* I should like also to call attention to a very sympathetic article by Miss Storm Jameson, "The Dualist Tradition," *Times Literary Supplement,* 6 August 1954.

14. Aron, chap. 9, "The Intellectuals in Search of a Religion," pp. 264-94; Erich Voegelin, *Die politischen Religionen* (Stockholm, 1939), pp. 39-42; Fritz Gerlich, *Der Kommunismus als Lehre vom tausendjährigen Reich* (Munich, 1920), esp. pp. 17-78.

Levellers and the Diggers of the English Civil War,[15] is an acknowledgment of the affinity, but is not evidence of a directly received influence.[16]

Perhaps the continuity of the millenarian outlook through many different situations arises not from a continuously handed-down tradition but from the recurrent attachment to its sources—the Book of Daniel, the Book of Revelation, the Sybilline Books, and the Johannine prophecy, which are available on the edge of our culture to all those who have a need for them. To these, time and again, persons with a yearning for the end of earthly injustice and the transcendence of time in a new and purer realm resplendent with harmony and love, have turned. In the past century, they have not had to go back to the original sources. Through the heirs of these sources, their transformations into the doctrines of contemporary ideological politics have been available in an idiom more acceptable to the contemporary mind.

Now, if this is no ordinary tradition, transmitted in the way ordinary traditions are transmitted, why then does it persist as such a recurrent theme in Western history? The answer must be sought in Christianity, which contains among its manifold potentialities the ever-present promise of a Second Coming and the unchanging imminence of the ultimate catastrophe which precedes the second coming of a Messiah. Although the central institutions of modern societies, out of the very necessities of their continuing existence and the nature of the human beings who live in them, preclude the widespread practice and observance of the ideological orientation, there are always some persons in these societies to whom the ideological orientation has an especial appeal. It is always there for those who have the ideological need to be in saving contact with the ultimate. Every society has its outcasts, its wretched, and its damned, who cannot fit into the routine requirements of social life at any level of authority and achievement. Max Weber said that salvationary religions are most commonly found among declining

15. Cf. Friedrich Engels, *The Peasant War in Germany* (New York, 1926); Karl Kautsky, *Communism in Central Europe in the Time of the Reformation* (London, 1897); Edward Bernstein, *Cromwell and Communism: Socialism and Democracy in the Great English Civil Revolution* (London, 1930); Ernst Bloch, *Thomas Münzer als Theologe der Revolution* (Munich, 1921).

16. The German working class movement of the 1840s and British working class radicalism did, it is true, thrive in areas which had been the scenes of Protestant sectarianism from the sixteenth to the eighteenth centuries. It is a plausible hypothesis that the ideological traditions of sectarian life made for a receptivity to revolutionary and radical ideas by virtue of their correspondences; in turn, aided by theorists more deeply dyed by the revolutionary traditions of the French Revolution and the Hegelian (and ultimately Christian) idea of history, the tradition of religious enthusiasm was transformed into an apparently secular heroic doctrine of ideological politics.

strata of handicraftsmen and small enterprisers. This proposition is capable of generalization. Those who are constricted, who find life as it is lived too hard, are prone to the acceptance of the ideological outlook on life. A society in which the lot of the many becomes more constricted, in which they feel more deserted and more uncared for as a result of the failure of their rulers, will encourage this proneness to seek realization.[17]

Naturally, not all those who live in a broken and disadvantaged condition are drawn equally by the magnet of the ideological orientation. Special personal qualities are required.[18] It takes a hypersensitivity to ultimate standards, to the sacred, and this is a quality which although rare in all populations, is found in some measures at all times and particularly at times of crisis. There are human beings who, by personal constitution, are sensitive to the ultimate grounds of existence, just as there are human beings with a need for and a capacity for abstract reasoning, for understanding the mysteries of the universe in accordance with the powers of their reason. Some become mystics, some become scientists, other philosophers. Others who are filled with the sense of injustice and of grievance against the earthly order in its various manifestations, political and ecclesiastical, as well as familial and sexual, reach out toward and seek fusion with the symbols of apocalyptic fulfillment.

17. Bengt Sundkler, *Bantu Prophets in South Africa* (London 1948); Georges Balandier, *Sociologie actuelle de l'Afrique noire* (Paris, 1955), pp. 417-86; and Peter Worsley, *The Trumpet Shall Sound: A Study of "Cargo" Cults in Melanesia* (London, 1957), show the connection between salvationary, messianic religion and the deprivations arising from the disruption of traditional institutions.

18. Professor Cohn declared that paranoid tendencies are a necessary condition for the expansion of millenarianism. His view is supported not only by the content of millenarian imagery and aspirations which his book so richly describes, but by contemporary experience of millenarian groups, religious and political. He does not claim that all members of such groups must be paranoid, but that the leaders must be such. "There are always very large numbers of people who are prone to see life in black and white, who feel a deep need for perfect saviours to adore and wicked enemies to hate; people . . . who without being paranoiac yet have a strong tendency towards paranoid states of mind. At a time when such tendencies are being encouraged by external circumstances, the appearance of a messianic leader preaching the doctrine of the final struggle and the coming of the new age can produce remarkable results—and that irrespective of whether the leader is a sincere fanatic or an imposter or a mixture of both. Those who are first attracted will mostly be people who seek a sanction for the emotional needs generated by their own unconscious conflicts. . . . These first followers, precisely because they are true believers, can endow their new movement with such confidence, energy and ruthlessness that it will attract into its wake vast multitudes of people who are themselves not at all paranoid but simply harassed, hungry or frightened" (pp. 311-12). There is much truth in this well-balanced picture, but it seems to me that he omits the religious or ideological sensitivity—the sensitivity to remote things—which is not necessarily connected with paranoia, any more than imagination or curiosity is connected with it.

That is why the ideological orientation so frequently draws to itself madmen full of hatred and fear—the paranoids who play such an important role in Professor Cohn's interpretation. Ideological sensitivity, even if it did not draw on the accumulated hatred and aggressiveness of its followers, would be separatist and in tension with the "world" of normal traditional society. Its utopianism and its quest for perfect harmony would put it at odds with the world of conflicting interests, half-measures, and self-seeking. The addition of the hatred and fear of those who feel injured and neglected adds a highly combustible fuel to its fire. For this reason, the ideological outlook is full of the imagery of violence and destruction, and its practice is often crowded with actual acts of brutality and a heartless asceticism, while preaching a message of an ultimate condition of love and peace enveloping all human beings.[19]

Ideological politics have their nerve in this need to be in contact with the sacred. They live from grievance and the feeling of injustice, and no conceivable society can attain the condition in which everyone could be permanently free from grievance and the feeling of injustice, any more than any society could live up to the standards affirmed by the most saintly prophets and maddest zealots of the apocalypse.

The tendency of intellectuals in modern Western countries, and latterly in Asian and African countries, to incline toward ideological politics does not, however, derive only from this permanent feature of the Judaic-Christian religious culture, which affects even those who do not accept its explicit articles of faith.[20] As intellectuals, they also live in the flowing stream of other traditions which are particular to them as intellectuals.

It is probably not an accident that most of the traditions of modern intellectuals seem to dispose them toward an ideological outlook. It seens to be almost given by their attachment to symbols which transcend everyday life and its responsibilities. Some of these traditions have arisen as effluvial by-products of specific intellectual activities, as, for example, scientism has arisen from scientific research and analysis. Others, like the tradition of bohemianism, have arisen from the age and mode of life of persons whose inclinations drive them toward an effort to be independent of

19. One need only read the pacifist press to see how the preaching of peace and love is combined with a pleasure in the contemplation of maimed bodies and universal destruction. Mazzini once wrote, "I am inclined to love men at a distance . . . contact makes me hate them." Bolton King, *Life of Mazzini,* (London [Everyman edition], 1912), p. 55.

20. Is it entirely an accident that communism in India has achieved its greatest success so far in an area where previously Christian missionary education had reached a larger proportion of the population than in other parts of India? It is not intended, however, to explain Indian leftism solely by an ultimate derivation from a secularized Christian outlook.

traditions and conventions and on whom their devotion to the symbols of artistic and literary creation, and the restricted market for the sale of their creations, enforces material poverty and uncertainty. And still others, like the tradition of romanticism, are the complex products of a profound movement of the human spirit, so intricate and multifarious that it seems almost inexplicable.

Let us consider some of these traditions of the intellectuals with regard to their contact with the ideological outlook and their inherent disposition toward ideological politics. Let us consider scientism first. Scientism entails the denial of the truth of tradition. It asserts that life, if it is to be lived on the highest plane, should be lived in accordance with "scientific principles," and that these principles should be achieved by the rigorously rational examination of actual experience, systematically confronted through the elaborate and orderly scrutiny and experiment which constitute scientific research. It regards the generally accepted traditions of society as impediments to the attainment of these principles, which are ultimately the principles immanent in the universe. As such, therefore, scientism constitutes a vigorous criticism of traditional and institutional life, and a refusal to accept authority on any grounds except those of scientific principle. It holds before mankind the ideal of a society in which scientists, and administrators and politicians guided by scientists, will rule and in which the ordinary citizens will hold no beliefs and perform no actions which are not sanctioned by scientific principles.[21] This rejection of the prevailing order and its central institutions and traditions, and the appreciation of an ideal order governed by the ultimate principles of science, obviously possess close affinities with certain features of the millenarian outlook. The hostility toward the barrier which received tradition raises between the human being and the ultimate principles of the universe, the dispraise of the authority of institutions, and the vision of an ideal order (infused by and conducted in accordance with the ultimate principles of universal existence) are only a few of

21. Cf. F. A. Hayek, *The Counter-Revolution of Science* (Glencoe, Ill. 1952), which provides the best account of one of the most important sources of scientism, that which derives from Descartes and which reaches its fullest elaboration in the work of Saint-Simon and Comte. B. F. Skinner, *Walden II* (New York, 1948), is an extreme contemporary statement of the scientistic position, to which there are numerous approximations, not the least the Marxist. Marxist scientism is best represented by Professor J. D. Bernal, who has written, "Science has put in our power the means of transforming human life to a degree at least as great as those provided by the technical developments of the origin of civilization but the change differs in one crucial respect in that they can be consciously undertaken. What we can see straight away is the possibility of the removal of most of the hindrances to full human and social life that exist in our civilization." "Science and Civilization," in C. Day Lewis, *The Mind in Chains* (London, 1937), pp. 194-95.

the lines of affinity which link these two traditions. It is therefore not difficult to understand how the acceptance of the scientistic tradition can prepare the way to the acceptance of a secularized millenarianism and thus lead on to ideological politics.

Romanticism too flows in the same direction, feeding into and swelling the sea of ideological politics. Romanticism too views any existing order as repugnant because it mediates, compromises, and deforms the ideal. The ideal of romanticism is the spontaneous and direct expression of the essential nature of the individual and the collectivity. Both the individualistic and the collectivistic variants of the romantic tradition placed great emphasis on the direct and full experience of the ultimate value of individual creativity or of the spirit of the community (folk or national or local). Like the millenarian outlook, romanticism regards immediate experience of the sacred as a touchstone of the good. Whatever is mediated by calculation or contrivance, by organization or compromise is antithetical to it. That is why modern large-scale society as it has emerged since the end of the eighteenth century is abhorrent to those who live in the tradition of romanticism. Civil society, which allows so much space for private concerns, and which permits neither the single individual nor the total community the complete realization of their essential potentialities, is seen by romanticism as a system of arbitrary repression in contrast with some ideal realm of freedom and fulfillment. Civil society requires compromise and reasonableness, prudent self-restraint, and responsibility, and these are all deviations from the unqualifiedness and spontaneity which romanticism demands of all action. Romanticism is, as a result, at war with civil society.

The influence of romanticism on the outlook of intellectuals runs far beyond those circles who knowingly acknowledge its sovereignty over them. It has become universally pervasive. It is a major determinant of the attitude of the intellectuals toward politics and the authority of institutions. And different though it is in content from the frightful and dazzling visions of millenarianism, they both work to the same end—the rejection of the existing order in the name of a pattern of existence more infused with the sacred.

In their spiritual genealogy, the tradition of bohemianism and populism are closely related to romanticism. Bohemianism had an older history before it developed an ethos of its own. The restless scholars of the medieval universities[22] and the homeless minstrels

22. Miss Helen Waddell, describing these forerunners of bohemianism, quoted the Council of Salzburg: "They go alone in public naked, lie in bake-ovens, frequent taverns, games, harlots, earn their bread by their vices and cling with inveterate obstinacy to their sect, so that no hope of their amendment remaineth." *Wandering Scholars,* 7th ed. (London, 1942), p. 188.

and minnesingers who lived from begging, thieving, and the hope of selling their artistic wares were the ancestors of the modern bohemian. They were footloose; they were not incorporated into the routines and responsibilities which filled most of the medieval European social structure. They would not accept the burdens of family and vocation, and sought only to serve their own creative impulse and pleasure.

The development of printing and the appearance of a body of writers trying to maintain themselves from the sale of their written product added a substantial body of persons in Western Europe whose uncertain existence and whose intellectual sensitivity forced them into an irregular course of life. Bohemian practice and bohemian ethos were well under way in London and Paris before the beginning of the nineteenth century. The widened range of education and the increased reading public, fed by the romantic idea of the creative man, the lonely genius who knows no law, made the café intellectual, the bohemian writer and artist into a major figure of life in all the great capitals of the Western countries. Paris was the center of this life, but London, Berlin, Munich, Saint Petersburg, Rome, and New York all had their bohemias. The traditions of the French revolutions of 1789, 1830, 1848, and the commune of 1871, and the tradition of anarchism, doctrinal and practical, found a warm reception in the Parisian bohemia, and, with varying degrees of attenuation and adaptation to national political traditions, they found acceptance in the bohemias of the other countries as well. Antinomianism—moral, aesthetic, and political—was at home there, and the political police kept their eyes peeled for revolutionaries in bohemian intellectual circles. Bohemians were at war with society,[23] some on well-thought-out grounds, seeking a free life less encumbered by traditional standards, others out of an incoherent and impulsive aggressiveness against any sort of authority, cultural or institutional, and an inability to live in a settled routine of work or life. There were many points at which bohemianism and millenarianism diverged. Bohemianism was usually against the Church as well as against Christianity; millenarianism was Christian and only hostile to the authority of the Church. Bohemianism was usually opposed to asceticism; millenarianism was often ascetic. They had in common, however, their repugnance for *mere* tradition and for the constituted authorities who were associated with it.

Populism—the belief in the wisdom and the supreme moral value of the ordinary man of the lower classes—is a new phenomenon. In some respects it was a creation of romanticism, but it was also an

23. Baudelaire once wrote, "Usefulness to the community always seemed to me a most hideous thing in man." *The Essence of Laughter and other Essays, Journals and Letters,* ed. Peter Quennell (New York, 1956), p. 178.

outgrowth of the moral egalitarianism of the Christian sects and of life at the peripheries of Western culture. By its praise of the uneducated and the humble, it places itself in opposition to the great and mighty of the earth; it denies their cultural creativity while imputing true creativity to the lower classes. Populism charges academic science and scholarship with a preoccupation with bloodless symbols unconnected with the essence of life. When it becomes political, populism asserts that the standards of the ordinary people should prevail against the standards represented by the authoritative institutions of society—the state, the law, the church, the universities. Thus the populistic tradition, too, like the other traditions cited, expresses a deep alienation from traditional culture and from the society ruled through civil politics and the equilibrium of power.

Populism and millenarianism share many significant features. Both repudiate the official traditions of learning, millenarianism declaring that the prevailing interpretation of sacred texts falsifies their true meaning, and populism charging the learned with the transfiguration of authority and with enmity towards the truth expressed in the popular will. Both oppose the mediation of contact with the highest values, by authoritative institutions, by priests, professors, and parliamentarians. Both are against the cold-blooded and impersonal rules of institutions; both are responsive to charisma. The conceptions of the people and of the proletariat easily merge, as do those of people and nation; so populism can turn without difficulty into an ideological political orientation.

These are not the only traditions of the modern intellectual, but most of the others have the same tendency. Of course, these traditions are not accepted equally by all intellectuals. They are most widely accepted among men of letters and academic scholars and scientists. Nonetheless, although an increasing proportion of intellectuals in the broader sense, i.e., persons who have passed through colleges and universities, are engaged in practical tasks in adminstration and technology which curb their ideological predispositions, the atmosphere in which they acquire their qualifications, and the traditions which adhere to their professions, give to many of them some impulsion in this direction. The impetus to an ideological outlook inherent in the very constitution of intellectual activities would probably not be enough to account for the upsurge of ideological politics of the past century and a half. It has required the confluence of numerous traditions and their common confrontation with the situation of modern society to release the flood.

IV

Traditions seldom die. They recede very slowly, yielding before new traditions which replace them by incorporating elements of their predecessors and assimilating them to new elements. The new traditions can grow only by attachment to older traditions which they expand and elaborate.

It seems excessively sanguine, therefore, for us to congratulate ourselves on the end of the ideological age. We would be more realistic to speak of its subsidence, rather than of its end. Old traditions, such as millenarianism, deep in the marrow of our intellectual bones, traditions such as romanticism, which are at the very heart of the modern age, are not likely to disappear so soon after the fury and the disillusionment of the first fifty years of this century.

What we may legitimately hope for in the coming decades is a condition of quiescence of ideological politics and of the ideological disposition from which it springs. This quiescence can be sustained only if an effective alternative is available. Civil politics are this alternative.

Civil politics are based on civility, which is the virtue of the citizen,[24] of the man who shares responsibly in his own self-government, either as a governor or as one of the governed. Civility is compatible with other attachments to class, to religion, to profession, but it regulates them out of respect for the common good.

Civil politics do not stir the passions; they do not reveal man at the more easily apprehensible extremes of heroism and saintliness. They involve the prudent exercise of authority, which tries to foresee the consequences of that exercise while appreciating the undeterminable limitations of human powers and the uncertainties of foresight. The civil politician must be aware of the vague line between the exercise of authority and the manipulation of human beings as objects outside his moral realm. He must shun that line and yet on occasion go over it, realizing the moral costs of such crossing over and the difficulties and the necessity of crossing back into the domain of legitimacy. He must maintain a sense of affinity with his society and share with his fellow citizens their membership in a

24. Civility has meant more than good manners, and it is an impoverishment of our vocabulary as well as a sign of the impoverishment of our thought on political matters that this word has been allowed to dwindle to the point where it has come to refer to good manners in face-to-face relationships. Two recent books by eminent British writers—*Traditions of Civility*, by Sir Ernest Barker (Cambridge, 1948), and *Good Behaviour; Being a Study of Certain Types of Civility*, by Sir Harold Nicolson (London, 1955)—show no awareness of the older meaning of the term.

single transpersonal entity, while bearing in mind their unresponsiveness to the ideal and their incapacity to sustain a continuous and
intense relationship with the sacred. He must maintain this sense of
substantial affinity while being aware of their lesser willingness to be
responsible for the common good and while keeping his own feeling
of responsibility for it alive and taut.

The difficulties of civil political conduct are great in democracies.
Their large size and the impossibility of direct contact between
politicians and their constituents are strains on the sense of moral
affinity which, lacking the support of personal relationships, must be
self-sustaining. Civility was rare in aristocratic societies, partly
because aristocratic virtue—the virtue of the warrior—and civil
virtue—the virtue of the citizen—are so far apart in their inner
constitutions, and particularly because aristocratic systems by their
nature restrict man's development of the empathic sense of affinity.
Liberal democratic regimes place great burdens on the civil sense
because they permit open conflict and acknowledge and thus
encourage partisanship. The common good is always hard to define,
but it is rendered even harder when it must gratify and reconcile
opposing interests and simultaneously attempt to guard values for
which no strong partisan contends, but which, nonetheless, are
essential to a good society. The politician must be partisan himself,
while civility requires a partial transcendence of partisanship as well
as an empathic appreciation of the other parties within the circle of
the civil political order. Partisanship must be carried on with the
simultaneous perception of the civil and moral order which embraces
both one's opponents and one's allies.

Civil politics—which are by no means identical with democratic
politics—are especially difficult in contemporary society. The complex tasks which governments undertake and which nearly everyone
thinks they should undertake, make so great the amount of material
that a politician who devotes himself to the matter must master, and
so many the obligations to which he must attend, that reflection is
deprived of the quiet and leisure which it needs to mature. The
complexity of the tasks renders easy understanding of them beyond
the power of most of the citizenry and encourages a depreciatory
attitude toward the capacities of the electorate, thus inhibiting the
vitality of the sense of affinity between citizens and leaders that is
essential to civil politics. The deep and increasing penetration of
populism in all countries results in a greater pressure on the
politician for the immediate satisfaction of class and sectional ends.
The development of techniques of mass communication and of
chemical, surgical, and psychological modes of controlling human
behavior presents continuous temptations to the politician to
respond to the incessant demands by manipulation. Not that he

always by any means yields or that the techniques would be successful if applied, but the mere existence of the putative possibilities creates an atmosphere which impedes the cultivation and practice of civility.

Civil politics entail judging things on their own merits—hard enough in any case where the merits and demerits in any complex issue are so obscure and intertwined—and they also require respect for tradition. Civility requires respect for tradition because the sense of affinity on which it rests is not momentary only but reaches into the past and future. As to the past, civil politics appreciate the factual reality of past achievements as well as the human quality of those who, by virtue of having once been alive, command our respect for their names and the things they valued; as to the future, civil politics see the unity, in essence, of the present generation and those which are to follow, not just in a biological sense, but in the order of value as well. The population of a civil polity is in its fundamental being a continuous procession of those living in the present, preceded by those who have lived, shading off into the obscurity of time past, and to be followed by those who have still to live, shading off into the even more shadowy obscurity of time still unelapsed.

The traditional consciousness is not, however, one which encourages the direct contemplation of the merits and demerits of things as they are. The utilitarian mind usually has little patience with the pastness of things and is even disposed to assume that the mere fact of having been appropriate to the past is a disqualification for relevance to the present and future. Yet both the need for continuity—i.e., the maintenance of affinity with the past—and the need to draw on the benefits of the intelligence and artfulness exercised in the past, render imperative an appreciation of tradition.

Above all, civil politics require an understanding of the complexity of virtue, that no virtue stands alone, that every virtuous act costs something in terms of other virtuous acts, that virtues are intertwined with evils, and that no theoretical system of a hierarchy of virtues is ever realizable in practice. It has been a major fault of ideological politics that they have made the mistake of thinking that a coherent systematic doctrine could guide conduct unfailingly along a straight line which made no compromise with evil. Ideological politics believed that the more strictly one adhered to a virtue, the more intensely one was attached to it, and the more completely one fulfilled it, the better would be one's actions.

This was the basis of the idea of the political spectrum which ran from the pole of virtue—be it left or right—to the other pole, the extreme and complete negation of virtue. The realism and circumspection of civil politics cannot accommodate such a simplification.

Practicing politicians do indeed manage to avoid the excesses which are inevitable in such simplifications. Professor Aron once said French politicians in the nineteenth and twentieth centuries, in one of the countries of the most extreme ideological politics among intellectuals, have in practice usually not been dominated by this distinction between "left" and "right."[25] Indeed, this has been one of the reasons why French intellectuals have been so alienated from the political practice of their country.

The practice of politics imposes some measure of civility, but it also stirs the temptation of demagogy and offers the easy solution of satisfying the most clamorous sectional interests. If intellectuals could settle down to a more reasonable political outlook, their concern for the more general and for what transcends the immediate advantages of particular "interests" would infuse a most precious ingredient into political life.

V

Is it plausible to expect intellectuals to renounce their attachments to antipolitical traditions in which they have lived for centuries? Can it be expected that intellectuals will be drawn down from the heights of the ultimate ideal so that they could, while still remaining intellectuals, tolerate the burden imposed by the vicissitudes of maintaining themselves as politicians who have invested their future in the unpredictabilities of politics, and by the task of keeping a society going? Can intellectuals be brought to appreciate politics which are concerned to keep society on a steady course, as much concerned to keep it from becoming worse as to make it better? Can they be expected to affirm a political practice which provides no final solution and which does not promise to bring society or the human race to a resting point of perfect fulfillment?

The civil politics which must replace ideological politics in the affections of the intellectuals have many competitive disadvantages. Their traditions are fewer and frailer. Cicero, who preached and tried to practice the virtues of civil politics, has been called an opportunist, and his assassination by the side with which he compromised has been regarded as evidence of his failure as a politician. Tacitus spoke on behalf of civility through his censure of its degradation in the Empire.[26] Clarendon's civil wisdom was put on paper in the

25. The avoidance of ideological politics is not synonymous with the practice of civil politics. Politics practiced in accordance with the prevailing constellation of interests is a third alternative, and it is one which is most commonly pursued by politicians. If the "interests" are intractable, then the civil order can be as badly damaged as it would be by ideological politics.

26. "So corrupted, indeed, debased was that age by sycophancy that not only the foremost citizens who were forced to save their grandeur by servility

rueful melancholy of exile and with the distrust of power which is the destiny of the disappointed and disregarded counselor to princes. The fate of More and Raleigh and the disillusionment of the humanists who sought to guide the conduct of princes have left bitter memories of the tribulations of the intellectual in politics. On the other side, the image of politics reflected by those "advisers to princes" whose names stand out in our minds, Machiavelli above all, Halifax, and others like them, have given an appearance of justice to the condemnation of politics which the intellectual, devoted to the ideal of his calling, has often expressed.

The intellectual who seeks the path of civil politics has little to cheer and fortify him in his quest. He has many of his own prejudices to overcome—the whole complex of the traditions of ideological politics, and, in America, his traditional aversion for the politics of the pork barrel and the patronage lists, and his image of the 42nd Ward Young Men's Democratic Club, with its smokers and its belching boorishness, and of the harsh selfishness of the Union League Clubs.[27] He has no feeling of standing in a great intellectual tradition. There is no equivalent civil tradition to counterpose to the subterranean pervasiveness of the millenarian tradition, to provide an atmosphere in which he can breathe. He has the memory of Woodrow Wilson and Thomas Masaryk, Disraeli and Gladstone, and Guizot, to set alongside the far more numerous intellectuals approving of bomb throwing and assassination, themselves engaged in wire pulling and plotting, impatient and contemptuous of the political profession.

If civil politics depend on an acceptance of the limitations of human powers, their establishment in the second half of the present century will not be rendered easier by scientific developments. The advances in physiology, biochemistry, neurology, applied mathematics, cybernetics, and the foolish propaganda made by some of the enthusiasts of psychology and the social sciences, can hardly induce a feeling of modesty in man, nor can they be expected to promote that fellow feeling necessary to civil politics.

Nor, for that matter, can the specialization of education which

---

but every ex-consul, most of the ex-praetors and a host of inferior senators would rise in eager rivalry to propose shameful and preposterous motions. Tradition says that Tiberius as often as he left the Senate House used to exclaim in Greek, 'How ready these men are to be slaves'" (*Annals*, book 3, section 65).

27. This is by no means confined to capitalistic America or to bourgeois politicians. Ferdinand Lassalle once said, "I have a real horror of workers' delegations where I always hear the same speeches and have to shake hard, hot and moist hands" (David Footman, *The Primrose Path* [London, 1946], p. 183). The intellectuals' attitude toward politicians, regardless of their class, is epitomized in: "I met Murder on the way. He had a mask like Castlereagh."

accompanies this scientific progress bring much support. Quite the opposite. It is not that the humanistic education of the past has provided much of a bulwark against the ideological outlook. Extreme specialization, however, adds a further strain to the weak sense of affinity. It is true that extreme specialization which reduces the contact of the intellectual with the broad range of traditions of the intellectual life of the past also restricts his relationship with many of the ideological elements in the traditions of the intellectuals. In many fields, however, and particularly in those of increasing importance, it exposes him more fully to the scientistic tradition. Thus, while it increases his matter-of-factness, it also increases his pride, his contempt for the past, and his confidence in the boundless superiority of the future, and these are not so congenial to civility.

If ideological politics thrive in conditions of danger, what are we to think of the chances of civil politics in an age in which peace is maintained by a conscious fear of cataclysmic destruction by nuclear weapons? These awful possibilities cannot avoid stirring up latent apocalyptic images and expectations. These real dangers make the sober, moderate, small-scale measures of civil politics appear excessively puny alongside the monstrous tasks which nuclear weapons impose on governments.

It should not be thought that civil politics can be stifled only by ideological politics, or that millenarianism is the decisive determinant of radical alienation. Radical transformations in society can be undertaken without millenarian impulsion. Western and Oriental antiquity have known revolutions without ideologies. Every social order, even the most just, will have some victims, and every population will contain antinomian personalities. These alone instigate tendencies towards a sort of proto-ideological politics, even when there are no ideological traditions living in the open or under the surface.

Finally, civil politics are not the only alternative to ideological politics for the intellectuals. They have in some instances entered upon political careers like professional politicians, given up their intellectual concerns and attachments, and devoted themselves to the conventional round of vote getting, interest representation, self-preservation, and self-advancement. They could yield to the customary temptations of the vain and egocentric, demagogy, flattery, and opportunism. They could, in short, conform to their own prevailing image of normal political life.

This, however, is not likely. What is far more likely is withdrawal—angry withdrawal or sad and serene withdrawal. The traditions of withdrawal among the intellectuals are among the profoundest in our intellectual inheritance. One can be antipolitical without being ideological. This was the dominant trend among American intellectuals from the Jacksonian revolution until the Russian revolution; and it is unfortunately, despite the charges of conformity, of "other-directedness," and of being "organized men," still prevalent among American intellectuals today. The valiant effort to embrace "our Country and our Culture" is not a resounding success as far as civil politics are concerned.[28] The repudiation of ideological politics has not led to the espousal or practice of civil politics. The life of American society is affirmed, but its political life and the civil element in its political life are not.

The situation in Great Britain is not very different. Great Britain has a better record in civil politics than any other country in the world, and its intellectuals have their proper share in that record. What is the situation today? The post-war idyll has ended in disenchantment. "Butskellism" has retreated. The "angry young men" are on the rampage. Even the most amiable Mr. Kingsley Amis, who said that he is, when he has to choose, a Labour Party man, cannot take politics seriously. His heart is not in it.[29] He, like those with whom his name is coupled, is distrustful of the "professional espouser of causes." The humiliation of the Suez fiasco and the danger of the hydrogen bomb have seriously damaged the British intellectuals' capacity for civil politics. Even a sober, responsible intellectual of long and honorable political experience, Mr. Christopher Hollis, told his fellow intellectuals that the main task before the British electorate is to discredit the two major political parties, even though he expects no serious "Liberal revival."[30] Mr. John Osborne, who has no such background of experience of political responsibility, is far harsher in his antipolitics. "I can't go on laughing at the idiots who rule our lives. . . . They are no longer funny because they are not merely dangerous, they are murderers . . . they are stupid, insensitive, unimaginative beyond hope, uncreative, and murderous."[31]

VI

Can the intellectuals reeducate themselves to a civil state of mind? Can they keep the traditions of ideological politics quiescent while they modify their own outlook? Can they bring forth and fortify the incipient impulses of civility which the harsh experiences of the past half-century stirred into movement?

28. Cf. Newton Arvin, et al., *America and the Intellectual,* Partisan Review Series no. 4 (New York, 1953).

29. *Socialism and the Intellectuals,* Fabian Tract 304 (London, 1957).

30. "What Shall we do Next Time?" *The Spectator,* no. 6765, 21 February 1958, pp. 225-26.

31. "They Call it Cricket," in Tom Maschler, ed., *Declaration* London, 1957, p. 67.

One condition of the success of this effort at "self-civilization" is that we should not think that we can or should completely extirpate the ideological heritage. There are valuable elements in that inheritance which are worthy of conservation in any political outlook which lays claim to our respect. The demand for moral equality, the distrust of authority and of the institutions which it conducts for its own continuance, the insistence on justice, and the call to a heroic existence, even the belief in the earthly paradise and the realm of freedom, all have some validity in them. To deny them will only lay civil politics open to the charge—not unjustified—of being philistine politics in the worst sense, without feeling or sympathy, unimaginative, timorously clinging to what already exists. The ideological element in our intellectual classes will not die out so easily and so soon that its successors will be able to escape unscathed while conducting politics which, while called civil, are merely concerned with the maintenance of order and keeping things as they are.[32]

These impulses in the human heart will not be disregarded. The fact that they have been forced to an extreme and cast into the framework of unrealizable hopes does not mean that they are in themselves immoral. The discredit into which their doctrinaire proponents have deservedly fallen should not be extended to them. Life would be poorer without them, and a political system which sought to proceed entirely without them or entirely against them would find the most sensitive spirits of its society once more drawn up in embittered and irreconcilable opposition.

It has not been the substantive values sought by ideological politics which have done such damage. Rather it has been the rigidity, the exclusiveness, and the extremity with which particular values have been sought. There is nothing evil about loyalty to one's community, national or ethnic or cultural, nor is there anything wicked in the appreciation of equality or the devotion to any particular ideal. What is so malign is the elevation of one value, such as equality or national or ethnic solidarity, to supremacy over all others, and the insistence on its exclusive dominion in every sphere of life.[33]

Civil politics therefore will have a better chance to obtain more

32. One of the dangers of the New Conservatism is that it fails to see that civil politics are as eager for improvement as they are ready to conserve what has come down from the past. Cf. Charles Parkin, *The Moral Basis of Burke's Philosophy* (Cambridge, 1956), chap. 6, pp. 109-30; also Mr. Kristol's perspicacious essay in the *Yale Review*, mentioned earlier.

33. Few writers have made this criticism of ideological politics, while retaining a compassionate sympathy for their ideals, as well as Conrad. Natalie Haldin says at the end of *Under Western Eyes.* "I must own to you that I shall never give up looking forward to the day when all discord shall be silenced . . . and the weary men united at last . . . feel saddened by their victory, because so many ideas have perished for the triumph of one. . . ."

enduring devotion among intellectuals if their proponents do not disavow all continuity whatsoever with the substantive values of ideological politics. Correspondingly, their chances for success will be enhanced if the prudence they extol is exercised in finding a just balance among the contending values rather than in merely seeking self-maintenance, which will degenerate into unprincipled opportunism.

A complete disavowal of every line of affinity between civility and ideology will not only be false in fact but would turn civility into an ideology. Civility would become an ideology of pure politics concerned with no substantive values except the acquisition and retention of power and the maintenance of public order and with absolutely no other interest. Civility would take upon itself the onus of the very same moral separatism for which it criticizes ideological politics, if it denied its affinity with the substantive values which the ideological outlook holds and distorts.

VII

How can intellectuals retain those elements of romanticism which prize spontaneity and genuineness of expression, and which aid the cultivation of individuality, while curbing their expansiveness? By excessive demands for individuality and the consequent exaggeration of the restrictions which institutional life imposes on it, romanticism will discredit any social order and turn the intellectuals against it and arouse the custodians of order against the intellectuals. The "imperialism" which the late Baron Ernst Seillière bemoaned in so many volumes can disrupt any social order, and above all a liberal order. A way must be found to retain many of the values of romanticism while restricting their expansiveness.

A renewal of the old idea, fundamental to modern liberalism, of a separation of the spheres is needed. It can, of course, be realized only very incompletely; economic life cannot be completely independent of government and politics, and vice versa; religion and politics cannot be completely separated; culture and politics cannot be completely separated. Nonetheless, while acknowledging and accepting their necessary collaboration and affinity, it is very important that the guardians, practical and intellectual, of each of the spheres should be aware of the desirability, in principle, of their separateness. This would be a bulwark against the romantic—and ideological—insistence on the universal application of a single set of standards. The separation of the different spheres of life would not please those ideological politicians and intellectuals who seek complete consistency. Without it, however, civility would be extinguished and our best intellectual traditions would be frustrated.

It should be quite possible in practice to realize a far-reaching separation of the spheres while maintaining their overlaps and affinities. This is in fact done to a large extent in societies of the West, however imperfectly and unprincipledly. The real difficulty is to bring about the intellectual's acceptance of it as a reasonable policy. There is not such a completely unbridgeable antimony between individuality and institutions as romanticism insists on although there must inevitably be some tension. The intellectual's distrust of the ongoing life in the spheres outside his own arises from the defects in his sense of affinity.

The nature of the sense of affinity which binds the members of a society together is a mystery. It seems somehow connected with the empathic capacities of the individual—not just his empathy for persons whom he encounters in concrete form, in person, or through written or plastic symbols, but for classes of persons who must necessarily remain anonymous. Up to a certain point, it goes hand in hand with individuality, and societies which do not know individuality also live without a sense of civil affinity. It is shriveled and shrunken by fear, and when it is restricted, it is in its turn conducive to fear of one's fellow men. If somehow the intellectuals could be got over their almost primordial terror of and fascination for authority, which, they fear, crushes their individuality, the movement for civility would make a tremendous advance.

Modern Western societies have witnessed a diminution in the moral distance separating the higher and the lower classes. This has in part been a result of the changes in the distribution of national income which have raised the lower strata and diminished the upper strata, so that standards of life are now very much nearer to each other than they have ever been before, however considerable the differences remain, and should, to some extent, still remain. But more significant, I think, is the change in the civil consciousness which has taken place in Western societies. This is in some measure a result of the inner development of the potentialities of the Protestant idea—the same complex of ideas and sentiments which has aggravated the millenarian disposition. The notion that every man has a spark of divinity in him, that all men participate in a common substance—sacred in the last analysis but civil in its concrete and mediated forms—has grown out of the conjunction of the modern national state and Christian protestantism. From this conjunction grew the idea of the citizen, and from it our modern idea of the civil order as a stratum of being in which all the members of a state participate.

The modest flowering of civility in the modern world is a new thing in history. Pericles' Funeral Oration foreshadowed its program. The great Roman forerunners were, however grandiose, no more than adumbrations of a human possibility, rather than indications of a well-functioning civility in ancient times. The growth of civility has been halting and very imperfect. Its growth has been attended by an exacerbation of ideology—and the two seem in the modern epoch to have some obscure and intricate interdependence. Yet it does seem that with the spread of individuality—imperfect now and never perfectly realizable—in the wider reaches of the population, the sense of civil affinity has increased its scope and power among the lower strata, who previously existed as objects of authority and economic power but did not dwell within the same moral and civil domain as their rulers. There is now in all strata, on the average, a higher civil sense than earlier phases of Western society have ever manifested—and this despite class conflicts and ideological separatism and irreconcilability. Even ethnic barriers seem slowly to be yielding to the rising tide of civility. Is it too much to hope that the intellectuals, who have provided such illustrious antecedents in the true "civilization" of politics, will themselves come more fully into this process, and thus, by one of the great continental drifts of history, bring the age of ideology to an end?

4 The Traditions of Intellectual Life: Their Conditions of Existence and Growth in Contemporary Societies

I

The rational-empirical outlook—the outlook of independent curiosity, openness to experience, disciplined inquiry and analysis, reasoned judgment, and the appreciation of originality—has been a major property of the intellectual in most countries in the nineteenth and twentieth centuries. It has been contained, in the most diverse ways, in most intellectual activities—in art, science, scholarship, and systematic thought. It has been the possession or the aspiration of the intellectuals everywhere in the contemporary world, and it has provided the criteria by which they have judged intellectuals and societies.

The rational-empirical outlook has grown up with the development of modern Western European civilization. From Western Europe it has spread in nearly every direction—into Russia, into the Americas, to Africa, to South Asia, and around Asia to all the countries of Southeast Asia and to China and Japan.

The rational-empirical outlook grew up under special European conditions of a stable but loosening Christian conception of the world. One condition was the approximate unity of the intellectual classes within each national society, through their association with church and state, and through their share in a unitary cultural tradition formed around a classical humanism in a Christian reinterpretation. Another condition was the high status of intellectual activity, connected with its association with church and state and the auxiliary and interconnected institutions of universities, aristocracy, gentry, and landownership.

Modern intellectual life was born in the polity of absolutism which in the course of modern history turned occasionally toward varying brightnesses of enlightenment, toward monarchy with limited powers, republican liberalism and democracy in different mixtures. It came into being in societies which were markedly hierarchical in structure. Most were peasant societies, monarchical, absolutistic, bureaucratic or feudal in their government. It thrived in these, as it did in mercantile patrician city-states and later in constitutional monarchies.

Previously published in a slightly different form in the *International Journal of Comparative Sociology*, vol. 1, no. 2 (September 1960), pp. 177-94.

The rational-empirical outlook, which is the modern intellectual outlook, in its early centuries was the work mainly of amateurs. It was an impassioned avocation to most of the great creators of modern intellectual traditions. It was not a profession from which one made a livelihood, and there was relatively little institutional provision for creative intellectual exertion.

The modern outlook has been protean in its form and in its content. It has assimilated the discipline of the universities, it has entered into the professional practice of art and literature despite their contamination by alien traditions. It has added new subject matters and changed the focus of its interest. It has reached into politics and acquired diverse substances in that contact with the various streams of political action and belief.

Modern intellectual life has, in its career of more than four centuries, grown steadily, consolidating and refining itself, expanding its techniques, deepening and ramifying its understanding, enriching its traditions and therewith giving new opportunities for their extension and transformation by the oncoming generation of creative talents. The problem which it now faces, on a worldwide scale, is whether it can live under conditions in which it has never had to live before.

The new conditions in which modern intellectual life must be carried on arise from changes within the pattern of intellectual life itself and from changes in its political, economic, organizational, and cultural environments. Some of these changes have taken place within the societies in which modern intellectual life had already reached a high level of creativity. Others arise from the extension of the practice of intellectual life into areas of the world where it is new, in which it is not a native growth, and where, unlike Europe, it has not emerged from an internal evolution of indigenous intellectual traditions.

II

Within the continuous flow of the tradition of modern intellectual activity, there has been a pronounced expansion of the systematically cumulative mode of intellectual work, and closely associated with that expansion has gone an increased density of scientific and scholarly activity. A larger proportion of a tremendously enlarged intellectual class now is engaged in forms of intellectual production which require a deliberate and specific articulation of their own work with what has just gone before. The greatly heightened application of the best talents of the society to science and, to a lesser degree, to scholarship—and the nature of scientific and scholarly progress and of the methods of training in research—have led conjointly to a gigantic multiplication of the amount of scholarly and scientific literature in every field which the members of the intellectual community must read and to which they must contribute. The point has long since been passed when a single person in the course of his lifetime could know the best works of the past and present in every field; we are already at the point where the individual scientist or scholar can scarcely read all that is relevant to his field of interest within his own discipline; if he also wishes at the same time to maintain his contact with the highest points of intellectual production of the past as well as with what is being done in fields other than his own, he must be very selective indeed. These necessities generated by the institutionalization and discipline of specialized work restrict the range of the intellectual's attention, narrow his interests, and loosen his attachment to the larger intellectual community and its traditions. Alternatively, they condemn an intellectual to a degree of dilettantism which is hardly compatible in most instances with creativity in those fields, notably science and scholarship, where the tradition to be mastered is highly articulated, compact, and intricate.[1]

This problem does not yet impose itself on the intellectual classes of those countries—underdeveloped and totalitarian or pluralistic—which are not at present conducting advanced scientific and scholarly research on a significant scale.[2] It is, however, beginning to appear in India, which is intellectually the most advanced of the pluralistic underdeveloped countries; it already exists in Communist China, the most advanced of the totalitarian underdeveloped countries. In the lives of the intelligentsia of the advanced totalitarian countries, such as Soviet Russia, Poland, Czechoslovakia, and the German Democratic Republic, the pressure of the vast bulk of the intellectual inheritance is as great as it is in the advanced pluralistic countries.

III

The changes in the environment of intellectual life are nothing other than the changes from the world of European princely absolutism and constitutional Whig and bourgeois liberalism to those very different conditions which exist today in Europe and everywhere else in the contemporary world. The changes are those of scale and moral atmosphere. The intellectual class of every country is much

1. The problem is less severe in those fields in which the tradition is less articulated and where a systematic and deliberate continuity is less imperative, as in literature and art.

2. Nor does it affect the creators of literary or artistic works except insofar as it affects the size and receptiveness of the audience which will be available for the consumption of their productions.

larger than it has ever been, both in absolute size and in proportion to the total population. More of the national income of every country is being spent on the maintenance and training of the intellectual class, and the institutional system for this maintenance and training is correspondingly larger and more complex. In moral atmosphere, the main change is a much more permeative populism which is expressed in a mòre open access to educational opportunity than ever before and a more urgent demand that the exercise of the intellect should serve the public good. The changed situation is visible in every sphere in politics, in economic life, in the organizational matrix of intellectual activity, and in the cultural cosmos which infolds it.

The major variants of the situation of the modern intellectual life are: (1) the pluralistic, mass society, democratic in its political constitution, industrial in its economy, individualistic, pluralistic, and increasingly romantic and populistic in its culture; (2) the totalitarian society, oligarchical politically, already highly industrialized or seeking energetically to become industrial, and attempting to impose rigorously a unitary ideological pattern on an elaborate modern cultural life; and (3) underdeveloped countries which range from totalitarian and military oligarchies to democracies in their political form, mainly agricultural economically but seeking to become industrial, and primarily traditional in their culture, with the bearers of the modern outlook more discontinuous in their culture from the rest of the population than is the case in the advanced countries of the West.[3]

In the Western countries, as in the most advanced totalitarian countries, the traditional patterns of intellectual life and the modern rational-empirical outlook are under strain in consequence of a disproportionate growth of the technological sector of the intellectual classes, which is characterized by highly specialized training and professional activities and a very attenuated contact with the inherited traditions of humanistic and scientific thought. In advanced pluralistic societies the organization of intellectual life has been changing, not as a result of ideological considerations (which are important forces in their own right in the advanced totalitarian countries) but because of the increased military and industrial importance of science, changing intellectual interests, new techniques of inquiry and the emergence of new forms and high scale of financial support. The latter group of factors are integral to all

3. Many of the totalitarian countries are underdeveloped; several of them resemble the pluralistic mass societies in their level of industrialization, in their occupational structure, and in the elaborateness of their intellectual activity and traditions. These latter countries—the Soviet Union, Poland, East Germany, and Czechoslovakia—all manifest marked tendencies to intellectual pluralism, which their totalitarian constitutions suppress or hold in check.

advanced societies whether they be pluralistic or totalitarian. In the advanced societies, furthermore, the rational-empirical tradition of intellectual life coexists with what has been called "mass culture," a vast body of mediocre and brutal culture of a type which has always existed but which is now greater in volume and immensely more visible and audible, as a result of the development of films, radio, and television, than it ever was in the past. The rational-empirical tradition is also confronted by expanded romanticism which is hostile to the disciplined and institutionalized features of the hitherto dominant tradition. Like mass culture, romanticism has a long history and it has indeed contributed greatly to the emergence of the rational-empirical outlook which has for most of the modern epoch been able to assimilate it to its own benefit. Overlapping with mass culture and the newest variants of romanticism is a widely spread and deepening populism. On the one side, populism brings with it an esteem for traditional rational-empirical culture and a desire to share in it; it also comes with a resentment against the alleged "elitism" of the modern intellectual tradition. The phenomenon of "mass culture" is more pronounced in the advanced pluralistic countries of the West and in Japan, where the level of economic development and the political regime allow it an ampler and more free expression. But in the more advanced totalitarian countries, and in the most urbanized sectors of the underdeveloped countries, the same sort of mass culture is stirring; but, because of the relative poverty of all these countries, and the centralized control of the culture of the totalitarian countries, mass culture has a more muted and harried existence. The same is true of the new romanticism and the new populism.

IV

In all advanced and underdeveloped societies, intellectual activity, feeding on the modern intellectual tradition, has acquired a functional importance greater than and different from that which it possessed in earlier centuries in the West. In the European Middle Ages and in other cultures before the modern age, the major service demanded by the earthly powers was legitimation. Intellectuals did other things, for they observed the heavens and they wrote plays, histories, and treatises for the purpose of illumination and expression in which the earthly powers were criticized. But legitimation was the main service rulers demanded. The situation is different in the second half of the twentieth century. In all countries, advanced and underdeveloped, which seek to live at the height of modernity, intellectuals have had thrust upon them tasks and responsibilities which they have been unable to refuse and which many of them have promoted. Those who exercised power in the state, the economy, and society have demanded their services and demand them even more for the future. The new demands have been met only in small part by the conversion of roles of intellectuals of established or traditional categories; the numbers of intellectuals available even if they were all converted to the service of the new demands would not have sufficed, and on the whole except in wartime, there was no need for such a rapid conversion. The need was met through the expansion of opportunity for advanced training and through the consequently increased number of new intellectuals trained for technology, management, research, and public administration.

A modern state could not exist without an elaborate system of higher education to create these new "functional" intellectuals—civil servants, applied scientists, engineers, accountants, teachers—that whole range of professional middle-class "tertiary" occupations which are integral to a modern economy, which are indispensable to a modern military establishment and which are essential in the functioning of state and society. Certain kinds of intellectual more specialized and less attached to the literary and philosophical traditions of earlier generations of intellectuals have been trained for the performance of these rational-empirical tasks, and their training has required a larger body of intellectuals of similar orientation to produce them in institutions of higher education.

In the advanced societies, institutions for the production of intellectual personnel already existed when the demand began to increase. There, the problem of these institutions has been their adaptation to the production of larger numbers and of new kinds of specialists. In the underdeveloped countries, the institutions through which these intellectuals are to be produced must be either newly created or built up from a very rudimentary state. There, even more than in the more advanced countries, the recruitment of teaching staffs which will be sufficiently in contact with the great intellectual traditions which nourish their subjects is a major problem.[4] The supply of highly qualified persons is bound to be small; and the worldwide increase in demand, together with the demand in each country for a numerically large output, accentuates the difficulty. The lowering of the standards of staff recruitment as well as the standards of admission and graduation of students is a constant threat under these conditions.

4. This problem is rendered more acute by the adduction of class origin in deciding on the appointment of staff, or ethnic or national or political or other nonintellectual qualities. It was for a long time a problem in totalitarian countries, both advanced and underdeveloped, and it is beginning to emerge as a problem in the newly independent underdeveloped countries, and in the advanced pluralistic countries as well.

In underdeveloped countries, at the moment of independence, the older generation of the stratum with modern intellectual training was very small. The extension of the range of recruitment has meant that new strata who have had little contact, prior to their formal training, with the modern intellectual tradition have been drawn into the corps of intellectuals. In the more advanced countries, which already had a large intellectual class, its further extension has often meant that a lower average capacity has necessarily to be drawn upon if all functional tasks are to be attempted and more or less fulfilled and if all the aspirations for a larger share in culture and higher status in society in consequence of the larger share are to be realized.[5]

Everywhere, the state has pressed by decree and by financial assistance for this numerical extension in the output of persons with the qualifications thought necessary for the performance of those functions which the state wishes to use or to have performed outside state institutions. Pressure for expansion is also exerted out of considerations of "social justice" toward sectors of the population previously not sharing in higher education. Large numbers and "forced marches" are repugnant to the effective implantation of the traditions of intellectual life, which is brought about through identification with a closely observed work. The creative impulsion of intellectual life, passed on by an osmotic process in a personal relationship between teacher and taught, between master and apprentice, is antithetical to this pressure of numbers which overwhelm such personal relationships. If the average receptive capacity which may be a function of cultural background, innate capacity and intensity of intellectual motivation is lower, then increased numbers make implantation and arousal more difficult.

The high degree of specialization which is believed to be appropriate in the practice of these rational-intellectual professions, and the repercussions of this demand on the courses of study, exercise a similar influence. Receptivity to intellectual traditions depends on the prior intimacy, such as is communicated in the atmosphere of an educated family, on personal qualities of sensibility and curiosity and on the breadth of the formal training which the oncoming generation of intellectuals receives. The extension in numbers and the social range of recruitment have placed a heavier burden on the formal training. Where admission is unselective, the lightening of the burden has been achieved by lowering standards of advancement at the undergraduate level or by high rates of withdrawal and failure. In some countries both results occur. Where, therefore, formal educa-

5. This statement applies more to the United States than it does, for example, to Great Britain or to Germany, where the proportion of the relevant age group attending higher educational institutions before the great expansion was very much lower than in the United States.

tion is compressed and specialized, as national necessity and the international development of many subjects require, the result is a specialist whose specialized culture is not embedded in a broader matrix of knowledge of the intellectual tradition and of sensitivity to its imponderable elements.

As the years of the present century pass, the proportion of the educated classes which is blind to the traditional literary and philosophical culture increases in all countries. In England, the weakened persistence of the aristocratic-gentry ideal of the cultured gentleman has offset this to some extent. In France, the humanistic component in the public opinion of the educated classes, resting on the stiffly classical element in the syllabus of the secondary schools, has also tended to offset it to some extent, just as in Soviet Russia the Victorian ideal of culture, of being *kulturny,* also makes for a partial resistance to this tendency towards a "deeper illiteracy" in the professional classes. Nonetheless, despite the resistances, the movement goes on. It will probably become even more pronounced in most underdeveloped countries, totalitarian and pluralistic, where a nationalistic emphasis on indigenous culture and a resentment against the remaining bearers and elements of the metropolitan culture are leaving an imprint on the syllabus, as are the politicians' insistence that higher education be useful and the radical critics' pressure for the extirpation of the cultural remains of the colonial epoch.

V

This demand for the services of intellectuals which is felt in all states, and which contributes to their increase, naturally gives the rulers an interest in what goes on in their higher educational institutions. In the advanced pluralistic societies this interest has tended to be confined to the scale of output of graduates rather than to be concerned with what they are taught; there too, however, rulers have been more inclined to support those studies which are thought to be more contributory to the intellectual-practical professions—engineering, technology, and chemical, latterly bio-medical research, cybernetics, certain branches of social science, etc., etc. On the whole, however, they have restrained themselves from intruding into courses of study, syllabi, or recruitment and promotion of teachers for political, ethnic, or class considerations.

The elites of totalitarian states, more concerned about the dangers of beliefs which deviate from orthodoxy, intrude more into recruitment and promotion, and into the content of courses of study.

This involves occasional attempts at intrusion into the process of intellectual production as well, or at least as close to its heart as an intellectually uncreative and external authority can ever come. Communist totalitarianism, perhaps even more comprehensively than National Socialist totalitarianism because of the greater elaborateness of its doctrine, has attempted to dominate the content of intellectual activity so that the results would correspond with its ideology. It has not just been a matter of assuring that intellectuals observe their civil obligations and avoid subversive actions and proposals, or that they produce works which will be useful to the state. It has rather been an effort to make intellectuals create in such a way that what they create will exemplify and affirm the ruling ideology.

To achieve this end, totalitarian elites have established a comprehensive system of control. They have attempted to organize intellectual life far beyond what is required either by the inner nature of contemporary intellectual activity or by the functional tasks which the state, the economy, and society place before it. In many fields, this political machinery prescribes a degree of uniformity which is incompatible with the indeterminateness which is inherent in any creative undertaking. Through the control of appointments, promotions, funds, and publication and distribution facilities, totalitarian elites have tried to predetermine the content of the output of their intellectuals, particularly in those spheres which touch most closely on the sacred ideology or on politically sensitive questions.

In pluralistic societies, both advanced and underdeveloped, intellectual achievements are judged preponderantly according to intellectual standards, and promotions, appointments, and success are in the main guided by these standards. Occasionally political, religious, communal, and personal considerations enter—they do so more in the literary sector of the intellectual class than in those sectors which are more institutionalized and more specialized. The political elite generally abstains from entry into such matters; it does so rarely even in the United States, where there have been more intrusions of political elites than in the United Kingdom. In totalitarian societies, the political elite tries to impose its own standards on the intellectual community by rigorous control over the educational system which produces candidates for intellectual careers, over selection, and over the right of publication.

This has entailed the intrusion of standards which are inherently foreign to intellectual creativity and to the elaboration and development of intellectual traditions.

This imposition can be carried out—to the extent that it is carried out—in some measure through the creation of a bureaucracy to supervise intellectual work and to check on its conformity with official expectations. Naturally this bureaucracy attracts, on the whole, persons of a type who have little sense of what is involved in intellectual creation. This hampers their capacity to supervise effectively—which in any case can never be done with complete effectiveness. The political-administrative supervisors of intellectual activity in totalitarian societies range from imperious bullies and subservient party hacks of no distinction at all intellectually to Janus-faced figures who try hard to please their political superiors while also protecting, as well as they can under unpropitious circumstances, the careers and freedom of creative intellectuals. Within the intellectual system itself, control over incipient deviants is exercised by the disposition of patronage in the form of grants for foreign travel, better housing accommodations, honors and advancement within the intellectual system. Those who exercise control on behalf of the political elite are themselves professional intellectuals and only amateur politicians, but this does not always make their standards of judgment less political.

VI

Intellectual life in the twentieth century has become much more subject to external demands than it was in the nineteenth century. It is more under pressure from political elites and administrators and more under pressure from various currents of opinion. These external pressures have contributed to a greater degree of institutionalization of intellectual activity. Even where the ideological pretensions of totalitarian and oligarchical elites have been absent, the widespread belief in the functional utility of intellectually qualified persons in any society of the contemporary world has caused much of modern intellectual activity to become bound to an organizational machine. A good deal of the organizational machinery arises from the dependence of intellectual institutions, and even of individual, uninstitutionalized intellectual activity, on the financial support of the state.

There has been an immense increase in the expenditures for intellectual activities in the budgets of practically all states. Universities in almost all countries are now dependent on their governments for financial support. In England, where the two older universities were almost entirely self-sufficient financially forty years ago, and where the modern universities received only a fraction of their funds from the state, the situation has changed profoundly. In the United States, the improved position of the state universities and the increased share of federal funds in the budget of the great private universities are accompanied, as in England, by a comparable increase in the conduct of scientific research supported by grants from civil and military branches of the government. Parallel developments may be seen in India, Japan, and Soviet Russia, which operate modern university systems and seek to accelerate scientific and technological research. In quite impoverished countries, with only a scanty apparatus of modern intellectual activity, the state is the chief provider since there is no private patronage to speak of and since even the most uninstitutionalized forms of modern intellectual activity require a steady income, which means regular employment.

The fiscal policies of modern states have contributed to the destruction of the classical type of Maecenas: in India, the maharajahs no longer perform the function of patronage, which was once one of their redeeming features. In Britain, death duties have eroded the great fortunes. Only in the United States does private patronage still occupy a prominent position in the support of intellectual work. There, an old form of patronage, the philanthropic foundation, has been adapted to modern intellectual life. It has been organized, freed of the element of personal clientage which was present in the classical patron-client relationship, and extended into nearly every sphere of intellectual creation.

Changes in the nature of scientific research in many fields have promoted institutionalization. The large scale which is characteristic of many contemporary scientific and scholarly inquiries has enforced the need for collaboration and administration in spheres where they were practically absent in earlier centuries of the modern age.[6] This change in modes of intellectual procedure has, in turn, added to this financial dependence on extra-intellectual institutions. The large scale of scientific and scholarly inquiries made possible by collaboration has called for large funds: not only do more research projects now require larger staffs than were conventionally required in the nineteenth century, when the professor and his research students supplied the necessary manpower, but scientific research has become prodigiously more expensive simply because it requires vastly more complicated apparatus. Reaching outward into the heavens, inward toward the particle, the instruments of science can no longer be paid for from the private purse of a landed gentleman, from the pocket of a professor, or from a small regular grant for the maintenance of a laboratory. The complicated apparatus requires a larger staff to handle it. The newer types of social and economic research—countrywide inquiries into consumers' budgets, studies of national income and industrial productivity, investigations of social

6. It is not that there were no large-scale "projects" before the present century. The great encyclopedias were works of immense collaborative effort; the monumental undertakings in the publication of historical and literary source materials entailed a great deal of collaboration over long periods of time. Nonetheless, the intellectual bureaucracies of past times seem to have been smaller, looser, and less specialized than are our contemporary intellectual-administrative bureaucracies.

and political attitudes on the basis of national samples—cost sums that would have been unimaginable to investigators in these fields five decades ago. The scientist and scholar cannot now, as easily as they did a century or a half-century ago, decide to follow a certain line of interest and then set about it forthwith, without consulting anyone else or seeking financial aid. Now they must apply for a grant from a government department, an academy, a foundation, or their own university, which must itself then turn to the government or to a foundation. This process is most advanced in the United States, but it has also made great strides in the United Kingdom, France, Germany, Japan, and India. For these same reasons, and additional reasons as well, it is perhaps more pervasive and dominant in the Soviet Union. On a proportionally smaller scale, it is equally characteristic of the poor countries of Africa and the Middle East. Indeed there are few modern intellectual activities outside literature which escape institutionalization.

These changes have given rise to a large bureaucracy which now administers the financial support and auxiliary services of intellectual life. The contemporary bureaucracy which looks after the administration, finance, and service of intellectual activity is much more elaborate and much more intimately linked with intellectual activity than were the ministries of culture and national education in the German, French, or other European states which exercised much power in the nineteenth and early twentieth centuries.

This bureaucratic transformation of intellectual activity—in which bureaucratic roles are filled by practicing intellectuals—affects the functions which the isolated individual inquirer once performed in the choice of problems, procedures, and substantive approach to intellectual works.

To these it has added the new task of selecting and assigning personnel and in gathering financial support. For the most part, the decisive powers in these institutionalized sectors of intellectual activity have remained with intellectuals even in countries where political elites and governmental administrators are very intrusive. The strength of will of the diverse sectors of the intellectual class in totalitarian countries varies. It has hitherto been strong enough in many vital spheres to resist pressure on the choice of problems, on approaches, and on the selection of personnel, but it has not always been successful. A new effort is being made now in the German Democratic Republic to turn university study into an adjunct of industry. It remains to be seen whether it will be more successful than Soviet research and development, which has tried to gain the ascendancy over Soviet pure sciences but with fluctuating success.

But even granted the toughness of intellectual traditions, the intrusion of political and administrative tasks presents a constant threat. In pluralistic countries like the United States, Great Britain, and the German Federal Republic, the external governmental bureaucracy which administers funds tries to avoid introducing political considerations and is generally ready to be guided by the most outstanding academic opinion. The simple fact of financial power remains nonetheless an always open opportunity for the introduction of an extra-intellectual component into decisions, which for the health of intellectual traditions should remain within the actively creative intellectual class.

VII

Thus far we have dealt primarily with that sector of the intellectual class concerned with science and scholarship and working in higher educational and research institutions. This sector, although its importance and its proportion have greatly increased in the present century, is by no means the whole of the intellectual class. Its members do not even exhaust the sector of the institutionalized intellectual roles, to say nothing of the freelance, independent intellectuals, rentiers, or self-supporting intellectuals, who still continue a traditional, at one time more preponderant, role.

The progress of technology in films, television, and radio, and the supplementation of journalism by the vast increase in governmental (and private) publicity and propaganda, have added to the numbers of corporately employed intellectuals. There is little difference in the direction of this trend in any of the three types of societies we are discussing except with regard to numbers, and the greater dominance in totalitarian countries of political-ideological considerations deriving from the preoccupations of the political elite in personnel policy and in the assessment of intellectual products, with the maintenance of a uniformity of opinion. The increase in the opportunities for employment has permitted many persons with intellectual propensities and training and with literary ambitions to find a regular income instead of the uncertain and fluctuating income from the sale of literary works. In underdeveloped countries where illiteracy and poverty restrict the market for literary works, employment in the information services absorbs many of those literary men who are not engaged in teaching or the civil service.

The private scholar and the independent author, free from the control of writers' unions and with free access to a variety of separate publishers, still exist in the advanced pluralistic societies. There, the diminished proportion of the institutionally unconnected rentier or freelance scholars and literary men within the intellectual classes still leaves, thanks to greater literacy and ampler purchasing power, a large enough market to support many independent authors.

In the underdeveloped countries of Asia and Africa, however, entirely independent or self-sustaining authors are relatively rare phenomena. In comparison with these, intellectuals employed in universities, schools, colleges, newspapers and periodicals, broadcasting systems, governmental and private administrative organizations or research institutions, form the vast majority.

In totalitarian countries, rentier intellectuals cannot exist; but literary men and artists who are self-supporting through their works certainly do exist, and many flourish. They do not, however, enjoy the same independence as writers in pluralistic countries, because their membership in the politically obligatory writers' association and their conformity with its demands govern their access to the public. Although the actual work of literary production inevitably —owing to the very nature of such creation—is carried on individually in totalitarian countries, a far-reaching institutionalization of the literary profession has been carried out. Opportunity, exhortation, praise, and censure are allocated by functionaries according to their interpretation of what they regard as the right policy; decisions to publish any work or to withhold it from publication are made in the same way and by the same standards.

There is no inherent necessity in modern, large-scale society for the high degree of institutionalization and control over the processes of literary and artistic creation which is characteristic of totalitarian countries. It is contrary to the internal necessities of such creative activity. Insofar as this institutionalization of the immediate environment of literary production is fully successful, it attains that success only by constriction of creative achievement. It should be added that efforts of unitary and pervasive control are seldom wholly successful because disagreements among those in control of literary institutions such as writers' unions, publishing enterprises, and periodicals do occur, and they follow different policies and offer their facilities to authors of different styles and viewpoints. Furthermore, authors are sometimes able to mask their attitudes to some extent, although this alternative, owing to the suspicions of the custodians, is only infrequently successful.

In the traditional modes of expression, the situation in the advanced pluralistic countries is radically different. There, too, however, the doctrinal whims of publishers and their editors might mean that authors of certain styles or standpoints find some difficulty in obtaining publication, while others whose accomplishments are slighter but whose outlook is more congenial to the majority of the publishing industry find it much easier to be published. Nonetheless, a wide variety of organs of publication exist, and there is practically no exclusion from publication.

In the mass media, which require much larger capital investments than book and periodical publication and which even in pluralistic countries are either under governmental control—as in the case of television and radio—or are regulated by the government, political criteria sometimes come into play in personnel policy or in the acceptance and production of certain kinds of works. Critics of the cultural and intellectual level of works presented or produced in the mass media in pluralistic countries have charged that the institutions of the mass media threaten the maintenance of intellectual traditions not by repression, exclusion, or prohibition as in totalitarian countries, but by the temptations of easy fame and fortune which the media present. These, they allege, cause intellectuals who otherwise would have adhered to the traditions of high culture to turn to the production of mediocre and trivial works of mass culture. Although the criticism might hypothetically be true, neither evidence nor principle confirm it. Some works of high cultural quality have been produced in the mass media, and adherence to the practice of the more traditional genres is no guarantee of the high quality of performance. Corruption and the diversion of aspirations from literary production to the gratification of stable income and chances of promotion and power undoubtedly do occur, but there is no reason to conclude that they affect those with strong motivation or outstanding literary and artistic talent.

VIII

The modern elites of the underdeveloped countries of Asia and Africa have come to the aspiration for modernity in a situation in which their own countries were largely devoid of any institutional framework for the conduct of a modern intellectual life. Their modern intellectual outlook was acquired through study in universities in the centers of Western civilization or institutions in their own countries founded by foreign missionaries and administrators. The provision of such opportunities was very sparse, as was the opportunity to employ this outlook in a vocation after its acquisition.

In these countries, except for India, the modern intellectual elite has been very small; its field of operation is confined in the main to government service, teaching, politics, journalism (which is often political), and the practice of law (also often a platform for political activity). There are few opportunities for modern scholarly or scientific research, and modern forms of literature have a tiny market and very few who could, or even now can, practice it professionally, unless their works can find a predominantly metropolitan reading public.

Except for a few centers in particular archeological, historical and linguistic subjects in India, Japan, and China, there were, until recently, few possibilities for advanced research and teaching in modern intellectual fields throughout those areas of the world. For most of Africa and South and Southeast Asia this is still the case. The scientific services of the government remain small, the employment of scientifically qualified persons in industry is slight, partly because there is little industry, partly because indigenously owned industry does not do research and development, and foreign-owned industry does its research and development in the metropolis.

The belief that one's country should become modern has included the belief that this could occur only through the creation of a corps of intellectuals. The existence of a class of highly educated persons is regarded as an essential constituent of a modern regime as well as a necessary functional prerequisite. This has necessitated the creation of a system of modern intellectual institutions where previously there were only scattered fragments such as a medical school here and a law of engineering school there. It has also entailed a sharply critical attitude toward the inherited structure of intellectual institutions and of the attitudes of the intellectuals staffing them or produced by them.

In striving to rectify these deficiencies, governments[7] have had almost a monopoly of initiative as well as a near-monopoly of the financial resources for taking such initiative.[8]

For these reasons, intellectual activities receiving the support, promotion, and surveillance of the state are more characteristic of underdeveloped countries than of the advanced pluralistic countries. The deliberate effort to cultivate and foster intellectual activity could occur only if some important part of the political elite took it in hand. In most underdeveloped countries, public opinion supporting the development of intellectual institutions and intellectual activities is borne by too small a section of the population and disposes over too small a fund of resources to contribute a great deal to the promotion of the intellectual cause. Its largest performance is the establishment of numerous poorly conceived and conducted colleges in India and Pakistan. For the vastly preponderant part, it is the state which must take the task in hand, if it is taken in hand at all.

Even in the promotion of an artistic and literary intelligentsia, governments of the underdeveloped countries of Asia and Africa have felt called upon to evince interest and to act through financial provision and intellectual establishment. Governments cannot write books or paint pictures; and where they do not wish to control

7. In some instances, the initiative was exercised by the colonial government in anticipation of the needs of the prospectively independent state.

8. As might be expected from the nature of the social structure in most underdeveloped countries, there has been, except for ecclesiastically supported institutions, relatively little private initiative in the promotion and financial support of intellectual activity other than undergraduate instruction.

content but to aid creation, they have sought to provide the conditions under which writing and painting could be done. This has also required organization to consider applications, administer grants, award prizes, facilitate publications, etc.

In research in science and scholarship, governments in most of the new countries have lavished attention—within the limits of their resources—on the extension and elaboration of the old institutions founded for such purposes by the foreign rulers before their withdrawal and on the creation of new ones. Since these activities, together with the production of qualified intellectual personnel, are among the first interests of governments, there is little reason to be surprised that the uninstitutionalized or independent intelligentsia occupies such a minor place in underdeveloped countries of Asia and Africa.

Governmental action and finance have been indispensable if anything at all was to be done. They have brought, however, the dangers of pressures for output (primarily of personnel and to a lesser extent of publications), of political interference in appointments policy and in the determination of teaching and research programs. Direct political interference, although striking instances can be cited from Singapore to West Africa, has been, by and large, not very frequent. More distracting has been abusive criticism from radical populistic politicians and radical populists within the staffs of the allegedly "neo-colonialist" culture of the institutions and their continued attachment to the culture of the metropolis.

IX

Despite the nearly universal diffusion of the modern intellectual outlook, and of the intellectual procedures it involves, its Western origin remains, in those countries of Asia and Africa where it has been incipiently implanted, a fact of more than historical importance.

In every country to which it came, there was an indigenous culture which dominated the lives of the vast majority of the inhabitants. In Asia, these indigenous cultures had a continuous history of long duration and great achievements, and this added weight to the compellingness which flowed from the fact of being indigenous. They were cultures of great intrinsic intellectual, moral, and aesthetic value; they were elaborate, coherent, and comprehensive. They had, in their priesthoods, in their monastic orders, and in their traditional teaching professions, intellectuals of their own.

The modern intellectual outlook and the traditions in which it grew were foreign to this indigenously traditional intellectual culture. Their foreignness was underscored by their association with foreign conquerors who imposed their hegemony on the indigenous society, supplanting or dominating the traditional political elites.

The modern intellectual outlook has exercised an irresistible fascination on certain strata of the societies outside the European center. In Asia, particularly, but also in Eastern Europe and in Africa, it has won adherence through its critique of tradition and its individualism, which would liberate man from the heavy burden of an individuality-suppressing culture. Since, however, its devotees, in the areas of the world to which it is not native, remained in important ways very attached to their traditional pattern of life, they came, because of this surviving attachment, to feel inferior to the foreign culture which attracted them so much and which they esteemed so highly. The situation was not made any easier to bear by the often explicit derogation of their own culture and society which they encountered among their foreign rulers and even in the works and attitudes of the intellectuals of the foreign culture which they so much admired.

This feeling of intellectual inferiority vis-à-vis the West still exists in the underdeveloped countries and, indeed, in almost all areas of the world. It survives in the Soviet Union; it was common in the United States in the nineteenth and early twentieth centuries and is not yet entirely dead there. Among the more backward totalitarian countries[9] and among the intellectuals of the underdeveloped countries of Asia and Africa, it is very strong. The preoccupation with the Western intellectual outlook has been strong even in those sections of the population which have become fervently nationalistic. The two conflicting attachments are very closely connected with each other. For political purposes as well as out of deeply rooted sentiments, certain sections of the political and intellectual elites of these countries assert the greater appropriateness of their own cultural tradition to their national life, and claim that the Western outlook in one way or another has a debilitating effect. There are those who say that it destroys all that was genuine and great in the past history of the society; there are others who say that its perspective prevents the society from moving forward into a future free from the bondage of colonialism. The radical reactionary, past-loving intellectuals and politicians and the radical revolutionary, future-loving intellectuals and politicians become identical at this point. At the same time, they seek to remodel their own societies so that they will conform more closely to the Western tradition.

9. The feeling of provinciality with respect to the metropolitan culture in these countries acquires an additional complication through the establishment of the Soviet Union as a cultural metropolis from which to draw guidance. It is at least the intention of the Communist elites in these countries to replace the West by the Soviet Union as their cultural metropolis. The effort, however, has not been successful, as developments in Poland and Roumania have shown.

The situation is made more involved by the fact that, in all the underdeveloped societies, the major languages for maintaining contact with the modern intellectual tradition must be Western languages. In Black Africa, past the very first years of school, a European language is the medium of instruction. Throughout Black Africa and in parts of the Middle East and Southeast Asia, at the higher educational level, a European language is frequently the medium of instruction. Where it is not, much of the reading of the students and the teachers must still be in books either printed in European languages or translated from European languages. The reality and the subjective experience of dependence on the metropolitan culture remain, and, with them, the tension between this dependence and the indigenous traditional culture also remains. It is likely to continue to be so until the modern indigenous intelligentsia, devoted to modern intellectual traditions, becomes creative in its own right, and produces its own literature, and its own scientific and scholarly research on a level which convincingly justifies the esteem which it demands. When this occurs, then the self-esteem of the intelligentsia which creates and consumes it will become well founded and it will transcend its provinciality.

X

The strains of provinciality and the struggle with their own indigenous and yet alien cultural traditions are not problems which confront the more advanced pluralistic countries, where the modern intellectual traditions are indigenous. The preoccupation with the metropolis was to some extent a serious problem in the United States, but even in its worst phase American culture was only a provincial culture vis-à-vis the metropolis of Britain, France, and Germany, and there was never an alternative cultural tradition, deeply different in substance, which exercised a pull in the opposite direction.

Another counterpressure against the modern intellectual tradition has begun to attract the attention of intellectuals in the advanced pluralistic societies, above all in the United States, and to a lesser extent Great Britian, France, and Germany. It has begun to emerge in distorted form as a preoccupation of communist ideologies in the more advanced totalitarian countries. We refer here to the mediocre and brutal cultural products presented on such a vast scale over the newer mass media of film, radio, and television and consumed by all classes outside the intelligentsia. Pornography is part of this brutal culture.

In all advanced industrial countries a higher standard of living and more leisure have released desires for simple, crude, and exhilarating pleasures in sections of the population formerly bound down by fatigue, tradition, and necessity. The result has been a consumption of "popular culture." In large cities of India and other under-developed countries, its first tinkles and rumbles can be heard. In the economically advanced totalitarian countries, the same tastes and aspirations exist, but they are repressed by the communist elite. A puritanical ideology, and resentment against the indulgence of their "masses" and their "youth" in pleasures imported from the West and not provided for by Marxism, account for the refusal of the communist elite to acknowledge the legitimacy of these strata of culture.

Many intellectuals in the Western countries look upon popular culture as a challenge and a threat to the inherited traditions of creative intellectual life. It does compete with works which stand in the superior intellectual tradition; in its aspiration for an expanded audience, it draws personnel from the circles which have been brought into contact with the great traditions; and by its visible and audible presence and its obvious popularity and capacity to give pleasure, it affronts the claims of creative culture to universal validity and universal acceptance.[10]

XI

The traditions of modern intellectual life have shown a high degree of adaptability. They have shown themselves able to withstand a quite considerable degree of involvement with corporate forms. Indeed, certain parts of these traditions have never flowered as they have within the structure of the universities. They have been able to withstand their dependence on the state for financial support and their occasional surveillance by the state. The great achievements of the French and German universities under state financial and administrative control in the nineteenth century, and the no less great achievements of the British universities since the entry of the state as their chief patron, are ample testimony to the capacities of certain strands of the modern intellectual tradition to adapt them-selves to new and uncongenial circumstances.

Nor has political tyranny such as the totalitarian states have exercised shown itself able to destroy the tradition of modern intellectual life. The impressive achievements of Soviet physics and chemistry, and the great vitality and curiosity which many observers

10. In the advanced communist countries, it is regarded as a form of American corruption, which infects those who have not been adequately penetrated by their own ideological tradition. In the underdeveloped countries, both traditional and modern intellectuals, both pro- and anti-Western, regard it likewise as a corruption which flows from an amoral industrial civilization. Even the modernizers wish to avoid it.

have noted among the younger generation of Soviet academic intellectuals, are evidence that political supervision and far-reaching demands for ideological conformity cannot be truly successful in their efforts to permeate and dominate intellectual fields in which a great tradition has been alive and which still attract creative talents of a high order. As long as some measure of autonomy is left to the acknowledged superiors in a field of intellectual work to choose and train their closest collaborators and their most intimate apprentices and to control what is published in their organs of communication, the tradition can live on despite temporary appearances of submergence. Even where, as in the field of literature, those who are made the custodians of the organs of communication—the publishing houses and the critical reviews—are conforming political placeholders and flatterers of the mighty, the extinguishing of a great literary tradition does not lie within the powers of the tyrants or their supine agents.

Within the advanced pluralistic societies, specialization which develops from the internal evolution of the intellectual disciplines constitutes a greater impediment to the growth of the modern intellectual tradition than do most of the external distractions arising out of those societies. Specialization postulates the unquestioning acceptance of an inherited framework of analysis and it often proceeds to forget it. Traditions grow not merely from the elaboration of the inherited framework but from its continuous transformation and deepening. It is not that specialization renders this type of growth impossible. It does, however, render it more difficult. Particularly as specialization becomes a common characteristic of the world of learning, mutual criticism across the boundaries of specialization is obstructed; and it is just at the boundaries that growth occurs.

It is unnecessary to stress the injury which extreme specialization does to the transmission of the intellectual tradition in its broader sense. Not only are the substantive content, the particular works of that tradition, forgotten, but the sensitization of the mind to the wider possibilities of thought that the modern tradition carries with it is diminished by the loss of contact.

If specialization continues unchecked and if institutional means are not discovered which can retain its intellectual advantages and prevent some of its harmful repercussions, there might be little hope of a continuing creativity at deeper levels. The great intellectual tradition will be transmitted haltingly and discontinuously. It will have to be recurrently rediscovered by the powerfully inquisitive mind which, with little direct help from the tradition, breaks out of the restraints which specialization imposes.

The constraints of tyranny, the tribulations of excessive administration, the dilutions and distractions of mass culture, the shrinking of specialization, are all, in a sense, barbarians at the border of intellectual life. The capacity of intellectual life to resist their invasion comes down, in the last analysis, to the strength of the tradition itself. This is not merely a tautology.

If the intellectuals of a given country feel themselves attached to the great models of intellectual work, if they have incorporated the standards implicit in that work into their own outlook, and embedded them in a sense of self-confidence about their own capacities to bring them actively into intimate contact with the universe, then we may say that the intellectual traditions are strong. Such intellectuals will be able to forestall the invasion.

Intellectual traditions undergo elaboration and transformation because human beings of a high degree of creativity become genuinely imbued with them, breathe and emanate them. The modern intellectual tradition is no unchanging substance, and reverent acceptance will bring it to a standstill. It can go on only if there is a mutual contact between itself and energetic minds who are capable of accepting its discipline as a point of departure and who can then come back from it from a newly attained standpoint and critically reassess and reformulate it. Such minds enliven sensibilities of young persons, mold and guide them in their own direction, and implant into them some of the lively relationship to tradition which they themselves possess.

This active, outgoing orientation toward an intellectual tradition becomes, in those who accept its discipline, a personal quality as tough, as rooted, and as unyielding to external pressures as the most constitutive quality of a strong, expansive personality. The fundamental qualities of such personalities cannot be changed or instigated or uprooted by exhortation or by the promise of rewards or by threats; and by the same token, the active orientation toward the intellectual tradition has great resilience and resistive powers. It is formed by the exercise of intellectual powers on a problem and a subject matter, and it is maintained through that exercise and through direct contact with those who share that orientation and through an intellectual conviality with their unseen presence.

The superimposition of a bureaucratic administration, the organization of an elaborate system of financial provision, and other distractions and temptations might draw the weaker away from intellectual work or cause them to temper their sails to the winds of grants, official favor, promotion, and the pleasures of ordering other people about. They do not break down the attachments of the firmly attached. They cannot enter into the intimate relationship between colleagues equally devoted to their tradition or between master investigators and their apprentices. Tyranny may crush men physically, it can thrust them into the outer darkness where they are unable to do their work, it can silence them, and it can corrupt them, it can rule its society with the aid of the police and the army; but it cannot destroy the intellectual tradition unless it also annihilates those who bear it. Modern tyrannies have never succeeded in doing this—though they have exiled many and sent many others to concentration camps.

As long as totalitarian regimes allow creative personalities who have had contact with the great intellectual traditions to work in libraries and laboratories, to have pupils, and to be in touch with each other through their published writings and through conversation, the continuity and growth of intellectual traditions are not seriously in danger. Somehow the mind finds its way and the stream flows onward.

This assumes, however, that the modern intellectual tradition is already there and that there are strong personalities ready to receive it. The situation of the underdeveloped countries, however, is not like this. There, the tradition has not yet taken root, and the major problem is its implantation.

The modern intellectual tradition can become implanted in the countries where the traditional culture is alien to it. For this to occur, however, requires some release of the creative potential, its emancipation at least partially from the discipline of its own indigenous tradition and its inflammation in its deepest reaches by the modern traditions. It requires genius and a position in the aspostolic succession which links genius to genius across generations and national boundaries. It requires the congeniality of an environment populated with strong and like-minded persons, free to go their own way. It requires a self-confidence which is genuine. In the underdeveloped countries, the modern intellectual atmosphere is attenuated, self-confidence is thinner, and the chances of ignition are correspondingly smaller. But they exist.

In such countries, the tyranny of bureaucracy, the counter-pressures of specialization and of the much denser and more permeative indigenous traditional culture are greater dangers than they are in the advanced countries. They are not, however, inevitably victorious. The success of the Japanese in assimilating and going forward with the modern intellectual tradition and the appearance of scattered geniuses in India in the present century are evidences that the essential ingredients exist. It is the task of statesmen to allow the sparks to turn into flames, and to avoid the temptation to smother them in elaborate and expensive structures of administration and incessant demands for immediate and useful results.

XII

Ultimately man is an incorrigibly wayward and willful creature. The "old Adam" cannot be expunged from the species. Neither can the active, curious, pushing, questioning, self-disciplining mind. Unlike the old Adam, who needs no tradition, the active mind does need its own traditions. Once such minds are enabled to find contact with those traditions which will guide and form them, and if they are allowed within their own intimate sphere a freedom of play and movement, we may look with assurance on the chances of the modern intellectual tradition to move ahead, to transform itself, and to continue to be what it has been. And all this under very different circumstances from those which presided over its birth and early years.

Part Two

Intellectuals in Modern
Societies

5 The High Culture of the Age

For centuries, in the great but, by present standards, not very populous societies of the past, the life of the intellect was carried on by very small numbers of persons. What can have been the number, in fourth-century Rome, of the producers of intellectual objects—poets, historians, moral and natural philosophers, grammarians, mathematicians, epigrammists, dramatists, speculators on the affairs of the commonwealth, teachers of law and rhetoric and all the other subjects a highly educated Roman was supposed to know? How many consumers of their works and ministrations were there—studious and reflective civil servants, lawyers and politicians, well-read landowners, great figures of the state who cultivated and patronized literary men?—All these together in Rome itself must have been a rather small circle of men. Five thousand persons at any one time might not be too outrageous a guess. It could not have been very great; the number of copies of each book was small, so that very few persons could have led a very intense and diversified intellectual life. There was not enough in quantity or diversity on which many could feed.

Let us take the whole of England in 1688. The inheritance was much richer and activities more diversified. The numbers of those who devoted themselves to intellectual pursuits were surely greater than in Rome, although the total population which could be drawn on was smaller. There were two universities, numerous grammar schools with educated teachers, a thriving theater, a book-publishing trade far larger in its output than the Roman book-copying systems. There was a national church with an administrative staff in which educated men could find a place. There were dissenting sects which took theological study with great seriousness. There were 10,000 clergymen, men of education and intellectual concern. The civil service might have been more dilapidated than the Roman bureaucracy of the third century, but the mode of recruitment meant that there were always likely to be some men of intellectual training and interests among them. There were 10,000 of these. There was a considerable gentry, of whom there must have been a considerable

Previously published in a slightly different form in *The Arts and Society*, edited by Robert N. Wilson, © 1964. Reprinted by permission of the publisher, Prentice-Hall, Inc., Englewood Cliffs, New Jersey.

minority interested in intellectual things. There was a legal profession of almost 10,000. There was a medical profession. There were playwrights and actors, writers trying to live from their writing of potboilers or from the patronage of the great. There were artists and musicians, composers and performers. Intellectually, England was the home of a group of the very greatest scientists in the whole history of science; philosophy and political thought saw some of their greatest achievements brought forth at this time. Modern historical scholarship was taking form. But the numbers of creative spirits were small. They, their audience, and the ranks of the less creative who helped to supply this audience with instruction and entertainment—although many times more numerous than the genuinely creative—were, taken all together, probably fewer than 70,000.

In any one of the great contemporary societies of the West, the United States or Great Britain or France or Western Germany, the situation is markedly different. The intellectual institutions, universities, technological colleges, research institutes, public and university libraries, bibliographic services, publishing houses, the better newspapers, reviews, and periodicals, sound broadcasting and television, learned societies and academies, all engage great numbers of highly educated persons, many at whom are very productive, some of whom are creative at the level of genius. They provide intellectual services for a vast audience of students, readers, viewers, and listeners, as well as for the narrower, but nonetheless very large, circle of the productive whose works must be assessed, selected, and graded to enable other producers and the vast audience of consumers to have an approximate map of the intellectual continent. College and university teachers, scientists, authors, journalists, artists must come to more than a half million in the United States alone. The audience is very much larger, since members of the professions and occupations from which the audience of intellectual work is generally constituted numbered more than four million in 1950 in the United States. The magnitudes are not too different in Great Britain, West Germany, and France.

The sheer volume and diversity of production in the intellectual (including expressive) domain are incomparably greater than in any other epoch. As compared with the middle of the nineteenth century or the beginning of the twentieth century, the stock of intellectual "goods" is enormous, and it goes on expanding in the second half of this century. The inheritance from the past is preserved, and the increment enriches the stock and adds to the intellectual wealth and burden of the oncoming generation of each successive decade.

But what of the quality of this outpouring? Does the quantitative increase automatically entail an improvement in quality? Is the truth of science in any subject simply a function of the amount of work done? Does history become truer and does it penetrate to the essentials better simply by virtue of the number of historians and the amount of work they perform? Is the quality of poetry improved as a result of an increase in the amount of poetry written and published? Although a proper answer requires some qualifications, a first approximation to an adequate answer may be made by saying, "Of course not."

Still, the overwhelming multiplication of the personnel, provision, and output of the intellectual activities of our society is not without some influence. Some persons would say, as Mr. Kingsley Amis has said of the expansion of the numbers of university students in the United Kingdom, "More is worse." There are others who, interpreting "more" as derivative of "modern," would go further and say that "modern is worse."

It almost seems that no sooner had "the Battle of the Books," "la querelle des anciens et des modernes," been won by modernity than some of the beneficiaries of the victory turned around and proclaimed its nullity. This diminution-in-growth had been traced by certain contemporaries to the very nature of modern society in its latest phase, to the nature of mass society. This concern is not a new one. Scarcely had modernity accredited itself than its derogation began in a new form. From the *Discours sur les sciences et les arts* onward, a clamorous flood has risen. The Parisian mob, comprised mainly of those alleged buttresses of order, the artisanat, set loose a specter which sensitive and ungenerous imaginations transformed into a pandemonium of culture-destroying devils. The years 1830, 1848, 1871 horrified many of the European high intelligentsia and made them fear the new age.

Today the detractors of mass society look upon that great and stuffy bourgeois age, which preceded the formation of "mass society," as a wonderful, irretrievably lost age of a genuine individuality and dignity of the mind. Some of the best spirits of the time, ancestors of the present anxiety, claimed even then to see the first erosion which the democratic flood was to cause to the culture of the educated classes. Their criticisms were not specific. They confused the philistine vulgarity of the bourgeoisie with the barbarity of the populace. They rendered no just comparison of their own age and some better past, and in some respects they did no more than repeat the ancient denunciations of the present as a sorry falling away from a better, more virtuous past. The recently prevailing conception of "mass society" in most intellectual circles is only the latest form of this unexamined devil whose mere existence degrades the culture of his betters.

Of course it is conceivable that our present high culture, viewed from a sure and detached standpoint, is poorer than the high culture of any comparable span of years in the past. There might be any number of reasons or causes for that deterioration. The distribution and efflorescence of genius are mysterious matters.

There may be waves of cultural movement which we cannot discern. It is conceivable, although not very likely, that our neural equipment is poorer than that of our ancestors. And even if it is as good, it might be argued that our cultural traditions have passed their point of culmination. It may be that our cultural traditions have reached exhaustion; that they contain no possibilities of further development, that they offer no point of departure even for creative minds. These are possibilities which must be considered if we conclude that our contemporary culture has sunk or is sinking below the level of those ages which have preceded us. But has high culture really declined in quality?

Has the culture of the past fifty years—which is the approximate age of "mass society"—deteriorated, as its detractors claim?

In our own time, we are surrounded by the easily visible debris of recent, unsuccessful aspirations to high achievement and by the newly formed rubbish of that mediocre culture which seeks no attainment higher than mediocrity. It takes many decades, perhaps a century, for this poor stuff to be washed away into the silt with which only research students, curio-hunting dilettantes, and scholarly investigators will concern themselves in the future. This process has already occurred for the output of the preceding centuries of the modern epoch, and those who regard themselves as the vessels of refined culture generally think only of the great classics when they think of something with which to contrast randomly selected instances of vulgar mediocrity. When, out of perversity or curiosity or for reasons of scholarship, they exhume the otherwise neglected trivia of the past, they know what they are doing. They know that they are dealing with what is inferior. They do not think that its mediocrity diminishes what is great in the age which they study. In contrast with this, films of the poorest quality, television silliness, journalistic beastliness are unqualifiedly presented as characteristic of the style of the present age and as significant of the whole.

Our present cultural cosmos, like any other, is far from homogeneous, and its coordinates and strata, cutting across us and surrounding us, do not form a determinate map in our minds. Regardless of whether the quality of our contemporary refined culture is superior to that of the past, the task of its location and assessment would be very hard.

The evidence of our decline is not, however, very impressive. It is likely that no one in our age can leap beyond the inherited stock in the way in which Galileo or Copernicus or Newton did in physics, or Harvey in physiology, or Boyle in chemistry, or Hobbes in political philosophy. Individual genius might be as great, but the vast and concerted effort and the density of achievement—which is surely on a higher level than it was in the greatest decades of the seventeenth century—make an equally striking advance more difficult to encompass. In all these domains of intellectual work in which there is in general a unilinear course of development, the state of knowledge is more advanced than it was a century or a half-century ago. The advance is not just an advance in the quantity of verified details, although this is not irrelevant. The understanding of the laws of the universe is more comprehensive, deeper, and more differentiated—we understand important things now that we did not understand then. The same obtains in fields other than physics or physiology or genetics. It is proportionately as true of the lesser disciplines like the study of politics or sociology. There is no Locke or Hobbes who has apprehended such a fundamental theme with such clarity and precision, or who has penetrated so deeply into one root of man's existence and then traced its ramifications. Yet, in a way we have advanced beyond them, and so the level of performance attained by the best of our age is in advance of that attained by seventeenth-century political philosophy, even if the magnitude of the accomplishment of any single individual thinker falls beneath that of the geniuses of the earlier century and even if some of the insights of the seventeenth century are not widely possessed among us.

Let us look at the United States, which is the cultural nightmare of those dreamers, European and American, who in their sleep produce the clichés which come from the surface of thought and from the depths of fear and animosity. Is American science on a lower level now than it was fifty years ago? Are the best of American literary critics less perceptive, less elegant in their interpretation, more superficial in their grasp of motives than their predecessors of the period before World War I? Is American painting now inferior to what it was then? Are our playwrights and novelists poorer than their like of fifty years ago?

It might be answered that things are culturally as good as they are in America today because we still draw so much from Europe—from distant models and from recent refugees and immigrants—and that America has gone forward by adding to itself what was extruded from Europe in its decades of self-destruction. Certainly American culture, which was first the creation of European culture, has continued to benefit immeasurably from the works of the most superior quality which still appear in Europe, even after the silence and desolation of two hideous wars. No American, even if he has completely emancipated himself from provincial fascination with the old metropolis, can afford to be ignorant of what is being accomplished by his colleagues in Europe, whether his field be physics, chemistry, sociology, anthropology, journalism, or literary criticism. It is right that such should be the situation. Participation as an equal contributor and beneficiary in the Western intellectual community implies no deficiency in creativity.

There are certain other features of intellectual life in the present period which call for attention when the quality of the age is placed in question. The present century has experienced an extension of its horizon and a fertilization of its sympathies of the sort which has never been seen in the Western world or in any great civilization. Indeed, it is in America that this new sensibility, disciplined by active research, has developed most uniquely. Of course oriental studies began in the eighteenth century and flourished in the nineteenth century; the great work of exploration and their chronicles began much earlier and continued as long as there were unexplored territories. Nonetheless, it must be acknowledged that the range of curiosity and the openness of sentiment have never been as great as they are now or, for that matter, more generously and discriminatingly intelligent than they are now. The artistic, social, and religious life of civilizations outside our own has never been studied so much or so soberly and humanely appreciated as it is in the past several decades. And all this is under conditions of very great difficulty, when the quantity of what there is to travel to, to see, to listen to, to read has never been greater—and when we are having to concede that our own civilization is not as ascendant in every regard as our immediate ancestors thought it was. In this new renaissance of oriental studies, America has had a great share and that largely in the years since World War II. It is no diminution of the reality of this accomplishment to acknowledge that the occasion has been the political transformations of the postwar world or that the wherewithal has come from a government involved in a cold war or from the munificence of a prosperous capitalistic economy.

Nor do I think that the standards of moral and civic integrity of the American intellectual classes have sunk particularly. It must be agreed that the thirty years after World War I saw degrees of insult and submission of intellectuals in very many countries, including the United States, which were appalling to those who had to submit.

There were, it is true, a few intellectuals who affirmed the will of their silly and not very effectual tormentors in America. A much larger number, coming out of an apolitical cocoon, became protagonists of doctrines which were injurious to intellectual life abroad and which bespoke a frivolous ignorance on their own part. Even the featherbrained leftism of the thirties was in a sense an advancement in moral sympathy and in the concern for justice. It was, moreover, accompanied by a growth in intellectual civility such as had been absent from the public life of the country for many decades. It is true that there has been an extraordinary abdication of common sense among American intellectuals since the middle of the 1960s, but they are only a little sillier than they were a half-century ago.

Simultaneously the influence and status of the intellectual classes have increased markedly. In the prosperity of their institutions and in the opportunities for research and publication the situation has never been more indulgent to the intellectual life of the country.

Nonetheless these latter considerations are peripheral to the immediate issue of the quality of contemporary intellectual life; their greater relevance will be made apparent later on.

II

Let us return to the consideration of the charge that out culture is in decline. It is a broad charge, very vague in its objects, and any rebuttal is bound to suffer from the grossness of the terms in which the problem is set. It is a criticism that intermingles without discrimination individual creative genius and the average level of production, the creators and their audiences, works and institutions, the general level of culture in the society and the cultural condition of the intellectual classes. It is a criticism characterized by the arbitrariness of its comparison of the bases of our own age with the heights of achievement in much longer periods of the past. Nor does the criticism bear in mind that in assessing contemporary culture it is comparing individuals who have not completed their careers with great figures of the past whose greatness is assessed on the basis of a completed career of great works. The argument for a decline is a poor argument and is more poorly put than it need be.

That there is a *consciousness* of decline is undeniable. Many intellectuals in Western Europe and the United States are beset by a malaise, by the malaise of a sense of isolation, of disregard or lack or sympathy, of a feeling of loss of an affective contact with that most important of all audiences, the audience formed by those who exercise power in society. The malaise takes the form of a probably unprecedented rancor.

But there is nothing new in this complaint. Romanticism antedates mass society, and in a multitude of shapes it is still far from dead. It still lives among us with full vitality and in many transformations. It was a cardinal tenet of romanticism that the creative person was cut off from his own society and that he was despised by its rulers. The contemporary romantic intellectual has, in addition, as a precipitate of revolutionary and populistic traditions, an acute sense of the cleavage between himself and "the people." Unlike his antecedents—even up to the 1940s—he does not seek to immerse himself in them (or at least, in his idea of them). He does not regard them as models or as repositories of the highest values, as many Asian and African intellectuals do. He is, instead, repelled by them. In the imagination of the present-day intellectual who has given up the substance of the revolutionary tradition while retaining its categories, the mass of the population is utterly alien to culturally significant things. It manifests the deficient sympathy with refined cultural things, the crudity of mind, the preoccupation with worthless matters, which he previously found in his rulers, particularly the new rulers of his country's economic life. In a way, the mass has acquired the character it had before romanticism and revolution took dominion over intellectual life, but unlike the writers of the seventeenth century, who attended to the populace only occasionally when it became turbulent, the contemporary critics of mass society cannot remove their minds from it as a continuous threat. The fierce partisanship for the "poor," the blacks, homosexuals, for the *Lumpenproletariat* and the outcasts of society, is of a piece with the revulsion against the mass of the population.

The too noisy, too visible, too tangible presence of mediocre and brutal culture, from which the mind can no longer be averted, has heightened their anguish. Whereas intellectuals of the earlier ages of modern society could remain indifferent to and ignorant of the impoverished cultural consumption of most of the members of their own society, this privilege is no longer given to contemporary intellectuals. Modern society is democratic, and the masses are on the minds of the intellectuals, particularly those who were once socialists who thought the working class was ready to become the heir of classical philosophy. Then, too, by virtue of their own role in the production and reproduction of these works of mediocre and brutal culture, and the evident and visible enjoyment of many of them by their consumers—including many intellectuals—intellectuals are as familiar with the manufacture of popular entertainment in the daily and periodical press, the films, and the television as their intellectual ancestors were with the heartless stinginess of patrons and the arbitrariness and frivolity of authority.

These interpretations of the motives and traditions of those who see the cultural inheritance and contemporary creativity menaced by the masses are not an adequate reply to their arguments, even though they rightly serve to set us on guard against them. The arguments themselves must be considered. Is the high culture of the ages really endangered by mass society? To what extent do such dangers as do exist differ from earlier dangers? To what extent do these dangers derive from mass society; to what extent from other sources?

High culture is not today, and never has been, the culture of an entire society. Even if it were to become the culture of the society to a much greater extent than it has ever been before, high culture must necessarily be in a state of tension vis-à-vis the rest of its society. If the producers and the consumers of refined culture see further and more deeply than their contemporaries, if they have more subtle and more lively sensibilities, if they do not accept the received traditions and the acknowledged deities as much as do their less creative and less sensitive contemporaries, whatever they say or believe or discover is bound to arouse a certain measure of hostility in some of their fellow countrymen.

Are intellectuals more endangered in mass society by the jealousy and distrust of the powerful than in other social orders? Censorship, arrest, and exile are nothing new. Can the occasional flurries of the interfering antiintellectualism of American politicians and business-men be placed on the same plane as the restraints imposed in Communist Russia and China, Fascist Italy and Spain, or National Socialist Germany, none of which are or were mass societies in the sense that the contemporary United States is or the United Kingdom, Western Germany, and France are becoming? Do the inane and exasperating intrusions of advertisers on the television screen represent a greater intrusion into the creative sphere than the prosecutions of Flaubert and Baudelaire in nineteenth-century France, the moral censorship which Mrs. Grundy once exercised so coarsely in Victorian Britain and America, or the political and religious censorship practised in eighteenth-century France? Athenian society was no mass society, and there were no advertisers there, yet Socrates was executed. I do not wish to belittle recent interferences with intellectual or artistic liberty in the United States and Western Europe, but I do wish to stress that they are not unique to mass society, that they are not more severe in mass society than in other societies, and that they do not even derive in most cases from the "mass" character of mass society.

There is one particular feature of mass society which does generate tension when confronted with refined culture. This is populism, which has been a recurrent element in the hostility of some American politicians toward intellectuals. There is no doubt that this is a distraction to intellectual life, both within the intellectual classes and outside their boundaries. But politicians, even the least populist and those who share authority with them, have never lacked legitimations for action against those whom they have regarded as guilty of lese-majesty or sacrilege. At bottom, these are the risks which intellectuals must run if they are to continue to be intellectuals. Thus, if there are intellectuals, the livelier among them must engage in the reinterpretation and transformation of the traditions which they receive from earlier generations and which they inevitably share in some measure with their fellow countrymen. Their fellow sharers do not enjoy having the tails of their sacred cows twisted by intellectuals, and that is so whether the society is a mass society or an oligarchical one. A mass society has its own special dangers, persecutory and corrupting, but I doubt whether the magnitude of the dangers places mass society in a uniquely destructive position.

It is sometimes asserted that the culture of mass society produces its insidious effects in roundabout ways that constitute a greater danger than the crude external pressures employed by the rulers of earlier societies. It seduces, it is said, rather than constrains. It offers opportunities for large incomes to those who will agree to the terms of employment offered by the institutions which are organized for the production of works of inferior value. Television, the films, the popular press, the advertising industry do attract to themselves considerable numbers of persons of some moderate intellectual quality. But does this opportunity, and even its acceptance, necessarily damage the high culture? There are two questions to be raised here. First of all, is the person with outstanding gifts destructible in any way other than physically? If his talents are accompanied by the strength of motivation and by the self-confidence which are so often associated with the successful exercise of talent, he is not likely to be drawn out of the category of activity in which his talents have found an adequate field of exercise. Even if he is tempted by money and fame and is drawn into another field—for example, from literature into films or from scholarship into journalism—his talents are very likely to show themselves there.

The argument against which I am contending implies that certain genres are incapable of offering an occasion for important achievement; entry into them is the equivalent of self-condemnation to ruin. The very fact that, here and there in the mass media, on television, and in the films, work of superior quality comes forth seems to be evidence that genuine talent is not inevitably squandered once it leaves the traditional media of refined culture to work in the mass media, which tend on the whole to present mediocre and brutal culture.

It is, of course, possible for men to waste their talents: to corrupt themselves for the pleasures of office, for the favor of authority, for popularity, for income, or for the simple pleasure of self-destruction. Qualitatively, the financial temptations of work in the media of mass communications are of the same order as the other temptations which intellectuals encounter. Quantitatively, they extend to more persons and offer more imposing rewards in extreme instances. There are many more opportunities now for intellectuals to earn large sums of money in the production of intentionally inferior cultural objects than there were before the development of the mass media. Literature is the field most likely to be affected by the temptations. There must be some unknown talents which were really distracted and ruined by the style of life and the commercial concerns of the film world. James Agee, Nathaniel West, and F. Scott Fitzgerald are the frequently cited instances; but it is excessively simplistic to attribute the miseries of these talented men to the frustrations of Hollywood alone, just as it is undeniable that, despite their miseries, they left behind works of genuine value. Poets and artists and other men have gone to the dogs before the temptations of Hollywood were invented, and there are many paths to the dogs which are followed now and which have little to do with Hollywood. Not all literary men, poets, scholars, painters, scientists, teachers have been tempted or have yielded to the temptation—even if we concede, which we do not, that their experience in the mass media prevents them from finding creative expression either in the mass media or outside them.

Popularization is something cited by the critics of mass society as one of the ways in which superior culture is being eroded. Popularization is, of course, not just a product of mass society. It is a product of a state of complexity in the development of a subject where it ceases to be directly or immediately intelligible to the layman. It is not just the ignorant brute or the passive one fixed before the television screen who is in need of popularization today. In so many fields of research in science and scholarship, the output is so large that it is difficult for an outsider—even a scientist or scholar—to penetrate into it even if he can get through the terminology. Without popularization, the ravages of specialization would be even worse than they are. Still, there is popularization and popularization, and perhaps the critics of mass culture have in mind popularization beneath the level of the *New Scientist* or *The Scientific American.* They have in mind presumably *Life* or *Reader's Digest* as organs of popularization. These are assuredly not parts of our high culture, but it is extremely difficult to see what harm they do. No person with a serious concern about intellectual matters draws on these magazines to sustain his mind, and most of those who do read them do not enter in the circle of the high intellectual activities of our society. Hence, if they are harmful, they are harmful only to the writers and editors of these journals, and, since some of these have serious intellectual pretensions and mingle with intellectuals, they might do harm in this way—or at least so the critics of mass culture could argue.

First let us consider whether writing occasionally for a popular journal or newspaper or broadcasting in a popular program is injurious to the intellectual or expressive capacities of a man or woman. To begin at the top, the late R. H. Tawney's scholarship and literary style certainly did not deteriorate because, at an early stage of his career, he was a tutor of the Workers' Educational Association. Professor Raymond Aron's thought has not become less subtle or less forceful because he writes occasionally in the *New York Times* and much more frequently in *Figaro*; Bertrand Russell suffered no intellectual injury from articles in *Look*; Professor A. J. Ayer is not a poorer philosopher nor Professor Fred Hoyle a poorer astronomer because they are such excellent broadcasters. There is no reason why an intellectual of preeminent gifts should become soft in the brain from writing articles, from time to time, for an audience unable to comprehend his usual level of analysis and exposition. An intellectual who devotes all his efforts to popularization would naturally, in the course of time, ceases to have anything of his own to popularize and would have to become a popularizer of the works of other persons. But there is no evidence whatsoever that persons who are capable of serious creative work, who are strongly impelled to it, and who do in fact devote a good deal of their energy to serious creative effort, are being unwittingly debilitated by occasional activities of popularization. The contact between a scientist and a popularizer with some scientific qualification does no harm to the scientific work of the former. American, British, and French science in the past forty years has certainly not been harmed by the development of the new branch of journalism called "scientific popularization." How many of our few outstanding political philosophers have been lost to their calling through becoming political analysts?[1] There is probably a process of selection which separates those who can create and who are strongly impelled to do so from those who, having been trained in a discipline, devote themselves to making its results intelligible to the inexpert instead of adding to its results.

But what about the popularizers themselves? What harm do they do? As far as I can see, they do no harm at all to those who read their work or to those whose work they popularize. They might do themselves a little harm; they might feel guilty of vulgarity because they share certain common prejudices of intellectuals. They might

1. Walter Lippman's name comes to mind at this point: Is *The Public Philosophy* a markedly poorer book than *Public Opinion* and *The Drift Diplomacy*? Are Professor Denis Brogan's later books *The French Republic* or *The Price of Revolution* markedly poorer than the books he wrote before he became a broadcaster and journalist? Bertrand de Jouvenel is one of the most eminent of contemporary political thinkers; he earns his livelihood by an intense journalistic activity.

feel inferior and unhappy because, quite reasonably, they regard their own category of activity as of a lower intellectual dignity than those whose works they popularize. They might make a few poor characters in the intellectual world jealous because they have not chosen the works of these persons to popularize. Neither they themselves nor their popularizing writings really afflict the main currents of the decisive forces of the subjects they touch. Has American sociology been made better or worse because Professor David Riesman appeared on the cover of *Time* or because Professor Robert Merton was the object of a *New Yorker* profile?

The production of works of inferior culture need not, however, the argument goes, destroy superior culture by striking directly at its producers, either constrainingly or seductively. It can deprive them of their market, and especially of the discriminating audience which they need to keep their skills at the highest pitch. The deformation of the taste of those consumers whose natural discriminatory powers are not so great that they can dispense with the support which a clearly ascendant and superior cultural environment provides, is certainly a possibility. There must be many people in all Western countries and certainly in the United States who would have a better content to their cultural existence if they had no choice of a poorer one. They might indeed have better lives if they were not allowed to sink to the level which at present, all things given, they enjoy more than the refined culture of their intellectual contemporaries. In other words, things could be, in one sense or another, much better than they are—or they would at least look better, like military piety under conditions of compulsory church parade—if the mass of the population were not allowed to expose themselves to the mass media.

The culture of the mass media might impede the improvement of public taste. The fact remains, however, that in the United States as well as Great Britain, discrimination in a small minority— probably larger in numbers than it was at the end of the nineteenth century—has been as perceptive as it ever was. The quality of literary criticism in the best American and British reviews is not less informed, penetrating, and reflective than it was fifty years ago in these two countries. The public for the works which are criticized in these reviews is probably larger than it once was. If it were much larger, the external cultural tone of these societies would be more seemly and these reviews would be a more severe assurance to creative intellectuals that the resonance which they need is present. But there is at least a minimal resonance, enough to help maintain a quite respectable standard of performance in the various fields of refined cultural production. There are certainly no grounds for predicting that it is bound to shrink in the future.

If no inferior cultural products were available, some of the thus liberated purchasing power might be spent on superior products. This would be to the economic advantage of those intellectuals who live from the market, and it might also raise somewhat more the general level of culture. This was the situation in Britain during World War II, and it is probably the situation in the Soviet Union today. In Britain, after the war, once inferior cultural objects became available in larger supply, the prosperity of serious book-sellers declined pronouncedly. The same would probably occur in the Soviet Union if a larger range of consumer goods, cultural and other, were to enter the market.

When, therefore, public demand is free to obtain the objects it desires, the market for refined cultural objects, given the present distribution of tastes, is restricted, and enterprisers with capital to invest will not rush in to use their resources in areas of the market where the return is relatively poor. Yet are there many manuscripts of books of outstanding merit lying unpublished today? It is true that if there is more money to be made in publishing or broadcasting works of poor quality, investors will not put their money into the production of better works for less remunerative markets. This is the principle, but for various reasons the principle does not quite work out in reality. There are investors whom irrationality or devotion to more valuable cultural activities commits to the acceptance of smaller returns on their capital. Many publishers pay for the publication of superior works with a smaller market from the proceeds of publishing less valuable works with a larger market. They do so because it has been the tradition of their trade to do so and because they are, although in business for profit, also concerned to adhere to the traditions of superior culture.

The relative unprofitability of the market for high cultural objects is compensated therefore by the existence of these enter-prisers who are motivated by considerations other than the largest possible return on their investments. It is possible that the newly developed interest of larger-scale investors who have not shared in the tradition of the book-publishing trade might change this for the worse. It remains to be seen; but meanwhile there is no certainty that it will in all cases. Some of them will want the prestige which is, in part, associated with the renunciation of profit, and they too will become assimilated into the traditional responsibilities which have never been absent from this branch of business enterprise.

The argument that the operation of the laws of the market results in the constriction of the superior cultural sphere is wrong in fact and problematic in its ethical postulate. It is problematic ethically because it implies that persons with inadequate cultural discrimina-tion should not be allowed to gratify their desires; it is also problematic because it implies that a coercively imposed superior culture would be the genuine thing. It is wrong in fact because the market is not so completely uncongenial to superior cultural goods and because superior culture does not depend, never has depended, and never should depend entirely on the market.

We often hear the old system of patronage praised by those who bemoan its passing and contrast it with the vulgar insensitivity of the rich of the present century. It is well to remember, however, what misery and humiliation the older individual patronage often imposed on its beneficiaries, how capricious and irregular it was, and how few were affected by it during the period of its greatest prevalence.

The direct private patronage of individual intellectuals by individual patrons still exists, but it plays a scant role. The place of the older form of patronage and subsidy has been taken by the universities, the state, and the private foundations, and with all their deficiencies they appear to be more liberal, more generous, and more just than their counterparts in earlier centuries.

It is only in modern times, with the growth of a literate public, that it has become possible for even a small number of authors to maintain themselves from the sale of their literary works, and for a larger number to supplement their not quite adequate literary or artistic earnings by teaching or by occasional journalism. Television and films have extended these supplementary opportunities. Just as good books with small circulations need the financial support of other and often poorer books with larger circulations, painters need the support of art schools, foundations, museums, churches, and private collectors. Scientists and scholars could never conduct their research for the returns they can get from the sale of their output. Only recently have scientists in certain countries begun to sell their services collectively to governmental bodies on a contractual basis, but the purchasers of their services (or their output) are not business enterprisers who sell the resultant scientific discoveries or inventions in a market.

So it does not seem to me that there is much to the critics' arguments about the corrupting effects of mass and commercial culture on the creators of high cultural works of the genres of higher culture, and the preemption of the market for such works. The situation of high culture is, however, far from perfect. There are many flaws and dangers, and it is to some of these that I shall now address myself.

III

The transformation of the role of the intellectual from the amateur pursuit of a rentier or landlord, or of a civil servant or courtier, to a profession has been accompanied by an increased production and distribution. Production—even if only for copying a manuscript by hand—has always required some organization, and the prodution of plays could not have come about without organization. But the practice of philosophizing, of writing poetry or history, and of conducting scientific research were individual efforts, bound into a social framework through the assimilation of a tradition, by study under a master, and by informal communication by oral discussion and correspondence. The writing of poetry is still that way; so is the writing of novels. But history is no longer that, and science is that way even less than history. Historical research nowadays entails an intricate system of training in historiography, elaborately organized archives, bodies which grant funds to scholars to enable them to travel to "their" documents; it requires a network of publishers, editors, and reviewers. Sometimes historical writing is even collaborative. Scientific research nowadays demands a tremendously elaborate and costly institutional system—science teaching at the secondary school level, university teaching, research training, the manufacture and procurement of very costly apparatus, a complex of journals with their editorial boards and referees; and the research itself is now often collaborative within a given laboratory and cooperatively competitive among laboratories over a far-flung territory. Painting and sculpture are still organizationally what they were in the Middle Ages and early modern times; commissioning is probably no more organized than it was, but the sale and distribution of paintings and sculptures are immeasurably more differentiated and dense than they were. The development of the devices of mechnical reproduction in film, radio, and television have bred a mighty bureaucracy into which the creator of the work being filmed, broadcast, or televised fits himself with various degrees of comfort or discomfort.

The greatest organizational changes have occurred in connection with the financial support and the administration of intellectual institutions. The diminution almost to extinction of the amateur scientist and scholar, great growth in the numbers of universities, and the increased proportion of all cultural life that they embrace, have meant that contemporary intellectual life is set in a far denser institutional matrix than it ever has been in the past. Applications, authorization, planned division of labor, scheduling, periodic reporting, all play a greater part now in culture than they did in an earlier age when deliberately coordinated action was unthought of or dispensable. Change in the nature of the tasks of intellectual activity, its greater dependence upon external financial support, as well as a change in the pattern of private patronage, have all helped to make the organization of financial provision more intricate than it ever was before. Culture has become more costly, and the intellectual worker is less capable of bearing its cost. It is carried on less frequently by rentier-amateurs or businessmen with intellectual interests. As a result, the producer must now be supported by the sale of his services as a teacher or as a research worker. But his salary as a teacher or research worker cannot pay for the material and equipment he needs to do his creative work, nor can it pay the other expenses, such as the travel, secretarial, and technical assistance, which is needed or which is thought to be needed. Equipment is much more complicated now than it once was, and far more expensive. Even in the social sciences, which up to thirty or forty years ago were like philosophy in their financial requirements, certain techniques of research, such as the sample survey and the use of statistical methods, have greatly increased the cost of a single piece of research. In the humanistic subjects, too, microfilming, the use of computers, and radioactive dating have introduced new financial necessities. All of these have called for an institutional machinery for receiving applications for funds from research workers and for assessing the applications and allocating funds. They have also required further organization to administer the funds in the institution to which they are granted. Committees are in frequent session to make decisions or advise on making them.

Since so much of this money comes from government and from a relatively small number of philanthropic foundations, it would appear that the direction and range of intellectual development is now subject to control from a small number of centers outside the intellectual community proper. In principle, this possibility certainly exists. In fact, it has hardly done so, even though it has changed the structure of decision making. Neither in Great Britain nor in the United States is the expenditure of the funds allocated by governments or private patrons for research and cultural activities in general independent of the control of members of the intellectual community. Through incumbency in the decision-making posts or through advisory functions, members of the intellectual community exercise a very far-reaching control over the direction which research and teaching will take. The diversity of governmental and philan-thropic sources assures also that, even if one group had a clear and firm idea of the direction into which it would like to steer a branch of cultural life, it could hardly do so because of the existence of alternative sources of funds. The volume of funds, too, and the desire to please also give assurance that only the most eccentric proposals will not find support—and even then the eccentricity which does find support is often amazing in its extremity. A new stratum of intellectual-political-bureaucratic roles has grown up as part of this situation. Persons of intellectual qualifications and achievements are drawn into administrative and policy-making roles in the intellectual community on a grander scale than ever before. In some cases the drawing off of these persons is a loss to intellectual creativity, but in others it represents a new stage in a career which was once creative and which has ceased to be creative. Since, on the whole, these persons maintain very intimate relationships with the intellectual community and depend for their sustenance and esteem on the opinion of the intellectual community, their ideas and standards—for better or for worse—are pretty much the ideas of their fellow members of this community.

Of course, in the increasingly important part of science which depends on governmental financial support, the preoccupation with national defense affects the direction of expenditure. Even within the limits of the direction, however, the free choice of the academic-scientific community plays a very important part through influential advisory functions and through a certain respect for basic research.

Scholarly and scientific creativity has, at least thus far, suffered no harm from the administrative incrustation brought about by its greater scale, cost, and division of labor. This observation applies to the universities which have been especially favored. But very much research is at present conducted by industrial and commercial enterprises as well as by governmental bodies. These are, in the main, concentrated on technological problems, and although the level of scientific skill is high, the problems on which the scientists work belong more to the realms of technology than to those of basic science proper. In this field, on the whole, the autonomy of intellectual work is foregone, but even here, not entirely. Certain institutions doing the most original work grant a great deal of autonomy to their scientists to choose their problems within the general field of common interest. Since recruitment is voluntary, the field of work chosen often corresponds to the dominant intellectual interest of the individual scientists. All this notwithstanding, this sector of the intellectual community is definitely one on which considerations of national power, private profitability, and public welfare have taken a place alongside and even superior to scientific curiosity and the internal directions of science itself.

The numbers of scientists employed in these types of institutions are likely to grow in the coming decades. What will be the impact of this growth of applied science on the quality of creative intellectual life? Applied science at present is largely derivative from university science; the university's standard of work remains uppermost, particularly in those laboratories with the highest aspirations and the highest prestige. The relationships of these latter laboratories to the centers of intellectual creativity will remain close, with the major universities continuing to have the upper hand. They will supply the leading members of the staffs, and their teaching and publications will provide the general theoretical orientations guiding technological research. Their pattern of organization—one in which the freedom to follow one's bent is predominant—will embody the standard by which the organization of governmental and industrial laboratories will be judged, by scientists inside and outside them and by responsible administrators of science. There appears, therefore, to be little likelihood that the scientific culture of the universities will be swamped by the outlook of more bureaucratically conducted institutions; the chances are better for an increased approximation to the university standard of organization on the part of the governmental and industrial scientific institutions.

This, however, is not the whole story. As the numbers of scientists in industrial and governmental laboratories increase, the universities will have the task of training their prospective staff members. This has for a long time been the case in chemistry; it has begun to be so in physics, statistics, mathematics, etc., as well as in much less developed subjects like sociology and psychology.

Will the greatly increased numbers of university students—which are a result of mass society in the sense that they are the product of a widely diffused expansion of the desire for enhanced dignity— damage the high culture of our society? There is indeed a general apprehension that they will do so. They need not do so if the newly recruited students are of an intellectual caliber equal to the students of earlier generations. There must certainly, in most countries, including the United States, be many young people of a university standard of intelligence who are not in the universities. Many lack the motivation and the culture to use their intelligence most effectively; they come from families which inhibit their social self-confidence and they are fearful of letting themselves go intellectually. Furthermore, in the United States especially, the quality of elementary and secondary instruction is such that capacities are not aroused or are permitted to atrophy. There are, in any case, even with the system of state scholarships and similar aids to the offspring of the economically poorer sections of the population, many who do not get into effective contact with the machinery of the higher culture of our society. There seem, therefore, to be veins of undeveloped talent which could enable the considerable quantitative expansion which is probably needed in the next decades to permit the maintenance of the present level of attainment.

Increased numbers might pull the cultural level of the peak downward if they afflicted all universities and every post within every university equally. But they will not do so. The greatest universities and even the fairly good ones are not going to let their best men be swamped by routine reaching and administration—and the best men would find a way around the efforts of students and administrators to engulf them.

The past fifty years offer further evidence that increased numbers do not inevitably cause deterioration. Those who claim that the high culture of this age had deteriorated never allow their minds to turn to the universities and to compare the American university now with what it was before World War I. The standard was not forced lower by the increased size of the student body.

Of course, the expansion of the numbers in universities would result in a lower average if the hitherto existing mechanisms of selection had worked so perfectly that there were no young people above a certain level of capacity and character who had been excluded in the past, and if all the previously admitted college and university students had been above that level of capacity and character. This was obviously not the case. The indolent, fun-loving undergraduates at Princeton or Harvard or Chicago or Berkeley fifty years ago were no different from the mass of the young men at the great state universities like Michigan, Minnesota, Illinois, or California today.

They are probably even a little better by virtue of having more sophisticated intellectual formation than their predecessors of a half-century ago. The American universities today are better institutions intellectually than they were fifty years ago, when their student bodies and staffs were much smaller. There are more American universities at which important scientific and scholarly research and teaching are done now than then, and the number of persons who are creative and not just productive is very much greater now than then. Numbers as such will not corrupt standards as long as the standard appropriate to the less gifted does not become the standard regarded as appropriate to the more gifted. It certainly need not become so. A self-respecting community of science and scholarship will be able to resist the pressure of the opinion of the indolent among the students and of the demagogic among the politicians to replace a more demanding standard by a slacker one.

The question is whether the communities of science and scholarship will be sufficiently self-respecting. Will their members have sufficient strength of character and devotion to their intellectual traditions to withstand an uncritical populism on the one side and the winds of frivolous doctrine which blow up from time to time among intellectuals on the other?

IV

The state and position of intellectual life in society are not merely functions of the quality of the works created. Intellectual life needs an audience to form the community within which creation can go on and in which those who are to transmit what is created to the wider society can receive the sustenance they need. Intellectual life depends, therefore, on institutions of communication through which the works can be assessed, selected, and disseminated. In the spheres of scientific and scholarly work, the contemporary situation is almost too prosperous. So many books are published, and journals go on multiplying past the capacity of any one human mind, even a moderately specialized mind, to survey and pass on their contents. The scientific and scholarly worlds have, however, met this situation by a mechanism of selection which protects the individual scientist and scholar from being inundated. An informal, vague, and loosely conceived hierarchy of journals, publishing houses, and research centers has become established in the opinion of the various scientific and scholarly subcommunities, and works which originate in or pass through these institutions are given more attention than others which do not. This is supplemented by the network of individual acquaintanceship and the distribution of publications along the paths of this network. Finally, more massively, as a final protection against the flood, there are the huge apparatuses of bibliographical indexing, abstracting, and information-retrieval services. By these means an international scientific community is maintained. But the audiences of especially scholarly and scientific work, except for marginal exceptions, are the scholarly and scientific communities. There is practically no laity for scientific work in the sense that there are religious, artistic, and literary laities.[2] The laity of scholarship within the United States, although probably not becoming smaller than it was, is not growing. The audience of scholarly works is increasingly becoming as sharply defined and as identical with the community of creators and reproducers as it is in the scientific sphere. The laity of art and literature and social and political analysis is what used to be called the educated public. The situation here is not what one would like to see.

2. The lay audience of science consists of the scientists who are not the specialists in a particular topic but who have a general intellectual and technical interest and who can follow technical expositions with some understanding. Beyond that is a more genuine laity, which needs popularized science: industrialists, government officials, military men, who depend on scientific advisers who tell them what and how the results, once attained, are utilizable for their various ends. The relationship of the scientist and the layman is a serious ethical problem to which scientists have not given sufficient attention.

Where, as in the United States today, there is a centrifugal tendency within the intellectual classes arising from their numbers, their spatial dispersion, and their professional specialization, there is too little focus to give a sense of intellectual community to our large intellectual classes. Without this sense of community, with the broadening of responsiveness which it carries with it, the educated classes will slacken their standards in those matters in which they are receptive rather than creative, and they will not exercise the collective influence which they should in the country at large or in their localities.

The organs of communication of arts, literature, and social and political analysis are the serious daily press and the reviews. In this category of intellectual institutions, the United States, which has done so much in the technology and organization of mass communication, seems to suffer particularly from the deficiencies of its system of intellectual communication. Other Western countries, with many imperfections, have a small, serious press which is not only serious and responsible politically, but also culturally. The same cannot be said for the United States, where the serious and responsible press, which does exist, is—unless the *New York Times* becomes a national newspaper—restricted in circulation to locality and region. The handful of good newspapers in the United States, such as the *Washington Post* and the *St. Louis Post-Dispatch*, are much more confined to their area of origin than is the *New York Times*. All these papers, moreover, are extremely feeble culturally. It is true that the *New York Times* makes some effort in this direction, but, especially in its literary assessments, it deliberately "writes down" to a presumptively unqualified audience. The other dailies are almost unmentionable culturally. Their book reviews are negligible in quality and quantity, and the level of the political and social analysis in their leaders and features, except for a very small number of syndicated features, is distressing. Chicago, San Francisco, Los Angeles, Philadelphia, New Orleans, Detroit all suffer from the intellectual nullity of their local press. There is, moreover, no regular making up of the deficiency by the radio or television or by the weekly reviews. The *Nation* and the *New Republic*, which some decades ago provided something more or less respectable, have been for many years in a condition of pathetic paltriness. Part of their misfortunes has arisen from their own poor editorial direction, their fellow-traveling, which persisted longer than that of their audiences, and the ineptitude of their efforts to make themselves competitively "popular."[3] Even had they been better,

3. *The New Republic* is now showing signs of recovery, but it has much ground to regain. It is here that the critics of the cultural consequences of a mass society do score a point. The intellectual weeklies were forced into

they might not have been able to withstand the drawing power of *Time*, which, with all its vices of prejudice, arrogance, and cleverness, has, in recent years, performed the function of supplying information about the larger world of politics and culture more satisfactorily than either of the two intellectual weeklies. However well *Time* were to perform its self-appointed task, its accomplishment would still be different from what a journal which aspires to sell only 100,000 copies and to reach one-third of a million readers should be. *Time's* conception of its audience, leaving out the distortions of snobbery, is inevitably different from that of a weekly with a more stringent standard. A proper weekly, in the tradition of the best weeklies of the century, must assume its audience to be highly intelligent, highly and broadly educated, well informed, and curious to know and pass a complex judgment about a wide variety of things.

The absence of a passable intellectual weekly[4] does damage to American intellectual life. The country is so large, the intellectuals are so scattered, and their superior training and practice are so specialized that a continuous and discriminating focus on a wide variety of cultural, social, and political matters beyond their immediate speciality would do much to raise the level of discourse and offset the philistinizing consequences of specialization. There is of course no shortage of ill-written, competent technical journals. For those, however, who would concern themselves with matters outside their professional specialities, the situation is very unsatisfactory. The highbrow reviews, insofar as they are not self-consciously "little magazines," are excessively academic (written by professors for professors and their research students),[5] and below them there is a nothingness until we reach *Saturday Review*, which is an organ for secondary school teachers, and the *New Leader*.[6] *Harper's Magazine,* the *Atlantic*, and the *New Yorker* are good enough in their way for the same audience as enjoys the *Saturday Review*, but their

---

an inferior position in the competition for editorial talent and for readership by the weeklies of mass circulation.

4. *Commonweal* exists on a higher intellectual plane than the two secular weeklies, but its Roman Catholic preoccupations have restricted the generality of its appeal.

5. The *New York Review of Books* too is written for actual and quondam academics. Its uniqueness lies in its combination of the literary pages of the *New Statesman* and the *Observer,* at greater length, with a fluctuating patronage of all the varieties of *bien pensant* New Leftism.

6. Oddly enough, the direct heir of what Trotsky called "socialism for dentists," *The New Leader* was, as a weekly, the best of them, but it was too often written for persons who were assumed by its authors to know nothing of the subject before reading their particular articles.

weakness becomes all too evident when they are compared with *Encounter.*

This situation is perhaps partly a result of the draining off of the best talents for intellectual journalism to the mass media on the one side and the university "human sciences" on the other. It is also a result of the high cost of production of intellectual goods in the United States and the greater capital resources of the mass media and the universities. In part, too, it is a result of the antecedent weakness of the wider cultural attachments of the educated classes in the United States. This is, in turn, a product of an unthinking rush into specialization as a way of correcting, at a later stage, the deteriorated state of elementary and secondary education and the slovenly inefficiency of so much undergraduate education.[7]

The unenthusiastic acceptance, which remains nonetheless an acceptance, of the local daily press and of the national periodical press in their present condition is the fundamental obstacle to the improvement of the extra-university intellectual institutions in the United States. Just as they have learned to exist without bookshops, so American intellectuals have learned to exist without a decent intellectual press. They suffer its ill effects, but they do not feel them. Their consciously perceived needs are met by their professional organs, by their university libraries and laboratories. As a result, alongside a very high level of proficiency and the occasional peaks of genius in intellectual production, the educated classes of the United States are, outside their specialized professions, philistines in their intellectual consumption and reproduction.

V

The boorish and complacent ignorance of university graduates and the distrust of or superciliousness toward high culture exhibited by university professors in the humanities and social sciences, in the medical and law schools of this country, outside their special subjects, and by journalists and broadcasters to say nothing of lawyers, engineers and physicians, cannot be denied except by those who share these qualities. The near illiteracy of so much of the American press, the crudity of judgment of our news commentators and our lawyers, the yawping vulgarity of our publishers, or at least

7. The poor quality of the earlier levels of the American educational system was a result of the rapid expansion of educational provision and has been supported by the populistic and antitraditional prejudices of educationists. The poor quality is not the result of the demands of the mass for a poorer education or of their insistence on a lower cultural level. They probably would not have resisted had they been offered something better.

those who write their jacket blurbs and their advertising copy, can give little comfort.

The political, economic, military, and technological elites are no better, but they at least do not allege that they are the custodians and practitioners of high culture, even though some of them are.

It is true that these are phenomena of the periphery of our cultural creativity. The center is very much alive. Its vitality, its curiosity, its openness are its virtues. They are the virtues of uninhibitedness, of letting oneself go, of being whatever one "is." This results in much trash and nonsense in the effort to be creative, as well as some brilliant originality. It also results in the culturally inert complacency of the consuming and reproducing intellectuals in the United States. This emptiness of the cultural cupboard of the educated classes outside the creative minority in the sciences, scholarship, and the arts is not simply disagreeable to contemplate; it is full of consequence. It is probably the main reason for the unseemly quality of much of the mass communication in America. Quite the opposite of what is believed by those who see mass culture, that is, the culture of the mass media, as an infection doing harm to the culture of the educated class, it is the poor culture of the educated classes which is doing harm to mass culture. It is the abdication of the educated classes that opens the way to the infiltration of so much mediocre and brutal stuff in our popular culture. It is not that a proper intellectual bearing within the educated classes would necessarily be accepted as a model by the less educated portions of American society. The latter would not necessarily accept what might be offered to them by a more solidary intellectual front dominating all the main positions from which cultural objects are distributed. Even in a situation without alternatives, they might be obdurate. Nonetheless, all these considerations are entirely imaginary in the present situation. At present there is no such unity of standards or such a cultural consensus between the creative center and the consuming and reproductive periphery. Why does this dissensus within the educated classes exist, and to what extent is it a consequence of mass culture?

It is to some extent a product of the sheer size of the educated classes and the multiplicity of intellectual institutions. A large intellectual class is inherently bound to be more dissensual in its standards and in its cultural substance than a small one. That much is to be attributed to mass society. Other determinants antedate mass society in their origins.

The dour-spirited Puritanism which looked on aesthetic expression as self-indulgence appeared in America and Britain long before mass society. The complacent and often rude provincialism of the

American middle classes, which originally distrusted the artistic and literary elements of high culture because they believed them to be Eastern, urban, and connected with an Anglophile patrician upper class, does not come from the culture of a mass society. It was found in all classes, in the plutocracy, in the mercantile middle class, in the small-town philistine physician, lawyer, banker, and merchant. If the term *mass* is not just a "cuss word" and refers primarily to the urban proletariat, as its originators intended, and to the "new middle class" of clerks which later critics added to the earlier meaning, then the bearers of that unpleasant provincialism were not of the masses at all. America was not a mass society in the nineteenth century—it was a differentiated society in which pronounced equalitarian sentiments often took on a populistic form. Mass society is its offspring, not the other way around. Much of its culture, although mediocre, sentimental, and brutal, was produced neither in the institutions nor by the professional personnel now producing the culture of mass society. The greatest achievements of this ungenteel high culture from Mark Twain to Theodore Dreiser were certainly not a product of mass culture any more than were its inferior and much more common manifestations.

The dominant high culture of nineteenth-century America was stained with the faded colors of the gentility of the cultivated classes of New England and the Middle Atlantic States. It did not enjoy a hospitable reception in the Middle West—in the common pattern of provincial hostility toward the metropolis. American provincial culture in the nineteenth century was a variant of the British provincial dissenting culture that Matthew Arnold disparaged in *Culture and Anarchy*. Whereas this mediocre provincial culture collapsed in England after the First World War, in America it survived in powerful form until very recently, and its traces are still with us.

In practically every differentiated society, high culture arouses some distrust, and the nature of the provincial Victorianism of nineteenth-century America and the sensitive zones in which revolt against it took place accentuated this distrust. Furthermore, American Victorian respectability was an integral part of a larger landscape in which rough manliness, rude patriotism, and touchy equalitarianism were no less important. The political and economic elites of American society were figures in this landscape, and very few of them indeed, until very recently, have felt any obligation to cover themselves with a thin covering of high literary and artistic culture such as their opposite numbers sometimes do in Great Britain and France.

Against this background of Puritan, populist, and provincial tradition and sentiment, the educational system of the United States in the past decades has created a scientific, technical, and scholarly intelligentsia of increasingly outstanding merit, which neither forms nor enters into a self-consciously coherent intellectual community. Whereas secondary education became less intellectual in its content, and undergraduate university and collegiate education for the most part was dissipated in courses of study of very low intensity and little discipline, very superior and vigorous systems of postgraduate education and professional training developed. In trying to make up for lost ground and in seeking to make as deep and thorough a penetration as possible into a rapidly growing body of knowledge, postgraduate training in each discipline has had to become highly specialized.

This impetus toward specialization has been heightened by the internal diversification of scientific knowledge and by the growth of the population pursuing postgraduate studies and conducting research as a profession. The natural development of science has greatly increased the volume of literature and the intricacy of detail which a student must cover in each discipline. The increasing number of students and the necessity for each of them to do a piece of research which no one has ever done before has tended to narrow further the concentration within the discipline imposed by the internal evolution of the subject[8]

The product of these educational and scientific developments has been a specialist who shares little of the inherited culture and whose views and tastes outside his own speciality are too often like those of a much less educated person with a lower income and a smaller responsibility for the guidance of his country and the care of its cultural and moral inheritance. Except for those strong and expansive personalities whose curiosity and sensitivity lead them to the discovery and experience of what their education has failed to give them, the well-trained and competent American scientist, scholar, or technologist possesses a very meager and miscellaneous knowledge outside his special subject. More important, perhaps, than the meagerness and fragmentariness of his knowledge is the indifference,

8. The romantic idea of originality, which claimed that genius must go its own *unique* way, has been transposed into an idea of originality which demands that the subject matter should be unique to the investigator. This led to much specialized triviality in humanistic and social science research, even before the present stampede of research workers treading down topic after topic. The increased number of university presses and their hunger for manuscripts have shown what is afoot. Authors otherwise incapable of life are revived and then reembalmed in public form. In the past, the dissertation very seldom became a book, and when it did it was usually as one of a series as much intended for the learned world as the most specialized periodical. The patriotism which led to the busy work of American studies is responsible for much of the digging up of once sealed and forgotten intellectual cemeteries. But the alternative of studying the monuments is equally problematic. How many more books can Herman Melville or Mark Twain or Henry James stand?

callowness, and indiscriminateness of his judgment about the very things for which the highly educated in any society have a special responsibility.

One might interject at this point the question whether it really makes any difference if there is so much specialization? Might not the problem be the product of a humanistic snobbery affronted by the growth of science and technology outside the influence of conventional cultural concerns? Is there any value in a community of culture within the educated classes, apart from the value for the individual, and for the entire aggregate of individuals, of understanding and experiencing the world at the levels made possible by the greatest geniuses. Is there any value in a coherent educated class? Might not the very setting of the problem be a prejudice derived from a false image and a nostalgic attachment to some past age, no more truthful than the image of early capitalistic society put forward by the critics of mass society?

My conception of the unity of the intellectual class is in part derived from eighteenth-century France and especially nineteenth- and early twentieth-century Britain when, especially in the latter, there was some approximation to the reality of a coherent educated class, not by any means unitary in its political or ethical outlook but unified by sharing a common culture and having some sense of affinity despite all opposition and antagonism. The unity of the educated class is desirable because it is important for the maintenance and diffusion of our cultural inheritance. It is important for improving the quality of judgment concerning ethical, political, cultural, religious, and social policies; it is important for establishing and upholding the authority of the educated classes in the formation of opinion throughout society.

If it be answered, especially to the last point, that it is undemocratic to think that the educated classes should enjoy a particular authority—entirely uncoercive and voluntarily assented to—then the answer is that it is not the sole function of education to produce experts and technicians. It is also the task of the educated to enlighten their own judgment, to make it more informed, detached, and disciplined, and to make that judgment heard and seriously considered throughout their respective societies. Their authority would be enhanced if they possessed more of a common universe of discourse, a more mutually intelligible idiom, which, despite inevitable and desirable diversity, would improve the quality of argument and enhance its persuasiveness.

A full solidarity of the educated classes and their closure vis-à-vis the rest of the society is unrealizable, and it is also not desirable that it should be fully attained. The unbroken unity of the highly educated in the face of the rest of the society would produce a hierarchy and a disjunction which would be very undesirable. There is, however, no danger of this at present in any country and least of all in America. The dangers of segregation consequent on specialization seem much more imminent.

In the present century we have experienced the dissolution of "the educated public," that coherent, although unorganized, public for the objects of high culture; the public which appreciates cultural objects which are not of immediate professional significance. The incorporation of so much of our higher cultural production and creativity into the universities represents a great improvement in the activity of our universities. It is a process which is more advanced in America, but it is already visible in Great Britain. It is part of the process of dissolution of a supraprofessional public for higher culture; it contributes to it, too, since the universities are among the most important agents of intellectual specialization and the professionalization which is very akin to it.

The ascent of the universities to preponderance in the life of high culture in the United States, and increasingly, though not yet to the same extent, in Europe, is a further instance of the segration which follows on specialization. Too much of the public for intellectual products in the United States is increasingly in the universities, among teachers, research workers, and postgraduate students. It is the same among the producers. Intellectual institutions are beginning to supply their own and each other's audiences, while the larger public which is not concentrating on intellectual things becomes the audience for intentionally mediocre culture and diversion and commercial advantage. Thus the university public is large and its quality is good, but it is in danger of being too isolated as well as too specialized for the cultural and social good of its own society.

The production of refined culture may be vocational without damage to creativity, and, in fact, certain types of such production, such as science and some branches of scholarship, must be vocational if they are to be carried on at all. It is injurious, however, to the fruitful impact of the universities on their society if they concentrate too much of the intellectual life of the country within themselves. It means that they reach a public of too limited an age range and largely of students' status. For the rest, their influence is exercised in advisory capacities to government and through popularization to a much less well qualified public. The larger public dries up.

It would, of course, be a disregard for the truth to overlook the extraordinary vitality of the contemporary American university, even fairly far down the scale. Vitality by its nature is diffuse and inflammatory. It is possible, therefore, that, despite the densely specialized clutter of the postgraduate system and the prevailing pattern of research which is partly a cause and partly a result of that system, this vitality will do more than withstand the pressures on the intellectual life in the universities arising from segregation. It is possible that the vitality will spread and ignite interest and curiosity and stringent standards along a broader front within the intellectual classes than their specialized training would indicate.

Specialization has lessened the coherence of the intellectual community. It has dispersed its focus of attention and thus left ungratified cultural needs, which the mediocre and brutal culture of the mass media have been called in to satisfy amidst the obscurity of private life. The consumption of inferior and mediocre culture is the consequence, not cause, of the desert which covers much of our educated classes.

This, however, is only one side of the picture. It is possible that the wastes of secondary and undergraduate education will be brought under lively cultivation through the vitality of the new generation of college teachers who are at present, together with the postgraduate students, among the chief consumers and reproducers of refined culture. But it is no less likely that the specialized training which they have recieved and the random character of their nonprofessional culture will make this new generation of university and college teachers so incompetent to judge large issues and so deficient in a reasonable perspective that when they are jolted out of their narrowness by some unanticipated events they will be as indiscriminate in their judgment as any uneducated person. The result might well be a desperate flailing about, an irrational susceptibility to useless nostrums, and a passionate espousal of unthought-out programs doomed to failure.

VI

The responsibility of the custodians and practitioners of the various genres of high culture—science, literature, art, scholarship, philosophy—is to do their work as well as they can. The job is a threefold one. The first is to discover or create something true, genuine, and important to perceive, experience, and express in a way which adds to the value of the stock of culture of the human race. The second task is the conservation and reinterpretation of the inheritance. The third is the maintenance and extension of the influence of high culture in the other sectors of the society. This third task entails, as do the former two, a stringent self-discipline; it requires too a deliberate refusal to pander to the laity or to take advantage of their respect for the learned.

The responsibility is the same in all differentiated societies. It is not just a responsibility which is attributed by an outsider to the practitioners of high culture, but one which is inherent in the intellectual's role and which is sensed in varying degrees wherever intellectual life is practiced. It is particularly felt by the more creative intellectuals. Not all three responsibilities are accepted with equal fullness or performed with equal integrity.

The effective performance of its first task is not entirely independent of the second, although the balance might vary. In our own society, for example, the emphasis lies more heavily on creativity than on conservation. Nonetheless, any sector of high culture, if it is to be creative, must look to the protection of its own *tradition* and its own *internal coherence*. The progress of high culture—and its continued self-renewal and expansion—require that there should be a continuous contact with tradition, not simply to reproduce it but to take it as its own point of departure. It is not that creativity would be entirely impossible without the platform of tradition on which to stand. It would, however, be so much less rich in its achievement if it were not enabled to avoid the false paths rejected by past experience and to take advantage of the openings indicated by what has gone before. Contact with tradition discloses new possibilities even to the most creative mind.

The reception of tradition in a manner which allows freedom to move about easily within it and away from it goes hand in hand with the internal coherence of the intellectual community or the sub-communities within it. This in turn is intimately connected with self-respect. The custodians, the reproducers, the teachers of the sciences and arts, must feel themselves to be performing a vital task, as indispensable to the well-being of the race as are the labors of manual workers or the exertions of administrators and technologists—and even more constitutive of its greatness.

It has not been easy to maintain such an attitude in the United States. The equalitarian moral tone of American society is not conducive to such an attitude; nor is the predominant tone of unfriendliness toward high culture which appears to emanate from the economic, political, and technological elites, however brilliant and important the exceptions.

The mood begins at the earliest stages of education. Children who come, as most necessarily do, from families in which there is little experience of high culture, acquire their first orientation from their teachers. Overworked, underpaid teachers, not well educated themselves, are scarcely capable of representing with persuasive conviction the high culture of their civilization. Even at the level of secondary education the situation is not especially favorable.

The influence of a populistic elite is obvious; recently other factors have come into play. The state of municipal finance, the armaments program of the federal government, the traditional conception of the separation of church and state, the diversion of so much talent into the mass-communications industry, the outlook of educational progressivism, are only a few of the factors which hamper the effective reception of the inheritance of high culture in American schools. The position becomes more favorable at the level of undergraduate education, but it is still extremely uneven, and the inimical traditions are difficult to weather. The result is a public opinion which is much too indifferent to the values of its inheritance of high culture, far too unconnected with it.

The prospect is uncertain. Sporadically, here and there, in television and in the widespread sale of paperbound books, in the alarm of an occasionally humiliated national pride, and above all in the great expansion of postgraduate education, which might soon manifest itself in an improved undergraduate intellectual life, there are signs that the situation is unstable and that it might indeed change for the better. Unless it does, one of the most vital supports of the system of high culture and of the formation of an intellectual community which cuts across the boundaries of professional specialization will be lacking in the United States. Not only will the public life of the country be poorer, but the quality of life as a whole in the society will be poorer. Opinion on political, economic, and social matters will have a poorer guidance, and the style of life of the mass of the population will be more frivolous and petty than it need be. The dangers are no less great for the intellectual classes themselves.

Yet, even failure in this sphere might still leave fairly unimpaired the capacity to meet the first obligation of an intellectual class, which is to do intellectual work creatively. The experience of the country since World War I would support the contention. The country is, moreover, committed to science and to higher education in a way which appears oddly incommensurate with its other dispositions. Thus at this superior level, despite the pressures and distractions of a populistic state of mind, the prospects of the maintenance of creativity are good. There is always the chance in the United States that a spotty resurgence of demagogic populism will harass intellectuals in the way it has done occasionally in the past. Yet, if experience is to guide our judgment, it should be remembered that the unpleasantness of the time of McCarthy did not derail the serious intellectual life of the country. It is true that the distractions often described by the critics of mass culture will exist, and they will lure away and spoil some talented persons. But they will not ruin all whom they attract, and some of them will surely continue and might even expand the present small amount of outstanding work done in those fields.

Serious intellectuals have never been free of pressure from other sectors of their society. The intellectual sectors, like any other sectors performing specialized roles, are always somewhat removed from other sectors of their society, and this is so, regardless of the role of the intellectuals in economic and political life. The external world is always jealous of the devotion of the intellectuals to their gods and of the implicit criticism that such devotion directs against the ruling values of the other sectors of society. Intellectuals have always had before them the task of continuing their own tradition, developing it, differentiating it, improving it as best they could. They have always had to contend with church, state, and party, with merchants and soldiers who have sought to enlist them in their service and to restrict and damage them in word and deed if they did not yield to their blandishments and threats. The responsibilities of intellectuals also remain the same—to serve the standards which they discern and develop and to find a way of rendering unto Caesar what is Caesar's without renouncing what belongs to their own proper realm.

It has not been easy for intellectuals to find the right relation to their society, whether it be a civil mass society, an aristocratic oligarchy, or a tyranny with populistic pretensions. In some respects the situation is more favorable than it has ever been in America. Public opinion and political opinion especially are firmly convinced of their need for the intellectual institutions which train specialized professionals and which do research. Intellectuals have, over the past three decades, come into positions of influence in the economy and polity, which the country had not known for about a century. They occupy powerful positions in the mass-communications system. For all this to bear the desired fruit in an adequate performance of the third function, which lies in the guidance of society, some greater degree of closure of the intellectual community as a whole is required. It must be a closure which transcends specialization. If this is attained, then the many channels of intellectual, social, political, and economic influence which intellectuals now occupy will make possible a very great improvement in the intellectual style of the wider reaches of our society. It will not however have been an improvement if the increased influence of the intellectuals is not accompanied by a more serious concern for general intellectual standards and the moral obligations they imply.

VII

The question has recently been raised as to whether the maintenance of high culture necessitates an avant-garde. An avant-garde, in the most general sense, is as necessary as it is inevitable, if the field of work continues to attract living human beings with creative capacities. It is given in the nature of creativity. Creativity involves a partial incorporation of tradition, but it also involves a partial rejection of tradition. The avant-garde, which tends to emphasize the element of rejection, very often fails to appreciate how much of the rejected tradition it is incorporating. The avant-garde may wear workman's caps or any other garb; it may conduct its personal relations in a bohemian fashion or in the most respectable manner. These types of behavior are quite irrelevant to the way in which the avant-garde performs its innovative, reinterpretative role with regard to inherited traditions. The avant-garde is as much a phenomenon of science and scholarship as it is of art and literature. It can become a danger to culture and society if the preoccupation with innovation becomes indiscriminate and if that indiscriminateness spreads throughout the intellectual class.

In all fields of culture, the reception and transformation of traditions are the essential things. Transformative powers are not equally distributed through the whole intellectual community. Many of its members are solely reproductive, may others seek to transform and reinterpret but fail, and only a few succeed in their efforts.

There is probably, however, some difference between the organization of innovation in the more institutionalized fields of science and scholarship on the one hand, and the less organized fields of art and literature on the other. In the latter fields, the young, especially, who conceive of themselves as an avant-garde—including both the successes and the failures—have tended since the eighteenth century to segregate themselves from the rest of the intellectual community, on the basis not of their achievements but of their aspirations. They have developed their own traditions, not all of which are essential to intellectual creativity and some of which even serve as a substitute in those who lack it. The self-segregation of bohemia is a good thing. Its expansion into the intellectual class as a whole, given the defenselessness of the specialist when judgments have to be made on problems of wider import, can have a derailing effect.

One of the more remarkable developments of recent years in the West is the assimilation of the culture of the avant-garde in the more routine and even philistine cultural circles. The enfeeblement of the institutions for the inculcation of the traditional or conventional high culture—and a rebellion against its diminished authority—opens the way as much to the penetration of often trivial avant-garde culture as it does to the penetration of an even more trivial mediocre and brutal culture.

The drawing in of left-wing horns in the United States in the

1950s has led to the question as to whether intellectual creativity—
or, as it is called in artistic and literary circles, the avant-garde—is
necessarily linked with revolutionary attitudes in political and
economic matters. From the standpoint of logical necessity or of
reasonable common sense, there is obviously no such obligatory link.
Why should an original feeling for color or form or a new conception
of light require the belief that the existing social order should be
transformed, that property should be brought under public ownership, women rendered equal to men, aristocracy abolished, and
kinship connections diminished in their importance? Nevertheless,
there has grown up an affinity between the avant-garde variant of
high culture and revolutionary dispositions, and this has not been
entirely an accident. There is some psychological linkage between
the rejection of tradition in the cultural sphere and the rejection of
tradition in the social and political spheres. It is an affinity which is
unnecessary to cultural creation—it is probably even damaging. This
affinity has had many merits and many lasting achievements to its
credit. It has given color to the cultural life of an entire century and
a half. It has sharpened our moral conscience and heightened and
distorted our sensibilities as to the nature of the society in which we
have been living. It has also added to the disorder of political life and
has aggravated the inevitably never perfectly harmonious relations
between high culture and civil society.

VIII

The need to maintain continuity with the past is not more important
than the need to maintain community among those now living in the
present. In some respects the position in the United States is
advantageous. In the new generation of literary men, there are many
who have had a wide range of experience in their late teens and early
twenties. They come, moreover, from beyond the limits of the
educated classes and so they have a more extensive range of
sympathy than their counterparts in Great Britain. Once, however,
they are underway in their careers, they tend to lose this wider
contact and to confine themselves inordinately to literary circles or
to universities or to literary circles within universities.

In the more formally disciplined intellectual activities of science
and scholarship, the range of external connections varies. Scientists
have come increasingly to concern themselves with the world outside
the laboratory. Not only are many employed in industry and
government, but even those who remain within the university have
developed a greater interest and a more active partisanship in politics.
They serve the government in many important capacities. Pro-

fessional social scientists are not confined to their cloisters but are out in society as investigators, which gives them a unilateral and unprecedented intimacy of a special kind with many parts of society. They, too, have become more civil than heretofore in their history. In most respects, the civility of American intellectuals has gone further than at any time since the Jacksonian revolution but it is still very frail and can collapse very easily.

All these improvements notwithstanding, there is no doubt that the main "political" tradition by which most of our literary, artistic, and social science intellectuals have lived in America is unsatisfactory. The fault does not lie exclusively with the intellectuals. The philistine, puritanical provincialism of our elites has contributed its share to the troubles. Crude and passionate irrelevance and disregard for the public interest have added to them, and nowadays the mere existence of nuclear weapons fastens onto the political elite a burden which is monstrously difficult to carry and of which it cannot divest itself. All these things have been repellent to intellectuals, for good reasons and bad ones. There have been bad reasons for being antipolitical or anticivil, and the American intellectuals have had their fair share in them. Until recently the intellectuals had not been forthcoming in their efforts to ameliorate the situation.

One of the responsibilities implied by the obligation to maintain good relations with the nonintellectual elite is the "civilization" of political life, that is, the infusion of the standards and concerns of a serious, intellectually disciplined contemplation of the deeper issues of political life into everyday politics. Our intellectuals have, in the main, lectured politicians from the outside, upbraided them, looked down their noses at them, opposed them, and suspected those of their fellow intellectuals who have become politicians of moral corruption and intellectual betrayal. The intellectuals who, in any country, have taken on themselves the care and cultivation of high culture are, by prominence, influence, and self-conciousness, part of the differentiated elite of their society. But in the United States they have not usually felt themselves to be bound, by an invisible filiation, to the political, economic, ecclesiastical, military, and technological elites.[9]

They have tended to feel isolated and have seldom brought their influence to bear in a way that would have continued the practice of the founding fathers, the practice in which philosophers and men of affairs collaborated in the formation of an enduring constitution. The civilization of politics, the infusion of the best that intellectual activity offers into the practice of politics and government, is one great

9. This is not a condition unique to the United States. Only Great Britain has managed to avoid it for most of the period since the French Revolution. (The past few years show that such good fortune does not always endure.)

possibility of modern society. Naturally, it can never wholly succeed. Politics are too strenuous; the machinery of power warps the sensibilities too much for the wisdom of detachment ever to dominate them completely. Deciding is different from contemplating the differentiation of reality, and the tensions of alternatives are always greater than they look from a distance. Still, some interpenetration is possible—certainly more than we have had in the United States. Such improvement is the condition of a better polity and of the better understanding which the intellectual community needs from the rest of society.

The "civilization" of political life is only one aspect of the "process of civilization," which is the expansion of the culture of the center into the peripheries of society. In this particular context, the "process of civilization" is the diffusion of some elements of high culture into the areas of society normally consuming mediocre and brutal culture.

Within the limits mentioned earlier in this essay, the prospects here seem to be moderately good. The mutual interpenetration, at certain points, of social classes has resulted in an expansion of the elements of high culture toward persons whose usual inclinations do not lead them to seek it out, just as it has increased the consumption of mediocre and brutal culture among persons whose equals in occupation, and income might in the past have been resistant to it. Popularization, which brings a better content, although eradicating refinements, helps in this. Not all of the expansion is popularization; much of it is the presentation (and consumption) of works of genuinely high culture. An improvement of our educational system at the elementary and secondary levels, which is entirely practicable, would also further this process of a broadening civilization. The better education of the passions, which a richer, less scarcity-harassed society can afford, the opening and enrichment of sensibility, which leisure and a diversified environment can make possible, a more fruitful use of available intelligence, can also push forward the "process of civilization." There is no guarantee that this will happen. It depends on the intellectuals. If they take seriously the obligations which are implicit in their best traditions, if they can avoid the temptations of self-indulgence in what appears to be creation because it rejects intellectual and moral discipline, then the chances are good. But will they be able to do it?

Thus, if the periphery is not to be polished while the center withers and becomes dusty, the first obligation of the intellectuals is to look after intellectual things: to concentrate their powers on the production and consumption of particular works of philosophy, art, science, literature, or scholarship; to receive the traditions in which these works stand with a discriminating readiness to accept, elaborate, or reject.

elaborate, or reject. Their other obligation is to remember what they owe to their society. These are not two separate and unconnected obligations. The overriding concern for truth is common to both of them.

6 British Intellectuals in the Mid-Twentieth Century

When Basil Seal joined the Commandos, Sir Joseph Mainwaring, an old Blimp. said, "There is a new spirit abroad. I see it on every side"; and Evelyn Waugh, who was himself invaded by the new spirit, closed the book with the words: "And poor booby, he was bang right."[1]

He was bang right. It was the end of two decades of rebellion against society, against the middle classes, against capitalism, against British institutions and manners. Even as the period came to an end, W. H. Auden—perhaps the leading figure of his generation— renounced his country and took up residence in America. There went with him one of the more talented writers of the period, Christopher Isherwood. Earlier, two of the most esteemed writers of the twenties, Aldous Huxley and D. H. Lawrence, had already expatriated themselves, one to California, the other wandering restlessly until his death. Other eminent British writers, e.g., Norman Douglas, Richard Aldington, Robert Graves, *et al.*, found life at home unsatisfactory and preferred to live abroad. English writers were on the move: travel books became a category of literature with a new intellectual significance. Who had a good word to say then for Britain among the intellectuals? Who had a good word then to say for British towns, where "every street [was] a blow, every corner a stab"; or for the British countryside and for English village life— those scenes of harsh inequality, of social snobbery and death- bringing gossip? "England's green and pleasant land" was the façade of iniquity, and the British past was an elaborate pretense.

T. S. Eliot was still the poet of those who felt contemporary England to be a waste land. Graham Greene, whose specifically political interests had become faint and enfeebled soon after their birth, portrayed a seedy, peeling, sinister, violent, and treacherous England, an England without faith and without order, while Evelyn Waugh's England was a contemptibly irresponsible, a painfully frivolous land in which silliness ruled. E. M. Forster was not a revolutionary, but his three cheers for friendship and his devotion to

Previously published in a slightly different form in *Encounter*, April 1955, pp. 1-12.

---

1. *Put Out More Flags* (1942).

"love, the Beloved Republic" took their place—a more refined place, to be sure—in the general alienation from institutions and traditions.

The capitals of the intellectuals' ideal commonwealths varied. For some it was Moscow, which held the hearts of more than members of the Communist Party; for others, it was Baghdad, or Paris, or Berlin, or Los Angeles—it was in any case not London. It was certainly not Manchester or Bristol or Liverpool or Glasgow. It might be in some other period or it might be in the realm of the imagination; it was certainly not in twentieth-century Britain. A dreary country, ruled by an "old gang," by philistines and middle-brows, where the muse lay dying or in chains—who could give his heart to it?

The thirties was the time of the Left Book Club, whose authors seized any stick with which to beat the British dog, and every pretext to announce its death; it was the time of *In Letters of Red*, of *Fact*, of *The Coming Struggle for Power* and *Forward from Liberalism*, and of the powerful movement of Marxism among British scientists. The London School of Economics was at the height of its reputation as a fountain of radical criticism of British life and institutions as well as a mine of scholarship. The hatred of British society was not a matter simply of the fervent revolt of adolescence and youth, nor was it just a criticism of particular aspects of British life while leaving the whole untouched.

Indeed, even when he loved his cottage, or his Regency house, or some little spot of English soil, the intellectual's love of Britain was overshadowed by a feeling of repugnance for its dreary, unjust, and uncultured society, with its impotent ruling classes and its dull and puritanical middle classes. It was not particular institutions or attitudes that were repellent but the whole notion of Britain or of England. This was not just the view of the communists or the aesthetes. It was the view of nearly everyone who, in the 1920s and 1930s, was considered worthy of mention in intellectual circles in Great Britain.

The alienation was by no means shared by all parts of the intellectual class—nor were the alienated uniformly and equally alienated. The intellectuals in the higher civil service were not swept off their feet, nor the whole of the journalistic world, nor everyone in the universities, new and old. The younger generation in the universities, in science and in literature, were more alienated than their elders, who remained more concerned with Empire and Commonwealth. Nonetheless, the prevailing attitude, in quantity and emphasis, was one of alienation. Divergence from this view was a sort of disqualification for being taken seriously. *The Times* and *The Times Literary Supplement* were the stuffy representatives of a deadening official culture; a writer like Arnold Bennett was as contemptible as a businessman. Those who were still proud of their country or who invoked its history and traditions were dismissed as Blimps.[2]

Rediscovering the Virtuous Britain

But in the forties and early fifties it was not at all like what I have just described. Deeply critical voices became rare. In 1953, I heard an eminent man of the left say, in utter seriousness, at a university dinner, that the British constitution was "as nearly perfect as any human institution could be," and no one even thought it amusing. Who criticized Britain then in any fundamental sense, except for a few communists and a few Bevanite irreconcilables? These were complaints here and there and on many specific issues, but—in the main—scarcely anyone in Great Britain seemed any longer to feel that there was anything fundamentally wrong. On the contrary, Great Britain on the whole, and especially in comparison with other countries, seemed to the British intellectual of the early 1950s to be fundamentally all right and even much more than that. Never had an intellectual class found its society and its culture so much to its satisfaction. It was inconceivable that any British literary period-ical—of the few that survived—would have had the audacity to publish, as *Horizon* did about ten years earlier, a series on "Where Should John Go?" in which the young Briton, bored and fed up with his country, had surveyed for him the wide range of possible places to which he could emigrate? (But even at that moment Mr. Connolly, very much a man of the thirties, was already out of touch with the times; Mr. V. S. Pritchett had recently attributed to him a mid-nineteenth-century Bohemianism.)

The postwar years, it is true, tarnished the patriotic enthusiasm of 1944 and 1945 for the new Britain. Socialism turned out to be less than some had hoped it would be; others found it more than they cared for. The merciless appetite of the Inland Revenue was complained about on all sides but it was not accused of injustice, and the public and the welfare services which impelled its action were not assailed in principle, even by their severest critics. The arbitrary and inflexible rulings of bureaucracy gave rise to a little restiveness, and the unforthcomingness of many of the beneficiaries of the bounties of the Labour government caused sardonic dis-gruntlement and crankiness. But criticism of the comprehensive schools from one side, of the American alliance in foreign policy from the other, and of many more details from all sides, never gave the impression of a deeply penetrating cleavage or withdrawal.

2. The chief admirers of British institutions during most of this period were the Germans, who found in England the ideal of the Christian gentleman and an austerely responsible aristocratic governing class.

Fundamental criticism of the trend of British society had become rare. Whereas in the interwar period Wyndham Lewis was distinguished only by his talent and his violence of expression and not by his fundamental negation of British society, in the decade which followed the war he was a rare bird.

The British intellectual came to feel proud of the moral stature of a country with so much solidarity and so little acrimony between classes.

The disapproval of public school culture—long a stock in trade—still cropped up from time to time, but it ceased to be of serious concern to either side. The public schools stealthily crept back into the hearts of the intellectuals, where they reposed more securely and more vitally than ever before. To cite only one of many examples, the *New Statesman*, in response to a recommendation by one of the younger M.P.s for the abolition of the public schools by legislative action, replied that they represented quality and not just privilege. It was not even embarrassed to say that "even the conscientious socialist with a little money is forced to send his child to a private school or to face the self-criticism that he has sacrificed his chances in life to a political prejudice." The "old school tie" ceased to be an accusation of British injustice; it was now taken as evidence of British quality.

Even India, that ancient sore on the conscience of the forward-looking, had become in retrospect a credit to Britain. Philip Woodruff's work on *The Men Who Ruled India* was everywhere and rightly acclaimed, but one is struck by the reviewers' tone of national self-congratulation for having produced such a class of men capable of ruling with such justice and humanity. Practically everyone agreed that it was proper to have withdrawn from India; at the same time, there seemed to be no question at all that the British Raj itself was something very great indeed—the very extreme opposite of that cause for shame which it was once alleged to be by the liberal intellectuals.

When, in 1942, the late George Orwell rehabilitated Kipling against the unjust denigration of "pansy-left circles" and praised him in particular for his identification with the official classes and for his sense of responsibility for the maintenance of an orderly society, it was clear that one of the extreme positions was being evacuated. Another had been evacuated from the other side in the previous year, when the poet of *The Waste Land* took on himself the task of reasserting the merits of that same "vulgar apologist" of imperialism.

While the welfare state had raised the floor of British society, the symbols of hierarchy and authority found increasing acceptance. Did the fifties have anything to match the refusal of a peerage by one of the greatest intellectuals of the twenties and thirties, R. H. Tawney, reported in Dr. Thomas Jones's correspondence? On the contrary, it could show an avowed anarchist and an ardent exponent of the avant-garde in art and literature accepting a knighthood.

What brought the intellectuals back to the nation? What made them, with all their complaints and grievances, conscious and proud of being British? What put them at ease with the symbols of sovereign authority? Why did they come once more to appreciate British institutions? What produced this extraordinary state of collective self-satisfaction?

II

As Sir Joseph Mainwaring sensed, it was with the war that the new spirit began. It was, however, really not a beginning. It was rather a renewal. The cranky antinomianism of the twenty years between the wars was more like a digression from the main course of the British intellectual class in its relations with British institutions. The intellectuals in the first half of the nineteenth century had never been as revolutionary, as aesthetic, as antibourgeois, as antipolitical, as hostile to the symbols of authority as their opposite numbers on the Continent. There had been lots of criticism and disagreement in the second half of the century, but the union of the intellectuals with the civil service, the church, the Houses of Parliament, the press, and the leadership of the political parties, through the ancient universities primarily but also through kinship and through the social and convivial life of London upper-class society, constituted a bond from which few could escape and which no other country could then or has since been able to match. Neither socialism nor the aesthetic revolt of the turn of the century ever bred a doctrine or practice of complete alienation. Many of the major figures in the twin, sometimes separate, sometimes joint, revolts of art and justice, were outsiders—Irishmen mainly. The British intellectuals might have appeared dull to the Continental firebrands and gypsies but they were dutiful and loyal.

This residual loyalty which had been beaten down by the rancor of rebelliousness, this civility which had been suppressed by aesthetic disdain, had been lying in wait all through the interwar period to be summoned back to ascendancy. It was embarrassing at first for many to perceive within themselves the stirring of national sentiments against which they had earlier set their faces and the denial of which had indeed been central to their outlook. Richard Hillary was one of the first to record his return to the bosom of the nation. He was not describing himself alone when he told of how anomalously uneasy he felt to act in the service of the symbols of a society which he had rejected and to which, despite his conscious rejection, he became aware of a genuine attachment below the surface.

Unlike the First World War of 1914-18, there was no butchery from thoughtlessness in the Second; there was boredom but there was little waste of human life in aimless, large-scale military operations. Two of the most eminent British generals of the 1939-45 war were renowned for their humane concern for their troops. The purblind unimaginativeness which sacrificed so many young men's lives in the First World War, and which contributed so mightily to the greatest alienation of the British intellectuals from civil society in the entire history of Great Britain, was absent in the Second World War.

Furthermore, the way against Nazism and Fascism made a little more sense to the recently ideological intellectuals, who were thus enabled more easily to disregard the suspect influence on their conduct of considerations of national interest and national loyalty. The alienation of the twenties and thirties was an alienation from the primordial institutions. It was an alienation from kinship, from tradition of tribe and land, from the established church and the civil state—all in the name of life, in accordance with principles freely chosen. It was a smoother passage to return to the objects of primordial attachment through what seemed to be a war for principles.

Then, too, the war gave much more for intellectuals to do as intellectuals. Not only the scientists but the historians, economists, linguists, philosophers, and other scholars found hospitality in official circles, in the Cabinet offices, in the Ministry of Information, in the Political Warfare Executive, in the BBC, in military intelligence, in the War Office Selection Boards, etc. These and others provided an appreciative audience for the intellectuals in their intellectual capacities—and it contrasted very sharply with the intellectual's image of official antiintellectualism of the period between the wars. British society too seemed to become more cultivated during the war. The Committee for the Encouragement of Music and Arts—the parent of the Arts Council—the concerts in the National Gallery, the increase in the sale of books and some corresponding increase in their reading, the flowering of discussion circles even under official auspices, as in ABCA and the National Fire Service, facilitated the growth among the intellectuals of the idea that the country was not hostile to them.

The Blurring of Ideologies

Of at least equal importance was the fact that the government during the war, despite inefficiencies and errors, gave the appearance of being just.

The WOSB was a direct refutation of the old complaint by outsiders and rebels that the public school system, in the words of Captain Grimes, "never lets one down." It disregarded breeding, accent, and background, and concentrated on what was necessary for the effective performance of the duties of an officer. Rumors, true or untrue, that Lord So and So's nephew or Sir This and That's son had been unable to meet the requirements of the Selection Board contributed to the impression that considerations of efficiency and justice had penetrated into a sphere which had hitherto been reserved for the old guard. The system of officer selection in the Second World War helped to dissolve some of the rancor against antebellum Britain.

No one seemed to be getting rich out of the war, and the nearly universal discomfort, squalor, and poor food were equated with virtue. There were black marketeers, but they were not seen as products of the moral deficiencies of the ruling class, and society was not to be blamed for them. Many thought they were foreigners.

The magnanimous wartime figure of Winston Churchill, above parties and especially above the old gang of vulgar businessmen, bloated Tories, and exploiting imperialists, was a reassurance that bourgeois Britain would not come back into the saddle after the war. The victory of the Labour Party at the polls in 1945 was a further reassurance that intellectuals could continue to regard Britain as their own country, where, in union with civil servants, they could either rule or feel themselves intimately affiliated with those who ruled. Clement Attlee, with his background in a professional family, his Oxford education, his respectable military record, and his almost exaggerated restraint in speech and attitude, kept the conservative intelligentsia from alienation, however much they disliked the expected consequences of some of the policies of his government. On the other hand, the mere incumbency of the Labour Party in the seats of authority reconciled many of its intellectual members, who were disgruntled on specific issues, to the society against which their doctrine and principles logically aligned them.

Responsibility, through their party, for the fortunes of the country curbed the oppositional mentality. Such responsibility at a time when the country seemed to be declining in power in the world, and to be in great economic trouble as well, reinforced the curb. The latent patriotism which had been partially suppressed when the country appeared safe and powerful came back to the surface of consciousness when the country was threatened. Those who had ridiculed and abhorred patriotism began to find themselves patriots. The emancipation of India, Burma, and Ceylon, which politically-minded leftist intellectuals had sought so long, had many repercussions. The feeling of being without an empire, a feeling of being bereft of something, a feeling of loss, enhanced the sense of national identity. Also, the nation seemed to be cleaner and more worthy of being embraced when it was divested of its immoral imperial appurtenances. Little Englanders could feel more comfortable in such a country and could love it more easily, and they could embrace its past without feeling that its present disgraced them.

Then, too, there was America. From a harmless, amiable, good-natured, powerful, ridiculous, loyal ally—a sort of loutish and helpful nephew—it suddenly seemed to develop into a huge challenging empire, willful, disregarding Britain, criticizing Britain, lording it over Britain, and claiming to lord it over everyone everywhere. Loyal British backs were arched at this peril, and the worrying economic crises of the second half of the forties accentuated impatience with America. Patriotism in this atmosphere was nurtured by anti-Americanism.

Animosity against naïve, boorish, and successful America heightened the gratification which British intellectuals derived from their national self-contemplation.

On the Continent, in the years after the war, France went without governments, and Italy and Germany were in ruins; the rich ate well, the poor rummaged in dustbins—and that too enhanced British self-esteem. Whereas in the great days of the Empire, imperialistic Britons thought Britain should be tutor to the world by moral ascendancy and the intellectuals denounced such arrogance, now former antiimperialists began to think of Britain as a model commonwealth, a paragon of how to do things without corruption, with public spirit, with a sense of responsibility, with respect for the past and an openness toward the future, free from ideological fanaticism, and without ambitions of self-aggrandizement. This imaginative self-transformation into an ideal commonwealth was fed by and made for patriotism.

There was another factor too in this process. Although the war, for the previously alienated intellectuals, had been a war of principle, the war itself, and the course of events in Britain and in the world at large since then, marked a downward path for ideology. As I have just said, the rediscovery of national sentiments in the wartime experience, and partly the state of siege in which Britain lived during most of the postwar decade, focused attention and feeling on the symbols of the nation. Symbols of party and class lost some of their power. Abroad and at home, meanwhile, an almost complete evaporation of the basis for a doctrinaire socialism was occurring.

British socialism has never been doctrinaire—except for inconsequential corners—and the vicissitudes of governing and the achievement of many of the socialists' most tangible goals had made it even less so. The practical conservation by the Conservative government of most of Labour's post-World War II innovations helped to blur the edges of the socialist ideology. The extremes of planning or of laissez-faire were not espoused in the Britain of the mid-fifties by very many intellectuals. There were still a few extremists who would underscore the differences, but for the most part there was not a wide difference between the intellectual proponents of liberalism and those of socialism. The differences were, moreover, not made into differences in fundamentals, in Weltanschauung, and a consensus of matter-of-factness had settled over most discussions of economic policy.

As a result of this evaporation of ideology, and of socialist ideology in particular, the range of dispersion of the British intellectuals was much narrowed. Without a doctrine which they could espouse, the handful of extremists were forced to confine their extremism to mood and disposition and to express it ad hoc. They could scarcely form a sect on such a basis.

One more factor may be mentioned: the fostering of cultural institution by public authority. How could a society which maintained the Third Programme, the Arts Council, the British Council, etc., with their numerous opportunities for the employment of intellectuals, be regarded as lacking in sympathy for intellectual things? On the contrary, such a society arouses the intellectual's appreciation as well as giving him a sense of responsibility for its support.

III

There was, however, something deeper than this. It was the vindication of the culture associated with the aristocracy and gentry, and its restoration, in the decade following the Second World War, to preeminence among the guiding stars of the intellectuals. It was a change which is not confined to the intellectuals. All English society had undergone this process of submission to the moral and cultural—but not the political or economic—ascendancy of the aristocracy and gentry.

For nearly a century, the culture of the aristocracy and gentry was in retreat. When their political power and their privileges were increasingly restricted and their economic strength damaged by American and Australian agriculture and the legislation of pre-1914 liberalism, their cultural power too seemed to be broken. It had been subjected to fierce criticism by the intellectuals. Nineteenth-century radicalism, the aestheticism of the end of the century and after, the diversified and penetrating denunciation by H. G. Wells, John Galsworthy, D. H. Lawrence, and G. B. Shaw made people distrustful of class privilege, of snobbery, of elaborate etiquette, of the display of power.

In contrast, bourgeois culture—the culture of the business classes—seemed slowly and steadily on the upgrade in the nineteenth century, both in London and the provinces—especially in the provinces. As long as Dissent lived in inner exile, excluded from the ancient universities, and excluded therefore from the opportunities to which those universities gave access, as long as it was shunned by the gentry and nobility because it was "in trade" or in manufacture, its culture maintained a high intensity in both its religious and secular forms. After or alongside of money-making it made the improvement of civil life its concern; it founded literary and philosophical societies, libraries; and above all, through its own benefactions and through the local government which it controlled, it raised its chief monuments, the modern universities—to show that it too, even though excluded and thought barbarous, could pursue truth and glorify the dingy cities in which its money was made. Living to itself, puritanical, pharasaical, proud, and excessively sensitive to the slights and denials of the traditional society, the bourgeoisie of the big provincial towns, partly from local patriotism, partly from a love of learning, created, before their submission, a genuine civilization—earnest, searching, and profound. Matthew Arnold, Ruskin, Carlyle, and the other great critics of the Victorian bourgeoisie which was Dissenting and provincial did less than justice to their victims.

However that may be, the businessman's Dissenting culture of the nineteenth and early twentieth centuries—the culture which founded the modern universities, the musical and literary institutions of the provinces—had been routed by the mid-twentieth century. Sons sent to Oxford or Cambridge, or into the army as professional officers, themselves removed southward and Londonward, the Chapel renounced for the Church—these were the signs of the surrender of the British bourgeoisie to its upper-class antagonists.

The London-Oxford-Cambridge Triangle

The movement toward London in the twenties and thirties was not merely a demographic fact. It was associated with the assertion of the cultural supremacy of London society—and with it, of Oxford and Cambridge—over the provincial centers.

The aristocratic-gentry culture came back into the saddle in the fifties, and with little to dispute its dominion. The twenties and thirties, which did it so much damage, did even more damage to the provincial bourgeois culture. The rebellion of the intellectuals was rather against bourgeois culture than against the aristocratic-gentry culture. The latter never abdicated. Some of its offspring might revolt against it, but they could not find anything to substitute for it except bohemianism and an utterly spurious proletarianism. Bourgeois culture, on the other hand, as soon as it came freely into contact with aristocratic-gentry culture, lost its self-esteem and its spiritual autonomy. It could not win the youth, even those brought up in its own atmosphere. It seemed paltry and mean alongside aristocratic-gentry culture.

This is not relevant solely to the description of the class structure of post-World War II Britain. It has the most significant consequences for the development of the British intellectuals because the change in the status and self-esteem of the classes was paralleled by changes in the status and self-esteem of the cultural institutions patronized by the classes. I shall illustrate this with reference to the relations between the ancient and the modern universities.

The modern British universities, which in scholarship and science take second place to none in the world, have—despite efforts of the University Grants Committee and many worthy men who had loved them—been belittled in their own eyes. They had never had a place in that image of the right life which had evolved from the aristocratic, squirearchal, and higher official culture. To those who accepted this image, modern universities were facts but not realities. As late as the 1950s, Oxford and Cambridge were thought of spontaneously when universities were mentioned. If a young man, talking to an educated stranger, referred to his university studies, he was asked "Oxford or Cambridge?" And if he said Aberystwyth or Nottingham, there was disappointment on the one side and embarrassment on the other. It had always been that way.

True, very many more persons were factually aware of the modern universities by the fifties than, say, thirty years earlier. They had established themselves as bulwarks of research in science and scholarship, and without them Great Britain would be poorer in every respect. Nonetheless, fundamentally the situation had scarcely improved. It had perhaps become even worse. The deterioration was revealed in the diminution in self-esteem which these universities had undergone among their own staff, graduates, and patrons.

The modern universities had by no means declined in relative intellectual stature. On the contrary, in some subjects the modern universities now took the lead. The differences in prestige, however, had probably been accentuated. There was less contentment in being in a modern university than there had been. It was becoming more difficult to get first-class younger men to leave Oxford and Cambridge—and London—for professorships in the provincial universities, however superior the traditions of the chair to be filled. It was more difficult to keep young men in the provinces; they were less contented with the prospect of a career in one of the great provincial universities, and looked on them instead as jumping-off places, as places where they could keep alive and wait until something better came along. They were, moreover, even quite open in disclosing their motives, as if that were and always had been quite the normal thing. And for the writers of the fifties who were setting out to show the humanity and vitality of provincial life—particularly Mr. William Cooper, Mr. Kingsley Amis, and Mr. John Wain—did not their heroes, on their different levels of talent, find their appropriate salvation in Oxford and London? Did not Dr. C. P. Snow's chronicle of the world of Lewis Eliot move southward and reach its plateau in the professional class in London and Cambridge, where, over sunlit polished tables on which stood old silver milk jugs, few appeared to do any hard work and all lived graciously and spaciously?

IV

The internal unity of the British elite has often been remarked. The reestablishment of amicable and harmonious relations between the intellectuals and British society was really the unification of the intellectuals with the other groups of the ruling elite; it was a resumption of friendly relations with the government, with the Houses of Parliament and the civil service, and with the complex of institutions around the central institutions of authority, the judiciary and the Inns of Court, the Church of England, the ancient universities, etc.

The culture which had now regained moral ascendancy was not an aristocratic culture in the sense that it was the present culture of an active aristocracy, nor was it the actual culture of the gentry. It was the culture traditionally inspired by those classes, the culture appropriate to certain institutions allied to those classes. Many of the aristocracy and gentry were quite ignorant and boorish, but when they became cultivated, their culture took that tone: moderate, unspecialized and unobsessed, civil, restrained, diversified, and personally refined.

The culture of the fifties was a pluralistic culture within itself: it had room for politicians, for sportsmen, for travelers, for civil servants and judges and barristers and journalists, for artists and writers of different persuasions. It was an unbourgeois culture, even though members of the bourgeoisie and their offspring peopled it most densely. It was an exclusive culture into which the rest of the society was rarely admitted except on the terms of the host. The "insideness" of the British elite was part of a great social machine for creating "outsiders." Its internal unity was intimately related to the tangibility of its external boundaries.

Their conquest, like all conquests, was incomplete. It left under the surface of the conquered a mass of sentiments and loyalties and suspicions which were far from dissolved. For years, the division of British society—on the one side, the society of the aristocracy and gentry and their allied institutions, and, on the other, the Dissenting bourgeoisie with their provincial, modern society—rendered possible and even easy the public expression of the cultural aspirations and social and aesthetic sensitivity of "the other nation." The reconquest by aristocratic-gentry culture rendered this expression more difficult, just as it obscured the persistent and effective division of the nation and gave a spurious impression of unity. Among the British intellectuals of the mid-twentieth century there were thickly scattered Judes and Leonard Basts and Bruce Truscotts, experiencing with distress, while hating to acknowledge, the line which separated them from the inside, from the charmed circle of cultivation, affluence, worldliness, and ease.

Earlier there was rivalry and even antagonism between the two nations of British culture, but there was little emulation. The bourgeoisie was too concerned with the intrinsic importance of its own cultural and philanthropic works, and too apprehensive of rebuff to worry itself profoundly about its conformity with the standards of the aristocracy and gentry. Indeed, the mere notion that the aristocracy and bentry prized one way of doing things led the business classes to follow another path. The small class of clerks, shop assistants, and self-educated workmen were not sufficiently in contact with, or near to, the uppermost classes in the social hierarchy to be substantially affected by their standards. When they studied at night, it was from sheer love of learning or to advance themselves in the knowledge required for progress in their own occupations.

The intellectual's desire to move in the aura of the aristocratic-gentry culture is only about half a century old; its first distinguished representative in the twentieth century was Leonard Bast, and only in the 1930s did such young people become noticeable in large numbers. The two wars with the opportunities which they afforded for great numbers of young men to be schooled as officers and gentlemen, the increase in the demand for professional and clerical skills, the increase in grammar school and university attendance between the wars and their tremendous increase after the Second World War, all created a public zealous for the culture of the refined classes.

Continental vacations, the connoisseurship of wine and food, the knowledge of wild flowers and birds, acquaintance with the writings of Jane Austen, a knowing indulgence for the worthies of the English past, an appreciation of "more leisurely epochs," doing one's job dutifully and reliably, the cultivation of personal relations—these were the elements in the ethos of the newly emerging British intellectual class after the Second World War. It was around an ethos of this sort that the new attachment to Great Britain was formed. It was in its attachment to symbols of a culture which have always been associated with a "stake in the country" that the British intellectual class was finding its way home. It was through the limited range of sympathy characteristic of that culture, elegant and admirable though it is, that the British intellectual of the fifties restricted his attachment to British society, and it was around that ethos that the misery and uneasiness of the incompletely assimilated were focused.

Insiders and Outsiders

The triumph of the mid-twentieth-century version of the aristo-cratic-gentry culture did not result in the complete assimilation of the intellectuals to the nation and its institutions. It only meant a reattachment to a sector of the upper classes. The aristocratic-gentry culture assumed and implicitly praised a considerable stratification of the British society; it made clear the inferiority of the business world, of the mere technician, of the practical man, and of the enthusiast—moral, religious, and political. It praised the authority which rests ultimately on the Crown and on the land, and it derogated authority which was unconnected with those two sources. It measured its praise in accordance with the proximity of a person to those sources or to the institutions associated with them. The acceptance of this ideal by the intellectuals, then, could not be without serious consequences for a society which was still a largely bourgeois society in its economic organization and which still possessed much more than traces of cultures other than the aristocratic-gentry one.

The reconquest had created the problems which are characteristic of situations in which a superior culture is superimposed on more backward cultures. There is a tendency towards "overassimilation"—becoming more genteel than gentility requires—on the part of marginal persons, and there is also much resentment generated within the minds of those who overassimilate. At the same time, on the top, there is a tendency for the beneficiaries of the superior culture to confine themselves to their own culture and its realm and to close themselves off from the rest.

Let us deal first with the latter consequence—the narrowness of the range of sympathy and curiosity of the British intelligentsia within its own society. Many students of English literature over the first half of this century have remarked on the limited scope of its subject matter. Novels of working-class life were certainly extremely rare, both in general and among the writers who succeed in being taken up by the arbiters of taste in the literary reviews, on the BBC, etc. If one surveys the works of the chief writers of the decade which followed the end of the war what does one find? In the writings, for example, of Anthony Powell, Julia Strachey, William Cooper, William Plomer,[3] Elizabeth Bowen, Elizabeth Lake, Antonia White, *et al.*, we do not find the working classes treated at all. Do we find shopkeepers, clerks, small businessmen? There is a little more openness there. William Sansom treated suburbia because its dull placidity is an excellent foil for diabolism. V. S. Pritchett came closer to a sympathetic depiction; nonetheless, *It May Never Happen*, effectively, and *Mr. Beluncle*, ineffectively, used a petit-bourgeois atmosphere to uncover amusing eccentricities, minor and fairly amiable madnesses. Businessmen did very poorly. The old-fashioned business brute whom Mr. Pritchett killed off in *Nothing Like Leather*, the cultured Northern business family so fascinating to the narrating outsider and so sympathetically described by Mr. Priestley in *Bright Day*, were as close as the British intellectual of the 1950s came to intimacy with the world of commerce and industry.

This is not intended as criticism of the English novel of the fifties but only as an indication of the spontaneous inclinations and the objects of aversion of the intellectuals. It reveals the very special area of attachment of the intellectuals to British society. Their very attachment, and the patriotism associated with it, blinded them to British society in its wider reaches. It did not, to be sure, breed hostility or bitterness or contempt toward the other classes in society; and the attachment to this culture made for a greater homogeneity within the class itself. While this was morally and politically an advantage, it was intellectually a disadvantage. It made them less good as intellectuals, among whose tasks—there are many others—is the truthful interpretation of their national society and its culture to their own countrymen and the world.

There was another consequence of the specialized affection of the intellectuals for British society. This was the invisible but painfully tangible ring *within* the intellectual class which shut off those inside the charmed circle from the fellow travelers and aspirants—which separated those who are thought to live fully in the culture of the aristocracy and gentry from those who admired them for doing so and who would do so themselves if they could.

It was manifested in many ways. Charges were made that there was a literary clique, an organized body of friends which dominates British literary life. This was an extreme manifestation, it is true, of that eternal affliction of the "outsider" in every society—namely,

3. William Plomer's *The Invaders* is an exception which argues that an effort to enter into contact with the lower classes will be hopelessly frustrated.

the belief that at the center of the magic circle a closed group schemes and rules to the deliberate disadvantage of the excluded. For years Dr. Leavis had assailed the wickedness of Bloomsbury, its coterie culture, its meretricious standards, and its improper influence via the BBC, the British Council, and other official organs; and his lament sounded once more as an overtone in the skirmishes of the new provincialism against the Oxford-Cambridge-London triangle. This preoccupation with an inner circle was, in the mid-fifties, very evident in the modern universities, where Oxford and Cambridge— and London, as far as the provinces are concerned—were invisible presences; in the common rooms, appointments and disappointments at Oxford and Cambridge were as real and immediate as if they were happening right there. Questions about students in the modern universities were very often met with a bitter complaint that the students at the local university were poor—with the addition that the good ones went to Oxford or Cambridge, and sometimes London was added in a sober afterthought. The desire to be at the institution as little as possible, and away as much as possible, was part of the injury done to corporate and individual self-esteem by the vestigial but persisting traces of the barrier between the two nations within the intellectual class—the nation of London, Cambridge, Oxford, of the higher civil service, of the genteel and sophisticated; and the nation of the provinces, of petit-bourgeois and upper working-class origin, of bourgeois environment, studious, diligent, and specialized.

The Unsolved Problem

The assimilation of the new intellectuals into the ideal pattern of the old intellectual class remained a terribly difficult task for at least a decade after the Second World War. On the surface, it appeared to go on merrily and cheerfully; the new intellectual rejoiced in every new cultural acquisition which brought him nearer the old—like the brilliant young university lecturer who, a few years before, could not tell grape juice from wine except by the aftereffects and who now took such pleasure in sparing no one from his knowledge of vintages and vintners—who even could tell the difference between the wines produced on two neighbouring California hillsides.

Underneath the surface, however, all did not go so well. At the very top of the profession, a man who had talent, genius, or good fortune, found acceptance by his peers and admission to their society. The strain of being an outsider was more painfully experienced in the young and in those who did not quite reach the pinnacle of achievement. The insecurity was not, by any means, just a matter of personal achievement; it was also affected by the status of the school and university through which this man had passed as a student, and of the institution of which he was a member. It was also in part a matter of his social or family origin although that was less important than the other factors mentioned. The man doomed to live at a provincial university felt it—he felt it if he was a graduate of a provincial university and he felt it worse if he was a graduate of an ancient university. Injured sentiments, memories of slights and rejections would accumulate, and fantasy would accentuate it all. Mostly, however, the sense of being in the outer circle was expressed in faint sniffs of distaste for students, in mockery and irony. It affected the young more than it did their elders and students more than their teachers.

Nor was it entirely a matter of the subjective creation of a barrier by those who felt themselves to be outsiders. Part of the exclusiveness of the aristocratic-gentry higher civil service culture arose not from the organization of a coterie but from the fact that it was a humanistic culture, hostile to unbalanced specialization and hostile therefore to those professions, the practice and traditions of which necessitate the preoccupations of specialization, and in which the modern universities are so strong. We see it still in the ambivalence toward postgraduate research at Oxford and Cambridge and in a more trivial way we see it in the attitude toward the academic titles of address of Professor and Doctor in those universities. Much more importantly we saw it in the long-drawn-out and unsatisfactory discussion about the development of institutions of higher technological studies. The training of technologists on this level was repugnant to the ancient universities and their proponents, who felt perhaps rightly that such studies were too practical and too "unhumane" to be admitted to their universities; at the same time, they also did not like the idea of independent specialized institutions of university rank where technological research and studies could be carried on as if they were on the same dignity as traditional university studies.[4]

Finally a word may be said on the influence of the coterie itself. It seemed to be no more important in England than in any other centralized country where the leading men in each field of intellec-

4. It has sometimes been said that the reason why scientists, especially in Great Britain, have been inclined toward political radicalism lies in the nature of the subject, which requires the use of reason unaided by tradition and which involves the manipulation of material things in accordance with rational principles. Quite apart from the dubious picture of scientific work which this explanation adduces, it seems to suffer from disregard of some simple facts: namely, that in mid-twentieth-century Great Britain, science which was less than pure science was *infra dig*, and that a disproportionately large amount of the best scientific work of Great Britain, pure as well as applied, was carried on in the modern universities which could confer on their numbers little prestige beyond what they could achieve by their work. Scientists, even pure scientists, and certainly applied scientists in Great Britain lived and worked in an atmosphere which made at least some of them regard themselves as outsiders.

tual activity come to know one another personally, either because they happen to have been at school together or because their eminence at the peak of their professions has brought them together. On the whole, although there occasionally seemed to be some odd goings-on made possible by anonymous reviewing, British intellectual life did not seem to be regulated internally by personal attachments to a much greater extent than in other countries. To a very considerable degree it seemed to be governed by impersonal standards that were in part standards which had been associated with certain restricted classes and institutions, themselves the objects of strong, if ambivalent, sentiment.

Those who had grown up inside the culture of these classes and institutions felt very much at home in them in the fifties. But those who had not were powerfully attracted by them and were yet put off by the implication of their unworthiness for not having been so born. It was not an accident that the *New Statesman* at that time, with its wide circulation, should have presented an apparently contradictory table of contents: cranky radicalism in its political pages and genteel culture in its literary and cultural sections; or that it should have combined Bevanism in politics with a special wine supplement.

V

The New Elizabethans, who were conjured up in aspiration at the time of the coronation as the carriers of British tradition, petered out into thin air after a couple of years. The culture of the new age was nothing like the old Elizabethan culture. The new Elizabethan age was an age of very notable talent but it was a talent of fine lineaments, of delicate but not deep voice, of restraint which bound no passion, of subtlety without grandeur. Outside the China of the mandarins, no great society has ever had a body of intellectuals so integrated with, and so congenial to, its ruling class, and so combining civility and refinement. The consensus thus achieved was remarkable. What were the costs?

Just as in the nineteenth century the public schools and the universities had the task of assimilating into the ruling classes the heirs and descendants of wealthy businessmen who had made the necessary concessions to the spiritual ancien régime, so mid-twentieth-century Britain had the equally important task of assimilating into its great traditions the new aspirants to the ruling classes, broadly conceived, who came from the lower-middle and upper-working classes. It was easier to assimilate newcomers when they were only a trickle and when the institutions of assimilation were thoroughly governed by the older culture. It became more difficult, when the numbers were greater and when many of the institutions themselves had only an ambivalent and uncertain hold on the older culture. The success of the new process of assimilation and refinement was achieved at the cost of a narrowing of sensibility and imagination, and of a hard conflict-engendering pressure on those who crowded the periphery.

7 Intellectuals and the Center of Society in the United States

I

The primary intellectual roles are constituted by: (1) the creation of patterns or symbols of general significance through the action of the imagination and the exercise of observational and rational powers and their precipitation into works, (2) the cultivation of the stocks of intellectual works, and (3) the transmission through interpretation of the traditions of intellectual works to those who have not yet experienced them. The secondary role is the performance of intellectual-practical (or intellectual-executive) actions in which intellectual works are intimately involved.

Each of these roles has a culture which may, for analytical purposes, be distinguished into a substantive culture, which consists of beliefs, categories of perception, and rules referring to the performance of the role, and a penumbral culture, which asserts beliefs about the value and dignity of the role and the works produced in it, and about the actual and proper relationship of the performers of intellectual roles and those who perform other roles in society.

Those who perform intellectual roles constitute the intellectual classes. The intellectual classes differ from society to society in composition and structure. They differ, for example, with respect to numbers or size; they differ in their distribution over the various types of intellectual roles and in the genres of works which they produce. They differ in their creative powers and in their knowledge of and attachment to the stocks and traditions of works; in their degree of internal differentiation and specialization. They differ too in the magnitude of their performance of secondary, intellectual-executive roles in their respective societies, in the degree of integration with other elites of their society, and in their influence on these elites and therewith on the working of their societies. The intellectual classes also differ in their penumbral intellectual culture, that is, their beliefs about intellectual actions and intellectual roles and about the proper place of intellectual actions and intellectuals in society.

Intellectuals exercise influence on their societies—on the predominantly nonintellectual institutions and elites of their own societies—through the works produced in their primary and the actions performed in their secondary roles. Their influence is a function of the attitudes of the nonintellectual elites—political, economic, military—toward intellectual works, intellectual institutions, and intellectuals; it is also a function of the reception of intellectual culture by the nonintellectual elites and of the establishment by the nonintellectual elites of secondary, intellectual-executive roles in the executive subsystems of society. The changes in the secondary roles of intellectuals in the United States and in their penumbral culture constitute the theme of what follows.

In most societies, prior to the present century, intellectuals exercised such influence as they did mainly through the creation of patterns of belief which permeated the outlook of the non-intellectual elites, usually very slowly and with long delay. They were enabled to do this by serving as tutors, courtiers, advisers and by their contribution to the creation of the intellectual ambience in which rulers moved. Through the preaching and exemplification of religious beliefs and precepts they also influenced the mass of the population more directly. When they performed intellectual-executive roles as civil servants or as ecclesiastical administrators, they acted in accordance with a code which was part of their secondary, penumbral traditions. Insofar as authority could be said to govern the working of their respective societies, they shared in this control. They were very seldom actually rulers, because ruling and the process of preparation for accession to ruling do not combine easily with the performance of the primary intellectual actions. (There have, however, been a few striking exceptions to this rule.)

The penumbral culture of intellectuals in the West, particularly in modern times, has included a marked distrust, and even abhorrence, of the nonintellectual elites in politics and in the economy. Institutions, established traditions, incumbents of positions of authority, and intellectuals who have accepted these have come in for severe criticism and rejection. This particular secondary, penumbral tradition has varied among western societies and in different epochs of each of these societies. Present-day American society is an instance of a society in which the intellectuals—literary, humanistic, and academic—for a century were alienated in sentiment and imagery from the nonintellectual elites, both national and local. They shared only slightly in the exercise of authority in American society, which reproduced itself and developed with minimal participation by its contemporary intellectuals. This structure changed in the second third of the twentieth century. The society became an increasingly "intellectual-based" and "knowledge-based" society. Education became an object of universal aspiration as a means to a better life and a higher social status. American society became a national society in which the distance between center and periphery was diminished through the formation of a common national identity, common foci of attention, and a common constellation of values. These major changes, which were not the only ones—nor were they by any means total and comprehensive in their extension into all sectors of American society—were accompanied by major changes in the structure and culture of the intellectual classes. Intellectual institutions proliferated, and the numbers of intellectuals grew correspondingly. As the number and proportion of intellectual-executive roles increased and with them the proportion of intellectuals formed in intellectual institutions and incumbent in such roles, the outlook of sectors of the nonintellectual elites absorbed many elements of the intellectuals' ethos.

The incorporation of intellectuals into the exercise of authority and influence in a society has usually been accompanied by their attachment to the central value system. The confluence of these two processes of incorporation into the central institutional system and of attachment to the central value system strengthened the former and secured internal peace, Naturally, it could not protect that society from all the vicissitudes of uncontrollable ecological and demographic changes, from the emergence of new centers of power outside itself and the inevitable ravages which are consequent on the limits of foresight, neglect, pride, rigidity of judgment, and un-adaptedness of conduct. In the United States, however, incorporation, having had a strengthening effect for a third of a century, has generated in the latter part of the sixties a regressive effect. In consequence of their expanded numbers, their more frequent incumbency of authoritative roles, and the great permeation of their ethos resultant from the increased prominence and predominance of intellectual institutions, the developmental and integrative processes of American society have been obstructed. Authority has been weakened; the center of society has been placed in a moral shadow.

II

From the Jacksonian revolution until the administration of Franklin Roosevelt, intellectuals, particularly literary and humanistic-publicistic intellectuals in the United States, found much to distress them in the actions and culture of the ruling groups of their society. The long persistent, indeed, still lingeringly persistent, preoccupation of American intellectuals—especially literary men and humanistic publicists—with Europe was part of an attachment to a culture in which they thought intellectuals "counted." The preoccupation with Europe was dominated by the fact that Europe was, in literature, in science, in scholarship, and in art, the very center of creativity. They were also awed, though sometimes resentfully, by European power—

that sheer economic and military might which was dominant, with only intermittent challenges, throughout Asia, Africa, and Latin America. In these three continents, paradoxically, the very success of the movement for independence corroborated the centrality of Europe. These features of cultural creativity and military and economic power of the European metropolis were very influential in the formation of the American intellectuals' image of Europe. They should not, however, obscure the utopian function of Europe for American intellectuals. Europe was, for American intellectuals a place where intellectuals were respected and taken seriously by those strata of society which exercised power.

When American intellectuals between the Civil War and the First World War looked at Europe, what did they see? In London, for much of the nineteenth century, politics and literature moved in overlapping circles. Disraeli, who was a famous novelist, had been a prime minister; other prime ministers, Gladstone for example, were classical scholars and students of theology. The British universities, above all Oxford, were the breeding grounds of famous politicians and the training schools for the highest class of the civil service both at home and in the empire.[1]

Dr. Maurice Dobb, the communist and economist of Trinity College, Cambridge, in a book published in Great Britain in 1928 ruefully compared Great Britain with the Continent, where revolutionary Marxism had found academic and otherwise learned proponents and expositors.[2] But to vaguely socialist American intellectuals of the time, the British condition at that time seemed almost paradisical. The Labour Party carried in its diadem such gems as Harold Laski, G. D. H. Cole, R. H. Tawney, and the Webbs—all intellectuals, some of them academic and all of them ostensibly influential. The Conservative Party, despite its serried ranks of "hard-faced businessmen who had made a good thing out of war," studiously maintained its Oxford connection. To many American intellectuals Oxford was as sustaining a pillar of conservatism and liberalism as the London School of Economics was of socialism— although socialism also had its Oxford adherents. Of France, it was known that **Painlevé** had been a mathematician and that Raymond

1. The American Rhodes scholars' image of Oxford in relation to British politics and the influence of this impression on American intellectuals' attitudes is a subject which deserves attention. Especially important in this regard are recollections of eminent British politicans coming to speak at the Oxford Union.

2. He cited "Labriola and Ferri in Italy . . . Kautsky, Bebel, Cunow and Luxemburg in Germany . . . Hilferding and Bauer in Austria . . . Struve and Plekhanov in Russia." Nor did Marxism "stir the waters of academic discussion in Oxford, Cambridge, and London, as it did in Berlin, Vienna, Rome, and Petersburg." (Dobb, *Russian Economic Development since the Revolution* [New York: E. P. Dutton & Co., 1928], p. 5).

Poincaré was the brother of a famous mathematician, that Jaurès had been a great historian, that Clemenceau had edited *l'Aurore*, that Anatole France, Henri Barbusse, and Romain Rolland were prized by Communist Party leaders. It was known that men of letters were honored by official distinctions and by banquets. It was known that in the Dreyfus affair a small circle of intellectuals had formed a party on behalf of the victim; the individual action of Emile Zola, one of the most important novelists of his time, undid a great injustice and delivered a staggering blow to the union of reactionaries who had wished, for various base considerations, to allow the earlier condemnation of Captain Dreyfus to stand.

The American intellectuals' image of Germany, vague though it was and very unevenly distributed, was much like their image of France. The academic intellectuals seemed to play a crucial role: the universities trained the higher civil service; the Verein für Sozialpolitik, crammed with professors, acted as if its declarations were respectfully listened to and seriously considered; learned lawyers sat in the Reichstag. Had not the Frankfurt parliament of 1848 been called the "professors' parliament"? Even the trade union movement was struggled over by intellectuals—a few of them university graduates and self-educated persons who vied with each other and other intellectuals in doctrinal disputes. Was not a great socialist intellectual, Lassalle, one of the fathers of the German trade union movement? Professors were sometimes nominated to be privy councillors (*Geheimräte*) and they were generally held in awe.

European artists too, despite their alienation in their respective societies, were regarded, from the obscurity in which American intellectuals thought they themselves were forced to live, as existing within the charismatic circle. European artists received commissions to adorn public buildings; there were officially maintained academies of art; modern art had its patrons among the wealthy and influential who were encouraged and educated by able dealers.

Even Russia, barbaric Russia, appeared to give a place to intellectuals which their American counterparts believed the United States did not provide. If it did not honor or patronize them, it at least persecuted them. Persecution was a form of attention. The greatest of all, Tolstoi, a count, which was not forgotten, criticized the czarist regime and Russian society for its moral degradation, and because he was so great and so famous internationally, the regime could do nothing to him. Dostoievsky had a halter put round his neck for having attended a meeting of the Petrashevsky circle, where Bielinsky's open letter denouncing Gogol's religious turn had been read. Turgenev, who had in the last part of the nineteenth century been regarded as second only to Tolstoi, was constrained to live abroad in exile. All this attention from czarist authority was regarded as a sort of honor.[3] Abroad, eminent intellectuals like Kropotkin and Vinogradoff denounced from visible positions the czarist autocracy. What was true of the Russians was true of other European countries: the revolutionaries were intellectuals. Engagement with the authorities, even subversive engagement, was at least a certain kind of intimacy. American intellectuals did not even have this gratification.

This in its roughest outlines was the map of the relations between intellectuals and the powers as it was perceived by many American intellectuals over the course of nearly a century, but particularly since the end of the Civil War. Looking around at their own situations, what did they find? Public life was a shambles, corruption rampant, mammon enthroned, and the muses rusticated, unregarded, disrespected, sometimes even, in spectacular cases, persecuted. The fate of *Leaves of Grass,* of Dreiser's early novels, the scandal of Maxim Gorki's "wife," the trial of Art Young, Max Eastman, and the editors of *The Masses* stood out as characteristic episodes. The trial of *Madame Bovary*, the humiliation and destruction of Oscar Wilde, the arrest of Bertrand Russell and his removal from his fellowship at Trinity College, the *Lex Arens*—these did not darken the American intellectuals' picture of the special relationship of European intellectuals and their powers.

American politicians appeared to their fellow countrymen to be very different from European politicians. Edmund Wilson epitomized a view which had been widely held when he wrote: "Our society has finally produced in its specialized professional politicians one of the most useless and obnoxious groups which has perhaps ever disgraced human history—a group that seems unique among the governing classes in having managed to be corrupt, uncultivated and incompetent all at once.[4]

The businessmen were of a piece. Among literary men, especially those who made the running from the Civil War onward, businessmen had a very bad press. There were very few like Dreiser who admired power so much that a figure like Cowperwood, the hero of *The Financier,* could be made acceptable by sheer force of character. The army offered no respectable career; the church was hopeless: the Roman Catholic hierarchy was the epitome of benightedness,

3. This masochistic yearning is still not dead. Only a few years ago, Miss McCarthy wrote in *The New York Review of Books* that the persecution of Siniavsky and Daniel by the Soviet government was evidence that literature was taken seriously by the Soviet government. She contrasted this with the example of the unworthy United States government, which demonstrated its indifference to letters by abstention from interference with the freedom of writers.

4. "An Appeal to Progressives" *The New Republic* 14th Jan. 1931, reprinted in *The Shores of Light: A Literary Chronicle of the Twenties and Thirties.* (London: W. H. Allen, 1952) p. 529.

and the Protestants ranging from the despicable stuffiness and sycophancy of the Espiscopalians and the Presbyterians in the presence of the mighty to the innumerable sects of ranters and Bible-pounders who had fallen out of the bottom of the Baptists and Methodists were no better. The civil service had never been an object of aspiration to American intellectuals:[5] here and there one of them was ingloriously employed in it, Melville as a minor official in the customs service, Whitman a clerk in the attorney-general's office, some sound scientists in the Department of Agriculture. The diplomatic and consular services, despite the xenotropism of the intellectuals, were tarred with the brush of government and politics. Few intellectuals sought their place in them—there were a few major exceptions, mainly from New England—and in any case the selection of ambassadors through political patronage gave intellectuals little opportunity.

The society at large appalled them. For the most part, American scholarly and literary intellectuals lived in a world they never made and for which they took no responsibility. But they were not immune to the claims of the primordial ties. They suffered from their membership in a society to which they were bound by an unexpungible identity and which at the same time revolted them. They were perverted patriots bound to a country from which they could not release themselves and which they could not love. The self-exiled Americans in Paris lived among other Americans. Few were able to denationalize themselves even by long residence abroad.

III

American intellectuals were pained by their membership in a society, the rulers of which seemed to have no need for them. This was partly a misunderstanding. They could not have come into existence in the United States had the government and the society been totally antiintellectual. Universities were maintained with increasing munificence after about 1880; periodicals with quite large audiences and of a respectable intellectual level existed, giving intellectuals, literary men and publicists places for the publication of their shorter and some of their longer works. There were publishing firms which produced their works and sold them to an American audience. It is true that there prevailed a puritanical attitude in the cultural and intellectual institutions, and these were not wholly sympathetic with

5. One of the major public actions of American intellectuals between the Civil War and the Spanish-American War was the campaign to reform the civil service. This would have entailed replacing the power which politicians exercised in the form of patronage by appointment on the basis of educational qualifications and performance in examinations.

the "advanced" views of the new European realism—which for that matter was encountering difficulties in Europe too.

There was a demand for intellectual services in the United States in the latter part of the nineteenth and the early part of the twentieth centuries. The federal government, despite the antiintellectualism of many politicians and the low estimate in which officials were held, probably employed more intellectuals than most European governments. Many intellectuals were hidden away in the Surgeon-General's Office, in the Geological Survey, in the Bureau of Indian Affairs, in the Patent Office, and latterly in the Department of Agriculture, which in time became a leading intellectual institution in agricultural economics and statistics. They were, however, obscure and they did not move in the circles of the powerful. They worked peacefully and quietly and they were unknown to the great world. They were specialists, and the literary and humanistic intellectuals had little sense of affinity with them. The country was huge and there were many colleges and universities; the literary and humanistic intellectuals did not usually pass through the same institutions as the scientific civil service. But even if a sense of affinity had existed, it would not have overcome the feeling of exclusion. The scientific civil servants were servants. They were not masters; they did not make major policies or associate with those who did. Although progressive politicians in the Northwest and in Wisconsin brought academic social scientists into their councils, the same did not happen on the federal level to any extent which the intellectuals cared to remark.

It was from the great world that the intellectuals felt excluded. It was in the great world—the center of society where it appeared that decisions were made and where the regalia reposed—that the intellectuals felt the cold wind of indifference and perhaps contempt.

And they were largely correct in this.

The political elite felt no need for the support or the collaboration of the literary and humanistic intellectuals and it did not seek their company.[6] For the most part, the political elite in the United States had come up through long service in the political machines, where in the rough and tumble of the ill-educated, they had learned the arts of compromise and combination and even more unsavory things. The American political elite was by and large the product of a populistic polity and had not, by origin or by association, acquired the refinements of European political elites drawn from the aristocracy and gentry and the professional classes.[7] The American political

6. Theodore Roosevelt was far more friendly with Rudyard Kipling than he was with any American literary men of comparable quality.
7. American intellectuals, particularly the humanistic intellectuals and some of the non-bohemian literary men, had for a long time a belief in the

elite by and large, and least of all at the municipal and state levels where political apprenticeships had to be served and support had to be elicited, did not think that they needed the company and still less the services of literary and humanistic intellectuals. Scientists were regarded by politicians as all right—in their place, which was not in the political arena. Nor did the intellectuals seek to enter politics: the hurly-burly of low company was not to their taste and without a capacity to stand such company, the chances of a political career were slight. What a contrast between this and the occasional British practice of patronizing a well-connected young man, freshly down from Oxford, and granting him an opportunity to stand for a parliamentary constituency! The American system was not judged favorably with respect to this difference.

Nor did the big businessmen think they needed university graduates, even scientists, in their firms. Only the chemical industry employed university graduates in large numbers; the chemists were kept in research and in production but they rose in management only after they had lightened their burden of scientific curiosity. Agriculture too made use of scientists in the state agricultural research stations. They had a significant part in the advance of American agriculture and they were respected by farmers. The agricultural scientists were, however, specialists. They were local and not national notables and they regarded themselves as scientists and not as part of a larger class of intellectuals. Iron and steel, coal mining, and the railways, on the other hand—the great industries of the industrial expansion of the half-century between the Civil War and the First World War were the industries in which the great free-booting capitalists operated—had no use for intellectuals. The technological and managerial innovations which gave these industries their central place in the American economy and which enabled the American economy to come to the forefront of the world, arose from within the industries themselves. They were not the products of research done by university-trained scientists and engineers. The great capitalists who patronized art patronized either long-dead painters or society painters, disesteemed by the intellectuals, who regarded themselves as custodians of the more advanced "European" culture. Even those plutocrats who were generous patrons of academic learning associated very little with scholars if they were

---

superiority of the genteel and the well-born. This lasted until well into the 1920s and it faded only with the Great Depression. This naturally nurtured a prejudice against the uncouth politician in his "long-johns," his galluses, his string necktie, and his chewing tobacco. Long after the respect for gentility has disappeared and the backwoodsman among legislators has become rare, the stereotype persists.

not also university presidents; they did not associate even that much with literary men.

Banking progressed without economists; the federal government likewise eschewed the knowledge and wisdom of economists, although Wisconsin and a few other progressive states drew on such knowledge as they possessed. Such social work as there was, was done by local politicians and by amateurs of the prosperous classes, some of whom were strong personalities and outstanding intelligences who became important humanitarian reformers. Only in the press, in the churches, and in the reformist politics of certain states of the Midwest and Northwest did a certain kind of intellectual hold his own among the incumbents of the central institutions. In the press, where the reportorial function was regarded as a proper training for a young man aspiring to become a naturalistic novelist, a certain robust class of intellectuals was to be found; in the editorial rooms were to be found intellectuals who felt no kinship either with European intellectual trends or with those Americans who did feel that kinship. Still, the interchange between the press and the literary and the humanistic intellectuals between 1890 and 1910 was more pronounced, above all in the muck-raking era, than that between the intellectuals and any other sector of the elite. In fact it was through the press that American intellectuals reentered the center of society—but they did so as an active counter-elite, depicting the degradations of corrupting plutocrats and corrupt politicians. Some of them stayed on to play a part in the reform politics of Theodore Roosevelt and Woodrow Wilson. By the 1920s much of this participation had disappeared, and it was recalled, by the generation of intellectuals which came to prominence after the First World War, as a failure. All that remained was the reinforcement of an anti-political, anticivil tradition. At the periphery of the Protestant churches, a certain kind of active, social-reforming, Christian intellectual was to be found, but, on the whole, literary and humanistic intellectuals had no affectionate connections with these circles. Theologians and ecclesiastical dignitaries, insofar as they had intellectual roles, were regarded as alien to the valid intellectual tradition. Those who had close connections with the plutocracy and the leading politicians were regarded by literary and humanistic intellectuals as traitors to the true cause of the intellect.

Thus, American society, although it was nurturing a vigorous and creative body of intellectuals of many diverse interests and talents, can scarcely be said to have been structurally dependent on their cooperation, and insofar as it actually was dependent, in agriculture, in the chemical industry and in the scientific civil service, these functions were invisible to those members of the intellectual classes—the literary and humanistic intellectuals—who designated themselves as "the intellectuals" and who had grievances against American society for its neglect of intellectual things. Through much of this period, many of the most accomplished literary and humanistic intellectuals were hostile toward the "practical" elites. They censured the indifference of these other sectors toward intellectual things and, by implication, toward intellectuals. They disapproved of American society because intellectuals were not actually incorporated into its symbolic ornamentation. They thought that a good society, quite apart from any merits it might have in the relations between rulers and ruled or among fellow citizens or in the conduct of parents and children or in the accomplishments of the practitioners of crafts and professions, must, in justice, accord a high status to intellectuals in the circle of rulers. As a result, many intellectuals lived in an "inner exile" and some lived in actual, voluntary exile.

Politicians and businessmen were well aware of this mainly silent, but sometimes harshly expressed, hostility. They paid the intellectuals back in their own coin. They despised them as effete and unmanly, as Anglophile and snobbish. They usually ignored their existence. When American universities began to bestir themselves intellectually from the 1890s onward until the 1930s, academics, mainly in the social sciences, were sporadically harassed, threatened, and dismissed from their posts for criticism of existing economic and political institutions and those who exercised authority in them.[8]

Yet American society prospered, this withdrawal of intellectuals notwithstanding. It was a rough and, in many respects, a callow society but it performed great things. It settled the open country, coped powerfully with nature, and drew great rewards; it attracted vast populations from among the wretched of the earth, assimilated them to a new way of life which prized individual exertion and accomplishment. Its conflicts—except for the Civil War—were not often deep or long-lasting, although they were frequently violent. New tasks were undertaken continuously, and very many were handled with considerable success. Government, despite a long period of pervasive corruption, was brought into increasing responsiveness to popular desires. A common culture was formed out of heterogeneous elements; an inclusive educational system was developed which not only diffused the common culture but also provided the early stages of what later became a prodigious scientific and scholarly creativity. A lively democratic political life was developed, with many glaring defects but generally democratic and competitive withal.

8. Cf. my: "Limitations on the Freedom and Research and Teaching in the Social Sciences," chap. 15, this volume.

All of this was accomplished with a relatively marginal and diffuse participation of the contemporaneous or recently-living highly educated or the intellectually most creative in the processes through which the society was maintained and developed. Technological innovation was the work of inventors rather than of scientifically educated scientists; the managers of business enterprises drew relatively little from the higher culture of society. The army likewise made little use of the academically trained intellectuals until the Second World War. The growth of the powers of the federal government owed much to the exertions of very strong personalities among legislators, mainly middle western and northwestern populists—usually men of no great culture but intelligent and of strong character, guided in two significant periods by presidents who were professional politicians of outstanding intellectual propensities—one of them Woodrow Wilson, being formerly a professor of political science and a university president as well. Business enterprisers, farmers, professional politicians, journalists, amateur social workers and religious and social reformers, labor leaders, civil servants, school administrators, and judges were the main architects of the growth of American society. The growth of American society was its transformation into an urban and industrial society, liberal and democratic generally in its political institutions and increasingly drawing its heterogeneous, newly entered ethnic segments into a national society and a common culture. Only the rural Negroes in the South as a relatively massive minority and a few small pockets of Red Indians in their reservations were omitted from this contraction of the space between center and periphery. The leading agents of this transformation included only a few intellectuals in crucial and prominent roles. Men like Theodore Roosevelt and Woodrow Wilson, Herbert Croly and Louis Brandeis, John Dewey and Alfred Mahan were very influential in guiding of policies and providing the ideas which led American society into its new form, but they did not affect the image of the antiintellectual character of American society which dominated the thought of American humanistic intellectuals.[9]

IV

The coming and conduct of the Second World War greatly widened and complicated the reincorporation of the intellectuals into the center of American society which had begun in the progressive era. The curve which had swung upward in the period of the New

9. Again the persistence of this view is manifested in Professor Richard Hofstadter's *Anti-Intellectualism in American Life.* Despite Professor Hofstadter's thorough and scholarly mastery of the facts, his important book permits it to be believed that the antiintellectual Yahoos have had the upper hand at all times.

Liberalism relapsed, following the First World War, into a trough as deep as any in the nineteenth century. Then in the 1930s at a time when the Great Depression was transforming American society in so many significant respects, the intellectuals reentered the center. The damage to the puritanical ethos which was previously un-challenged, in principle, except for a very small number of reformers and bohemians; the assimilation of Jews into the center; the raising of expectations concerning the creative capacities of governmental action, were among the major effects of the Great Depression. All of these involved the intellectuals, touched on their interests, gave them new opportunities to assert themselves.

Ordinarily, a crisis like the Great Depression disintegrates a society and discredits its elite. In part this is what happened in the United States. The business elite was discredited and so was the incumbent Republican administration. The clergy, associated with the reigning economic and political elites, saw their authority diminished at the top although, at the level of parish and congrega-tion, their devotion and solicitude was a compensation for the diminution of prestige of the higher ecclesiastical authority. The decentralized character of Protestant ecclesiastical organization in the United States helped to save the status of the religious elite. Municipal and state political elites on the other hand would have suffered a further diminution of their already not very high prestige had the new national administration under Franklin Roosevelt not acceded to power. As a result of the indomitable personality of President Roosevelt in the face of every vicissitude and every failure, and the appearance and, to some extent, the reality of effective action by his administration, the legitimacy of the authority of the state governments was saved—undeservedly.

But the chief beneficiaries among the elites of the policies of the Roosevelt administration were the central political elites themselves and the intellectuals. The numerous reforms instituted by or credited to the federal government—first, and most symbolically, the National Recovery Act itself—the reforms in agriculture which halted and reversed the course of the disasters suffered by the entire rural population, the enactment and implementation of the new social security arrangements, the guarantee of bank deposits, the encouragement and protection given to trade unions of the semi-skilled workers, the various public work schemes, the salvaging of youth through the Civilian Conservation Corps and the National Youth Administration—all of these contributed to the restabilization of American society in a new structure after the disaggregation which had been going on since the end of 1929. The vital personality of President Roosevelt, his moving eloquence and patient com-passion, his confident castigation of the failed elites and his imaginative deployment of the constitutional powers and the financial resources available to him offset the previously rising and still very strong current of real deprivations being suffered by most sections of the population.

The traditional structure of recruitment to the higher civil service and the great expansion of governmental activities permitted and necessitated a very large-scale recruitment of civil servants from outside the existing cadres. In a very short time and in a way they did not expect or demand, the aspirations of the civil service reformers of the last quarter of the nineteenth century were brought into reality. The British and German practice of recruitment of the administrative elite from the universities—so much admired for so many years by American intellectuals with civic concerns—was given an approximate American counterpart.

The "Brains Trust" of the presidential campaign of 1932, which drew primarily on Columbia University social scientists, was a foreshadowing of the role which intellectuals were to play throughout the remainder of the Roosevelt administration. President Roosevelt was a loyal Harvard graduate, and he was always ready to permit himself to be identified with the universities. From the very beginning of his term of office, academic intellectuals, primarily professors from the law faculties of the major universities, economists and political scientists as well, were called to the highest offices in practically every new administrative agency. Professors and historians were sent abroad as ambassadors; the National Planning Board, although its chairman was the president's uncle, was replete with academics. The National Academy of Sciences began to move into the role from which it has never since receded. There had never been anything like it in the history of American universities, never anything like it in the history of the American intellectual classes since the formation of the Republic and the drafting and promulgation of the constitution.

Some of these intellectuals were given major administrative responsibilities; on the whole, however, they did not become administrators. Many who were appointed as legal counsel to departments and agencies were assigned the tasks of devising substantive policies to be espoused by the president and to be enacted into legislation by Congress. Even where they had administrative posts, their tasks were to think about policy on behalf of the president. They formed an extended, informal personal cabinet around the president, superseding the actual cabinet.

The outbreak of the war in Europe was followed by a gradual movement toward American participation. The "lend-lease" legislation brought in more academic lawyers and some economists. The entry of America into the war produced a vast proliferation of new organizations. The greatest of these was the Manhattan Project, which drew scientists of many sorts and of the highest quality into government service on a scale never undertaken before in any country or in any epoch. There were many other major scientific projects. Other new organizations which drew on intellectuals to fill their ranks were the Office of Strategic Services, the War Production Board, the Board of Economic Warfare, the Office of Price Administration, and the Office of War Information. Older departments expanded their activities; the Department of State, the Department of Justice, and others added new functions, provided places for intellectuals: university teachers of law, economics, history, geography, and even political science and sociology. Anthropologists and linguists, even teachers of French, German, and English literature and practically every other discipline of the human sciences served in minor policy-making and in important intelligence and administrative capacities in civilian and military organizations. The physical and biological scientists were absorbed to a probably greater extent—there were more of them and there was more precedent and basis for their services. Mathematicians and statisticians were heavily drawn upon. For the most part, these academics were glad of the vacation from teaching and they enjoyed the excitement of proximity to great events and to great authority as well as the occasional exercise of power on their own.

The war was in part a contest of industrial strength and skill. Industry and agriculture in the two decades preceding the war had become much more "science-based." From chemistry and agriculture, science extended its dominion into the communications industry and its industrial supplements. Engineering in its various branches was becoming more and more scientific and therewith more intellectual. Statistics began to be more widely used in many branches of economic life and in government; the Roosevelt administration greatly increased the scale of statistical services of the federal government, although the Hoover administration had already shown the way forward from the stimulus given to it by Hoover himself when he was secretary of commerce in the Coolidge administration.

Nonetheless, it was war production itself which extended so much the domain of the "science-based" industry. The war therefore became a contest of mobilized intellect working through or on the basis of research.

The combination of opportunities to carry on work which was a continuation of their peacetime activities with immeasurably greater resources and in contexts which excited by their proximity to power together with their affirmation of the general purpose of the war, brought American intellectuals into solidarity with the political and even the business and military elites of the country. Many who had been fellow travelers of the Communist Party in the 1930s rallied to the government after the period of embarrassment which lasted from the signing of the Ribbentrop-Molotov agreement in September 1938 to the German invasion of Russia in June 1941. It is true that those with firm Stalinist attachments gave only a conditional affirmation to the government, but they too shared even if only superficially and hypocritically in the general consensus of the intellectuals. In contrast with the First World War, when many Americans had expressed reservations about America's engagement in the war, there were few pacifists or conscientious objectors. Isolationism among intellectuals—which had been slight enough in any case—almost disappeared during the war.[10] Those who were pro-German or pro-Japanese or pro-Italian were infinitesimal in number, and those who served the enemy directly, as did Ezra Pound abroad or George Sylvester Viereck at home, had no audience among American intellectuals in their traitorous activities.

V

When the Second World War ended, the unanimity of intellectuals was broken by the reemergence of the Stalinists and their fellow travelers maneuvering for protective cover behind Henry Wallace and by small circles of Trotskyites and miscellaneous non-Stalinist sects. There remained a very comprehensive consensus. Most of the leading intellectuals in the natural and social sciences and the humanities who had been in governmental and military service, returned to academic life, but they did not give up their sense of being at the center. Many of them retained an active relationship with the government, either with the Department of Defense or with other governmental or quasi-governmental bodies, which wished to retain the connection with intellectuals formed during the war, with such happy results. New research institutions were established, living mainly from government research contracts, and some of them were able to attract natural and social scientists of a very high quality. This too maintained a sense of affinity with the center.

The end of the war saw the emergence into public light of a new phenomenon in the United States: pressure groups of scientists seeking to influence governmental policy through public agitation, representations to legislators and to the highest levels of executive branch. The Szilard-Einstein letter to President Roosevelt was the first

10. Stalinists, prosperous German-American businessmen, congressmen who remembered the inquiries into the munitions industry, and some Irish-Americans were the main opponents of America's aid to Britain after the fall of France. Robert Hutchins and Charles Beard, who stuck to their isolationism until the very declaration of war, did not have many sympathizers among intellectuals.

step in this process. The atomic scientists' movement, of which the *Bulletin of Atomic Scientists* and the Pugwash meetings are the monuments, was a remarkable expression of civility in a sector of the American intellectual classes, which except for a slight rash of Stalinism in the 1930s, had never concerned itself much with politics.

The expansion of the universities greatly increased the opportunities for teaching and research appointments and salaries increased. There were more graduate students to work with, and libraries improved. For many university teachers, especially those who had completed their studies early in the Great Depression and who had, despite the niggardliness of those times, survived, the situation seemed beyond the dreams of avarice. Carrying out scientific and scholarly research did not seem incompatible with serving the government; there seemed to be an identity of interests. It did not seem anomalous that the government should support these activities. Its goodwill towards intellectuals—despite McCarthyism—appeared to be self-evident. Through an elaborate system of federal government support, scientists at their universities did research in which the military was sufficiently interested to provide financial support—although it should be emphasized that much of this research had only the most tenuous connection with military practice. The profusion of opportunities and resources turned many heads and bred a state of mind in which all things seemed possible because the reign of scarcity appeared to have ended.

Industry and commerce had learned from the wartime experience of the government and from the conduct of the war and they too sought the services of the intellectuals—mainly chemists, physicists, mathematicians, statisticians, and economists. The tremendous expansion of television and advertising absorbed many literary and artistic intellectuals or provided supplementary income for them. The affluence of the country enabled literary men to benefit from the prodigality of private foundations; grants for young and established writers became common, and the shift of emphasis at the undergraduate level of the universities to expression rather than learning and to presentness rather than pastness gave literary men an entrée to the universities such as had been previously unknown.

American intellectuals were now honored in their own country. They felt honored. Even literary intellectuals who had not enjoyed the enormous prosperity of the academic intellectuals felt their tradition of alienation being eroded.[11] Some tried to remind

11. The two symposia conducted by the *Partisan Review* were expressive of what was happening among the chief heirs of the tradition of alienation among literary and humanistic intellectuals. Cf. Arvin, Newton, et al., *America and the Intellectuals,* PR Series no. 4 (New York, 1953), (originally published as "Our Country and Our Culture." *Partisan Review,* 1952). Cf. also Agee, James, et al., *Religion and the Intellectuals.* PR series no. 3 (New York, 1950).

themselves that it was not their calling to affirm the principles embodied in the practices of their society, Others were well aware of the dilemma created by their new functions and the larger intellectual consensus in confrontation with the traditions in which they had grown up. The general revulsion against Stalinism as practiced in the Soviet Union and the "people's democracies" and by the Communist Party of the United States made it easier for intellectuals who had in the past been uncompromisingly anti-capitalist to reconcile themselves to postwar America.[12]

By the end of the 1940s, America had become the center of the world. The increasing number of American intellectuals—academic and literary—who went abroad, thanks to the largesse of their government and the private philanthropic foundations, were made aware of this. The bitterness of the anti-Americanism among foreign intellectuals only testified to their preoccupation with America; not only were foreign societies being "Coco-Colonized" but their intellectuals could not resist the fascination of America. American intellectuals were even less able to resist the attractive power of the centrality of the United States. From the condition of being peripheral in a society which they believed was culturally provincial, American intellectuals came to see themselves as effective members of the center of an intellectual metropolis. Their earlier feelings of

12. By the end of the 1950s, the truth about the Stalinist purges had been accepted by most intellectuals in the United States. Khrushchev's revelations of February 1956 at the 22nd Congress of the Communist Party of the Soviet Union was only a final and authoritative confirmation of what had already been generally recognized. Attachment to the center of American society included awareness of the moral value of material well-being, individual freedom, and a pluralistic structure of society. None of these had been attained in the communist countries, where the two latter had been deliberately suppressed on the ground that their suppression was a necessary condition for the attainment of the former, which had nonetheless remained unattained. The issues raised by the Soviet Union dominated the international perspective of American intellectuals after the war, in part because in fact the communists had mounted a very vociferous intellectual campaign before the war which had touched the conscience and influenced the cognitive maps of many American intellectuals. In any case, the evident superiority of the United States to the Soviet Union in the very categories which communists insisted should be applied to the assessment of the merits of societies, and the disillusionment about the Soviet Union among those who had once been enthusiasts, made for readiness to appreciate American society.

There was one rift in the lute. This was the first McCarthyism which disturbed the atmosphere of the decade after the war, harrying fellow travelers, doing considerable damage in a small number of instances, intimidating communists and quasi-communists, and discrediting American society in the minds of men who would have wished to reaffirm their connection with it. Much more lastingly damaging was the impediment which it formed to the healing of the breach between American literary and publicistic intellectuals who had grown up in a tradition of alienation and American politicians at a time when so many other factors tended to erode this tradition. McCarthyism reinforced it.

provinciality had not been experienced as a happy condition. They embraced with enthusiasm the escape from peripherality in a province to centrality in a metropolis.

The gratification over incorporation into the center probably derives some of its impetus from the fact that many of the intellectuals of the generation which came into prominence from the 1930s onward were of Jewish, mainly Eastern European Jewish, origin. They were the first generation of the offspring of the immigrants who came to the United States in such great numbers between the mid-1880s and about 1912. Intellectual aptitude and intellectual passion were coupled with social ambition. The white Anglo-Saxon protestant ascendancy was still publicly unchallenged, and to move in their company was regarded by many Jewish intellectuals, however radical some of them were, as a good thing. The attainment of that ideal, in association with and through intellectual accomplishment, could be a cause of self-congratulation.

But at the root of this affirmation was the reality of a strong state. Although the dominant, most visible tradition of American intellectuals of almost all kinds has been that of distrust toward the regnant political and economic powers, it has ever since the 1880s at least, been associated with a tradition which asserts that the ills of society can be cured by a strong and virtuous authority. Long before American intellectuals became socialists, Stalinists, Trotskyists or whatever, they believed that "the state should do it." When the idea of planning, very simplistically conceived, came upon the scene, it was seized upon as the right solution. It was no wonder that at a time when the mythology of planning was most flourishing, so many intellectuals came under Stalinist influence. They were, however, only sharers in the common intellectual culture. A strong state was their ideal. The strong and active state of the long administration of President Roosevelt gratified this desire.

VI

Education has always been regarded as a good thing in America. The state universities and the land grant colleges as well as the universality of public education without fees and the late school-leaving age were evidence of this. Science, too, had been spoken of in terms of awe and in anticipation of benefits. But pure science, abstract thought and the life of letters tended to be treated with levity and disparagement. In the period after the Second World War, higher education, scientific, technological, and, to a lesser extent, humanistic research and belles lettres, were all elevated—although not uniformly. In this period what had been esteemed became more esteemed; what had been disparaged or taken lightly was treated more seriously and in good earnest. The munificent support of higher education and research in private and state universities by federal and state governments and the readiness of businessmen to support higher education and research in private universities, both bespoke the widespread conviction of the nonintellectual elites of the value, practical and glorious, of the intellectuals. The intellectuals were of the same view. It appeared as if an old dream had come true.

Through the length and breadth of the academic and non-academic intellectual classes, particularly in the natural and social sciences, this self-serving view was espoused. Grants and subsidies for study and research were available, and even those who were in principle opposed to the government and "the system" were able to avail themselves of such benefits and were eager to do so.[13]

There was little dissent by the intellectuals from the obligation laid upon the universities to educate and train persons who could fill all the various roles in the higher level of government and business administration and technology thought to be needed for the further development of the American economy. It was taken for granted by the critics of the "organization man" no less than by others that the universities should do this and that the government and businessmen should provide the money for it. The doctrine of the "multiversity" was only a precipitation of what was already general policy and belief.

This had in fact been done by the American universities in earlier decades, but it was done on a much grander scale in the two decades immediately following the Second World War. Those responsible for the institutions were delighted to have their services so tangibly appreciated. University teachers were equally pleased—the expansion provided more students to train in research and for teaching careers. It also represented an approximation toward the ideal of equal access to higher education, thus meeting one of the standing grievances of the populistic and radical wing of the alienated intellectuals against the universities, namely that they were for the offspring of the rich.

There were many new roles for intellectuals which had scarcely existed before the war: scientists in the Department of Defense and in the national laboratories of the A.E.C., economists in the Council of Economic Advisors, a scientist as chief scientific advisor to the president,[14] the entire apparatus of the National Science

13. It is against this background that the one original contribution of the "student revolution," the expectation of a state-subsidized "revolution," is to be understood.

14. The agitational, critical role of the scientists in the first years following the war shriveled as scientists became advisors, members of grant-awarding panels, etc. The high point was reached when the American section of Pugwash was nearly assimilated into the Disarmament Agency.

Foundation. In the Policy Planning Board of the Department of State were academics and historians and political scientists, together with such distinguished professional diplomat-intellectuals as George Kennan and, at a somewhat lower level of the intellectual hierarchy, Paul Nitze, Charles Bohlen, and Louis Halle; in the Department of Defense, which became more science-based than any other part of the government or part of any government, a series of eminent scientists occupied the office of assistant secretary with responsibility for guiding the immense research activity of the armed services; an academic economist became the dominant spirit in the reorganization of the procurement policy of the Department of Defense. Private organizations like the Rand Corporation performed research on contract for the air force on matters at the very center of military policy. There were many roles filled by intellectuals in the two decades after 1945 which had not as much as existed previously.

Old roles became more influential. In the Federal Reserve system, which had become more important than ever before in the maintenance of the economy in its state of stability and growth, academically trained economists retaining intimate relations with the academic economic professions were more numerous, more prominent, and more influential than previously. Professors of law outside the government played an important part in the selection of their best students to serve as clerks to justices of the Supreme Court. Congressional committees invited intellectuals to testify before them with higher frequency than before, and several staff directors of certain important committees such as the Senate Foreign Affairs Committee have been intellectuals of reasonable stature—an unprecedented development. At numerous points where policies were made, intellectuals shared in varying degrees in the process of decision making. High officials turned repeatedly and frequently to the universities for assistance, enlightenment, counsel, guidance, and personnel. This structure of collaboration between the government and the intellectuals was the achievement of the Democratic administrations—and the intellectuals had always had, at least since the Wilson administration, a penchant toward the Democratic Party as the relatively antiplutocratic party and the party of the ethnic outcasts and therewith a party closer to an alienated outlook. The practice was not, however, notably reduced by the Republican administration of President Eisenhower.[15]

The Kennedy administration continued the collaboration, begun

15. The great weapon in the verbal armory of the New Left—"industrial-military complex"—was given to the nation as a parting gift by President Eisenhower, but he in his turn had it entrusted to him by one of his court intellectuals, an academic social scientist.

under President Roosevelt, in a more spectacular way and reached out more energetically toward the literary and artistic intellectuals as well.[16] The White House court became a nest of singing birds, although they sometimes sang, as almost all nonscientist intellectuals do nowadays, the songs of social science. With varying external fortunes, the Johnson and the Nixon administrations continued the dependence. Although the alienation in sentiment of American intellectuals in the two latter administrations has been in many respects more vehement and acrimonious than it has been since the 1920s and perhaps than it has ever been before, the number of complainers being greater and the language more rancorous than ever before, Patrick Moynihan and Henry Kissinger, President Nixon's two chief advisors—both with cabinet rank—in domestic and foreign affairs are among the most distinguished intellectuals in the country. Professor Milton Friedman's ideas have probably had more direct influence in the Nixon administration than those of any economist in any major country since John Maynard Keynes. The list is indefinitely extensible.

So much for the incorporation of the intellectuals into roles of authority and influence in American society.

VI

It would require more space than I can take here and more knowledge than I have at my ready command at the moment to trace in detail the consequences of the enlarged and more central roles filled by intellectuals in every sphere of the life of American society in the twenty years following the end of the Second World War. It was certainly large, very ramified, and very pervasive; the United States became to an unprecedented extent an "intellectual-based" country. It was a major change for a society which intellectuals had asserted was the society most uncongenial to the life of the spirit of any great society known in history.

Let us take the major changes and attempt to estimate the part intellectuals played in them. First of all: the relatively easy transition from war to peace, the demobilization, then the continuing growth and stability of the economy; then the remarkable integration of American society—twenty years of internal peace, of the moderation of political conflict, of strikes without violence; the continuous improvement in the condition of the Negro; after the end of McCarthyism and of the persecution of the shriveled remnant

16. Despite the elevation of Robert Frost to an equivalent of poet laureate, no literary intellectuals attained the intimate and influential position which had been held by Robert Sherwood in his relations with President Roosevelt.

of the Communist Party, a greatly broadened tolerance of political dissent, a greater freedom of individual action, particularly in the private sphere, the further attenuation of puritanism; a reduction in ethnic hostility except in the southern states,[17] a reduction in the traditional animosity among Roman Catholics, Protestant, and Jews.

To some extent, these accomplishments were the fruit of older ideas—the Keynesian economists of the 1930s, the liberal ideas of equal justice before the law and of equality of opportunity, the idea of the moral equality of all human beings drawn from certain strands of Protestant Christianity and from the Enlightenment. The main general feature of all these changes was the narrowing of the distance between center and periphery through a reduction of the moral ascendancy of the center. In large measures this was made possible by the extraordinary productivity of American agriculture and industry, which was in some considerable measure the result of the work of the agricultural research stations connected with the land grant colleges, and of the scientific and technological research in chemistry, metallurgy, food processing, electronics, industrial management, etc. The affluence of American society helped to change the self-image of the mass of the population in the working classes and the lower middle classes by permitting their standard of living to improve, by permitting them to receive more education and to live in a more "appropriate" style which was an adaptation of a middle-class style. The development of the technology of mass communications contributed to the creation of a single national society with a common focus of attention and to some extent, a common culture. The direct agents of this common culture were literary and artistic intellectuals—just as its indirect ones were scientific and technological; sometimes the former were of outstanding quality, although more frequently they were mediocre and derivative.[18]

The economic growth and stability of the period undoubtedly owed something not only to the scientific and technological research to which I have already referred, but to the vigorous empirical research and elaborate theoretical analyses of economists inside the

17. The "backlash" among whites has amounted to very little outside the south. The growth of antiwhite sentiment among Negroes is largely a phenomenon of the last half-decade following the period to which I refer above.

18. The "intellectualization" of the mass media was evinced in the weekly periodicals of mass circulation. *The Saturday Evening Post* and *Colliers* among the deceased, and *Life* and *Time* among the still surviving, all became more and more "intellectual" in their most recent phase. Works of great art and superior literary and culture became a large part of their stock-in-trade. Even the ocean of triviality and meretriciousness which constitutes much of this common culture is the product of intellectuals—many of them intellectuals *manqués* who resent their self-exclusion from intellectual grace.

government and outside it. The improvement in the condition of the Negroes—much of which was a function of their urbanization and northward movement in response to the growth in the employment opportunities in industry—was certainly affected by the change in opinion to which judicial decisions and a more humane public opinion contributed; these in turn were affected by the research done by sociologists on the situation of the Negro—epitomized and summarized just at the end of the Second World War by Gunnar Myrdal's *American Dilemma*. Even the villainous McCarthyism, although it continued an older tradition of nativism and populist antiintellectualism, certainly owed something to the evidence of ex-communist intellectual turncoats like Whittaker Chambers, J. B. Mathews, et al. It should also not be forgotten that McCarthyism in the broadest sense owed something to the fact that intellectuals like the late Henry Dexter White and others, who had risen to high positions in the federal government, had apparently become involved in communist espionage.[19]

The attenuation of puritanism had been moving apace with the urbanization of American society, but its models and legitimators who had fought for it a long time were literary and humanistic intellectuals. If the whole country has been turned into a macrocosm of what used to be found only in Greenwich Village and among the bohemians of Chicago and San Francisco, the model provided by one sector of the intellectuals has certainly played a part. (To this should be added the shattering blow given to puritanism by the "pill," which was the product of elaborate research by biochemists and physiologists.)

The general culture of impulse owes much of course to the weakness of authority in the family and in society. This certainly cannot be accounted for without reference to the long intellectual tradition of the restriction of the legitimacy of authority from the seventeenth century onward. The popularization of psychoanalysis through Margaret Mead, Erich Fromm, Karen Horney and many others less gifted, the research of Arnold Gesell, and the educational doctrine of John Dewey, all led to Dr. Spock's famous handbook of child rearing. It is not by accident that humanitarian and liberal attitudes toward children and their rights began and is still most widespread in families in which the parents are more highly educated. Assertions about the power and influence of intellectuals should not disregard this.

19. McCarthyism was itself a response to the greatly increased prominence of intellectuals in government service. Its greatest accomplishment was the elaborate degradation of Robert Oppenheimer. The antiintellectuals had never before had such a grand intellectual in government service to persecute.

VII

The affirmation of American society and culture and participation in its direction and orientation at the center and in numerous subcenters did not absorb all American intellectuals—nor was the affirmation unqualified in those who were engaged in it. Alongside of and intertwined with the acts of affirmation in practice and in statement was a continuous denial. The alienation of American intellectuals had always been strongest among literary and artistic intellectuals, and it never died out, even in the period of the greatest measure of affirmation. There was an illustrious and honorable line of direct descent from the aesthetic alienation of Edgar Allan Poe and Henry James, the moral alienation of Herman Melville and Theodore Dreiser, the patrician alienation of Henry Adams, the bohemian alienation of Floyd Dell and Art Young, the socialist alienation of Jack London, Upton Sinclair, and John Dos Passos. In the 1920s these different currents of alienation crossed each other, and there were partial fusions. H. L. Mencken, Ernest Hemingway, Sherwood Anderson, Eugene O'Neill, Edmund Wilson, and many others continued this line through the 1920s and into the 1930s.

The Communist Party and its agents who conducted the *New Masses* attempted to amalgamate these various kinds of alienation and to exploit them by giving them the status which Dante gave to Virgil, namely that of annunciations of the comprehensive alienation of Marxism-Leninism. They were, however, hampered by their guilefulness and their need for political purposes to appear to be something which they were not. The *Partisan Review,* following its removal shortly after its birth from the control of the fellow travelers and agents of the Communist Party, was a more genuine heir and representative of some of the diverse traditions of the alienated American intellectuals.

The Communists lost their hegemony during the war. Having renounced their identity in the larger cause of the Soviet alliance with the Western powers, they could not recover significantly after the alliance ended. Their line was blurred by internal conflicts, then by a new form of popular front tactics, and their organizations further enfeebled by the persecutions to which they were subjected by congressional investigative committees and the prosecutions under the Smith Act. The alienation of those who had traveled with the communists went out of sight under the pressure of intimidation by congressional committees and the Department of Justice and unpopularity among the large majority of intellectuals. Their confidence was shattered by the latter as much as by the two former, whereas before the war they had bullied, censored, and defamed the characters of their critics and acted generally as self-confident cocks of the walk. In publishing and literary circles they were shunned after the war. Their friends took cover. But while the communists and their friends took cover or changed their external guise, a more honest alienation was expressed in the *Partisan Review* and in *Politics*. The *Partisan Review* became the organ of a miscellaneous bundle of alienations and it could not withstand the delights of being at the center. Its Trotskyist anti-Stalinism tended to fade into American anticommunism. Alienation and reluctant affirmation mingled in its pages. *Politics*, on the other hand, was for the pure in heart; in a more humorless and a more self-righteous way, it continued in the traditions of the *Masses* and the *Liberator*.

The main criticism of American society of the alienated intellectuals of the late 1940s and most of the 1950s—the critique of mass culture—had its seat there. The self-destructive tendencies of capitalism and the baseness of the politicians yielded their place of honor in the alienated intellectuals' image of American society to the vulgarity of American culture and to the damage which this mass culture did to the high culture. This critique, which had a multiple ancestry in patrician disdain, aesthetic revulsion, puritanical disapprobation and a high-brow Marxism, did not have a wide adherence. Literary publicists and a handful of sociologists under the influence of German *Edelmarxismus* were its chief carriers. It was probably shared in a fairly inert manner by the academic humanists whose preconceptions were directed by the older tradition of aesthetic alienation and the abhorrence of the genteel classes for money-grubbing and the baser pleasures.

The critique of mass society and of mass culture did not have a long life. It was swept away by a new current. Many of its proponents, eager to swim in a new, more turbulent stream, jettisoned it for something stronger and more fashionable.[20] Others forgot it as they withdrew to higher ground.

VIII

Since the middle of the 1960s a pronounced change in the relations of American intellectuals to the center of their society has occurred. The tiny rivulets of twenty years earlier have turned into a broad and shallow river which seems to have no banks and which has inundated nearly all the reclaimed intellectual terrain, turning it into a muddy marshland. The change set in shortly after the accession to power of President Lyndon Johnson. The first triumphs of the Negro civil rights movement had raised hopes and these led to frustrations. The

20. One could not go on inveighing against "mass culture" while praising a new radicalism which includes hipsterism, the Beatles, pot and acid rock, and being covered with buttons like a "Pearly."

"poor" were discovered—not the working classes, who remained written off as the brutish enjoyers of mass culture and who were now regarded as gross, unthinking supports of the existing order—but the *Lumpenproletariat*, who had never enjoyed such a good press as in the past five years. The flowery rhetoric and ill-natured bearing of President Johnson reawakened the dormant animosities of the American intellectuals toward the plebeian professional politician. The failure of the military leadership of the country to bring the war in Viet Nam to a successful conclusion broke the attachment to authority which had grown up among American intellectuals when American power appeared supreme in the world.

The withdrawal from the center was symbolized by the agitated euphoria of certain circles of literary and publicistic intellectuals in refusing the invitation of President Johnson to attend a series of ceremonial festivities at the White House in 1965. Under President Kennedy, when such festivities had been inaugurated, the invitation to the company of the mighty of the earth was the final seal on the union of power and intellect. The seal was a very fragile one and of very brief duration. The affirmative attitude which had been so common in the period just preceding was not solely a product of the perception in American society of values—moral, aesthetic and political—which were part of the intellectuals' internal traditions. It had also been the result of the attraction of strong and effective power which has always been characteristic of intellectuals. At a time when America was only a province of the great European world and when the political and economic elites were indifferent and even sometimes hostile toward literary and humanistic intellectuals, American intellectuals saw no merit in those who ruled American society. When, however, they were taken to the bosom of those who exercised power and when the latter seemed to be the most powerful elite the world had known, American intellectuals found much to be pleased with in their situation and in the situation of their country. Once the power began to falter, however, to be not merely unsuccessful in action but perplexed and lacking in decisiveness and self-confidence, large numbers of intellectuals—literary publicistic, scientific, and humanistic—decided that the American political elites were no longer worthy of their affection. No condemnation could be strong enough. It was not simply the older accusations of vulgarity and venality and indifference to "life's finer things." The accusations were more bitter. The accusation of "genocide" became the coin of the intellectuals' realm—"genocide" at home and abroad. In its more extreme forms, in the view of Noam Chomsky for example, any performance of a governmental service was culpable.

What was striking about the hyperbolically acrimonious and embittered criticism of the post-1965 alienation was its relationship to the older traditions of intellectual alienation. The first initiators of the new alienation had been either socialists of the tradition who had abstained from the incorporation into and affirmation of the center—*Dissent* and Michael Harrington—or Stalinoids like Paul Sweezy, the late Leo Huberman, and I. F. Stone, who had survived the hard times of the late 1940s and the 1960s. The new alienation in contrast, once it was in full spate, found many of its main bearers among those who had little connection with the older tradition of alienation. No less striking was the durability and toughness of the non-Marxist tradition of alienation which came back into a strength fuller than ever after a period of attrition which had lasted for more than a quarter of a century.[21]

Bohemianism has long been associated with revolution. The recent advance of aesthetic sensibility has greatly extended and modified the social sources of affiliation to the movement of alienation. Jazz commentators, mod. journalists, television comedians, packagers of fun goods, specialists in pornography, cartoonists, interior decorators, "young people" in publishing, advertising executives—all these so responsive to fluctuations in style—are new recruits to alienation. To these are joined the "new class" of college and university teachers, clergymen, black intellectuals, liberating women, and the university and college students—the very vanguard of the whole thing.

The clergy in the United States, leaving out the self-designated preachers in store-front churches and those who bash the Bible and froth at the mouth in berating the Devil, form an important component in the present-day disorder of the intellectuals. Having with the aid of Deweyan naturalism, "demythologization" and existentialism, disposed of their deity or at least placed him in a weak position, Protestant clergymen in the United States have been suffering from the intellectual equivalent of technological unemployment. Superior in attitude toward their benighted flocks, displaced by atheism and psychiatry from the cure of souls, they were for a long time at loose ends. The tradition of "social Christianity" did not arouse their enthusiasm. With the Negro civil rights movement, however, they found something to do; with the war in Viet Nam they found much else to do. Reinforced by restless Roman Catholic priests from whom the hand of authority had been lifted and by a rabbinate of doubting piety—all fearful of not being in tune with the

21. It is true that there has been a small revival of Marxism, but that has come in a roundabout way rather than through the direct filiation of tradition. It is in part a consequence of revival to half-life of the Communist Party which has made the writings of Marx and Engels available through its publishing house and partly as a result of the diversity and intellectual randomness of the younger left. It is also a product of the elevation to fame of Professor Marcuse, whose sexual doctrines seem more attractive than his Marxism.

times—the clergy has reentered the public life of the intellectual classes. They have not been a steadying element.

Negro intellectuals for the first time in American history have gained the attention of the white intellectuals. In the past, worthy Negro intellectuals knocked in vain at the doors of American intellectual life but, outside socialist and communist circles, few attended to them. Then in a short time a handful of Negro intellectuals—a few of them of some genuine talent, most of them of little talent and the beneficiaries of a forced levy—appeared on the scene. Their passionate abuse of American society could not have come at a luckier time; without the audience of white intellectuals they could not have been so encouraged.

Finally, the students in higher educational institutions should be mentioned. In an age which praises youthfulness with fewer qualifications than devout Marxists used to praise the working classes, and in a situation in which intellectuals had become convinced of their indispensability, university and college students got whatever benefits there were in being both youthful and intellectuals. The students' hostility against authority—characteristic of adolescence, and in America adolescence is prolonged—was reinforced by their elders' chorus of denunciation of authority, including their own, and by the supineness of authority, academic and governmental.

When one looks over the various kinds of radical activists, one finds that many of them share one major characteristic of the amateur politician pointed out by Max Weber, namely, they are "wirtschaftlich abkömmlich."[22] Many are not employed at all, or employed irregularly. They have no fixed hours of work in general; they come and go as they please. They are more prosperous than the lawyers without briefs and physicians without patients whom Marx saw as the supporters of his rivals. They have much leisure and much flexibility in their work schedules, where they work at all. They belong to the free as over against the workaday sector of society. From this comes some of their sense of affinity with the *Lumpenproletariat*. It also renders them easily available for their characteristic political techniques, the demonstration and the mass meeting.

The consequence of all this is a spiral of mutually reinforcing animosity against their own society, combining withdrawal and aggressiveness.

These new recruits to the espousal of the intellectuals' traditions of alienation, diverse and novel though they might be, have only a loose connection with the intellectually substantial parts of that tradition. Bohemianism never had much intellectual substance, and that is the part of the tradition to which many of the new recruits

22. Weber, *Politik als Beruf,* 2d edition (Munich and Leipzig: Duncker and Humblot, 1926), p. 16.

give their allegiance. The very looseness of their connection with a definitive and elaborate doctrine such as Marxism is part of the larger paradox of their outlook. Despite their hostility toward the intellectuals who were in the forefront during the period of incorporation and affirmation, the new recruits to the movement of alienation continue some of the culture of those they revile.

The period of incorporation and affirmation generated two convictions among the intellectuals who participated in it. The first of these—bred by experience and propaganda—was that intellectuals were indispensable to America's functioning. The second, based on this, was that intellectuals were in a crucial position because in a variety of ways the authorities of society were dependent on them. From having felt unwanted and unused, intellectuals moved to the opposite extreme of a conviction of indispensability. The conviction of indispensability has been fully compatible with hostility toward those who seem to deny the rights which come with indispensability.

IX

The movement from a sense of nullity in making decisions to a sense of weightiness has not been undone by the movement from denial to affirmation and back to denial. Civility has made progress even though its name is momentarily darkened. For one thing, a great many intellectuals have not made the return journey to denial; many have remained in the positions of authority in decision making at or connected with the institutional centers of American society. Economists and scientific advisers are firmly entrenched and they cannot be done away with. They are, however, simply continuations of positions and outlooks consolidated during the years between 1933 and 1965.

The persistence of the civil attitude is also evident in its deformation. The denial of the legitimacy of authority shows traces of the period of civility through which it has passed in the last third of a century. Those who hate authority and deny its legitimacy now think that it is plausible to require that authority should yield to their demands. The new relationship of the deniers to the authority which they deny includes their giving orders to it which they think they can force it to implement and which it should implement. The passionate deniers think that they should be part of the existing central institutional system. This is unique in the history of the critique of authority. Furthermore, the expectations of the deniers are rendered plausible by the fact that they have in fact benefited by some partial success in establishing their own view of the matter at the center where the authority is exercised.[23]

23. I cite at random the recent opinion of Judge Wyzanski on conscientious objection and the numerous pronouncements of Mr. Justice W. O. Douglas.

An "intellectualization" of public life has taken place in the United States. Some of the values of the alienated intellectuals have become established in the circles of authority. The centuries-long process of the "civilization" of authority, which entailed authority's becoming modest in its self-legitimation, restrained in its public declaration of its claims, responsive in its sensibility to the demands of those it ruled, has now gone a step further. Elites now quail before the charges of "elitism." The exercise of authority and the management of affairs are now disguised as "decision making." The maintenance of law and order and the eforcement of law which political and administrative elites have always in the past taken as their first charge, and which are indeed inseparable from the maintenance of society and the protection of its members, have become matters about which those who rule have become shame-faced. The prevention of riots or their restraint, suppression, and dispersal when they do occur, have become thought of as inadmiss-ible—although in practice they remain drastic and sometimes harsh. Judges and publicists acknowledge a right of violent demonstration as part of the freedom of expression and as a legitimate procedure when constitutionally provided procedures are unsatisfactory or not immediately effective. In principle—and to a great extent, in fact— the legitimacy of dissent, derived from the freedom of expression, is granted even where it involves coercive action and the disruption of institutions.

The penetration of the aggrieved intellectuals' outlook occurs in a twofold process. The first, the recruitment of intellectuals of alienated outlook, is part of the general process of the increased recruitment into intellectual-executive roles. Since the alienated anti-authoritarian outlook is so widespread among the younger generation of intellectuals and those in humanistic and social sciences from which the recruits were drawn, it is only to be expected that in the mass communications, in the universities, and in government too, despite the persistence of the practice of "security clearance," the new recruits bear with them some influence of the alienated outlook. Through their influence as speech writers and as "idea men," as research workers and as staff members of special investigative commissions, authority has come often to speak—if not equally often to act—in accordance with the voice of the aggrieved intellectual.

But the penetration goes further than the incumbency of the bearers of the outlook in the roles of greater functional importance and of greater numbers. There has also been a penetration into the outlook of incumbents of traditionally authoritative roles who them-selves are not intellectuals or who, even if intellectuals, have up until recently espoused outlooks conventional to those in authority, the crucial element of which is the belief in the legitimacy of their own authority. For one thing, the sociological sciences have come since the 1950s to dominate this idiom of discourse on public events, not only the terminology but the conceptions of causation and motivation as well as the implicit political outlook of workers in these fields. In addition to this, intellectuals in the United States have become demonstrators, not by rational argument, but by standing in public places, by covering themselves in buttons and badges, by signing petitions and public declarations. They have come to fill the air and the press. Politicians have been in some measure responsive to this clamor. They have been increasingly deferential to intellectuals ever since the end of the war and the atomic scientists' movement. It was noticeable ever since the Second World War in the deference accorded scientists when they testified before congressional committees—the McCarthy procedures were rearguard actions in this respect. Social scientists have now slipped into place alongside scientists. The American politicians' attribution of greater importance to clamorous demand than to reasoned argument and the quiet preferences of the mass of the population, the fear of the politicians of being out of step with the view which they think to be prevalent, gives resonance to the demands of the aggrieved intellectuals.

Since the alienated intellectuals, like ideologists and radicals everywhere, cannot be completely alienated, their claims take the form of the intensification and underscoring of certain elements already present in the central value system of American society. The values of substantive equality are intensified at the expense of the value of an equivalence between reward and exertion. The value of majority rule has long been transformed, by a clamorous insistence, into the supremacy of the uncriticizably virtuous "people" (meaning, in the vocabulary of those who clamor, a number of Negroes, Puerto Ricans, discontented females, and rebellious university students).[24] The value of individuality has been intensified into the value of the immediate gratification of spontaneous impulse.

24. "The people," those bearers of virtue and touchstones of policy according to the principle of populistic democracy, have yielded place to "people." This disappearance of the definite article is not just a linguistic quirk characteristic of a generation which has been brought up to express its sentiments but which has lost contact with the traditions of English speech. There is more to it than that. "The people" used to mean the mass of the population: the majority. But the majority are now in bad odor among aggrieved intellectuals. The majority are now the industrial working classes, truck drivers, office workers, etc., lawyers and doctors, government employees, conservative, complacent, hedonistic, looking after their own pleasures and comforts. The majority are now the "scissorbills," sunk in the morass of bourgeois society. "People" on the other hand are any minority of outcasts who are impoverished, unemployed, on relief rolls, and in need of support by the welfare services of the state. They are also those who make demands on their behalf.

Because of this affinity between the central value system and the ideologically exacerbated interpretation of certain elements of this system, the political and publicistic elites who are often not very subtle, and who are sometimes easily disoriented, regard these claims as plausible and consistent with what they believed before.

There is more to it than this. Many politicians—omitting the cavemen—feel inferior to intellectuals. They might behave rudely toward them as President Johnson often did, but the same President Johnson following his retirement said that he had not felt qualified to lead the country effectively because he had not gone to one of the major universities. He implied that because of this he could not command the respect of those who had done so.

The mass communications show a similar success for their intellectuals. Although aggrieved radicals in all countries in the twentieth century have criticized the conduct of the media of communication—whether privately or governmentally owned—where they have had the freedom to express their views, the situation nowadays is much different from what it was before the Second World War. Although there is still much criticism of the privately owned press in the United States, there is also a very strong representation of aggrieved intellectuals within the institutions of public opinion. In television there is a similar situation. The professional tradition of muckraking, the tradition of reportorial vigor, the tradition of sensationalism and of the maxim that "good news is no news" all mean that disorder, failure, catastrophe are given the greatest prominence. Delight in disorder, occasional sympathy with its perpetrators and the cause which it purportedly serves, cause the disorder to be much attended to in the mass media.[25]

In book publishing, which is centered mainly in New York, practically all publishers and editors and other intellectuals who are members of the industry are permeated by the aggrieved outlook either from conviction or from the desire to be stylish or because of the belief that that is what the spirit of the age requires. The far-reaching relaxation of censorship and the inclusion of sexual polymorphousness and publicity as part of the culture of the new strata of the alienated intellectuals as well as some of their older outriders and followers, give the intellectuals in the publishing industry a commercial interest as well as a cultural one in being

25. It is in the nature of the present movement of hostility against the center of society that it is driven by hunger for publicity. Its violence is in part propaganda of the deed: its main political actions are extra-institutional as well as anti-institutional. The brief civility of the organizations for Senator Robert Kennedy and Eugene McCarthy quickly exhausted their resources. Demonstrative politics, intended to gain attention rather than to modify institutions, have replaced it.

"with it."[26] Many are reluctant to publish any book which is critical of the aggrieved view of American society, again out of conviction or out of fear of being out of fashion.[27]

The universities, as has been indicated, have become the scene and seedbed of the intellectual life in the United States. Not only do they carry on the traditional functions of the universities of training for the learned, practical-intellectual professions and conducting pure research, but they have accepted the burdens of applied research for government, trained for numerous not so learned occupations, performed numerous tasks which governments should properly have performed themselves, provided the support for little magazines and for other activities which in the past were in the sphere of bohemia. All these miscellaneous actions, encouraged and applauded on the outside, led to and fed on a form of *Grössenwahn* among university authorities. All this expansion should, one might have thought, been the work of strong characters. Nothing could have been more erroneous. Many of the great university and college administrators who presided over the vast expansion of universities in the indiscriminate service of American society have turned out to be characterless weathervanes facing whichever way the wind blew.

The release of animosity against authority, beginning with the murder of John F. Kennedy, first manifested itself on a trivial issue at the University of California in Berkeley. The University of California, after its recovery from the ravages of the loyalty oath controversy, had been one of the major pillars of the new structure of cooperation of authority and the intellectuals. Its administrators and teachers were full of pride, justified pride over their accomplishments. Yet, with the first onslaught it fell into disorder. The teachers fell out with each other, the presidents and deans were thrown into confusion. The "rightfulness" of the students' cause called forth much support, and those who denied it could not bring the university back to where it was. Similar events occurred with increasing frequency over the ensuing half-decade. Finally, even Harvard, which had rebuffed McCarthy, fell before its students. It was only to be expected that the universities which had helped to generate so much of the new culture should be so riddled by it. Presidents, deans, professors, from conviction or cowardice, fell for

26. The Grove Press combines the culture of the literary avant-garde with the heritage of Mr. Girodias' Olympia Press. It is also the agent of Fanonist and other phantasms of a morally purifying destructiveness.

27. Professor Mathew Hodgart's Swiftian parable of the events at Cornell University in 1969 was refused by twelve American publishers before it was finally accepted. The book had already been accepted for publication in Great Britain. Professor Hodgart is a very reputable scholar, but his letter to the *Times* (London) describing and passing reasoned judgment on the Cornell events aroused the disapprobation of the *bien pensant* aggrieved intellectuals in the American publishing industry. This is not the only instance.

obviously nonsensical arguments. No authorities under attack had ever gone so far in flattering and beslavering their insatiable antagonists and attempting to placate them.

X

The new renunciation of civil collaboration by the American intellectuals began even before the failure of effective power in Viet Nam, although much of the weakening of belief in the effectiveness of the American political and military elites is attributable to that. The civility of the American intellectual would have had a hard row to hoe even if things had gone more favorably for the United States in Viet Nam and if President Kennedy had not been assassinated, both of which events showed the vulnerability of power.

American intellectuals, even more than most intellectuals in most other countries, have inherited an antipolitical tradition. What they have received from their intellectual forebears and what they themselves teach and believe outside scientific research fosters an antipolitical, anticivil outlook. The very favorable structural circumstances of three decades—indulgence by the center, occupational opportunities at the center, and centrality in the world—had put this tradition into the margins of the mind. The first and the third of these circumstances were modified by the deterioration of President Johnson's demeanor in consequence of the resultlessness of the war in Viet Nam. The tradition reasserted itself when the major politician of the country was rude in tone and ineffective in action. But whereas the older tradition was one of antipolitical withdrawal, the new disposition, while remaining antipolitical, has been far more active. One variant of it resembled, after the outburst of civil political energy on behalf of Robert Kennedy and then Eugene McCarthy, the new politics of the intellectuals under Franklin Roosevelt. The politics of the intellectuals under the New Deal were not electoral or party politics but rather political activity carried on in advisory and counseling capacities under the auspices of a powerful political personage. Political activists among intellectuals do not now seek electoral office any more now than they did then. They seek programs and grants paid for by the public treasury to work against the government.[28] This paradoxical antipolitical civility is a novelty, although it has superficial resemblances to the communist technique of "boring from within."

Another variant of the new antipolitical politics is part of an older tradition: namely demonstration. The technique of demonstration was not an intellectual's device until the intellectuals and the

28. Compare the role of the most brilliant young graduates of the major law schools nowadays with those of the period of the New Deal and its successors!

communists came together under the auspices of Willi Münzenberg. Demonstrations have now been given up by the working classes since they have trade unions to represent their interests; demonstrations have become once more part of the technique of those who regard themselves as outside the central institutional system in which interests are represented and compromised.

The activist element is at its most extreme in violent, disruptive demonstrations, where the aim is to prevent an institution, usually a defenseless one like a university or a church, from functioning in a normal manner. Although there is much talk of power in intellectual circles, the new politics of the intellectuals do not seem to aim to accede to positions of authority in the existing system or in a new revolutionarily established system. Hating it and denying its legitimacy as they do, they still seem to acquiesce to its factuality. They seem to count on its continued existence and they anticipate its responsiveness to abusive influence, rather than to influence within consensus. In that sense, the new revolutionary intellectuals— there are some exceptions of course—seem themselves to be the victims of the tentacular powers of the center.

XI

Can a modern society maintain a stable and orderly structure when the political elites and those other sectors of the elite who share power with them have lost their self-confidence and are dominated by a clamorous hostility against that society and those who rule it? An elite which wavers and abdicates the responsibility which is inherent in the roles which it fills becomes uncertain of its entitle-ment to legitimacy. If it cannot claim legitimacy for the actions it undertakes, its actions will be ineffective. Ineffectiveness on the part of an elite breeds disrespect and the refusal of legitimacy. No society, least of all one as complicated as present-day American society, and so difficult to govern under the best of circumstances, can survive in its ongoing form, nor can it develop peacefully from that form if its central institutional system has lost its legitimacy. American society is a noisy and a violent society, even in good times. In bad times like the present, it strains the capacities of even the best of governments.

The containment of conflict in a culture so consecrated to the gratification of demands has always been difficult. The institu-tionalization of class conflict—a by no means perfect institutionaliz-ation—was one of the great accomplishments of the Roosevelt and subsequent administrations. Its continuation depends on the con-tinued legitimacy of authority in government, business enterprises, and trade unions. The evaporation of legitimacy renders the continued institutionalization more problematic than it has been for about a third of a century. Inflation and the demonstration-effect of the successful pursuit of expanded demands places the machinery of collaboration of classes under a heavy burden. The sight of successfully affronted authority is a great stimulant to antinomian impulses.

The ineptitude of governmental institutions in the face of ethnic conflicts—an ineptitude arising from serious disagreements within the government on the merits of the claims and how to treat them, diminished self-confidence in dealing with violence, particularly violence by some thousands of university students and by a section of the Negro population, the legitimate moral claims of which have been usurped and exaggerated by a small, violently inclined group— has further eroded legitimacy.

The inconclusiveness of the war in Viet Nam has damaged the legitimacy of the federal government more than any other factor. The Russian czarist government, incompetent and ineffective though it was in a time of peace, was shaken by revolution (in 1905) only after military defeat at the hands of the Japanese. It was finally overthrown following its disasters on the battlefield in the first two and a half years of the First World War. The agitations and the terroristic activities of a small group of conspiratorial intellectuals from 1825 onward would undoubtedly have come to nothing had the czarist government not experienced those two shattering military defeats in little more than a decade. The Habsburg monarchy was a ramshackle political system but it decomposed only after defeat in the First World War. The Hohenzollern regime in Germany was one of the most stable in the world until its defeat by the Allies in the First World War. The German revolutionaries were feeble indeed— witness the weakness of their creation, the Weimar Republic—but the ancien régime had lost its legitimacy. Similarly the legitimacy of the National Socialist regime, which had been so firm in 1943, began to falter when the German armies suffered their first great reverses at Stalingrad and in North Africa. Thereafter, as defeat followed defeat, the Nazi regime which had exterminated or paralyzed all opposition began to crumble within, and, when it was totally defeated in 1945, it lost practically all domestic support. In short, governments which lose wars are governments which have undertaken to do more than they can. A war is an undertaking which involves national identity and, as such, it touches on the deepest roots of the acknowledgment of legitimacy. The loss of a war endangers the real and the symbolic existences of the entire national community and it thereby weakens the readiness to acknowledge the right to rule of those who have taken to themselves the care of the name and safety of that national community. Among those whose inclination to acknowledge the legitimacy of rulers is—for all sorts of reasons and motives—already weak, such failure is a further ground for denial.

The situation of the American government is different. It has not lost the war. It has, however, not won it, and that is almost as bad in some respects because it has dragged on and brought with it an inflation which injures most classes of the population and above all those who are otherwise the most faithful devotees of the legitimacy of government. It also exacerbated class conflict through the continuous demand for higher wages, resulting in strikes and the disruption of services. All this has weakened the legitimacy of government by further revealing and emphasizing its ineffectiveness.

In this situation of weakened legitimacy, the alienation of the now pervasive intellectual classes is of consequence. Had intellectuals continued to be as marginal as they were forty years ago both in their functional roles and in their symbolic prominence and appreciation, their alienation would not concern any one by themselves and students of their attitudes. As it is, however, the question merits further scrutiny.

The first thing to be said is that the alienation in question here is not universal among intellectuals. Large sections of the intellectual classes do not share in it. Those in the practical-intellectual professions are less alienated than those in the primarily intellectual professions. Those in the scientific and technological professions are less alienated than those in the social science, literary, and humanistic professions. Even in the latter professions, among the social scientists, for example, the economists and the political scientists are less alienated than the sociologists (and anthropologists); in the humanistic subjects it is those concerned with English and American literary studies who are most alienated. Certain Negro intellectuals are among the most vociferous, but there are many who do not receive publicity and who are less alienated although no less critical of the traditional treatment and position of the Negro in American society. The younger generations, especially students in higher educational institutions, are more alienated than the older generations, although there is a wide spread of opinion among them also. In each of these sectors of the intellectual classes, the tide of aggressive alienation seems to have ebbed, and the more aggressive are separating themselves from the rest.

The diminution of the volume of echo which white intellectuals give to the most radical Negroes is likely to diminish, partly because those who do the echoing are creatures of fashion and do not sustain any fashion for long. If this occurs, the more radical Negro intellectuals will have less resonance, and their pressure on the more moderate ones will decrease. Their isolation will have the same effect on the whites that the isolation of the white extremist intellectuals will have on their Negro counterparts. They will shrink into conspiratorial circles and will be subject not to the laws of movement of intellectual opinion but to those of the security services. These developments depend in part on the capacity of the political and administrative elites to regain control of their nerves and to discriminate between destructive actions and reasonable demands for improvement. They depend on the avoidance of exciting rhetoric. They depend most of all on the restoration of effectiveness and on the image of effectiveness on the part of the government. They depend very much on bringing the war in Viet Nam to an end, and in managing this without generating in sectors of the political elite and in the society at large a "stab-in-the-back" legend.

The intellectuals, sensitive as they are to power, would respond by a renewal of their sense of affinity, as they did under Franklin Roosevelt, even though there is a strong prejudice against any Republican administration. In addition to this it should be pointed out that at present, in the ranks of the alienated intellectuals, the most alienated are primarily concentrated in the functionally most marginal roles. Economists and engineers are more important to society than students and teachers and research workers in sociology and English and American literature. Their danger to social stability arises more from their role in the mass communications than from any "direct action" they can take from the inside as incumbents of executive roles or from the outside as demonstrators and bomb throwers. Nonetheless, in the present period when intellectuals possess so much prestige and many politicians are inclined to listen to them so deferentially, the most vociferous and most demonstrative, especially in the Negro-white collaboration—are capable of making demands and accusations which rattle the established political and administrative elites and cause them either to lose self-confidence or to react in an extremely aggressive and repressive manner. Either of these responses threatens to weaken the legitimacy of the established elite among those intellectuals who are inclined to give it the benefit of the doubt; it neutralizes them, weakens their civility, or makes them more sympathetic with the more extremely alienated.

Yet, the fact remains that the American economy—despite the burden of inflation—continues to operate with a most impressive effectiveness. The business elite, despite concessions here and there to the mounting lunacy, is more archaic in its sentiment and ethos. The leaders of the trade unions continue with an unruffled "business as usual" demeanor. It comes down therefore to the question whether the political elites in the federal government and in the big cities can reequilibrate themselves, regain their equanimity, reassert themselves by placing confidence in those sections of the population which support them, show initiative in bringing about some noticeable improvement, and in so doing, resume a steady course.

It is a far from easy task. It is encumbered on one side by an alliance with politicians of an irreconcilable outlook, particularly regarding ethnic questions; it is encumbered on the other by many within its own ranks who have been overrun by extremely alienated intellectuals—not as extremely alienated as the bomb throwers but extremely alienated nonetheless—who claim to speak on behalf of "people." What is called for is the reestablishment of a sovereignty deriving ultimately and through representative institutions from "the people" and the reduction of the direct ascendancy of "people," i.e. the "plebiscitary" democracy of a small minority. But that sovereignty cannot be reasserted unless it is done by those who have accepted the rewards and responsibilities of leadership in representative institutions.

XI

The growth to prominence of the intellectual classes in American society has been a function of changes in the function of the political and administrative elites and the changes in the character of physical and social technology from empirical to "scientific." Intellectuals became more prominent in the minds of the nonintellectual sectors of the elite as the technological procedures in American society came to require systematic study for their practice and development. In consequence, the number of intellectual roles in the society increased greatly, the number of intellectual institutions for training incumbents for those roles increased, and the number of persons filling the roles—practical-intellectual and intellectual—involved in the practice of the technology and training for it grew disproportionately.

The political, administrative, economic, and military elites, who had in the past not been notably appreciative of intellectual works and intellectuals, thus came to take an active part in the promotion of the institutions where such intellectuals were to be trained and in the recruitment of intellectuals so trained into their own institutions.

In the past the distance which the nonintellectual elites had maintained with respect to intellectuals was reciprocated. American intellectuals, particularly those concerned with the production and cultivation of literary and humanistic works, were hostile toward those in positions of authority in American society. They believed themselves to be disesteemed by them and they avoided entry into roles which entailed service and close association with the authoritative elites of their society. The intellectuals developed a penumbral tradition, which is seldom far from the surface of intellectual activities in general and was perhaps even stronger in the United States than in any other advanced country of the nineteenth century. This penumbral tradition prescribed distance from and disparagement of those in authoritative roles. Although the tradition was not developed in an equally extreme form among scientific and technological intellectuals in the nineteenth century, of whom there were not so many, they too shared in it. The intellectuals in the last two-thirds of the nineteenth century had practically no positive influence in American society. Even if their sense of alienation was caused in part by this exclusion from influence and authority, their hostility made little difference because of their lack of influence.

The transformation of American society in which authoritative roles came to be linked more intimately with intellectual roles had two major consequences: it brought about the partial suspension of the hostility of the intellectual elites toward the nonintellectual or authority-exercising elites, i.e. toward the executive elites in the broadest sense of the term. It also brought about the incorporation of the intellectuals into a closer, more collaborative relationship with the executive elites. In the course of this, intellectuals came in a variety of ways to have great influence on American culture and social structure.

The incorporation of the intellectuals into the central institutional system is now integral to the structure of American society. The penumbral traditions of the intellectuals have, however, retained their vitality despite their several decades of submergence, and in the recent troubles of the political, administrative, and military elites, the tradition of alienation has been reactivated. This time, however, as a result of the structural incorporation of the intellectuals into the center of American society, their cultural influence has been great. As a result, the legitimacy of the executive elites—a cultural phenomenon—has been impaired, and the effectiveness of these elites has been further damaged with a resultant further deterioration of their legitimacy.

The stability of American society has thus come to depend upon a sector of the society which lives in a tradition of alienation, part of which, in its extreme form, is historically contingent and part of which is almost self-generating in the primary culture of the intellectual role. At the same time, it should be observed that the primary culture of the intellectuals is increasingly generated in academic institutions, where there is a delicately poised and not always equally stable balance between, on the one hand, a discipline which acknowledges at least the authority of its own traditions and of the institutions which sustain them and, on the other, a more antinomian and expressive culture. The latter has a long and deep tradition, which developed before it came within academic confines. The stability of the larger society depends, therefore, on the maintenance, within the culture and the institutional system of the intellectuals, of the predominance of that element which accepts an objective discipline and the integration of academic institutions into the central institutional system of American society.

8 Freedom and Influence: Observations on the Scientists' Movement in the United States

I

In 1944 a new current of thought and action could be felt among American scientists. It originated within the Manhattan Project and arose from the depths of a troubled concern about the application of their scientific work. It raised no moral question about the rightness of their own actions in the realization of the atomic bomb, but it insisted that their will be consulted about its applications. For about two or three years there pulsated—with an intensity which varied with institutions, age, and the state of international relations—a current of anxiety, political alertness, and the desire for original and courageous action to prevent the harmful use of the achievements of science.

Its novelty lay not only in the considerable scale on which it touched the life of American scientists but also in its content. The earlier interest of American scientists in the social repercussions of their work had not only been isolated and scattered, but it was part of a radical, more or less Stalinist, criticism of American society; it was less interested in the integrity of science than in the derogation of the existing social order. The American Association of Scientific Workers, which embodied this tendency, never found an echo in the sentiments of American scientists. The new movement, organized in the Federation of American Scientists and expressing its views in the *Bulletin of the Atomic Scientists* though it swept or drew into its ranks many who had once shared the Leninist-Stalinist view and some who still did, did not concern itself with a radical criticism of America. Whereas the A.A.Sc.W. had complained of the suppression of science by capitalism, the new movement was impelled rather by the fear of the ways in which science had been and might be applied. Most of their leaders had had no contact with public life previously, and their desire to call to the attention of the public and its constituted authorities consequences which might arise from the presence of nuclear weapons was not the product of any doctrinal prepossession. The gradual realization of the bomb and then the two detonations in Japan had shaken them into a worried conviction that they alone possessed an awful knowledge which, for the common good, they must share with their fellow countrymen and, above all,

Previously published in a slightly different form in the *Bulletin of the Atomic Scientists*, vol. 13, no. 1 (January 1957), pp. 13-18.

with their political leaders. Free from the technocratic fringe of left-wing scientism, the movement which emerged never had a program which would make rulers out of scientists. It accepted the general structure of government and of scientists in it and sought only in an informal way, and amateurishly, to transmit to legislators, administrators, publicists, and civic leaders the awareness which their scientific experience had given them.

Beginning with the campaign for the development of a feasible scheme for international control of the uses of atomic energy and the elimination of its military application, and at the same time for civilian control of atomic energy, the scope of their interest gradually broadened as new issues arose. What was first conceived as an emergency, in which a few specific problems required resolution, established itself as a chronic condition. Loyalty and security policies, the genetic consequences of atomic bomb and hydrogen bomb tests and the political desirability of such tests, the estimation of the destructive power of nuclear weapons and the possibilities of civil defense, the nature of nuclear warfare and the possibilities of maintaining peace in the age of nuclear weapons, the economic development of backward areas of the world and the contributions of science to this, and, increasingly, the discovery of the optimal relations between scientists, scientific work and institutions, and the rest of the community, provided a natural agenda for the movement.

Problems had to be pursued into areas of social life which might have appeared earlier to be unconnected with the interests of responsible scientists. The interest in the international control of atomic energy, which was at first their exclusive concern and which, in fact, was the original contribution of the movement to public discussion, led to the study of the more general features of disarmament and then to the whole range of foreign policy. The study of the significance of atomic bombs led the scientists' movement to attend to matters of military technology and military strategy and planning; the concern with civil defense led into the problems of industrial location and the psychology of the family; the development of atomic power forced the scientists' movement to consider the advantages of private as compared with public enterprise, of monopoly and competition; the desire to protect the integrity of science and the status of scientists required reflection about the status of intellectuals and intellectual activities of all sorts in modern societies, liberal and totalitarian. So the simple and urgent problems of ten years earlier had, by the mid-fifties, become knottily involved with nearly every aspect of society. The decision of the *Bulletin of the Atomic Scientists* to add to its title "A Magazine of Science and Public Affairs," and the fact that it even considered changing its title to *Science and Public Affairs*, accurately recorded the broadened scope and permanence of the emergency once considered to be no more than a transient and grave distraction.

The clamorous flood of problems and the limited resources of the scientists to deal with them gave little time for thought about fundamentals or a general philosophy. There was no trace of a political affiliation in the American scientists' movement although there was probably a disposition in the direction of the Democratic party. The movement scarcely had an ideology; such an outlook as it had, had nothing to do with any prevailing current of political ideology. Here and there one or another of its leaders might have expressed the belief that the scientific mode of thought provided a specially valuable preparation for public life and for judgment on questions of public policy and that therefore scientists had more than their distressing knowledge to contribute to American politics. The scientists' movement was, however, remarkably free from the delusions of "scientism," from the scientific variant of the idea of the "philosopher-king." Every issue had to be confronted on its merits, and the humane and flexible viewpoint, at once liberal and realistic, which emerges from the pages and deeds of the scientists' movement is the precipitate of numerous discrete actions. No principles to govern the relations of science and society were promulgated; instead, a more differentiated judgment was schooled, and a more realistic understanding of the obduracy of the facts of social and political life was developed.

II

The Federation of American Scientists, with its headquarters in Washington and its local branches and affiliates at a few universities and national laboratories, and the *Bulletin of the Atomic Scientists* were the products and generators of this movement. They have lived from hand to mouth. They were run by amateurs who remained scientists and scholars, on scant time grudgingly torn from their own scientific and academic work. Unlike the trade unions of scientists, they never interested themselves in questions of salaries, hours, tenure, or conditions of work. When they spoke on behalf of the rights of the scientific profession, it was always for its right to pursue the truth and, in doing so, to be free from irrelevant intrusions.

The small groups or clusters of groups which constituted the scientists' movement in the United States in the fifties were bound together only in a loose and ill-coordinated organization. The two major organs had no formal connection. The real link which bound the two organs together and which bound the small network of the more intensively and actively interested with the sympathetic matrix of the scientific profession was an informal consensus. The movement was neither a party nor a sect, nor was there ever any serious effort to turn it into such. It was the more articulate expression of a widespread mood of scientists who were unable to give literary form to their sentiments or who grudged the time required or who lacked self-confidence for the public representation of their views on questions of policy relating to science. Those at the center of the movement knew that they were the objects of the hope, the projection of the aspirations, of many with whom they had no contact, and this sustained them.

The center, the actual life and work of the movement, drew on a very small number of persons with very small funds and very little time and energy at their disposal. Active collaboration in writing, editing, organizing, making representations, raising funds, investigating, etc., was probably the product of the efforts of little more than one hundred persons, with active but less intensive support from not many more. Despite its epoch-making novelty and its eminently meritorious achievements, the movement did not succeed in enlisting the vigorous participation or even the explicit attachment of the scientific profession in the United States.

III

What were its accomplishments? The movement definitely made a mark on American life in the decade after its initiation. The Federation of American Scientists and, even more, the *Bulletin of the Atomic Scientists*—even though they could claim only a few specific victories (and no complete victory on any major problem) —could justly declare that they had installed themselves into the conscience and intelligence of the upper levels of American public life, and that, through the latter, their influence had radiated outward toward the whole politically interested population. The most important publicists of press, radio, and television who were writing on matters connected with science in the mid-fifties heeded with some measure of respect what the scientists said through their two organs. Many senators and representatives, especially those on the relevant congressional committees, turned an interested and sometimes even hospitable ear to what the scientists associated with or sympathetic to this movement had to say. The executive branch of the government, although it seldom obeyed, listened with discomfort and respect to what the organs of the scientists' movement said, and it felt the need to reply and to adapt its conduct to render it less vulnerable to the scientists' criticism. When the Gray committee decided that Dr. Oppenheimer was a security risk, it also felt it had to defend itself against the kinds of criticism which would come forth from the scientists' movement. When, during the 1956 presidential election, the Republican administration wished to support its then current position on hydrogen bomb tests, it recognized that it had to appear to have the support of leading figures in the scientific community in order to undo the impression created by other members of the scientific community. In vital matters of national policy, the support of scientists was sought by both of the contending parties.

In brief, the scientists' movement in the United States—and the stirrings in the great professional scientific associations which these two groups, by their incessant and dignified activity, occasionally engendered—introduced a new element into American public life. On almost every issue which aroused the interest of the scientists' movement, something arising from the efforts of the scientists touched and deflected the course of political or administrative action toward what was almost always a more reasonable course— through prodding, reminding, pointing out, through the embodiment of an outlook or state of mind which reasserted the values of detachment and generosity of judgment, of freedom from tyrannous passion, and of objective inquiry and of calm reflection. To these efforts, the *Bulletin of the Atomic Scientists* brought assurance and support. The small circulation—15,000 by the mid-1950s—sent its ripples far beyond the zone of its regular readership. The resonance which it found in the American and foreign press helped to imprint in the American public an awareness of its independence, its detachment, its reasonableness. Many who would otherwise have been more reconciled to iniquities, were stiffened in their inner resistance by the feeling that there was someone who was thinking on these problems; some few were even encouraged to express their views in public places. Backbones were stiffened and hearts were cheered in many quarters by the scientists' movement, and many minds were made more thoughtful on all issues of public policy in which science is involved.

IV

This very cursory survey of the American scientists' movement produces some observations concerning the place of science in the system of public life.

The first observation emerges from the fact that this movement was not only unique in the history of the United States, it was unique in the contemporary world. No other country witnessed such a phenomenon. Perhaps none could. There were other countries where in the decade following World War II, intellectual liberties were placed under the shadows, but none of these gave rise to a scientists' movement. In the totalitarian countries, where liberty was not merely threatened but actually subverted, there were no such movements, nor were there any such movements in any of the countries where the encroachments on the autonomy of the scientific community were slighter than they were in the United States.

It is a paradox that the decade 1945-55, during which the uproar of antiintellectualism and of distrust for scientists was louder than it had ever been in America, was also the decade of the greatly enhanced influence of scientists within public bodies and of a moderate but nonetheless unprecedented effectiveness of scientists outside the government seeking to influence opinion and policy. Both facts testify to the increased esteem in which scientists came to be held in the country—and the hostility toward scientists which appeared to contradict this assertion can indeed be reasonably interpreted as the Parthian shots of an adversary in retreat.

During the embroilments in the fifties with McCarthy and his fellow travelers only small numbers in the membership of the scientific profession were willing to exert themselves to speak or write in public or to make representations to administrative and political authorities. The scientific profession was one of those most affected by the loyalty-security mania and the distrust of intellectuals, but their response in overt behavior was not massive. Most scientists preferred to stick to their work, to carry on with their ordinary routines, and to confine their disapproval, which was nearly universal, to embittered comment among their colleagues. In this respect they were not very different from their colleagues in countries where there is no scientists' movement and where there are problems aplenty for such a movement. Efforts to stir these American scientists into writing their opinions or experiences for the *Bulletin* were frequently unsuccessful. On ceremonial occasions, or when some part of the government behaved with especial crudity, a few of the more eminent occasionally spoke out in strong tones. For the most part, it was in the younger generation of scientists that the earnest and disinterested sentiments which supported the scientists' movement were found.

It is noteworthy that the American scientists' movement found little response among a vast sector of an academic profession which prides itself on being scientific—namely, the social scientists. Practically every problem dealt with by the scientists' movement called for knowledge of social and political institutions, of economics and law, but, despite some outstanding exceptions, social scientists remained aloof, indifferent to or disdainful of the lay social science of the leaders of the scientists' movement. This was almost as true for the action of social scientists concerning loyalty and security problems as it was for the other problems of policy in which the scientists' movement became engaged. The same could be said of the rest of the American intellectual community.

Why do crises of intellectual freedom find the academic profession, in its majority, so supine and complaisant? Why are the great battles for academic freedom fought by—and, when won, won by—a heroic handful?

The position of academic freedom is almost always delicately poised. One of the sources for this instability is the indifference of the academic profession itself to its own freedom as a community within the larger society.[1] Only if their own freedom or that of their immediate colleagues is infringed, would most scientists or scholars in most countries bestir themselves, or even pay attention to issues of academic freedom, and then they would do so in a narrow perspective.

There are good and reasonable reasons for this. Scientists do not enter science and cannot do good scientific work if their concerns lie elsewhere than in science itself. A true passion for science or scholarship does not necessarily carry with it a concern for justice and liberty.

Furthermore, scientists respect scientists. They do not respect busybodies and gadabouts and those who spend their best hours working on nonscientific subjects. The young scientist who spends his time on such matters is not likely to advance in his career, not primarily because his seniors dislike such activities but because they think he is showing insufficient scientific zeal. Nor for that matter can the young scientist really spend much time on extrascientific affairs and still do outstanding work in his subject.

Then, there is sheer cowardice, the desire for safety which can be given an honorable face. No one who has witnessed his own behavior or that of his colleagues in situations threatening to academic freedom will contest the contention that this phenomenon is very common. When the force of cowardice coincides with the pressure of professional specialization and the scientist's love of his subject and his distrust of the dilettante who meddles in realms beyond its boundaries, the defenses of intellectual freedom are bound to be feeble.

1. While obviously everyone worth his salt wishes to be free to teach what he thinks true, to do the research which interests him, and to report his results as he finds them, there are quite a few academic persons who are more than willing to do what is proposed to them because they wish to please or because they have no ideas of their own and no independent intellectual curiosity.

V

Academic freedom and academic influence rest ultimately on opinion and on that particular opinion called respect or esteem. There are many institutional safeguards, but none is significant if there is not a substantial body of opinion which tolerates or supports academic freedom because it respects intellectual work and those who do it.

In the United States too many of us in the struggle through which we passed in the fifties overstressed the utilitarian argument for intellectual freedom—the argument that the harassments which the enthusiasts of loyalty and security sought to impose on the intellectual community were injurious to military defense and economic welfare. We did not stress sufficiently that these impositions wounded the dignity of one of the most important spheres of human action. We failed to stress the inherent value of our sphere of life, not because we did not believe in the intrinsic importance of it, but in part because of our lack of confidence in the will to understand among the sections of the population to whom we addressed our arguments. We felt a great cleavage between ourselves and the others, and we felt too little common ground to believe that an affirmation of the values we espoused would carry any weight with those we sought to persuade.

In the last analysis, academic freedom and academic influence rest not on university constitutions or on financial resources or on laws or formal advisory bodies but on the esteem in which intellectual life is held in any particular society. The worst arrangements for filling a university council or board of governors with businessmen, lawyers, civil servants, and politicians are compatible with the utmost academic freedom, if the relevant sectors of that society highly esteem intellectual activity and academic institutions. Likewise the best constitution guaranteeing academic self-government is hopeless if the political and economic powers of a society despise intellectual activity and deny the value of those who carry on this activity. And the esteem in which intellectual activity is held by those outside the intellectual community is to a significant extent a function of the esteem in which those within the intellectual community hold themselves.

9 The Scientific Community:
Thoughts after Hamburg

In the rebuilt free city of Hamburg, from the 23rd to the 26th July 1953, 119 scientists and scholars from nineteen countries met to discuss "Science and Freedom."[1] The theme of the congress was intended to summon the attention of the world to the damage done to science by totalitarianism. But wisely the conveners of the conference sought to utilize the critique of the oppression of science to contribute to the clarification of our own appreciation of the freedom of science and the conditions of its maintenance. It was the intention of those who called the conference not only to denounce the harassment and deformation of science, above all, of genetics, in the Soviet Union but also to make Western scientists and scholars more fully aware of what is entailed in the claim to freedom for the pursuit of truth.

Underlying the program was a tacit agenda which sought comprehensively to treat: (a) the structure of the autonomous scientific community; (b) the institutional preconditions of scientific freedom, particularly with respect to the mode of financial support for universities and research; (c) the methodological presuppositions of freedom in science, i.e., the conception of science underlying the demand for the freedom of scientific activity; (d) the foundations in our political and moral outlook of the demand for freedom in science.

I think that it is just to say that though the discussions sometimes seemed to wander rather far afield—especially when methodological issues raced hare-like across the field—there was scarcely a moment when the agenda was exceeded. The coherence of the discussions is enhanced in retrospect when the unspoken agenda and its central theme have become more visible and the excitement of the discussion dissipated.

The program began with the problems arising from the practice of pure science, from the development of applied science and the

Previously published in a slightly different form in the *Bulletin of the Atomic Scientists*, vol. 10, no. 5 (May 1954), pp. 151-55.

1. The meeting was held under the auspices of the Congrès pour la liberté de la culture. It was organized by Professor Michael Polanyi, then of Manchester University, and the late Alexander Weissberg, the Austrian physicist who had worked in the Soviet Union for a number of years. (Dr. Weissberg's reminiscences of his last years in the Soviet Union are to be found in his *The Conspiracy of Silence*.)

large-scale organization of modern scientific research and publication, which have in turn resulted from the discovery of the practical utility of science for industry and war. This led to the question of how the freedom of science could be guaranteed when governmental subvention was necessary. The debate then moved toward a miscellany of subjects concerning methodology, the impact of class and national identification on social science, and the disposition of scientists and scholars to espouse extreme ideologies. Throughout there struggled toward clarity a still very inchoate theory of intellectual freedom—the conception of the autonomous scientific community functioning in a pluralistic society.

II

The first day's discussion of the papers of Professor M. Polanyi on "Pure and Applied Science and Their Appropriate Organization,"[2] John R. Baker on "Scientific Authority and the System of Scientific Publication," Professor Samuel Allison on "Academic Freedom and State Security," and Professor J. Thibaud and Professor L. Raiser on "Academic Freedom and Governmental Financial Support," gave rise to lively discussion but little passion.

Professor Polanyi's paper set the theme of the conference. In attempting to distinguish pure science from applied science and to justify the freedom of the former while allowing for the incorporation of the latter in the network of practical actions, he described the form of the social organization through which science works and develops. Polanyi assimilated the structure of the scientific world to the free market in the economic sphere. In neither is there any centralized coordination of decision: the determination of what is to be produced, how much and at what price, and, correspondingly, of what is to be investigated and which lines of inquiry are to be followed up by further research, are arrived at through a system of institutions operating through multitudes of individual decisions freely made.

In the world of pure science, each important scientist makes his own decision as to what he will work on and how, and when he completes his research he communicates with other scientists informally and through the various journals that are available to him. His colleagues and peers pass judgment on his work, freely accepting or rejecting it without any reference to any prescription by an institutional authority.

J. R. Baker followed Polanyi's pattern of analyses with an argument for the freedom of the press in scientific publication.

2. Professor Polanyi's paper has been reprinted by the Society for the Protection of Freedom in Science.

Allison departed widely from his prepared paper, which had dealt with the menace to intellectual freedom in America. Instead, he gave the conference a vivid account of the wide freedom which university scientists have been able to maintain even under conditions of government financial support.

The picture of a scientific community, with its own institutions, its own rules, its own authorities—effective without coercion and through their own achievement in accordance with generally perceived and acknowledged standards—was beginning to emerge. Both Professor Allison's paper and his talk set the stage for the next problem: How can this community, which requires autonomy for its survival and progress, withstand the pressure of political fanatics and doctrinaires on the one side, and the ties of financial dependence on interested governmental bodies on the other?

To the former problem, an entire session was devoted on the third day of the conference. To the latter problem Professors Thibaud and Raiser addressed themselves. Both recognized that the increased cost of equipment for scientific research and the absence or insufficiency of endowment rendered necessary some financial dependence on government. Thibaud saw difficulties arising from political wire-pulling by certain scientists who enjoyed the favor of the ruling political group; Raiser's extensive survey of the different types of finance of universities found none fully reliable as a guarantor of the autonomy of intellectual work. Direct appropriation by legislative action could be dangerous. So could direct appropriation by administrative bodies such as ministries or government departments. The British University Grants Committee seemed the best because it placed the responsibility on a quasi-academic body, which was granted the funds by Parliament and stood between the universities and the government. Although there can be no absolutely secure protection of the freedom of learning, Raiser pointed out that the self-esteem and the self-confidence of the universities and of individual scientists was one of the factors most conducive to the situation in which the state can be dealt with as "an equal partner" to the extent that partnership is necessary. Without "communal responsibility and self-discipline" among the members of the university community, nothing can be done to assure academic freedom.

The need to accept money from governments conflicted with a distrust of government. No one questioned the need—not even John Millet in his paper which was circulated but not discussed—or denied that scientific research today needs government aid on a large scale. There was not much inventiveness shown in the discussion—perhaps there are no alternatives to the present main methods—and the only addition to the prevailing methods was Millet's suggestion that governmental aid should come to the universities through the subvention of large tuition fees. The absence of originality in the suggestion of new methods of financing research was offset by the importance of Thibaud's and Raiser's emphasis on the increased need for steadfastness in the devotion of the scientists to the standards of their community—the scientific community. One might commend also Raiser's repeated reference to the partnership among equals which he recommended as the right relationship of the scientific community and the political community. The conception of the nature and conditions of intellectual liberty which the congress fostered would have been impossible if these propositions were disregarded.

III

Against the background of this anxiety about financial dependence on government, the arguments about the moral responsibility of scientists for the care and observance of the transcendent standards of their discipline took on especial poignancy. The problem was real, but the formulations were archaic and they often threatened to lead the discussion into bypaths. Yet even on its bypaths, once one grasped the drift of the discussion in the direction of the idea of the scientific community, one could begin to see how the traditional philosophical discussion of the problem of the moral responsibility of the scientist and scholar had really been an attempt to define and defend intellectual liberty. One could also see how the traditional philosophical discussion of the matter had been deficient in its neglect of the social, economic, and political relations of the scientific community to the other communities. The failure of the traditional views was apparent also in their disregard of the internal social structure of the scientific community.

The discussion was often carried on with the kind of eloquent pathos which we associate with German professorship. The German idealistic view of the individual responsible for his own moral relation with his highest values, independently of any institutional mediation, somehow seemed to obstruct the progress of thought. It seemed to interfere with deliberate consideration of the urgent problem of how to prevent encroachments on the autonomy of intellectual life and institutions, at a time when the state demands so much of science and when politicians are so doctrinaire or so boundless in their aspirations.

I think it had not been intended to raise these deeper moral and sociological questions until later in the conference but the matter-of-fact scientism of Professor Mehlberg at the third session stirred a tempest of excitement among the antipositivists. The sobriety of the earlier sessions was succeeded by an atmosphere of strenuous excitement. The passionate moral fervor of Professor Theodor Litt, the cool irony of Professor Mehlberg, the vigorously unquenchable voice of the Enlightenment speaking through Sidney Hook, the grave religious tones of Professors Jores and Mitscherlich, the histrionic declamations of Professor Fedor Stepun, stirred the members of the conference to vivacious applause and tempestuous disagreement.

It must be said again that the continuity of the discussion was disrupted, and the development of the idea of the scientific community, which was the intended and the effective rationale of the conference, was diverted by the too early emergence of the problem of moral responsibility before the social, political, and psychological aspects of the problem had been adequately treated.

The whole conference was antistatist in disposition, very antitotalitarian, and for the most part (but not entirely) free from any element of scientistic utopianism. Against this background of agreement, there were very marked differences. The Germans argued that more than the cognitive processes and powers of man were involved in scientific research and that, by virtue of that fact, the scientist accepted moral responsibilities and a fundamental moral orientation which was given by the very nature of his work as a scientist. The scientist had to be concerned for the consequences of his work; he also had to be concerned for the institutions and values which the pursuit of truth presupposed. Moreover, the fact that the scientist did not exhaust his intellectual activities and responsibilities in observation and induction meant that these processes so highly prized by the positivists could not be placed above all other intellectual activities, etc. But the main point which emerged from this was the antagonism of the idealists to any form of scientism which, due to their superior scientific knowledge, would give preeminence to scientists in the making of political and moral decisions. It would probably have been easier for the basic agreement which existed among the participants to come to the surface if it had not been for the excitation of prejudice aroused by the battle cry of empiricism versus theory.

Both the idealists—led by Litt, whom they all acknowledged as their spokesman—and the positivists—Tarski, Mehlberg, et al.— revealed a major gap in our thought about the conditions of intellectual and academic freedom. For the former, scientific truth is the product of the whole man, and its establishment assumes a whole constellation of values which are more than cognitive or intellectual. For the positivists, truth can be guaranteed by excluding every trace of noncognitive, emotional, religious, or metaphysical thought or sentiment, by restricting ourselves solely to the use of our powers of observation and ratiocination, and by being guided in our judgment by them alone. For the moment, neither group remembered the reality of the scientific tradition and its authority in science. The positivists, by their deification of the individual investigator, made it appear as if each investigator by himself questions and simultaneously observes and rationally analyzes every component of his hypothesis. The idealists failed to acknowledge that the scientific tradition is unlike other traditions in that in the course of time and in principle every single element in the tradition—which is a system of thought—is subject to critical appraisal, and its authority at any given time is a function, not just of its conformity with our individually experienced values, but of its acceptance by our peers in the scientific field whose accomplishments have entitled them to our confidence. They could have found a common ground in the notion of the scientific community.

The aspirations of the positivists for the hegemony of the scientific method among all our intellectual processes and thus by implication for the supremacy of scientists among our legislators was combated with much emotion. Mitscherlich, in a deeply moved expression of aversion for what the Nazis had done in their medical experiments, and many others, in a torrent of eloquence and moral idealism, denounced the desire of scientists to supply the moral standards for the guidance of individual conduct and social policy. But there was no voice that responded to Hayek's and Rabinowitch's effort to focus the discussion on the scope and limits of what scientists could contribute to public policy and the capacity in which they could make that contribution. Looking back one sees how continuously the remarks of the discussants skirted about the theory of the scientific community and of its possible and proper relations with the other spheres of life in a pluralistic society.

Despite its frequent centrifugal flights it was extremely impressive how time and again the discussion moved back toward the seldom articulated central theme. For example, from many points of view, the communal nature of the traditions of science was touched upon and its features explored. There was general agreement that the tradition of science does not consist only in the propositions and current hypotheses and its codified procedures—the professional ethos of the scientist was viewed as a vital element, both tough and fragile, without which scientific work could not go on. Not only in the statements of Polanyi, Hook, and myself on the first day was this stressed but even in the discussion on the fourth day of the damage done to genetics by the Soviet policy of interference into the stream of scientific inquiry, the emphasis on the vitality of an autonomous, partially self-maintaining tradition of scientific and scholarly research was clearly evident. In Gitermann's and in Rauch's papers, in which the speakers did not close their eyes to the truth-deforming intentions of the Soviet authorities on all matters touched on by their doctrinaire prejudices or touching on the legitimacy of their authority, we could see that somehow, in the personal relations of masters and pupils and among peers in the scientific and scholarly professions, a love of truth still survived under the surface of official requirements and resulted in great works of scholarship and science. In the robust comments by Alexander Weissberg, drawing on his own experience as a scientist in the Soviet Union and as editor of the Soviet "Journal of Physics," the same point was made. The real scientists, those in Soviet Russia no less than elsewhere, do not allow the doctrines of the ruling political group to intrude into the heart of their studies. They are willing to compromise in externals—compromises which do no immediate injury to the dignity of their realm and to the channels of impersonal communication by which the field as a whole subsists; they will yield, for example, to the extent of publishing general articles about the scientific fruitfulness of dialectical materialism. But they do not deform their own minds by attempting to believe in dialectical materialism, and, to the extent that they do, they do so only segmentally so that the vital nerve of their own scientific work remains unaffected. As Weissberg said, "They just don't believe it." Raymond Aron, in his paper on "The Idea of Class or National Truth in Social Science," and I, in my discussion of it, made the same point: no scientist who has made any contribution to science or who aspires to do so believes at all seriously in the totalitarian contention that there are truths peculiar to classes, races, etc. Such notions are the property of propagandist demagogues, toadies in the academic world who seek promotion by flattering the prejudices of their political superiors and honest philosophers who muddle themselves into a relativistic confusion. No scientist really devoted to his work and well incorporated into the ethos of his profession believes in the theory of "two truths"—of one truth for the ruling classes and another for the working classes. The very act of participating in scientific work and accepting thereby membership in the scientific community is intrinsically incompatible with this dogma. The strength of the tradition of scientific life and scientific institutions reaffirms itself against the claims of ideology, and must do so as long as scientific work of a high intellectual caliber is allowed to go on.

No one claimed of course that ideologically motivated intrusions into scientific institutions could be without influence. Indeed, the first day's discussions on institutional relations and the subsequent discussions of moral responsibility showed how much the members of the conference thought the danger must be guarded against. John Baker's talk on the first day, taking up the lead given by Polanyi, showed how important for the development of scientific opinion is the free, competitive operation of scientific publications within a framework of norms of respect for truth and moral integrity. Other speakers pointed out how the pressure of ideological prejudices on the part of rulers and of conformity on the part of scientists could dam up, divert, and muddy the stream of science. The comments which stressed the reality of the tradition of science did not contend that it could live on, independently of the society in which it had to exist; it was generally acknowledged and indeed forcefully emphasized that the tradition could be painfully hurt by the doctrinaire or excessive demands of external powers. Nonetheless, it seems to me that one very valuable contribution of the whole conference was the gradually developed notion that scientific activities—institutional and individual—form a kind of social and cultural system with its own powers of self-maintenance and self-regulation and that this system must of necessity be relatively autonomous. With this was associated the view that in this autonomy a very major role is played by the internal tradition of science, in general, and of the particular scientific discipline as well—a tradition which runs from investigator to investigator, which lives on in memories and anecdotes as well as in scientific communications, and none of which is irrelevant to keeping alive the conviction of the supreme value, within that tradition, of scientific truth.

The analysis of the ideologies which would lead science astray—which pseudophilosophers and politicians offer to scientists—was not among the more useful parts of the conference. I am quite sure it would have contributed more to the clarification of the emergent theme of the conference—namely, the autonomy of science and the conditions of its maintenance—if, instead of the refutation of a philosophy which very few people really accept in the scientific world, more attention had been paid to the problem of why scientists and scholars sometimes espouse philosophies and political judgments which in the course of time lead to the wounding and deformation of science. This problem, which, in the very distorted form given to it by Senator McCarthy, had been harassing us since the disclosure of the misdeeds of Nunn May and Fuchs, was unfortunately treated in only one brief but compact paper by Professor Helmut Plessner of Göttingen. Professor Plessner, by quietly opening the problem of how certain strands in the traditional culture of the educated classes in Western society have nurtured an antagonism toward civil society, touched what seems to me to lie at the root of much of the present agitation against scientists and intellectuals generally. Plessner asked why scholars and scientists are inclined toward the acceptance of extremist political views—historians in Germany particularly toward reactionary extremism and natural scientists toward leftist extremism. Part of the explanation of the extremist dispositions, which are by no means universal or of equal incidence in all countries, derives from the modes of thought which are practiced in each field. Empathic, organismic thought in the historical disciplines, critical ratiocinative antiauthoritarianism in the natural sciences color the atmosphere and make for a readiness to move to an extreme position. It would have been good if Professor Plessner had been able to distinguish more sharply than he did the intrinsic and the extrinsic traditions of the learned and the scientific worlds. There is an important difference between the traditions which have arisen accidentally as far as the pursuit of science is concerned—from the social origins of the persons working in scholarship and science or from the conflicts between ecclesiatical authority and scientists. The latter, although not essential to science or scholarship, have entered into the heart of the traditions of the scientific world and have contributed greatly to the formation in the minds of intellectuals of the belief in a necessary conflict between free intelligence and public authority, etc. Professor Plessner's paper was only a beginning but it is a beginning which should be followed up from within the learned world itself—and not from within the circles of crackpots or wayward journalists and demagogues who have been the main custodians of this theme in recent years. Such a study or series of studies would augment our understanding of some of the numerous ties binding together the scientific community and the various sectors of the larger community. It would show how the inner equilibrium of this very special kind of community—the scientific community which lives in the wider world while maintaining its own life—becomes disrupted. By virtue of this, it would contribute to the equilibrium of the scientific community and its relations with the extrascientific sectors of society.

10 The Intellectuals and the Future

One of the major streams of our contemporary intellectual traditions has long declared the present to be not the best of times but rather the worst of times. This tradition has been with us since the last part of the eighteenth century and especially strongly since early in the nineteenth century. A subsidiary proposition of this tradition asserted that the past was a better time, a season of light, a spring of hope. Quite recently there has flowed into this stream another one, carrying on its shallow waters a whispered message that the future will be even more the worst of times, a season of darkness, a winter of despair.

For most of the two centuries of a growingly embittered and comprehensive denial of virtue to the present, many of those who thought it a poor time also foresaw a better time ahead, prescribed by the powers of reason and the good potentialities of man's nature, or, more often, by the necessities of the unfolding of history and the force of a possessing idea. Some of them foresaw and hopefully recommended an elaborate picture of the state of affairs which might be brought into existence in the future.

This utopian hope was condemned and replaced, in a more scientific age, by "scientific socialism." Scientific socialism spurned these cheerful and detailed delineations of the future state but affirmed its confidence in a profoundly disjunctive, globally transforming improvement which the future would bring. Marxism refused to write "the recipes for the cookshops of the future"; it shifted its attention to the laws and techniques which would lead necessarily to the establishment of those wonderfully nourishing cookshops. It was certain that they would come and that their products would be ample and tasty.

Even the contemptuous efforts of the founders of Marxism could not suppress the yearnings of their followers to know what the ennobling future would look like, and a number of Marxists such as Kautsky and Ballod squinted hard to detect the outlines of the object of their striving. Once the Russian Revolution occurred, it was no longer possible or politic to deny this desire to know the physiognomy of the future. "I have seen the future and it works."

Previously published in a slightly different form in the *Bulletin of the Atomic Scientists*, vol. 23, no. 8 (October 1967), pp. 7-14.

The Soviet Union was the acknowledged prefiguration of the future. It was no longer necessary to write utopias. Fantasies purporting to be realistic accounts of what went on in the Soviet Union met the need to know what the future would be like and to be certain that it would be a very good thing indeed.

Throughout the 1920s, except for irreconcilable social democrats and reactionaries who for different reasons, worthy and unworthy, found Bolshevism abhorrent, the pattern of Bolshevik society seemed to be the best possible approximation to the heights to which mankind might reasonably aspire. Liberals and socialists, who felt no loyalty to the leaders of official social democracy, so vehemently abused by the Bolsheviks, thought that the chief characteristic of the Bolshevik elite was its unrelenting determination to leap into the future, carrying the Russian people with it, mainly through inspiration.

It was taken for granted that the Bolsheviks knew what the future would be l like, and how to get there. There were no costs except exertion. I remember particularly discussions of the restrictions on civil liberty in the Soviet Union at that time. Those who were unofficial socialists and radicals in general, though they were aware of the abolition of public discussion, thought that it was all right because it was plainly necessary to protect the economic system of a socialist society from its "class enemies." The "class enemies" were not members of the essential community which was to inherit the future. They were alien to the constitution of a socialist society, and their losses were not to be counted among the costs. Once the socialist society was attained, civil liberties would be restored undamaged to a community which had voluntarily and deliberately renounced them. The incarceration or extermination of "class enemies" was not a "cost." It was part of the suffering and purification which were prerequisite to entrance into the transfigured future. They were sanctifying actions. The past was wholly bad; what was discontinued was no loss. Tsarist society was wholly bad; its institutions were entirely dispensable. The only cost in discarding them was the exertion required to be made against "class enemies" who tried to protect those institutions. There were, of course, well-wishers of the Soviet Union who admitted that there were real costs incurred in the movement through the pre-future condition; they argued, however, that tragic sacrifices had to be made because of the unquestionable value of the goal. They conceded that valuable things might be lost through the undifferentiated eradication of the precipitates of the past. But such well-wishers were relatively rare.

In the 1930s, when the then present sank markedly in value, the future took on a new and more urgent attractiveness. The availability of a model of the future made subscription to it more feasible. The existence of the model and the character of the present both changed the content of the future. Whereas in the 1920s the future as represented by the potentialities of the Soviet Union had borne the general features of the idealistic utopia centered about the *freier Mensch auf freiem Boden*, in which the ordinary man would stand as high as Aristotle, in the thirties the economic features of the future condition were underscored more heavily. The Great Depression in the West was contrasted with "the land without unemployment." The optimism which the enduring idea of progress still sustained was given an additional force and intensity by a newly generated or reactivated sympathy with the outcasts and wretched of the earth. This uncritical and energized optimism was rendered even more uncritical and optimistic about the costless attainability of the goal by the zealously practiced dishonesty of the communist politicians and intellectuals of the period. Once more, as in the twenties but more densely, it was argued that the only costs were those involved in the protection of the future from the destructiveness of those with vested interests in the bad past and present. The frustration of the destructive exertions of the enemies of the future entailed no costs other than the maintenance of secret police. The losses of their victims did not count as a cost. The resources for the future were the hitherto unused energies of those who were to be drawn into the collective effort. Additional exertion was heroic; sacrifices were renunciations made by individuals when their intensified exertions diminished their private gratifications. No one sacrificed anyone else, only himself, and that was ennobling.

In contrast with a present in which everyone paid for the gratifications of a few, there was juxtaposed a fantasy of harmony in which all particular interests were dissolved and in which all values were simultaneously realizable. Even the simplest propositions about renunciation of present consumption for purposes of capital accumulation were passed over without comment. It went without saying that the remote and endless future was entitled to the sacrifices of the present.

All this is now changed. Very few intellectuals still believe that the future has settled in Soviet territory. The simple and arrogant optimism has faded. The great dream of socialism is like a moonbeam at noon. Khrushchev's secret speech of February 1956 made it clear that the future had not taken up residence in the Soviet Union. Socialism has shriveled into a problematical scheme for the organization of industrial and agricultural production; it has lost its allure. The proponents of what was once an anticipation of a transformation of all of human life have lost the assumption of their own superiority. The true discovery of the Soviet Union and the people's democracies of Eastern Europe has made those who saw them as the desired end to the baseness of the present less confident of the rightness of their alternative.

The hedonism which was integral to socialism has turned out to be more gratifiable in capitalist economies than in socialist economies. The chaos of the planned economies of Eastern Europe and the utterly prosaic character of the nationalized industries of France and Great Britain on the one side, and the affluent society in America and the "economic wonder" in Germany of the other, although not endearing them to their beneficiaries, have weakened attachments to the central feature of socialism. It was not the question whether the goal was worth the costs which caused socialism to fade. It was rather that the goal turned out to be a phantasm. Socialism and the future had become so amalgamated that a future without socialism seemed only an empty zone in the extension of time, not a fulfillment of time.

The future has sunk into a swamp. Who now speaks of it as the locus of a happy life? The future and discourse about it have become the domain of experts in computers, automation, and information systems. It cheers no one except those who see the future as a theater for the exercise of their technological virtuosity. The inevitability of automation is accepted, but the emancipation of man from arduous labor is not welcomed. The provision of an income not earned by work is not thought of as a wonderful opportunity but as a desperate welfare measure. The idea of a workfree existence is attended by more than a tremor of apprehension. It is definitely not a future which quickens the steps of those who are forced to approach it.

Some of those who formerly saw the future's embryo in the Soviet Union, having given up their old friends and retained their old enemies, no longer defend their old ideals or its early vessels; they only heap abuse on the heads of those who criticize the old ideal. Recently we have heard it said that sabotage and subversion have never been more called for—although the invoker felt that the existing powers were too impregnable to allow them! Even though the blood in hardening arteries pulsates a little more quickly at the reminiscence of cell meetings and talk of barricades, there is no confidence that anything could come of them. The future has become empty or indeterminate—impossible of access or no better than the present. It no longer beckons or enchants. And the approach to it is through the techniques of meliorism—the extension of the franchise, the extension of educational and occupational opportunities, the improvement of the quality of education, the promotion of civility. It is right to call these movements "radical," for even though some of them like to think of themselves in the vocabulary of revolution, they have gone back to the techniques and ends of the radical reformers of the nineteenth century.

Even this flowering of youthful radicalism—admirable and moving as it is—does not burn with conviction about the future. The new radicalism is radical in its criticism of the present but also accepts a lot of it, and it has no certainty. It sees no open roadway over which to march toward the future. It moves tentatively. Toward authority it has the sentiments of rebellion. The older Marxist ideology, which had the future as its center and revolution as its approach, is discredited, and although the new radicalism sometimes appears to seek an ideology, it cannot accept the discredited one and must therefore content itself with the "piecemeal social engineering" which used to be repugnant to the ideological orientation. While it speaks out against "meliorism" and uses the old large words such as "power" and "the poor," and older ones like "fraternity" and "community," it cannot relate its actions to anything more comprehensive or fundamental than particular reforms. Perhaps it has been too closely embraced in the arms of the universities; perhaps its wings have been clipped by too much study of contemporary sociology. A sporadic praise of violence, a brief rash of bombing, or withdrawal to shut out the evil of the present are the alternatives to particular reforms with new names. They do not resuscitate the image of an inevitable and happy future.

The most vital force among contemporary social movements, which has aroused other, subsidiary movements and set echoes and memories reverberating in dilapidated ideologies, is directed toward the integration of the Negroes and the derelicts of our society into the moral and civil structure in which most of the population already lives. Those whose ears quiver faintly, like old hunting dogs dozing before the fire, when they hear of civil unrest and the echoes of a violent delivery of the future, cannot overcome their imprisonment by the present. There are some who say that a revolution is necessary, but what they have in mind is often not more than control over the dismissal from employment of persons engaged in automated occupations, desegregation in schools, voluntary associations among the lumpenproletariat, and similar things, for which the despised liberals and reformers have also been contending. Thus, we have come to a turn in Western civilization in which the bearers of that intellectual tradition which has taught the rest of the world to think about the future and to act for it has lost its self-confidence. "Futurology" and the new evolutionism of a small group of sociologists predict only an extension of the recent past into a future which gives no cheer.

II

In the underdeveloped world, revolutionaries are in an uproar against neocolonialism. Their hatred of their former foreign rulers and of their present indigenous rulers is so strong that the contentlessness of their goal does not inhibit their ardor. In the Western world, the emptiness of the future, or its prospectively distressing content, disarms many who have a lingering affection for the rhetoric and clatter of revolution. The inheritance of utopianism and the wisdom of the schools convince them that it makes no sense to aspire toward a contentless goal. They do not believe that "the end is nothing, the movement everything." Unlike the underdeveloped world, the inheritance of the West and its recent disillusionment are too strong to permit hatred and aggressiveness to take unquestioned command; there must be an ostensibly positive, factual legitimation for movement; actions must be seen to stand in a chain of means and end.

Just as governments nowadays, however incompetent and hypocritical, must have policies and cannot permit themselves to appear satisfied simply to remain in power, so critics of governments and the societies which they govern must also have a remote and elaborate goal which is the ideological equivalent of a policy. The aversion of attention from the future cannot endure, even if utopia continues in attrition.

Preoccupation with the future has seized the minds of modern men. They must strive towards it. If they do not, they must be discontented with themselves for being less than they would be. But the whole thing is easier for governments; they only concern themselves with futures which are five or ten or fifteen or twenty years away, and within these brief spaces their imaginations are confined to segments of the world. They think about particular resources, about particular regions, about particular educational outcomes or particular economic variables such as gross national product or per capita income. The intellectuals' tradition, which is heir to much of the tradition of revolution, faces a different and more difficult task.

This revolutionary tradition has tended to think of a total order of life at the end of time, of a condition totally different from the present, running on indefinitely. The distance to be traversed is maximal; action might reduce to an instant the time which must pass before it is brought to realization.

Governments, unless they are severely demoralized and extremely disorganized, are forced by the pressures of the incumbency of office to think about the tasks which are imposed on them, which their constituents or subjects force on them or which the culture of their age and the professional traditions of their personnel generate.

They might do poorly what they undertake but they cannot evade the actual responsibility for doing things which must show short-term results. They have at their disposal whatever resources their societies can provide, but since the resources must come from a stock which might otherwise be used by private individuals or subgroups of the society who are therefore "paying" for the immediate future, governments must think of the costs of their actions more than outside critics must do.

Revolutionaries, and especially those who without being revolutionaries inherit some of the revolutionary tradition and express it in criticism of their society, have a more difficult situation with which to deal. They do not exist within an organization in which the very incumbency of office provides tasks involving the management of society. As outsiders they have no resources for organizing the future condition. Not being politicians, who must make the various groups in society pay for the installation of the future and who must receive their consent or toleration, they need not think of the renunciations which will have to be made. What the revolutionaries aspire to do is to get into the position which the government occupies so that they can avail themselves of its resources—but for the time being they have nothing except their beliefs and sentiments to drive them onward, and beliefs and sentiments are insufficient to impose discipline of judgment. The revolutionaries' beliefs are beliefs about the positive potentialities of the future and occasionally detailed images of what the future will be like. They are not beliefs about what will have to be paid to get there.

Revolutionary critics of the existing society in America or Britain or France or Western Germany or any other advanced country, or those who, without being revolutionary, inherit these traditions, are therefore very handicapped in the performance even of their traditional functions. The handicaps lie both in the loss of persuasiveness of their earlier images of the future—even more fundamentally in their loss of conviction about the positive potentialities of the future—and in the fact that governments also have begun to think about the future in a competitive way.

We are thus in the paradoxical situation in which we have become more conscious of the coming of the future and at the same time the shape of the future is more opaque or appalling. Holding operations and straightening of the line rather than offensives into or conquests of the future seem to be the order of the day.

This loss of confidence in the image of the future contained or implied in the revolutionary tradition is a large part of what is meant by the end of ideology. This situation is an untenable and unsatisfactory one. The future is not rendered impossible because some people have ceased to believe in the certainty or desirability of a future they once predicted. Nor is the human race going to give up its preoccupations with the future. No society can live exclusively in the present. Sentiments about and images of past and future, near and remote, are essential in the constitution of the mind. It is certainly difficult for me to believe that the thousands of years of life of Western traditions, of theological and humane reveries about the future, can have left a precipitate so faint that they will not continue to shape the inherent propensity to think of the future.

Furthermore, our growing scientific accomplishment and pride make us think of the future. Arrogance about the powers of the disciplined imagination and intelligence and the expansion of the aspiration for a self-governing individuality extend the will to self-determination into the future.

III

It must be admitted that our success in prediction has not hitherto been great. There are scattered successes such as those of Herzen and Tocqueville about the future dominion of Russia and the United States. There are the anticipations of H. G. Wells. But there are not many. Most of our predictions are extrapolations of past trends. Our social sciences, whatever the chances for development in the future, have not sufficient achievement to their credit to render plausible their predictive statements, although if their present modes of work are legitimate, they may reasonably be expected to contribute to rendering the future more subject to prediction than it has been. The development of computers to deal with many series of data should be able, as is now possible in demography, to delineate a variety of plausible futures and to assert what is compatible with what else. It is, of course, quite likely, that the predictions made by very powerful analytical processes employed on vast quantities of well-ordered data might still turn out to be not very successful.

The future might well turn out to be impenetrably obscure over longer stretches of time. It is certainly so at present, just as it has always been, despite the readiness of men from the eighteenth century onward to say what it would turn out to be. The creative powers of man in science and technology and in religion—the very powers necessary for prediction and control—seem to be recalcitrant to prediction. It is conceivable that the creative powers of the species have reached an end and that after the further development of computers and of social science they will have become exhausted. There is no reason to think that this is so—certainly there are no grounds for thinking that these sciences are absorbing all the available genuinely creative powers of the human race or that they will do so in the foreseeable future. We may take it therefore that our predictive accomplishments will always remain imperfect. This should not, however, lead to the conclusion that no successful prediction at all will be possible within smaller stretches of time and within particular spheres of life.

Predictive exercises as embodied in contemporary techniques of planning and linear programming are bound to have a by-product at least as important as the predictions at which they aim—a rather equivocal undertaking in any case. Predictive exercises foster a mode of thinking about the future which requires that the preconditions of each subsequent stage be specified. In other words, the problem of what it will cost in resources is brought to the forefront of attention. If, for example, so and so many university students are to be produced by 1985, then it becomes imperative to determine how many children at anterior points in time must pass through high school, how many must pass through elementary school, how many teachers there must be in high schools and elementary schools, how much provision must be made in school buildings, equipment, administrators, etc. If it is desired to produce so and so many university graduates in particular fields such as medicine or engineering, then similar and more differentiated estimates must be made concerning the numbers of children and young people required in particular courses of study at the pre-university level, and the numbers of teachers of physics, biology, mathematics, etc., which will be required, and so forth. Constants like wastage rates at each stage, teaching techniques at each stage, must be constructed. There will be large margins of error at each stage and in the global predictions, but as experience is gained in the technique of such predictions, a precipitate of "cost consciousness" will be formed. Facility in thinking about the future, not in making global prophecies but in thinking the conditions (costs) under which particular goals can be attained, will develop.

The shorter the time span over which a determinative prediction is made, the greater the likelihood of its verification, its realization, and its accuracy. The concern of governments with shorter time spans and the presumably continuing feebleness of the antigovernmental, revolutionary, utopian predictions and determinations—for the reasons given in the first part of this paper—will render short-term determinative predictions and cost estimations more widely accepted. The need for futurity which many people feel and will feel increasingly—once the terror of the future diminishes—will be satisfied by these short-term determinative predictions.

There seems to me to be another reason for thinking that, quite apart from the discrediting of the traditional revolutionary orientation toward the future, orientations toward the remoter future will become less appealing. There is a growing realism about the variability of tastes and desires through time. Even if long-term predictions were demonstrably accurate, which they are not, it is now coming to be seen that each generation has its own tastes and that the tastes of the next generation neither are certain to be ours nor necessarily should be ours. To carry out a policy calling for thirty or forty years of continuous effort in the same direction requires also an iron-willed, invincibly ignorant elite of a long life span and unerring accuracy and control in the choice of its successors. The juvenocentric ethos of the times as well as experience of the foibles of dictatorships discourage efforts to saddle future generations with detailed long-range programs of earlier generations. They also discourage any impulse which we might have to entrust so much of our capital to schemes which will require the concurrence of the unborn for their fruition and which, if fruitful, will confer their outcomes on generations which might not regard them as appreciatively as our own generation does.

It is coming to be understood that there is no sense in sacrificing the present generation to future generations. Outcomes are too uncertain; future generations might not want what we think is good for them. The cost is too great to the paying generation, and the motives of those who would sacrifice the present generation to future ones have become profoundly suspect.

There is still another reason why we may expect a change in the attitude toward far-off goals, and their replacement by goals much closer to the present and more consensual. It was characteristic of far-off goals that, insofar as the technique of their realization was considered at all, only the additional exertion of those who affirmed the goals, and the dispossession or extermination of those who did not, seemed to be involved. The balancing of costs and benefits did not often enter. If the goal was worthwhile, then the problem of costs did not arise. This attitude was fostered by the alienated situation of the proponents of the remote goals—alienated whether they were outside the central institutional system or were in its key positions. The deprivations inflicted on others—loss of income, loss of opportunity, loss of liberty, or loss of life—were not taken into account except in an ecological sense, the way in which agriculturalists employing an insecticide might consider the effects on the insects at whom they aim their poisons. Since in the classic form it was believed that the resources for progress already existed but were being allocated and managed in a way which restricted their fruitfulness, it was only a matter of taking them away from those whose use of them restricted their productivity. Since their unjustified possessions had no moral status, there was no moral cost to their expropriation.

Modern society has seen an extension of the range of consensus, and this has affected the consiousness of costs. The attenuation of class conflict in the Marxian sense, the "bourgeoisification" of the proletariat, the incorporation of outcast elements into society—of which the Negro civil rights movement has been one very dramatic instance—all these and many others have testified to the trend toward a moral unification of society. The process is very imperfect at present, but it has advanced sufficiently to the point where it has made a difference. One of these differences is that those whose weakness in the past forced them to pay the price of progress have now begun to be considered. They have acquired a voice which compels itself to be heard, and those who recommend progress are now more inclined to hear their unspoken words when they are silent. Their losses must now be considered among the costs of progress, and its advantages must now be balanced against what they forego. The burdens which would be put upon them on behalf of very remote goals now seem to be less justifiable.

We may expect that in the next years preoccupation with the future will be preoccupation with relatively short-run futures. A good deal of that preoccupation will be found in government and expert circles. The preoccupation will be less prophetic than it was in the great age of revolution. It will be less global. It will be piecemeal and contextual—more concerned with particular problems but more concerned, too, with the ramifications and preconditions, over a wide area, of the alternative solutions to particular problems.

IV

What will be left, under these conditions, of the tradition of revolutionism? What will there be for critical intellectuals to do in a situation in which enthusiastic attachment to remote goals has been attenuated, when great expertise will be applied in the estimation of costs and benefits, and when much of the estimation will take place within governments? Do our Western societies stand in need of the traditional revolutionary ideological orientation? Do we need a renewal of ideology?

No simple, single answer is possible. In the first place a renewal of the ideology of Marxism seems most unlikely, even if it were desirable. It has been too thoroughly undermined by the realities of the Eastern European countries which were achieved under its auspices. Modern social science, all its niggling puniness and triviality notwithstanding, has diminished it, eroded it, and disclosed the crudity of its way of seeing things. No other equally comprehensive, systematic, "scientific-ethical" ideology, oriented toward action and appropriate to an alienated outsider's position, is available. The depth of the imprint left by Marxism, with its long history in which many strong personalities have collaborated, is so great that no alternative ideology seems capable of emerging and claiming credence. No alternative arising from a different source appears to be in germination. No fully grown alternative exists.

Although a yearning for such an ideology does exist, I do not think that the yearning is very widespread or deeply rooted. To some extent the yearning is to be found among those who retain an ideological frame of thought from which the Marxist picture has been removed. The tradition of ideology has become so associated with vigorous criticism of existing social arrangements that some of those who practice the latter think that they should also acquire the former.

This ideology-less situation which obtains at present need not persist. Some new variant of an ideology with a Marxist ingredient— it is hard to think of one entirely without it, so deeply engrained has it become in the tradition of stringent criticism of society—might well arise again. What could be the calling of such an ideology?

As an ideology it would probably be doomed, like all ideologies, to be broken by experience and attenuated by its subsequent recipients, who do not share the impulsions of its originators. But like Marxism, it might color the moral tone of its time and heighten sensibility to the imperfections of society. It might be effective through pointing out deficiencies and, by exaggerating them, make sensitive people aware of the defects of their society and cause them to try to find remedies.

Ideologies are only accentuations and intensifications of certain elements in existing patterns of value orientation. There is no reason why the proponents of an ideology of diminished intensity—which is therefore in that sense less of an ideology—cannot be in a continuing dialogue with the protagonists of the central institutional and value system in a way which Marxism was only very infrequently and yet not entirely ineffectively. It is only in its more Manichaean phases that an ideology cuts its proponents off from effective dialogue with the rest of their society. If the intensity of an ideology is moderate, its alienating power is checked. Its carriers then become and act as members of the civil polity and they thereby contribute to the moral vitality of the center of their society.

There is another sense in which the proponents of ideology have a part to play if they can avoid the tendencies in ideology toward alienation from the central institutional system and toward the global Manichaeism which accepts nothing short of perfection and which regards all else as worthless. These features of the ideological orientation arouse antagonism and disrupt communication. Yet communication between a comprehensive, ethically sensitive, realistic, and informed outlook and a specialized, technical expertise is a necessity to the humanity of our contemporary and prospectively emerging societies.

The cost-and-benefit-calculating welfare state which is now coming into being has called and will continue to call for a high degree of professional expertise. The process has been in movement for decades now in our society and it has been strengthened by the growth of science, the multiplication of its literature, and the creation of numerous fields of specialized study and practice. These taken together with the decay or inanity of American secondary school education and the flaccidity of the undergraduate courses of study in most colleges and universities, especially in the humanistic and social science disciplines, have resulted in the present situation. This situation is one of high professional proficiency in many fields, each talking to itself; a highbrow, more or less literary-political culture tinctured by Marxism, isolated from the rest of the culture and fearful of contamination by it, and also speaking only to itself; and over all this a layer of unserious philistinism.

One of the major features of American intellectual life in the present century is the attrition of the "educated public." The emptiness and then specialization of education are its major causes. One of the consequences is the absence of an informed, matter-of-fact sense of responsibility for the whole society. The intellectuals outside the more specialized technological professions have not remedied this deficiency although they are the recipients of a tradition of general culture and a widely ranging concern. The alienation of American literary and academic intellectuals from American public life is a phenomenon of long standing, but it too has been aggravated by specialization. The reception of Marxism furthered this lack of interest in the whole and in the proximate future.

Marxism contains a global view of society but it rejects the concern for particular changes in the proximate future in favor of an uncompromising espousal of an ultimate and "total transformation." The totality with which it is seriously concerned is located remotely in the future. The critical and solicitous care for the whole in the proximate future must be the charge which American intellectuals take on themselves if American society is not to become the victim of the parochial preoccupations of specialized technological experts. If academic social scientists and freelance publicistic or amateur social scientists are not analysts on behalf of the whole society over the reasonably foreseeable future, no one else will be.

Specialists do estimate certain costs of social change. They calculate the costs of any policy in terms of the variables with which those who are expert in its promulgation and administration deal. Specialists in education estimate the financial costs of increasing the school population and the school teaching staff. They are less qualified and less interested in the ramifications of an increase in the number of schoolteachers, in what this does to the family life of women teachers who return to service or to the supply of persons for other professions such as research scientists or laboratory technicians. This is only a trivial illustration of the tasks which run beyond the jurisdiction of specialists in our society.

Authority has always to be scrutinized; its policies must be assessed with respect to the worthwhileness of its goals and of the ends to which these goals contribute, and the costs of pursuing those policies must be scrutinized. It must always be asked whether there are less costly ways of attaining the same end, assuming for the moment that the end is acceptable or desirable.

Insight into the complexity of society, the interdependence of its parts, the elements which foster its cohesion and cleavages, the mechanisms by which the past lives into the present and survives in the future, are essential to an effective concern with the whole. The present situation calls for a prudence which assumes custodianship for the protection of traditions and which is at the same time continuously ready to initiate, encourage, and support courses of action contrary to the prescriptions of tradition.

Our cities are the unintended consequences of numerous particular paths of action which seemed reasonable to those who traversed them, but have the disagreeable results which we see; and our society as a whole shows the defects arising from the same pattern. No one looks after the whole. Planning is only part of the solution to these difficulties. No government, however virtuous and devoted to the common good, can or should be entrusted with the exclusive care for that good. Governments are pluralistic internally as well as responsive to the conflicting pressures of a pluralistic society. Of course compromises among the special interests of government departments and of private groups are necessary for a good society, but often these compromises are made at the expense of weaker groups or of values for which no single group or coalition of groups cares sufficiently to insist upon.

There should, if our society is to be improved, be groups or circles who are concerned to protect not only the weak but the whole society and the values which are not the particular interest of any group. It is desirable for some to concentrate on the weak so that they can be made stronger and able to look after their own interests. But that is no solution to the problem of the interests of the entire society and to the cognate problem of criticizing and guiding government in its role as implementer and compromiser of departmental and private interests.

Who is to do this? Who can serve as the conscience and

intelligence of the whole? Everyone should do it to some extent, but this cannot be counted on. The higher judiciary has the power to serve as the conscience of the country and to some extent it has done so. The legal profession has the knowledge which would enable it to be the intelligence of our society and the rhetoric to be the conscience too, but the prizes offered by the service of private interests and to a lesser extent of government limit the fruitfulness of its activity in this respect. Newspaper and television journalists can and to some extent do—and sometimes brilliantly and courageously—but the level of American mass communications inhibits and deflects them. With this we are brought back to the academic and amateur social scientists—highbrow journalists, literary critics, novelists, even poets—those who are interested in society in a disinterested way, who have no significant interests other than an intellectual and moral interest in the way in which contemporary society works.

The difficulties in the assumption of this responsibility are several and serious. Many of the academic social scientists are narrowly specialized, and their objects of study are often—but not invariably—trivial. They live, moreover, in narrowly constricted circles. They write for journals and reviews which they and few others look at and they often write in a laborious way which is difficult for laymen to assimilate. Furthermore, many of them with interest in the global society are the recipients of an alienated and unrealistic tradition which hides reality from them and makes them indifferent to the present except as evidence of its own worthlessness.

Nonetheless, the scene is not homogeneous. There has always been a current of American social science concerned with the immediate and proximate problems of American society. From the Great Depression onward, the perspective within which this tradition has operated has broadened and become more sophisticated. It has, moreover, come to accept itself as part of American society, a little detached from it by its university position but feeling responsible for its possible future courses and the moral criteria for choosing and judging those alternatives. Increasingly it has come into the public arena. What it lacks above all are organs through which its rhetoric can be formed by expression and its judgment sharpened by dialogue.

The amateur social scientists suffer, many of them, from a different sort of isolation. Their isolation is more like a holier-than-thou attitude, which has grown from a highbrow aversion for the vulgarity of American life and a persisting adherence to a Marxist ideology in which they scarcely any longer believe but for which they have no acceptable substitute.

I think that they are wrong to await or seek a substitute ideology.

They ought to renounce, insofar as it is possible for them to do so, the belief that total transformation is the standard by which every action or policy must be judged. They should renounce their belief in the feasibility of long-term predictions and intentions. They should retain their ethical sensitivity and their sensitivity to the entire society. Freed from their belief that one particular class is the repository of virtue and promise and that it alone can be the agent of significant progress, but still attached to the idea of a better society, the unspecialized character of their knowledge provides a matrix in which a genuinely valuable civility can grow. In partnership with the academic social scientists, they could constitute the forum of assessment which American society needs.

11 Mass Society and its Culture

A new order of society has taken form since the end of World War I in the United States, above all, but also in Great Britain, France, Northern Italy, the Low and Northern European countries, and Japan. Some of its features have begun to appear in Eastern and Central Europe, though in a less even manner; more incipiently and prospectively so in Asian and African countries. It is the style to refer to this new order as the "mass society."

This new order of society, despite all its internal conflicts, discloses in the individual a greater sense of attachment to the society as a whole, and of affinity with his fellows. As a result, perhaps for the first time in history, large aggregations of human beings living over an extensive territory have been able to enter into relatively free and uncoerced association.

The new society is a mass society precisely in the sense that the mass of the population has become incorporated *into* society. The center of society—the central institutions, and the central value systems which guide and legitimate these institutions—has extended its boundaries. Most of the population (the "mass") now stands in a closer relationship to the center than has been the case in either premodern societies or in the earlier phases of modern society. In previous societies, a substantial portion of the population, often the majority, were born and forever remained "outsiders."

The mass society is a new phenomenon, but it has been long in gestation. The idea of the *polis* is its seed, nurtured and developed in the Roman idea of a common citizenship extending over a wide territory. The growth of nationality in the modern era has heightened the sense of affinity among the members of different classes and regions of the same country. When the proponents of the modern idea of the nation put forward the view that life on a contiguous, continuous, and common territory—beyond all divisions of kinship, caste, and religious belief—united the human beings living within that territory into a single collectivity, and when they made a common language the evidence of that membership, they committed themselves, not often wittingly, to the mass society.

An important feature of that society is the diminished sacredness of authority, the reduction in the awe it evokes and in the charisma

An abridged version of an article previously published in *Daedalus*, vol. 89, no. 2, pp. 288-314. Reprinted by permission from *Daedalus*, Journal of the American Academy of Arts and Sciences, Boston, Massachusetts.

attributed to it. This diminution in the status of authority runs parallel to a loosening of the power of tradition. Naturally, tradition continues to exert influence, but it becomes more open to divergent interpretations, and these frequently lead to divergent courses of action.

The dispersion of charisma from the center outward has manifested itself in a greater stress on individual dignity and individual rights. This extension does not always reach into the sphere of the political, but it is apparent in the attitudes toward women, youth, and ethnic groups which have been in a disadvantageous position.

Following from this, one of the features of mass society I should like to emphasize is its wide dispersion of "civility." The concept of civility is not a modern creation, but it is in the mass society that it has found its most complete (though still very incomplete) realization. The very idea of a *citizenry* coterminous with the adult population is one of its signs. So is the moral equalitarianism which is a trait unique to the West, with its insistence that by virtue of their sharing membership in the community and a common tongue men possess a certain irreducible dignity.

None of these characteristic tendencies of mass society has attained anything like full realization. The moral consensus of mass society is certainly far from complete; the mutual assimilation of center (i.e., the elite) and periphery (i.e., the mass) is still much less than total. Class conflict, ethnic prejudice, and disordered personal relations prevent the tendencies I have described from exceeding a historically unprecedented but still very limited degree of realization.

Mass society is an industrial society. Without industry, i.e., without the replacement of simple tools by complicated machines, mass society would be inconceivable. Modern industrial techniques, through the creation of an elaborate network of transportation and communication, bring the various parts of mass society into frequent contact. Modern technology has liberated man from the burden of physically exhausting labor, and has given him resources through which new experiences of sensation, conviviality, and introspection have become possible. True, modern industrial organization has also been attended by a measure of hierarchical and bureaucratic organization which often runs contrary to the vital but loose consensus of mass society. Nonetheless, the fact remains that modern mass society has reached out toward a moral consensus and a civil order congruous with the adult population. The sacredness that every man possesses by virtue of his membership in society finds a more far-reaching affirmation than ever before.

Mass society has aroused and enhanced individuality. Individuality is characterized by an openness to experience, an efflorescence of sensation and sensibility, a sensitivity to other minds and personalities. It gives rise to and lives in, personal attachments; it grows from the expansion of the empathic capacities of the human being. Mass society has liberated the cognitive, appreciative, and moral capacities of individuals. Larger elements of the population have consciously learned to value the pleasures of eye, ear, taste, touch, and conviviality. People make choices more freely in many spheres of life, and these choices are not necessarily made for them by tradition, authority, or scarcity. The value of the experience of personal relationships is more widely appreciated.

These observations are not meant to imply that individuality as developed in mass society exists universally. A part of the population in mass society lives in a nearly vegetative torpor, reacting dully or aggressively to its environment. Nonetheless, the search for individuality and its manifestations in personal relations are distinctly present in mass society and constitute one of its essential features.

The Culture of Mass Society

The fundamental categories of cultural life are the same in all societies. In all the different strata of any given society, the effort to explore and explain the universe, to understand the meaning of events, to enter into contact with the sacred or to commit sacrilege, to affirm the principles of morality and justice and to deny them, to encounter the unknown, to exalt or denigrate authority, to stir the senses by the control of and response to words, sounds, shapes, and colors—these are the basic elements of cultural existence. There are, however, profound variations in the elaboration of these elements, for human beings show marked differences in capacity for expression and reception.

No society can ever achieve a complete cultural consensus: there are natural limitations to the spread of the standards and products of superior culture throughout society. The tradition of refinement is itself replete with antinomies, and the nature of creativity adds to them. Creativity is a modification of tradition. Furthermore, the traditional transmission of superior culture inevitably stirs some to reject and deny significant parts of it just because it is traditional. More fundamental than the degrees of creativity and alienation is the disparity in human cognitive, appreciative, and moral capacities. This disparity produces marked differences in the apprehension of tradition, in the complexity of the response to it, and in the substance of the judgments aroused by it.

Thus a widely differentiated "dissensus" has become stabilized in the course of history. The pattern of this "dissensus" is not inevitably unchanging. The classes consuming culture can diminish in number, their taste can deteriorate, their standards become less discriminating or more debased. On the other hand, as the mass of the population comes alive, when its curiosity and sensibility and its moral responsiveness are aroused, it begins to become capable of more subtle perception, more appreciative of the more general elements in a concrete representation, and more complex in its aesthetic reception and expression.

For present purposes, we shall employ a very rough distinction among three levels of culture, which are levels of quality measured by aesthetic, intellectual, and moral standards. These are "superior" or "refined" culture, "mediocre" culture, and "brutal" culture.[1]

Superior or refined culture is distinguished by the seriousness of its subject matter, i.e., the centrality of the problems with which it deals, the acute penetration and coherence of its perceptions, the subtlety and wealth of its expressed feeling. The stock of superior culture includes the great works of poetry, novels, philosophy, scientific theory and research, statues, paintings, musical compositions and their performance, the texts and performance of plays, history, economic, social, and political analyses, architecture, and works of craftsmanship. It goes without saying that the category of superior culture does not refer to the social status, i.e., the social status of the authors or of the consumers of the works in question, but only to their truth and beauty.

The category of mediocre culture includes works which, whatever the aspiration of their creators, do not measure up to the standards employed in judging works of superior culture. Mediocre culture is less original than superior culture; it is more reproductive; it operates largely in the same genres as superior culture, but also in certain relatively novel genres not yet fully incorporated into superior culture, such as the musical comedy. This may be a function of the nature of the genre or of the fact that the genre has not yet attracted great talent to its practice.

1. I have reservations about the use of the term "mass culture," because it refers simultaneously to the substantive and qualitative properties of the culture, to the social status of its consumers, and to the media by which it is transmitted. Because of this at least threefold reference, it tends to beg some important questions regarding the relations among the three variables. For example, the current conception of "mass culture" does not allow for the fact that in most countries, and not just at present, very large sections of the elite consume primarily mediocre and brutal culture. It also begs the important questions as to whether the mass media can transmit works of superior culture, or whether the genres developed by the new mass media can become the occasions of creativity and therewith a part of superior culture. Also, it does not consider the obvious fact that much of what is produced in the genres of superior culture is mediocre. At present I have no satisfactory set of terms to distinguish the three levels of cultural objects. I have toyed with "high," "refined," "elaborate," "genuine," or "serious"; "vulgar," "mediocre," or "middle"; and "low," "brutal," "base," or "coarse." None of these words succeeds either in felicity or aptness.

At the third level is brutal culture, where symbolic elaboration is of a more elementary order. Some of the genres on this level are identical with those of mediocre and refined culture (pictorial and plastic representation, music, poems, novels, and stories) but they also include games, spectacles (such as boxing and horse racing), and more directly expressive actions with a minimal symbolic content. The depth of penetration is almost always negligible, subtlety is almost entirely lacking, and a general grossness of sensitivity and perception is a common feature.

The greatest difference among the three levels of culture, apart from intrinsic quality, is the tremendous disparity in the richness of the stock available in any society at any given time. What any given society possesses is not only what it creates in its own generation but also what it has received from antecedent generations and from earlier and contemporaneous generations of other societies. Superior culture is immeasurably richer in content because it contains not only superior contemporary production but also much of the refined production of earlier epochs. Mediocre culture tends to be poorer not only because of the poorer quality of what it produces in its own generation but because these cultural products have a relatively shorter life span. Nevertheless, mediocre culture contains much that has been created in the past. The boundaries between mediocre and superior culture are not so sharp, and the custodians of superior culture are not so discriminating, as always to reject the mediocre. Furthermore, a considerable amount of mediocre culture retains value over long periods; and even though mediocre taste varies, as does superior taste, there are stable elements in it, too, so that some of the mediocre culture of the past continues to find an appreciative audience.

At the lowest cultural level, where the symbolic content is most impoverished and where there is very little original creation in each generation, we come again to a great, if much less self-conscious, dependence on the past. Games, jokes, spectacles, and the like continue traditional patterns with little consciousness of their traditionality. If the traditional element in brutal culture has been large, this is due to the relatively low creative capacities of those who produce and consume it. Here, until recently, there has been little professional production, machinery for preservation and transmission is lacking, and oral transmission plays a greater part in maintaining traditions of expression and performance than with superior and mediocre cultures.

The quantity of culture consumed in mass society is certainly greater than in any other epoch, even if we make proper allowance for the larger populations of the mass societies at present. It is especially at the levels of mediocre and brutal culture that an immense expansion has occurred, but the consumption of superior culture has also increased.

The grounds for this great increase, and for the larger increase in the two lower categories, are not far to seek. The most obvious are greater availability, increased leisure time, the decreased physical demands of work, the greater affluence of the classes which once worked very hard for long hours for small income, increased literacy, enhanced individuality, and more unabashed hedonism. In all these, the middle and the lower classes have gained more than have the elites (including the intellectuals, whatever their occupational distribution).

The consumption of superior culture has increased, too, but not as much as the other two categories, because the intellectual classes were more nearly saturated before the age of mass society. Moreover, the institutions of superior culture—the collections of connoisseurs, academies, universities, libraries, publishing houses, periodicals—were more elaborately and more continuously established in the pre-mass society than were the institutions which made mediocre and brutal culture available to their consumers.

Thus in mass society the proportion of the total stock of cultural objects held by superior culture has shrunk, and correspondingly the share of mediocre and brutal culture has grown.[2]

Note on the Value of Mediocre and Brutal Culture

Mediocre culture has many merits. It often has elements of genuine conviviality, not subtle or profound perhaps, but genuine in the sense of being spontaneous and honest. It is often very good fun. Moreover, it is often earnestly, even if simply, moral. Mediocre culture has its traditions too; many of the dramas and stories which regale the vulgar have a long history hidden from those who tell and enjoy them. Like anything traditional, they express something essential in human life, and expunging them would expunge the accumulated wisdom of ordinary men and women, their painfully developed art of coping with the miseries of existence, their routine pieties and their decent pleasures.

There is much ridicule of kitsch, and it *is* ridiculous. Yet it represents aesthetic sensibility and aesthetic aspiration, untutored, rude, and deformed. The very growth of kitsch, and of the demand which has generated the industry for the production of kitsch, is an

2. This change in the relative shares of the three levels of culture has been distorted by contrast with the preceding epochs. The cultural life of the consumers of mediocre and brutal culture was relatively silent, unseen by the intellectuals. The immense advances in audibility and visibility of the two lower levels of culture is one of the most noticeable traits of mass society. This is in turn intensified by another trait of mass society, i.e., the enhanced mutual awareness of different sectors of the society.

indication of a crude aesthetic awakening in classes which previously accepted what was handed down to them or who had practically no aesthetic expression and reception.

The Reproduction and Transmission of Culture

In medieval society, the church and, in a less effective and more limited degree, the schools (which were immediate or indirect adjuncts of the church) brought the culture of the center into the peripheral areas of a very loosely integrated society.[3] Protestantism and printing led to a pronounced change, which showed the direction of the future. The cheapened access to the printed word and the spread of a minimal literacy (which became nearly universal within European societies only at the beginning of the present century) resulted in an expansion of each of the three strata of culture. In this expansion, the chief beneficiaries were mediocre and brutal culture.

The increased wealth, leisure, and literacy of the lower classes, and the flowering of hedonism which these permitted, would undoubtedly have produced the great expansion in mediocre and brutal—as well as superior—culture consumption, even without the further technological developments of communication in the twentieth century. This technological development did, however, supply a mighty additional impetus. The popular press of the last decades of the nineteenth century showed the way. The development of new methods of graphic reproduction in lithography and in both still and moving pictures, new methods of sound recording, and the transmission of sound and picture increased the flow of communication from the center to the periphery. Where previously the custodians of superior culture and its mediocre variants had nearly a monopoly— through their quasi-monopoly of the institutions of transmission— the new methods of mass communication have transformed the situation.

The quest for a larger audience, which would make it feasible to obtain a subsidy (in the form of advertising) to cover the difference between what the consumers pay and what it costs to produce cultural objects, has been of the greatest importance to the interrelations of the various strata of culture. The dependence of the subsidy on greatly extended consumption would in itself require a reaching out toward a heterogeneous audience. The increased overhead of communication enterprises in television, for example, as compared with book printing, has intensified the need for large and heterogeneous audiences.

3. A society which was far less "organic" in its structure and outlook than the critics of modern society allege, and less "organic" also than the modern society, which is so unsympathetically assailed by these critics.

Before the emergence of the most recent forms of mass communication, with their very large capital requirements, each stratum of culture had its own channels and institutions. As long as books were the chief means of impersonal cultural transmission, the cultural segregation of the classes could be easily maintained. The drive toward a maximum audience has helped change this, and the change has had momentous repercussions. The magazine is the embodiment of this new development. The form of the magazine is an eighteenth-century phenomenon; but the enlargement of its role in the reproduction and transmission of culture is the product of the latter-day need to gain the maximum audience, one in its turn impelled by the economic necessity of the subsidy. To speak to the largest possible audience, it has been necessary to make the content of what is transmitted in a single issue as heterogeneous as the audience sought.

The general principle of providing something for everyone in the family became well established in the first decades of the popular press. The principle was developed to the point where every class which could possibly increase the total audience was offered something. This principle has not succeeded in dominating the entire field. There are still specialized organs and institutions which seek to please only one particular stratum of consumers, and in Europe the tradition of a unitary public still persists—but even there not without making very substantial concessions to the new principle. Even the universities (which do not necessarily seek large numbers) in Europe, although not as much as in America, have diversified their programs in order to meet the diversified demand. In popular periodicals like *Time, Life, Look, Picture Post, Paris-Match, Der Spiegel, Esquire,* and in distinguished daily newspapers like *The New York Times* and recently, in a cumbersome way, *The Times* of London, there has been an intermixture of superior, mediocre, and brutal culture which is historically unique. The same can be observed in television and, of course, in the film: a single network presents a wide variety of levels, and films of genuinely high artistic and intellectual merit may be produced in the same studio which produces numerous mediocre and brutal films.

The Consumption of Culture

In modern society, the number of consumers of superior culture has never been very large; in premodern societies, it was even smaller. The chief consumers of works of superior culture are the intellectuals, i.e., those whose occupations require intellectual preparation and, in practice, the application of high intellectual skills. In the contemporary world this category includes university teachers, scientists, university students, writers, artists, secondary-school teachers, members of the learned professions (law, medicine, and the church), journalists, and higher civil servants, as well as a scattering of businessmen, engineers, and army officers.

Outside the intellectual occupations, where the largest numbers are found, the consumers of superior culture are spread thin and at random. This situation has probably never been different, even in periods when the princes of the church were patrons of painting and sculpture, or when in most grand bourgeois households one could find sets of Goethe, Nietzsche, Fielding, the memoirs of Sully, or the letters of Mme de Sévigné.

The political, technological, military, ecclesiastical, and economic elites have not usually been intellectuals, even though some of them have had intellectual training and followed intellectual careers before entering their particular profession. Politician and intellectual come closest to each other in regimes just established by revolution or by a successful nationalist movement (their quality as intellectuals, however, is usually not particularly distinguished). In established political regimes, although there may be a significant number of politicians who were once intellectuals of a respectable level, over a long period the demands of the profession of politics leave little time, strength or sensitivity for the continued consumption of intellectual goods.

Among the leading Western countries, it is in the United States that the political elite gives a preponderant impression of indifference toward works of superior culture. The situation is probably not very different in Great Britain, France, Germany, or Italy—though in those countries the political elite, living amidst aristocratic and patrician traditions, possesses an external gloss of intimacy with high culture. In the United States, however, despite Woodrow Wilson, Franklin Roosevelt, the Plutarch-reading Harry Truman, and the *De re metallica*-editing Herbert Hoover, the political elite gives a definitely unintellectual impression.

The same is true of the American plutocracy. As a body of collectors of the works of painting and sculpture and as patrons of learning, some wealthy Americans will take an outstanding place in the history of the great Maecenases; yet the dominant impression is one of indifference and inhospitality to intellectual work. The great industrial system of the United States has required a large corps of engineers and applied scientists, men of great imagination, and even high creativity; yet their cultural consumption (not only of superior culture but also of mediocre culture) is rather small. The vigor and preeminence of these sectors of the American elite, and the conventions of the media of information through which their public image is formed, fortify intellectuals with the sense that they alone in their society are concerned with superior culture.

Among the middle classes the consumption of the traditional genres of superior culture is not large. Popular periodicals, best-selling novels, political books of transient interest, inferior poetry, inspirational works of theology and moral edification, and bio-graphies—these made up and still make up the bulk of their consumption. More recently, the films and radio, and most recently, television, have provided the substance of their cultural consumption. Their fare is largely philistine—mediocre culture and brutal culture. Nonetheless, because of exposure to the "mass media," e.g., periodicals like *Life* and a narrow band of the output on television, film, and radio, a larger section of these classes has come into contact with and consumed a larger quantity of extrareligious, superior culture than has been the case throughout the course of modern history.

Finally, the industrial working class and the rural population remain to be considered. Together, these classes consume almost nothing of the inheritance and current production of superior culture. Very little mediocre culture of the conventional genres reaches them except in such periodicals as *Life, Look,* and the *Reader's Digest*. Much of their culture as transmitted by mass media is brutal—crime films and television spectacles, paperbacks of vio-lence, pornographic oral and printed literature, and the culture of the world of sports.

It would be a mistake, however, to think that the culture possessed by these classes is exhausted by what comes to them through the mass media. A large amount of traditional religious culture (and of sectarian variants of traditional religious culture) flourishes in all the nonintellectual classes. Much of regional and class culture, maintained by family, by colleagues, neighbors, and friends, and by local institutions, survives and is unlikely to be supplanted by the larger culture which emanates from the center. The places limits on what is incorporated from the current flow of the mass media.[4]

A special stratum of the population that cuts across all classes and gives a particular tone to mass society is the younger generation, the maligned and bewildering "youth." The coming forth of youth in contemporary society rests on primordial foundations which exist in all societies. In most societies, however, the institutional structure and the niggardliness of nature have kept youth in check. In modern times, romanticism and increased wealth and (more deeply) the expanding radius of empathy and fellow-feeling have given youth

4. Also, it should be added, this persistence of traditional and orally transmitted culture renders fruitless the effort to diagnose the dispositions and outlook of a people by analyzing what is presented to them through films, television, radio, the press, etc.

opportunities never before available. The enhanced productivity of the economy of Western countries has, on the one hand, allowed young people to remain outside the hard grind of work for a longer time; it has given them opportunities to earn and spend substantial individual incomes. The resulting cultural manifestations are largely responsible for what is called "mass culture."

Before the advent of mass society, a small proportion of the youth were rigorously inculcated with superior culture; the rest were exposed to the brutal culture of their seniors. It is one of the marks of mass society, however, that youth has become a major consumer of the special variants of mediocre and brutal culture that are produced for transmission through the mass media. An extraordinary quantity of popular music, mediocre and brutal films, periodical literature, and forms of dance is produced for and consumed by youth. This is something unprecedented, and this is the heart of the revolution of mass culture.

Most of the "youthful mass" comes from strata of society which have had little connection except through religious education with high or superior culture. Not yet enmeshed in the responsibilities of family and civic life, and with much leisure time and purchasing power, youth constitutes both an eager and a profitable public, which attracts the attention of the mass media. Where the political elite does not grant this eagerness the right of direct expression, but seeks instead to divert it into ideological channels or to dam it up, it still remains powerful and indomitable. Where the political order allows this passionate and uncultivated vitality to find a free expression, the result is what we see throughout the Western world.

The Production of Culture

A differentiated creative intelligentsia is the oldest stratum of Western society with a set of continuous traditions. Such a stratum still exists today, far broader than ever before, far more extended, and with international ties exceeding that of any other section of our or any other society.[5] There is today more internal specialization than in the past: it is impossible for any one man to be fully conversant with the inherited and currently produced stock of cultural objects. The productive intelligentsia is perhaps less intensely like-minded now than in the past, when it was smaller and the body of what it had to master was smaller. Nonetheless, despite changes in society, in the modes of financial support, and in the

5. The internationality of the medieval church and of the European aristocracy in the eighteenth century was thin and parochial in comparison with the scope and intensity of that exhibited by present-day intellectual classes.

organization of intellectual life, this creative stratum is constantly reproducing and increasing.

The modern age, however, has seen growing up alongside this creative intelligentsia a much larger stratum of producers of mediocre culture. In the seventeenth and eighteenth centuries, when letters and the arts began to offer the possibilities of a professional career, thanks to the advance of printing and to an enlarging public, there emerged, besides those whose creative capacities achieved the heights of greatness, a wider group of writers, artists, and scholars. From these were recruited the residents of Grub Street, who while still trying to reach the highest levels, had to live by producing for a less discriminating public. The nineteenth century saw the stabilization of the profession of mediocre culture. The popular press, the film, radio, and television have deepened and extended their ranks. The enlargement of university populations and the corresponding increase in the number of university teachers, the increased opportunities for careers in research, in the applied natural and social sciences, have similarly added to the producers of mediocre culture.[6]

The professional practitioner with a mediocre culture has developed traditions, models, and standards of his own. More frequently than in the past he engages directly in the professional production of mediocre culture without first essaying the production of works of superior culture. He can attain an excellence within his own field that often brings him satisfaction and esteem. Indeed, in certain genres of mediocre culture that are new or at least relatively new, he can reach heights of unprecedented excellence, to the point where, if the genre is admissible, his work can take on the lineaments of superior cultural achievement.

Yet despite this approximation to autonomy, the autonomy remains incomplete. The producer of mediocre culture is exposed to the standards of superior culture, and he cannot entirely escape their pressure. If he prospers, and his colleagues on the level of superior culture do not, then he is guilt-ridden for having 'betrayed" higher standards for the sake of the fleshpots.

This troubling juxtaposition of two consciences is rendered more acute by the physical juxtaposition of the two levels of cultural objects and the social contact of their producers in the media through which mediocre culture chiefly finds its audience, namely, the media of mass communication. The professionals of mediocre

6. The increase in numbers of persons in intellectual occupations and those that require intellectual training might well be pressing hard against the supply. The supply of high talent is limited; improved methods of selection and training can somewhat increase it, but they cannot make it limitless or coterminous with the population of any society. Hence, as the numbers expand, modern societies are forced to admit many persons whose endowments are such as to permit only a mediocre performance in the creation and reproduction of cultural works.

culture cannot, even if they would, forget the standards of superior culture, because they mix with persons who often attain them, because the media from time to time present works composed according to those standards, and because critics continually refer to them. These factors provide an increasing stimulus to an awareness of and a concern for high standards, even when they are not observed.

The producers of brutal culture confront a quite different situation. They have neither a similarly compelling historical past nor the connections with superior culture which their "colleagues" in the field of mediocre culture possess. They do not, so far as I know, justify their performance by reference to the great masters of their art. There are some exceptions among crime-story writers, boxers, jockeys, and certainly among a few of the best sports writers. But these are new professions. Their practitioners feel no continuity with their forerunners, even though the objects they produce have been produced for a long time. Brutal culture therefore has only recently developed a differentiated professional personnel.

Brutal culture has not shown great potentialities for development. Nonetheless, certain genres of brutal culture have produced works of great excellence, so that these reach through mediocre culture into the outer confines of superior culture; some horror stories have done the same, as have the chronicles of sports. Since brutal culture is by no means restricted to the uncultivated classes for its audience, works of brutal culture which reach a form of high refinement also make their way upward, and with them their producers move in the same direction. In the main, however, there is a wall which separates the producers of brutal culture from the producers of superior culture. Even where they find the same audience, the tradition of superior culture is such as to erect a barrier to a massive interpenetration.[7]

A few words should be said here about another kind of cultural production: the anonymous production of folk art and literature and linguistic innovation. In its highest manifestation, the production of these arts was probably never very widely spread. They grew on the edge of craftsmanship, of religious worship, and of brutal entertainment. Considerable creative talents must have impelled them into existence. Their creators must have been men of genius, working with subterranean traditions that scarcely exist any more and that had only a small direct connection with the great

---

7. The bohemian sector of the high intelligentsia, past and present, is an exception to this generalization. The mingling of poets and cutpurses has a long and special history, which runs down to the contemporary highbrow glorification of the criminal-turned-author, the plain criminal and bank robber.

tradition of superior culture. Insofar as they were inspired by craftsmanship, machine production has greatly restricted their production; the traditions which sustained them have atrophied.

It is sometimes asserted that the anonymous cultural productivity of craftsmen and peasants in the Europe of the later Middle Ages and of early modern times has been destroyed by the growth of mass culture. This is possible, but it is not the only possibility. If we assume that the proportion of geniuses and outstandingly gifted intelligences and sensibilities in any population remains fairly constant (not an unreasonable assumption) and that modern Western societies with their increasing cultivation of science, literature, art, enterprise, administration, and technology have been drawing more and more on their reservoirs of talent, then it appears quite plausible to assert that the talents of the type once manifested in the anonymous productions of folk culture have been recruited and diverted into other spheres and are active at different levels of culture and social life.

The Position of Superior Culture in Mass Society

Has the culture created in the past fifty years—the approximate age of mass society—deteriorated as much as its detractors claim? The task of assessment is most difficult.

Let us for the moment grant that contemporary refined culture may be poorer than the superior culture produced in any comparable span of years in the past. There may be any number of reasons or causes, totally unrelated to the development and impact of mass society on culture. For example, the distribution and efflorescence of genius are matters that still await full understanding. It is conceivable, if unlikely, that our neural equipment is poorer than that of our ancestors. And even it is as good, it is also possible that our cultural traditions have passed their point of culmination, that they contain no possibilities of further development, that they offer no point of departure even for creative minds. Another important consideration is whether the alleged deterioration is being evaluated in the light of standards that are applied equally to other periods. We must be sure to comprehend in our assessment the whole range of intellectual and artistic activities. We must remember that the genius which is expressed in refined culture may be of diverse forms, and that it can flow into some domains in one age, and into other domains in other ages.

Yet these might be idle reflections. The evidence of decline is not by any means very impressive. In every field of science and scholarship into which so much of our contemporary genius flows (in physics, chemistry, and in mathematics, in comparative religion, in Sinology and Indology), outstanding work is being done, not only in the older centers not yet afflicted by the culture of mass society, but in the United States as well, that most massive of all mass societies. Linguistics seems to be in a more vital and powerful state than it has been for several centuries. Economics proceeds on a high level, higher on the average than in past periods; sociology, barbarous, rude, and so often trivial, offers at its best something which no past age can match in the way of discovery and penetration. In political philosophy, in which our decay is said to be so patent, we have no Aristotle, Hobbes, or Bentham, but there are probably only a half dozen such masters in all human history. On the other hand, in France and America, there are a few writers who are nearly as deep and rigorous in their analysis of central issues as John Stuart Mill or Walter Bagehot or Tocqueville were. In the novel, we have no Tolstoy, no Stendhal or Dostoievsky or Flaubert; still, the peaks of achievement are high. In poetry and in painting, there may indeed have been a falling-off from the great heights; in drama there is no Aeschylus, no Shakespeare, no Racine. But these are among the highest peaks of all human history, and the absence of any such from our two-thirds of a century can scarcely constitute evidence of a general decline in the quality of the products of superior culture in our own time.

That there is, however, a consciousness of decline is undeniable. Intellectuals are beset by a malaise, by a sense of isolation, of disregard, of a lack of sympathy. They feel they have lost contact with their audience, especially that more important of all audiences: those who rule society.

Puritanism, Provincialism, and Specialization

If the arguments of those who attribute to mass society the alleged misery of contemporary culture are not sound, there is no gainsaying the fact that the consumption of superior culture does not rest in a perfectly secure position in the United States. The culture of the educated classes, who in America as elsewhere should be its bearers, leaves much to be desired. One is distressed by the ignorance of university graduates, by the philistine distrust of or superciliousness toward superior culture which is exhibited by university professors in the humanities and social sciences or in the medical and law schools of this country and by journalists and broadcasters. The political, economic, military, and technological elites are no better. The near illiteracy of some of the better American newspapers, the oftentimes fatuous barbarism of our weeklies and our one widely circulated fortnightly, the unletteredness of many of our civil servants, the poverty of our bookshops, the vulgarity of our publishers (or at least those who write their jacket blurbs and their advertising copy) can give little comfort. The laudation of civil and sexual perversity among literary men and academics in the "human sciences" is no improvement on the philistinism which it has to some extent replaced.

There is undeniably much that is wrong with the quality of culture consumed by the more or less educated classes in America. Very little of what is wrong, however, can be attributed to the mass media, particularly to the films, television, radio, and popular magazines.

It is not that the cascade of mediocre and brutal culture which pours out over the mass media is admirable. Quite the contrary. The culture of the mass media is not, however, the reason that the distribution and consumption of superior culture disclose (alongside so many profoundly impressive achievements) many things that are repellent.

What is wrong, is wrong with our intellectuals and their institutions and with some of our cultural traditions, which have little to do with the culture created for and presented by the mass media.

The dour puritanism that looks on aesthetic expression as self-indulgence did not grow out of mass society. Nor does the complacent and often arrogant provincialism that distrusts refined culture because it believes it to be urban, Anglophile, and connected with a patrician upper class. America was not a mass society in the nineteenth century; it was a differentiated society in which pronounced equalitarian sentiments often took on a populistic form. Certain tendencies which have culminated in a mass society were at work in it. However, much of its culture, although mediocre and brutal, was not produced by the institutions or by the professional personnel now producing the culture of mass society.

Refined culture in nineteenth-century America, reflecting the taste of the cultivated classes of New England and the Middle Atlantic States, did not enjoy a hospitable reception in the Middle West, as a result of the usual hostility of province against metropolis and against those who became established sooner. American provincial culture in the nineteenth century was a variant of the British provincial dissenting culture that Matthew Arnold criticized unsparingly in *Culture and Anarchy*. Whereas this culture collapsed in England after World War I, in America it has continued powerful almost up to the present.

Populism as an ethos and as a political movement was hostile to some aspects of superior culture but not to all. It did however antedate the large-scale production of the works of mass culture and it did not prevent the flourishing of American literature between the Civil War and the First World War.

These are some of the special reasons for the present uncongeniality of superior culture to so many Americans. It springs from a general distrust that superior culture often encounters in many societies. In this country it expresses itself with greater strength, virulence, and freedom because the political and economic elites of American society feel little obligation to assume a veneer of refined culture, as in Great Britain and France.

Against this background of tradition and sentiment, the development of education in the United States in the past decades has created a technical intelligentsia that does not form a coherent intellectual community. While secondary education became less intellectual in its content and undergraduate education dissipated itself in courses of study of very low intensity and little discipline, a very superior and vigorous type of postgraduate education developed. In trying to make up for lost ground and in seeking to make a deep and thorough penetration into a rapidly growing body of knowledge, postgraduate training in each discipline has had to become highly specialized.

This impetus toward specialization has been heightened by the natural development of science and by the growth of the percentage of the population that pursues postgraduate studies. The development of science has greatly increased the volume of literature a student must cover in each discipline; the increasing number of students and the necessity for each to do a piece of research no one has ever done before have tended to narrow the concentration within the discipline imposed by the internal evolution of the subject.[10]

The product of these educational and scientific developments has been the specialist who is uncultivated outside his own speciality. Except for those strong and expanisve personalities whose curiosity and sensitivity lead them to the experience of what their education has failed to give them, even the creative American scientist, scholar, or technologist often possesses only a narrow range of mediocre culture.

The ascent of the universities to preponderance in the life of superior culture in the United States, and increasingly (though still not to the same extent) in Europe, has meant that trends within the university are trends of intellectual life generally to a much greater degree than in earlier periods of modern society. As the universities have become more internally differentiated and specialized, superior cultural life has also tended to become more specialized.

What we are suffering from is the dissolution of "the educated public," coherent although unorganized, with a taste for superior

10. The romantic idea of originality, which claimed that genius must go its own unique way, has been transposed into one that demands that the subject matter should be unique to the investigator. This has led to much specialized triviality in humanistic research.

cultural objects with no vocational import. The "universitization" of superior culture—most advanced in America but already visible elsewhere—is part of the process of the dissolution of the body of consumers of superior culture.

Specialization has lessened the coherence of the intellectual community, comprising creators, reproducers, and consumers; it has dispersed its focus of attention and thus left ungratified cultural needs which the mediocre and brutal culture of the mass media and of private life have been called in to satisfy. The consumption of brutal and mediocre culture is the consequence, not the cause, of developments which are quite independent of the specific properties of mass society.

The Prospects of Superior Culture in Mass Society

The problems of superior culture in mass society are the same as in any society. These problems are the maintenance of its quality and influence on the rest of the society.

To maintain itself, superior culture must maintain its own traditions and its own internal coherence. The progress of superior culture (and its continued self-renewal and expansion) require that the traditions be sustained, however much they are revised or partially rejected at any time.

Respect for the traditions in one's own field, together with freedom in dealing with those traditions, are the necessary conditions for creative work. The balance between them is difficult to define, and it is no less difficult to discern the conditions under which that balance can be achieved and maintained. Of great importance is the morale (in its broadest sense) of the intellectuals who take on administrative and teaching responsibilities for the maintenance and advancement of high culture. Within this section of the intellectual class, there must be an incessant scrutiny of every institutional innovation, with regard to its possible impact on intellectual morale. An essential element in this internal state is a balance between respect and freedom in relation to the immanent traditions of each field of intellectual work.

Serious intellectuals have never been free from pressure on the part of sectors of society other than their own. The intellectual sector has always been relatively isolated, regardless of the role of intellectuals in economic and political life. Intellectuals have always been faced with the task of continuing their own tradition, developing it, differentiating it, improving it as best they could. They have always had to contend with church, state, and party, with merchants and soldiers who have sought to enlist them in their service and to restrict and damage them in word and deed if they did not yield to temptations and threats. The present situation has much in common with the past. The responsibilities of intellectuals also remain the same: to serve the standards they discern and develop and to find a way of rendering unto Caesar what is Caesar's without renouncing what belongs to their own proper realm.

There is no doubt in my mind that the main "political" tradition by which most of our literary, artistic, and social-science intellectuals have lived in America is unsatisfactory. The fault does not lie exclusively with the intellectuals. The philistine puritanism and provincialism of our elites share much of the blame, as does the populism of professional and lay politicians. Nonetheless, the intellectuals cannot evade the charge that they have done little to ameliorate the situation. Their own political attitudes have been alienated; they have run off into many directions of frivolity. The most recent of such episodes in the 1930s and 1960s were also the most humiliating, and temporarily the most damaging, to the position of intellectuals in American society.

One of the responsibilities implied by their obligation to maintain good relations with the nonintellectual elite is the "civilization" of political life, i.e., the infusion of the standards and concerns of a serious, intellectually disciplined contemplation of the deeper issues of political life into everyday politics. Our intellectuals have, in the main, lectured politicians, upbraided them, looked down their noses at them, opposed them, and even suspected those of their fellow intellectuals who have become politicians of moral corruption and intellectual betrayal.

The intellectuals who have taken on themselves the fostering of superior culture are part of the elite in any country; but in the United States they have not felt bound by any invisible affiliation with the political, economic, ecclesiastical, military, and technological elites.[11]

The "civilization" of political life is only one aspect of the "process of civilization," which is the expansion of the culture of the center into the peripheries of society and, in this particular context, the diffusion of superior culture into the areas of society normally consuming mediocre and brutal culture.

But if the periphery is not to be polished while the center becomes dusty, the first obligation of the intellectuals is to look after intellectual things, to concentrate their powers on the creation and reproduction and consumption of particular works of philosophy, art, science, literature, or scholarship, to receive the traditions in which these works stand with a discriminating readiness to accept, elaborate, or reject. If that is done, there will be nothing to fear from the movement of culture in mass society.

11. This is not a condition unique to the United States. Only Great Britain has managed to avoid it for most of the period since the French Revolution, yet there, too, the past few years have not provided notable examples of Britain's good fortune in avoiding this separation.

12 Daydreams and Nightmares: Reflections on the Criticism of Mass Culture

I

The well-wishers of the human race who laid the foundations of our present outlook looked forward to a time when man would be free from the brutish ignorance and squalor in which he then lay, and from the shadows which darkened his mind. The easing of burdens, a more universal opportunity, a heightened respect would, they thought, open man's spirit to the great heritage of literature, philosophy, and art. Revolutionaries, Marxist and otherwise, extended and made more intense this dream of philanthropic liberalism.

The present century has, at least for the time being, belied these hopes. Universal education, the alleviation of physical misery, the drift of equality have not brought with them that deepening and enrichment of the mind to which liberals and revolutionaries alike aspired. The silliness of television, the childishness of the comic strips, the trivality of the press, the meanness of the luridly bound paperbacks are now taken as signs that Western humanity has turned off the road which for a time seemed to lead into the broad sunlit uplands of a discriminating appreciation and is rushing into the swamps of vulgarity. Beyond the swamps many now perceive the sea of a base and unredeemable vulgarity. The sea has never been in such flood, and never has it so threatened not only the lowlands in which the populace lives but the heights of the high culture of the West.

In the United States, in Great Britain, on the continent of Europe, or at least in the parts of Europe where the custodians and consumers of the traditional culture of the educated classes are free to express their views, there is a feeling of consternation and bewilderment, deliberate complacency, guilty enthusiasm, and apologetic curiosity about the phenomenon of mass culture.

II

Between the wars, the voices were few and their focus was scattered. The late Wyndham Lewis and Ortega y Gasset, and Dr. F. R. Leavis and his circle criticized the culture of neoliteracy and for their pains

Previously published in a slightly different form in *Sewanee Review*, vol. 65, no. 4 (October-December 1957), pp. 586-608.

they were either called fascists or were passed over in silence. Since the end of the Second World War, the criticism has gained in force, volume, and coherence of focus. The majority of the writers are now resident in America where popular culture has made itself more visible to the educated, but British and Continental authors have been no less alarmed.

The earlier critics of mass culture were aristocratic and aesthetic in their outlook. Wyndham Lewis, Ortega y Gasset, and the Leavises feared the preponderance of poor taste and judgment. Ortega's viewpoint was only a subtle extension into the moral and aesthetic sphere of a conception of the coarseness and indiscipline of the lower classes which had prevailed among the opponents of political democracy since early in the nineteenth century. The Leavis argument had nothing political about it; it was entirely concerned with the obstacles to the diffusion of discrimination in literary judgment. The new critique of mass culture takes over many of the aristocratic and aesthetic arguments and the antibourgeois attitudes of nineteenth-century Europe. Its point of departure is, however, different.

It is not accidental that most of the recent critics of mass culture are, or were, Marxian socialists, some even rather extreme, at least in their past commitment to the socialist ideal. Mr. Dwight Macdonald,[1] who, as editor of *Politics,* did more than any other American writer to bring this interpretation of mass culture to the forefront of the attention of the intellectual public, was a former Trotskyite communist whose zeal had waned and since then has entirely disappeared. Professor Max Horkheimer,[2] who is the leading exponent of the "critical" philosophy of the Frankfurt circle, is an apolitical Marxist whose Hegelian sociological terminology obscures his Marxism. Professor T. Wiesengrund-Adorno[3] and Professor Leo Lowenthal,[4] the former at Frankfurt University, the latter at the University of California, have both been leading adherents of the school in which a refined Marxism finds its most sophisticated expression. Dr. Erich Fromm[5] was a psychoanalyzing Marxist. Karl

1. Dwight Macdonald, "A Theory of Mass Culture," *Diogenes* no. 3, reprinted in *Mass Culture: The Popular Arts in America,* ed. Bernard Rosenberg and David White (Glencoe, Ill., 1957).
2. Max Horkheimer and T. W. Adorno, *Dialektik der Aufklärung* (Amsterdam, 1947), and Horkheimer, "Art and Mass Culture," *Studies in Philosophy and Social Science,* vol. 9 (1941).
3. T. W. Adorno, "On Popular Music," *Studies in Philosophy and Social Science,* vol. 9 (1941); and "Television and the Patterns of Mass Culture," *Quarterly of Film, Radio, and Television,* vol. 8 (1954), reprinted in *Mass Culture.*
4. Leo Lowenthal, "Historical Perspectives of Popular Culture," *American Journal of Sociology,* vol. 55 (1950), reprinted in *Mass Culture.*
5. Erich Fromm, *Escape from Freedom* (New York, 1941).

Bednarik[6] is an Austrian Socialist. Czeslow Milosz[7] is a Polish poet who served the Stalinist Polish government as a cultural official for some years, then adumbrated the break-up of Polish Stalinism by quitting his post and going to live abroad while still adhering to the ideals which made him a communist. Richard Hoggart is a socialist of the Labourite persuasion. Irving Howe and Bernard Rosenberg[8] are socialists in the tradition of Trotsky, and moving spirits of *Dissent.*

None of these socialists and former socialists is an orthodox Marxist, and some of them no longer think of themselves as Marxists at all. The names and terminology of Marxism scarcely appear on their pages. Yet Marxism has left a formative imprint on their thought about mass culture. Their earlier economic criticism of capitalistic society has been transformed into a moral and cultural criticism of the large-scale industrial society. They no longer criticize the ruling class for utilizing the laws of property and religion to exploit the proletariat for the sake of surplus value; instead they criticize the "merchants of kitsch" who are enmeshed in the machine of industrial civilization and who exploit not the labor but the emotional needs of the masses—these emotional needs themselves produced by industrial society. They no longer criticize modern society for the hard life which it imposes on the majority of its citizens. They criticize it for the uninteresting and vulgar life which it provides. They criticize the aesthetic qualities of a society which has realized so much of what socialists once claimed was of central importance, which has, in other words, overcome poverty and long arduous labor. The indissoluble residue of their Marxism shows itself particularly in the expectations which form the standard of judgment which they apply to mass culture.

As Marxists they once thought that the working classes—as Engels said of the German proletariat—were destined to be "the heirs of classical philosophy," by which was meant that the working class had a special receptiveness for the highest manifestations of the "objective spirit." They shared the Feuerbachian conception of man elevated to the conditions of full humanity, in which all share in the greatest discoveries and creations of the human mind. They believed that in the "realm of freedom," which socialism would bring about, the freedom of each man from the dominion of others and particularly from the dominion of the propertied, and the sufficient

6. Karl Bednarik, *The Young Worker* (London, 1955; Glencoe, Ill., 1956).

7. Czeslow Milosz, "Bielinski and the Unicorn," *Papers of the Milan Conference on the Future of Freedom,* Congress for Cultural Freedom, Paris, 1955.

8. Bernard Rosenberg, "Mass Culture in America," in *Mass Culture,* and Irving Howe, "Notes on Mass Culture," *Politics,* 1948, reprinted in *Mass Culture.*

wealth and leisure which the realm of freedom would carry with it, would emancipate the mind, free it from prejudice and superstition, and make it master of itself. Knowledge would be universally diffused, and taste would be refined. Their hopes were the hopes of Trotsky, who while Marxism was descending from its heroic phase to the depths of tyrannical and bureaucratic dogmatism, still retained enough of the old spirit of the French and German Enlightenment and of German idealism to envisage a future in which "the average human type will rise to the heights of an Aristotle, a Goethe or a Marx. And above this ridge, new peaks will rise."[9]

Now they are affronted by the waywardness of the mass of the population in whom they once thought they found the chief agent and the greatest beneficiary of progress. That section of the population from which they expected heroic action on behalf of great, far-distant goals has turned out to be interested in wasting its time in self-indulgent and foolish pleasures. Instead of reading Shakespeare, Goethe, and Tolstoi, it reads comic books, sensational newspapers, and magazines which concentrate on illicit sexual activity and crimes of violence. The classes from whom intellectuals expected a heroic awareness of grandiose events and an eagerness to participate in them concern themselves at best with the routine philistine life of bourgeois politics, and often not even with that. Instead of high aspirations they immerse themselves in their immediate situations or in cultural creations which are either only slight extensions of their private situations or else wholly unrealistic dream-worlds. Those from whom it was believed a hitherto hidden appreciation of the sublime and the beautiful would emerge are, on the contrary, attracted by the trivial, the sensational, and the gruesome.

The working classes, even where, as in Britain and Germany, they have become socialists, or as in Italy and France, communists, are uninterested in revolution, in the moral transformation of themselves and the rest of the human race. Instead of rising to the highest levels of the human spirit, to which their prophets had summoned them, they are satisfied to take life as it comes and to seek pleasures which are alien to the great dream of a transfigured humanity.

The indulgence in mass culture is not only aesthetically and intellectually degrading but, according to its critics, it prevents its victims from striving to achieve the socialist ideal. One of the gravest charges against mass culture is that it deadens and deforms the capacity to conceive of a better world, i.e., to participate in revolutionary movements.[10]

9. Trotsky, *Literature and Revolution* (London, 1925), p. 256.
10. "Wherever revolutionary tendencies show a timid head, they are mitigated and cut short by a false fulfillment of wish-dreams, like wealth,

It is assumed by many of these ex-Marxists that there is really only one reasonable social ideal—namely, socialism. All activities which do not strive to establish socialism, if they are not of the stuff of high culture, are "escapist."[11]

Few of the critics of the new culture of the lower classes have had firsthand contact with those classes; their hopes were derived from an image which was almost entirely doctrinal. Writers like Richard Hoggart are exceptional for their vivid and affectionate firsthand recollections of lower-class life. These give an especial poignancy to his regrets for the fading of an independent and lively pattern of life. But since the hopes were the same, the disappointment is essentially the same. He, as well as the more doctrinal critics of mass culture, is disappointed that, instead of ascending to the heights of the greatest cultural achievements of aristocratic and bourgeois societies, the working classes are content to accept the infiltration of the advertising man's culture, cheap films, machine-fabricated popular songs, the insipid or sensational entertainment of television.

There is a shock of pain in their perceptions and an element of revenge in their disclosure of the corruptibility and actual corruption of those whom they once loved. Part of the preoccupation with mass culture is the obsessiveness of the disappointed lover who, having misconceived his beloved when their love was blooming, now feels that she deceived him and he has no eye for anything but her vices and blemishes. Her present vices are magnified by the past exaggeration of her virtues, and she cannot be forgotten.

The transmogrified Marxism of the disappointed manifests itself in another way. They still believe, as they once believed, under the auspices of their pristine Marxist outlook, in the existence of a crisis of culture. Creative high culture is still endangered by the pressure of society, but whereas before it was the specific pressure of the contradictions and crises of capitalism, now it is the result of modern industrial society—namely, mass culture—which endangers high culture. The once prospective heirs of high culture have turned out to be a menace to its survival.

---

adventure, passionate love, power and sensationalism in general." Leo Lowenthal, "Historical Perspectives in Popular Culture," in *Mass Culture,* p. 55.

11. Nothing shows the persistence of puritanical Marxism in the writings critical of popular culture as much as the idea that popular culture is "escapist." Underlying it is the belief that man's first obligation is to understand his environment in order to transform it into the socialist society. Expressive dispositions, the need for fantasy, the play of imagination are disregarded by this standpoint. The same hostility against "art for art's sake" which was characteristic of Marxist literary criticism reappears here in another guise and context.

Mass culture threatens to destory high culture. Mr. Dwight Macdonald, Professor van den Haag, and the others are at one in their diagnosis of the dangers. Mass culture, by its remunerative market, exerts a great pull on artists who are nowadays "more market-oriented than taste-oriented. They create for anonymous consumers rather than for the sake of creation."[12] The opportunity to write for the films, television, for *Readers Digest*, or *Life* is so attractive that artists become corrupted in their standards. "There are some," Professor van den Haag concedes, "who doggedly insist on being themselves but the temptations are infinite, infinitely disguised and insinuating. The psychological burden of isolation has drawbacks affecting creation. The ability and will to create are impaired if there is no public and the defense against the temptations of popular culture uses much of the energy needed for creation. The artist who by refusing to work for the mass market becomes marginal, cannot create what he might have created had there been no mass market." Mr. Macdonald, believing that "all the cultures of the past were elite cultures," thinks that there is little chance for high culture to survive in America, where class lines are blurred, stable cultural traditions are lacking, the intellectuals as a group are incoherent, and the manufacture and distribution of kitsch has so much greater resources. There is something "inexorable" in the mechanism by which mass culture is killing high culture, and only a few heroes can hold out.[13]

Of course, the frustration of socialist expectations is not the sole reason for this aggrieved preoccupation with mass culture. It is obstrusive, garishly visible, and blatantly audible and one would have to be blind and deaf and very withdrawn not to be aware of it—especially in America. There are also some other important reasons why it draws the attention of intellectuals. The institutions of mass culture offer well-paid employment, which many accept, in advertising, radio, television, films, and market research, and this troubles the conscience and disturbs the equanimity of those who are inside as well as outside these institutions. Some of the most savage criticism of mass culture is produced by those who are enaged in creating or promoting it.[14] There are of course other more

12. Van den Haag, in *Mass Culture*, p. 520.
13. Dwight Macdonald, in *Mass Culture*, p. 71.
14. And on the other side, some of the defensive literature is no more than special pleading by persons who, having found a niche in life in the professions connected with mass culture, seek to give respectability to their work. Often they are a little guilty because neither they nor the intellectual circles in which they grew up really approve of mass culture, and yet because they are very well paid or because they have an intense pleasure in what they disapprove of or simply because it is what they are doing, strive to give their work and pleasure a dignity which they sometimes inwardly doubt.

free-floating students of the subject who, like Professor Riesman,[15] defend mass culture, but they do so largely because it is looked down upon by European anti-American intellectuals and by American xenophile intellectuals; they defend mass culture because they resent mere empty snobbery and they feel that the usual grounds of condemnation of mass culture are conventional and unreflective. Neither Professor Riesman nor Professor David White[16] nor the greatest friend of popular culture among intellectuals, Mr. Gilbert Seldes,[17] approves of the content of most of popular culture as it exists at present. Either they select certain elements of high culture which appear in the channels of mass consumption, such as superior paperback books, or long-playing records of serious music, or Shakespeare on television, etc., or they criticize its critics for being undemocratic or unrealistic. For the bulk of popular culture, however, even those who oppose its opponents have very little to say.

There are, of course, among highly educated persons a considerable number who enjoy science fiction, comic books, and television programs of all sorts, as a continuation of childish pleasures; and there are others who feel that liking them and developing a connoisseurship in matters of mass culture makes them "folksy" and flaunts their rebellion against the rigor and aridity of the higher culture and the tradition which their parents, teachers, and the culturally ruling classes once sought to impose on them. The interest of the former is the result of educational and professional specialization, which leaves those aspects of the person which are not subjected to specialized education in a state of juvenile underdevelopment. For the latter, the interest in popular culture is an alternative to political radicalism which involves "going to the people" without courting risks to hopes or careers. These educated enthusiasts for popular culture write little; they are satisfied to enjoy it.

Hence, the bulk of the literature which defends popular culture shares many of the convictions of the more hostile criticisms. It regards the widespread pleasure which television, films, radio, comic strips and books, and novels of violence bring, as a misuse of leisure time. It asserts that the great audience does not know how to use its leisure time properly and that the producers of popular culture do not, on the whole, serve it well. It thinks that the masses are ill advised to spend their time in the way they do. The great difference

15. David Riesman, *Individualism Reconsidered* (Glencoe, Ill., 1954), pp. 179-270.

16. David White, "Mass Culture in America: Another Point of View," in *Mass Culture,* pp. 13-21.

17. Gilbert Seldes, *The Great Audience* (New York, 1951), and *The Public Arts* (New York, 1956).

between the negative and the affirmative standpoints is that the former regards mass culture as an unqualified catastrophe, the latter as a misfortune which still has a chance of correction and which in any case does little harm. They agree in morals and aesthetics but they differ in their fundamental political expectations.

III

The critical interpretation of mass culture rests on a distinct image of modern man, of society, and of man in past ages. This image has little factual basis. It is a product of disappointed political prejudices, vague aspirations for an unrealizable ideal, resentment against American society, and, at bottom, romanticism dressed up in the language of sociology, psychoanalysis, and existentialism.

If one were to take seriously the two fountainheads of the interpretation of mass culture, namely, the Frankfurt Institut für Sozialforschung led by Professor Horkheimer, and *Politics* under the editorship of Mr. Macdonald, one would believe that the ordinary citizen who listens to the radio, goes to films, and looks at television is not just *l'homme moyen sensuel* known to past ages. He is something new in the world. He is a "private atomic subject," utterly without religious beliefs, without any private life, without a family which means anything to him;[18] he is standardized, ridden with anxiety, perpetually in a state of "exacerbated" unrest, his life "emptied of meaning," and "trivialized," "alienated from his past, from his community, and possibly from himself," cretinized and brutalized.[19] The ordinary man has, according to this view, been overwhelmed by the great society; he had lost his roots in his organic communities of territory and kinship, craft and faith. Man in modern society lacks individuality and yet he is terribly lonely. Instead of developing the rich individuality for which his well-wishers idly hoped, he has lost his apparently once-existent individuality through the anonymity of modern institutions. He has been depersonalized and degraded to the point where he is a cog in an impersonal industrial machine. The mass-produced nature of his culture—which is necessary if he and his kind are to be satisfied in sufficient quantity and cheapness—prevents him from developing his tastes and intelligence. Instead of rising to the heights of sensitivity and awareness, as socialist doctrine led its adherents to expect, the majority of the population voluntarily impoverishes its own existence, welcomes the "distractions from the human predicament"[20] which mass culture provides, and yet it finds no contentment.

18. Max Horkheimer in *Mass Culture*, pp. 292-94.
19. Bernard Rosenberg in *Mass Culture*, pp. 4, 5, 7. The words are Mr. Rosenberg's but the ideas are the common property of the critics.
20. Irving Howe, in *Mass Culture*.

Modern man is incapable of having genuinely affectionate relationships with other persons. He can no longer love.[21] Mass culture is welcomed by this unfortunate being because it "adjusts" him to an unworthy reality by "helping us to suppress ourselves."[22] Lacking religion, man can find surcease from his burdens only in the movie theaters.[23]

This interpretation of life in modern society has a corollary in the picture of society before modern industrialism burst in upon us. Art and the works of culture in this legendary time were vitally integrated into everyday life, the artist was aware of his function, man was in a state of reposeful self-possession. The mass of the population naturally did not have access to the works of high culture but it had its own art, namely folk art, created by itself and genuinely expressing its own relationship to the universe. Peasant society and aristocratic society had no problem of mass culture. They were societies in which nothing factitious or meretricious existed. Taste had nothing vulgar about it. The educated classes were genuinely educated, and, despite the rigors of a fundamentally exploitative society, religious faith was genuine, artistic taste was elevated, and important problems were thought about with true sincerity. Men did not seek to "escape." If we are to believe what Professors Horkheimer and van den Haag say, premodern man was autonomous; he was spontaneous; his life had continuity and distinction. His existence felt none of the pressures which are dehumanizing modern man.[24] Genuine individuality flourished, in which there was no alienation of man from man or of man from himself.

What is the source of this picture of the past and present of the American and European sections of the human race? Is it systematic firsthand observation, is it historical scholarship, is it a wide experience of life, or a facility to enter into intimate contact with all sorts and conditions of men? It is none of these.

Its intellectual history can be traced to the early writings of Marx and to German sociological romanticism.[25] The transformation of

21. Erich Fromm, *The Art of Loving* (New York, 1956), pp. 83-106.
22. Irving Howe, in *Mass Culture*, p. 498.
23. Ibid., p. 497. This, it should be noted, comes from a leftist without sympathy for religion. Mr. Howe accepts, however, the conventional romantic sociological critique of modern society which stresses among other things its religious faithlessness. He notes no contradiction between that and his socialist convictions which are entirely "secular."
24. These fantasies about the qualities of the happy pre-mass culture have been very fairly and cogently criticized by Professor Denis Brogan: "The Problem of High Culture and Mass Culture," *Diogenes* no. 5 (Winter 1954), pp. 1-13, and by Mr. Henry Rabassiere, "In Defense of Television," in *Mass Culture*, pp. 368-74.
25. The criticism of popular culture, and the outlook from which it is derived, have much in common with the criticisms of modern society which

Hegel's philosophy of the spirit into a doctrine of criticism directed against the existing institutions of civil society laid special stress on the phenomenon of alienation, on the condition of man when he is not permeated by the "spirit." German sociological romanticism, which found its decisive expression in Ferdinand Toennies' *Gemeinschaft und Gesellschaft* (1887), in Georg Simmel's numerous works, especially in *Die Philosophie des Geldes* (1900) and *Über soziale Differenzierung* (1890), and in Werner Sombart's early quasi-Marxist writings on capitalist society, had at the very center of its conception of the world a picture of premodern peasant society, in which men lived in the harmonious mutual respect of authority and subordinate, in which all felt themselves integral parts of a community which in its turn lived in continuous and inspiring contact with its own past. Traditions were stable; the kinship group was bound together in unquestioned solidarity. No one was alienated from himself or isolated from his territorial community and his kin. Beliefs were firm and were universally shared. This is the fantasy which lies at the basis of the criticism of modern society which allegedly hard-headed publicists and scientific sociologists have accepted without critical examination. This idyll was juxtaposed against a conception of modern urban society which is much like the state of nature described by Hobbes, where no man is bound by ties of sentimental affection or moral obligation or loyalty to any other man. Each man is concerned only with his own interest, which is power over others, their exploitation and manipulation. The family is dissolved, friendship dead, religious belief evaporated. Impersonality and anonymity have taken the place of closer ties. This is the picture of life in the great cities of the West which flourished in German sociology from the time of Ferdinand Toennies and Georg Simmel, and it found many adherents in America[26] and France. The refined Marxism of the earlier, more romantic writings of Marx and Engels formed a perfect companion piece to this academic romanticism. It was left, however, for the Institut für Sozialforschung, attached to the University of Frankfurt before 1933 and to

---

emanate from other intellectual milieux. The Roman Catholic romanticism of Chesterton and Belloc, the French monarchists, the classicism and the admiration for heroic violence of T. E. Hulme, the Southern Agrarians, the heroic puritanism of George Sorel come from intellectual sources as diverse as Cobbett, Proudhon, Comte, Le Play, and Jefferson. The common feature is their dislike of urban society and of bourgeois individualism and hedonism. They were all ideologists, hostile to human beings as they are, and this they shared with Marxism.

26. In American sociology, it found its fullest expression in the writings of Robert Park, who had been a pupil of Simmel, and in "Urbanism as a Way of Life" by the late Louis Wirth. (The latter essay is reprinted in *Community Life and Social Policy* [Chicago, 1956].)

Columbia University during the late thirties and early forties, and to the *Politics* circle which came under its influence, to effect the synthesis. The Marxism of the Institut was never the Marxism of the parties. In a series of important collaborative works which included *Autorität und Familie* (Paris, 1934), *The Authoritarian Personality* (New York, 1948), and a variety of other equally characteristic books like Fromm's *Escape from Freedom,* Neumann's *Behemoth,* Horkheimer's *Eclipse of Reason,* and most recently Marcuse's *Eros and Civilization,* an ingenious, courageous, and unrealistic point of view was promulgated and applied to modern society. A fusion of Hegelian Marxism, psychoanalysis, and aesthetic repugnance for industrial society, each freely and imaginatively adapted to the underlying philosophy of the Institut, dominated their point of view.

The Institut's point of view was formed in its most general outlines in Germany and in the first years of exile in Europe but it developed into a critique of mass culture only after the immigration to the United States. Here its members encountered the "mass" in modern society for the first time. Their anticapitalistic and, by multiplication, anti-American attitude found a traumatic and seemingly ineluctible confirmation in the popular culture of the United States. Whereas in Europe an educated person of the higher classes could, and even now still can, avoid awareness of the life of the majority of the population, this is impossible in the United States. What is a vague disdain in Europe must become an elaborate loathing in America.

The Institut had responded to the terrible experience of the rise and temporary triumph of National Socialism with a strenuous effort to understand why it had happened. It tried to discern trends toward the spread of totalitarianism to other Western countries. Orthodox Marxism, to which the Insitut had in any case never been bound, was not adequate to the task. It might explain why the property-owning classes welcomed National Socialism but it could not explain why there was so much voluntary and enthusiastic submission on the part of those who might have been expected, on the basis of an attachment to the ideals of liberalism and socialism, to resist. Why had the working classes not been true to the revolutionary vocation with which Marxism had endowed them? Here German romanticism, brought up to date by sociology and psychoanalysis, appeared to offer an answer.

It was because man was alienated and uprooted that he so eagerly accepted the cruel and spurious ethnic community preferred by National Socialism. The same factors which led them to National Socialism are responsible for modern man's eager self-immersion into the trivial, base, and meretricious culture provided by the radio, the film, the comic strips, the television, and mass-produced goods. It is therefore to be expected that the mass culture which has been created to meet the needs of alienated and uprooted men will further the process, exacerbate the needs, and lead on to an inevitable culmination in fascism. According to Mr. Rosenberg, who is not a member of the Institut but who speaks with its voice, "mass culture threatens not merely to cretinize our taste and to brutalize our senses," it paves "the way to totalitarianism."[27] The fact that fascism triumphed in Germany, Italy, and Spain before the "masses" in these and other countries began to enjoy the benefits of mass culture, raises no questions in the minds of these writers.[28]

IV

These arbitrary constructions emerge from the minds of speculative sociologists, existentialist philosophers, publicists, and literary critics. The chaos of motives and the lack of intellectual discipline render understandable the arbitrary and melodramatic nature of their conclusions. But empirical sociologists are also involved in the analysis of mass culture. Do they not bring a sobering influence into the discussion? Do they not control their observations and judgments by a systematic discipline?

The reply must be equivocal. Precise and orderly as their observations might be, they are made outside a matrix of intimate experience, without the sense of emphatic affinity which would enable the events which they observe to be understood as they actually occur in the lives of those who experience them.[29] One frequently feels in reading the sociological reports on the cultural interests and activities of the populace that the observers are from Mars and that they know only of the listening or viewing or buying activities of their subjects. Their other interests and activities fade into the background, not because they are actually inconsequential, but because the particular techniques of inquiry bring the contact with mass communication so sharply into the foreground.[30] The inquirers often, and the interpreters of the inquiries not less frequently, go far beyond the limits set by their observations and assume that reading or seeing is evidence of a close correspondence

27. *Mass Culture*, p. 9.

28. Nor does the fact that the United States, where mass culture is so developed and where according to research of Professor Adorno and his collaborators in *The Authoritarian Personality* so many Americans are protofascists, is the scene of a thriving democracy arouse any doubts about their theory of the nature and consequences of mass culture.

29. Not that intimate experience alone is a guarantee of truth!

30. One should perhaps except from this the report by Mr. Leo Bogart on his inquiry into the response of adult readers to comic strips (*Mass Culture*, pp. 189-98).

between the content of what is seen, as interpreted by the sociologist, and the mind of the person who comes into contact with it. Most of the discussion goes even further and assumes, without any basis, the full assimilation into the depths of consciousness and unconsciousness of the latent content of films, radio, and television broadcasts. Too often the observations are very limited in scope, and the "interpretation," which goes far beyond them, introduces utterly baseless prejudices.[31]

"Content analyses" are regarded by many students of popular culture as providing a direct and unquestionable path of entry into contact with the depths of the mind. The nature of the person who reads or sees or hears some work of popular culture is inferred from the content of the work, on the assumption that every image, every event corresponds to some deep and central need in the personality of the reader, viewer, or listener. There is no reason whatever to think that this is so, and yet this assumption lies near the heart of much of the treatment of mass culture.[32]

Orderly and realistic sociological research could tell us much about "modern man" and his relations with the roaring ocean of "mass culture." It is still to be undertaken. There is no reason at present to believe that men and women in modern Western society or that Americans in particular have much resemblance to the picture of them presented in the works of contemporary social

31. For example, Mr. Leo Crespi reports (in *Mass Culture,* pp. 418-22) on card-playing activities and concludes that they demonstrate that in modern society intimate personal relations are in a crisis. Card-playing is alleged to be a substitute for personal relations. Thus a perfectly matter-of-fact set of observations on card-playing is put into the context of German and American sociological romanticism, for which there is no evidence. German and, after them, American sociologists got it into their heads that personal relations had broken down in modern urban society and they contrasted this, sometimes implicitly, sometimes explicitly, with the cultivation of refined and lasting friendship from antiquity to the end of the pre-capitalist era. They have never considered why so much of the ancient and early modern literature on friendship is devoted to the faithlessness of friends, the distinction between true and false friends, the common dangers of flattery and deception by ostensible friends, etc.

32. It would be more conducive to the understanding of the sources of the content of mass culture if sociologists, psychologists, and critics were to examine the producers of the works of mass culture—the film writers and producers, the authors of radio scripts, etc. Much of value concerning the producer's attitude toward his prospective audience and his underlying sentiments about his fellow countrymen would emerge from such studies. It is quite conceivable that they would reveal the circularity and the arbitrariness of much of the concern about mass culture. The producers and authors of works of mass culture make certain assumptions about the needs and desires of their audience, and then produce the work. Sociological investigators then proceed to study the works and from this draw inferences regarding the nature of the personalities who listen to it. These analyses then enter the atmosphere of intellectual opinion and provide allegedly scientific evidence to those who promote such production that their assumptions are correct.

scientists. There is far too much arbitrariness in these inquiries, far too little direct and intimate contact, far too little empathy in a matrix of a feeling of affinity to justify in any convincing way the general and melodramatic interpretations which are made by the critics of mass culture. The sociological study of mass culture is the victim of the culture of sociological intellectuals.

V

It would, of course, be frivolous to deny the aesthetic, moral, and intellectual unsatisfactoriness of much of popular culture or to claim that it shows the human race in its best light. The major error of the analysts of popular culture, however, is their belief that it has succeeded to something which was intrinsically worthy, that man has sunk into a hitherto unknown mire because of it, and that this is a necessary prelude to the further degradation, and perhaps ultimate extinction, of high culture.

Most of the analysts of popular culture make a mistake when they fail to see the great volume of output of popular culture as more than the expansion of a stream which has never been absent from Western society. They forget that up to the nineteenth century, when a great change was brought about by the confluence of economic progress, a new sentiment of the value of human life, and the efforts of liberal and humanitarian reformers, the mass of the human race lived a degraded life. It is sheer romanticism when Professor van den Haag says "industry has impoverished life."[33] The contrary is true. Hunger and imminence of death, work such as we in the West would now regard as too burdensome even for beasts, over very long hours, prevented the development of individuality, of sensitivity or refinement in any except those very few in the lower classes who were either extremely strong personalities or extremely talented or extremely fortunate in forming a connection with the aristocratic or mercantile classes, or all three together.

The culture of these strata, which were dulled by labor, illness, and fear, and which comprised a far larger proportion of the population than they do in advanced societies in the twentieth century, was a culture of bear-baiting, cock-fighting, drunkenness, tales of witches, gossip about the sexual malpractices of priests, monks, and nuns, stories of murders and mutilations. The story of Sweeny Todd, the demon barber of Fleet Street who ran a profitable business in meat pies made with the flesh of the victims dropped through the trapdoor of his barber shop, is not a creation of modern mass culture. It dates from the Middle Ages. The *fabliaux* were

33. Van den Haag, in *Mass Culture*, p. 531.

about the best that folk literary culture could offer in the Middle Ages and they were certainly not very salubrious. The *littérature du colportage* was not a literature in the style of Jane Austen or Gustave Flaubert. It was much closer and much inferior to Eugene Sue. The present pleasures of the working and lower-middle classes are not worthy of profound aesthetic, moral, or intellectual esteem but they are surely not inferior to the villainous things which gave pleasure to their European ancestors from the Middle Ages to the nineteenth century.

Only ignorance and prejudice, impelled by a passionate and permeative revulsion against their own age and their own society, can explain why contemporary intellectuals, who pride themselves on being socialists or liberals and democrats, wish to believe that the aristocracy and gentry in European societies of the seventeenth and eighteenth centuries lived an elevated cultural life, or that the spiritually numbed peasantry had a coherent and dignified existence. Only a very small minority of the upper classes of the first four centuries of the modern era read a great deal, and a great deal of what they read was worthless from any point of view except that much of it was harmless. No one who has spent many hours in old libraries or in antiquarian bookshops can evade the conclusion that the vast majority of books produced in the seventeenth and eighteenth centuries, to say nothing of the nineteenth century, were of no consequence from an aesthetic, moral, or intellectual point of view. The high culture of the seventeenth century included not only Shakespeare, Jonson, Bacon, Hobbes, Racine, Pascal, La Rochefoucauld, et. al., but a far greater number of absolutely worthless writers, authors of spurious philosophical works, of foolishly mean-spirited and trivial theological treatises, of tales as vapid as the choices of the Book of the Month Club, and of poems which would try even the insensate patience of a PhD candidate in English literature. It was not different in the eighteenth and nineteenth centuries.

This is not to take the modernist side in the battle of books, or to claim that our contemporary philosophic, artistic, and literary genius is as rich as it was in the three preceding centuries. It is intended only to correct the utterly erroneous idea that the twentieth century is a period of severe intellectual deterioration and that this alleged deterioration is a product of a mass culture which is unique in all respects to this unfortunate century.

Indeed, it would be far more correct to assert that mass culture is now less damaging to the lower classes than the dismal and harsh existence of earlier centuries had ever been. The reading of good books, the enjoyment of superior music and painting, although perhaps meager, are certainly more widespread now than in previous centuries, and there is no reason to believe that it is less profound or less genuine. Only the frustrated attachment to an impossible ideal of human perfection, and a distaste for one's own society and for human beings as they are, can obscure this.

The root of the trouble lies not in mass culture but in the intellectuals themselves. The seduction and corruption of intellectuals are not new, although it is true that mass culture is a new opportunity for such degradation. Intellectuals are not required to read comic strips and then to blame others for doing so. They can skip the first and accept the second as an inevitable manifestation of "the old Adam." It is not popular literacy and leisure which forces university professors to spend their leisure time in reading crime stories or looking at silly television programs. If they lower their own standards, they should not blame those who have not had the privilege of living within a tradition of high standards such as they themselves enjoy or could enjoy if they cared to do so.

Intellectuals do not have to work in the mass media, and even if they do, there is no unavoidable requirement for them to yield their standards as easily as they do, either in their work or outside it. Much but not all the wretched quality of the products of popular culture is a result of the producers' and authors' contempt for the tastes of the prospective audience and of their own *nostalgie de la boue.* There are certainly limitations in what the producers and authors in these occupations can accomplish because their employers are often convinced that only intellectual and aesthetic products which we regard as inferior will find a large audience; there are probably also inherent limitations in the capacity of the audiences of the working and lower-middle classes to respond appreciatively to works of good quality. It is far from certain, however, that the range of those limits has been definitely established and that the best possible has been done within them.

The uneasiness of Mr. Macdonald and of Professor van den Haag is not entirely without foundation. Populism, popularity, commercial criteria, expediency, are all impediments to good, if not to great, cultural achievements. But there are other factors which have little to do with mass culture and which are at least as important, and they do not consider these. Excessive educational and professional specialization seems to me to be more injurious to the cultural life of the educated classes than popular culture, and indeed it prepares the way to resort to popular culture. The squandering by our educational system of the opportunities for creating a foundation for general cultural responsiveness among our more gifted boys and girls and young men and women between the ages of five and twenty-one is certainly far more damaging to high culture in America than the availability of popular culture to the mass of the less gifted. The readiness of university teachers and literary publicists to lower their own standards in their teaching and writing is more pernicious in its effects on high culture than Hollywood or the radio industry.

Naturally there are intellectuals who feel guilty for not acting up to the standards of cultural life which they know to be right. That is no reason why they should take it out on others who come from strata which only now, in the twentieth century, have for the first time in history the possibility of becoming full members of their society, of living a human life with some exercise of cultural taste and the means to acquire or to come into contact with the objects of their taste. Nor are their own shortcomings a good reason why intellectuals should, with such *Schadenfreude*, proclaim and encourage the dilapidation of the high intellectual tradition to which they claim to be devoted.

Finally, it should be said that the strata which have just emerged from an immemorially old, clodlike existence cannot be reasonably expected to have good taste or discriminating judgment. It is quite likely that the majority never will be able to develop such taste and judgment. It is also, however, quite possible that a substantial minority, after several generations, will be assimilated as producers or consumers into one of the various traditions of high culture, and that they will serve as a leaven among their fellows. The chances for this to occur will naturally diminish if the bearers of high culture strike their own flags and scuttle their own ships. All the more reason, therefore, why intellectuals should not, out of impossible political zeal or out of furtive indulgence in pleasures which they know to be unworthy of their own traditions, blame these newly-born strata for ruining what is neither yet ruined nor necessarily ruined. The seed of the cultural health of the intellectuals lies within themselves.

13 Plenitude and Scarcity: The Anatomy of an International Cultural Crisis

Western European and North American student rebellions in the present decade are more comprehensively and more fundamentally hostile toward authority than they were three and four decades ago. They are more hostile in principle toward authority as such, whereas their predecessors were hostile only to particular authorities and submitted enthusiastically to others. They act now without the sponsorship of external adult organizations, and they feel little sympathy with most of them. Where they seek to collaborate with outside organizations such as trade unions or even political parties they seek to do so as equals, and they do not do so often or regularly. They have very little attachment to any section of the population outside their own generation.

The innovators in the present generation of student radicals are antinomian; whereas, when their predecessors of more than a third of a century ago rejected authority, their rejection was sustained and limited by a legitimating authority outside themselves. They did not venture so far or so independently from adult authority as the most advanced student radicals do nowadays. The present-day student radicals act without the legitimating authority of older figures: their middle-aged courtiers who offer their legitimatory services are offering something which is neither wanted nor needed. From Sartre and Marcuse to Paul Goodman and Dwight Macdonald, they provide agreeable but unsought applause. When the student radicals group themselves around an older figure he is of their own creation as was the case of Senator Eugene McCarthy—who was made into a charismatic person by the student radicals' need for one. The adults most closely associated with the student radicals are usually young teachers little older than themselves, and they function more to affirm than to guide and legitimate. The "big names" of present-day student radicalism—Mao Tse-tung, Fidel Castro, Che Guevara, Frantz Fanon—are remote in space or dead. They have no commanding power over them; what they offer to the student radicals is a quasi-bohemian, free-floating, anti-institutional aroma. Even where their older heroes govern tyrannically it is their anarchic element which appeals to the radical students. Castro's period in the Oriente province, his conduct of the affairs of his high office in cafés at 3

Previously published in a slightly different form in *Encounter*, May 1969, pp. 37-48.

a.m., and the generally impromptu air of his tyranny, attract just as the image of Mao Tse-tung owes much to the period in the caves and "the Long March." Neither of these two living amulets is in charge of an organization which the student radicals must obey. It is their inspiration to rebellion abroad rather than their domestic regime which recommends them.

The intellectual "prophets," too, are freely chosen and tolerated and can be dismissed at will by the student radicals. The writings of Professor Herbert Marcuse are useful sources of phrases, not authoritative texts. Professor Wolfgang Abendroth is a self-appointed ambassador of student radicalism to the adult generation; he exercises no authoritative function.

How are these major differences between student radicalism of the 1920s and '30s on the one hand and student radicalism of the '60s on the other to be accounted for?

The New and the Old

The turbulence of student radicalism now has the appearance of being worldwide. Alongside the formal international federations of students, which appear to be of scant significance for the more dramatic activities of the student radicals, there is a spontaneous and unorganized or, at best, an informal identity of sentiment and outlook of the student movement which forms a bridge across national boundaries. In 1968, student radical movements seemed to be synchronized among a number of countries and were uniform in content and technique to an extent reminiscent of the monolithic phase of the Communist International and its subsidiary organizations in the '20s and the '30s.

Student radicalism is no longer the exclusive possession of small, relatively closed sects within larger student bodies; on the contrary, it reaches out toward the sympathy of a very large minority, occasionally even the majority of students, at particular places and for limited times. Its organizations within each country, despite numerous ups-and-downs, are more persistent in their action and have a larger following than they used to have. They show a self-confidence reaching to arrogance in their dealings with hostile authority, and they are aware of the transnational scale of their undertaking. Nonetheless, the movement is not unified internationally; it is certainly no conspiracy. Synchronization is a function of a generally identical mood, not of concerted organized action.

There are major differences between countries and continents. In India, for example, where until the outbursts in Japan in 1960 and in Western countries since 1964 the university student populations were the most turbulent in the world, the student agitators do not as a rule make the structures of the larger society and of the university objects of a general critique. Indian student agitation declares no fundamental criticism of its society; it has no schemes for the reconstruction of Indian universities. It does take stands on public issues, e.g., on behalf of the construction of a steel mill in Andhra Pradesh or on behalf of or in opposition to the use of English as the medium of instruction in higher education—the nearest it has come to taking a stand on some element of a general policy for higher education. The Indian student agitation is "occasionalist"; it responds to particular stimuli, local, regional, or national, but grievances do not become generalized and are therefore not persistent. India, however, is exceptional in its relatively apolitical agitation.[1] In Indonesia student radicalism is, contrarily to India's, wholly—and over the past few years continuously—political. Internal university conditions, terrible though they are, scarcely engage its attention; its interest is in the public realm, where in collaboration with but not under the dominion of the army it was important in the reduction and ultimate undoing of former President Sukarno.

Elsewhere in Asia (omitting mainland China[2]), in North Africa[3] and, to a lesser extent, in black Africa, and in Latin America student agitation follows the conventional nineteenth-century pattern of nationalist agitation against the repressive character of the incumbent government and its insufficient devotion to the national cause (even though the foreign rulers have departed, in some cases very long ago). In Spain, the incessant student agitation of recent years has for the most part been concerned with one narrow issue at the periphery of university organization, namely, the right of students to have their own student organization and not one which is dominated by an official body outside the university. (In the past two years, the Spanish students have become more political, have reached out toward the "workers' commissions" and begun to express more general political attitudes about the regime and about international problems.)

In all these countries, actions are larger, more vehement, and

1. Commentators on the indiscipline of Indian students often explain the dissatisfactions of the Indian students by saying that the political leadership presents no acceptable ideal to the student generation, that it is corrupt and purposeless, etc., and therefore is unable to inspire the students. The students themselves, however, seldom refer to the general features of contemporary Indian society. See my article, "Indian Students," *Encounter*, September 1961.

2. Where the recent form of the student movement appears to be a more moblike variant of youth movements of the Soviet Union, Fascist Italy, and other countries where state and party authority have dominated student action.

3. The countries of the Maghreb still, as in colonial times, have the seat of their most virulent oppositional student organizations located in the former metropolis.

more frequently recurrent than they were in the earlier period but, except for the magnitude and intensity of the manifestations, they have not changed. They agitate against restrictions on freedom of organization and propaganda and against their government's moral corruption and its alleged subservience to foreign powers—in most cases nowadays the United States. Hostility toward "neo-colonialism" is now widespread in most student movements but it is not new. It is only a shoddier version of the Marxist-Leninist analysis of colonialism and imperialism which was a fairly common possession of the nationalistic student movements in Asia during the 1930s or of the African student movements in France and England during the '40s and '50s.

Nonetheless, despite these similarities with their earlier outlook and despite marked national differences, the student movements in most of the countries of the third world, like those in the advanced Western countries, have broken away from the pattern of their antecedents by becoming independent of adult organizations. They have practically no significant older political figures from whom they take their commands. In the underdeveloped countries of Asia and Africa the leaders of an earlier generation of students are in power or apolitical, dead, or in exile. They are, whether dead or alive, out of the question as the leaders of an effective opposition. In those countries of Asia and Africa, where political opposition is currently impracticable, aggressive student radicalism is forced to stand alone, to the extent that it stands at all. In India, where public opposition is still permitted, the student agitation has also, by and large, lost its connection with a dominant organization of adult politicians. Although in many particular instances party politicians are able to manipulate some of the disruptive capacities of Indian students, the organizational links are loose or nonexistent. In India, too, there is no larger adult political movement of which the students regard their own movement as a part, and this is one of the main reasons why the Indian student agitators have practically no general political outlook.[4]

In Eastern Europe, particularly in Poland and Czechoslovakia, courageous students have agitated against tyranny in the larger society and on behalf of the traditional freedoms of thought, expression, and assembly and for the rule of law—and with some of the same nationalist, anti-Russian accompaniment which was characteristic of their nineteenth-century antecedents. And they do these things alone, except for the patronage of a few literary men and professors. Even in the brief periods of liberalization in Poland and

---

4. This is true even for West Bengal. Considering the widespread restlessness of the students, relatively few of them are willing to subordinate themselves organizationally to the Moscow or Peking Communists.

Czechoslovakia, the students acted independently *with* the "liberalizers," not *under* them. In Yugoslavia, in 1968, the students acted entirely on their own, although once the outburst had begun, they received the blessings of some of their teachers. The administration and functions of the university do not worry the liberal students of the "camp of peace and democracy" except in so far as party tyranny and favoritism manifest themselves there.

In its independence of adult oppositional organizations, Western European and North American student radicalism resembles that of the third world. In Britain, the once oppositional Labour Party is ingloriously in power; in Western Germany, the Social Democratic Party is part of the Grand Coalition. In France, the socialists are futile and the communists in their odd way, and despite what General de Gaulle claimed, are pillars of the existing order in the face of student "provocation" and "adventurism." In Italy, the socialists share government responsibility, and the Communist Party has scarcely more sympathy than the French Communist Party has with the student radicals, whom it regards as Maoist *provocateurs*. In the United States, the major parties are abhorrent to the student radicals, and the only adult opposition to the major parties is a racist known-nothingism. In North America, the major parties have never shown any interest in student support, and those parties which did—the Socialist and the Communist parties—have been negligible and have dwindled in size and in moral standing. Official Marxism is unaccredited or discredited, and there is no authoritative ideology ready to hand for student radicalism.

The student radicals in the advanced countries of the West have no adult political masters; they act on their own. Those sections which maintain organizational relations with adult parties or groups are either in a state of conflict with their elders or are relegated to positions of despised insignificance by their radical contemporaries. The discrediting of the Communist parties, the moderation of the Social Democratic parties and the eclipse or disappearance of Fascist and Nazi parties in Western Europe have left the student without either a parent organization of elders or an authoritatively promulgated doctrine to which they can give their loyalty or adherence. A "natural" Castroism, amorphous, passionately hostile to organization, forms a powerful, profound undercurrent of sentiment and of vaguely formulated belief.

The large increase in the scale of agitation has not been accompanied by any striking novelty in doctrine or in organizational technique. In Eastern Europe, the efforts of students to liberalize their communist regimes, to abolish censorship, to introduce a system of several parties, and to "humanize bureaucracy," admirable and courageous though they have been, have not been accompanied by any intellectual innovation. In India, *hic et nunc* protests against very particular features of university and college administration and against very particular deprivations represent a retreat from the variety of nationalist, Marxist, and Gandhian creeds and ideologies of the 1930s. For the rest, the student movements in Africa, Japan, Indonesia, and Latin America have added nothing fundamentally new to the intellectual repertoire of the student movements. The sources of their imagery are themselves only echoes: Frantz Fanon was only an eloquent Sorel; Marcuse, a weak Marxist adulterated by Friedrich Schiller and Wilhelm Reich.

Students commandeer trucks, use "bullroarers," confront the police armed in helmets and bearing shields; they smash windows, break furniture and lights, but technologically they are mainly borrowers. They have adopted Molotov cocktails from the Russians they despise and the Spanish loyalists they have forgotten, and the "sit-in" from the American automobile workers' union with which their sympathies are minimal. The aerosol spray only permits them to do more ineradicably what used to be done by chalk and paint brush. Even their main tactical innovation, buffoonery, is a continuation of the older bohemian maxim: *épatez le bourgeois.* Nor have they been original organizationally; even the specter of a worldwide movement, which has been created for them and from which they profit through the heightening of their self-consciousness and confidence, is the work of the bourgeois press and television.

Nonetheless, there is a fundamental respect in which radicalism at the beginning of the '30s differs from that of the '60s. Far more important than the differences such as the far-reaching organizational independence from adult parties or the criticism of the universities are the differences in fundamental beliefs about the self, about authority, about institutions, and about what is "given" by the past and the present.

Mood, Ideology, and Doctrine

University students were a far smaller proportion of the population at the beginning of the 1930s than they are now. They were less noticed by the public at large or by politicians and they did not conceive of themselves as an independent estate of the realm. Even in Latin America, where they were constitutionally incorporated into university governing bodies, they did not apparently conceive of themselves in their capacity as students as a "permanent interest." Being a student was thought by students and others to be a transient condition, subordinate to or derived from other statuses, from prospective roles at a later stage in life, from parental status, and from identification with a particular college or university.

Most university students in most countries came from the

relatively privileged classes of their societies. Even in the United States, with its open state universities, students formed a small proportion of their generation and they came from the well-off and from the respectable less well-off who believed they had a "stake in society" or wished to acquire such a stake. They expected to enter into the better-paid occupations and professions. The radicals among them did not regard themselves as "representatives," even if unchosen, of all students. They were radicals or revolutionaries, not "radical students" or "revolutionary students." They did not regard the "student class" as an entity central to their respective societies, and they did not regard their student status as an aspect of themselves significant enough to raise revolutionary issues about it. Their parental social class, the social class to which they sought entry through their studies, the ethnic group of which they were part, or the political party under whose guidance they acted were the "powers" of their societies, and they formed their image of themselves from those sources. These collectivities and aggregates are still very important in society and they are still very important to most students but they are not so important to student radicals as they used to be. Why?

Students in the late 1920s and early '30s were at university for a variety of reasons; some were ambitious to learn more, some wished to ascend in society, to earn more than their coevals who did not go on to university. Some attended university because their parents had done so and because it was the "normal" thing to do for full membership in their stratum of society. Others attended university for all or any of these reasons and because it was pleasant and exciting to be there. The pleasures of friendship and discovery and the excitement of sports were available there. It was a way-station on a variety of paths of life.

It was generally regarded in that time that to be able to go to university was a privilege, an advantage in itself and for the future. It was an experience and opportunity open to relatively few. It was to be exploited for the immediate pleasures of intellectual acquisition, convivial experience, and the prospective rewards which it rendered available. The privilege was of a special kind; it implied no present ascendancy over teachers, officials, politicians, or elders in general; it was a privilege in a subordinate role which adumbrated a more substantial and central privilege at a later stage of life. It was a privilege in an inequalitarian society and in an inequalitarian institution where those at a particular level in the hierarchy accepted the ascendancy of those at higher levels. The privilege of attendance at university was the privilege of entry into the middle classes and perhaps even into the upper class—either to enter it for the first time in the history of one's own family or to enter it as one became an adult at a level approximately similar to that of one's own family. In any case, being at university was very much a middle and upper-middle class condition. The life lived at university was of a pattern thought to be appropriate at that particular stage of life to the style of those classes, and completion of a course of studies there was regarded as a major qualification for subsequent membership in those classes. Even in India, Japan, and Germany, where it had become difficult for university graduates to find suitable employment, this conception of the potentialities of university education still prevailed.

Society before the Great Depression and the Second World War was much less equalitarian than it has since become. Among the main criteria for distinguishing the strata from each other was their respectability, their diligence and dutifulness, their capacity and readiness to persist faithfully in a given task, and their willingness to submit their performances to the assessment of authorities they regarded as legitimate. Most university students, however idle or uproarious or however rebellious, accepted this set of arrangements; they thought it just, insofar as they thought about it at all. They expected to enter it and to take superior places in it. Of course, the prospect, except for the minority of the "highly born," was a strenuous one, but the strain was accepted as "given" in the nature of things and as a precondition for the privileges to be enjoyed later. The necessity and the justice of examinations were generally accepted, even in India.[5]

There were among the students some rebels—nationalists, fascists, socialists, communists, aesthetes, and bohemians—who were not wholly reconciled to the university system. Variously, they thought the larger social system unjust, or they were appalled by the philistinism of their fellow countrymen, or they disapproved of their moral conventions and, insofar as they perceived some of these qualities in the universities, they were against them. The fascists and nationalists usually disapproved of ethnically alien rule or of the presence in the middle classes and in the university of ethnically alien elements. They wished to expel the foreigners from their countries or at least from positions of high authority and reward; they therefore criticized the universities where they thought that the aliens were benefiting from them or controlling them. But all of these objectionable qualities did not raise any question concerning the ideal nature and function of universities. Their function as a preparatory stage to the professions and toward the superior occupations was accepted. Their role in the transmission and extension of

5. Students sometimes rebelled against a particular examination in India; occasionally individuals cheated in an examination in the United States, but even the delinquents did not revolt against the institution of examinations.

knowledge and appreciation was accepted. Their methods of government, their use of the resources available to them, the substance of what they taught, the research they did, were not regarded by students as "their business"; these matters were the universities' business, and the students were only there as transient, present or prospective beneficiaries of what they offered. Particular teachers might be disliked, insulted, and in a few cases assaulted; some students might absent themselves from classes and try to prevent other students from attending them. Other students might have little interest in what was taught and would do the minimum of study but they did not challenge the "system." The university system was unimpugned and its place in society unquestioned. This was so even in Germany and India, where the students were fervid with nationalistic political passions and where Jews and Englishmen held prominent positions in the universities. They wished them to go, but they accepted the structure of the university and its place in society and the modalities which flow from its tasks. The politically radical and revolutionary students of this earlier period thus not only accepted the authoritative structures of their radical and revolutionary elders but they also accepted the university as an institution in the society against which they rebelled.

Their beliefs about the nature of society and the rights and privileges of men also showed this same duality. The beliefs of student radicals and revolutionaries were received beliefs, knowingly shared with those of their elders who led and spoke for the larger movement to which the student organizations were affiliated. They were beliefs which had an authoritative promulgation in the programs of parties and in the writings of doctrinaires. They stood generally in an alienated tradition which heightened the authority of the elders to whom the students looked for guidance. The rebellious students were ideologically disposed and they had an ideology made available to them. Marxism (in one or another of its Leninist, Social Democratic, Trotskyite, or Stalinist variants), national socialism, fascism, monarchism, Gandhism, etc., were in their diverse ways the accomplishment of sometimes learned and sometimes genius-like intelligences and of charismatic madmen. None of them was as systematic or as elaborate as Marxism, but most of them had their literary or theoretical classics and all invoked an intellectual past.

The new generation of student radicalism is by contrast relatively unideological. They are ideologically disposed but they have no elaborately and systematically promulgated set of beliefs. Except for small Maoist and Trotskyite groups they do not accept the ideological services which are available to them and they have constructed no ideology of their own. Their own anarchistic inclinations do not lead them to seek the guidance of the writings of Prince Kropotkin or Elisée Reclus and to espouse their ideas. They have affinities with Fourier and Proudhon but they do not look to them for an intellectual construction of the future. Lukács is singularly not in demand, Habermas has been rejected, Lucien Goldmann has never been accepted.

Instead of ideology, they have a mood which a strong systematizing mind could cast into a coherently formulated ideology for wide acceptance. The world burgeons with potentialities for such an ideology. Marcuse, Louis Althusser, R. D. Laing, Foucault, Norman Brown, Fanon, Paul Baran, Ernest Mandel, and others all offer some of the ingredients of an ideology. They are all minor prophets whose prophecies overlap with each other because they all contain the basic mood. A pervasive intelligence might articulate the mood into a doctrine.

Of Evil and Perfection

The germinal element in student radicalism in Western Europe and North America is a relatively novel moral mood. Like apocalyptic and manichaean revolutionaries in the past they demand a total transformation—a transformation from an undifferentiated totality of evil to an undifferentiated totality of perfection. Evil consists in the deadening of sentiment through institutions and more particularly through the exercise and subordination to authority in particular institutions and in the state. Perfection consists in the free expansion of feeling and the fulfillment of desires. The highest collective good is "participation." "Participation" is a situation in which the individual's desires are fully realized in the complete self-determination of the individual and which is simultaneously the complete self-determination of each institution and of society as a whole. In the good community, the common will harmonizes individual wills.

The SDS in the United States spoke about "participation" long before General de Gaulle's proposal in June 1968 of the participatory solution as an alternative to the solutions of "totalitarian communism" and "competitive capitalism." Lucien Lévy-Bruhl spoke about it before either, and he referred to the extension of the boundaries of the self—among other objects—to include within it objects which to empirical common sense appear alien to it. Lévy-Bruhl's idea of participation entailed a transcendence of boundaries. Contemporary student radicals critize modern society and its institutions, particularly the university, because they resist the aspirations of a limitless expansion of the boundaries of individuality. Individualities as they expand embrace each other in the seamless unity of the community.

The contemporary proponents of participation do not distinguish between the baser will of empirical individuals consisting of actual and immediate sentiments, impulses, and desires and the higher wills which are fused into a common will. The common will is not the resultant of the rationally arrived-at assent of its members, it is not an actually *shared* act of decision; it is certainly not the outcome of consent to a compromise arrived at by bargaining and exchange. It is not the product of rational argument. It refuses to accept anything less than what is immediately desired. Participation is the transformation of expanding sentiments and desires into reality in a community in which all members realize their sentiments simultaneously. Anything less is repressive.

This is why the advance guard of student radicalism is so resolute in its reaction against repression. It is resolute not just against the violent and often brutal repression by the police; it is just as resolute against the moderate repression which is entailed by the application of the principle of *in loco parentis*. It is against the "repressiveness" of the rules of the game of parliamentary politics and of distributions of rewards in accordance with a criterion of merit. It is against "institutional repression" or "institutional violence" by which is usually meant the discipline of a practicable consensus in a regime of scarcity. Whatever hampers the fulfillment of whatever happens to be desired at the moment—whether it is a student housing arrangement which stipulates the hours of visiting in halls of residence, or an examination, or a convention regarding dress, or sexual behavior in public places—is repressive. And, as such, it is part of an undifferentiatedly repressive system.[6]

Academic intellectual life is repressive too. It has a tradition which must be assimilated before it can be criticized and corrected. Those academic subjects which have the least imposing, least demanding traditions have the most appeal to the hypersensitive young persons who cannot tolerate any demands which do not flow out of themselves.

Sociology and political science are subjects with ill-ordered, unauthoritative traditions. Architecture and the study of English literature in the United States, *Germanistik* in Germany, have broken with their own classical traditions of philological and historical scholarship. Certain kinds of sociology and political science are obsessed by fantasies of the concentration of power, by

6. Student radicals in France, Germany, and the United States do not know that their frequent denunciations of the "system" are of a piece with the Nazi abuse of the Weimar Republic, called *"das System."* This is only a minor instance of their contempt for history and of the past experience of mankind. History being "little more than the register of the crimes, follies, and misfortunes of mankind," there is nothing to be learned from it. More important, however, is the belief that any inheritance from the past is a curb on present potentialities and a hinderance to creativity.

the romantic imagery of the atomized *Gesellschaft*; architecture, English, and *Germanistik* increasingly aim to foster the student's creativity in contrast with helping him to assimilate a tradition of learning. They are "soft options" as compared with mathematics and physics. In general, factual studies are regarded as much inferior to theoretical studies. (The sociology of knowledge, that stillborn offspring of Karl Mannheim, has again become an object of student interest—not, however, as a systematic study of the relationship of institutions to intellectual traditions and their development but as a means of "unmasking" the real and problematic motives of academic knowledge and of showing the vanity of aspirations to objective truth.)

It is no wonder that the New Left sociologists and political scientists criticize quantitative sociology. Statistics have to be studied. They have a structure which is external to the individual student and to which the student must subordinate himself before he can use them. They constrict the free outward movement of the self and they are, therefore, evocative of scarcity. Economics is about scarcity. It is also very demanding of selfless study; it has no interest as an academic subject to the student radicals.

The Sacredness of Sentiment

The conception of a life in which desires cannot be completely realized at the moment they are experienced is part of a larger view of existence as a realm of scarcity. It is a tradition with the longest history in the moral repertoire of mankind. The acknowledgment of the fact of scarcity has been an essential element in the outlook of mankind over most of its history. Poverty and injustice, illness and the brevity of life, the limitations on the possibility of gratifying desires and impulses have been regarded as inexpungible elements of the situation of mankind, and ethical patterns and theodicies have been constructed to justify or to censure—and to integrate—this inevitable condition. The opening of the self and its elevation was confined to festivities, carnivals, and rites; but everyday life was marked by constriction imposed by nature, society, and the moral powers of the personality. It consisted in limits on experience, the selective suppression of experienced impulse, the "avoidance of temptation" to impulses not yet experienced but known to be capable of coming forward into consciousness or conduct. Poverty, ignorance, fear, and oppression through most of human history and for most of the human race have been the preconditions for the constriction of individuality. A few great personalities transcended these limitations and made their lives into "works of art."

Christianity (particularly in its dissenting Protestant form), the growth of wealth, the spread of literacy, and the gradual recession of the primordial categories and criteria of assessing the meaning and worth of a human being have in the course of centuries worn away some of these individuality-suppressing and -constricting conditions. A profound revolution was worked by romanticism, which spread more widely in intellectual circles the conception of "genius" which need not regard the laws of society and its authorities and which aimed only to be guided by the inner necessities of the expansion of the self—to embrace new experiences, to enrich itself by the opening of its sensibilities.

The First World War and the Great Depression were the watershed. The erosion of the bourgeois ethic and of the puritanism of diligence, respectability, and self-restraint for the sake of prospective results which rendered one respectable was greatly aided by the Depression. The vanity of self-restraint was made evident; saving and striving were discredited; sexual self-restraint had been undermined by popular psychoanalysis and its literary popularization in the period between the wars. More or less liberal, tolerant, and constitutional political elites had been shown to be incompetent by the prolonged slaughter of the First World War and by their failures in dealing with unemployment during the Great Depression. The regime of scarcity with which they were associated was discredited when their own legitimacy diminished. The same happened to the virtues of abstinence and self-discipline preached from the pulpits. Ecclesiastical authority had been under a steady pressure of rational disbelief and indifference. Its legitimacy was further undermined in intellectual circles because of the association of the churches with the earthly regimes of external constriction and internal restraint already under assault from other sources.

The Second World War was followed by an efflorescence of material well-being in the advanced countries on a scale never previously experienced. Particularly for the educated classes, there seemed to exist a relatively unbounded vista of opportunity for interesting employment, for travel, and for freedom from the restraints of impecuniousness, boring toil, and confinement. Full employment, the welfare services, inflation, made unrealistic the conception of a rainy day for which to save. At the outermost reaches was the perpetual threat of extinction in a war fought with nuclear weapons. The anxiety about the latter accentuated the attachment to pleasures of the moment. The heir of these developments was the generation born after the end of the Second World War.

In a variety of ways, this was a uniquely indulged generation. Parents who were in a state of unprecedented prosperity were persuaded of the merits of hedonism and were capable of giving some reality to its precepts in the raising of their children. They were convinced of the beneficence of a life free of repression and inhibition, and they treated their offspring with a concern and affection which seemed to confirm the prediction made by Ellen Key at the beginning of the twentieth century that this was to be the "century of the child." Expanding incomes and unceasing freedom from the threat of unemployment—for the middle classes at least— made for a readiness to believe that scarcity had been expelled from human existence. A life beyond the dreams of avarice seemed to have become accessible to those whom the fortunes of birth—in time and status—had favored. They were moreover, an increasingly larger proportion of the population.

The postwar generation has grown up, too, in a society in which authority has been deprived of its sacredness. As the center of society expanded, those in positions of authority acquired a new conception of their obligations. Democratic elections, moreover— and a populistic outlook even where there were no democratic elections—have made rulers believe that they have to justify them- selves by realizing the desires of their citizenry. The expansion of individuality and the appreciation of the self, intricately related to enhanced self-esteem in many Western societies, have diminished to some extent the arrogance of authority. The range of dispersion of dignity between the highest and the quite low has narrowed. It is certainly true that all Western—and all other—societies are far from the fulfillment of an ideal of equality. Power is unequally distri- buted, wealth is unequally distributed, income is unequally distri- buted, but the deference system of modern societies strains toward equalitarianism. Of course this "moral equality" is far from being realized; the strength of inherited beliefs and the presence of such tremendous concentrations of authority in the state and in great economic organizations—public and private—stand in the way of its realization.

Nonetheless, the younger generation—living in the midst of the culturally juvenocentric society which Huizinga discerned already in the 1930s—is experiencing this moral equalitarianism to a far- reaching degree. New methods of pedagogy and exclusion from the labor market—as far as middle-class young persons are concerned— have reduced the amount of experience with severely hierarchical and repressive institutions. They are thereby spared direct contact with the very painful features of the condition of scarcity. But as much as the arrogance of authority has diminished, it has still not disappeared. Its diminution, moreover, has been more than balanced by the increased intolerability of what it seeks to impose. Sensitivity to the impositions of authority has greatly increased, and almost every impingement on it from the outside—unless voluntarily chosen as part of the expansion of individuality—is painful to the point of unsupportability.

Basic in all this is the view that every human being simply by virtue of his humanity is an essence of unquestionable, undiscriminatable value with the fullest right to the realization of what is essential in him. What is essential is his sensibility, his experienced sensation, the contents of his imagination, and the gratification of his desires. Not only has man become the measure of all things; his sentiments have become the measure of man. Provision for the growth of the capacity for unconfined sensation is the measure of the value of an institution. The goodness of a life consists in its continuous enlargement of these sensations and of the experiences which give rise to them. Institutions with their specialized and prescribed roles, their restrictions on individual wilfulness, the crystallization of traditions and their commitments which bind the future by the past are repugnant to this aspiration toward an individuality which creates its temporary boundaries only in response to its internal needs. Authority is repugnant too, and all that tradition brings down and imposes from the past.

All this is old stuff. This is what the romantics taught us. But romanticism was only a literary and more or less philosophical movement; it did not become a widely pervasive outlook and style of life for many persons. Writers, artists, and bohemians espoused and embodied it, but its consistent following was small. The desacralization of authority, the productivity of the economy, the growth of moral equality, and the spread of enlightenment and educational opportunity have resulted in the diffusion of a much more consequent romanticism throughout a much broader section of each Western society. The more prosperous classes are the recipients of its diffusion; the offspring of these classes are their purest products.

University students in Western countries, despite an increased recruitment from among the offspring of the working classes, still come largely from the middle- and upper-class families. Many of those who have not come from these classes live in a cultural atmosphere of hedonistic expectations for the present and the future as much as do those who have come from families in which such expectations are to some extent realized. Many are supported from the public treasury, at the expense of taxpayers. The availability of opportunity to attend university is still interpreted by many students as it was in the past—as a first step into a less constricted future. Attendance at university, which was once regarded as a stroke of the good fortune of birth or the result of exertion and which offered its beneficiaries a chance to diminish to some extent the rigors of the regime of scarcity, is now, however, regarded by student radicals as itself part of an actual realm of plenitude. Anyone should have it for the asking, and, once admitted, no further demands should be made except where the person on whom the demands are laid is also the one who makes them.

University students, in the view of forty years ago, appeared to be on a straight road into a future which, in the light of the standards of the Enlightenment and in view of the immemorial fate of human beings, seemed to be extraordinarily rich in the possibilities of a better life—at least for themselves if not for all the other members of their own societies. The student radicals of today have a quite different view of the matter; they do not wish to live in a society in which "the danger of death by starvation is replaced by the danger of death by boredom." The denunciation of the "consumers' society" is the common slogan of the French and West German student radicals; less explicitly but no less pervasively, the same view obtains among the American and British student radicals. They do not wish to be part of a "repressively tolerant society" which seduces by its favors. They wish their universities to be "restructured" to become the microcosms of a total revolution, from which, in moments of exhilaration, they think that the rest of the society can be no less totally transformed. The universities must become "participatory," and from there onward their "societies" must become "participatory." They wish to choose their own teachers, form their own syllabi, and, as a concession to a reality in which they do not wish to believe, they will accept examinations if they themselves participate in their construction and administration. By control over their universities, by "occupying" them, they give expression to sentiment. The mere expression of sentiment is an end in itself and the beginning of the transformation of society by the power of feeling. The slogan "imagination takes power" was indeed the appropriate maxim of a "revolution" constituted by taking asylum in university buildings with occasional sorties outward to hold "demonstrations of sentiment" and to fight with the police without any substantial objective such as the seizure of an arsenal, communication or transportation centers, or any of the institutions crucial for the revolutionary seizure of power. Acts of feeling and states of mind are crucial.

Against Boundaries

The student revolutionaries criticize their universities for having become "integrated" into their respective societies but they are otherwise completely for integration. They believe that everything is integrated with everything else and that dispassionately acquired knowledge is an impossibility. They insist that "objectivity" and "neutrality" are simply masks which conceal the intention to serve "the system." They do not wish their universities to become "ivory towers"; they refuse to acknowledge the differentiation of tasks or a division of labor among institutions. There is no task which they would not have their institutions undertake in the transformation of society; only the disciplined transmission of knowledge[7] and disciplined discovery are left unmentioned by them.

The slogans of "student power" (Great Britain and the United States), *cogestion* (France), and *Drittelparität* (West Germany) disregard the particular tasks of universities and the functions which these tasks qualify them to perform. The idea that there is a measure of inequality which is constitutive in the university's transmission of knowledge from those who possess more of it in particular spheres to those who possess less of it in those spheres is alien to their conception of the right order of life. For the same reason, equally alien is the idea that different institutions have different functions to perform. The very notion of differentiation and specialization in a division of labor among individuals and among institutions is repugnant to them.

They demand—at least in the United States but also in France —that their universities cease to be connected with government— except presumably to be supported financially by it. At the same time, in the United States and in France they insist that the universities take the responsibility—financial, primarily—for forming "participatory" communities in their own neighborhoods. They wish their universities to be open to everyone; they are resolutely opposed to *selection*, to *numerus clausus*, and to the restriction on the use of university facilities and amenities to those who are its inscribed members. The "openness" or boundarylessness of institutions for which they contend is paralleled by their insistence on the openness of individual existence to new experience and new sensations. Hence, within their universities, the rebellious minority wish to be rid of all remnants of the institutions which embody the principle of *in loco parentis*. No restraints on their conduct are to be tolerated; neither restraints on their living arrangements, on their sexual associations, or on their consumption of narcotics. They insist on an expanding series of subsidies for whatever activities they wish to engage in.

These views of life, society, and the university are not by any means shared by the entire generation of students today in the Western countries. Most of the students in most universities still share in the older culture. Nonetheless, the new "communitarian," "participatory" culture—which is really the romantic hunger for

---

7. They seem to think so poorly of the transmission of knowledge as a university task that they insist that all learning must be through "dialogue" and "contestation." They assume that the past has accomplished nothing, and that those who are ready to transmit the fruit or record of its accomplishments are simply repressive of the essential individuality of each student.

282 Intellectuals in Modern Societies

Gemeinschaft[8] on a more grandiose scale—pervades a substantial minority of the intelligent, sensitive and hyperactive students.

The Limits of Flattery

Why should all this have occurred on such a scale since 1964? It is now almost twenty-four years since the end of the Second World War. Most of today's undergraduates were born in the late 1940s, most of the more advanced or graduate students were born during or just after the war. They were raised during the prosperity of the 1950s; they came to such maturity as they possess after the thaw of the Cold War.

In most of the countries of Western Europe and in North America, a considerable state of consensus has obtained between the ruling party and the bulk of the opposition. Socialist parties of aggressively radical bearing have been lacking, the Communist parties, as in the United States and Great Britain, have nearly disappeared, or in countries where they are strong, they have gradually, as in Italy and France, become domesticated to bourgeois society. Therewith they have lost the attractive power which Communist parties had for young antinomians in the heroic period of the Communist International. The hypersensitive student radicals of the past few years came, as they left adolescence, face to face with a "reactionary mass" formed by the major parties, the leading politicians, leading trade unionists and businessmen, leading journalists, leading academics and scientists, all committed to "the system." This "reactionary mass," so hated, has until recently not responded reciprocally.

I am speaking only of moderates, liberals, and conservatives, not of the chorus of bourgeois highbrows like Abendroth, Enzensberger, Touraine, Mahler, Tynan, Macdonald, Jacobs, and countless others who flatter the student radicals and assure them of how right they are in whatever they demand. Many members of this flatterers' chorus are middle-aged adults who seek the ardors of their youth in the vicarious exhilaration of "sit-ins" and strikes. Old memories of revolutions dreamed of in cafés and salons are revived, embittered recollections of the Moscow trials and of the Hungarian revolution of 1956 are dissipated by the thought of the new revolutionaries in the universities. One would have expected them to sympathize with these self-proclaimed revolutionaries. What is surprising is the chorus of appreciation which especially in the United States has come

8. I should like to take this opportunity to call attention to a forgotten book which deserves to be recalled and studied for its sober assessment of an earlier form of the present *Gemeinschaftsschwärmerei*. It is Professor Helmuth Plessner's *Grenzen der Gemeinschaft: eine Kritik des sozialen Radikalismus* (Bonn, 1923).

forth from university administrators, clergymen, university teachers, editors, and others who do not have to vindicate their revolutionary illusions.

Great pains have been taken to appreciate their "just demands," as well as the legitimacy of their complaints about the vileness of life, the hypocrisy and lack of ideals of their parents, the terrible world which their parental generation is bequeathing to them. Above all, the "sincerity" and "idealism" of the student radicals are praised. Great exertions are made to "understand" them and to discern what is valid in their discontents. Up until recently, scarcely a single politician has proposed that the lowering of the voting age to eighteen should be deferred until the student disturbances abate. The occasional but increasingly frequent voices which demand the withholding or withdrawal of grants, scholarships, etc., from public funds have called forth from the despised agents of consensus and unideological politics strong words and often successful efforts to prevent such sanctions from being applied.

The moral self-abasement of a large part of the French literary and academic intellectual class in the face of the student "revolution" in May and June 1968 expressed a disposition which is to be found in nearly every Western country. The students have for the time being replaced the "working classes" at the highest point of the pantheon of the "progressive" intelligentsia. There is no evidence that student revolutionaries are impressed by this. As far as they are concerned it is only an attempt to moisten a flood.

Weak and compliant authorities occupying the highest positions in institutions which, by their nature and task, require the exercise of authority do not arouse respect or instill fear. They do not reconcile those who refuse (or are unable) to distinguish them from genuine reactionaries. They only generate contempt and hostility, particularly when they themselves seem to believe so uncertainly in the legitimacy of their authority. Split, disunited, temporizing, half-hearted authority which repeats against itself the charges made by the student radicals serves only to encourage more hostility. It must be said on behalf of the student radicals that they take with a large admixture of salt the flattery and self-abasement of their elderly admirers. But the feebleness of those whom their fantasy expects to be strong gives courage to their hostility. The absence of effective positive models and the faint-heartedness of those who oppose them open a free field for their aggressive dispositions.

In the advanced Western countries the governments are nowadays generally humanitarian in their sympathies and progressive in their domestic social and economic policies. In many particular instances, their conduct diverges from these norms but on the whole, as compared with the constitutional governments of earlier decades—to say nothing of the fascist and communist governments—they are very liberal; they respect the freedom of expression, they legislate for the extension of welfare benefits and educational opportunity and submit to the insults and abuse directed toward them. By and large, they seldom order security forces to shoot looters and depredators: they generally attempt to restrain their agents in the face of rioters, and they are usually successful in doing so. Chicago, it is true, was an exception, but it would be as wrong to deny its exceptional character as it would be to deny its excess.[9] They are even more yielding and conciliatory in speech. They find it hard to refuse the claims to rightfulness of the students who are against them. At most, they denounce the malfactions as the work of a "tiny minority of extremists" while acknowledging in many respects the legitimacy of the demands of the student radicals. What is true of governments is even more true of university administrations.

Despite all this, the existing authorities do not abdicate their authority; they are only liberal in social policy and compliant before the denial of their own legitimacy. Despite their conciliatory statements that the students are right in this or that, despite their forbearance, they still go about the business of conducting their governments. They maintain and use their armed forces, they impose burdens of national military service, they administer regimes of scarcity which cannot provide enough for everyone.[10] The same is true in universities; the teachers continue to occupy their professorships (and associate and assistant professorships), to receive their salaries, to set, administer, and mark examinations, pass judgments on dissertations, and grant or withhold degrees and diplomas. Presidents and rectors of universities might make speeches and write articles explaining that much of the criticism which student radicals

9. The roughness of American and French police is notorious, but in all of the student demonstrations of last spring in Paris only one young man was fatally wounded during an altercation between demonstrators and police and he was the victim of a knife wound which has not been attributed to the police. And in the United States, the behavior of the police in Chicago in front of the Hilton Hotel in August 1968, utterly incommensurate with the intended and real provocation, was also a deviation from the prevailing pattern. Recollection of American police conduct in labor disputes and toward radicals over the past century would soon disclose the relative domestication of the police in the past few years in dealing with "dangers to public order." All I contend above is that the agents of public order are much less harsh and repressive than they were during the 1920s and '30s in Western Europe and North America—and in many other places in the world.

10. The ineffectiveness of authority is a stimulus to aggressiveness against it. A deprivational, scarcity-administering authority puts itself into a difficult position when it acts ineffectively. If the United States government had been able to fight the war in Viet Nam successfully (even using the same technology it is now using in fighting without a positive outcome), I venture to say that it would not have aroused such animosity among student radicals as it has in the past few years.

make of the ideal-less, faltering, contemporary, liberal society is just; but they do not dissolve their universities and they do not resign. They continue to operate their universities, which, despite permissiveness and flexibility and flattery, continue to be selective institutions in a world of scarcity.

The Ordeals of Scarcity: Examinations

The radical students are opposed to competition and the scarcity which necessitates it. Scarcity is constriction imposed by the structure of the world outside the self. The ideal of the expanding self, of impulse and desire realized at the moment of conception, of "participatory democracy" in which all selves are simultaneously and fully realized would come to nothing in a regime of scarcity. The ethos of student radicalism is the ethos of a regime of plenitude; but they know too that their societies are regimes of scarcity. Their critique of present-day society is directed against the scarcity which they allege it creates and imposes. They sometimes claim and always assume that a regime of plenitude is possible. In the world of their fantasy, the good life is a life lived in plenitude. But they know that scarcity exists and they are fantastically horrified by its continued existence. They are entranced by a vision of plenitude of which they also disapprove when they conceive of it in its present approximation as the "affluent society" or *société de consommation* or the *Konsumgesellschaft* but which has nonetheless become an essential part of their construction of reality. They also know that they live in a world of scarcity run by adults whose legitimacy they do not acknowledge and whose ascendancy they hate; they deny the inevitability of the realm of scarcity and at the same time they know that they themselves will not be able to avoid it. They know too that if they do not accept the rules of the regime of scarcity they will go to the wall. Dean Marc Zamansky, himself one of the acclaimers of student radicalism, told the striking students of the faculty of sciences in Paris, when they were debating the boycott of examinations, that even "a socialist society must be selective." A bourgeois society can hardly be any less so. Honors are scarce, first places are scarce, research grants and stipends are scarce, professorships are scarce, appointments in the higher civil service are scarce, so even are interesting appointments in the film industry, in television, and in market research! They are of course all more available than they used to be, but the student rebels do not know the past any more than most other young persons and they do not take seriously what little they do know of it.

The examination system is the focal point of the repugnance for the regime of scarcity, particularly in the European universities where they are so concentrated in comparison with the dispersion of the American examination system. In the United States, however, as if to compensate for the attenuation of strain by the dispersion of examinations, there is the other strain of having to obtain marks high enough to qualify for admission to an eminent graduate school and then the serious strain of postgraduate work. The radicals among American undergraduates are also those disposed to go on to graduate school for no other reason than that it is less obnoxious than the bourgeois world outside. It is to those better universities with famous graduate schools, which are also more liberal and therefore more popular with student radicals, that admission is sought. Places in such universities are scarce and their regime is severe for those who succeed in entering. In American universities, postgraduate studies, to make up for the lightness of undergraduate courses, are densely organized. Many of the students are married and feel the pressing proximity of philistine life—family, job, routine responsibilities, assimilation into the great machine where ideals are only a fragrance; and hard decisions in the allocation of scarce resources to alternative ends must be made. The long-drawn-out proceedings of acquiring a postgraduate degree—several sets of examinations and an elaborate research dissertation—and a real or imagined dependence on the good will and sponsorship of one's supervisor for financial support and then for appointment to a teaching or research post on completion, add to the strain. All this underscores the discrepancy between the ideal of a regime of plenitude and the "hard facts of life" so often and so rightly referred to by older critics of student radicalism. It all comes at the worst possible time—at the point of passage which separates the open life of the expanding individuality from the dreaded knuckling under to authority.

It is not for nothing that the French "revolutionaries," once they occupied the Sorbonne and other university buildings and distracted their minds from examinations by the exhilaration of meetings of action committees and fighting with the police from behind barricades of largely symbolic function, soon began to worry about their examinations. Nor is it for nothing that the German student radicals—sprung from a breed famous for putting off the dreaded examinations—should demand that students sit on examining bodies and that the examination system be transformed.

It does not therefore seem to me to be accidental that the outbursts all over Europe and the United States reached their height in the spring of 1968 just at the time when students normally begin their first preparations for examinations. It was fitting that within a short time after the occupation of the Sorbonne, examinations— whether they should be boycotted, put off, abolished, transformed or, in the last resort, taken—came to occupy the center of the revolutionaries' attention.

I do not contend that examinations and examinations alone are the cause of the present student unrest,[11] and that they provide an exhaustive explanation of why the disorders occurred on such a grand scale in the first half of 1968.

Issues and Non-causes

To understand why 1968 saw such an expansion of radical student activity it is not sufficient to consider, for each country taken singly, the feelings of grievance which have a loose connection with the causes and the issues which have been made of the grievances. The condition of youth in each country, the domestic and international political situation of each country, and the state of higher educational institutions in each country cannot provide an adequate explanation of the outburst.

It is certainly true that every society has its own history and its own boundaries, and in each of the countries there have been processes and institutional practices which have in a sense lives of their own. Furthermore, these processes and institutional practices are fairly similar to each other across national boundaries and these have made for similarities of response. The growth of affluence has been common; the growth in the numbers of university students; the lag (except in Great Britain) of facilities behind numbers; the large size of many universities in the United States and on the Continent; the trends in the development of the idea of the expanding self; the war in Viet Nam; consensus politics of the major parties; etc., etc., are elements common to almost all the major Western countries, but they do not explain why so much happened within a relatively short period.

It is also true that in France, Italy, and Germany conditions in the universities became aggravated by the neglect of necessary reforms in university government and structure.[12] But the same could not be said of Great Britain or the United States.

The internal domestic regulations and disciplinary arrangements

11. Examinations and their appurtenances are among the main occasions of student disorder in Indian higher education. The confrontation of a kinship-dominated culture of diffuse expectations, such as that of the student in his familial *foyer*, with the culture which demands specific performances as conditions for prospective rewards such as examination marks, appointments to particularly desirable positions, etc., creates much tension.

12. The French academic session of 1967-68 began late by about two weeks because of insufficient facilities. The students were already apprehensive in October and November 1967 about whether they would be held responsible in the examinations for material omitted because of the shortened period of teaching.

of American universities are certainly irksome to some students, as have been the occasional arrogation of power and its unthinking use by professional university administrators (e.g., the withdrawal of the "speakers corner" at Berkeley in 1964); and sensitivity to this has also become sharper and more reactive in the past few years. Above all, there is the continuation of the war in Viet Nam in all its cruelty and its unending ineffectiveness and the menace of conscription into the most individuality-constricting of environments; draft card burning, Dow Chemical, C.I.A. and Army recruiting officers, Institute for Defense Analyses affiliations, and the Reserve Officers Training Corps are all part of the Viet Nam complex. Finally, the agitation of Negro extremists in the United States has increased as the moderate leadership has become depleted, and with it the idiom of violence has become more widespread and more permissible. At the same time the number of Negro students in the universities has increased and with it an increasingly obstinate intransigence in their demands for segregation in residence and curriculum and for Negro student power. The reluctance of the Negro students to collaborate with the white students has caused the radical white students to be more radical in order to show how fervent they are in the Negro cause.

For British radical students there are Rhodesia, Mr. Enoch Powell, the supply of arms to Nigeria, the tacit, uncomfortable and negligible support of the British Government for American action in Viet Nam, "co-residence," college gate hours, biological warfare research, etc.

In the German universities, reforms in the system of academic self-government have made slow and unsteady progress while radical German students have intensified their extraacademic concerns. For German students, there have been the Springer press, the Shah of Iran, the alliance of the Federal Government with the United States, the recognition of the East German Democratic Republic, the emergency legislation of the spring of 1968, and the legalization of the German Communist Party. For French students, there has been very little since the end of the war in Algeria except for anti-Americanism and unlimited visiting between the sexes in university cities. From time to time specific issues like the free distribution of *cours polycopiés* arose and passed away. There were also fights with the extremist *Occident* but these did not lead to large-scale demonstrations or strikes.

In Italy, there were many fights between antagonistic extremists of various designations but until recently these did not precipitate a "confrontation" with the authorities on a broad front. Although university conditions have continued to be very poor and the government and parliament have been very laggard in the promotion of reform, student agitation in Italy only became acute in connection with the Venice Biennale, the Milan Triennale, and examinations. In Spain, the conflict between students on the one hand and the authorities in government and the university on the other has been unremitting, and the original domestic issue of "free student syndicates" has been increasingly supplemented by anti-Americanism (Viet Nam, American aid to Spain) and fitful collaboration with the illegal "workers' commissions."[13]

The intervention of the police in student disturbances within or outside universities has inevitably and everywhere become a major issue, which has drawn into the wake of student radicalism large numbers of students previously relatively indifferent to the concerns of the radicals.

It is impossible to establish a pattern of precipitating causes operating in each country in 1968 to account for the flood of student radicalism in that year. It appears more reasonable to assert that in the major Western countries there has developed among a minority of students a common political culture, a common image of the world nurtured by a common fundamental ethos—the ethos of the expanding ego and of a regime of plenitude in a situation which receives a common interpretation. The common situation is one of weak authority, elaborate and demanding organization, a wide consensus around the center of society, a high level of affluence through most of the society, and the loss of *élan* of traditional revolutionary and radical parties and doctrines.

Many of the issues around which the passions of the radical students focus are not seriously or deeply cared about. What does the German SDS care about Iran or about the protection of civil liberties in Western Germany? The accusations of anti-Negro prejudice against the newly appointed director of the London School of Economics, for example, were frivolous. The accusations of indifference to Negro needs on the part of the Columbia University administration were a little better based but they were not quite as the SDS alleged. The concentration of effort to frustrate the Dow personnel officers was much ado about nothing.

13. The Japanese disturbances are recurrent and of fluctuating intensity and scale. The issue there is the Japanese defense agreement with the United States, and particular issues appear from time to time such as the visit of a United States naval vessel or a trip by the Japanese prime minister to the United States. On the whole the Japanese movement has not been synchronized with that in Western Europe and America; although it was only moderately active in the first half of 1968, it assumed very large proportions only in the latter part of the year, when the European movement had reached its peak and then somewhat abated.

In Mexico, a long period of quiet was followed in 1968 by extraordinary demonstrations and violence, originating in no easily discernible academic or political issue.

The insulting of M. Missoffe, the Minister for Youth and Sport, when he opened the swimming pool in the faculty of letters at Nanterre, was a confrontation pure and simple; M. Missoffe was a harmless figure and the swimming pool could do no harm either. But he was a minor member of the government of France and he had been invited by the authorities of the university. He was simply the occasion for expressing hostility against governmental and academic authority. The protest against the visit of the Shah of Iran (which was the occasion of the death of Benno Ohnesorg at the hands of the police) was not a serious issue for the West Berlin students; it was the occasion for a confrontation in which authority could be abused and discomfited. The striking thing about all of these precipitating issues is how soon they disappeared under the onrush of subsequent responses.

At the London School of Economics, the merits and demerits of Dr. Adams were forgotten in favor of resistance to the disciplinary actions threatened by the authorities of the School following the death of a porter. The long "sit-in" disregarded Dr. Adams; it was concerned with the removal of the penalties against the suspended students. At Columbia, protests against the action of the university administration in summoning the police and against the police for their unnecessarily harsh action soon dwarfed protests against the university's policy to build a gymnasium in Morningside Park and even against its relationship to the Institute for Defense Analyses. At Wisconsin, protests against the university's use of police and against the conduct of the police placed the prior protests against the Dow Chemical Company in the shadows. In West Berlin, the agitation following the death of Benno Ohnesorg consigned the Shah of Iran far into the recesses of radical student memory. In Paris, even the issues of visiting rights of the two sexes in university cities and of the disciplinary proceedings against Cohn-Bendit and his colleagues were put aside in favor of amnesty of those arrested during the demonstrations and skirmishes of the nights of May.

All these issues are very disparate and they do not tell us why they should have emerged with such an uproar this year. The earth is a vale of tears but it was certainly not much worse in 1968 than in other years in the past century-and-a-half. The horrified resistance of those possessed by fantasies of the regime of plenitude to the oncoming pressure of the regime of scarcity does not explain why the outburst occurred this year. Nor does the war in Viet Nam and student hostility to it explain it. Certainly the lagging of university reform on the Continent does not explain it either.

Center and Periphery

We are far from living in a single world community but the rudiments of a world society do exist. The international scientific community is the most international of all the elements of this rudimentary world society. Learned and scientific periodicals, international scientific societies, and the universities are the most elaborated and most internationally coherent parts of this rudimentary worldwide network of institutions. They do, at least at their peaks, have common standards, common heroes, and a unifying sense of affinity. Students through their membership in universities share in some of this, and their sense of sharing in it is accentuated among a fluctuatingly small group by an acute sense of generational identity.

Although international student organizations are of little significance in the concert of action of 1968, and although students have nothing like a major scientific or scholarly press which creates a common focus of attention and a common awareness of leading accomplishments and personalities, they have an effective surrogate in the mass media—the newspaper press, radio, and television. Information flows rapidly without a student international, without the use of a cumbersome system of couriers and coded messages such as international revolutionary organizations had to use. The radical students have not created this organ of their movement but they have been responsive to it and, indeed, being aware of its value, direct their actions to it. They value television publicity as much as do the figures of the entertainment world or of politics, and they are as sensitive to it. Their generational identity, the large radius of their attention, and the internationality of the academic system render them very reactive to what the mass media bring to them. The students are members of the rudimentary international society.

This rudimentary international society is no more equalitarian in fact than are the various national societies. This is as true of scientific distinction as it is of wealth and political power. The scientific world has its centers and its peripheries just as any national society has, and so does the sphere of student radicalism. What happens in the periphery does not radiate to the center, the movement is in the contrary direction. When the Indian students erupt as they have been doing quite continuously for about twenty years, Western students do not attend to that. They attend to it even less than their teachers in biochemistry or sociology attend to what is being done in biochemistry or sociology by their colleagues in the Indian universities. When the Spanish students contend with their academic and governmental authorities or when they fight with the police, that too goes unnoticed. For years Latin American students have been participating in the government of their universities and striking and fighting with the police, but that too has gone unnoticed in student circles in Western countries. In the Sudan, student demonstrations precipitated the fall of the government of General Aboud. That went unnoticed. In South Korea students helped to bring down President Syngman Rhee; that caused no stir among European or American students. The accomplishment of the Turkish students in the face of the Menderes regime found an equally inattentive audience among Western students. Even a more powerful country like Japan produces little demonstration effect. When the *Zengakuren* went on a rampage to prevent President Dwight Eisenhower from visiting their country, the facts became known but they did not become exemplary. When the Indonesian KAMI helped to bring down the unspoken coalition of Sukarno and the PKI, what they did was admired but not attended to. When the gallant students of the *Po Prostu* circle helped to bring about the short-lived and now dead Polish October, the students of Berkeley and London found no inspiration there. When, however, in 1964 the University of California students in Berkeley began their "revolution," the radiation from the center outward began. It was like the radiation of the revolution of February from Paris in 1848, when all of Europe felt the repercussions.

The Berkeley model was diffused to West Berlin. One of the original instigators of the events of West Berlin was Ekkehard Krippendorf, who had been a graduate student in political science in the United States at the crucial time. Until the "Krippendorf affair" (arising from Krippendorf's allegedly insulting behavior toward the rector of the Free University), the West German students had not been rebellious. When agitation in West Berlin became chronic and intense, it spread to the rest of Western Germany; from Berkeley, it also spread to the London School of Economics, employing the same idiom and the same tactics, and it spread—very lightly and unevenly—to other British universities. From Western Germany, it spread to Nanterre through the personal embassy of Daniel Cohn-Bendit. With the emergence of the movement in Nanterre, the tone and vigor of student radicalism changed markedly. The 22d of March Movement spread to the Sorbonne only in May after the great student strike at Columbia in April, and after the anti-Springer demonstrations and riots which followed the attempted assassination of Rudi Dutschke in the same month. For a time, in a way not pleasing to General de Gaulle but in conformity with the main direction of his desires, Paris once more became the center of the world. (He would have been even less pleased than he was, however, had he reflected that the technique of those who made Paris momentarily into the center of the world of *chienlit* had been imported from the United States, where it had first been used by automobile workers in Michigan and later by Negroes in the Southern states.) From Paris it spread to such peripheral academic backwaters as Brussels, Rome, Florence, Milan, and Dakar.

Why 1968?

The transience of initial issues testifies not the forgetfulness of the student radicals but to the fact that, however passionate they might be at the moment, they are not serious about the objects of their protest. But they are serious about something. They are serious about authority. Whether they really wish to destroy it is another matter. A small number are really revolutionary in their intentions and look forward—rather vaguely, it is true—to the elimination of existing authorities and their replacement by new authorities who will be committed to the realization of the revolutionaries' utopia. Some are really anarchists who wish and believe it possible to eliminate not only presently incumbent authority but all authority. But most of the student radicals are neither revolutionaries nor anarchists in the sense of meaning business. What they want to do is to annoy and frustrate authority, to bewilder it and enrage it. They wish to taunt it and cause it to lose control over itself and thus to show their own ascendancy over it. They wish to humiliate authority and degrade it.

This brings me back to the general predisposition and immediate precipitation of last year's outbreaks. In West Germany, Great Britain, and the United States, 1968 was a poor year for governments. In the United States in particular, the image of the ineptitude of President Johnson, exemplified in the faltering and failing conduct of the war in Viet Nam, the inability to bring the disturbances in Negro districts of the big cities to an end, the enfeeblement of urban public order in other respects, and the lack of spectacular results from the poverty program, has made government authority into an easy target. The possibility that he could be succeeded by Senator Eugene McCarthy made for an even greater aggressiveness against incumbent authority. In Great Britain, the recurrence of the crisis of sterling and the devaluation, the failure to compel admission into the Common Market, and powerlessness in the face of the Smith regime in Rhodesia, as well as the flagrant impropriety of the government's treatment of the East African Asians who held British passports, have darkened the visage of the Labour Government. For different reasons, the Federal German Government is in the same position. In France the mounting criticism of General de Gaulle from the ineffective opposition parties and the immobility of the General's government, as well as the small majority by which he was returned in the general election which preceded the crisis, had similar consequences. These were aggravated too by the absence of the two most powerful figures in the government (General de Gaulle in Rumania and M. Pompidou in Afghanistan) when events were cascading—the image of a strong and effective authority was replaced by one of feebleness and abdication. Where authority abdicates through failure, ineptitude, and weakened self-confidence, it invites aggression against itself. That is what happened in the spring of 1968.

If this complex of factors accounts for the concert of confrontations in the advanced Western countries, how do we account for the magnitude and especially for the speed with which movements of *groupuscules* became "mass movements"?

Wherever authority is confronted and takes aggressive even if limited counteraction, there are some victims. The repressive actions—police action and intrauniversity disciplinary proceedings—always enlarge the size of the student group drawn into the confrontation of the second stage. The students whose sensibilities are affronted by repressive action are much more numerous than the student radicals; they are drawn into confrontation on an issue which is quite different from those on which the smaller group of radical pioneers took the initial steps of challenging authority. The issues become transformed, and the newly involved protesters are drawn from a different stratum of opinion among the students. This is when amnesty becomes the main issue.

Why is the second and usually much larger group drawn in? Originally, they were more moderate and kept their distance from the extreme, particular, and sometimes fairly specific demands of the pioneering nucleus of disturbance. Yet, when the issue becomes the redemption of those subjected to discipline or injury, they become as involved, as adamant, and as daring as those whose initial confrontation was the prelude to their own involvement. It is also usually among these somewhat more responsible elements that demands for *cogestion* and *Drittelparität* obtain some honest support.

The rapidity with which repressive measures by authority galvanize a larger support among students previously inactive indicates that there is moral consensus within the student generation deeper than that about the particular and often trivial and transient issues the tiny minority of extremists invoke. In one form or another, this consensus centers on a belief in the rightfulness of the free expression of sentiment and impulse; it works through a quick expansion of empathy to the victims of authority. The strength of the belief is not so great that is is continuously prominent, but constrictive and repressive activities by authorities shock it into salience. This ethos of the expansive ego, free from constraint and from sanctions—from all that scarcity imposes in the world—is the bond which unites the extremist *groupuscles* and the larger circle around them. The difference between them is that in the former it is intense and continuous, in the latter attenuated, only intermittently intense and easily subsided. It spreads through what used to be called "contagion" by old-fashioned students of the dancing manias of the Middle Ages or of the tulip craze. Involvement in a confrontation is a state of mind difficult to describe. It seems to entail the departure from the daily categories of perception and judgment. The focus of attention is changed; the assessment of what is important is changed; routine tasks disappear from consciousness, at least for a time. Enthusiasm, exhilaration, exaltation are the more vivid features of discourse and conduct of those swept into a confrontation. In my limited experience, I have also been impressed with the fluency of young persons who in ordinary academic situations speak with deliberation and hesitation. The fluency serves a repertoire of clichés, most of which refer to the virtues of the expanding ego, the deadness of the past, the continuous rebirth of the self. Schemes proliferate endlessly. Glossolalia is the only name I have for it. The mind falls into the possession of the daemon of plenitude, and the tongue speaks with the daemon's language.

A precondition for possession is the extraordinary generational self-consciousness of university students and perhaps of all young persons in contemporary advanced societies. Their sense of kinship, class, and national identity seems to be less than in preceding generations. In contrast with this, there has been a very pronounced increase in the sense of affinity with other persons of the same generation. There is a sensitivity to the equal vitality of others at the same stage of physiological development which makes for empathy and entry into a paradoxically ego-transcending community. That is why the spirit can spread and take possession so rapidly.

The Future of Student Enthusiasm

What of the future? Will the present enthusiasm die away and will the student body return to its ways of forty or sixty years ago? Or, at the other extreme, will the present trend of sentiment continue to spread so that universities as we have known them will cease to exist and will be replaced by perfervid communities in which all is dialogue and little or nothing is taught and nothing discovered except the vacuum of the expanding and contentless self?

I think that the former alternative is unlikely. That, however, is not necessarily to be feared. Universities have changed in structure in the past; they have changed the content of what was taught and they have also changed their structures of government. Of course, they cannot become what the proponents of dialogue in a community governed by student power think they wish them to be.

The renewal, intensification, and expansion of utopianism will not go away without leaving a trace. The fantasy of plenitude and the belief in the sacredness of the immediately experienced impulse and sensation will not disappear—it is too much a part of a cosmic development which, fused with received beliefs and categories of judgment, will be entirely tolerable and perhaps even mark a step forward in the evolution of the human spirit. In the extreme forms in which they are fragmentarily adumbrated today, however, they will not be able to subvert the existing academic order—any more than revolutionary Marxism succeeded in the course of the nineteenth and twentieth centuries in subverting any of the advanced societies of Western Europe and North America. But this possibility of withstanding the ravages of the "possessed" is not a certainty. It will be stayed only if those who have taken positions of responsibility in the universities everywhere in the world stand firmly by traditions of teaching, training, and research as the proper task of universities and do not allow themselves to be swept away by the desire to be "with it," to relive their lost youth, or to prolong their fading youth. If vice-chancellors, rectors, deans, presidents, professors, lecturers, and all those who are senior members of universities know how to adhere to their academic traditions and are not afraid of being condemned as "purists" or "elitists," then they will be able to preserve the universities. They will, by adhering to their central traditions and making modifications on secondary matters, stiffen the morale and restore the good sense of the large number of their students who waver when their elders divide and falter. When they do so, they will isolate the charismatic antinomian destroyers. Nothing dismays and disheartens charismatic types like the disappearance of their audience and the cohesion of their enemies.

The present state of possession will ebb. Widespread enthusiasm has never persisted before in human history, and it is not likely to do so in the future. Most students will return to their studies and will reenter the body of moderates, variously diligent, variously interested in their studies, variously deep and original. Some student consultation in the government of academic institutions will occur and it will be, as the student radicals fear it will be, "incorporated" into the governing system of most universities.

The ideal university of the realm of plenitude will never come into existence. There will be eccentric "free universities"—there have always been odd institutions at the periphery of higher educational systems.[14]

14. There might even be black studies "faculties" with "black teachers" chosen by "black students" teaching "black perspectives" in some ill-guided American universities and colleges, with the same academic qualities and standards as departments of home economics, physical education, hotel administration, or chiropody. The American higher educational system is enormously heterogeneous, and it has shown in the past a remarkable ability to tolerate the academically most degraded kinds of activities alongside excellent teaching, training, and research.

The isolation and disheartening of the zealots will not cause them to vanish. Cells will continue to exist. They might even exist within universities although care will have to be taken to render that difficult. As a phenomenon, on the scale of the past few years or perhaps on a somewhat larger scale, their future is poor. Nonetheless, even though their influence is diminished they will have their successors. They are the creatures of the dream of a regime of plenitude. They cannot be conjured away and they cannot be gratified by flattery from elders.

In the United States, the war in Viet Nam will be brought to a halt, and the Negroes will be treated with a greater measure of indifference to their color. The universities will be somewhat reformed in France, Germany, and Italy; the Spanish Government might allow students to have their own unions—it is already moving haltingly in that direction, although perhaps the moment has passed when it could do it without cost to anything but its obstinate pride. If the parents who are still legally responsible for their minor offspring agree that university should not stand *in loco parentis*, then that feature of Anglo-American university life will be modified. Students everywhere outside the communist countries are likely to be granted consultative powers in certain university decision-making bodies, and in some matters they will be given a share in the making of decisions.

All these changes, desirable or undesirable, will not, however, resolve the deeper tensions between a cultural tradition which fosters individuality and the vision of a realm of plenitude, and a society the institutions of which require efficiency, competence, selection on the basis of past and prospective accomplishment, and differential rewards. The task is to contain the extreme, ideological manifestations of the former while enabling the latter to benefit from its attenuation.

14 Observations on the
American University

The British university seems like a determinate, well-defined—perhaps too determinate and too well-defined—institution when it is placed alongside the American university. Whatever the cleavage between the ancient universities and the modern, between the English and the Scottish, the range of variation of the British universities from the highest to the lowest is very narrow in comparison with the American. New foundations do not change this. The students seem less variegated, the conception, however ambiguous, of the tasks of a university more severe and inflexible, more resistant to criticism and questioning. The students are there. It is their duty to study and to learn. The teachers are there. It is their task to teach and to do research. Increasing numbers do not change this. Here and there, there are criticism and dissatisfaction, occasionally an eagerness for innovation, an eagerness accompanied by awareness of the uncongeniality of the environment to innovation.

How different the present scene in America! It often looks like a vast "buzzing, booming, confusion." So many students, so many very different kinds of students, brilliant, imaginative, dull, enthusiastic, routine, distrustful, curious, dutiful, unwilling, positively recalcitrant—covering a variety which seems to be wider and more multifarious than the British student body. So many universities and colleges, small and gigantic, conventional and radical, intellectually

Previously published in a slightly different form in *Universities Quarterly*, vol. 17, no. 2 (March 1963), pp. 182-93.

These remarks have their point of departure in *The American College: A Psychological and Social Interpretation of the Higher Learning*, edited by Nevitt Sanford (New York and London: John Wiley and Sons, 1962). The work of thirty collaborators and of an editorial committee of eight, the book is a remarkable achievement. It is remarkable for the indefatigable ramification, sometimes subtle and differentiated and sometimes simply callow, of its analysis of the social processes which go on in classrooms, in the relations of students with each other and with their teachers. It is remarkable also for its summary of past research and its introduction of the results of a certain amount of new research. It is finally remarkable for its "student-centeredness." The student and his "needs" seem throughout this book to be the touchstone by which academic things are to be judged. It is not just because so much research and reflection on student motives and responses and on student culture are to be found in the book that one gets this impression. It is rather the constant recurrence of the preoccupation with the full development of the student's personality which underlies this impression. Indeed, the authors seem to regard universities as someting like adolescent personality formation institutions and they pay only the most unconvinced and unconvincing lip-service to the obligation of a university to do serious intellectual work.

backward and intellectually great, colleges which are an evening shambles and universities as great as any in the history of science and learning, privately endowed and privately conducted institutions, colleges and universities conducted by Roman Catholic religious orders and by Protestant sects and churches, some impoverished, some wealthy, some attended by the *jeunesse dorée,* others attended by those for whom it is just an appropriate stage of life and with little other purpose, and still others by the worn out and distracted who work most of the day or night in offices, shops and even factories. There is no central authority which grants charters, there is no central body to promulgate standards to which the universities and colleges of the country must conform, no central body provides financially for them. The most diverse "experiments" are carried on alongside the most reactionary conventionality.

All this heterogeneity and dispersion notwithstanding, the different streams of culture and the different strata of American society which characterize the American academic cosmos are gradually being formed into a new unity. The unity is imposed in part by the fact that the whole affair exists within American society and is accordingly influenced by the common traditions of American culture, of beliefs in the desirability of self-improvement and, therewith, of a closer approximation to the center of society. The unity of the university system is coming about also from the unification of the country, arising from the speed and ease of travel and communication, and the enhanced authority of all government, above all, the authority of the central government. The leading universities are becoming the universities of the whole society and not merely a small pluto-aristocracy of the major cities, such as the Ivy League universities and colleges were for a long time, and still are, to some extent. The lowering of the barrier separating Roman Catholics from the rest of American society, and the diminution of Protestant sectarian fervor, at least in the more or less educated sectors of the population, have opened the colleges of church and sect increasingly to the influences of the intellectual community at the center of the society.

The university system is unified, too, by its own interior development. The advance of research as the major concern of a university and the closely related requirement of the Ph.D. for appointment even to fairly junior teaching posts, have led to the ascendancy of the graduate school within the university. The labor market for scientific and academic personnel has become more national than ever before. Directly as a result of these developments, a relatively small number of universities have become the chief sources of personnel, a standard of assessment and the model of what is academically correct. A hierarchy which was simply a matter of status in earlier years, has now become a hierarchy of intellectual authority and a system of the "circulation of elites."

The relatively centralized system of elite (i.e. Ph.D.) production has produced common foci of attention, common heroes, and a common body of problems and literature, appreciated and explored with different intensities, but avoided with difficulty. At the peak, a certain competitiveness of individuals for preeminence within the same fields, and of institutions for distinction of personnel and activity, heightens mutual awareness; at the less exalted levels of the hierarchy of institutions, there is a correspondingly greater, more acute, awareness of the center than there used to be when colleges existed to teach a small number of students according to conventional syllabi, and could go their own way without thought or fear of being old-fashioned.

The growth of this national system has two faces. The central universities of the country have established their predominance as research universities. Their eminence comes from the quality of the research published by their staff members and by the subsequent achievements of their Ph.D.s in research. The standard for judging the quality of an institution is the research which its members publish. Productivity in research and publication becomes the standard by which university and college teachers judge themselves and are judged by others. Accomplishment as a teacher, unless it is as a teacher of research workers, is likely to be less noticed and, if noticed, less appreciated. Administrators, trustees, and teachers who are ambitious to elevate the reputation of their institution do it through devices which shift the emphasis steadily toward research and publication. The teacher of undergraduates is slighted; the value of teaching undergraduates is estimated lightly. The public intellectual functions of the university, beyond the conduct of research and the training of future research workers, university teachers who will, in their turn, be primarily research workers, and lawyers, physicians and engineers, are passed over without discussion.

Meanwhile, the number of undergraduates increases. To have a B.A. for all sorts of ill-understood reasons becomes a goal of the multitudes which many attain; and as they do so, those through whose hands they must pass to reach that goal care less and less about it. The teaching of undergraduates is coming to be regarded as the activity of juniors, of misfits, and of eccentrics who enjoy it. The bachelor's degree is regarded as nothing in itself, as being only the floor from which real life progresses. Undergraduates are thought of increasingly as an affliction or as a reservoir from which promising young men and women can be selected for the career of research.

One of the sources for this disregard for undergraduate teaching is a belief that the undergraduates are too immature for "serious" work. Many American university teachers think of their students as "kids" incapable of, or not inclined to do, interesting intellectual work. The poor quality of so much of the American secondary education from which the undergraduates have come sustains the view that the student is not capable of intense or prolonged intellectual exertion and that his absorptive capacities are not great. The result is a syllabus which is adapted to a very slack intellectual life.

The expansion of the general education movement, meritorious though this has been in many respects, has probably accentuated this tendency toward the lightening of the burden which is laid upon the undergraduate. Only exceptional students discover their real interests before their third year, largely, I think, because they have not been pressed or inspired to dig into any subject with an intensity sufficient to arouse their curiosity or to give them a sense of achievement. Consequently, many students who develop an interest in a subject late in their undergraduate years decide to become graduate students in order to learn more about their subject which has interested them. Many of them do not wish to make their careers in research or even to be trained in research techniques, but since this is the condition of their further penetration into the subject of their belated interest, they are pushed willy-nilly in this direction. The multiplication of research students is thus, in part at least, a complex consequence of the neglect of the intellectual side of the undergraduate education, and contributes to its further neglect. Such seems to be the situation in some of the greatest of the private and state universities of the country.

It is not universally the case. There are undergraduate colleges in the United States where teachers are not only devoted but demanding and the undergraduates are sufficiently well educated so that when some of them subsequently become graduate students in the great universities, they make the dissatisfying discovery that they have already been over the ground. (The impressive density of the American graduate syllabus is the counterpendant to the intellectual sparseness of the undergraduate course.)

Are numbers inevitably at the root of this evacuation of the undergraduate syllabus? Are the undergraduates worked so lightly because they are incapable of anything better? Do large classes necessarily attenuate the intellectual intake of the students? As the universities grow in size, the teaching of undergraduates is in danger of becoming more perfunctory and not just because, as is said, "more means worse." The increased size of the teaching staff, which must accompany this increase in the number of students, and which is recruited by the newer criterion of a completed Ph.D., will probably be accompanied by a considerable decline in interest in the teaching of undergraduates and a further increase in interest in research. Research, in the mass university, is a sort of island in which intellectual intensity and integrity can be preserved in the midst of a flood of anonymous students whom one cannot come to know because they are seen so transiently and in such large numbers.

The national labor market for university teachers, to which I have referred above, and the competitive search for institutional and departmental distinction—which is perforce a search for distinction in research because there is at present no way for a distinguished teacher to be known except by the legends which are created about him—have parallel effects. They pass over the man who is primarily a teacher. There are brilliant and beloved teachers of undergraduates in the American system. They are not, however, sought out by important universities, when they make new appointments, nor, in fact, do they themselves usually seek to reenter circulation in the larger world. They are unknown except to former pupils and to friends and immediate colleagues. Outstanding teachers of undergraduates move in a sort of confidential underground; there is no way in which their reputation can be established except through word of mouth. Such teachers are heroes to undergraduates; but they are "local gods." They are often unknown outside the environment in which they were formed.

The growth of the national system has another result, beneficial in some respects, injurious in others. Many institutions which were content to perform local services by producing graduates for local employment, and to provide local entertainments in the form of football, track sports, and basketball, have since the Second World War raised their sights. They do so partly because the younger generation is now more serious and because alumni of the type described by James Thurber in *The Male Animal* are passing from the scene; they also do so because their new staff members have been formed in the national system and have their minds focused on research and high intellectual matters. The senior administrators have decided too that things could not go on as they were. As a result of this, football has been "de-emphasized" and research has attained a new dignity.

Colleges and universities founded by religious bodies have become more sensitive to their tradition of isolation from the main currents of intellectual life in the country and they have ceased to be content with it. Their own expanding numbers of students have entailed enlargement of their teaching staffs and this has meant difficulty in recruiting from religious orders or from communicant members of their sponsor-church or sect, sufficient staff members who are proficient in their subjects as well as religiously orthodox.

Agricultural and engineering colleges have been transforming themselves into universities, again partly in response to the growing numbers of students, partly in response to the conviction that a narrowly professional, technical education is inappropriate. This "metropolitanization," this effort to enter into the national system has been impelled by and impels the desire to do research on a scale appropriate to gaining national attention and appreciation.

The parochialism of engineering and agricultural colleges, of state universities, and of Roman Catholic and Lutheran colleges, was not a good thing from the point of view of the intellectual growth of the country or the intellectual development of their graduates. The growth of a metropolitan ideal and the culture of the "center" has, in general, raised the intellectual level of these institutions. It has given them staff members who feel themselves to be part of a larger intellectual culture which goes beyond their own religious body, their own technical specialty, and their own local responsibility.

The growth of the national system has also added to the pressure on outstanding liberal arts colleges to become like universities, to have on their staffs many men and women doing research and training their own students to do research rather than to prepare them with the best possible intellectual foundations for fruitful careers in the professions and in research. The young recruits to the staffs of the best liberal arts colleges have usually taken their advanced degrees at the major centers; they are usually "research-oriented." They do not invariably find the vocation of teaching on a high level to undergraduates, which is a very demanding vocation, sufficiently rewarding in the way in which they would like to be rewarded. Opportunities for research in these colleges are bound to be poor because they do not have research libraries and because their laboratories, planned for undergraduate teaching, are not equipped for large-scale research. The sheer fact of availability of funds and the awareness that colleagues elsewhere receive them are temptations to do research. Quite apart from the intrinsic appeal of the research problems themselves, they are drawn by the prospect of grants from the Atomic Energy Commission, the National Science Foundation, the United States Public Health Service, the Rockefeller Foundation, etc., etc., and they hope ultimately to return to the "big leagues." The absence of an imminent prospect of doing so causes them to think of changing their own institution into a microcosm of the metropolis.

Certainly in a system as large as the American system there are bound to be young deviants who, for whatever motives, perhaps not always admirable, wish primarily to be teachers, who do not want to do research or do not wish to do it on the scale and with the intensity and exclusiveness of some of their colleagues. Some of these might be very good teachers. There is a natural harmony of interest between these people and the tasks of undergraduate education. The outstanding liberal arts colleges like Reed, Oberlin, and Swarthmore manage to obtain a sufficient supply. There is no reason why an effective system of allocation, which would discern and direct these people into posts in colleges and universities throughout the country which require primarily the teaching of undergraduates, could not function if the great universities did not permit themselves to be so dominated by the ideal of research that they regard those who seem reluctant to pursue the ideal path as being beyond redemption.

Most university and college teachers in the United States do teach undergraduates and some of them do it very well, but it is a mark of elevation in one's career and a liberation from inferiority to reach the position in which one can, also or exclusively, teach graduate students. Unless even the better liberal arts colleges watch themselves carefully in this regard, they will also become the victims of this trend. The teaching of undergraduates in the United States is today a defensive operation in which there are many Trojan horses within the walls. The dignity of an institution is enhanced, in this equine conception, by its provision for the training of graduate students, by its "Ph.D. program." The struggle to provide oneself with a postgraduate audience, short of changing one's place of employment, leads directly in the direction of creating postgraduate departments and offering postgraduate degrees.

Observers of this process in the United States have not failed to see the intellectual evacuation of the undergraduate phase. They avoid a head-on collision with it by stressing the extraintellectual functions of higher education, the development of the personality, the "enlightenment of conscience," "freeing of impulse," "differentiation and integration of the ego."

Some simply shrug their shoulders and speak of making up the lost time in graduate school. One of the most recent writers on the subject justified the waste by referring to the lengthened lifespan.

The loss of these years is serious, especially in a country which neglects its adolescents intellectually. It is not only a waste of precious years; it is also harmful to the public intellectual tone of the country. For the time being, however, it is hard to see where the impetus for the change will come from in the United States. The amount of work demanded of the student is pathetically small. The student is not forced to extend himself, and, not being forced to do so, only those who are driven from within by their curiosity and love of their subject or from the compulsiveness of their characters, drive themselves hard. In consequence of this, the amount that any student knows about any particular subject, even after having specialized in it as an undergraduate, is meager.

The improvement of the quality of the culture of the under-graduate in the United States is at present taking the form of general education, and more specialized schemes of undergraduate educa-tion, which were never as specialized as they are in Great Britain, have been allowed to go by the board. I do not think that the broadening is incompatible with a greater intensity—there is so much slack—but this is not the general view.

These years can be recovered if the postgraduate schools could find an honorable place for prospective teachers as well as for prospective research workers in their outlook. It is not so much that the specific content of postgraduate training should be different as that its cultural intention should somehow be modified so that undergraduate teaching would be viewed as an intrinsically worth-while activity—no less important than research—and not just some-thing that one must do in order to be able to do research in the most congenial atmosphere. Deans and presidents will not be able to bring about the change, while liberal arts colleges will probably be unable to do more than hold their own. Yet if such a change does take place—and there is no inherent reason to think that the movement of academic opinion is inevitably unilinear—it will find many allies.

The renaissance of a more intense and demanding undergraduate education in the American university system is impeded by some of the same reasons that have helped the research side to gain such ascendancy in recent decades. Research is a public accomplishment, visible nationally and internationally as soon as, or immediately after, it is published. Teaching is one of the few relatively private things left in the world, although it is conducted in public. Colleagues do not go to each other's lectures, except rarely. The testimony of students, either direct or by their examination results, is not very conclusive. The sense of gratitude which students express and their achievements in life come too late and are too difficult to assess to provide the basis for appointment and promotion. Even if appointing bodies had an adequate idea of what is desired of a teacher, and were ready to give it due weight in their decision, it would not be easy to decide about the merits of a particular person as a teacher because of the confidential character of his performance in the past.

Our ignorance of the quality of the past teaching performance of any individual candidate—disregarding extraordinary defects which come to public attention—is matched by our indifference about the possibility of learning how to teach. Although at first glance the very idea of teaching a prospective university teacher how to teach is repugnant, there is really nothing to be said against it in principle. A man learns to do research under supervision, in collaboration with and by the criticism of his supervisor. Is teaching of necessity less routine or less creative than research?

Even though we might accept the principle that the art of university teaching could be in some sense be taught, it is something which has not been done in any self-conscious or deliberate way. Certainly there is no systematic body of psychological or sociological knowledge from which we could draw any more certain directives than we can from reflection on individual experience. In principle, however, this does not mean to say that such systematic psychological and sociological knowledge might not be acquired by the systematic study of the process of teaching. The subject could scarcely be said to be in its beginnings at present.[1]

The as yet unharvested fruits, even the unsown seeds of sociological and social psychological research into teaching and learning at the university level, can hardly expect it to be a decisive factor in bringing about the needed change in the trend of the relationship between research and teaching in American universities and colleges. A deeper change of opinion will be needed and the emergence of this change is as yet not at all tangible. Still not all the passion for research is a passion for truth. Some of it is just fashionable, and fashions, by their very nature, change. It might, therefore, be that within the not too remote future we shall witness such a change in fashion. It is also possible that the dissatisfaction with the state of public culture in the United States at a time when particular arts, sciences, and humanistic disciplines are flourishing, might cause the leaders of intellectual opinion to see that a richer and more intense undergraduate syllabus could contribute to the diminution of the mixture of vulgarity and philistinism which is so often found in the United States alongside the most brilliantly creative performances.

1. The section of *The American College* devoted to teaching and the curriculum shows how difficult the matter is, and how much more has yet to be done before it will be possible for these disciplines to contribute significantly to the training and the selection of teachers.

15 Limitations on the Freedom of Research and Teaching in the Social Sciences

I

The central interest of this essay is in the use of sanctions against social scientists in colleges and universities in the United States whose scientific and pedagogical work runs counter to the evaluations dominant in their institution or in the wider community. Restrictions on the *public* utterance and activity of the social scientists, however widespread and important these restrictions are, are not of direct concern, and come in for consideration only as they have a bearing on teaching and research activities. Nor are we to deal with the numerous disputes in academic life arising out of questions of tenure, advancement, rivalry among the faculty, and administrative conflicts, except as they are directly relevant to the freedom of research and teaching. Heavy teaching burdens, inadequacies of staff and equipment, and financial hindrances, though they are certainly very significant as obstacles to research in the social sciences, will not be brought into this discussion unless they appear as consciously used implements of a policy oriented toward the prevention of the investigation and the pedagogical exposition of certain subject matters and problems.

In short, we shall treat here only one segment of the broad complex of situations designated as academic freedom, namely, restrictions on the freedom of research and teaching in the social sciences in the higher schools, understanding by the freedom of research and teaching the probability of the non-invocation of sanctions against persons treating particular subject matters, propositions, or problems at the level of average competence obtaining within the discipline in question.*

Previously published in a slightly different form in the *Annals of the American Academy of Political and Social Science*, vol. 200 (November 1938), pp. 144-64.

---

* It should be borne in mind that this article was written before the Second World War. In the period dealt with, the social sciences, including economics, did not enjoy the prestige within universities or in American society at large which they later came to receive. The older American tradition of imperious presidents, interfering ecclesiastical and lay governing bodies, a callow orthodoxy, and a considerable touchiness among businessmen regarding the sanctity of the existing order of things combined to place academic social scientists in a weak position.

II

In a society lacking an inclusive consensus, numerous groups strive to create a consensus which will guide the actions of the other members of that society in a manner conforming with the values of the groups in question. Practically all of the politically, economically, and culturally relevant values of the validity of which they attempt to persuade nonmembers are based not only on certain ultimate valuations but on certain assumptions about the factual structure of the social world. It is the peculiar situation of the social sciences that the objects of their investigations are those very conditions and relationships toward which, in a variety of ways, a central part of the program of every group is evaluatively oriented. This is true whether the group has already "arrived" and is seeking to maintain or to consolidate its position, or whether it has not yet attained the status or goods which it desires. Purely factual propositions, established with the best techniques now available and asserted with the most impartial intentions are subject to attack from interested parties who feel that some of their claims have been shown to be either less practicable or less legitimate than they had hitherto claimed because the facts are not as they say they are.

Every scientific proposition which has a bearing on practical issues tends to become "someone's" proposition. A scientific analysis of the structure of a political party will soon enter public circulation, either through the channels of that party itself, if it happens to discover and present facts which will make that party the object of favorable evaluations, or through the channels of the opposing parties if it presents facts which are likely to cause the analyzed party to be judged negatively by the public for whose support the parties compete. Analyses which reveal the impracticability of certain norms are fortunate if they pass unopposed.

The same is true of scientific analyses which diverge from certain conceptions concerning historical personages or events, from an identification with which certain groups believe that they derive their status and moral value as well as the security of their economic position. "Facts" have indeed become all the more crucial, since with the more or less universal acceptance of a system of hedonistic humanitarian values as the ultimate source of legitimation, conflicting groups (insofar as they do not resort to violence) must appeal to the "facts" to legitimate their divergent immediate ends.

It is for these reasons that the reprisals, obstructions, and criticisms which have been directed by various groups against the social sciences throughout their existence as academic disciplines in the colleges and universities of the United States, have by no means been aimed exclusively at the assertion of value judgments which many social scientists have felt were included in their pedagogical and civic obligations. They have been aimed equally at the factual analysis of situations, particular conceptions of which are regarded by interested parties as essential to the validation of their preferences and the fulfillment of their "factual" expectations or plans. Of course, often the allegations about pernicious doctrines taught and obnoxious objects investigated were in fact instigated by disapproval of statements made in public places outside academic confines.

III

Restrictive action may be taken in almost any social science field, but the highest concentration of such cases has, in the last years, occurred in such fields as the sociology of the family, social disorganization, social psychology, labor economics, race relations, and social origins (social evolution). Restrictions motivated by dogmatically held values such as those involved in religious beliefs and sexual and racial attitudes are likely to be directed not only against specific propositions but against a subject matter as a whole. Restrictions motivated by pragmatically held values, on the other hand, tend to disregard subject matters, and to be alert for specific propositions within the subject matter field, and the way in which they are asserted. Depending on the social context, objects which are responded to on a pragmatic basis at one time and place, may be treated dogmatically at another.[1]

The more dogmatic the manner in which the values touched on in a given field of scientific work are held, the greater is the probability of interference. Furthermore, it might safely be said that the greater the dogmatism of the social environment, the earlier in the process of intellectual production will be the interference. Thus, for example, in cases where inquiries into sexual attitudes were interfered with, the restrictive action took place immediately upon discovery; whereas in economics, toward which usually a more pragmatic attitude is maintained, restrictions largely occur after several years or at the point of publication (as in the Levine-Montana case discussed below).

---

1. It should be noted that objections rooted in highly affectively toned attitudes and "final" values (as in the case of sexual and religious matters) may be expressed and legitimated in very pragmatic terms. We shall, nevertheless, consider these as instances of dogmatic, rather than pragmatic, obstructions to teaching and research. This does not, of course, exclude recognition that such objections may at times have a distinctly pragmatic motivation in addition.

Economics

Economics, thanks to the increased explicitness of ethical neutrality in the field and the increased capacity for instrumental as over against dogmatic thinking on the part of influential businessmen, has experienced a decrease in the proportion of attacks made in response to threats to the mores. Pragmatic interest in the teaching of economics has led to attempts at restrictive action whenever the position of the predominant groups in our society has been so threatened that vigorous defensive measures were deemed necessary by them. The limitations on academic freedom in economics have passed through three high points: (1) the first great attack on the plutocracy at the end of the last and the beginning of the present century (Populism and muckraking); (2) the post-World War period when the fear of communism was at a maximum; and (3) the deepest period of the post-1929 depression and the years immediately following, when the plutocracy organized against the New Deal reforms.

Since the labor situation has been continuously in the forefront of attention, it has been the social scientist specializing in labor problems at whom sanctions of varying degrees of severity have most frequently been directed.

However, monetary and other problems have frequently been the center of discord. In the period of public concern with the bimetallism issue, proponents of free silver coinage did not escape unscathed. The cases of Professor Edward A. Ross at Stanford University, President E. B. Andrews at Brown University, and Professor John R. Commons at Syracuse stand as testimony to the severity with which the dominant classes of the period met this challenge.

Similarly, economists dealing with public utilities in a manner which, given the reigning values, would be conducive to an unfavorable judgment have often found themselves in unpleasant situations. Professor E. W. Bemis in the first decade of the existence of the University of Chicago and Professors Leo S. Rowe and E. J. James at the University of Pennsylvania at the end of the last century were among those whose conclusions regarding public utilities stimulated sharp opposition. (The late Professor J. L. Laughlin denied that the Bemis case was one of reprisal for statements within his principal sphere of competence, and other informants have agreed that it was not just a case of interference with freedom of research and teaching. What is relevant here, however, is that the personal issues involved would probably not have risen to the surface had Bemis not held the views that he did about the Chicago traction franchises.)

Recent instances of reprisal for assertions on this subject have not come to the attention of the investigator.[2]

The fiscal policies of governments as objects of study have also met with resistance when the policies which research implied were regarded as dangerous. Illustrative of this type is the case of Professor Louis Levine and the University of Montana in 1919. Professor Levine had completed a series of studies on state tax problems which indicated that the mining enterprises bore a dispro-portionately small share of the state tax burden.[3] Although he had had the support of the university administration and a promise of university assistance in publication, he was informed that it would be inadvisable to publish the results of his research. Although no evidence can be given as to the precise number of such cases, there can be little doubt that the treatment of fiscal problems has been relatively free from extrascientific control.

Sociology

Perhaps because of the diversity of attitude among members of the academic profession and between the academic and the layman as to what is factually correct and politically practicable in socio-logical analysis over the country as a whole, there are more instances of interference in that field than in economics. Sociology is as yet a discipline in which professional consensus is rather restricted and in which there is a great divergence between what is generally accepted within the field and what is insisted on by lay persons whose conceptions of society are derived from traditional definitions of the situation or from interests which are still too unsophisticatedly viewed.

Thus, while economists are usually attacked (for pragmatic reasons) by businessmen and by groups supported by businessmen or those who identify themselves with businessmen such as politicians and university administrators, sociologists are open to attack from

2. In the twenties, agents of the public utilities seem to have shifted their tactics from protests to university authorities, once objectionable statements were made, to a more aggressive preventive type of action. The National Electric Light Association solicited textbooks which presented the "facts" as they preferred to have them seen. One of these texts by Professor M. G. Glaeser of the University of Wisconsin was "submitted to the National Electric Light Association, which suggested extensive emendations. Glaeser testified that he had made some 'corrections and changes of argument' after receiving the utility criticisms, but only such as were deemed valid. He denied that he had submitted the manuscript to the N.E.L.A., and accused Prof. Ely or Macmillan of having done so." H. K. Beale, *Are American Teachers Free?* pp. 556, 562-63; cf. also Jack Levin, *Power Ethics* (New York, 1931), pp. 81-86.

3. American Association of University Professors, *Bulletin,* vol. 5 (1919); *New Northwest,* March 14, 1919. Cf. also Louis Levine, *Taxation of Mines in Montana* (New York, 1919).

any individual or group which abhors what is taught in sociology and fears that it will bring about a departure from established ways of thinking and acting (dogmatic and pragmatic considerations).

Further, since there is such a great cultural difference between city and country, between metropolis and small town, and between the North and the South, it is not surprising that sociologists trained in advanced departments of sociology in the great private and state universities should encounter difficulties when they take up posts in the less liberal areas. Professor Howard K. Beale has observed that "in many communities conservatism, either religious or economic or political, is so strongly intrenched that no graduate of a liberal university can obtain a position. This has long been true of the University of Chicago in fundamentalist parts of the South, because it allegedly destroys the religion of its students."[4]

In this connection we may cite the complaint of one sociologist teaching in the South, that a book which is completely acceptable in the North was objected to by his superior. Classical sociological works such as W. I. Thomas' *The Unadjusted Girl,* Shaw's *The Natural History of a Delinquent Career,* and others have created tense moments for some sociologists. Teaching institutions are dominated by strict mores regarding the mentionability of sexual subjects.

What is taught about the Negro and about race relations by the best contemporary sociologists has not been acceptable to every part of certain Southern college communities, and at least one teacher of sociology has been "put on the carpet" for the assertion that there was no evidence of biological deterioration due to intermarriage between Negroes and whites. The pedagogical procedure of student tours through various sections of the city for purposes of sociological observation has contributed to the dismissal of at least two well-known sociologists and has embarrassed others.

Sex

Inquiry into sexual attitudes has frequently been an object of repressive measures. Thus, two persons were dropped from the faculty of Oklahoma Baptist University for using a questionnaire containing what President W. W. Phelan called "a vile set of questions on sexual life."[5] Similar action was taken against members of the University of Missouri faculty for participation in the distribution of a questionnaire on sex mores.[6] A specialist on the family, preparing a work on divorce, encountered the displeasure of

4. *Are American Teachers Free?* p. 518.
5. *New York Evening World,* April 25, 1929.
6. American Association of University Professors, *Bulletin,* vol. 6 (1930), pp. 143 ff.

his colleagues because he interviewed divorced persons. Another sociologist, at a large privately endowed institution, found his situation becoming difficult due to his prosecution of a study of homosexuality. When ·he finally published it in a foreign journal, resentment rose even higher. The author of a reputable book on prostitution was regarded uneasily by the administration of the eminent Southern university where he taught, and the chancellor insisted on examining the reading lists for his course on social disorganization. The author of a highly competent book on divorce was the object of suspicion at a large Western state university.

> The president has objected to any discussion of sex matters in my courses on "Social Pathology" and "The Family." For example I was asked if I could not omit the chapters in the text by Queen and Mann, *Social Pathology,* entitled "Prostitution" and "Illegitimacy." The President took out of the College Library last year several books which I had the Library order for parallel reading in connection with these two courses, because he considered them improper for students, especially girls.

So writes a professor of sociology in a small college in the South.[7] The number of illustrations could be multiplied.

Social Evolution

Social scientists whose activity involves a relativization of modern beliefs and institutions, as is, for example, required in the study of social evolution, have at times been subjected to severe attacks. This is notably the situation in the South and in small denominational schools where the attachment of the administrators, the trustees, and the community at large to the biblical version of the early history of human society is still intense.

The case of Professor J. M. Mecklin at Lafayette College provides an especially pointed illustration. Professor Mecklin was dismissed in 1913 from his Presbyterian college for applying the "genetic and functional method" to the history of religion.[8] One trustee stated that the objection to Dr. Mecklin's teaching was based upon his use of the doctrine or theory of evolution in his discussion of the growth of religion.[9] A correspondent said that the president of the college had declared, "the doctrine set forth in certain textbooks adopted by Professor Mecklin, viz., Angell on Psychology, Dewey and Tufts on Ethics, McDougall on Social Psychology, and James on the Psy-

7. Letter to L. B. Milner, March 28, 1933.
8. *Journal of Philosophy, Psychology and Scientific Method,* vol. II, no. 3 (Jan. 29, 1914), pp. 76-77.
9. Ibid., p. 77.

chology of Religious Experience, were a departure from the doctrines that had been taught in the college."[10]

The consequences of this cultural differential are nowhere more clear than in those instances where conformity with the tenets of a particular theology is demanded, either explicitly or implicitly, of all staff members. Conflicts over the early course of social development are especially likely in denominational schools,[11] although it should be recognized that many denominational schools do not require a rigid adherence to their theological principles. Nonetheless, the study of the early condition of mankind and of the morally relativistic analysis of the moral codes of non-Christian societies has often caused teachers to be brought to book. One has the impression that as late as the 1920s college teachers were still being warned to desist from such views. The incidence was especially great in the South and in undenominational colleges in the Middle West.

It seems safe to say that within the larger universities, this attitude, which was characteristic of the nineteenth century, has already been transcended, so that interference on such grounds is now highly improbable. At the same time, the increased secularization of the formative centers of public opinion in the metropolis makes outside interference in this respect almost negligible.

IV

Thus far we have considered taboos erected out of moral, religious, political, economic, and "personal" considerations. Quite different in characteracter are those taboos which are exercised on intellectual-doctrinal grounds. In a university where metaphysical first principles are espoused by the controlling administrators, empirical research such as has been carried on in the social sciences in the past two decades is frowned upon. In social science faculties where historical and general speculative work is carried on, precise statistical investigations limited to rather specialized subjects of a con-

10. Ibid., pp. 75-76.
11. President E. D. Soper of Ohio Wesleyan University, one of the more liberal denominational schools, has said that a member of the faculty of such a school "should be a Christian in the essential meaning which is conveyed by the word. . . . A Christian is a man of deeply reverent spirit whose God is the one personal creative spirit at the center of the universe, a God who can be in significant contact with personal beings through prayer. He is one who has caught the meaning of Jesus Christ and who sees in him and his way of life the hope of social righteousness and the assurance of personal emancipation." *Schools and Society,* vol. 30 (Oct. 19, 1929), p. 525. When a faculty member can no longer accept these views, President Soper believes he should leave the institution.

temporary character do not meet with favor, and in other faculties where exact quantitative research is favored by those in authority, broadly conceived studies not relying exclusively on statistical procedures are discouraged.

Such situations are perhaps generally infrequent and are most improbable in disciplines which have developed to the point where the various contending methodologies and techniques have had an opportunity to demonstrate their fruitfulness in such a way that consensus obtains among the recognized leaders in the field. In the less well-established disciplines, where a methodological anarchy tends to prevail, this situation is more likely to emerge. It may also be expected where personal rivalry exists. The operation of sanctions that maintain these "taboos" does not culminate in dismissal or threat of dismissal or in intimidation. The sanctions consist, however, in the creation of an "atmosphere" and in the provision of models to which students who seek advancement conform.

What is taboo in one type of institution is, as has been seen, by no means necessarily taboo in all others. And the same type of research or teaching or publication is not always equally outlawed in all departments of a given institution. The threshold of prohibition fluctuates in height from one situation to another. A large state or private university with a liberal tradition, such as Chicago, Harvard, or Minnesota, will only rarely invoke sanctions against members. Yet during crisis situations, as in war time, persons who have been a minor source of irritation to the administration or to civic groups during peace time will be proceeded against under justification of the emergency situation. The level of instruction is also a relevant factor. Prohibitions are almost always confined to the undergraduate level of instruction, so that teachers of the social sciences feel less constrained and apprehensive in graduate instruction.

A large city, and especially a metropolis, is more favorable to freedom in the social sciences than a smaller community. The research activities of the social scientist are much less likely to become the object of off-campus gossip in a big city where the college or university is not in everyone's eye than in a small town where most of the population is in one way or another connected or familiar with the school. The larger the city, the greater are the opportunities for off-campus contact for the faculty, and the fewer are the opportunities for that particular form of intrafaculty surveillance and gossip which has an inhibiting influence on the study and teaching of unpopular subjects. But on the other hand, the large cities offer the threat of sensation-mongering or red-baiting press campaigns, such as those to which the country was treated by the Hearst papers in 1935.

Among the conditions which are relevant in determining whether or not sanctions will be invoked against a given utterance, is the manner of exposition. The cultivation of special forms of obscurity which permit the assertion of what would otherwise cause consternation seems to have been pursued by Thorstein Veblen. Other persons have succeeded in escaping restriction through a careful avoidance of the dramatic. Matter-of-factness and absence of rhetorical emphasis seem to be indispensable accompaniments of the maintenance of freedom of teaching and research in certain institutions.

V

No discussion of the varying conditions under which prohibitions are made effective may disregard the "mixed case." Reference has already been made to cases in which the research or pedagogical activity in itself would not alone have led to punitative action. Persons who transgress in only one way, and who are entirely respectable in every other phase of their activity, are still relatively secure. A Marxist who teaches sociology and who is a "good fellow" has a more secure position than a Marxist who is equally scholarly and competent as a teacher but who is not so pleasing socially. A Marxist who participates in outside organizational activities is less secure than one who attends exclusively to his academic concerns. A man who investigates taboo subjects can less well afford to disregard the moral or social conventions of the campus community than those who do not.

An associate professor of economics in a Southern university was engaged in a study of liquor consumption during the twenties. There was originally some resistance to his appointment and later a threat of discharge because of this investigation, but the threat was suspended when an agreement was reached that his title as a member of the university in question would not appear in the printed report. Certain students who wished to avoid his course started rumors about him, and this revived the threat of dismissal. A colleague summarized the situation as follows:

> I am also of the opinion that the officers of the University were greatly biased by the prohibition study and that they were to a degree awaiting an opportunity to dispose of Mr. X. . . . An overt act not appearing, they decided to take advantage of the manufactured student unrest, and expressed it in terms of not "fitting in." I am also of the personal opinion that the failure of Mr. X's wife to "fit into" the women's community was a prejudicial factor. Mrs. X has been teaching at a Negro School in the community, and she is

lacking, apparently, in certain social qualities that faculty wives demand.[12]

Professor E. A. Ross's caution to the independent-minded academic seems to provide an adequate characterization of the situation:

> You'll have to live much more straightly than your harmless colleagues. You'll have to pay your bills promptly, be content with your wife, shun "wild" parties, give your students the best you have, meet your classes with clock-like regularity, avoid rows with your colleagues, conform to all the university rules, tell good stories, be able to laugh at yourself, and stand "razzing" good-humoredly.[13]

In brief, the degree to which one may deviate from accepted viewpoints or interests varies with the standing of the particular person. The higher the scientific, personal, or "social" status, the greater the range of freedom in specifically intellectual activities. For those who do not have the requisite esteem of their colleagues and the community, statements which would pass unremarked in the case of more widely accepted persons might well lead to disaster.

VI

In the "mixed cases," the precipitating factor often also provides the necessary public justification for the sanction when it is thought inadvisable to make explicit the original and central consideration. In denominational schools or in other institutions where the administrators are not entirely devoted to the freedom of research and teaching, they feel no necessity for dissembling their motives by claiming that the person in question did not conform with standards the binding character of which is conceded by everyone.

Where administrators do feel an obligation to refrain from interference with heterodox research or teaching, or where they perceive the existence of such an attitude in influential sections of the community, they attempt to avoid charges which point at nothing more than intellectual heterodoxy. Under these conditions, the application of sanctions is likely to involve charges that the person is "incompetent," "a troublemaker," presents "personality problems," does not have a "scholarly attitude," is "disloyal" and "generally disharmonious." Curtailment of the budget also can offer a justification for dismissing teachers who are not entirely agreeable.

On the whole, however, it appears that the more dogmatic the

12. Letter in A.C.L.U. files.
13. E. A. Ross, *Seventy Years of It* (New York, 1936), p. 86.

manner is in which values are held, the greater the probability is that restrictive actions will be legitimated directly in terms of those values. On the other hand, when values are held pragmatically or instrumentally, and scientific assertions are regarded as pernicious not in themselves but rather in their repercussions, there is greater probability that restrictive actions will be legitimated in terms of other values (masking).

Masking is especially probable when the repercussions of a scientific investigation or classroom statement are likely to be distasteful to a special group but not to the public at large. In such cases, those who feel their interests threatened and consequently seek to invoke sanctions against the investigator or teacher are especially apt to disguise their motives by an attack on other matters about which the public can be aroused. Recourse to pretexts which are actually of secondary importance is likely in areas where attitudes of intellectual tolerance are widely diffused in the relevant sections of the public, and where accordingly restrictive actions against intellectual activity would arouse some resistance and ultimately a withdrawal of support.

Another factor which influences the chances that the justification for restrictive action will be masked rather than avowed is the degree of ethical neutrality prevailing in a field. Where ethical judgments are explicitly asserted in the classroom, the administrator might feel a greater justification in taking action against a teacher than where the teaching is purely analytical, even though distasteful. In tolerant communities, there is apt to be an especially strong aversion for the invocation of sanctions against strictly analytical work, and the administrator who wishes to take action must find a legitimation which will be more acceptable publicly. Accordingly, charges like "incompetence" and "administrative necessity," which find a universal acceptance, are the ones most likely to be used.

When masking is required, the "incompetence" charge is preferred where the degree of intellectual consensus within the field is relatively low, while "administrative necessity" is chosen where consensus is high and where accordingly charges of incompetence would soon be denied by an important section of the profession.

VII

Every effective prohibition involves a sanction. This section of the report will analyze the various types of sanctions (*methods*) and the *agencies* by which they are initiated and administered. Steps taken against social scientists may be classified into (a) primary, i.e., those which operate directly on the individual in the sense that they represent official or unofficial punitive measures of the administration or faculty of the school directed against the "guilty" one, and (b) secondary, i.e., those which are initiated by groups other than administration or faculty, but which operate directly as sanctions through intimidation and indirectly through transformation into primary sanctions. Secondary sanctions, which comprise newspaper agitation, complaints of individual alumni, parents, and students, and the activities of civic, religious, political, and legislative bodies, usually aim at the initiation of a primary sanction.

Dismissal

Of the primary sanctions, dismissal is the most decisive. Dismissal is especially likely to occur when pressure from outside sources is very great. Agitation from outside the institution for punitive measures almost always calls for dismissal. The period elapsing between the time at which the decision to dismiss the faculty member is arrived at and the point at which his connection with the institution is completely severed varies from a few days to several years. A rather frequent procedure is to inform the person to be dismissed that his teaching duties are to cease at the end of the current academic year, but that his salary will continue through the following year.

This type of consideration seems usually to be reserved for those who have attained a rank beyond instructorship and who have accordingly already served for a number of years. It is highly likely, furthermore, that such financial considerateness is a luxury which more impecunious institutions cannot afford, and these, therefore, simply notify the person in question that his services will not be required after the current academic year.

Abrupt dismissal in mid-term is a practice which can be indulged in only by administrators who have no reputation for judiciousness and liberalism to maintain. Accordingly, such dismissals are most infrequent in the large, wealthy institutions with established positions as centers of intellectual eminence and administrative restraint.

Finally, in institutions which would seem otherwise immune from the practice of precipitous dismissal, a severe crisis which is thought to threaten the entire society is likely to be the condition for dismissal without more than a few days' notice.

Threat of Expulsion

The threat of expulsion is also employed as a means of silencing a particular viewpoint. Instances of this which have been discovered are confined to small institutions which are not outstanding for either their educational or their scientific standards. Such procedures are usually followed only by tactless administrators lacking in experience. They usually involve teaching, since the institutions in which such actions are taken do not allow much time or opportunity for research by their faculties. In none of the more important universities which are famous for the social research done under their auspices has such a barrier been encountered. Intimations that it would be tactically unwise to investigate certain aspects of homosexuality and divorce have been found in one large university, but the sanctions did not proceed further than general social unpleasantness.

Schools like the University of Pittsburgh, which maintain a system of annual reappointment delayed until some time after the customary date of reappointment, use this system as a means of keeping their faculty members in leash. "As is to be expected, the evidence shows that it (the obtaining system of reappointment) has brought into the lives of the men and women of the faculty . . . acute anxiety, worry and fear."[14] This insecurity is aggravated by the fact that the renewal notification sometimes has appended to it a very menacing and ambiguous note which says nothing specific but which intimates that the coming year may be the recipient's last year at the University of Pittsburgh.[15]

Nonpromotion

The blocking of the normal course of the teacher's and investigator's career by withholding promotion and financial advancement is an additional technique. This technique has precedence over dismissal in institutions where attitudes of toleration are not entirely absent in matters of intellectual disagreement or where there is an intense aversion for the unpleasant type of publicity which usually accompanies dismissals. Where neither of these preconditions is present, it is necessary that the degree of heterodoxy should not be extraordinarily large if nonpromotion is to be preferred to dismissal as the sanction.

Promotions may be either refused entirely or granted only after a

14. American Association of University Professors, *Bulletin,* vol. 21 (1935), p. 256.

15. Occasionally these notices of appointment carry with them an ominous postscript which in effect conveys to the recipient in rather vague terms the information that at the expiration of his present appointment he may not be reappointed. There is evidence that a large number of professors find such disturbing postscripts added to their regular letter for the annual reappointment. Many of the professors testified that these postscripts are usually phrased and worded in such an equivocal manner that it is impossible to construe their real meaning.

"Thus in the case of Prof. C. Professor C. has regularly been reappointed and promoted. . . . Then one year he received his renewal contract with the following postscript: 'Further, in view of the probable decrease in the attendance, a reduction of the number of faculty may be imperative. The administration, therefore, wishes to notify you at this time that you may not be reappointed to the faculty at the expiration of this appointment.' " Ibid., pp. 257-58.

much longer lapse of time than is customarily the case. In both cases, but especially in the former, nonpromotion is to be regarded as an implicit notification to modify one's intellectual conduct in the direction of greater conformity with orthodoxy or to look elsewhere for employment. While nonpromotion and the perception of the possibility of nonpromotion are important factors in extending the academic territory ruled by orthodoxy, they are not infallible devices; for if an instructor or an assistant professor decides that the results of his analyses or the problems that interest him are worth more to him than a promotion to a higher position, and if the school which employs him, though obviously intolerant, is not so intolerant as to dismiss him for his pertinacity, he may continue to expound his views and to investigate conventionally unapproved subjects or problems.

Selection

The process of determining what ideas shall come to expression and what shall remain unexpressed is, moreover, at work even before the teaching stage of the career is attained. From the stimulation and recognition offered in the first year of graduate studies to first appointment as a faculty member and subsequent promotion, a process of selection goes on which, other qualities being equal, offers the best chances for ascent to the man whose ideas are in conformity with those held by his superiors. The choice of graduate fellows and the distribution of assistantships always provide the possibility for eliminating the student who deviates from some of the intellectual conventions of the academic social sciences.[16] When new appointments to a faculty are to be made, it is only to be expected that the candidates will be carefully scrutinized and that those who promise to be embarrassing to the institution will be looked upon less warmly.[17] In consequence, very many teachers in American colleges are able to feel that their freedom is unlimited, simply because the process whereby they and their colleagues arrived at their present

16. It should be remarked that this possibility is somewhat reduced by the fact that the main centers of graduate training are also the main centers of research, and are in general characterized by the highest degree of tolerance to be found anywhere in the country. Consequently, the selection of fellows is made by the men whose capacity for detached judgment is more than average.

17. "There is one even more important question which hardly comes under the name of academic freedom. It refers to the fact that while a man is fairly well protected once he has gained a permanent position in a first-class university, it may easily be true that men whose opinions are unconventional are handicapped in securing such positions. If university teaching is in general biased on the side of conservatism—and I do not grant that it is—it is because of the way in which selection rather than elimination works." From a letter from the late Professor Allyn A. Young to Roger T. Baldwin, April 25, 1924. Cf. also Norman Foerster, *The American State University* (Chapel Hill, 1937), pp. 166-67.

positions operated in such a way as to select out persons to whom the intellectual actions which might lead to sanctions do not have the slightest appeal.

Intimation of Sanctions

Intimation of sanctions rather than their actual application is another method which frequently produces compliance. Taking the form either of *warning* or of *counsel*, it is often sufficient to remind a transgressor of the dangers involved in his present tendency in order to secure greater conformity. This is sometimes done through a conference in which either an order to desist is issued by the administrator or the matter is merely discussed by the administrator indicating the sources of his uneasiness and advising a certain moderation. The degree of formality can, however, be much slighter and the sanction no less effective. A remark from the head of the department or from an older colleague who is in no way officially inspired but who has had long experience in the academic world, may sometimes suffice, and a word of caution from a friend on the staff who points out the fate of a more recalcitrant person at the same or another institution, may be all that is necessary to increase conformity. The following statement by Dr. Louis Levine, in connection with the prohibition against publication of his taxation study, is illustrative of this procedure:

> Chancellor Elliott did not claim that his new policy gave him the right to forbid me to publish my monograph privately. He argued with me that it would be better for me not to publish it. He told me that "The Interests" were determined to crush out all liberal thought, and that if I published the monograph, an attack would be made on me generally: that the newspapers of the State would not give me a fair hearing . . . that the very fact of my being brought up for trial would ruin my professional reputation and would make it impossible for me to get another position anywhere in the country. . . .
>
> The chancellor claimed that he wanted to keep me at the university and that he was advising me not to publish my book in order to protect me.[18]

Uncordiality

A general "social unpleasantness" manifested toward those who have broken the taboos is an occasional instrument for obtaining conformity. In one university the members of a department of sociology were advised to shun one of their colleagues who had investigated a forbidden subject. The one person in the department

18. *New Northwest,* March 14, 1919.

who refused to follow this advice endangered his own position. This lack of cordiality sometimes takes the form of open though unofficial hostility when the man's colleagues feel that his failure to conform to the values of the community has placed the institution in a difficult situation and made their own positions less secure against outside attacks. The boycott is not likely to be applied to persons who enjoy high status among their colleagues. Naturally, the extent to which this uncordiality does silence the transgressor depends very much on the psychic dependence of the person involved, on the environment, and on his devotion to his scientific views.[19] Accordingly, the chances for the success of a boycott are affected by the size of the community and the opportunity which it affords for convivial relations outside the faculty.

Obstructions

Of a more official sort among the primary sanctions, and likewise more substantial in character, are those actions coming under the head of obstructions. In research, this appears chiefly as a withholding of funds. However, it so happens that the institutions in which funds are available for social research are probably the most liberal in the country. In the limited investigation possible for this report, only one attempt to withhold funds from an applicant on extrascientific grounds was discovered.[20] Decisive action by an influential member of the committee quickly quashed this attempt. Here too the possibility exists for repressive measures based on doctrinal or scientific-theoretical considerations,[21] the chances for such withholding being greatest in those fields or disciplines where professional consensus is slightest. The monopolistic attitudes of individuals or departments toward research on certain subject matters sometimes presents a danger to freedom of research on these

19. A professor who was dismissed from the University of Minnesota during the First World War summarizes the process of intimidation as follows: "Usually the intimidation of a professor is so veiled and vague that he hardly knows what is wrong. A certain significant remark, dropped at the right time, a certain coldness of attitude, failure to be included in certain social affairs, a certain slowness to get well-earned increases, granted with gusto to others, many other little hints that his views do not meet with favor in certain quarters serve to curb many a man with wife and babies to provide for. For instance there were a score or more called before the regents at the time I was. . . . Some of these men told me they had to lie or starve their wives and babies, and they took the easier road." Letter quoted in Upton Sinclair, *The Goosestep* (Pasadena, 1923), pp. 214-15.

20. The applicant in question had written several authoritative studies the conclusions of which may be regarded as conducive to an unfavorable judgment of the reigning system of economic organization.

21. The determination of the extent to which funds have been withheld from research on "dangerous" subjects would necessitate an analysis of the decisions on every resquest to research committees for financial assistance. Such detailed investigation was not possible in this report.

subjects by younger colleagues or by persons in neighboring disciplines.

Heavy teaching schedules are sometimes mentioned in popular discussion as a type of obstruction designed to interfere with research on taboo subjects. No evidence of this has been turned up, and the presumption is against it, since in the larger universities where considerable research is carried on, obstructions to research activity rarely occur, while in the smaller colleges very little research work is done, and teaching burdens are usually heavy for other reasons.

There have been cases where courses teaching "unsound doctrine" have been scheduled for hours inconvenient for students or have been made to run at exactly the same hours as certain courses required of all students. The consequence of this is of course exactly as intended: the students are kept from "infection," and the instructor comes to appreciate that he is not one of the favored sons of the institution.

Secondary sanctions are effective either by galvanizing into action the formal administrative machinery of the college or university or by bringing into play the more informal "coordinating" procedures such as counseling, cautioning, avoidance, intimidation, and "self-coordination."

Patriotic Organizations

The most forceful form of secondary sanction is the campaign waged by civic, religious, business, and patriotic organizations. Of these campaigns there is no scarcity. Patriotic organizations are perhaps the most vehement and energetic. These organizations react even in situations where the trustees of a small denominational college would find no cause for alarm. Stimulated by and stimulating the sensation-seeking press, these organizations seek to focus the attention of the authorities—be they state legislators, the trustees, or the university administration itself—on what they consider derelictions within the institution.

The movement for loyalty oaths, although by no means aimed exclusively or even primarily at research activities, is only one phase of the repressive activity of such groups as the Daughters of the American Revolution, the American Legion, the Veterans of Foreign Wars, and other patriotic organizations.[22] A protest by the Sons of the American Revolution against Professor R. E. Turner was a contributing factor in bringing Chancellor Bowman to a decision to

22. Cf. *The Gag on Teaching* (2d rev. ed., New York: American Civil Liberties Union, May 1937), pp. 22-26; *Depression, Recovery and Higher Education* (New York, 1937), pp. 445-46.

dismiss him.[23] Professor William Schaper was dismissed from the University of Minnesota on the basis of "information" supplied by an informant of the Public Safety Commission, a patriotic society of the war period.[24] Veblen's *Nature of Peace* was assailed by Henry A. Wise Wood, chairman of the Conference Committee on National Preparedness who declared that "professors like Veblen must be driven from the colleges."[25]

Other Outside Forces

Other important outside sources of interference are to be found in the parents of students and in alumni and businessmen and ministers unattached to the school. Chancellor Bowman of Pittsburgh charged that the complaints which caused him to dismiss Professor Turner came principally from parents and ministers.[26] When Professor H. A. Miller was dismissed from Ohio State University, the recurring complaints of parents and others were put forward as among the reasons for the action. "From his very first year here, complaints were received from parents of students in his classes and from others about his teaching on the relations between classes and on domestic relations."[27]

The Illinois State Legislature investigation into the University of Chicago in 1935 was precipitated by a prominent local businessman and the zeal of the Hearst press. Businessmen who feel that the bases of their existence are being questioned at the university, and ministers, especially fundamentalists, who become agitated by the naturalistic analysis of social development and social organization, are among the most sensitive to any laxity in the reinforcement of conventional social ideas. They are quick to bring their misgivings to the attention of the authorities of the institution, as well as to carry on an outside agitation. Alumni whose induction into the detached scientific outlook during their student days was left unperfected are also to be included in the list of those who have at times demanded the silencing of teachers and investigators in the social sciences. The businessmen alumni of one of the greatest American universities were so perturbed by the economics taught to the undergraduates that they organized a committee to prepare a textbook to be used in undergraduate instruction there. The economics department of that institution is, however, still governing itself.

There is no evidence as to whether the alumni tend to be more

23. American Association of University Professors, *Bulletin*, 1935, p. 228.
24. Letter from Governor Elmer Benson of Minnesota to Mr. Lewis Lohman.
25. *New York Tribune*, Feb. 25, 1918.
26. American Association of University Professors, *Bulletin*, 1935, p. 233.
27. From a statement by President Rightmire in *Columbus Evening Dispatch*, May 27, 1931.

326 Intellectuals in Modern Societies

sensitive to deviations in institutions which are located in large cities and where consequently a larger proportion of the alumni are quite close to the school after graduation, or whether they are more responsive in schools in smaller "college towns," from which they are usually further removed but to which they are often bound by primary group ties.

VIII

Movements for sanctions initiated outside the college or university vary in the extent of their success. Occasionally some are able to bring about dismissal; others have been instrumental in the decision of legislative or administrative bodies to conduct inquiries into the content of faculty teaching. The Walgreen-Hearst Illinois Senate investigation of the University of Chicago in 1935 was of this character, and on this particular occasion the president of the university and some of the professors made very pronounced statements in defense of their teaching practices and emphatically denied the charges made against them. The university was exonerated, but two of the professors were censured. What was significant here was the action of the president and administrators of the university in defending its staff members. In contrast with this situation was that at the University of Missouri, where neither the president nor the administration attempted to defend several members of the staff who were attacked by the press and civic bodies.

A similar differentiation in response is to be found in the treatment of complaints coming from individuals. In some schools they are taken at their face value and made the basis of censure or even more far-reaching action by the authorities of the school. In a small college town in New England the members of the board of trustees received an anonymous letter charging several of the economics instructors with radicalism. One member of the board of trustees sent this to the president suggesting that one of the men in question be silenced or dropped from the staff. The president advised the instructor to avoid such utterances in the future. In another school an extrauniversity complaint was made the basis for immediate action without even an adequate hearing being given to the accused faculty member, or any serious examination being made of the reliability of the complainant.

In some schools, in contrast with the above, complaints from the outside are carefully sifted[28] and, when considered worthy of

28. The president of a large university writes regarding rumors and criticisms circulating on the outside: "When I have endeavored in the past to get substantial evidence from an individual, the complaint melts away and no

answer, are brought to the attention of the person complained about, who then has the opportunity of vindicating himself. In other instances, the head of the department himself prepares a statement to meet the charge. An excellent example of a statement in which the chairman of the department comes to the defense of his younger colleagues is contained in the following excerpts from a letter written in response to a request by the university president for information relative to a complaint which had reached his office:

> You say that "sometimes an instructor is critisized as being very loose in his thinking and very irresponsible in his statements and sometimes even immoral." All these terms are, of course, relative, and in the absence of definite charges, with accurate quotation of the instructor's remarks, can only be set aside as "loose talk" on the part of irresponsible citizens. No citizen who is himself judicially minded and free from preju-diced sentiments will make vague charges of this kind, since he knows or should know both that they may be unfair and that they cannot be substantiated if specific evidence is lacking.
>
> I wish very much that when you get any complaints about an instructor in economics, or about what is taught or said in an economics class, you would refer the complainant either to the Dean or directly to me. . . . it might in a measure discour-age irresponsible and uninformed complainants if they knew that they had to make good their criticisms directly to the Dean and the department head concerned. In most cases, I believe, a tactful conference with the complainant would help him to see that no instructor is perfect, that many things will necessarily have to be talked about in the classroom and many views expressed of which he would not approve from his own point of view, that he cannot have education in the social sciences at all unless both teacher and student—and student's parents—are tolerant and "reasonable," that in the social sciences we are not "teaching," that is inculcating, any specific doctrines but are trying to get the student to think for himself and to give him data as objective and unbiased as we can on which to do his thinking, and that our fundamental aim is to give the student opportunity to choose his own values.
>
> The sad part of this whole question of propriety in the classroom and of "outside" complaints that this or that

one has given me any definite statements which he would be willing to stand for. Loose talk apparently is carried on outside, but something tangible is brought forward only on the rarest occasion." "Economics and Sociology in the University," *School and Society,* vol. 42, no. 1096 (Dec. 28, 1935), p. 893.

instructor is "radical" in his teaching is that so few of the middle class public, from which college and university students preponderantly come, have an intelligent idea of what a college or university is for.[29]

Factors Affecting Sensitivity

In connection with all such actions by private individuals or civic groups, it would seem that the intensity of their influence depends to a large extent on the intimacy of contact between themselves and the school administrators. Close personal acquaintance between university or college authorities and persons who are concerned about the contents or the problems of teaching and research is apt to increase the effectiveness of complaints. This is especially likely to be the case in municipal colleges and in state universities which are located in the capital of the state, where the higher frequency of personal contact between the administration and those who control its funds creates a high sensitivity to complaints.

A further factor which helps to determine whether a given complaint will be heeded is the status of the complainant and that of the institution to which the complaint is made. Thus, whereas a complaint from an individual small businessman might be disregarded, one from a leader in the economic life of the community would probably be looked into. Correspondingly, while a given complaint to a smaller less opulent institution might find a respectful audience, a complaint coming from a person of the same status would, in the case of a more wealthy institution, have a good chance of being passed over with no more than a courteous acknowledgment.

The trustees are important in so many of the methods of applying sanctions that it is worth while to single them out from the other agencies for special attention. They are in the first place the only authorities in the institution whose major occupational activities are regularly nonacademic, and because of their economic position they may well be regarded as the representatives, in the councils of the college or university, of the dominant strata. They are furthermore, as we have seen, not merely representatives of their stratum, but also continuous channels through which protests can pass from the various centers of influence in the larger society to the administration of the school itself.

But despite the extensive class homogeneity, considerable variation in attitudes exists among trustees. These variations are probably

29. Ibid., pp. 893-95. The compliance of the administration with pressure from the outside is perhaps greater where appointments, dismissals, and other matters of academic policy and administration are centralized in the president or dean than in those institutions where there is a high degree of decentralization of authority among the various departments.

functions of educational experience, family tradition, and urbanization. The larger, wealthier, and more eminent schools recruit their trustees from the higher ranks of the plutocracy and from those segments of the professions which are closely associated with the plutocracy. Schools of the second rank in wealth and prestige draw their trustees from the lower fringes of the wealthy classes, depending much on local business leaders.

The longer the lapse of time between the first acquisition of a sizable fortune and service as a trustee, the greater is the likelihood of an attitude of tolerance and sympathy for intellectual values. The schools which are most successful in obtaining as trustees persons on whose families wealth has resided for several generations are accordingly less likely to have restrictive measures emanating from the board of trustees. In parts of the country where such trustees are more difficult to obtain the chances for such interference are correspondingly greater.[30]

But whatever the characteristics of the trustees themselves, the traditions of the institution itself as a center of science and scholarship and of tolerance toward intellectual variety are of prime importance in restraining the actions of trustees who in other roles are rather more conservative.

IX

One other phase of repressive action arising from outside complaints which merits attention is the hypersensitivity of university administrators during fund-raising campaigns. The possible alienation of potential donors because of unorthodox teachings of members of the faculty is a constant source of worry to university presidents, and in periods of straitened finances this fear and, consequently, the tendency to comply with imagined demands are especially great. Whatever sanctions might be imposed here are not necessarily consequences of intellectual or doctrinal intolerance as such, but rather of a concern for the financial well-being of the institution.

Nor is the apprehension itself always necessary, since it appears probable that in some cases, at least, the administrator projects his own intolerance on the environment.

It is not necessary to maintain that wealthy patrons of educational institutions attach service conditions to their gifts.

---

30. There is no evidence that there has been much improvement since the time when the late President Charles W. Eliot wrote: "In the newer parts of our country, it has of course been impossible to find at short notice men really prepared to discharge the difficult duties of educational trusteeship; and it will take generations yet to bring these communities in this respect to the level of the older states and cities." C. W. Eliot, *Academic Freedom* (Ithaca, 1908), p. 7.

It is a notable fact that this is rarely the case. It is much more commonly the fear on the part of faculty and managing boards that frank utterance will lessen the income from gifts which really impairs the freedom of teaching.[31]

An outstanding liberal American educator with many years of experience as a fund gatherer stated that in his opinion many donors of large sums would not be pleased if they knew of the restrictive measures taken by administrators in order to assure themselves of the donor's favor. The wealthier a school is, and accordingly the less its dependence on any single donor, the lower will be the degree of anticipation of assumed demands for compliance. With this, the probability of freedom is considerably enhanced.

X

Restraints are maintained not only by the punishment of those who have already deviated. Self-intimidation or *self-coordination,* by which we mean the more or less deliberate renunciation of any intention to investigate or teach subjects which are forbidden or which are thought to be forbidden,[32] operates against those who have not yet deviated.

A decisive action, as, for example, dismissal or a state legislative inquiry against a colleague at the same university or at another university, has often produced conformity among persons who under less dangerous conditions would have presented the views they actually held. There are, furthermore, numerous instances of the feeling that it is necessary to "soft pedal" the treatment of certain subjects. In schools where there is a strong and clearly formulated student opinion on public issues, there may exist a tendency for instructors who do not like to face opposition to accommodate themselves to the prevailing outlook, and sometimes out of no other consideration than that of student popularity, an instructor may find himself enunciating views which he did not previously hold. This is especially true in the smaller schools and in the less urbanized communities, where an incautious or misunderstood statement might give rise to distasteful gossip and ultimately perhaps to direct sanctions. Continued avoidance of potentially embarrassing issues renders self-restraint easier to bear. After a time the insight and interest which had to be repressed are lost, and the teacher comes to regard his situation as totally free from restriction.

31. Elmer C. Brown, "Academic Freedom," *Educational Review,* March 1900, p. 230.
32. It is, of course, necessary in this case to draw a careful line between conformity with intellectual standards on the basis of intellectual conviction, and conformity or self-coordination out of career-consideration. It is only the latter that concerns us here.

There is no indication that self-coordination is extensive in the sphere of research, since the institutions which are large enough and wealthy enough to provide time and money for research are also likely to be sophisticated enough not to interfere with the research done by their staff members. There is occasional self-coordination of interest by applicants for financial assistance in order to make a grant more probable. There is also self-coordination in the choice of research subjects by candidates for the doctorate, although again no evidence is available as to the extent to which it obtains. There is usually a wider range of political viewpoints among graduate students as compared with faculty members, and consequently a feeling that it is necessary to find a thesis subject which will be agreeable to the faculty members, on whom, of course, their academic career frequently depends.

XI

We now turn to a brief examination of the possible consequences of restrictions on the freedom of teaching and research. Insofar as they affect teaching, restrictions obviously limit the range of knowledge and of possible interpretation which is made available to the student, and whether one believes that the function of the university or college is to educate "whole men," citizens, specialized technicians, or humanistic scholars, this cannot be looked upon as other than a serious deficiency. Restrictions which are peculiar to the undergraduate level and to smaller schools are negated in some measure if and when the student continues his studies as a postgraduate student at one of the larger and more outstanding institutions.

On the side of research, limitations on freedom do not seem to play any very significant role, since the great centers of research are on the whole quite free. But the sanctions which deter teachers from dealing with "dangerous" subjects in the classroom carry their force over into the research field by focusing the attention of the student and future research worker and channeling his interests in such a manner that when he begins his research career he will out of "trained incapacity" skip over important problems requiring investigation which he would be quite free to work on if he so chose. It is not far from correct to say that a considerable amount of the narrowness of many American social scientists is the result not of any explicit restrictions or fear of possible sanctions, but rather of the narrow undergraduate training which they received (in less advanced institutions) at the hands of teachers who themselves were trained in a period when even the greatest of the American universities were considerably less free than they are today.[33]

33. These remarks do not pretend to offer a complete explanation of the range of selection of research problems which obtains today in American social science.

To the extent that restrictions on the freedom of the academic person determine the choice of problems, and therewith the development of social science, there is cause for concern. One does not have to hold the view that the social sciences ought to develop according to some immanent pattern of scientific advance in order to appreciate how detrimental can be a choice of problems which is in a certain sense dictated by persons who are themselves not competent in the field in question. This should not be understood as implying that the social sciences should not study "practical" questions at the suggestion of persons outside the academic profession. Quite the contrary, since some of the most important ideas in the social sciences have arisen in the attempt to comprehand some practical issue. Furthermore, a social science which disregarded controversial or "practical" issues would suffer the danger of running off into a sterile byzantinism and triviality. It should be recognized, however, that this type of developmental course is quite different from one which is determined by a restrictive fiat, which would deliberately leave certain areas uncultivated, not because they are of no intellectual interest but rather because they are of too much "practical" interest.

XII

It is to be expected that lay detractors of certain types of politically or socially unwelcome research and teaching should attempt to bring about its suppression, insisting on the incompetence of the investigators and especially of the teachers in question. It is, of course, presumptuous in most cases for nonprofessionals to attempt to pass on the competence of professional persons, and most mature academic men will readily admit this in a general form. There are, however, numerous concrete instances in which the autonomy of judgment within the social science profession is renounced in response to some attack from the outside. At such moments, it is often all too easy to forget that intellectual and pedagogical competence should be the sole criterion for admission into or exclusion from the academic circle, and to slip into an attitude of apathetic or even aggressive conformity with nonacademic judgments on scientific matters. The intellectual integrity of the social sciences can, however, be maintained only to the degree that every responsible scientist himself succeeds in distinguishing his judgment of a colleague's scientific competence from his agreement or disagreement with his political, economic, and moral views. Such integrity within the profession (toward one's colleagues and toward oneself) is the foundation stone for the protection of the social sciences from whatever limitations outside groups—administrative, governmental, and private—might seek to impose on their freedom.

Part Three

Intellectuals in Underdeveloped
Countries

16 Toward a Modern Intellectual Community in the New States

I

To be modern, a society requires at least a rational administration which extends its jurisdiction to the territorial boundaries of the state. It requires a rational outlook about economic matters and a rational organization of its economic activities. It requires a relatively rational legal system, and institutions of public political action. It requires a government concerned with more than the conduct of war, the maintenance of order, and the prevention of sacrilege. A modern government operates the educational system, takes responsibility for communication and transportation, and seeks to foster economic growth. It has policies which require implementation, not just decisions which require enforcement.

These are minimal requirements. They do not refer to the mass of population, but only to the elites of the major institutional subsystems of the society—the economy and the polity. Each of these subsystems requires an elite appropriate to its tasks. Rational administration requires higher civil servants, lawyers, judges, scientists, and technologists. A rational economic system requires enterprisers and managers, economists, accountants, chemists, agronomists, lawyers, and experts in transportation and marketing. Public political life requires politicians, party officials, editors and reporters, professors and social research workers, radio engineers, and producers. These professions can be neither staffed nor carried on without a modern intellectual system. By an intellectual system I do not mean a system of ideas but rather a set of intellectual institutions in which persons are trained for or perform intellectual roles.

The elites of any society that reaches this level of modernization are also bound, willy-nilly, to have and desire a modern intellectual system. They might, it is true, wish to use some of their intellectual apparatus to glorify their traditional culture, but this purpose will not be the sole ground for their aspiration. The elites' desire for a modern intellectual system will rest in part on the fact that they already possess to some extent a modern culture which they will not want to see eradicated; it will also come from the belief, widely

Previously published in a slightly different form in *Education and Political Development,* edited by James S. Coleman (Princeton, N.J.: Princeton University Press, 1965), pp. 498-520. © 1965 by Princeton University Press.

shared by the elites of the new states, that a modern culture, and particularly its intellectual institutions, are technically, or functionally, necessary for the modernization of the polity and the economy. Finally it will come from the belief that the elements in an institutional system of modern intellectual action—universities, scientific research institutions, learned bodies, literary publications, libraries, and the cultural productions that are generated by these institutions—are as essential to a modern sovereign state as an army equipped with up-to-date weapons, an airline, and a flag. They are part of the constellation of symbols that a state must have nowadays to merit the respect of those who have created and run it, and, as they think, of the outside world. The strength and direction of the desire for a modern intellectual system varies, of course, among the different sectors of the elite. Intellectuals have practical and ideal interests in expanding such elements of the system as already exist. The interests of practicing politicians might emphasize the practical, technological and national status aspects more. Nonetheless there is general agreement that intellectual institutions of many sorts are necessary.

Those who assert the necessity of such an institutional system are correct. Persons qualified through an elaborate educational experience are necessary. The technical knowledge prerequisite to the tasks of modernization does require systematic preliminary formation. Obviously scientists and technologists must have learned the rudiments of their subjects before they begin to work on them. Accountants and agronomists, lawyers and economists can scarcely learn on the job what they need to know to meet a moderate standard of proficiency. The higher educational system of a modern or a modernizing society must make provision for the preliminary formation of such skills. There must therefore be a body of persons capable of reproducing and transmitting this pattern of technical and specialized knowledge and skill. A body of persons, different in the substantive content of their intellectual culture but having parallel functions, is no less necessary for providing the education prerequisite to administration and public discussion. Anterior to these, teachers and supervisors and authors of text books for the primary and secondary levels of education are needed, and education must be provided for at least some of these.

Alongside these institutions for the formation of skills, the guidance of dispositions, and the preliminary exercise of the capacity for judgment, there are also the institutions in which these skills, dispositions, and capacities are to be brought into serious operation. Scientific and technological research institutions, institutes of economic and social research, government scientific services, scientific advisory committees, professional and learned societies, universities and other institutions of higher learning, museums and libraries, the machinery of communications (i.e., radio, newspapers, and periodicals), the publication of books, the machinery of their distribution, conferences, clubs and exhibitions— the list tails away as it ranges from the more massively organized to the more informal and spontaneous collectivities through and in which the actual work of productive and reproductive culture is carried out.

It becomes manifest that, as we move from the central institutions of the cultural system out toward the peripheral ones, the intellectual culture of a society consists not only of universities and research institutes in which people are trained for and perform intellectual work. It becomes no less manifest that the peripheral institutions are as much an integral part of the complex as those closer to the center. Without the former, the latter make little sense. There must, in other words, be roles and institutions in which the skills, dispositions, and capacities formed in the central institutions can be used. There must likewise be roles and institutions which, although apparently only ancillary, are indispensable conditions for the effectiveness of the central institutions. Libraries, publishing enterprises, bookshops, learned societies, periodicals, and so on, must exist. Institutions which link the production and transmission of knowledge to its practical application are necessary. Otherwise the social system of intellectual life will be incomplete and the need for completeness inherent in the system and in the exigencies of the life of the society as a whole will require supplementation by foreign institutions. Alternatively, the central institutions will languish or wither away.

Furthermore, the social system of intellectual life must have a culture of its own. I refer here not just to the articulated culture of specific propositions, the culture that consists of the contents of particular books, the knowledge and practice of the sciences and the arts. I refer to that stratum of culture which underlies and permeates the specific culture. This stratum belongs more in the sphere of generalized dispositions and deeper categories; it is more a matter of standards of judgment, of the unarticulated criteria which distinguish the essential from the unessential. At the bottom of this culture lies the motivation that impels intellectual action: above all, curiosity, the desire to learn something new, the self-confidence in one's right and capacity as an individual to know and experience. Here we should also list the pleasure in contemplation of reality at whatever level of concreteness, and the desire to go beyond any particular level of concreteness to a deeper or more general understanding. Also relevant is the experience of intellectual conviviality, of being in contact with other persons of similarly directed curiosity, together with solidarity with such persons in one's own sphere of action, both at home and abroad.

The new states have in varying degrees made substantial progress in the establishment of the central institutions of intellectual life. In the former colonial territories—and those which were never colonized—there are numerous universities and university colleges. Some were established before independence; others have been founded or reformed since independence. Even the few affiliated with a metropolitan sponsor are full-fledged institutions with a full complement of departments covering the major fields of interest to modern universities. Moreover, many of them conform to a respectable standard of administrative and intellectual performance.

Beyond these institutions, the intellectual systems of the new states are hardly adequate to the requirements of a modern intellectual system. Museums, libraries, publishing houses, periodicals and newspapers, the opportunities for meeting a wide range of colleagues in one's own or neighboring fields, through their publications or through face-to-face encounters, are few. The intellectual systems of the new states suffer not so much from isolation from their own societies—the most common complaint against them—as from their isolation from colleagues and like-minded persons, whether within or outside their own societies. Most of the new states lack an intellectual public outside the universities, the higher civil service, and the journalistic and broadcasting professions, and these categories are so small that they do not provide sufficient differentiation and diversity. The stimulation of a diversified intellectual environment scarcely exists. Moreover, the networks of intellectual communication are so slightly developed that what small productivity there is has no internal channels through which it might be transmitted. The number of persons available to stimulate and fortify the adherence to standards, either through competition or through fellow-feeling, is too small to be effective. The paucity of local writing and publishing and the meagerness of the social-intellectual environment either result in desultoriness and slackness of intellectual exertion, or force continued dependence on the intellectual life of the metropolis. In any event there would be a marked dependence on the metropolis, because in many areas of endeavor, metropolitan societies are presently exhibiting a high degree of creativity. The similarity of pattern of the institutions of higher learning and those of the metropolis, the paths of communication between metropolis and province, as well as the presence of many metropolitan expatriates in the local universities, all tend to focus attention on the continued intellectual output of the metropolis. Furthermore, it should be stressed that no country can ever be fully self-sufficient in its intellectual life; to aspire to be so is an aspiration to intellectual suicide. Nonetheless, the internal structure and the level of institutional development of intellectual life in the new states make for far-reaching dependence on the metropolis. Even efforts to break away, as in Ghana, only introduced other metropolitan centers of dominance. This close relationship inhibits the emergence of motivations for a high quality of local performance.

It might be argued that what I have been saying applies only to intellectual structures, and that it has little to do with the process of political modernization. After all, what a society needs for modernization is a good corps of civil servants, engineers, and technologists; all the rest is trimming. Colleges, universities, and higher technical institutes are sufficient, and the rest is just a highbrow demand. I do not share this view; I think that a creative intellectual stratum is an indispensable element which no society can forego on its path toward modernity. The very establishment of a society on a national scale, coterminous with the scope of sovereignty, requires a sense of national identity which, at least in part, focuses on a cultural activity concerned with the past, the present, and the future of its society. The existence of cultural monuments inherited from the past, either by physical survival or by traditional transmission, requires interpretation. To interpret them either by physical survival or by traditional transmission, requires interpretation. To interpret them, methods of universal validity, regardless of the parochiality of the subject matter, must be available. The inherited culture is not rich enough in itself either to serve as the cultural complement of a modern society or to engender the self-respect demanded by modernity. Cultivation of folk arts and of traditional medicine will not satisfy the elites of the new states, however traditionalistically they wish to present themselves on ceremonial occasions. There must be creativity in specifically modern genres, in literary and artistic production, in scientific research, in the social sciences, in history, and in the study of literature, language, and art. Self-discovery on a large scale is an essential part of the formation of a translocal or national society, and to this end humanistic and social research is necessary. It must be a self-discovery in which fictitious and mythical elements are treated dispassionately and sympathetically, for otherwise they will be despised by intelligent people, even by those who use them demagogically. The modern techniques of research are indispensable for this purpose.

So much for the value of modern cultural achievement in the creation of the symbolism of a modern society. If the standards in operation in universities and colleges are slack and the performance is poor according to universal criteria, the quality of the graduates produced will be poor. Scientists, engineers, technologists, and civil servants will be agents of modernization more in name than in performance. Their works will decay too soon, and their moral and economic competitive power will be low vis-à-vis their counterparts in countries whose agriculture is more efficient, whose commercial procedures are more orderly, and whose public and private administration is more trustworthy. Journalists will be less knowledgeable than the standards of the profession require, and politicians will tend to be of poorer quality, being less well informed and less realistic in their judgments. (Knowledge and realism, of course, are not the sole prerequisites to the effectiveness of politicians.)

The political public, unattached to any standards of judgment other than those provided by ethnicity, locality, party, or passion, will lack the capacity to pass judgment on the merits of policies, both for the very immediate present or the more remote future, and will be useless to the political culture of a modern society. Their culture will be a political culture in the worst sense of the term. Political development requires some limitations on politics. Excessive politicization is a degenerate form of political development. The poorly educated, proud and sensitive about their singular status, will be a source of perpetual political disturbance. No group exhibits this tendency more clearly than politicized university (and sometimes secondary school) students. The hyperexcitability of these youths, although it may sometimes be valuable in helping to overthrow a tyranny, is more often expressed in political procedures and on behalf of political ends that are not conducive to the formation of a pragmatic point of view or to the nourishment of a political culture capable of growth. An excessively politicized political culture helps to demoralize intellectual institutions and dooms them to effectual mediocrity.

II

India is a case in point. No other new state of Asia or Africa is so well situated as India with respect to the scale of higher education and, indeed, to its entire institutional apparatus of intellectual activity. No other new country is so capable of providing its own academic and intellectual personnel to staff its many institutions. No other new state is so well able to get along without the services of expatriates. In few other new countries is the number of university graduates large enough to meet the country's needs. No other new state can show so many persons capable of outstanding intellectual achievement.

The modern sector of Indian society is a powerful and impressive structure. Much of it is the creation of the Indian educated class, or at least its continuance is the work of that class. If the traditional sector of Indian society is like an ocean, broad and deep, the modern sector is like a well-settled coastal civilization, deeply affected by its oceanic environment but rich enough and ramified enough to lead, to some extent, a life of its own.

Whereas practically all other new states, such as those of Africa and the Middle East, arrived at independence with a flimsy or nonexistent modern intellectual system, India already possessed, at least quantitatively, a fairly well-elaborated system of intellectual institutions. India has had universities for more than a hundred years, and colleges for even longer. In the twentieth century, well before independence, India possessed many learned societies, research institutes in the natural and social sciences, a number of outstanding scholarly libraries, a dizzying proliferation of periodicals, a well-established and sober English-language press, a few scientists and scholars who were honored the world over, and two Nobel Prize winners.

Contemporary India, although its well-wishers and critics lament the state of affairs, has not marked time since independence insofar as its intellectual system is concerned. The country has a journalistic profession which is outstandingly good with respect to probity, freedom, and corporate spirit, although it is still deficient in such matters as reportorial curiosity and initiative. Owing to the in-adequacy of resources, derived from the smallness of the reading public and the insufficiencies of private advertising, the press has structural defects. A fair number of publishing houses issue books in English and in Indian languages. The country is beginning to have a few which publish books in English of a decent standard, and a few are of comparable quality in the Indian languages. India has many bookshops with large stocks, and in this respect exceeds the countries of Black Africa or the Middle East.

At the center of the Indian intellectual system stand the Indian universities—now numbering more than fifty—with more than a million students and more than thirty thousand teachers. There are about thirty government scientific and technological research labora-tories, a number of private research institutions in the natural and social sciences, and a very large output of scientific and scholarly publications. Indian research students are found in the major universities of Great Britain and America, where many of them do good work and some are outstanding. A growing number of Indian scientists hold posts as teachers and research workers in universities outside India. Many Indian research students abroad defer their return home indefinitely because they are able to obtain and hold appointments in research or industrial organizations. Most of these persons, acknowledged as competent by even the highest standards, have had their undergraduate training in India.

All these accomplishments notwithstanding, the Indian intellectual system is subject to severe criticism. One of the most common complaints is that the system is out of touch with India; that, having inherited the university from Great Britain, it has not adapted it to Indian needs. Its failure to do so is sometimes alleged to be damaging to India; it is also adduced to explain the public disorders in which Indian college and university students participate. Another criticism, less frequently voiced officially but often asserted privately, is that the quality of university education is poor.

Let us consider first the charge that Indian universities have not adapted themselves to the new conditions of independence. Presumably this criticism censures them for retaining too close an affiliation with the intellectual life of the former ruling power, for not teaching in Hindi or in the local Indian language, and for not paying due reverence to Indian traditional culture. It must be acknowledged that there is a certain xenophilia among Indian university teachers; indeed, it could hardly be otherwise when so much of their intellectual sustenance comes from abroad. Many textbooks used in Indian universities have been written by British authors, although Russian and American textbooks are beginning to achieve recognition. The scientific and scholarly literature read by Indians, particularly the former, is written almost entirely in English. Nontechnical books and periodicals are written mainly in English. A disproportionately high percentage of the best Indian research students receive their advanced training in Britain and America.

Yet Indian problems and Indian subject matter are not overlooked by Indian universities. In every university classical and modern Indian studies, linguistic, literary, and historical, have a prominent place in the curriculum. Science, engineering, agriculture, genetics—subjects claimed to be necessary for Indian economic development—are taught and investigated. The social sciences, too, are amply represented. And, although British and American textbooks are used more frequently than Indian textbooks, Indian material is by no means neglected, despite its relative mediocrity. In certain subjects, it is true, syllabi and required and recommended books contain much that is out of date, and out-of-date material tends to be more British than Indian. On the whole, Indian universities, which owe their origin mainly to British inspiration, gain far more than they lose from their factual and sentimental xenophilia. It would be better if they could be more independent, and could introduce innovations more conducive to their effectiveness. In view of the absence of initiative, xenophilia keeps standards higher than they would otherwise be.

Other aspects of the charge that Indian universities are not sufficiently Indianized have little merit. The demand for teaching in the Indian languages has recently made steady progress because the students' knowledge of English has collapsed; most of the progress in that direction has proved to be more injurious than beneficial. The demand for a deeper reverence for the Indian cultural inheritance is superfluous, because it has already been met. Indeed, individual staff members have done more than the government, with its sparing financial provisions for research and publication on classical Indian subjects, to inculcate respect for cultural traditions.

It is ridiculous to assert that the Indian university is a rootless institution, a foreign establishment on Indian soil. One could as well say that the Indian administrative service, the Indian army, and the system of parliamentary government are foreign institutions. The proposition makes sense only if, by India, one means traditional India, and if one regards anything modern as a rootless intrusion. It is impossible to argue that India should be modernized while at the same time denying that the universities are right in pursuing a course that implies adherence to standards of universal validity.

Universities must, in order to be universities, teach and investigate what is of universal validity; they must also teach and investigate what is of parochial value, either because it is practical or because it cultivates the parochial (or national) cultural tradition. The Indian universities serve all these purposes; their great deficiency is that they do not serve them well. There are outstanding exceptions. For example, the impressive young people who are recruited into the Indian administrative service, and the handful of outstanding young scholars and scientists, have almost all had their undergraduate training in India. Yet, despite these exceptions, Indian universities are on the whole doing a poor job intellectually; to the extent of their failure, the quality of performance of their graduates is bound to suffer. The public life of India will suffer accordingly. There will always be enough gifted persons to staff the upper grades of the administrative service and to provide a few brilliant scientists. Nevertheless, India runs the danger of having too small a supply of that solid stratum of B+ persons so necessary for the efficient functioning of any complex organization, be it administrative, political, or intellectual.

It is not that Indian universities teach the wrong skills, or skills that are irrelevant to India's problems. There are perhaps more persons trained in law than are really necessary, or more than can earn a decent livelihood from the practice of law. India does not suffer from a pronounced shortage of scientists and engineers; in fact, there is scarcely enough employment, most of it very ill paid, for those who are available. (For this reason many who have traveled overseas wish to remain overseas.) Nor is it that Indian university education is too old-fashioned, in the sense of being humanistic and literary, to the exclusion of scientific and technical aspects. The distribution of Indian university students is fairly well balanced. Particularly in view of the higher costs of a scientific or technical education, as compared with a liberal arts education, and of Indian poverty, the balance is quite reasonable. Furthermore, the arts subjects have served India well in the education of civil servants, politicians, and journalists, and there is no reason to suppose that the arts curriculum (including, of course, the social sciences) should not continue to do equally well by India in the future.

The deficiencies of the Indian university are deficiencies of teaching and research and of intellectual morale. The dismal pedagogy of the universities and colleges of India is a result of the teachers' poverty, their distraction by routine, and their feeling that they cannot do their work well under the present conditions. They feel meanly treated by the leaders of Indian society and the top officials of their own institutions; they are ill at ease and unhappy. Yet higher salaries and lighter schedules, the improvement of academic administration, and less interference by politicians in the internal life of universities and colleges, however desirable and imperative such reforms may be, would not necessarily remove one very important source of the present malaise. These improvements would not be sufficient to arouse the Indian universities from their intellectual doldrums.

At present, not enough teachers and research workers take intellectual work seriously; not enough of them do serious study of their own, either in research or in teaching. Too many of those who are engaged in research projects of their own do the work in a perfunctory and indifferent manner without real conviction as to its worthwhileness, or do it on "assignment." Many of those who once had an interest in research have given it up, though they may still go through the motions. It is common for teachers to have so little interest in their subjects that their classroom presentation has become boring to themselves and to their students. Few manage to keep up with new developments in their respective fields. The same antiquated lecture notes are used year after year. (Better preparation and the use of more up-to-date literature are not easy, given the poverty of the teachers and the deficiencies of most college libraries.)

A teacher who has no love of his subject matter cannot communicate such love to his students; the indifference of the students only increases the teacher's boredom. Teacher and student are caught in a vicious circle which, if it breaks at all, goes into a downward spiral because of the student's difficulties in understanding English lectures and textbooks. It has often been observed that the English of university students is not what it was before independence. True, but then there were only a hundred thousand students, the majority of whom came from urban, educated, and professional families, whereas today there are a million students, many of whom come from rural and uneducated families. The number of students who know English well must be as large now as it was thirty or forty years ago, but now they are in a minority and cannot set the tone of the college or university. The alternatives are lectures in a regional language and good textbooks in English, which consequently would be even less intelligible, or pot-boiled, paste-pot-and-scissors textbooks in the regional language, the number of which is increasing. Neither of these combinations would make for lively teaching or for a sympathetically responsive student audience.

The ineffectiveness of the teaching staff stems in part, of course, from overwork, anxiety about the economic situation of one's family, which is universal in the lower middle class, and the lack of adequate research facilities at home or in the college. Poor preparation, especially among some of the younger men in smaller colleges, contributes its share. Yet all these factors are insufficient to explain why brilliant and often promising young men, as many Indian college and university teachers were at the start of their careers, sink into boredom, intellectual dullness, and sterility.

It is by no means uncommon to encounter a tired and hopeless Indian university teacher in early middle age who, as a young man in an Indian or a British university, was full of enthusiasm for his work, impelled by bright and sometimes profound ideas, which he pursued with intense industry and even dedication. By early middle age he has accomplished practically nothing with his talent or his training. He has failed, as the years passed, to go forward with the line of inquiry he began as a research student, and he has undertaken no new study. If asked what has happened, he tells a melancholy tale. He began his career full of life but after a time his vitality faded. The head of his department was resentful of his qualifications and his intellectual vivacity. He could not get the books or the equipment he needed, or he got them so long after applying for them that he had lost interest. His colleagues, who had gone further in the process of stultification, offered neither the stimulation of their own ideas nor an understanding and responsive audience for his own. Bit by bit, under the weight of growing family responsibilities and the allures of college and university intrigue, his mind wandered away from the problems that had once fascinated him. The result is one more depressed, saddened, or embittered middle-aged teacher, who in his turn will lead other bright young men of the succeeding generation on the path to intellectual dullness and indifference, and who will bore the restless to distraction.

In India, the livelier young man, on joining a college or university staff, is thrust into isolation from the company of other interested research students and of inspiring, or at least exacting, supervisors. It is not that he is physically alone—in fact, he can hardly ever be alone. But the filament that binds minds together into an intellectual community has gone dead, or has been ruptured. The new teacher loses contact with minds interested in his field of research; he misses contact with superior minds in other fields which, quite apart from any substantive interest, have the electrical quality of intellectual brilliance.

There are, of course, geniuses who will do the work of genius whatever the immediate environment. For gifted men, as many young Indian university and college lecturers are, or could be under more favorable circumstances, it is intellectual death to be a member of so depressed a class. To do competent work, a teacher should be a member of an Indian and an international intellectual community, a community of peers who share a devotion to high standards and a common tradition. As it is, the Indian college or university teacher is not a full-fledged member of either an Indian or an international intellectual community.

India hardly has an intellectual community. Regional parochialism operates in intellectual as it does in political affairs. People in the academic world of India are astonishingly cut off from one another. There is little intellectual interchange among them, except within small circles linked by personal ties or by common memories of Cambridge, Oxford, or another university. Such is the circle that helped to make the *Economic Weekly* so interesting and so rare. Circles marked by vivid intellectual interaction are rare. Workers in a given field of research are often surprisingly ill informed about related work in other parts of India; sometimes they know more about what is being done in Britain or America. Sometimes there is a tendency to disregard Indian work. The means of intellectual communication in India are poor, although they are improving. Most Indian scholars and scientists still prefer to see their work published in a foreign journal rather than in an Indian one. A scholar who does publish in India fears that his work will not be noticed by colleagues in India or abroad; Indian journals are not accorded respectful attentiveness because scholars do not expect to find first-class articles in them. The attitude is understandable, but, as long as it persists, the creation of a coherent all-Indian intellectual community in science and scholarship will be inhibited.

Moreover, there is no all-India market for intellectual manpower except in a few subjects, such as physics or anthropology. People tend to stay, and to find their contacts, in their regions of origin. Instruction in regional languages at the university level will simply stabilize, or even extend, this situation. This intellectual Balkanization is pernicious because it obstructs the emergence of intellectual Indian leadership in science and scholarship. Without such leadership to set higher standards and instill confidence in Indian capabilities, intellectual endeavors in India will continue to be second-rate and derivative.

The University Grants Commission could adopt measures that would improve the situation. India could be well served by institutions like the Institute of Advanced Study at Princeton or the Center for Advanced Study in the Behavioral Sciences at Stanford in the United States, or by a system of research fellowships like those at British universities, which give able and promising young men a few years of free time in which to continue and deepen lines of inquiry first investigated in their work for advanced degrees in India and abroad. Indian institutions, conducted on a more modest scale, could be much less expensive than their counterparts abroad.[1] A small beginning, on a restricted scale, has actually been made in India in the direction of research fellowships, in a desperate attempt to recall some of the able young men who have shown a preference to remain in foreign countries where there are greater opportunities. It is absolutely necessary that the recipients of such awards be chosen by a highly qualified body from which the ordinary "stuffed shirts" of the Indian academic world are excluded, and that applications be rigorously scrutinized by the selection committee without regard to the caste or regional community of the applicant. It is necessary, above all, that applications be made without the approval of vice-chancellors, deans, or heads of departments of the institutions which employ the applicants. Otherwise, the same deadening hand of the mediocre middle-aged which is already responsible for the sterility of much of India's university life will be felt once more. India has already made a start in the Tata Institute of Fundamental Research in Bombay, the Gokhale Institute of Economics and Politics, and the Deccan College Research Institute in Poona. If suitable adaptations were made, these bodies could effectively contribute to the enlivening of Indian academic work.

Another helpful measure would be the establishment, on a restricted scale at first, of intensive refresher courses for college and university teachers in their thirties and forties. Such courses might be devoted to single subjects, such as mathematics or linguistics or

1. The Indian Institute of Advanced Study in Simla is an effort in this direction. It is too new for its merit to be assessed, although one already hears severe criticism of its performance.

sociology. Ideally, they would extend through an academic session. A program of lectures and seminars could be supplemented by reading, writing, and informal consultation. Outstanding workers in various fields, Indian and foreign, would bring a carefully selected group of Indian college and university teachers up to date in their respective subjects and try to stimulate them to do creative and original work in the future. Such measures would also serve to bring younger men with enlivened minds into contact with each other. Intellectual amity would be formed which would stimulate the participants to continued exertion. The awareness that there are other persons in one's own generation with similar interests and high standards would strengthen intellectual resolution.[2]

As a more radical measure, the University Grants Commission might concentrate its resources so that a few already somewhat better universities could be made much better than they are. The commission has already started the commendable practice of concentrating on certain special subjects by developing a system of "centers of excellence" in various research fields. Under the present proposal it might go further, and concentrate its program on a few outstanding institutions, such as the University of Delhi, which has high standards in many fields and is independent of any state government, or the University of Poona, which is fairly free of state interference and possesses a number of distinguished constituent institutions. It would be politically difficult to take this step, but in the long run Indian intellectual and political life would probably benefit from it.

One major advantage of concentration would be that it would terminate, or at least lessen, the tragic waste of gifted human beings which is characteristic of Indian higher education. If the best young men and women in each field were brought together, they would interact upon one another and achieve more intellectual progress. In so doing they would prepare a seedbed which would cultivate individual talents and thus provide the personnel for other Indian institutions. In the course of time, intellectual standards would rise. Such university centers would perform the functions that Oxford, Cambridge, and London performed for the modern provincial universities in Britain, until the latter got underway. If these specially improved university centers were genuinely national institutions, drawing students and teachers from all over India, their chances of influencing the other universities throughout the country would be enhanced. They could supply high-grade teachers in sufficient proportions to have a stiffening influence, and this would

2. Such courses have recently been undertaken on a considerable scale. Those who participate in them seem to value them highly.

also further the process of forming a genuinely all-Indian community in a variety of fields of research and scholarship.

This concentration would, above all, create within India itself institutional models for other Indian colleges and universities. They would become the centers of an Indian intellectual community, radiating the standards embodied in their research and in their graduates. The center of gravity of Indian intellectual life would be brought into India itself. If India is to assume full citizenship in the worldwide intellectual community, she must have an intellectual life of her own, centered within her own borders.

III

The really marked amelioration that would come as a result of improving the quality of the Indian university would be in the sphere of civil culture. India is, of course, much better off than any other new state in this regard, but it is not so well off as it might be in view of its greater political experience and its richer institutional and cultural inheritance from the former ruler and its own ancestors. Within the Indian university population, political hopelessness and alienation are common among the staff, and rebelliousness is rife among the students. The student, of course, is not likely to remain rebellious when he ceases to be a student, except possibly during the period of unemployment encountered by at least 10 percent of India's new graduates. Among these unemployed graduates, rebelliousness might become more intense, and might even be lifelong. For the most part, however, it will fade, as adolescent turbulence fades everywhere else in the world. Furthermore, the center of gravity of Indian political opinion rests among adults. Unlike his counterpart in some other parts of the world, the Indian adolescent or youth does not get the upper hand over his elders in politics. For these reasons, the turmoil within the Indian student body, expressed in demonstrations, riots, strikes, and other types of collective insubordination, is quite unlikely to disturb Indian political development in a direct way.[3]

Indirectly, however, Indian student indiscipline, through its propensity to demoralize the teaching staff, impairs the dignity and the effectiveness of Indian universities, which suffer accordingly in public esteem. This additional weight on the negative side of the scale further depresses the position of the university, and prevents the powers that rule Indian society from taking the university or its members seriously.

3. The Naxalite movement, especially in West Bengal, recruited as it is to a large extent from the student population, does increase the turmoil in that already very turmoilsome state.

Yet for Indian society to strengthen and expand its modern sector, the universities must supply manpower, ideas, and judgment. They will, in any event, supply manpower, some of which is bound to be good, but to supply the ideas and the judgment that are needed to enliven political life, the universities must be respected and self-respecting. They cannot reach this goal without genuine improvement in the performance of their constructive tasks—the teaching and discovery of truths—both Indian and universal in their reference and validity.

The major task in the development of the Indian intellectual community is the promotion of its intellectual creativity. The emergence of a number of points of creativity in Indian intellectual life—scientific, technological, scholarly, literary, and publicistic— would have the effect of providing models and forming circles around those models. This would "Indianize" Indian intellectual life in a profound way, much more profoundly than the deliberately and officially sponsored promotion of Indian subject matters. Once creative minds take hold of a subject matter or a problem and proffer a new solution or a new formulation, this will be bound to give it an Indian cast. Those who work on Indian history or Indian society or Indian economic and technological problems will make these subjects more fascinating, more engaging of the intellectual vitality of their coevals and their juniors. Those who work on more abstract and universal subjects will "Indianize" them by freeing them from xenophilic motives. General theories in sociology, economics, and politics will acquire an Indian substance. When this happens, people, except for a few hyperpatriots, will cease to worry whether or not their intellectual life is "Indian."

The real question refers to how this enhancement of creativity so necessary for a self-esteeming, self-sustaining intellectual community can be achieved. The answer, paradoxically, is that it requires the prior existence of some sort of intellectual community, in which good minds can support and challenge each other, in which a fruitful spirit of competition can operate. The human resources are there in India. They must be brought into frequent and free contact, in an environment of adequate material and institutional resources.

The criticism that Indian intellectual life is remote from the people, if it has any rationale at all, arises from the undistinguished quality of so much of Indian intellectual performance. The xenophilia which it attacks is only a symptom; it is a symptom of a weak intellectual morale. That morale can be strengthened only by accomplishment which will make Indian intellectual life less dependent on its foreign sources and models, and less responsive to their foreignness. When Indian intellectual life becomes more creative, it will live without self-consciousness and simultaneously in a universal culture and in the context of immediately interesting Indian problems.

The formation of an effective intellectual community in India must, for the foreseeable future, be confined to the nonliterary fields of activity. There is little prospect of a national literature, directed toward common models and studied and judged on a national scale, as long as novels, drama, and poetry are written primarily in the Indian regional languages. It might be better for India if it had a national literary language, but that is among those things about which nothing can be done at present. Yet as far as the other sectors of the intellectual community are concerned, the obstacles are not insuperable. They have the common language, they know they must acknowledge common standards, they can know each other's work and discuss it.

Moreover, the intellectual community is sufficiently internally differentiated and specialized that the absence of one major sector from the total community, although it is a disadvantage, need not paralyze intellectual life in other spheres. Science and scholarship are not directly dependent on *belles lettres.* The "two cultures," or rather the complicated system of specialized branches of knowledge, creation, and discovery to which that simplification refers, exist in India as well as in the West. (It is a testimonial to India's membership, however subordinate, in the worldwide intellectual community that it does.) The specialized subcommunities are more dependent on their substantively neighboring subcommunities than they are on the remoter ones.

Thus, the separation of the humanistic and scientific-technological cultures is no more a problem for India than it is for other more advanced intellectual communities, although its situation is somewhat more complicated by virtue of the linguistic problem. There is, however, another line of cleavage in the structure of the Indian intellectual system which is more injurious and about which something can and should be done. I refer here to relative isolation of the universities from other sectors of the Indian scientific and technological institutional system.

Whereas in the more advanced countries, the universities are the major centers of research and have a close connection with industrial research—the two together producing the main bulk of the research output—the Indian arrangement is different. There university and industrial research produce relatively little, and research in separate research institutes receives the lion's share of financial support and produces most of the research. This is injurious to the achievement of Indian research. The universities, by virtue of their training functions and their capacity to do fundamental research, should occupy a more central position in India. Until the position is rectified, the formation of an intellectual community will be hindered.

I say this not merely out of a prejudice in favor of universities as such. Universities must be central to a modern intellectual community, especially in the sectors concerned with natural and social science and technology, because everyone who later enters the intellectual community must pass through them for an extended sojourn. But more than that, they must be in vigorous multilateral contact with those who use their personal and intellectual products. A university system which is not integrated with the executive—economic and administrative—sectors of its society is bound to be a withered growth.

A new charter is needed for the intellectual community in India, and in that charter the universities must come to occupy a more central position than they do at present.

IV

What are the paths which Africa should travel in order to benefit from what has happened in India? What are the problems with which the new states of Africa must cope in order to make their intellectual life fruitful?

The first feature of the African intellectual which strikes one, in contrast with India, is sheer paucity of numbers. The African universities, unlike their Indian counterparts, are still unable to staff themselves indigenously, and the expatriates whom they engage cannot under present circumstances see themselves as having a lifelong career in Africa; expatriates on short-term appointments, however excellently qualified by talent and training, cannot really "Africanize" themselves intellectually, and, even if they do, it is hard for them to have a lasting influence. A rapid rotation of expatriate university teachers puts a heavy burden on the still small number of African university teachers. Their rapid promotion to senior responsibilities in the process of Africanization might mean that promising young men, full of intellectual vigor, are burdened prematurely with administrative responsibilities which interfere with their intellectual productivity. The growth of the civil service means, too, that the universities and other intellectual institutions must face severe competition for outstanding young graduates. The numerous tasks of government which fall on the shoulders of the civil service reduce the leisure for avocational intellectual activity. The situation is further aggravated by the present necessity for Africans who wish to do advanced work, to do it abroad, so that the stimulus which they might contribute is, at least for the time being, removed from Africa.

All this means that the sheer number of man-hours available for creative intellectual work in all the various fields is seriously limited. Political concerns further reduce the time and energy available. How are these to be husbanded to secure the maximum effect? How can able and well-trained men be enabled to use their talents in ways which will be intellectually productive at a high standard and which will be useful to their fellow countrymen?

Concentration of the sort which has been considered above for India is entirely out of the question for Africa. The political obstacles which are at once apparent within a single country like India are even greater in a continent with a multiplicity of sovereign states to which their universities are important evidences of progress toward modernization. Quite apart from such considerations, the universities have too many national obligations, even local obligations, to permit amalgamation into a smaller number. It is not as in India, where there are already so many universities and so many teachers that concentration involves only differentiation in the allocation of resources, not the loss of identity of individual, already existing institutions. The latter is unthinkable for Africa because it is not only impracticable; it is undesirable as well.

The alternative procedure for overcoming the isolating consequences of small numbers is to foster opportunities for regional and continental contact. Conferences, seminars, meetings of small groups with common substantive interests would present such opportunities. Intra-African intellectual association, initiated from within Africa by persons who wish not just to form an organization but to discuss the problems on which they are working or on which they wish to work, might have the effect of contributing to a sense of intellectual community in Africa and diminish the sense of intellectual isolation within Africa and intellectual dependence on the metropolis. Financial support from abroad might be necessary, metropolitan participation is desirable, but the initiative and the setting of the problems must be African.

Such meetings, which need not be elaborate conferences on a grand scale and which might involve only ten or twenty persons working on similar problems of African life—social, economic, medical, technological, etc.—do not, of course, preclude other forms of collaboration. The exchanges of teachers and students among the African universities, the conduct of joint research projects entailing collaboration of universities and of governments, of regional research institutions, continental and regional learned and scientific societies, are all desirable.

Africa has not yet reached the position of India, in which the universities have become isolated from other intellectual activities. This is partly a result of the undeveloped condition of intellectual institutions outside the universities. Nonetheless, the problem must be faced in Africa as it must be faced in India. Nonuniversity intellectual institutions exist in Africa and will become more numerous. Research in agriculture, medicine, engineering, social sciences, and social welfare is underway in Africa and must continue to grow if Africa is to develop economically and socially. The isolation of the "producers" of manpower and knowledge from the "users" of that manpower and knowledge will be as injurious to the growth of an African intellectual community as the isolation of the producers from each other. Unless there is close and mutually appreciative contact between "producers" and "users," the intellectual community, even if it overcomes the isolation of its constituent elements, will feel itself peripheral to the life of its own society. It might even attain considerable intellectual distinction, but its morale—and its capacity for creative intellectual work—will suffer. It will be susceptible to the painful self-accusation of not being a part of an ongoing and growing national life. It will also be subject to the charge by politicians and journalists of being a costly luxury, more a part of the outside world of metropolitan culture than an integral part of its own society. An intellectual community must be both. Its failure to be creative in either regard will hamper its creativity in the other.

The custodians of the intellectual communities of the new states must therefore bear constantly in mind that the precipitation of a new and indigenous intellectual center of gravity within their own countries requires simultaneously the cultivation of good relations with the intellectual community outside and with the authoritative, executive sectors of their own society.

17 Metropolis and Province
in the Intellectual Community

In every social system, there is a center from which authority emanates and to which deference is granted. This is equally true of groups as small as a handful of persons, of great societies, and of the relations among great societies. Some measure of inequality in the distribution of the properties of personality, role, and performance which call forth deference is inevitable in practically all social systems. Inequality brings forth the distinction between center and periphery. The center is constituted by those persons, roles, and actions which demand attention and elicit deference. Even those who reject or disregard the legitimacy of that center and who, deliberately or indifferently, yield no deference to it, acknowledge its centrality. (No center of any large society is ever completely unitary, but to those outside the center it often presents the appearance of unity.)

The center of any society tends to possess a particular territorial locus.[1] The center is not identical with the administrative, political, economic, or cultural capitals, but because deference goes toward authority and creativity, coincidence is likely. The more the different capitals coincide, the more probable is their common seat to be the point in space which weighs most gravely in the minds of the members of the society. The center is, however, not necessarily a city or town. It might be a cluster of towns, a region, or even, for those outside it, a whole country or a continent.

Previously published in a slightly different form in *Changing India*, edited by V. M. Dandekar and N. V. Sovani (Bombay and London: Asia Publishing House, 1961), pp. 275-94. Reprinted by permission of the Gokhale Institute of Politics and Economics and Asia Publishing House.

1. In the first third of the present century, American students of human ecology studied the phenomenon of metropolitan dominance, by which they meant the provision of professional services by an urban center for a wider area, the spatial location and scope of major decisions in the process of production, the exercise of financial power over an area, the area of the circulation of information from a center, etc. With the decline of human ecology as a subject matter of fashionable sociological interest, there occurred a shift toward the study of inequalities in power and status. In part because the national society was not studied, the territorial correlates of inequalities of power and status dropped from sight. Thus, the phenomenon of provinciality, and of the status of mind of being a provincial, which is partly a feeling of class status and partly one of the dignity, or indignity, of the province in which one lives, was overlooked.

The center or metropolis—which I prefer because it has a territorial connotation and can refer to an area more extensive than a single city—is profoundly different from its hinterland or province. The difference between metropolis and province embraces but is not identical with the difference between town and country. It has an approximate correspondence with the difference between rulers and ruled, between classes of higher social status and those of lower status, between the richer and the poorer, between the more educated and the less educated, between industrial, professional, administrative, and political occupations and agricultural and extractive occupations. These relationships of city and country, of governors and governed, of industry and agriculture, of the wealthy and the poor, are, however, only diverse manifestations of the more fundamental relationship of center and periphery. The responses which they arouse are the fundamental responses to center and periphery.

Every person has a "map" in his mind. It is a more or less vague image of the "world" which is significant to him. It is one of the ways in which he "locates" himself; it helps him to establish his own essential quality by contrast and identity with the objects of *his* environment. It is a cognitive map but it is not an emotionally neutral matter. It is a map which not only classifies but locates in a spatial sense. Its content varies widely among individuals and classes within any society. In some minds the map might be worldwide in scope, in others it might be confined to a very small area. For many persons, and especially for the more sensitive and the more widely experienced, a major feature of the map is its portrayal of their qualitative proximity to or distance from the metropolis.

Very few human beings in any society are continuously and wholly absorbed in the round of parochial life, in the life of their family, neighborhood, and the immediate tasks of work-place and locality. They have some perception of the center, some response to it, even though the community which is organized around it is marginal to their own existence and sensibility. Those persons whose "maps" have been widened by education, experience, and a more open and active curiosity are much more disposed to see "their" center as a metropolitan space of which they might be a part and toward which, in any case, their attention and respect are drawn. For them, it is the residence of the vital, of the "life giving." The metropolis is the place where "important" things happen. It is the stage of those actions which fascinate by their intrinsic vitality, by the creativity which commands deference and emulation or resistance.

The metropolis is a center of vitality. It is a seat of creativity. The residence there of power, political and economic, to which creativity is attributed, strengthens the disposition to respond to the centers of creativity; the exercise of authority from that center reinforces the inclination to heed whatever emanates from it. A quality, additional to the persuasiveness arising from the intrinsic value of idea or deed, grows simply from the fact of emanation from the metropolis. The connection with the metropolitan center confers on an object or a symbol a quality of its own quite independently of any inherent features, so that much of what comes from the center, even though it might be no better in itself than what originates in the province, profits from the special nature of its place of origin.

The opinion which asserts the primacy of the metropolis regards life in the provinces as dull. From this standpoint, provincial existence is rude, unimaginative, awkward, unpolished, rough, petty, and narrow. It is believed to lack the freshness, the openness, and the refinement of the culture of the metropolis. It is thought to be rustic and boorish because it lives in complacent isolation from the culture of the metropolis. It is true, as the metropolitan view declares, that in the provinces mental "maps" are often very local in scope and contain within their boundaries most of what interests, pleases, and displeases many a provincial. This, indeed, is what arouses the censure of those who speak of the "idiocy of rural life."

Not all who live in the provinces, however, accept the idiocy of provincial life. Belief in the idyll of rustic self-containment, humble or smug, gentle or gross, is not universally characteristic of those who reside in the provinces. The province has another face. It shows this when it gives up its self-sufficiency and enters into contact with the culture of the metropolis.

The provinciality which responds to the metropolis experiences an acute awareness of its distance from the vital and the "life giving," from the "really" important events which are thought to be important because they are metropolitan. Provinciality, insofar as it seeks to transcend sheer rustic ignorance and indifference, is burdened and impelled by the belief in the unsatisfactoriness of its immediate environment and of its own qualities. Sensitive provinciality produces a feeling of its inferiority to the metropolis; it feels the necessity and obligation to acknowledge the standards— moral, cultural, intellectual and political—which are believed to obtain in the metropolis. Provinciality in any sphere of life, once it has outgrown preoccupation with the immediate and the local, involves preoccupation with the "goings on" in that sphere in the metropolis. The belief that one's own quality will be elevated by the assimilation of certain features of metropolitan life is one response to the sense of the inadequancy of one's own provincial culture. (No less significant are the deliberate rejection of the standards of the metropolis and the consequent effort to stress the creativity of the provincial.)

Metropolis and Province on an International Scale

The relationship between metropolis and province is not confined within the boundaries of a given society. It extends across the boundaries of particular societies into the larger universe, into the society of societies. Whenever any particular society expands in power and prestige, through commerce, arms, or culture, beyond its own boundaries, the relationship of metropolis and province emerges. It is seldom so dense as the relationship of metropolis and province within a given society, because of the wider disparity of religious and cultural traditions, the ethnic differences, and the lesser frequency of contact. Nonetheless, a common value system begins to emerge from the system of authority and the minimal establishment of cultural institutions.

As Western Europe expanded into Eastern Europe, Asia, Africa, and America, it became the center of a rudimentary world society, universal in scale but neither entirely comprehensive nor all-embracing in the permeation of its dominion. Links were formed which united a dominant Western Europe with Eastern Europe, Asia, Africa, and America, which, to the extent that they became modern, looked to Western Europe as their model. In the eighteenth century, Paris not only dominated France; it also imposed itself on the princely states of Germany, on Moscow and Saint Petersburg; London, Milan and Madrid too came to feel its ascendancy in taste and thought. In the nineteenth century it extended its influence further eastward into the Balkans and into the Middle East.

With the growth of the modern intellectual stratum in the second half of the century, London, and Oxford and Cambridge, which came later on the scene, extended their magnetic power beyond the British Isles, reaching Hamburg and Frankfurt, Toronto, Bombay and Calcutta, Singapore, Boston, New York, and Philadelphia, and even obstinate Chicago, to say nothing of Accra, Baghdad, Khartoum, and Ibadan. With the unification of the Reich and the growth of Germany as a world power, German academic culture laid claim to the allegiance of the American, Russian, and Japanese universities. In a sense, by the end of the nineteenth century all the rest of the world became a cultural province of the Western European metropolis.

By the second quarter of the twentieth century the centers of cultural creativity in the United States became major parts of the Western metropolis, which therewith ceased to be any longer exclusively European. New York has, indeed, in many respects shaken the preeminence previously monopolized by London and

Paris. New York, and the culture which it transmits and symbolizes, now holds in fief the Middle West and Texas, and lays claim to the resistant affirmation of Paris, London, Berlin, Tokyo, and Bombay as well.

The heterogeneity of the center and the multifarious composition of the province prevent the complete ascendancy of any single metropolis on a world scale. A center might be such with respect to one sphere of action but not with respect to others. Very often there are likely to be several competing metropolises. Different sectors of the population might be drawn toward different metropolises. As in nineteenth-century Russia, some were drawn toward Paris, others toward Berlin, so in some of the new states of Asia and Africa, Paris and London on the one side, Moscow on the other, incorporate alternative models. For that matter, even within a particular society it is unlikely that there is ever complete consensus with respect to its metropolis (inside or outside the country). Nonetheless, the facts of the metropolitan-provincial relationship remain, despite all their ambiguity, their historical instability, and the imperfection of their fulfillment.

The Intellectual in the Interplay of Metropolis and Province

Those engaged in intellectual performance, either as producers or as consumers, are joined together in a social system or community. They are bound together by common standards applied to common objects of attention, by personal and corporate ties, and by participation in the same network of institutions through which intellectual life is conducted. This community exists in space in partial indifference to the limits of nations and states. This *Gelehrtenrepublik*, this community, because it lacks coercive power and a specifically defined territorial base, is of a much looser tissue, more fragmentary and less comprehensive than territorially bounded national states with their own machinery for the maintenance of order. The transnational intellectual community is split by specialization and by linguistic barriers and national loyalties, but it is not thereby obliterated or disintegrated. It is a community, and there is no likelihood that it will cease to be one as long as intellectual work is carried on. As universal consciousness and the practice of modern science, scholarship, and art develop and spread over the face of the earth, the worldwide character of the intellectual community comes more and more into evidence. The international movement of students is on a grander scale than ever before. Scholars and scientists, artists and literary men come into contact increasingly with their opposite numbers in other countries. They scrutinize each other's works. They people each other's imaginations. They form a dispersed but real audience which is addressed even when it is absent and scattered and even when it is not thought of consciously. They serve for each other as an audience which sets standards and guides judgments.

The intellectual community, within a society and among societies, is no more a community of equals than any other community. Within any given society, the first inequality in the intellectual community is between those who create and those who consume. Within the circle of the creators, there is a steep hierarchy ranging from the highest levels of creativity, passing through those who create within the framework set by the most creative persons, and ultimately reaching down to the merely reproductive. Within a particular country, there are points of creativity, which might be scattered in space, or which might be concentrated at one place in a single laboratory or university or research institution. Centers may be only relatively central; they may themselves be derivative from worldwide metropolitan centers. There are also provinces which are doubly provincial, which are provincial with respect to both the worldwide metropolitan center and their own national metropolis.

A restricted, but only seldom unitary, circle of workers in any intellectual field sets the pattern of subject matters and problems which are regarded as appropriate. A similarly restricted circle embodies and enunciates the standards by which achievements are judged. A restricted number dominate publishing houses and editorial boards of journals and thus decide what should be allowed to pass from the very narrow environment within which a writer or scientist creates into the broader arena where the public, which in specialized fields consists only of colleagues, can read his works. A restricted circle influences the content and sets the direction which dominates intellectual work throughout its particular sector of the intellectual community.

The order of the intellectual community is not an entirely spontaneous consensual order, nor is it the order of the market, an order of mutually adjusting sectional interests. Authority works through example, which sets standards and affirms certain basic beliefs; but it also works through the allocation of rewards which include status, monetary payments, appointments, opportunities for publication, honorific and ceremonial distinctions, etc., all in recognition of conformity with those transpersonal standards.

The inequalities of the intellectual community are not just the inequalities of individuals. The inequalities of institutions such as universities, research institutes, journals, and publishing firms, and of fields of intellectual specialization, derive from their association with the varying average levels of individual creativity. From the unequal distribution of these claims on attention and regard, emerge the intellectual metropolises and the intellectual provinces.

There are, of course, numerous other, and intellectually extraneous, factors which determine rank in the hierarchy of intellectual institutions within the intellectual community: past intellectual creativity; the social status of their individual and corporate members; the connections of the institutions with political and ecclesiastical authority; and—in the worldwide intellectual community—the linguistic accessibility of the work done by any national intellectual community and the political and military power of the states within which any national intellectual community performs. The importance of these extraneous factors is probably not notably smaller than that of actual present creativity in determining the location and boundaries of intellectual metropolises and provinces.

The same structure of initiation and emulation obtains in the other fields of intellectual work as well—in poetry, in the novel, in literary criticism—and these too have their institutional counterparts. There are certain publishing houses and journals the publications of which establish and maintain the prevailing standard or which generate new standards. To have one's works published by these firms or journals commands attention and confers prestige.

Within any single country the hierarchy of intellectual metropolis and province is far from absolute. There is no clear and universally acknowledged consensus, and those who begin in the provinces are not precluded from creative participation in the intellectual community and from thus becoming part of the national metropolis. Those who, regardless of location or provenience, succeed in conforming with the rules, can overcome the handicap of their provinciality. In the course of time, the metropolis within a country may shift from one place to another with changes in the distribution of creativity—although fact and acknowledgment are by no means in perfect correlation. Nonetheless, the distinction between metropolis and province in the intellectual community persists.

The leading circles of individuals and institutions—the intellectual metropolis—of the leading societies constitute the metropolis of the worldwide intellectual community. The rest of the intellectual world lives in their reflected light, drawing what inspiration and self-esteem they can from their efforts to conform with the model and to come thereby closer to the center.

The hegemony of the two ancient universities in Great Britain, shared to some extent with London and, to a lesser extent, with Manchester and perhaps one or two others of the modern and new universities, the predominance of the University of Paris in the academic intellectual life of France, and the ascendancy of about half-a-dozen universities in the United States, all testify to the inequalities which exist in the academic world within particular countries. These universities supply much of the staff of their national system of intellectual institutions; the works which emerge from them are the most noticed; gossip about what goes on in them is cherished in the intellectual community. The learned organs and societies which persons connected with these universities dominate reinforce this inequality.

The hegemony of certain centers within particular countries is an approximate microcosm of the worldwide intellectual community. The metropolises of a few countries become the metropolises of the world at large. Nor is the phenomenon a new one which has arisen only in connection with modern imperialism.

In antiquity, Greek schools, Greek philosophers, and Greek dramatists set the standard to which Roman intellectuals looked. In the later Middle Ages and early modern times, Italy was the intellectual metropolis, and the rest of Europe was the province—and until the sixteenth century a very thinly populated province indeed. In the nineteenth century, America was an intellectual province of Europe, first of England, and to a lesser extent of France. Then, in the last third of the nineteenth century and in the early twentieth century, at least in the sciences and in scholarship, it was an intellectual province of the German universities. (Neither France nor England was then completely excluded from influence, and Anglophilia and Francophilia have persisted longer than the once preponderant subjugation to German academic influence.) When Japan was opened to the world, it became an intellectual province of Germany in most matters. In the nineteenth century and in the early twentieth century, Russia, despite its powerful creative achievements in literature, was an intellectual province of Western Europe, particularly of Paris in the literary sphere, and of certain German and Swiss universities in science and scholarship. India was, and remains, an intellectual province of London, Oxford, and Cambridge; latterly Harvard, M.I.T., and Berkeley have entered into the Indian center. The areas of Africa once or still ruled by the British have become intellectual provinces of the British centers (and, in various ways, of Liverpool, Durham, Edinburgh, etc.). Africans in the formerly French-governed territories are still provincial vis-à-vis Paris. Indonesia, when relations with the Netherlands were very rancorous, sought to suppress similar relationships with Amsterdam, Leiden, and Utrecht, but did not succeed in doing so entirely. (Indeed, one of the difficulties of Indonesian intellectual life, in its provinciality, has been its lack of firm attachment to a major intellectual metropolis.)

In each of the provinces, the possession of a degree from a metropolitan university is a claim to respect and to preferment for an appointment in government or in education. The universities in the provinces tend to be modeled on those of the metropolis, down to the syllabi or courses of study, the required textbooks, and sometimes even the questions on examinations. In some cases they were linked by ties of constitutional affiliation; in others, by the recruitment of personnel. But even when these ties have ceased, the deeper bond remains.

The attachment to the symbols and realities of the metropolitan universities is accompanied by attachment to metropolitan publications. In general culture, political and literary, the *Times Literary Supplement*, the *Manchester Guardian Weekly*, the *New Statesman*, the *Economist, Encounter*, the *New Yorker, l'Express, France-Observateur*, etc., are read throughout the intellectual world by those who would overcome their intellectual provinciality. In the scientific sphere, *Nature,* the *Transactions of the Royal Society,* the *Physical Review,* the *Cambridge Mathematical Journal,* the *Journal of the American Mathematical Society,* etc., play a similar role. It is the required thing to read them or to be aware of their contents. Publication within their pages is a distinction.

It is not merely in externals that the attachment of province to metropolis functions. Much more significant, both for good and for ill, is the fundamental orientation which provincial intellectual life seeks to acquire from the metropolis. The selection and promulgation of problems to be studied, the concepts and techniques of their study and the fixation of certain models of achievement exhibit the real links of the universal system of metropolis and province in the intellectual community.

The Response to Intellectual Provinciality

The blissful seclusion of the provincial who knows and cares nothing about the metropolis, and whose interest in life is consumed in affairs within a narrow radius, is a privilege seldom granted to the educated person. Natural intellectual curiosity, the extension of awareness through travel, study, and ambition, the environment in which he moves, make the educated person in the provinces attend to the larger world. Provincial intellectuals might share the dullness and naïveté attributed to life in the provinces, but, if they do, the consolation of their fellow provincials is not readily available to them.

Intellectual performances, however feeble, lay claim to a measure of universal validity. They automatically translate their performer into an arena broader than his locality. Whereas a businessman or a craftsman or a farmer can be content with being a fish of whatever size in a small pond, the intellectual's realm, by his very engagement in intellectual activities, is oceanic. The more comprehensive and more open sensitivity which prior selection finds and which training elicits in the intellectual, and the need to place his productions on a scale which refers to achievements everywhere, inevitably put the intellectual into a network, the standards of which he cannot lightly disregard or deny. His wide-ranging sensitivity commits him to self-assessments based on achievements in a race in which his colleagues throughout the world compete. Furthermore, these self-assessments also derive, in a not very differentiated fashion, from such criteria as the status of the subject studied in a scale as large as the whole intellectual cosmos; the status of the institutions in which the intellectual has studied, taught, or done research, and of the institutions with which others in his field have been associated; the international status and might of the state within which he dwells, etc.

For these reasons the provincial intellectual is at a disadvantage. The handicap of being out of direct personal contact with the center of intellectual creativity is accentuated by the secondary disadvantages of provinciality which impose on it an inferior status. Sensitive provinciality cannot rest in contented self-containment. Either it must seek to transcend itself according to the model proffered by the metropolis, or it must find some means of defense against the criticism which the existence of the metropolis implicitly levels against it and which persons intimately connected with the metropolis explicitly assert.

The tension of the provincial intellectual with his eye immovably or intermittently fixed on the metropolis is a major component of modern intellectual life. It is unlikely that it could be otherwise as long as intellectuals form communities aspiring to a validity which commands assent governed by more universal standards.

In nineteenth-century Russia, the provincials' sense of isolation from what is truly important was repeatedly expressed in literature, and with especial poignancy in Chekhov's stories and plays.[2] Whereas the peasant and the boorish squire could find sufficient objects for their passions in an area of narrow confine, it could not be so with intellectuals, whether they were producers or consumers. It was not just in *belles lettres* that it was expressed. The pull within Russia was one component in a larger fascination with Western Europe.

The entire intellectual history of Russia in the nineteenth century can be interpreted in the categories of metropolis and province on the international scale. German intellectual achievement and, above all, German philosophy exercised a tremendous fascination on the young Russian intelligentsia; and then, in the forties, this was

2. Cf., for example, his *Three Sisters*, where Irina cries, "Oh, to go to Moscow, to Moscow." "There is nothing in the world better than Moscow" speaks for the century.

supplemented by the attraction of French socialism. The famous dispute, which ran in diverse forms for more than half a century, between the slavophiles and the Westerners dominated almost every aspect of Russian intellectual activity.

The issue was the permanent issue of judgment in the light of universal standards against judgment impelled by particularistic loyalty. And, as always in such conflicts of standards, the attractiveness of power and glory adds their weight to the scale. Intellectuals, no less than anyone else and perhaps even more, are responsive to the reality and symbols of authority; the mightiest countries inevitably intrude into and sometimes dominate their consciousness. The fascination with military, political, and economic strength reinforces the submission to intellectual achievement and the acceptance of the standards inherent in that achievement. Russian discontent with Russia in the nineteenth century was a product of both these motives. The uneasiness persists, however, independently of the reality with which it was once connected. The preoccupation in the Soviet Union with equaling and exceeding the West, the eager worriment over what the West is doing, go far beyond the exigencies of prudence.

In France, too, metropolis and province were major themes of intellectual preoccupation. The belief in the saving grace of the metropolis, in contrast with the demoralizing triviality of the province, was expressed by nearly every major author. Balzac, Stendhal, and Flaubert were all unsparing critics of the life-destroying emptiness of provincial society. Flaubert's designation of *Madame Bovary* as an account of the *mœurs de province* epitomized the French intellectual's conception of the provinces as the home of a hateful philistinism against which any soul of the slightest sensitivity had to rebel.

On the international scale, however, French intellectuals did not face the same problems as the intellectuals in countries at the periphery. In the nineteenth century, France, despite the defeat in the Franco-Prussian War—which was so deeply disturbing to its intellectuals—was at the peak of majesty. It was rich, mighty, expansive. No one exceeded it in the total sum of its glories; and French intellectuals, feeling themselves at the center of existence, had little sense that there were metropolises outside France to which they should give their allegiance. (It is only in the twentieth century that many French intellectuals, dismayed by weakness and impressed by strength, have begun to find foreign capitals to which to give their hearts.)

The situation of Great Britain has been much like that of France. Britain came later than France into the center of the world. Once it arrived there, it shared that center with France. The tension of metropolis and province in Britain has, therefore, been largely domestic. There, however, it was very acute. Throughout the nineteenth century and through much of the twentieth century, a major line of division in British intellectual life has been that which separates the radical, dissenting intellectual, largely sustained by the North, and the intellectual who has passed through Oxford or Cambridge, who is closely connected with London and the established institutions of the Church of England, the higher civil service, the bar and bench, Parliament, and the universities. It has been the triangle of London-Oxford-Cambridge against the rest. From Dickens and George Eliot to Kingsley Amis and John Osborne, from James Mill to F. R. Leavis, on the one side, and from the later Wordsworth and Coleridge to Virginia Woolf and Lord Snow, from Disraeli to A. L. Rowse, on the other, British intellectuals have been almost obsessed with the distinction between center and periphery, between metropolis and province. The outburst of resentment in the second half of the fifties against the "Establishment"—another name for center or metropolis—is only one more engagement in the long conflict between the "insider" and the "outsider" in British culture.

Rather than being assuaged by the democratization of educational opportunity and the entry of the once excluded into zones once—and still—part of the sacred center, bitterness persists. The "outsiders," although they are no longer kept outside, now give a freer expression to their resentment. The diminution of British power in the world, which the "outsiders" once decried, has only aggravated their anger and intensified their censure of the internal metropolis. The Anglo-French intervention in Egypt in 1956 disrupted the reconciliation with the internal metropolis which the war and the welfare state had encouraged.

Nonetheless, looking back in anger against the "Establishment," vehement denunciation of the "glittering coffin" of the London-Oxford-Cambridge culture, have not broken the domestic self-containment of the British intellectuals. Their belief that their own culture is at the center of the intellectual universe has been shaken but not shattered. An attraction to Paris since the nineties of the last century, toward Russia in the thirties of the present century, and a tendency toward the acknowledgment of American power and achievement in the past decade, represent only small variations on the fundamental self-containment of a worldwide metropolis.

The great states of the West which came later onto the scene—Germany and the United States—resemble Russia more than they resemble France and Britain as regards the issue of metropolis and province. Both internally and externally, with the former as a partial function of the latter, the alternatives of provinciality and metropolis have engaged the minds of American and German intellectuals.

For many decades after the French Revolution of 1789, German conservative intellectuals attacked those who saw France as the source and fountainhead of whatever was worthwhile in intellectual and public life. The Soviet abhorrence of "rootless cosmo-politanism" had its forerunner in the German romantic repugnance for the liberal, rationalistic transcendence of national boundaries.

German National Socialism drew support, among other sources, from the provincial intellectuals who hated Berlin as the epitome of metropolitan corruption and wickedness. The excoriation of the "asphalt intellectuals," i.e., the intellectuals of the big cities, was always a theme of the Nazi assault on modern culture.

Some similar manifestations are to be found in the United States. American populism and its intellectual revolt against the political and economic dominance of the Eastern seaboard and the culture of the genteel tradition was a beneficiary of the animus of a provincial antimetropolitan intelligentsia. Thorstein Veblen and John R. Commons, John Dewey, and a host of naturalistic novelists were all part of the refusal of the American intellectuals to reconcile themselves to the intellectual dominance of England over America, which was the core of the genteel tradition. This revolt found a political medium in the populism of the Northwest, the pro-gressivism of the senior La Follette, and finally in the New Deal. The more recent agitation which passed under the name of McCarthyism was a hostile response to the xenophilia of many American intellec-tuals. Even now, when American intellectual life is at the height of its powers, and of its awareness of being a world metropolis, large numbers of American intellectuals in many fields still feel toward Britain—and especially toward Oxford, Cambridge, and London— what Roman intellectuals in antiquity often felt toward Athens. Some sort of feeling of inferiority to what they believe to be still a culture of greater refinement, greater subtlety, greater profundity, manifests itself from time to time—even among those who almost deliberately cultivate a populistic "grassroots" attitude. In the United States, too, provinciality—despite the tremendous change of fortune—remains a wound. Provinciality is not what it was, but intellectuals still struggle to alleviate its pain.

For the intellectual of the underdeveloped countries of Asia and Africa, provinciality is especially stressful. The very profound dis-junction between the metropolitan culture and the provincial culture (the intellectual's indigenous culture) heightens his provinciality by rendering him more sensitive to the difference. In Western countries, the distinction between the province and the metropolis is mollified in many ways by a common language and a more or less common educational system, a common history which everyone shares, as well as more or less common religious traditions. Moreover, the historical record of Europe is full of instances of provincial creativity, especially in countries like Italy and Germany which became unified modern states rather recently. The intellectuals of underdeveloped countries do not, however, yet possess a tradition of creativity in modern science, modern scholarship, or the modern forms of art which could fortify their self-esteem. Hence the intellectuals of the new countries of Asia and Africa—so attached to the standards of intellectual modernity—must suffer their provinciality without the consolation afforded by the moral ties which in the advanced countries bind metropolitan and provincial intellectuals into a single nation, or by the awareness of the past achievements of their own ancestors in spheres which they deeply and genuinely respect.

The modern culture of the intellectuals of the underdeveloped countries, even in those with the longest history of modern culture, is very largely derived from a metropolitan culture. But the metropolis lies outside their own countries. The metropolis is, furthermore, invariably a state or a region which has previously dominated the intellectual's own country and humiliated his fellow countrymen by the elementary fact of foreign rule and by many actions which insulted and frustrated them.

There is no easy remedy, because, despite its painfulness, the culture of a foreign metropolis is the only modern culture he possesses. If he denies that culture, he denies himself and negates his own aspiration to transform his society into a modern society.

The textbooks from which he studies in college are usually from the metropolis. Some of his most respected teachers have been educated there in fact or in spirit. In many of the new states, the language in which he is educated is the language not of his own people but of the metropolis. He comes to appreciate the value of going to the metropolis for further studies—under the urging of kinsmen and teachers who perceive the advantage which it confers and who also feel that it is intrinsically valuable to be "foreign returned." Much of the literature he reads, the science he studies and practices, the principles of administration which he applies, the economic policy which he recommends or seeks to carry out, all come from the foreign metropolis.

Yet this metropolitan culture, his share in which evokes so much deference, is an implicit criticism of the provincial culture in which the intellectual of the underdeveloped country, however emancipated and modern, is deeply enmeshed. His mere living in the midst of the admixture of traditional indigenous and provincial modern culture is a pressure for commitment to it; its inescapable proximity arouses and maintains attachments to it formed in childhood and kept alive by kinship and affection. He cannot escape to London in the way in which a young man from Leeds or Nottingham or Cardiff can escape, assimilating himself in it with the reasonable expectation that, after a few years, he too will have ceased to be provincial. If he rebels against it, he has to turn to an alternative culture in which he does not really believe. His fate destines him, for the time being, to provinciality.

The Intellectual Struggle Against Provinciality

The feeling of being provincial, of being inferior in intellectual matters, is not a comfort. It creates a stress from which release must be sought. An easy and common release, and a very worthy one in certain forms, is to divert attention from the objects which determine provinciality. The concentration of effort on immediate tasks of social reform, of administration, and the care of students—these are gratifying occupations which merit and elicit respect, and satisfy, in a legitimate way, the obligations of teacher and citizen. There are less agreeable variants of this resolution: namely, the diversion of energy into academic intrigue, the persecution of vigorous younger persons who possess better contacts with the metropolis and evince signs of creative adherence to its standards. Self-blinding, the obscuration of one's field of vision, the withdrawal from active intellectual work, the cessation of reading and intellectual discussion, the clinging to the routine minimum of one's work without questioning or curiosity—all these are, in part, responses to the difficulties of being provincial. They are, of course, all aided by the already so numerous obstacles to serious intellectual work in the new states—poverty, overwork, public indifference and political hostility, isolation from stimulating contact which keeps fresh the awareness of stringent standards.

There is another way to try to overcome provinciality: this is the assiduous cultivation of the models afforded by metropolitan intellectual life. Reading the books which are read in the metropolis, talking of the books written and published there, subscribing to metropolitan periodicals, and concerning oneself with the intellectual personalities of the metropolis, with the gossip of the metropolitan universities and literary circles, are the paraphernalia of this cultivation. These do not go to the heart of the matter; but, on the other hand, they are not so injurious to autonomous intellectual development as the emulation in intellectual performance. The reproduction of the themes and problems of research, the copying of literary and artistic styles, and the imitation of university syllabi are almost a deliberate deadening of the pain of provinciality; but they are an equal deadening of the possibilities of creative intellectual achievement.

A third alternative, which proclaims the dignity of indigenous traditions, seems to me to be scarcely more fruitful. At first glance, the promulgation of the principle of the African personality or of the Indian heritage commends itself by its aspiration for continuity with the past and by the desire to be authentically oneself instead of a poor copy of a metropolitan model. Yet the intellectual of the new states of Asia and Africa is committed by his situation to be more than a manifestation of his autochthonous tradition. He is a modern man, not only in his externals, but in his aspirations and in his culture. His espousal of his autochthonous culture is insufficiently authentic because it is an espousal of only a part of himself and because it is a defensive reaction and an evasion of something that he genuinely experiences, which is his attachment to the metropolis and the standards of the metropolis. No intellectual in the new states will be content with the mere reproduction of the past achievements of his culture unless he takes refuge in a doctrinaire revivalism. Most intellectuals, however distrustful they are of the allures of the metropolis and however critical they are of their fellow intellectuals' concessions are themselves too affected by the prospect of modernity to enclose themselves in what they can find in their own indigenous tradition. They are, for better or for worse—I think for the better—involved in the tradition of modernity, the tradition which has its seat and origin in the metropolis. Their problem is the creative extension and enrichment of their indigenous tradition by the creative assimilation and adaptation of the metropolitan tradition. This is the way toward the transcendence of their provinciality.

The Transcendence of Intellectual Provinciality

The true cure for provincialism is creativity. The metropolis, and the creativity which helps to create it, are capable of dispersion—as the history of science in modern times, and not least in the present century, shows. There is nothing inherent in the economy of intellectual life which requires that the metropolis must be concentrated in one part of the world. Even though inequalities will always exist between genius and those who, however worthy, fall short of genius, there is no reason to believe that intellectual creativity in the various fields of modern knowledge and expression need be confined to Europe and the European settlements overseas. Nor is there a fixed quantity of intellectual creativity in the world which inevitably condemns whole areas of the world to a permanent provinciality.

There are serious obstacles to the awakening of creativity in science, letters, scholarship, and art; and some of these are functions of the inherent constitution of the traditional non-Western cultures. Some of these obstacles might take a very long time to be overcome. Others might pass more easily. It will be only when these have been overcome that the present division of the world into intellectual metropolis and intellectual province will be superseded by an extension, on a universal scale, of the network of creative centers which is now a feature of Western intellectual life.

The distinction between metropolis and province will still exist. It will exist as long as there are levels of creativity within any society. The distinction will, however, obtain more within societies than among them. Indeed, a necessary condition for the dispersion of centers of creativity over wider spaces is the creation of intellectual communities within large countries, and within regions made up of small countries—in spaces where, at present, there are no real intellectual communities at all. The emergence of a coherent intellectual community in an Asian or African country or region will involve the emergence of metropolitan intellectual centers in those areas. These centers will be linked across national boundaries in the way in which they are now linked in the West, as a linkage of peers. They will begin to form national or regional intellectual communities when they settle down to do the intellectual work which they and their societies respect, when they begin to ponder and penetrate the problems which are really problematic to them and not just to their models in the Western metropolis.

When this happens, the intellectuals of Asia and Africa will no longer be inclined to seek their intellectual and political inspiration in a metropolis, the specific territorial location of which will be an important determinant of their attitude toward it. When they become fully accredited members of their own national or regional intellectual community, and therewith of the worldwide intellectual community, they will cease to be its dependents. They will cease to be so painfully or deadeningly provincial. With this, their preoccupation with the status of their nation in the eyes of the "major powers" will diminish, and they will be more capable of devoting their capacities to the pursuit of truths which to them have the appeal of an intrinsic interest, and to the realistic confrontation of the problems of their own societies. They will study and act on problems which are their own, regardless of whether they are of transcendent scope and universal validity, or particular to the territory inhabited by their own societies. They will pursue the former because they will share fully in an intellectual tradition which confers significance on the problems themselves; they will attend to the latter out of the obligations of citizenship in a civil community in which they will be fully at home.

18 Asian Intellectuals

The intellectuals of Asia, like their counterparts everywhere, are defined by the relative elaborateness of their intellectual activities, professional and vocational, such as those of university teachers, scientific research workers, literary men, theologians, and journalists; or avocational, such as are sometimes found among businessmen, politicians, civil servants, physicians, and engineers. The level of development of the intellectual classes, and their intellectual institutions, differ profoundly from country to country in Asia. At the one extreme is Japan with its many universities and research institutions, and with a vast output of science and scholarship, an impressive literary productivity, a tremendous and prosperous press and publishing industry, and a dense and well-organized bookselling business. Next in stature are India and Pakistan with great numbers, occasionally high quality and a profuse though disorganized system of intellectual institutions. Then come Burma, Indonesia, and the Philippines, and the smaller countries like Laos and Cambodia, which have small bodies of intellectuals and very motley institutional systems.

The Asian intellectual classes of all countries, including even Japan, have in common the recent and exogenous origin of their modern culture. All the Asian countries, unlike most of Africa, have a rich tradition of religious-philosophical culture, well developed in written form and cared for by a class of professional custodians. In Asia the modern culture, introduced from the West, had, by the early part of the twentieth century, developed an elaborate set of institutions, universities, learned societies, periodicals, etc., through which modern culture was reproduced and applied to indigenous problems and traditions. Together with these there developed a considerable indigenous personnel, well schooled in the techniques and outlooks of modern culture. Japan and India were in the forefront. In Japan, of course, the initiative was Japanese; in India, Indian and British initiatives were intermixed. In China too, mixed initiatives were giving rise to a modern intelligentsia, academic, journalistic, and literary. In the other parts of South and South-east Asia under foreign rule, numbers were much smaller, but still some persons with a modern education—mainly lawyers and businessmen—

Previously published in a slightly different form in *Asia: A Handbook to the Continent*, ed. Guy Wint (London: Anthony Blond, 1963).

existed to express an indigenous demand, to serve as a pressure group for the establishment of advanced modern higher educational institutions and as a public for modern intellectual works, preponderantly of metropolitan origin. These intelligentsias, large and small, with institutions well equipped and well functioning or poorly equipped and poorly functioning, a century old in their rooting in Western culture or relatively recent, all faced, and still face, certain common problems and have certain common responses. Nationalism, populism, xenophilia and xenotropism generally, xenophobia and nativistic revivalism, inferiority feelings, curiosity and resentment in the face of the metropolitan culture are found throughout the continent. Countries like Japan, which retained their sovereignty throughout, as well as those which were ruled by Western powers, manifested these attitudes.

The Scientific-Technological Void

In their occupational structure, the intellectual classes of the formerly colonial territories still bear the marks of their colonial inheritance as well as of the present economic backwardness of their countries. In the colonial period, except in India, the highest administrative posts were reserved for expatriates, but the middle ranks of administration afforded numerous opportunities for indigenous, educated persons. High posts for scientists and technologists in industry and in governmental technical services were and still are few in number. There was little advanced scientific research and teaching; the poverty of the population meant a low effective demand for medical services. Outside the service of government, the main opportunity for the educated to deploy their skills with a prospect of substantial financial reward was in the legal profession. As a result, the educated classes in almost all the Asian countries, except Japan, are markedly skewed in the direction of the arts subjects—literature, languages, history—and the social sciences, while the scientific and technological categories are rather poorly represented. Japan and, latterly and incipiently, China are the only Asian countries which, possessing a modern industrial system and a more or less modern system of mass communications, have an intellectual class in which the technological component resembles that of the advanced Western countries.

The governments of most of the Asian countries have, in recent years, tried to establish or develop further technological education, medicine, and scientific research. Yet the fact remains that indigenously established industry, except in Japan and, to a much lesser extent, China, is both rudimentary and reluctant to give a prominent place to technologists, scientists, and engineers. (In India, for example, which is one of the more advanced countries of Asia, one-third of all engineers are employed in industry and two-thirds in government departments, whereas in some Western countries the proportions are four-fifths in industry and one-fifth in government departments.)

Since government departments are still the major employers of highly educated persons, the old tradition persists. It is, indeed, reinforced by the simple fact that the powerful drive for education, so characteristic of the new states of Asia, encounters no resistance from the arts faculties—more students can always be crowded into the lecture halls, and standards are less exacting—whereas the scientific, medical, and technological departments limit admissions more or less proportionately to the space available in laboratories. (Furthermore, since the latter are much more expensive to construct and equip than lecture halls, the expansion proceeds more slowly.)

Discouraging Conditions

In income and wealth the Asian intellectual is generally a very poor man. Recruitment into the intellectual professions in Asia, although markedly biased in favor of persons of middle-class origin, is really too wide to remain a monopoly of the offspring of the wealthy classes. Intellectuals are therefore dependent on their earned income—often gained in several occupations concurrently practiced—and in support by kinsmen in accordance with the traditions of the extended family system. Civil servants at the level of permanent secretaries and other members of the highest categories, some very successful physicians and lawyers, a handful of journalists and university professors, a small number in business, similarly small numbers of literary men, especially those who write for films, have incomes which permit them to live in what could be called, according to Western criteria, a middle-class manner. The mass of journalists, secondary-school and college teachers, literary men who write in the vernacular, most lawyers and doctors, although much better off than the masses of their countrymen, live in relative poverty. In their housing they are crowded far past the point where privacy of any sort is possible; they are unable to purchase books. Those with regular employment and income in the profession of their choice are the fortunate ones. At the bottom are the educated who have never been able to find a position corresponding even to very modest aspirations. About a tenth find no employment at all on the completion of their university studies, and this period of unemployment may persist for several years. Great numbers of the educated unemployed ultimately do find posts which, even though they are not what was sought, are sufficient for a scant livelihood. This is common to all the underdeveloped countries of Asia, and even Japan, as a result of the tremendous expansion of university studies, has a moderate amount of intellectual unemployment.

This situation is most pronounced in India, which had numerous universities before independence and a corresponding surplus of graduates. It has also become true of countries whose higher educational system has taken definite shape only since independence. Few governments have taken any steps to cope with the unemployment of the educated. In all these countries, intellectual unemployment is an urban phenomenon. Unwillingness to accept posts as village teachers and community development workers because of the lack of the amenities and low salary, is fostered by the extended family system.

The traditional intellectuals—monks, priests—live in their traditional mendicant poverty, perhaps even less well than they lived under the colonial regime because of the diminution of patronage and charity resultant on reforms in land ownership and the diminution of the princely orders. Despite the political concessions made to them by governments in Pakistan, Ceylon, and Burma and the flattery which, almost everywhere except Japan and the communist states, is directed toward the traditional culture and its custodians, Asian governments have done very little to improve the economic or even the institutional provision for traditional intellectuals.

Intellectual Institutions

The three major Asian countries, Japan, India, and China, are the only ones which have a relatively highly developed system of intellectual institutions. The Japanese system is the only one which has a full range of well-working universities, technical colleges, secondary schools, teacher training institutions, scientific and technological laboratories, libraries, museums, bookshops, broadcasting and television services, daily and periodical press, scientific press and book reviewing system.

The Indian system of intellectual institutions is, by virtue of its differentiatedness and amplitude, the most advanced of any underdeveloped country. It is less self-sustaining than the Japanese; it depends, like that of practically all underdeveloped countries, on government subvention and sponsorship. This is a consequence of the small size of the public willing and able to pay for intellectual goods and services. The literary market is very much smaller in India than it is in Japan. The supportive capacity of this small market is further diminished by the fragmentation of the country into a multitude of heterogeneous noncommunicating cultures. The situation is no better in many of the other countries, in contrast with Japan where the public is linguistically homogeneous. For these reasons, journalism and literary institutions, which suffer in any case from inadequate professional, commercial, and technical traditions, are further impeded by poverty.

The universities of most Asian countries are usually overcrowded and understaffed (often by part-time teachers); their libraries are small and spotty. The scientific research carried on in universities almost everywhere except Japan is scant in quantity and seldom important in quality. The publication of books and periodicals is ill organized and often unscrupulous; the system of book distribution is haphazard. Scientific research outside Japan, China, and India is very poorly provided for. Relatively little was inherited from the colonial regimes, and, although the new governments have created many research institutions, their performance has generally been meager— as could have been expected in situations where the tradition of modern scientific research has not been well implanted and where highly qualified personnel have been in short supply.

The Composition of Asian Culture: Modernity and Tradition

The culture of the intellectual classes of most of the Asian countries is of a threefold composition. There is, first, the modern culture, which involves an appreciation of the validity of science and of a rational, nonmagical approach to the problems of individual life and social organization; it involves knowledge of some of the main works of modern culture in science, literature, history, and a continuous contact with some stream of modern culture. The second culture is a mixture of the traditional and indigenous with the modern. It is a culture which entails familiarity with the lately metropolitan language and an acquaintance with some of the main works in it; much of this second culture is in the indigenous language. The products of this culture are an unstylized, matter-of-fact inter-mingling of indigenous traditional and exogenous modern. The third culture is the traditional religious-philosophical culture.

Higher civil servants, the more important university teachers, scientists, engineers, outstanding lawyers, physicians, editors of leading newspapers and their more prominent correspondents, some politicians, are the major participants in the modern culture. The second, mixed culture, is shared largely by elementary and some secondary school teachers, particularly in rural areas and small towns, journalists in vernacular newspapers or in the provincial press, middle- and lower-rank civil servants, most politicians, particularly those outside the central political elite. The traditional culture is carried by priests and monks, practitioners of indigenous or folk medicine, and religious teachers; although the bearers of the first and second cultures are increasing their share in certain selected aspects of the third culture.

Since the acquisition of independence by the newly sovereign states, the balance has shifted somewhat more in the direction of the second class from the first class which for so long, jointly with the foreign ruler, had played so vital a part in the implantation of the seeds of modernity in their societies. Even now the first class still occupies the central position of influence in their respective societies, in the higher civil service, in the law courts, in the leadership of the political parties, in the army, in journalism, and in the universities. But the new regimes of Asia being either democracies or populistic oligarchies, the second class and the third too have come forward to greater prominence and influence. In Japan, however, even the extremes of nationalism and hostility toward the West among the intellectuals have not in recent years resulted in any marked upsurge of cultural revivalism.

Of course, in no Asian country is even the first class, the modern or "Westernized" intellectuals, so modern and "Westernized" that they preserve no traces of the indigenous traditional culture in their outlook, in their tastes and social relationships, in their self-identification, or in their loyalties. At the other end of the continuum, there must be very few in the third class who do not respond in some way to their challenge.

The first class is often referred to as a class of "brown Englishmen" or "brown Frenchmen" or "brown Sahibs," as "uprooted intellectuals, suffering from schizophrenia," as men "suspended between two worlds and belonging to neither." They are alleged by their critics, often less educated politicians or litterateurs from their own circles, as being "out of touch with the people."

These criticisms notwithstanding, most of the Westernized intellectuals in the Asian countries retain in their outlook, in their family relationships, and in their tastes, a great deal of their indigenous culture. Many of them know a great deal about their indigenous culture too, often more than the less well-educated politician, whose education, such as it is, was also a modern Western education and whose indigenous culture is more a matter of espousal than of knowledge. The "Westernized intellectuals" of Asia usually know more about the higher content of the traditional culture than do their peasant fellowcountrymen, with whom they are so often and so unfavorably compared. They are also more attached to the national idea than most of the rest of their fellow nationals in their country; they are likely to be less sectional, less regional, less communal, less caste-bound. Not that the "Westernized intellectuals" are entirely free from these sectional attachments; they are just more free than most of their fellow countrymen.

Ambivalence and Its Consequences

Their attachment to their country and their appreciation of its past and its traditions, generally coexist with some disbelief in the traditional, indigenous view of the world and of man's place on earth. They are generally more secular in their understanding of the world, more hedonist in their conception of a good life, more equalitarian in principle, more accepting of science, technology, progress, and the potentialities of human initiative in changing society. This complex of beliefs has proved to be fairly compatible with a considerable degree of embeddedness in traditional familial institutions and the retention of indigenous elements in their style of life. Internal strain and conflict, at least on the level of consciousness, do not always result, nor need they do so. Yet, so deeply has this self-image of a "split personality," alienated from its society, penetrated into the consciousness of the modern Asian intellectual that it has become a secondary malaise. Their feeling of being *à l'écart* with respect to populistic and demagogic politics since independence has led many to accept as true the charge of "being out of touch with the people."

The intellectuals of the second class are much less afflicted by this problem. They do not possess so much modern culture that they feel themselves under attack when "uprooted intellectuals" are being criticized. Most of their cultural life is lived in the medium of their mother tongue and its literature. So much of their professional activity as school teachers, local officials, journalists, and authors is carried on in it, and so unintense is their concern with the modern culture conducted in English or French, that they feel no conflict or remorse. It does not occur to them to look on themselves as alienated. They are too concerned with local problems, which always have an indigenous accent.

The traditional intellectuals, at least the more sensitive and more alert among them, feel themselves on the defensive, under pressure from the secularizing tendency of the "Westernizing" intellectuals and higher civil servants of the big cities. Even where Buddhism or Islam is established as the state religion or where the state is designated as a Buddhist or Islamic state, the traditional intellectuals know that this has been achieved against the resistance of the political, administrative, and intellectual elite of the country. The conflict in which they are engaged is an external conflict, not an internal one within their own minds.

Creativity and Intellectual Independence

In its modern culture, much of Asia is still uncreative. In Japan the novel flourishes; in India there are some literary men of genuinely high quality. There are some interesting painters. On the whole, the tendency is toward reproduction rather than creation. In mathematics and the natural sciences, Japan has become a fully modern culture. In India there has been some work of high quality in physics, and Indians abroad have done distinguished work in this and in related fields. In India, research in the natural sciences is carried on on a large scale, but the quality of the scientific output in India throughout practically all the fields of science, is not generally thought to be up to a very high international standard. The situation in Pakistan seems even poorer, both quantitatively and qualitatively. In both of these countries, which, with Japan and China, are the most advanced in modern culture in Asia, there is a very marked tendency for some of the ablest young scientists to emigrate from their countries, temporarily if not permanently, to Western Europe or North America. Throughout Southeast Asia, scientific research scarcely exists. In the social sciences, creative and even routine work at a high standard of proficiency is still scant. Valuable work is being done in the historiography of the region and in the study of the indigenous traditional cultures. In these fields, the leading Asian scholars are now beginning to enter into relations of equality with metropolitan scholars.

The modern intellectuals of most Asian countries depend for their intellectual sustenance on the output from Western Europe and North America, and the level of intimate knowledge of this output is often very high. It is perhaps even too high for its own dignity, being impelled sometimes by a preoccupation with the culture of the old imperial metropolis almost as much as by a love of its intrinsic substance. Even in Japan, which in many fields of work is a full-fledged member of the world intellectual community, there is a strong xenotropic tendency. This preoccupation with the West as an intellectual metropolis is intimately connected with the continuation of substantive intellectual dependence on the West. Except for Japan, which has a very productive modern culture, nearly as self-sustaining as any modern culture in the world, Asian intellectual life continues to suffer from a many-faceted intellectual dependence on the old metropolitan centers.

The problem becomes acute in connection with the medium of instruction in the universities and the availability of textbooks. Practically all the other countries must still use textbooks in English or French or textbooks which are translations and adaptations of European or American textbooks. Since, except in Japan, China, and Indonesia, the medium of instruction has in the main been the metropolitan language, the situation could scarcely be otherwise. The introduction of a local medium of instruction, for which there is powerful motivation, is moving ahead. National self-regard, persistent preoccupation with colonialism, considerations of populistic politics, and a conviction of the anomaly of the high culture of the country being conducted in a language foreign to the mass of the population, all give impetus to the drive; and only strong determination by educators and high administrators is able to hold it in check, while slowly yielding to the inevitable pressure.

The present and the oncoming generations of students face a situation in which either they must conduct their higher education in a language which they have very imperfectly mastered—owing to unsatisfactory language instruction—or, if they are instructed at a university in their mother tongue, they must depend for their reading on literature in a foreign language or on a very inferior kind of literature produced in their mother tongue. The consequences of this linguistic interregnum for the quality of culture of the Asian intellectuals are apparent. Their contacts with the more creative metropolitan culture will be attenuated before their own cultures have become creative. The high points of intellectual cultivation and urbanity attained in the Asian societies by a small proportion of the intellectual class will undoubtedly be maintained, but the proportion of those at the heights will be reduced while the proportion of the second class of intellectuals will increase very markedly, and many of the latter will therefore have to be drawn on to occupy roles such as university teaching, journalism, and higher civil service.

The linguistic interregnum must, for a time, hamper the creativity of the indigenous modern culture, and thus will prolong the period of dependence. At the same time the metropolitan culture which comes to the Asian countries is dilapidated by the promotion of indigenous culture and the ramshackle quality of schools and universities, bookshops and libraries, periodicals and newspapers.

This cultural dependence has always carried with it overtones of inferiority. The response to this inferiority almost everywhere among Asian intellectuals has a propensity toward revivalism. This has entailed, in the new states, an effort to rehabilitate the indigenous culture, to make it more prominent and more appreciated. Among the most Westernized intellectuals there has been a quickening of interest in the traditional artistic, architectural, and religious inheritance. Here and there are efforts to modernize by reformulation in the modern idiom and to discover points of continuity between the cultural inheritance and the aspirations toward modernity.

Intellectuals in Politics

The political life of the Asian states, except Japan, is in many important respects the creation and the affair of the modern educated class. The political elites of the new states of Asia were constituted almost exclusively from the parties and groups which had been in opposition under the colonial regime. The longer history of the Indian political movement and the relatively early and large supply of educated and cultivated lawyers, businessmen, publicists, and social workers permitted the formation of a political elite of mature men. Similarly, the longer experience of the Indian move- ment for a larger share in government—ultimately for self- government and its much larger scale—permitted the emergence of a differentiated body of specialized politicians, party organizers, and "bosses." In the other countries of Asia, the movement was of more recent growth and tended to draw on a younger generation, particularly from the student population.

The political leaders in Asia—except for Japan, where an older aristocracy and plutocracy could provide personnel for politics— were drawn from the modern intellectual class. There were, indeed, few other groups from which a political elite could be drawn. Landowners and merchants lacked civic spirit and national concerns; the latter were often alien in race and culture, and they and the landowners prudently sought to avoid incurring the displeasure of the colonial rulers. Teachers in government schools and colleges and civil servants were barred from public political agitation, unless they were ready to give up their coveted stability of employment. Hence, malemployed, educated young persons, some of the prosperous lawyers and physicians and more of the less successful lawyers with time on their hands, supplied the personnel of political agitation. The tradition, endemic in the oriental religions, which authorizes the religiously learned and devoted to eschew the daily comforts and routine responsibilities of this world and to live from the charity of others, both impelled many of the intellectuals to turn toward the higher cause of politics and enabled them to live in a calling which offered no significant income.

The political intellectuals of Asia, particularly those who came into politics after the First World War, were, to a man, nationalist and antiimperialist. Antiimperialism tended almost automatically to be anticapitalist and therefore, by implication, socialist. Asian intellectual politics have also become increasingly populist; the more insistent on complete independence, and the less inclined toward the piecemeal enlargement of the sphere of self-government, the more populist it tended to be. For the most part it was culturally modernist and antitraditional as well, although the need to provide a cultural legitimation for nationalist political aspirations led to a more affirmative attitude toward selected elements of the traditional indigenous culture. Finally, the politics of the intellectuals in Asia before independence were oppositional and agitational and often merely obstructive, since, with the exception of a short period in

India in the second half of the 1930s, there was no constitutional possibility for a nationalist political movement to assume power as long as the foreign ruler remained.

With the attainment of independence, the political outlook of the intellectuals retained much of its earlier content. Those who took over the responsibilities of government became professional politicians to a greater extent than before. As members of the government, they had regular incomes. They also had to pay more attention to their party machinery; this entailed for the major parties, to a greater extent than before independence, the creation of a party apparatus, which required full-time, regularly paid political employment.

A fissure developed in the ranks of the intellectuals between those who now had a stake in the new government and its supporting institutions and those who remained outside. The former soon lost their oppositional disposition; the latter retained it and even deepened it.

The routines and the pitfalls of governing have produced a type of man and a type of rhetoric which fit poorly with the Asian intellectual's reverence for selflessness and for a pattern of life in accordance with a high, quasi-religious ideal. The result has been disillusionment with politics. In some cases the disillusionment is accompanied by a greater realism and a resigned reconciliation with the breed of politician available and with the rigors of the politician's tasks; in others disillusionment has led to alienation from politics, not only in action but in sentiment and belief. Depoliticization is the end product.

What is striking about the Asian intellectuals, given the importance of the political culture of the European thirties which is so important in their political tradition, their antiimperialism, their collectivistic outlook in economic matters, and their fluctuating anti-Western impulses, is that so few of them have become active communists or even sympathizers with the communist parties in their countries. Fellow traveling is certainly common among Asian intellectuals—it is in a sense the "natural" political outlook of the Asian intellectual—but membership and active support of communist parties, legal and illegal, is certainly not widespread.

No discussion of the politics of the Asian intellectual can overlook the importance of the university student and even of the high school student. In the independence movements they supplied many of the lower-rank agitators. Demonstrations, which are an essential part of Asian politics, almost always draw on student support.

To cite a few instances: the Japanese students are of an extreme and passionate turbulence, of which the wild demonstrations prior to the projected visit of former President Eisenhower to Japan gave only one instance. In Burma, the government of General Ne Win felt called upon to destroy physically the Student Union because it was a nest of student agitation. The restless demonstrativeness of the Indian students has often been noted in political as well as non-political events. In Pakistan, the students, even in the more repressive phase of General Ayyub's military government, reconciled themselves to the regime less passively than any other section of Pakistani society. In South Korea, student demonstrations played an important part in bringing down the government of Dr. Syngman Rhee. In Pakistan too the students helped to bring down General Ayyub's regime.

The tradition is an old one, as old as the independence movements and modern higher education in Asia. Adolescent rebelliousness, the decline of traditional authority, the impoverished conditions of student life, the lack of prospects, economically, of the students on graduation, youthful idealism, have been significant factors. The deliberate machinations of party politicians, especially among the opposition within and outside the ruling parties, aggravate the situation.

Prospect

In the coming decades, the intellectuals of the Asian countries are bound to increase in number. The rapid expansion of the university population throughout Asia guarantees that there will be more university teachers, and that from among the growing number of graduates there will be an indeterminate number who will follow intellectual occupations or who will develop and pursue intellectual interests avocationally. It is also likely that the governmental cultural bureaucracy—in communications, in the administration of academics, etc.—will increase. The belief in the need for technologists and applied scientists will also increase facilities, create posts, and undoubtedly attract many persons.

The vocational opportunities will undoubtedly be outnumbered by the aspirants with the formal qualification of university degrees and diplomas. The rate of economic development of the Asian countries is not likely to be great enough to absorb all who aspire to follow an intellectual occupation. There is bound to be an increase in those in lesser administrative and clerical posts and a large number who feel themselves misemployed.

The large numbers who enter into government service in one form or another will not greatly enhance the status of the intellectual in Asia. Government service, aside from the security it confers, is not such a claim to deference now as it was before independence. There are too many people in it with marginal economic existence; it is no longer believed to be the only proper place for young men of the highest intelligence, and the low esteem in which politicians are held will not enhance the reputation of those who staff their governments.

Teaching in colleges and universities is likewise not likely to increase in prestige, insofar as income and dignity of employment are sources of such prestige. The large numbers of students, the indifferent quality of the instruction which they seem destined to receive in the near future, and the undistinguished intellectual output of the universities staff will also not enhance their position in their respective societies.

What then are the chances for greater creativity where there has been little recently, or for the development of a higher standard of performance, which, even though not creative in a deep sense, would markedly raise the average level of intellectual attainment? Regarding the former: in literature, in painting or in the arts generally, such a development is not inconceivable. The improvement of performance in the nonartistic spheres of cultural life, of scientific and scholarly research, of university teaching, of journalism, of the learned profession, is more subject to policy, and therefore to wise policy, than in the artistic sphere. Much depends on the leadership of the universities. The difficulties which the near future will inherit from the present will be very great. Throughout India, Pakistan, Burma, the Phillippines, and Indonesia, the universities are in a bad way. In China, they have no opportunity to exercise leadership. Only in Japan have some universities managed to distinguish themselves from the motley of mediocrity, and therewith maintained, at least in certain fields of science and scholarship, a standard which reminds even the deficient of their deficiencies. Yet in the rest of noncommunist Asia the situation is not hopeless. The human material is there. Many outstandingly intelligent young Asians manage, despite their university systems, to come through, to qualify themselves, and to do excellent postgraduate work overseas. (Many, of course, are so poorly trained that, when sent overseas, they are incapable of doing competent work.) Many of them who do good work overseas are wasted in all sorts of ways when they return home. Sheer difficulty in finding fitting employment is one source of waste; another is life in an unstimulating intellectual environment in isolation from other talented men and women of their own generation and interests. There are no reasons, other than political hesitation, bureaucratic indifference, and the jealousy of older mediocrities in prominent positions, why this waste of talent should be allowed to go on. A little more courage by politicians, a little more alertness on the part of bureaucrats, a little more generosity on the part of the elders, would make it possible for one or a few high-grade universities in the more populous countries, one high-grade regional university in the French-speaking countries of Southeast Asia, to emerge. It would not be necessary, to attain this end, to change the open admissions policy which is now followed and which is one of the factors in the dilapidated condition of intellectual life of this area. All it would require is a little determination to concentrate resources more circumspectly than is done at present. Such a concentration helps to explain the superiority of Japanese intellectual life. If this were done, there would be grounds for hope that the intellectual life of the Asian societies would find a new center of gravity. The civil service, which depends on the universities, would be immensely benefited, economic policies would be improved, public criticism would be better informed and more realistic. The formation of a highly qualified specialized corps of scientifically trained technologists would be furthered. Science and scholarship would become sufficiently productive, and small but effective intellectual communities would grow up. Intellectual dependence and provinciality would begin to fade. The Asian intellectuals would begin to become equal members in the world-wide intellectual community.

19 Intellectuals in the Political Development of the New States

I

The gestation, birth, and continuing life of the new states of Asia and Africa, through all their vicissitudes, are in large measure the work of intellectuals. In no state formations in all of human history have intellectuals played such a role as they have in these events of the present century.

In the past, new states were founded by military conquest, by the secession of ethnic groups led by traditional tribal and warrior chiefs, by the gradual extension of the power of the prince through intermarriage, agreement, and conquest, or by separation through military rebellion. In antiquity, the demand that subjects acknowledge the divinity of the emperor was no more than a requirement that the legitimacy of the existing order be recognized.[1] The interests of dynasty and kinship group, the lure of majesty, considerations of power, aspirations for office, and calculations of economic advantage have been the components of political decisions and the grounds for pursuit of power in the state. It is only in modern times in the West that beliefs about man's nature, his past, and his place in the universe, and about the ethical and metaphysical rightness of particular forms of political order—the concerns of intellectuals—have played an important part in public life.

In the West in modern times, however, politics—particularly civil politics—have never been a preserve of the intellectuals. Well-established aristocrats and landed gentry with ample leisure have provided much of the personnel of politics, both oligarchical and democratic; clergymen and high ecclesiastical officials and, above all, businessmen—the former earlier, the latter more recently—have likewise added to the pool. Retired army officers, trade unionists, and of course mere professional politicians of diverse occupational

Previously published in a slightly different form in *World Politics*, vol. 12, no. 3 (April 1960), pp. 329-68. © 1960 by Princeton University Press.

1. The maxim of the Peace of Augsburg, *Cuius regio, eius religio*, was the beginning of the specifically modern view that a political order must be based on articulately affirmed beliefs. It, too, however, was more concerned with the protection of dynastic interests and the guarantee of public order. The substance of the religion was less important than its acceptance, and in this way it differed from the more intrinsically ideological orientation toward politics that is characteristic of the modern intellectual.

backgrounds have also been among the incumbents of or contenders for political office and the leaders in the agitation surrounding selection and decision. Intellectuals, too—professors and teachers, scientists, journalists, authors, etc.—have had a substantial share in all these activities. Radical, much more than conservative, politics have been their province, but there too they have had to share the territory with politicians and trade unionists who were not intellectuals. Modern revolutionary politics have been a domain very much reserved for intellectuals; even those who were not intellectuals by training or profession have been almost forced into becoming so by the ideological nature of modern revolutionary politics.

The prominence of intellectuals in the politics of the new states of Asia and Africa arises in part from the special affinity which exists between the modern intellectual orientation and the practice of revolutionary or unconstitutional politics, of politics which are uncivil in their nature. But even in the small space allotted to civil politics before the new states' acquisition of sovereignty and in the larger area since then, intellectuals have had a prominent position. They have not had to share their political role to the usual extent with the other participants in the building and ruling of states.

It was the intellectuals on whom, in the first instance, devolved the task of contending for their nations' right to exist, even to the extent of promulgating the very idea of the nation. The erosion of the conscience and self-confidence of the colonial powers was in considerable measure the product of agitational movements under intellectual leadership. The impregnation of their fellow countrymen with some incipient sense of nationality and of national self-esteem was to a large extent the achievement of intellectuals, both secular and religious. The intellectuals have created the political life of the underdeveloped countries; they have been its instigators, its leaders, and its executants. Until Gandhi's emergence at the end of the First World War, they were its main followers as well, but this changed when the nationalist movement began to arouse the sentiments of the mass of the population.

One of the reasons for the political preeminence of the intellectuals of the underdeveloped countries is a negative one. There was practically no one else. In so many of the colonial countries, the princely dynasties were in decay; their powers and their capacities had withered even before the foreigners appeared. Chiefs and princes squirmed under foreign rule; they intrigued and schemed and at times even resorted to arms, but they organized no political movements and they espoused no ideology. They sought only, when they protested, to retain or regain their own prerogatives. In most of the colonial countries there were no great families producing, in generation after generation, courtiers and ministers who with the emergence of modern forms of public politics could move over into that sphere as of right, as they did in Great Britain from the seventeenth to the nineteenth century. The traditional intellectuals, the custodians of sacred texts, usually—with a few great exceptions like al-Afghani—had no political concerns. They were interested in keeping their traditional culture alive, and this traditional culture had little political content other than to recommend leaving authority to those who already had it. They were ready to adapt themselves to any ruler, native or foreign, who left them alone to carry on their scriptural studies, their traditional teaching, and their observances.[2]

Moreover, there was generally no military force either to fight the foreign ruler once he was established or to supply the educated personnel for a modern political movement.[3] There was no military officer class except for a few subalterns in the jealously guarded army of the foreign ruler. There were many professional soldiers, but they were noncommissioned officers and other ranks and had no political interest whatsoever. The movement instigated in 1881 by the Egyptian colonel Ahmed Orabi Pasha[4] had no counterparts until the tremors and tribulations of independence began to be felt. There was no profession of politics which men entered early, usually from other professions, and remained in until final and crushing defeat or the end of their lives. There were very few merchants and industrialists who out of civic and "material" interest took a part in politics on a full- or part-time scale—although many of them contributed substantially to the financial support of the nationalist and even the revolutionary movements. Prudence and the narrowness of their concerns kept businessmen out of politics. The "foreignness" of many business enterprises in underdeveloped countries had further diminished the significance of this class as a reservoir of political personnel. There was and there still is scarcely any endogenous trade union movement which produces its own leaders from within the laboring class, and there have been practically none of those self-educated workingmen who helped to give intellectual tone to the European and American socialist and revolutionary movements in their early years. There was no citizenry, no reservoir of civility to provide not only the audience and following of politics but the

2. The religious reform movements like the Brahmo Samaj, Arya Samaj, the Ramakrishna Mission, and the Muslim Brotherhood which contributed so much to national consciousness were primarily movements for the purification of religious life and for the reform of social institutions. Their political significance was either indirect or an afterthought.

3. The practitioners of the guerrilla warfare and terrorism which have been carried on in various parts of Asia and Africa against the European rulers have always included a significant admixture of intellectuals.

4. It was, in any case, more of a protest against unsatisfactory service conditions than a political movement.

personnel of middle and higher leadership. In short, if politics were to exist at all in underdeveloped countries under colonial rule, they had to be the politics of the intellectuals.

The intellectuals did not, however, enter into the political sphere merely because other sections of the population foreswore or abdicated their responsibilities. They entered because they had a special calling from within, a positive impetus from without.

II

We deal here with the modern intellectuals of the new states—not with traditional intellectuals. Whom do we regard as modern intellectuals in the new states? The answer, in a first approximation, is: all persons with an *advanced modern education*[5] and the intellectual concerns and skills ordinarily associated with it. For a variety of reasons, the present definition of the intellectuals is a less selective or discriminating one than we would use to designate the intellectuals in the more advanced countries. This is in no way condescension toward the new states. It is only an acknowledgment of the smaller degree of internal differentiation which has until now prevailed within the educated class in the new states, and the greater disjunction which marks the class off from the other sections of the society. It is also a recognition of a means of identification employed in the new states by the intellectuals themselves and by others.

In the new states, and in colonies which are shortly to achieve independence, the intellectuals are those persons who have become modern, not by immersing themselves in the ways of modern commerce or administration, but by being exposed to the set course of modern intellectual culture in a college or university. Passage through this course of study is the qualification for being regarded as

5. This definition is ceasing to be adequate because the extension of opportunities for higher education is changing the composition and outlook of the group of persons who have availed themselves of these opportunities. Furthermore, the increase of those with an advanced technical or scientific and specialized education is creating a body of persons whose interests are narrower than their predecessors' in their own countries and whose contact with the humanistic and political tradition of the hitherto prevailing higher education is becoming more attenuated. They themselves will not merely be different from the conventional political intellectuals of the colonial or recently colonial countries, but will also less frequently identify themselves as "intellectuals." This will make a considerable difference. In this respect the underdeveloped countries will begin to approximate the more advanced countries.

This definition is not intended to deny the existence of a class of traditional intellectuals, largely religious in their concerns. Nor does it seek to obscure the influence of traditional intellectuals in political life (like the Muslim Brotherhood, the Darul Islam, etc.) or of traditional ideas on modern intellectuals.

an intellectual, just as the possession of a diploma is regarded as a qualification for practicing a profession which is the prerogative of the intellectual. The "diplomatization" of society to which Max Weber referred, although it exists on a smaller scale than in Germany or Great Britain because there are fewer posts available, is as impressive in underdeveloped countries as in the advanced ones. It is not, however, the diploma which makes the intellectual. It is his prolonged contact with modern culture[6] which does so. The diploma is only an emblem, however valuable, of a part of his outlook which he and others regard as vitally important. The possession of a *modern intellectual culture* is vital because it carries with it a partial transformation of the self and a changed relationship to the authority of the dead and the living.

Occupational Structure of the Intellectuals

The professions of the intellectuals in underdeveloped countries are civil service, journalism, law, teaching (particularly college and university, but also secondary school teaching), and medicine. These are the professions in which intellectuals are to be found and which require either intellectual certification or intellectual skill. (There are other professions with similar qualifications of certification and skill, such as engineering and accounting, which have usually been regarded as marginal to the circle within which the intellectuals dwell.)

The occupational structure which intellectuals enter in the under-developed countries is notably different from that of the more advanced countries. The occupational distribution of the intellec-tuals in underdeveloped countries is a function of the level of economic development and of their having only recently been colonial territories. Because they were impoverished countries, they lacked a fully differentiated middle class. They lacked and still lack a stratum of authors who could live from the sale of their literary products.[7] They have only a very meager class of technical intellec-tuals (electrical engineers, technologists, industrial chemists, statisti-cians, accountants). They have lacked the higher levels of scientific and humanistic personnel, the physicists, biologists, geneticists, historians, and philosophers who carry on the intellectual work

6. This does not mean that all intellectuals in underdeveloped countries who possess diplomas are intellectually equal, or that all intellectuals possess diplomas.

7. By very rough methods I estimated that there might be as many as one hundred professional literary men in India who are able to maintain them-selves by their writings. The director of the *Sahitya Akademi* thinks that there are only fifty. Think then of the size of this stratum in Ghana, Nigeria, Egypt, or the Sudan!

which is the specific manifestation of the modern intellectual outlook.[8]

They lacked nearly all of these latter professions under colonial conditions, and most of the underdeveloped countries still lack most of them today under conditions of independence. In the colonial era they lacked them because poverty and the absence of a significant development of industry prevented the emergence of demand for technical intellectuals, because illiteracy prevented the emergence of a market for literary products, and because the higher levels of modern intellectual creation and inquiry received no indigenous impulse and were too costly for poor countries to maintain. As a result, persons trained in those subjects found little opportunity for employment in their own country, and few therefore attempted to acquire these skills.[9]

Under colonial conditions, the underdeveloped countries lacked the effective demand which permits a modern intellectual class, in its full variety, to come into existence. Persons who acquired intellectual qualifications had only a few markets for their skills. The higher civil service was by all odds the most attractive of these, but opportunities were restricted because it was small in size and the posts were mainly preempted by foreigners. (In India in the last decade of the British Raj, there were only about 1,200 such posts in the Indian civil service and of these a little less than half were filled by Indians. In other countries, the number of posts was smaller and the proportion held by persons of indigenous origin was also much smaller.)

Journalism, as a result of generally widespread illiteracy, was a stunted growth and provided only a few opportunities, which were not at all remunerative. Journalism under colonial conditions was much more of an unprofitable political mission than a commercially attractive investment, and most of it was on a rather minuscule scale.

The medical profession was kept small by the costliness of the course of study, the absence of an effective demand for medical services, and the preemption of much of the senior level of the medical service by the government and its consequent reservation for foreigners.

Teaching at its lower levels was unattractive to intellectuals

8. India is a very partial exception. It is practically alone in its possession of a large corps of intellectuals, a fair number of whom work at a very high level. This is partly a function of the much longer period than modern intellectual life has existed in India. The British stayed longer in India and exercised greater influence there than any other European power did in its colonial territory, and as a result many more modern intellectual institutions came into being.

9. There are other important reasons, growing out of the culture of these countries, which precluded interest in these fields. We do not deal with them here since our interest lies primarily in the political sphere.

because it involved living in villages away from the lights and interests of the larger towns, and because it was extremely un-remunerative. Nor were there many opportunities in it. On the secondary and higher levels, opportunities were also meager. Of all the underdeveloped countries, only India had an extensive modern college and university system before 1920; after that date, the additions to the Indian system of higher education came very slowly until the eve of the Second World War and the chaos that accom-panied it. Outside of India there were at most only a few thousand posts available in institutions of higher learning in all of colonial Asia and Africa, and some of these were reserved for Europeans (and Americans, in the two American colleges of the Middle East). Thus opportunities for teaching on the upper levels of an extremely lean educational system were few. Where the authorities sought to maintain a high standard, they were very particular about whom they chose to employ. (It should be added that political considera-tions, at this time of nationalistic, anticolonialist effervescence, likewise restricted the chances of entry, since many able young men disqualified themselves by the highjinks of adolescent politics during their student days.)

The Legal Profession

For these reasons, many of the intellectually gifted and interested who had also to gain their livelihood entered the course of legal study and then the practice of the profession of the law. Entry to the legal profession was not restricted on ethnic grounds; the course of study was short and inexpensive and could be easily undertaken. There was, moreover, a considerable effective demand for legal services.

The colonial powers were concerned with order and justice and, in their various ways, had attempted to establish the rule of law in the colonial territories. The wealthy landowning classes and the newer wealthy merchants were frequently engaged in litigations in which huge sums were involved, and the possibility for lawyers to earn handsome fees gave an éclat to the legal profession which only the higher civil service otherwise possessed.

Furthermore, in countries like India, Egypt, or Nigeria, for example, what else could a university or college graduate do with his qualifications if he did not wish to settle for a clerkship in the government or in a foreign commercial firm? The law schools were therefore able to attract throngs of students. Once the legal qualifi-cation had been obtained, the young lawyer went into the nether regions of the bar, where he had much time for other interests. The leisure time of the young lawyer was a fertile field in which much political activity grew.

This existence of a stratum of underemployed young lawyers was made possible by their kinship connections. The aspirants to the intellectual professions in the underdeveloped countries were almost always from the more prosperous sections of society. They were the sons of chiefs, noblemen, and landowners, of ministers and officials of territories in which indirect rule existed, and of civil servants and teachers in countries under direct rule. In some countries they occasionally came from prosperous mercantile families, though seldom in large numbers.

These social origins, against the background of the diffuse obligations accepted by members of an extended kinship system, meant that even where the income gained from a profession was inadequate to maintain a man and his immediate family, he could still continue to associate himself with the profession. The deficiencies in his earnings were made up by his kinsmen. Unlike teaching, the civil service, and most journalism, where membership in the profession is defined not merely by qualification and intermittent practice but by actual employment, a person need not earn a living by legal practice to be a lawyer. This is why the legal profession in nearly all the underdeveloped countries has been, before and since independence, crowded by a few very successful lawyers and a great number of very unsuccessful ones.

These are also some of the reasons why the legal profession supplied so many of the outstanding leaders of the nationalist movements during colonial times, and why the lawyer-intellectuals form such a vital part of the political elites of the new states.

Students

No consideration of the intellectual class in underdeveloped countries can disregard the university students. In advanced countries, students are not regarded as ex officio intellectuals; in underdeveloped countries, they are. Students in modern colleges and universities in underdeveloped countries have been treated as part of the intellectual class—or at least were before independence—and they have regarded themselves as such. Perhaps the mere commencement of an adult form of contact with modern intellectual traditions and the anticipation—however insecure—that acquisition of those traditions would qualify one for the *modern* intellectual professions conferred that status on university and college students and, derivatively, on secondary-school students.

The student enjoyed double favor in the eyes of his fellow countrymen. As one of the tiny minority gaining a modern education, he was becoming qualified for a respected, secure, and well-paid position close to the center of society, as a civil servant, teacher, or lawyer. As a bearer of the spirit of revolt against the foreign ruler, he gained the admiration and confidence of those of his seniors who were imbued with the national idea.

Formally, the student movements in the colonial countries began their careers only in the 1920s, but long before that the secondary schools, colleges, and universities had been a source of personnel for the more ebullient and aggressive nationalistic movements. Since the beginning of the present century, students have been in a state of turbulence. This turbulence flowed more and more into politics, until the students became vital agents in the national independence movements. The secondary schools, colleges, and universities attended by the students of underdeveloped countries became academies of national revolution. It was not the intention of the administrations and teachers that they should become such; rather, the contrary. Nonetheless they did, both in their own countries and in the metropolitan centers of London and Paris, where many of the most important architects of independence were trained, and where they found the intellectual resonance and moral support which sustained them in lean years.

The London School of Economics in particular has probably contributed much more to the excitation of nationalistic sentiment than any other educational institution in the world. At the School of Economics, the late Professor Harold Laski did more than any other single individual to hearten the colonial students and to make them feel that the great weight of liberal Western learning supported their political enthusiasm.

However, it was not only in the universities of London and Paris, but in shabby clubs and cafés, cheap hotels and restaurants, dingy rooming houses and the tiny cluttered offices of their nationalist organizations that the colonial students were educated in nationalism, acquired some degree of national consciousness, and came to feel how retrograde their own countries were and what they might be if only they became their own masters and modernized themselves. Personalities like Mr. Krishna Menon, Dr. Nkrumah, and Dr. Banda were themselves formed in these milieux, and in turn formed many of those who were to play an active part in the movement in their own countries.

The political propensities of the students have been, in part, products of adolescent rebelliousness. This has been especially pronounced in those who were brought up in a traditionally oppressive environment and were indulged with a spell of freedom from that environment—above all, freedom from the control of their elders and kinsmen. Once, however, the new tradition of rebellion was established among students, it became self-reproducing. Moreover, the vocational prospectlessness of their post-university situation has also stirred the restiveness of the students.

The Unemployed Intellectual

In most underdeveloped countries during the colonial period, the unemployed intellectual was always a worry to the foreign rulers and to constitutional politicians, and a grievance of the leaders of the independence movements. He still remains a problem in the under-developed countries which have had a higher educational system for some length of time and which are not rapidly expanding their governmental staffs. In Ghana or Nigeria there was a shortage of intellectuals, and all graduates could find posts; in Pakistan, which inherited only a very small part of the higher educational system of British India, the government attempted to restrict entrance to the universities, especially in "arts" subjects. In India and Egypt, however, despite rapid expansion of opportunities for the employ-ment of intellectuals in government, there has been a more than proportionate expansion in the number of university graduates, and the problem remains as acute as ever.

Yet the difficulty is not so much "intellectual employment" as under- and malemployment. Most of the graduates, sooner or later, do find posts of one sort or another, but they are not posts which conform with expectations. They are ill paid, unsatisfying in status and tenure, and leave their incumbents in the state of restlessness which they experienced as students.

III

The nature of the political movements which preceded independence and the indigenous traditions of the underdeveloped countries both forced political life into charismatic channels. Charismatic politics demand the utmost from their devotees.

When the intellectuals of the colonial countries were ready to engage in politics at all, they were willing to give everything to them. Politics became the be-all and end-all of their existence. Those who were not restrained by fear of the loss of their posts in government schools and colleges or by the material and psychological advantages of their jobs became highly politicized. Some of the intellectuals who graduated in the years of nationalistic fervor did not even attempt seriously to enter upon a professional career but went directly into agitational and conspiratorial politics. Their middle-class origins and the economy of the extended family system, together with the relatively few needs of charismatically sensitive intellectuals, helped to make possible this consecration to politics. For these reasons and because an autonomous intellectual life in the modern sense had scarcely taken root in any of the underdeveloped colonial countries, politics of a very intense sort had the intellectual field largely to itself.

The high degree of political involvement of the intellectual in underdeveloped countries is a complex phenomenon. It has a threefold root. The primary source is a deep preoccupation with authority. Even though he seeks and seems actually to break away from the authority of the powerful traditions in which he was brought up, the intellectual of underdeveloped countries, still more than his confrère in more advanced countries, retains the need for incorporation into some self-transcending, authoritative entity. Indeed, the greater his struggle for emancipation from the traditional collectivity, the greater his need for incorporation into a new, alternative collectivity. Intense politicization meets this need. The second source of political involvement is the scarcity of opportunities to acquire an even temporary sense of vocational achievement; there have been few counterattractions to the appeal of charismatic politics. Finally, there has been a deficient tradition of civility in the underdeveloped countries, which affects the intellectuals as much as it does the nonintellectuals. Let us consider each of these aspects.

The intellectual everywhere is concerned with his relations to authority. In underdeveloped countries, where authorities have tended on the whole to be more unitary, and where alternative authorities, and the authority of alternative traditions, have not yet emerged because of the small size of the primordial community and its relatively low degree of internal differentiation, the preoccupation of the intellectual with authority is all the greater. It is difficult for him to escape from a sense of its presence and a feeling of dependence on it. Such continuous presence, and the unindulgent attitude of traditional indigenous authority, once childhood has passed, breed resentment and antipathy which are submerged but not dissolved in the obedience required for the continuance of daily existence in the primordial community.

The external air of submission hides a deeper and unceasing enmity. Distant authority, which has force at its disposal, which is impersonal, as bureaucratic authority must be, and which is not suffused with any immediately apprehensible charisma, provides an easy target for this enmity.

When one shares in authority, when one "is" authority, as a leading politician of the ruling party or as a civil servant, the antagonism toward authority is curbed by the counterbalancing need to be absorbed into it. For an intellectual in an underdeveloped country, authority is usually something into which he must be absorbed or against which he must be in opposition. It is seldom something about which he can be neutral while he goes about his business. The very structure of the underdeveloped countries, both in their primordial and in their wider aspects, both during the colonial period and during independence, is such that one can never be indifferent about authority. It cannot be overlooked; one's "business" cannot be carried on without regard to it.

Distant authority carries with it none of the compensations and urgencies of immediately present and permeative authority. Distance does not make for indifference among the politicized, among those whose passions are strong and no longer bound down by the weight of primordiality and tradition. The distance of authority renders revolt against it psychologically more practicable. Distant authority is "alien" authority. Even when it is ethnically "identical" with those over whom it rules, this "alienation" exists in those societies which are used to being ruled by visible and proximate authorities. (When distant authority is also ethnically alien, whether it be of the same general racial and cultural stock or as alien in color, cultural tradition, provenience, and physical appearance as the colonial authorities were, the impulse to revolt is all the stronger.)

The revolt against authority cannot, however, be complete and unequivocal. The need, from which no human being can ever wholly liberate himself, to be a member of an authoritative, transcendent collectivity remains. The individual, striving to emancipate himself from his primordial collectivity, must feel himself a part of some other more congenial, alternative collectivity. It must, moreover, be an authoritative one, a charismatically authoritative one. Where, in an underdeveloped society, with its relative churchlessness, its still feeble professional and civil traditions, and in the face of persisting particularistic loyalties, both subjective and objective, can the modern intellectual find such an authoritative collectivity? It is really only the "nation" which is at hand, and that organized body which represents the "nation"—namely, the "party of national independence."

This is one reason why the intellectual immerses himself, at least for a time, in intense political activities; it is why he seeks a "cause," an encompassing ideal. It is also the reason for the oppositional character of the politics of the intellectuals who themselves do not share in the authority. The belief in the efficacy of political action and in the political sources of evil and the remedies of evil also finds some of its explanation here. This is why the relatively unpolitical intellectual, or the intellectual who is indirectly connected with political affairs, the most specialized intellectual who wishes to work within his own professional intellectual tradition and to exercise his influence in the public sphere over the longer run and beyond the immediate disputes of the parties, is regarded as not being a "genuine intellectual" and even as a traitor to the ideals which the intellectual is properly called to serve.

The intense politicization of the intellectual is accentuated by the provision, through politics, of opportunities for individual effectiveness and achievement. In a society where status is traditionally determined by such primordial qualities as kinship connection, age, sex, and rank order within the family, the possibility of achievement, of making a mark on events by one's own actions, is minimal. In the larger society of the underdeveloped countries, although the narrower primordial determinants of status are to some extent transcended, the possibilities of achievement remain small. The opportunities for the satisfactory employment of an educated person under conditions of colonial rule were meager as long as the most authoritative positions in the civil service and in commerce were reserved to foreigners. They remain small under conditions of sovereignty as long as the economy is backward and posts integral to the modern part of the economy are relatively few, and as long as opportunities for specifically intellectual employment or the scale of the products of creative intellectual work are restricted.

The educated person acquires some degree of emancipation from the predominantly primordial tradition of status determination. The content of this modern education, and its dissolution of the hold of traditional cultural standards and the traditional patterns of life, arouse in him the need to determine his status and his self-esteem by his own achievements. Where can such a person make his mark in a society which gives him little room to do so?

The political movement with its demands and challenges is almost the only arena open to him. A political movement, unlike a business firm or a university or a government department, can absorb as many people as apply to it. It can give a man tasks to perform, and it can thereby offer him the possibility of seeing the effects of his actions. By shouting, demonstrating, marching, agitating, threatening and bullying, fighting, destroying, obstructing, helping to organize, running errands, distributing handbills and canvassing, he can see some effects and can believe in the importance of his deeds in thwarting or coercing a distant impersonal bureaucratic authority, or in serving the will of the new charismatic authority to which he gives himself.

Especially during the period of late adolescence and youth, when the impulses of self-assertion and the striving for individuality and creativity are at their height, and before the traditional system of status has reasserted its empire over him, politics seem to be the only field in which he can act with some expectation of satisfying effectiveness.

Once independence has been attained, the need for effectiveness and achievement does not die away. Politics remain a major alternative to apathetic idiocy or regression into the acceptance of the traditional pattern of life. Politics will in fact remain a major alternative open to the intellectuals for achievement and for absorption into a wider, no longer primordial collectivity as long as the underdeveloped societies remain underdeveloped. Only when they have become more differentiated occupationally and when they have developed a sufficiently large and self-esteeming corps of professional intellectuals, carrying on the specifically intellectual professions with their own corporate traditions and corporate forms of organization, will the passionate sentiment and energy flow into channels other than the political.

Nationalism

The nationalism of the intellectuals usually made its first appearance alone, free from the complications of socialist and populist ideas. Only in those underdeveloped countries where the nationalist movement has come more lately on the scene has it been involved in other ideological currents which are not necessarily integral to it.

The nationalism of the intellectuals of the underdeveloped countries emerged at a time when there was little sense of nationality among the peoples whose nationality the intellectuals were proclaiming. Its first impetus seems to have come from a deepening of the feeling of distance between ruler and ruled, arising from the spatial and ethnic remoteness of the foreign rulers and the dissolution of the particularistic tie which holds ethnically homogeneous rulers and ruled together. The identification of oneself, as a subject of an unloved (however feared and respected) ruler, with others who shared that subjection was one phase of the process. The discovery of the glories of the past, of cultural traditions, was usually but not always an action, ex post facto, which legitimated the claims asserted on behalf of that newly imagined collectivity.[10]

The assimilation of modern culture, which, historically, was a foreign culture, was an essential element in this process. The first generation of constitutional politicians in most underdeveloped countries were relatively highly "Westernized." The usual antagonism toward the older generation made the next, younger generation more antagonistic toward Western culture, and encouraged their rudimentary attachment to the indigenous traditional culture to come forward a little more in their minds. This provided a matrix for the idea of a deeper national culture and, therewith, of the nation

10. The stirrings of religious reform and the effort to rehabilitate the dignity of the traditional religious culture became political only when there was an alliance of religious leaders with a politicized modern intelligentsia.

which had only to be aroused to self-awareness. It was neither a simple attachment to their indigenous culture nor a concretely experienced love of their fellow countrymen which made the intellectuals so fervently nationalistic. These would have presupposed a prior sense of affinity, which for many reasons was lacking and often still is. In fact, however, "fellow countrymen" became so to the modern intellectuals primarily by virtue of their common differentiation from the foreign ruler. Fierce resentment against the powerful, fear-inspiring foreign ruler was probably a much more significant factor than either a sense of affinity or a conscious appreciation of the traditional culture.

The resentment of the modern intellectual grew from several seeds: one of the most important was the derogation implied in the barrier against entry into or advancement in the civil service. The other, closely related to this, was the feeling of injury from insults, experienced or heard about, explicit or implicit, which the foreign rulers and their businessmen fellow nationals inflicted on the indigenous modern intellectuals. Lord Curzon's derogatory remarks about the educated Bengali in his famous Calcutta University convocation address were only among the more egregious of an infinite multitude of such slights, injuries, and denigrations. The belittlement extended into every sphere of life, cultural, intellectual, religious, economic, political, and personal. A sense of distress and of anticipated insult became part of the indigenous intellectuals' relationship with foreigners for a long time. Even now in independence, the alertness to insult and the readiness to perceive it persist. They were at their height in the early period of nationalism.

The situation was rendered all the more insufferable by the genuine and positive appreciation which the native intellectuals often felt for the foreign culture, and their feeling of the inferiority of their own in comparison with it. Nationalism of an extremely assertive sort was an effort to find self-respect and to overcome the inferiority of the self in the face of the superiority of the culture and power of the foreign metropolis.

It was therefore logical that prior to independence the politics of the intellectuals, once the movement for constitutional reform had waned, should have been concerned with one end above all others: national independence. It was generally assumed by most politicized intellectuals that any other desiderata would be automatically realized with the attainment of that condition. The actual attainment of independence and of a condition in which the tasks of political life have become as demanding and as diversified as they must inevitably become in a polity where the state takes unto itself so many powers and aspires to so much, has not greatly altered the situation. Nationalism still remains one of the greatest of all motive forces;[11] it underlies many policies to which it is not really germane and serves as a touchstone of nearly every action and policy.

The socialistic and the populistic elements in the politics of the intellectuals of underdeveloped countries are secondary to and derivative from their nationalistic preoccupations and aspirations. Economic policies have their legitimation in their capacity to raise the country on the scale of the nations of the world. The populace is transfigured in order to demonstrate the uniqueness of its "collective personality." The ancient culture is exhumed and renewed in order to demonstrate, especially to those who once denied it, the high value of the nation. Foreign policy is primarily a policy of "public relations" designed not, as in the advanced countries, to sustain the security of the state or enhance its power among other states, but to improve the reputation of the nation, to make others heed its voice, to make them pay attention to it and to respect it. The "world," the "imperialist world," remains very much on the minds of the intellectuals of the new states. It remains the audience and the jury of the accomplishments of the nation which the intellectuals have done so much to create.

Nonetheless, despite the preeminence of the nationalistic sensibility, it does not rest upon a tabula rasa, cleared of all other attachments. The intellectuals of underdeveloped countries are not as "uprooted," as "detribalized," as they themselves sometimes assert with so much melancholy, or as, with more spite, their foreign and domestic detractors often allege. They have remained attached in many ways to their traditional patterns of social life and culture. These deeper attachments include parochial attachments to their own tribes and ethnic and caste communities, and almost inevitably seek expression in public policies and in domestic political alignments. The presence of these attachments is a supplementary generator of nationalistic sentiment. It is against them, and in an effort to overcome them—within themselves and in their fellow countrymen—that many intellectuals in underdeveloped countries commit themselves so fervently to intense nationalism.

By a similar process, the extensive use of a foreign language in daily intellectual life also feeds the force of nationalism. The intellectuals' very large amount of reading in French and English and their feeling of continued dependence on these cultures, their continuing and still necessary employment of French or English for their own cultural creations and even for political, administrative, and judicial purposes, and their awareness of the slow and painful course through which their nation must pass before its own language

11. Although it is by no means the chief reason, this nationalistic concentration is a significant factor in accounting for the poverty and uniformity of the intellectual life of the underdeveloped countries.

becomes adequate to the requirements of modern life, cannot avoid touching their sensibilities. The constant reaffirmation of their nationalistic attachment is an effort to assuage this wound.

Socialism

The socialism of the intellectuals of the underdeveloped countries grows, fundamentally, from their feeling for charismatic authority, from their common humanity, and from the antichrematistic traditions of their indigenous culture. More immediately, it is a product of the conditions and substance of their education, and of their nationalistic sensibility.

The intellectuals of underdeveloped countries are, in general, devotees of authority, even though they may be inflamed against some particular authority. They regard the existing distribution of authority as the source of present economic and social inequities and they seek a new distribution of authority as the instrument to abolish them. Their critical view of the state as it exists at present in their own country is partly a manifestation of their distrust of impersonal authority and of their faith in a more charismatic alternative.[12] They do not believe in the capacities of businessmen to increase the well-being of the nation. They have little sympathy, conscious or unconscious, with the man who is engaged in the pursuit of wealth.

None of the great traditional cultures gives a high rank to the merchant; even when they revolt against the traditional culture or slip away from it unwittingly, the intellectuals usually retain that part of it which allots no high place to the businessman. In their mind, the life of the businessman is unheroic; it is untouched by sacredness and they will have none of it. Intellectuals very seldom seek careers in private business; when necessity forces them into it, they are ill at ease and restless. The intellectual who works for a private business firm lays himself open to the charge of having deserted his calling, even though he has deserted it no more than a civil servant or a lawyer. The notion of an economic system ruled by the decisions of businessmen, out to make a profit for themselves, is repugnant to the intellectuals of underdeveloped countries—even more than it is in advanced countries, where the businessman does not fare very well either at the hands of the intellectuals.

As long as the intellectuals of underdeveloped countries pursued the paths of constitutional reform and confined their attention to administration and representation, these deeper dispositions whose source was the traditional indigenous culture did not enter into their politics. They accepted most of the existing regime. When, however,

12. *Vide* the Gandhian socialists and the Bhoodan movement in India.

they began to direct their attention to the society and the nation, when they ceased being politically "superficial" and began to touch on politically "sacred" things, the socialist potentiality of their fundamental orientation became more manifest.

These inner developments within the intelligentsia of underdeveloped countries coincided with the upsurge of socialist thought among the European intellectuals. To this, the intelligentsia of the underdeveloped countries felt drawn. The attractive power of the metropolis was enhanced by the cogeniality of intellectual socialism. From the 1920s to the 1940s, the example of the late Professor Harold Laski elicited and fortified the socialistic disposition of many young intellectuals of the English-speaking underdeveloped countries; Jean-Paul Sartre has played a parallel role among the French-speaking intellectuals from 1945 onward.

The spread of socialistic ideas was aided by the large-scale migration of Asian and African intellectuals to Europe for further study and professional training. The great stream of Asians to European educational centers began in the 1890s; their intensive politicization, in the 1920s. The stream of the African students began in the 1920s and became much wider after 1945. From the end of the First World War and the Russian Revolution, the young Asians and Africans, impelled by events in the world and at home, found themselves in an atmosphere which gave the encouragement of a nearly universal assent to their socialist aspirations.

The association between socialism as a domestic policy and hostility toward an imperialistic foreign policy—a connection which is inherent in the postulates of socialist thought and its Leninist variant, although not all socialists have at all times shared it—made European, and especially British and French, socialism even more acceptable to the Asian and African students who came to the intellectual capitals of the European metropolis.

To these factors, which made socialism appear such a bright ideal, should be joined the nature of large-scale business enterprise in the students' own countries. In practically all instances, large-scale business enterprise in the underdeveloped countries was owned and controlled by foreign capitalists. Not just the Europeans, and latterly the Americans, owned large firms in Africa and Asia, but Chinese, Syrians, Lebanese, Parsees, Armenians, Greeks, and Italians, away from their own countries, showed exceptional enterprise. Encountering few indigenous competitors, they built up extensive organizations and ample fortunes in underdeveloped countries. The ethnic diversity and separateness of the peoples, even within large, centrally governed countries, often brought about a situation in which private businessmen who were of the same "nationality" as those in the midst of whom they lived and conducted their affairs, but who were of a different "community," were regarded as outsiders who had no moral claims on the loyalty of the intellectuals. Businessmen, by the nature of their calling, could never be part of the "people," their ethnic distinctness was a further justification for treating them as alien to the "people."

On the other side, a socialistic economic system conducted in accordance with principles which are of intellectual origin, guided by persons who are imbued with these "principles," seems to be the only conceivable alternative to a privately operated economy. The intellectuals who dare to differ from such obvious conclusions constitute a small fraction of the intellectual classes in most of the underdeveloped countries, both colonial and sovereign.

The socialism of the intellectuals of underdeveloped countries, it should also be stressed, is a product of their pained awareness of the poverty of their own countries. The heightening of national sensibility led perforce to the discovery of the "people." Agitational activities brought them into contact with the "people," the vague doctrine of nationalism, even in its liberal form, brought the idea of the "people" into the consciousness of the intellectuals. Often, too, on return from a period of foreign study where they had encountered socialist ideas and experienced a heightened national consciousness, the sight of their impoverished fellow countrymen had a traumatic force. Confrontation with the poverty of their country evoked anguish and desperation in many intellectuals. They have been humiliated by their sense of the backwardness of their country. They have learned how gradually the advancement of the Western countries has moved, and they have heard of the speedy progress of the Soviet Union from a backward country to the status of one of the most powerful industrial nations of the world. What could be more harmonious with their present perceptions, their aspirations, and their background than to espouse a socialist solution to their unhappy problem? And if to this is added the fact that their countries have been held in subjection by capitalistic countries and that the socialist countries proclaim their hostility to imperialism, the disposition toward socialism receives another impulsion.

Populism

The populism of intellectual politics in underdeveloped countries has a familial affinity to the populism of the intellectuals of more advanced countries during the past century and a half. It is a part of a universal process consequent on the emergence of an incipient and fragmentary worldwide intellectual community. It is a phenomenon of the tension between metropolis and province which arises from the trend toward that worldwide intellectual community.

The populism of the intellectuals is German in origin. It was a critique of the feebleness of the petty elites of the system of *Kleinstaaterei*, alongside the grandeur of the Holy Roman Empire, and of the Germany which could emerge if the regime of the princelings could be abolished and all of Germany unified. It was a critique of the central institutional system, and particularly of the claims of the state, of the universities, and of the ecclesiastical authorities to embody what was essential in their society, and of their insistence, on that basis, on their right to rule over it. It was a rejection of the urban bourgeoisie. It was a denial that the "nation" could be found in existing authoritative institutions and an assertion that the root of the future lay in the "folk."

In Russia, populism was a product of a similar situation, aggravated by resentment against a prevailing enchantment by the West, which was more pronounced than the Francophilia of the princely courts against which the first generations of romantic German populism had been a reaction. In Russia, the intellectuals had carried on a passionate love affair with Western Europe, and many had been disappointed and had even come to feel guilty for deserting their "own" for foreign idols. Alienated from their own authorities of state, church, and university, hostile to their own mercantile bourgeoisie, disillusioned with Western European socialism after its failures in the revolutions of 1848, it had nowhere to turn except to the "people," whom it glorified as a repository of wisdom and as the source of Russia's salvation.

American populism was not very different in its general origins. It, too, was the product of a reaction against the Anglophile intellectual elite of the Eastern seaboard and the political and industrial elites who ruled the country from the Eastern cities. In America, too, therefore, it was an effort to find a firm foundation for intellectuals who were alienated from the authorities in their society and from their xenophilic fellow intellectuals. In America also it was a phase of the struggle of province against metropolis.

In the underdeveloped countries, the process has been essentially the same. Alienated from the indigenous authorities of their own traditional society—chiefs, sultans, princes, landlords, and priests—and from the rulers of their modern society—the foreign rulers and the "Westernized" constitutional politicians (and, since independence, politicians of the governing party)—the intellectuals have had only the "people," the "African personality," the "Indian peasant," etc., as supports in the search for the salvation of their own souls and their own society.

The "people" are a model and a standard; contact with them is a good. Esteem and disesteem are meted out on the basis of "closeness to the people" or distance from them. It is common worry of and an accusation against the intellectuals of the underdeveloped countries that they are "out of touch with the people," uprooted, *déracinés*, "brown" or "black" (as the case may be) "Englishmen" or "Frenchmen," etc. Many make the accusation against themselves, most make it against their fellow intellectuals.

Factually, it is usually quite untruthful. Most intellectuals in underdeveloped countries are not as "cut off" from their own culture as they and their detractors suggest. They live in the midst of it; their wives and mothers are its constant representatives in their midst; they retain close contact with their families, which are normally steeped in traditional beliefs and practices. The possession of a modern intellectual culture does remove them, to some extent, from the culture of their ancestors, but much of the latter remains and lives on in them.[13]

The experience to which the allegation of being "cut off" from the "people" refers is not to any serious extent a real result of the intellectuals' acceptance of the "foreign," modern culture. It rests rather on their own feeling of distance from the rest of their fellow nationals, which is a product of the ethnic, tribal, kinship, and caste particularism of these underdeveloped societies and of the consequent lack of a true sense of civil affinity with the rest of their fellow countrymen. It is the resultant of the superimposition of a nationalistic ideology, which demands fellow-feeling, on a narrower particularism, inharmonious with it and psychologically contradictory to it. There is a genuine feeling of strain; all the burden of this strain is put upon the fact that they possess some elements of an exogenous culture.

The frequent reiteration of the charge testifies to an awareness of this tension, and the choice of the foreign culture as its focus is a manifestation of a desire to find a way out which will conform to the requirements of ideological nationalism. Because the intellectuals assert it and, to some extent, believe it, they often try to make amends for it by some form of nativism, which extols the traditional ways of the people and juxtaposes them with modern and thus "foreign" ways.

This nativistic reaction accentuates demagogic political tendencies, and fosters a race among contenders for the distinction of being more "for" the "people" or more "akin" to them. It accentuates prejudice against the educated and a hostility against the modern education which the intellectuals of the new states need if they are to perform intellectual functions in a productive way, and

___

13. Much of the intellectuals' self-accusation rests on the populistic assumption that the "people," not being distracted or corrupted by modern culture, are the bearers of the traditional culture in its fullness and its glory. This assumption is probably an error; the "people" are quite unlikely to be in more than fragmentary possession of the corpus of traditional culture.

without which they would not be intellectuals and their countries would flounder and sink.

Nonetheless, despite this preoccupation with the "people," the populism of the intellectuals of underdeveloped countries does not necessarily bring with it either intimacy with the ordinary people, a concrete attachment to them, or even a democratic attitude. It is compatible with them but it does not require them. It is equally compatible with a dictatorial regime which treats the people as instruments to be employed in the transformation of the social and economic order, and their culture and outlook as a hindrance to progress.

Populism can be the legitimating principle of oligarchical regimes, as well as of democratic regimes and of all the intermediate types. The "people" constitute the prospective good to be served by government policy, and they serve as the emblem of the traditional culture which is thus glorified even while it is being eroded and its traditional custodians disregarded or disparaged.

Oppositionalism

The populism of the intellectual is a product of opposition to the authorities who rule at home and to the foreign culture which fascinates him and his fellow intellectuals in his own country. It is one facet of an oppositional syndrome.

The origins of this inclination to oppose constituted authority seem, at first glance, easy to locate. Practically all politics in the colonial period, once the constitutional phase had passed, consisted and still consist of root-and-branch opposition. Whether they took the form of conspiracy, sabotage, riots, assassination, clandestine or open journalism, public meetings, boycotts, demonstrations and processions, civil disobedience, or uncooperative participation in representative institutions, opposition and obstruction of the foreign ruler were the main aims. Where it was impossible to share in the responsible exercise of authority, opposition was in fact the only alternative.

The degree of alienation from the constituted authority varied but it was almost always deeper and more drastic than the opposition which exists in advanced pluralistic societies.[14] It was the opposition of politicians excluded or withdrawn from the constitutional order, who accepted neither the rules nor the ends of the prevailing system. It was, therefore, the opposition of politicians

14. Its only parallel in the West is the conduct of the Irish members in the House of Commons in the latter part of the last century and of communist members of European parliaments when they were a small minority and did not seek a popular front. The "Irish members" had considerable resonance in India, and their influence still survives even where its origin has been forgotten.

who refused in principle to consider the problems of the government as real tasks needing resolution. It was an opposition which was convinced by situation, temperament, and principle that it would never share authority with the foreign ruler. The only authority to which it aspired was complete and exclusive control of the entire machinery of state. Until that point was reached, its only policy was opposition.

The oppositional attitude of the intellectuals has another point of origin far removed from the political experience of a colonial situation. In most underdeveloped countries the traditional character of the culture sustains diffuseness in the exercise of authority. Diffuse authority, omnicompetent in the tasks facing the society, at least according to legendary beliefs, derives its legitimacy in part from its comprehensive effectiveness. Even though the substantive actions performed by such diffuse traditional authorities are no longer respected by intellectuals, the older pattern of expectation persists. Specific, delimited, impersonal, constitutional authority gives the appearance of being a weak authority, an unloving one which possesses no inner relationship with the ruled. The diffuseness of a charismatic authority is desired, and the bureaucratic rule of the foreign power or of its sovereign indigenous successor arouses little enthusiasm or even willing acknowledgment of any deeper legitimacy. The intellectuals of underdeveloped countries, despite their immersion in modern culture and their overt acceptance of modern political principles, are at bottom averse to a relatively weak, self-limiting government, even when that government is their own, bound to them by common ethnic ties, a common culture, and comradeship in the struggle for independence.

This is one of the underlying grounds for the widespread disillusionment which overcomes so many intellectuals in underdeveloped countries after independence. It must be remembered that, whatever has happened since, practically every new state of the postwar world began as a modern constitutional regime of representative institutions and public liberties. They have all had to employ modern bureaucratic methods of administration, even when they lacked the requisite personnel. They have tried to operate the rule of law. They all began as remote, impersonal machines, exercising authority without the diffuseness of charisma or tradition. Their equilibrium depended on an ostensibly charismatic personality who, at the peak of the governmental mountain, offset the distaste for bureaucratic-legal rule.

Thus, the establishment of a tradition of opposition in political life has, as has happened so often in almost every sphere of life in underdeveloped countries, coincided with a fundamental disposition resting on an indigenous cultural tradition.

It would be wrong, perhaps, to claim a universal validity for a generalization which could be drawn from Max Weber's criticism of Bismarck and the paralyzing influence which his autocracy in the Reichstag exerted on the opposition parties of that body. It was Max Weber's view that the irresponsible opposition which the Bismarckian regime and its Wilhelmian successor evoked would make the opposition parties incapable of responsible, efficient rule when they were given the opportunity to govern. He also asserted—and this is more important for our present discussion—that they would become incapable of conducting themselves as a responsible opposition, working within the rules of the parliamentary game. In certain of the underdeveloped countries this generalization does not seem to be applicable. In India, for example, certain of the intellectual politicians, and above all the first prime minister, Jawaharlal Nehru, have shown great adaptability in turning from a condition of complete and irreconcilable opposition to a responsible, hard-headed exercise of authority, and some of the socialists and independents conduct their opposition in a most intelligent and responsible manner. The same obtains in varying degrees in Ghana and in Tunisia. Certain intellectual politicians have shown considerable capacity to rule, even though they have not been as democratic or liberal as they once aspired to be or as Mr. Nehru succeeded in being. Not a few firebrands of the days of the independence movement have turned out to be responsible parliamentarians of the highest order.

Nonetheless, much truth remains in Max Weber's proposition. The intellectuals of the underdeveloped countries since they acquired independence, insofar as they are not in authority, do incline toward an antipolitical, oppositional attitude. They are disgruntled. The form of the constitution does not please them, and they are reluctant to play the constitutional game. Many of them desire to obstruct the government or give up the game of politics altogether, retiring into a negative state of mind about all institutional politics or at least about any political regime which does not promise a "clean sweep" of the inherited order.

Incivility

Although the intellectuals of the underdeveloped countries have created the idea of the nation within their own countries, they have not been able to create a nation. They are themselves the victims of that condition, since nationalism does not necessarily become citizenship. Membership in a nation which is sovereign entails a sense of affinity with the other human beings who make up the nation. It entails a sense of "partness" in a whole, a sense of sharing a common substance. This feeling of being part of the whole is the basis of a sense of concern for its well-being, and a sense of responsibility to it and for it. It transcends ineluctable divisions, softening them and rendering them tolerable to civil order, regarding them as less significant than the underlying community of those who form the nation. In political life, these dispositions form the virtue of civility.

Civility has hitherto not been one of the major features of the politicized intelligentsia of the underdeveloped countries. An intense politicization is accompanied by the conviction that only those who share one's principles and positions are wholly legitimate members of the polity and that those who do not share them are separated by a steep barrier. The governing party in many sovereign under-developed states, and those intellectuals who make it up or are associated with it, tend to believe that those who are in opposition are separated from them by fundamental and irreconcilable differences. They feel that they *are* the state and the nation, and that those who do not go along with them are not just political rivals but *total* enemies. The sentiments of the opposition are, mutatis mutandis, scarcely different. These are the fruits of intense politicization.

The incivility of the politicized intellectuals has a history which precedes their birth. Traditional societies, based on kinship and hierarchy, are not civil societies. They do not know the phenomenon of citizenship, since rights and obligations are not functions of membership in a polity determined by territorial boundaries. The primordial qualities of traditional societies—kinship, age, sex, locality, etc.—are not qualities which define the citizen. In a pluralistic society they are not by any means incompatible with citizenship. In the more unitary traditional society, they suffocate incipient civility.

The moral structure of the independence movement has enabled this uncivil tradition to persist. The independence movement conceived of itself as the embodiment of the nation, and after its victory it became and conceived of itself as identical with the state. Given the oppositional dispositions which come to the surface in parliamentary and journalistic circles not attached to the government party, there often appears to be a semblance of justification for the belief of an impatient and hypersensitive government that the opposition is subversive of the state and cannot be reconciled to it.

This does not imply that there are not civil intellectuals in every underdeveloped country, some of them in the government, some of them in opposition, and some in journalism, the universities, and the other liberal professions. They are, however, in a marked minority. The traditions by which they are sustained, although they do exist in some of the states, are frail.

IV

The politics of the modern intellectuals in underdeveloped countries have evolved in three stages. The first efflorescence occurred roughly between the years when India was recovering from the trauma of the Mutiny and its repression and the First World War. In the few countries where there was anything of a class with a modern education and a certain amount of political stirring, these were the years of constitutional liberalism, eloquently and courteously argued. This first stage came considerably later to Black Africa, and lasted a shorter time than it did in British India and the Middle East. In Southeast Asia, too, the course of development was greatly telescoped. The backwardness of Southeast Asia and Black Africa in the construction of modern cultural and legal institutions, and the smaller numbers of persons who went abroad for higher studies, resulted in a much smaller intellectual class than in India and a later, briefer, and feebler life of constitutional liberalism. Where the intellectual class scarcely existed, politics could only be embryonic.

This was the stage of the politics of lawyers and journalists. Their politics were the politics of *honoratiores*. They were well-educated men, many of whom had studied in the metropolitan countries; they had absorbed and appreciated something of the metropolitan culture and the liberal constitutional political outlook, which, in the circles in which they moved in the France and Great Britain of that period, appeared to be almost unchallenged.

They were not revolutionaries and they did not always aspire to independence, at least not in the immediate future. One of their main grievances in this earliest phase was the restriction of the right of entry of their fellow countrymen into the civil service which ruled their country on behalf of the foreign sovereign. They also desired that legislative institutions should be a little more representative of persons like themselves. These two concerns could be interpreted crudely as a manifestation of a narrow class interest, but they were actually broader and better than that.[15] There were serious grounds, in their own self-image, for their claim to share in the administration of the country and for a vote in the determination of the budget.

15. Nor were these their only interests. They proposed the liberalization of the legal system, greater equity in its administration, and certain liberal social reforms such as the improvement of the legal position of women, the provision of more ample educational facilities, etc.

Obviously, there was some element of "class" and "self-interest" in some of their demands, such as the insistence that imported foreign manufactures should not be allowed to enjoy any advantages over indigenously produced industrial goods. The interest of the whole society, of one class and of an individual might all coincide on particular issues. This is probably the most that can be credited to the charge against the first generation made by the actors who came on the political stage a little later.

They had been brought up in a hierarchical tradition in which the landowning classes and the learned, in their own view and that of others, were the possessors of a "stake in the country." Insofar as it was a country, they felt it to be "theirs," and "theirs" almost exclusively. Many came from families which had in the past exercised great influence and which, in the countryside, still continued to do so. It was therefore part of their conception of the right order of things that they should share in the ruling of their own country, under a sovereign whom they were not in the main inclined to challenge in principle.

The liberal constitutional ideas which they acquired in the course of their mainly legal studies fitted in with their conceptions. Europe was boiling with democratic agitation—the labor and socialist movements were in process of formation. In the main, however, the very small trickle of Africans and the larger numbers of Asians who before the First World War went to the metropolis for advanced studies did not come into contact with these circles. They wanted a liberal governmental and legal order in the administration of which they could share.

Since they were largely lawyers, they developed the rhetorical skills and the self-confidence in dealing with authority which are an indispensable part of the equipment of the modern politician.[16] The structure of legal practice also gave them the time and the resources to absent themselves from their professional activities. As the occasion demanded, they were able, while still continuing to practice their professions, to devote themselves to public agitation, to attend and address meetings, to write books, pamphlets, and articles for the press, to meet representatives of their rulers from time to time in order to argue their claims, and to participate in consultative and representative bodies.

Side by side with this form of lawyers' politics, a daily and periodical press struggled to come into existence, largely in the metropolitan language but also in the indigenous languages. The journalists were not professionals. They were often political lawyers who had either left their profession or practiced it alongside journalism; there were also among them men who had been teachers, or who had aspired to join the government service, or had actually been in governmental employ. They were usually well-educated men, with the gravity of the Victorian and Continental bourgeois liberals whom they admired. All this gave dignity and decorum to the political life of that stage of political development.

16. It seems to me not accidental that even now the highest flights of Indo-Anglian prose have the rhetorical quality of high-grade lawyers addressing a court or a parliamentary body.

As journalists, they were not following a career in the material sense of the word. They were not trying to become rich. They were not interested in being purveyors of news and diversion. They were not seeking a livelihood in journalism. Where they could not gain their livelihood from journalism or from their auxiliary professions, they unquestioningly relied on the support of their kinsmen and patrons. They were journalists because there was a small literate public which could be reached and rendered coherent and articulate on behalf of the ideal of constitutional government in which the best-qualified of the ruled would have some hand.

These journalists and lawyer-politicians had few followers other than themselves, i.e., like-minded men in similar stations of life, such as liberal businessmen or princes, chiefs, and landowners. Leaders and followers together constituted no more than a small group. Only in India were the absolute numbers fairly large. In the Middle East they were fewer, and in the rest of Africa and in Southeast Asia, their numbers were negligible. Nonetheless they created, by their activity, the foundations of a still surviving tradition of the modern intellectuals in politics.

They did not have the field to themselves, even at the time of their greatest preeminence. They were being challenged by a more aggressive group, less complaisant toward their Western rulers and toward Western culture. These new rivals claimed that constitutional tactics led nowhere. They were the forerunners of the political type which came to the center of the political arena in the second stage. During the first stage, however, there was also another trend of intellectual activity which profoundly affected subsequent political developments, though it was not in itself primarily political or even political at all.

An impassioned effort of religious and moral self-renewal accompanied the development of political life of the underdeveloped countries during their colonial period. It was at first a feature of the countries which possessed conspicuous evidence of great indigenous achievements in the past—i.e., of the countries with a literary and architectural inheritance which in the midst of present degradation could remind contemporaries that their country had once been great. It was therefore also a characteristic of countries with an indigenous traditional intelligentsia made up of the custodians of sacred writings. Thus it was that in India and in the Middle East, through much of the nineteenth century, the protagonists of the traditional cultures, and particulary of the religions of Hinduism and Islam, sought to purify their inheritance, to restore it to its pristine greatness, or to fuse it with modern elements. Both in India and in the Middle East, the aim was to reinstate the dignity of the traditional religious culture and the society which was based on it, and thereby to establish its worth in the face of the encroachment of Western culture and religion.[17]

This movement to evoke a national self-consciousness, through the renewal of cultural traditions which had been allowed to decay, was not directly political. There was not much contact between the modern men who represented constitutional liberalism, and the energetic, pious traditionalists.[18] The two movements seemed to run almost independently of each other; there was no antagonism between them, often little mutual awareness.

The agents of moral renewal were not secular social reformers. They were not modern intellectuals in the sense of the word used here. They were men of the traditional culture who were sufficiently sensitive to the impact of modern culture to feel the need to reaffirm their own.[19] Their task was the cleansing of the cultural— and this meant largely religious—inheritance of their society from what they claimed were historically accidental accretions which had brought it into disrepute among modern men and allowed their country to sink in the world's esteem and in its own and, particularly, to appear enfeebled and unworthy in comparison with Western achievements. They claimed that what was essential in their religious traditions could—by restoration and cleansing or by syncretism—be reformulated in an idiom more appropriate to the modern situation, and that if this were done, it would recommend itself to their fellow countrymen who were needlessly and even perniciously enamored of Western culture. They were not unqualifiedly fanatical enemies of Western culture. They claimed that much of what it had to offer—particularly science, technology, and forms of organization— were necessary for the improvement of their countries and the reestablishment of their greatness among the nations. They insisted, however, that their countrymen must not lose their own souls to the West. They must instead rediscover their own essential being by the acceptance of a new and purer version of their own cultural tradition.

The older generation of modern "Victorian" intellectuals did not pay much heed to these preachments, although they were not hostile. In the next stage of political development, this effort of moral rediscovery and self-renewal had very profound repercussions. When, in the second stage, constitutional liberalism seemed to

17. Movements to "rehabilitate" the reputation of African civilization also appeared very early.

18. There were, of course, exceptions like al-Afghani, Mohammed Abdou, and M. G. Ranade.

19. Their influence made itself felt, however, in both India and the Middle East, primarily among modern intellectuals. They exerted little effect on their fellow traditional intellectuals, who persisted in their torpor.

disappear or to be confined in a very narrow space, the movement of moral and religious reform was taken up and developed into a passionate nationalism. Now, even where the religious element in the traditional culture is passed over, praise of the essence of the traditional culture has become a plank in the platform of every movement for independence and of every new state.

From constitutional liberalism and religious-moral renewal, the intellectuals of the colonial countries passed to a second stage—that of a fervently politicized nationalism. With this shift, there also occurred a shift in the mode of political action and its audience.

India was the first of all the underdeveloped colonial countries to execute this movement; it was the one in which the traditional indigenous culture was richest and most elaborate and in which that culture had developed most systematically and comprehensively. It was also the country where the foreign rulers had been longest established in a thoroughgoing way and where the contact of the indigenous intellectuals with a metropolitan Western culture had given birth to a longer and richer modern tradition than was possessed by any other country of Asia or Africa. It was the country with the largest and most differentiated modern intelligentsia. The first long phase of fascination with the West had already begun, in the India of the 1880s, to produce from within itself a reaction in favor of more purely Indian things.

This was also the time of growing strength in the socialist movement in Europe and of the growth of anarchism. Terrorism was in the ascendancy in Russia and Ireland. Tales of the Russian underground spread in Asia, together with the repute and glory of the bold deeds of the "Nihilists" in Russia, Sinn Fein in Ireland, and the Carbonari in Italy. Mazzini, Stepniak, and Kropotkin were names well known among the younger generation of Indian intellectuals. Yeats was becoming a figure of weight among the literary intelligentsia, and along with this went a feeling for the Irish renaissance and a belief in the possibilities of a comparable Indian renaissance. The writings of these *rishis* became known in India, imported from England; some of them appeared in Bengali translations.

The new generation which came to the surface of public life around the turn of the century was no longer content with constitutional agitation, or with such limited goals as more places in the Indian civil service and more consultative and deliberative institutions in which Indians would be better represented. Indian traditional culture was being revived through the Ramakrishna Mission and the Arya Samaj, and a new Indian self-consciousness took hold of young men who, while not deeming themselves religious, were possessed by a profound resonance toward traditional

Indian symbols. The Maharashtrian and Bengali terrorists gave no thought to the kind of social and political order which they wished to see established. They wished only to have India free of foreign rule, free to be itself in its own Indian way.

Parallel developments a third of a century later could be seen in areas as far apart as the Gold Coast and Egypt. A half-century later, they began to appear in East Africa. The same pattern was visible in more foreshortened form in Syria and Iraq. The proportions and the tone of the movements in these smaller countries, with much smaller intelligentsias, have been roughly what they were in India.

In these smaller countries, too, there was a tendency to regard the older generation of liberal constitutionalists and piecemeal reformers as excessively subservient to the foreign rulers and as excessively bemused by their foreign culture and their foreign forms of government. The later, populistic phase of intellectual politics, which in a variety of forms continues into the present, only intensified and made more complex and luminous an already established pattern. The generally socialistic orientation of the politics of the Asian and African intellectuals, which took form after the First World War and became preponderant after the Second World War, in a similar fashion only elaborated the inherent potentiality of intense nationalism.

The intensification of political concerns was the outgrowth of the earlier political interest, in fusion with the more acute sense of nationality which the heightened awareness of the traditional indigenous culture had helped to arouse. The politics of the "second generation" touched a very much deeper chord than that which the earlier generation had reached; it is a chord which still vibrates. The greater depth of the new political movement meant also that it was more passionate, more in the complete possession of politics. The fundamental politicization of the intelligentsia of Asia and Africa led to the discrediting of the first liberal generation. The politics of cultured and urbane gentlemen, speaking French or English to perfection, interested in much else besides politics, was not for this generation.

The politics of the second generation received a further powerful impetus from its participation in a cosmopolitan movement, in which *foreign*, Western countries were involved. The intellectuals of the second generation, like those who preceded and those who have followed, were also held by their attachment to Western culture. The extremist nationalist movements in Asia and subsequently in Africa had a Western legitimation for their strivings. They drew inspiration and comfort from abroad; they felt that their actions were one with a mighty surge all over the world, a surge toward a new order of freedom with possibilities unknown and unregarded.[20] This sense of being a part of the larger world infused into the politics of the second generation the permanently bedeviling tension between province and metropolis, and added, as it always does, the heat which arises from conflicting loyalties.

When the second generation was still in its youth in India, and only in conception in other Asian and African colonial countries, the Russian Revolution took place. Only a little while thereafter, M. K. Gandhi established his ascendancy over the political scene in India.[21] These two events precipitated the populistic consciousness, which had been only latent in the exacerbated nationalism which had preceded them.

The early leaders of the second generation had been deferential to "ancient traditions," in contrast to the liberal, moderate, and progressive attitude of the earlier constitutional politicians, who had not given political significance to indigenous cultural traditions. The "people" had, however, not yet acquired the eminence which was later to be their due in the political outlook of the intellectuals. Now, under the guidance of Gandhi and an attenuated Leninism, they ascended to a central position.

Socialism was no further away than a step of the imagination. The preceding generation had been neither socialist nor anti-socialist. The issue had never arisen, as long as civil service personnel policies, the extension of representative institutions, and criticism of the "drain" had been the main objects of political debate.[22] Politics now became "total politics," and its claims on those who gave

20. The role of exiles and expatriates living in the metropolitan centers of Great Britain, France, Germany, and Switzerland helped to maintain a continuous link between the revolutionary and radical tendencies of the metropolis and those in the underdeveloped countries. These exiles and expatriates provided a sort of training school for young Asians and Africans who had gone abroad to study, and they constituted a continuous representation of the interests of their countries before the public opinion of the ruling metropolis.

Like exiles and expatriates everywhere, they also were more "uprooted" than their countrymen who either stayed at home or returned home after a few years. This "uprootedness" did not, however, diminish the intensity of their politics. Rather, the contrary.

21. And with it, he began his march toward ascendancy over the Western colonialist conscience. A skeptical attitude about the rightfulness of imperialism had already existed in the West for a long time, but it was Gandhi more than anyone else outside the European socialist and the communist movements who impressed it on the consciousness of the Western educated classes. As a result, a body of Western allies was formed, and its existence was a reassurance and a stimulus to the politicized intellectuals who continued to stand in need of a sustaining tie with modern "Western" culture.

22. In Africa after the Second World War, nationalism, intense politics, socialism, and populism came into life almost simultaneously, as if they were inseparably involved with each other.

themselves to it became all-embracing. Politics in colonial countries became a vocation, without becoming professionalized. Many came to live "for" politics, but few lived "from" politics in the way in which professional politicians live from it. The politics of the colonial intelligentsia became in a sense more profound; that is, they came into contact with the deeper layers of the intelligentsia's existence. The politics of the intellectuals became charismatic politics.

As one might expect from charismatic politics, a tremendous pull was exerted on the youth. Leadership still lay with the lawyers and a few who had once served in government as officials and clerks[23] or had been tempted sufficiently to prepare themselves to do so. A large and important part of the following, however, consisted of students—college and university students in countries with colleges and universities and high school students where these were absent. A great deal of the clamor and volatility of the politics of the second generation of intellectuals came from the students.

The third stage of intellectual politics sees the intellectuals in power in a sovereign state ruled by an indigenous elite.

With this stage the intellectuals who have reaped the fruits of the struggle become dissociated from the intellectual class. A schism occurs in the corps of intellectual-politicians. One sector comes into power and takes to it like a fish to water. The exercise of authority—which is not identical with the efficient exercise of authority—seems to be almost as natural as breathing to those intellectuals who are in power. To an increasing extent, they see themselves as different from the intellectuals who do not share the power and whom they chide as naggers, unreasonable critics, backsliders from the great national cause. The intellectuals in power feel themselves less continuous with the intellectual class than they did during the struggle for independence. As the burdens and challenges of office preoccupy them, and as they spend so much of their time with party bosses and machine men who have never been or who long since ceased to be intellectuals, their own image of themselves as intellectuals wanes and they become more sensitive to the antipolitical dispositions of their old companions.

This drift toward schism is aggravated by the fact that the opposition becomes the magnet which draws the intellectuals. Although within the political elite at the peak of government there are many who were once intellectuals by education, vocation, or

23. Where there were few indigenous lawyers or others with higher education, leadership was exercised by clerks with secondary or elementary education. The educated, the *évolués,* have kept the lead, the highly educated when they have been available, the less well-educated where the former were lacking.

disposition and who have now become hardened politicians, no longer paying any attention to things of intellectual interest, those who remain intellectuals in vocation and disposition seem to find their natural habitat on the opposite benches. There—and in common rooms and cafés—gather the intellectuals who in their outlook, in their studies, and their self-identification, remain intellectuals.

The transformation of the intellectuals in power discloses the duality of the oppositional mentality. The hatred of authority is often no more than a facet of the fascination and love that it evokes. When they come to power, intellectuals who have hated it quickly allow the identification with it, against which they struggled previously, to come into full bloom. They attach to themselves the regalia of authority and feel that they and the state are now identical. Whereas during the struggle for independence they felt that they represented the nation and that all who disagreed with them were outside the national community and had allowed their souls to be possessed by the foreigner, now that they are in power they regard themselves and the state as identical and all those who disagree with them as enemies of the state.[24]

On the other side of the floor, where it is allowed to exist, the oppositional mentality retains all of its old forms. Bureaucratic administration is criticized as too remote and too impersonal. The government is charged with corruption; it is alleged to be "too distant" from the people and to be the betrayer of the national idea. It is accused of damaging the reputation of the country in the world, or of turning the country over to a new form of foreign control.

The oppositional mentality of the third stage, however, possesses one feature which the second did not possess—i.e., disillusionment. Whereas the opposition of the second generation imagined an amorphously happy condition once their antagonists were removed, the oppositional mentality of the postcolonial period has no such utopian euphoria to assuage its present melancholy.

Oppositionalism, which was so involved in an intense politicization, tends among some of those who are out of power to shrivel into an antipolitical passivity. It is not that politics no longer engages the attention. It still does, but among many intellectuals it has become a source of despondent inaction.

Among others, a quite substantial bloc, it flows into a more rigid form of activistic extremism. In some instances this extremist

24. Mr. Nehru was something of an exception, although he too regarded the opposition as an unavoidable pestilence, as an inconvenient part of the community which remains, notwithstanding, as much a part of the community as he himself was. At the other extreme was that other intellectual in politics, Dr. Nkrumah, who regarded any criticism or disagreement as *staatsfeindlich*.

alternative to passivity takes on a traditionalistic guise; in others it assumes a Leninist visage. Both of these foster the intense and total rejection of the muddled, compromising, and often compromised, incumbent government, in the name of a higher ideal.

V

Practically every new state has begun its career with a commitment to a regime of representative government and public liberties. Whatever might be the democratic and consultative elements in the indigenous tradition of government, the particular constitution which was actually chosen to give form to self-government is evidence of the role of intellectuals in the establishment of the new states. It was only through the influence of the intellectuals in contact with the modern political ideas which circulated in the larger world that this decision could have been made. This alone would be sufficient to testify to the still living inheritance of the notables who peopled the first stage of modern political life in the then colonial countries.

The fate of the new states, whether they persist and flourish as democracies or whether they regress into more oligarchical forms of government, is as undeterminable as anything which lies in the future. As long, however, as they do not disintegrate into tribal and local territorial sovereignties, and as long as they at least aspire to be "modern," the intellectuals will go on playing a large role in the fulfillment of whatever possibilities fortune allots to their societies.

In most of the new states the intellectuals still constitute a notable part of the ruling political elite, although their position is no longer as preponderant as when politics were a charismatic movement. Politics, as the new states were consolidated, became a profession and ceased to be a calling or a mission. The emerging professional politician, military or civilian in origin, is forced to be less of an intellectual in his outlook. The inevitability of the formation of a political machine has meant, and will continue even more to mean, that organizers with little intellectual disposition, interest, or sympathy will move into a more prominent position in the political elite. Back-benchers and party functionaries will include a very considerable proportion of place-holders, and the tasks they will have to perform will not be very attractive to intellectuals living in the traditions of modern intellectuals.

Nonetheless, even on the government benches, if the regime continues to be more or less democratic there will remain some readiness of the professional party leaders to receive and sponsor intellectuals. The prestige of modern education will continue to be high, and any political party and government will therefore wish to draw on its beneficiaries. Furthermore, the reservoir of persons available for political leadership will continue to be limited in the foreseeable future; this will force the party leaders to look in the direction of the intellectuals, however reluctantly. At the same time, however, the oppositional tendencies of intellectuals and the hypersensitivity to criticism on the part of politicians of any sort—and of the politicians of new states in particular—will add to this reluctance.

Opposition parties, insofar as they are allowed to exist, will certainly draw on intellectuals for their critical ideas concerning the government and for leadership and following. Such parties are their natural home.

As the underdeveloped countries become completely oligarchical and are ruled by a military junta or a single party, the role of intellectuals in political life in the narrower sense will certainly decline. The diminution of public political life will tend to narrow the area permitted to intellectuals. Even then, single-party regimes are likely, because of their ideological nature, to find a place for some intellectuals within their leading circles.[25]

Regardless of the fate of democracy in underdeveloped countries, intellectuals will undoubtedly continue to be called upon for the civil service and for higher education. There will be increasing scope for intellectuals as the governments expand the range of their activities and as the demand grows for highly qualified persons for engineering, teaching, publicity and propaganda, health and social services, and research in social and natural sciences.

If the new states avoid the fate of the Latin American countries in the first century of their independence, and progress economically and socially, then indifferently of the political regime which rules them, the intellectual classes will become larger and more differentiated, and more fully incorporated into their own cultural institutional system in a variety of technological, administrative, educational, and therapeutic capacities.

This incorporation of the intellectuals into their own societies will depend to a large extent on the establishment of an equilibrium between the demand for and the supply of intellectuals. If there always is such a surplus of university and college graduates that their salaries are low and many of them have to take posts which they

25. The professional army officer in the new states is to a certain extent an intellectual since he, especially in the technical branches, is the recipient of a modern education. In fact, the intrusion of the military into politics, in the Middle East at least, may be partly attributed to their attachment to modern ideas about order, efficiency, and probity in government, ideas which are not part of the indigenous tradition of government and which come to them through their modern training. The military coups d'état which have occurred in many of the new states may be interpreted as, at least in part, revolutions of the technological intelligentsia acting on behalf of modern ideas of efficiency and progress.

regard as unsuitable, the process of incorporation will be obstructed. Instead, the oppositional mentality will go on reproducing itself. Where a public political life is permitted, there they will be a perpetual source of unsettledness.[26]

Let us imagine that the economies of the new states develop toward greater productivity and that a measure of liberal political life survives the burdens under which the new states now labor. The intellectual classes will become more diversified than they are at present as they find employment in applied science and technology, in governmental, industrial, and commercial administration, in scientific and scholarly research, and in the profession of letters. With this diversification there will be less unity of sentiment, less sense of a common identity among them.

There will be more specialization, more philistinism, and a less general cultural sympathy in the new intelligentsia than in the old. The new intelligentsia will also be much less political in its outlook and more practical and professional. Each intellectual profession will, as it has long since done in the advanced countries, nurture its own traditions and ways of working. As in the past, these traditions will draw on the more differentiated and more elaborate intellectual traditions of the advanced countries. Creativity will come to be more appreciated, and one necessary condition for its realization will thus be provided. The intellectuals of the underdeveloped countries will cease in the course of this process to be as dependent and provincial as they are now. They will become, as some already are, full citizens, with completely equal status, in the intellectual community of the world.

The opportunities for fruitful and satisfying employment of the skills of the intellectuals in the various spheres of civil and economic life and the establishment of absorbing and guiding traditions of an autonomous creativity in intellectual life proper will foster an attenuation of ideological dispositions. It can never eradicate them but it can reduce the commonness of their occurrence and mollify

---

26. This, in turn, would increase the demand for an ideological oligarchy, from outside the government, and would also impel the government itself to adopt oligarchical measures.

There is also the opposite danger of a disequilibrium in the relations between the intellectuals and the central institutional system arising from an excessive demand for intellectuals in technological and administrative roles. In countries which entered upon independence with an insufficient supply of qualified intellectuals and a very scanty complement of intellectual institutions, it is definitely possible to draw practically all of the best intellectuals into executive and technological roles, leaving too few for civil and intellectual functions. The rapid growth of the public services and the general trend toward the governmental preemption of so many diverse functions might well result in too small a proportion of the intellectual classes being left free for independent creative work and for vital activity in that publicistic borderland between the intellectual and the political.

their asperity. Many with political interests will no longer feel the urgent obligation to participate directly in day-to-day political life. More of them will be content to play an equally vital but less immediate part in the formation of the life of their countries. They will concern themselves less than they do now with the issues of the here and now, and will deal with problems which are of longer-run significance, more remote from the immediate issues of party politics and of the prospects and favors of the incumbent political elite. The indirect influence on politics which comes from the cultivation of the matrix of opinion, and from the provision of the personnel and the institutional conditions of long-term development, will bring satisfaction to a larger proportion than it now does, and politicians will perhaps learn to appreciate the equal and perhaps even greater value to the community of this kind of activity on the part of intellectuals.

Their direct participation in politics will probably continue to have a radical bent. The traditions of the modern intellectual are too deeply rooted and the tendency is too intrinsic to the exercise of intellectual powers for this to be avoided—even if it were ever desirable. The radicalism of the intellectual's politics need not, however, be revolutionary or ideological; it can also work within the civil order. In the espousal of this standpoint at the center of political decision, in party councils, in parliaments and in cabinets, the intellectual will continue to have a unique and indispensable role, the abdication of which cannot be compensated for by purely intellectual creativity or the efficient performance of executive, technological, and educational functions. In order, however, for this possibility to exist, the political society—the civil order itself—must first come into existence.

This brings us to one of the prototypical paradoxes of political development. For the intellectuals to inherit their true estate, they must live in a political society. But this civil order cannot be achieved unless the intellectuals, who would be among its greatest beneficiaries, help, against the greatest difficulties, to bring it about. Some of these difficulties reside within the intellectuals themselves, within the political and cultural traditions which enter into their constitution. The outcome then depends on whether those intellectuals who speak for civility in a modern society will by their talents, virtue, and good fortune be able to outweigh their own inhibitions, the dense incivility of their fellow intellectuals, and the rocky obduracy of the traditional order.

20 Intellectuals, Public Opinion, and Economic Development

Economic development in the West proceeded, until the latter part of the nineteenth century, without the aid of intellectuals. Neither the innovators in technology nor the enterprisers and managers of industrial firms were highly educated; nor were they generally interested in intellectual matters. The world of finance contained a few exceptions to this proposition, such as David Ricardo, Samuel Rogers, and George Grote, but it, too, moved without the aid of economists or other professional or avocational intellectuals. The graduates of universities stood aloof from the practical work of commerce and industry in their countries; they went into scholarship, into theology and the church, into administration (first in Germany and then gradually in the rest of the countries of Europe), into medicine and the law, but they did not enter into the central stream of the economic life of their countries. Even in Great Britain, where the intellectuals' interest in economic life was greatest, their participation in the conduct of economic affairs was minimal. In France, a little was owed to a handful of important businessmen with Saint-Simonian sympathies, but that was about all. In Germany, a higher education and intellectual interests were practically guarantees against sympathetic participation in creative economic activity; and in the United States, the great enterprisers were neither educated nor intellectual.

Fortunately, at the time there was no need for intellectuals in economic life. A tradition of inventive and artful craftsmanship, especially in the engineering trades and those closely related to it, and indomitable ambition and resourcefulness among businessmen provided the motors for the enormous economic progress of Europe from the sixteenth to the end of the nineteenth century. Here and there a great physicist or mathematician invented a machine which found application in industry, but for the most part their mechanical inventions were toys; by far the great majority of practical technological innovations was produced by men who worked within the traditions of a trade, as entrepreneurs or employees. The nurture of technological development through the deliberate cultivation and

Previously published in a slightly different form in *World Politics*, vol. 10, no. 2 (January 1958), pp. 232-55. © 1958 by Princeton University Press.

application of science came only at the end of this period. It was only in the present century, above all in the chemical field, that the graduates of institutions of higher learning began to play a significant part in industry, by virtue of the specific knowledge and the scientific outlook which were absorbed by them in courses of technological and scientific study. Only in the twentieth century have great laboratories of scientific research, pure as well as applied, been established by large corporate enterprises and trade associations. Plastics, synthetic fibers, light metals, jet propulsion—these and many other advances characteristic of modern industrial technique have been made through research conducted by graduates of departments of physics, mathematics, chemistry, metallurgy, aeronautics, etc., of the great universities and technical colleges. Important innovations in industrial and commercial organization have been promoted by engineers and scientists trained in the laboratories of such institutions. Even so, a large part of the driving force of contemporary industrial development in the countries which are improving their efficiency and are substantially raising the standards of living of their people—for example, Canada, the United States, Belgium, Italy, and Western Germany—still comes from outside the educated classes. Enterprise still draws its ethos from traditions which are not widely shared by the intellectuals.

The situation of the newly emerged countries, such as India, Indonesia, Burma, Malaysia, Ghana, and Ceylon, is rather different. These countries are without innovating craftsmen in industry or innovating, risk-taking, industrial entrepreneurs. Their craftsmen, however skillful, work within definite and restrictive traditions and require close supervision when confronted by new problems; their industrial entrepreneurs on a larger scale have been chiefly foreigners, while their own big businessmen find their talents drawn to commerce and finance. The dramatic initiative for industrial development in these countries draws little sustenance from the strata which in Europe and America created an industrial ascendancy. The most enthusiastic support for industrialization and modernization comes from those who have been in contact with the West, either in Europe or America or through Western intrusions and representatives in their own countries. The accepted contact with the West has been predominantly through Western educational institutions and Western-founded or Western-inspired colleges and universities at home. The type and scale of industry which the educated seek are those now existing in the West (including the Soviet Union). The undramatic germination of small-scale industrial enterprises from the efforts of ambitious independent craftsmen arouses neither their attention nor their admiration. The proponents of industrialization and modernization—although not necessarily the sole or even most effective agents—are largely intellectuals, and their conception of industrialization is largely that of intellectuals without technological education or experience of economic responsibility. In most of the new countries, prevailing opinion does not believe that industrial development will come about through the processes that produced it in the West. Planning, governmental initiative and even management, the deliberate application of scientific outlook and procedure to industrial problems—these are the means which are expected to raise the level of industrial output and efficiency. This view rests in some measure on a derogatory conception of business-men as either exploitative foreigners or money-grubbing, short-sighted, native manipulators of financial combinations. There is no confidence in their constructive powers and in their willingness to take risks, or even in their readiness to add to their wealth through industry. In fact, of course, this disesteem for business enterprises derives from a deeper disesteem for their function and activity as such. The intellectuals' traditional distrust of the man of business is in part a religious matter, in part a product of the scope and strength of the kinship system. Whatever the source, it seems clear that the ruling groups in new countries are not inclined to entrust much of the responsibility for their industrial advance to private businessmen.

The alternative source of personnel for industrial progress there-fore must necessarily be the intellectuals—the university-trained government official, the scientist, the economist, the engineer with a systematic training at a technological college rather than an empirical training at the workbench.

Economists well trained in both theoretical and applied eco-nomics are even more integral to the promulgation and execution of schemes for economic development in the newer countries than they are in long-established countries with a large stratum of experienced and forceful businessmen. A country like the United Kingdom, which decided to launch itself into governmentally planned economic life after the Second World War, could supplement an able civil service with a substantial body of experienced businessmen, and it could draw into government service a group of university-trained economists who had hitherto been engaged in teaching, research, and writing, in universities and independent research institutes and for economic periodicals. The poorer countries have no such resources. The more fortunate among them have a small number of high-grade economists taken from the universities and the civil service. They have very few businessmen to enlist into their service (and even if they had them they would be reluctant to use them). The less fortunate lack nearly all these resources. Their most vigorous personalities have chosen politics as a career. Their most acute minds are already in administration. They have very few industrialists conducting large-scale operations.

Most of these countries could use more highly qualified economists, economist-administrators, and statisticians than are available at present. Their vast schemes of construction—hydroelectric installations, factories, railways, etc.—all require engineers trained in higher technological institutions. The improvement of their agriculture requires research and extension work which will demand men with appropriate university training. Moreover, the aspiration in almost all the new countries for a "welfare state" can be met only if there are far larger numbers of well-trained teachers at every level from primary to university, whose activities will range from rarefied intellectual analysis to extramural work in villages in the hinterland; of physicians and social workers; and, as literacy spreads, of journalists, scenario writers, authors, and critics. Programs of economic and social progress will thus depend for their fulfillment on the executive action of large numbers of intellectuals.

Perhaps never before in world history have intellectuals had such responsibilities and opportunities for the exercise of authority and creativity within the central institutions of their own societies. The need is for men of practical judgment and factual curiosity, with a capacity to appreciate small increments of growth and to understand the complexities and intractabilities which creative economic activity confronts. Yet the qualifications of the intellectuals for these grandiose tasks and possibilities are problematic. There are ample lawyers, bachelors of arts with moderate literary interests, and a fair number of polemical and hortatory publicists. Among the numerous intellectuals there are scattered a small number of men who are first-class by the highest standards. They work against great disadvantages.

II

The newly emergent countries in Asia are the heirs of a powerful intellectual tradition, predominantly religious. The religious sage has thus enjoyed the highest esteem, and the religious conquest of the self, or individuality, has been one of the highest goods, if not the highest. Nonattachment to the objects of this world and purification of the spirit by avoidance of the gratifications offered by contact with living and nonliving material objects have been central features of the tradition of intellectual activity in these countries. Moreover, because the religious component has been so preponderant in the cultural tradition, much of the most refined intelligence has been devoted to the interpretation of texts. The traditional institutions of learning have concentrated on the exegesis of sacred texts. The experience of everyday social intercourse, the experience of the craftsman and reflection thereon, and curiosity about the world of natural phenomena, physical and biological, have been absent from the range of activities of the traditional intelligentsia in these countries.

At present the traditional intellectuals, such as the *pandits* in India, are looked upon with condescending pity or outright contempt by the modern intelligentsia in these countries. What the traditional intelligentsia regards as sacred, its modern counterpart regards as superstition or triviality. There is little contact between these two sections of the intellectual classes. Their modes of life, their intellectual satisfactions and curiosities seem to be poles apart. Nonetheless a deeper affinity exists between them, with important implications for economic development.

The affinity is evident in the theoretical and literary tendencies of the modern intelligentsia in the underdeveloped countries. There are many reasons why the novel has not flourished in non-Western countries other than Japan, but one reason is a deficiency in the sense of concrete, everyday reality. Naturalistic description of ordinary situations and concreteness of recall are both scantily developed in novels and biographies in the economically under-developed countries. This is one expression of a state of mind that reaches far beyond the literary world. How few study engineering or natural sciences, especially the experimental biological and physical sciences, in relation to those studying humanistic subjects! The readiness to immerse oneself in empirical enquiry—which has enough of its own dangers, as we see in America—and especially in the disciplines that require fieldwork, is strikingly scant among the best minds in the educated classes in most underdeveloped countries.

This situation is in part attributable to the impact of the West. The Western rulers created secondary schools, universities, and colleges in countries like India, Burma, and Indonesia, to supply the needed middle- and lower-level civil servants, the highest positions being reserved for their own nationals or for persons of local origin who had met the highest intellectual requirements of the metro-politan university system. Subsequently, when colleges were founded by local initiative, before and after independence, they were of the same sort. These colleges were not intended to make men into scientists and engineers. This was so in part because in the nineteenth century the chief colonial power, the United Kingdom, did not produce scientists and engineers in its own universities and did not think that it was the task of universities to do so. It was also a result of the absence of employment opportunities for native engineers and scientists. To the extent that the then dependent countries were industrialized, their higher technical personnel were imported from the metropolis. There was no incentive or stimulant to the growth of a technological sensitivity in the educated classes, and so no scientific or engineering tradition could find support.

The origins of the relative indifference toward the intellectual and practical mastery of nature and of the relatively weak feeling for concrete reality can thus be seen to be rooted both in the older traditions of each country and in recent traditions established by the method of domination employed by the foreign ruler. Because of these traditions, the educated classes of the underdeveloped countries, however much they believe in the saving graces of science and technology, have a largely literary or rhetorical relationship to them.

Moreover, although there has been a revival of appreciation for the inherent qualities of traditional art, music, sculpture, and religious philosophy, there is still more prestige attributed to a thorough familiarity with the culture of the West, even in India and other Asian countries possessing traditional cultures of universal value. It is not only the man who has studied at Oxford, Cambridge, Heidelberg, or Paris—or even Cambridge, Massachusetts—who is deferred to, but the person who, whether he has studied abroad or not, is intimate with the contents of the *New Statesman* and the *Economist,* who knows about Bertrand Russell, T. S. Eliot, Hemingway, Sartre, Graham Greene, Camus, Auden, and Faulkner, who is at home in the conflicts within the British Labour Party and in the plays of Samuel Beckett. Even among scientists in Asian countries, work seems to be done for an invisible jury of scientists in England, the United States, and Germany, while other scientists working in the same fields at home are less frequently thought of or referred to. This location of the intellectual center of gravity in foreign, indeed Western, countries, might—and to some extent should—be attributed to a more realistic or more refined appreciation of the superior quality of scientific, literary, and philosophical work in the West. This is, however, by no means the only reason for the displacement of the intellectual center of gravity; if it were, it would not injure the cause of national improvement and economic development. It is because this displacement fundamentally arises from xenophilia that it harms the culture, science, and economy of the underdeveloped countries.

The coexistence of xenophilia with fervent nationalism does not diminish its distracting consequences. Indeed, extremist nationalism is often an unconscious expiation for guilt-generating but status-enhancing xenophilia. The harmfulness of xenophilia does not lie in its alleged "separation of the intellectuals from the people," for which the intellectuals in backward countries are often criticized by intellectuals themselves, by political leaders who are antagonistic to them, and by foreign observers.

Intellectuals in all countries are "separated from the people," and so they should be. No society can have its indispensable division of labor if the different skills which it requires are not also associated with differentiated tastes and outlooks. No society would be worthy of even the slightest respect if it did not allow people to be somewhat separate from each other; even totalitarian regimes, which demand homogeneity of taste and outlook, must permit some of these differences and separateness, however unwillingly. Xenophilia is injurious because it manifests and fosters a severely deficient empathy for the states of mind of one's fellow countrymen, a lack of intimacy with the social and material environment, and thus, at bottom, a form of blindness to the capacities and incapacities of one's fellow countrymen, to their problems, and to their disposition to rouse themselves to do something about them. It expresses and reproduces the feebleness of the sense of affinity that unites a population into a modern nation. This "social scotoma" is not in the first instance a product of Westernization; it is a product of a hierarchical society in which the higher castes and classes have little feeling for those beneath them; it is furthered by the still undissolved cleavages which are generated by an overwhelmingly strong system of extended kinship. It is also a product of the religious tradition of nonattachment, which the more advanced religions of Hinduism, Buddhism, and Islam praise as the highest good, and which their vital existence in still very tangibly religious cultures renders into a frequently encountered reality.

III

Fruitful economic development, which will not only result in increasing the absolute numbers of metal lathes or planing machines or shipping tonnage, but which will contribute, through a self-generating, autonomous process, to raising the productivity and standard of living of the society, requires—in addition to capital and skilled manpower and natural resources—adaptable and realistic judgment in economic enterprise and, in the criticism of economic development through planning, an emphasis upon the adequacy of planning and administrative personnel. This is a just emphasis, and the first part of this article has been directed to an examination of certain inherited obstacles to such adequacy. But sufficient attention has not been paid to the machinery and personnel for critical evaluation of what the planners and administrators have done. Insofar as this problem is treated at all, it seems to be taken for granted that the government will do its own evaluation, or that foreign experts will be called in by the government to assess the effectiveness or the balance of various development projects or even the scheme of development as a whole.

This is insufficient. The government should not be its own sole judge. Such it will be, however, if it monopolizes the machinery, personnel, and opportunity for factual evaluation of past activities and prospective plans. Nor can foreign experts be relied upon for such assessments. They will usually lack the concrete sense of the situation without which there can be no realism, and, furthermore, they will too often flatter the government in that disingenuously condescending way which Western experts have of patting the heads of their colleagues in the economically underdeveloped countries. This means that evaluation and criticism must be carried on by independent organs within the country, staffed by independent personalities of the same culture as those they criticize.

It is not sufficient that the planners and executors of the plans should be well educated and hard headed, well schooled in economic theory and experienced in economic administration. With all these qualities and with good will, too, those who make plans and try to carry them out acquire a vested emotional interest in what they are doing. They tend to gloss over their failures, to overlook obstacles, and in general to avoid the self-criticism necessary for better action in the future. There are extenuating reasons for this: the senior officials with the experience and the vantage point which would enable them to formulate a coherent and realistic view are ordinarily so very heavily burdened that they have neither time nor energy to muster unaided the detached and comprehensive outlook required. (There are not enough highly qualified men to go around, and the vast overstaffing at the lower levels of the government service does nothing to mitigate this.)

Furthermore, practically all of the higher civil servants and economic advisers are intellectuals by training and disposition. They are modern in their outlook and Western in their cultural orientation (if not necessarily in their politics). As such, they tend to be distrusted by the politicians, who though often intellectuals themselves are more populistic and even demagogic, and therefore critical of those who have studied abroad, who live in a more or less Western style at home, and whose university and intellectual attainments are often higher than their own. In addition, the administrators are often at a psychological disadvantage vis-à-vis the politicians, because while the politicians were fighting for national independence, many of the higher administrators were serving the foreign ruler in the civil service or in educational institutions dominated by foreigners. The administrators are sensitive to the commonly held and frequently expressed criticism directed against them on these grounds, and this weakens their will to oppose the often unrealistic aspirations of their political superiors. For all these reasons, effective self-criticism within the government is bound to be insufficient. And since so many of the new countries wish to move in a more or less socialistic direction, the criticism which the competitive market and bankruptcy provide in the system of private capitalism cannot be effective. Hence, detailed and constructive criticism from outside the government—in other words, an effective public opinion—is an imperative condition of sound and not merely quantitative economic progress.

Although the economic planning in the Soviet satellite states of Eastern Europe failed in part because of the burden of Soviet exploitation of these "colonial" economies, the failure was aggravated by the fact that the planners and higher administrators were deprived of the benefit of independent criticism which might have made them more aware of their errors and the means of overcoming them. This kind of critical public opinion needs freedom from government control or censorship—and in most of the new countries outside the area of communist rule, this freedom exists sufficiently. It also needs something more than freedom from external sanctions. It needs well-trained intellectuals who are interested in politics whatever their professional expertise; it needs shrewd economists and sharp-witted, actively inquiring minds with a sense of responsibility, with practical acumen, and a strong devotion to the well-being of their country which stops short of doctrinairism and fanaticism. Such people are in short supply everywhere, and especially so in underdeveloped countries. It needs, moreover, the institutions of critical opinion—an economically independent press, sound research organizations within and outside universities, and civic and interest associations, as well as a parliament which by its debates and inquiries will inform that part of the citizenry which is concerned with affairs beyond the tip of its nose. These institutions too are inadequately developed in the new and economically underdeveloped countries.

In almost all these new countries, the short supply of talented and trained intellectuals is accentuated by the large-scale operations of the governments. The best are taken into the government at larger salaries, with higher prestige and better conditions of service than they could find in universities and colleges, on newspapers and reviews, or in native-owned private business. In consequence, the instructed public opinion in the middle classes and in the country at large is disarmed at its very center, when, thanks to the heritage of cultural and political traditions, that center was weak enough to begin with.

The chief organs of an instructed public opinion—of a critical attitude which shares the general objectives of the government, feels a tie of solidarity with it, and wishes it well as one wishes oneself well—are the press, parliament, the universities, and civic and interest associations. Where the radio broadcasting system is in the hands of the government or a public corporation, it requires a great deal of subtlety and sophistication on the part of the broadcasting administrators to attain a stage where criticism of government actions is permitted; this stage has not yet been attained in underdeveloped countries. The press—both the newspaper and periodical press—must carry the heaviest burden of responsible criticism and the instruction of public and governmental opinion.

The other burdens of the press in these new countries are so great, however, that they can scarcely carry the last straw, which is the government's preemption of so many of the best publicists, actual and prospective, and their consequent removal from journalistic circulation. Some of the other burdens are perfectly well known—for example, the high illiteracy rates and the poverty of the mass of the population, which restrict the circulation of newspapers and therewith the income from sales and advertising by private business. Newspapers, as a result, exist usually on a very narrow margin and come to depend on government advertisements or announcements for a larger share of their advertising revenue than is the case in the West. One resounding instance of sanctions imposed by a provincial government against a single critical newspaper by withdrawal of advertising goes a long way: most other newspapers become extremely cautious about criticizing the government on points about which it is sensitive. It also makes for circumspection in inquiring closely into such subjects. Even the economically strongest newspapers are cautious about giving the hospitality of their columns to well-informed critics, however responsible and cogent, when they wish above all not to have trouble with the government.

The poverty of the press also means that, for the vast majority of journalists, salaries are poor. The press consequently finds it difficult to attract and retain high-grade young men. Staffs have to be kept small, with the result that there cannot be sufficient specialization to develop the expertise necessary for useful evaluation and criticism of economic programs. In addition to these immediate impediments to the formation of an instructed, constructively critical, responsible public opinion, there are others which are more deeply rooted in the past. In the first place, the state of nonattachment to the objects of the phenomenal world, a product of the great traditions of some of the new countries, is expressed in journalism as factual uninterestedness. It is not that false facts are deliberately presented—although that is not infrequent; rather there is lacking that avidity for facts, that deep curiosity to know "what, where, when," which marks the good journalist and also the high-caliber analyst and commentator on current events.

This unfactual disposition is reinforced by journalistic traditions inherited from the period of the struggle for national independence. Aside from the foreign-owned and foreign-edited newspapers and periodicals, the main style of the press during the time of foreign rule was hortatory and polemical. The meticulous search for details and matter-of-fact analysis were not regarded as necessary or appropriate, except among a restricted band of liberal nationalists whose patrician liberalism was swept away with the rest of the Victorian inheritance by the more populistic nationalism which came to the fore in the second quarter of the present century. Denunciation in rhetorical grandeur and perpetual complaint about all manner of iniquities were poor preparation for discriminating appraisal and criticism. The outsider who does not face the possibility that his party might come to power does not develop the empathy for the concrete problems which afflict the person holding the responsibility of office. Journalism in colonial countries was the service of a higher cause, not a profession or a business, and the journalism of the underdeveloped countries bears that mark today. Editors do not on the whole expect their reporters to dig for facts, even if they wanted them to do so. Reporters do not think that they are called upon to unearth facts as part of their job; they feel their explorations are over when they have been given a briefing or a "handout" by a government press officer. As a result, the press tends to be stuffed with reports of speeches by cabinet ministers and members of parliament, and with the substance of official releases. Leaders and turnover articles are not based on ample study of the details of governmental or private economic policy and activity. They tend to be very general and either affirmative or denunciatory, without differentiated argument. Even significant reports, very factual in character, by parliamentary inquiry committees find no response in the press because they are not in harmony with the tradition of the profession, which still finds it easier to write about Western foreign policy and the misbehavior of white people toward colored people than about the day-to-day problems of the societies themselves.

It should also be said that the governmental machinery for making detailed information available is not always very useful. The reports of parliamentary proceedings take a very long time to appear in print. Reports of governmental departments and public corporations appear only after much delay and are hard to come by. The government is certainly at least reluctant to have its actions critically analyzed, thus continuing the practices of the foreign rulers.

There are other obstacles to the emergence and effectiveness of responsible criticism of governmental policies in the new countries. Even if the full supply of facts were accessible, responsible sympathizers with these policies would be reluctant to criticize the government in public. The most secure as well as the most unstable of the new states are feeling their way amidst great difficulties, and some of their more circumspect intellectuals appreciate their national independence too much to wish to give the appearance, above all to foreigners but also to their own public, of "letting the side down" by public criticism. They are aware that their new state rests on weak foundations which are recurrently shaken by traditionalistic and communal loyalties, and on an impoverished and depressed peasantry, and they wish to avoid anything that would enfeeble the authority of the government or hamper its efforts to create a vigorous consensus in support of its steps to improve the economic life of the country. This reserve on the part of some of the very best informed and most intelligent intellectuals in the newly established nation is accompanied by the hierarchical traditions of the society, which endow those in authority with charisma and thus make it unthinkable to criticize them. (This traditional attitude, which heightens sensitivity to the charismatic component of authority, is also responsible in a great many cases for much irrational, unfactual criticism, since the new ruling institutions are bureaucratic and untraditional and therefore lacking in the preponderantly charismatic quality which is prized in religious cultures. This is one of the important sources of conflict among the politically interested intellectuals.)

In the press of the new countries, there is no dearth of abusive criticism. Some comes from sensation-mongers, some from those who wish ill to the government, some from disappointed idealists whose struggle for national independence was motivated by deep ethical feelings and an ideal of a dignified national existence which has not yet been realized. Practically none of this criticism is matter-of-fact or well informed about the dreadfully difficult problems of trying to govern a disunited, traditionalist population by methods appropriate to modern unified countries. Abusive criticism is like the barking of an ill-natured dog; it is heeded only when it is expressed by a party or an interest group strong enough to do political damage. It is never looked to as a source of welcome and helpful guidance. The hostile critics, even those who share the general aims of the government, lack both the factual sense and the facts themselves on the basis of which realistic assessment could be made and constructive suggestions offered. The governments of the new states respond to this criticism by suppression and persecution. They promote their own press, which says what they want to hear.

Against this background it will easily be seen how little opportunity the planning officials and administrators have to receive
sympathetic and thoroughly informed criticism from intellectuals,
who, although outside the government, are not so much outside the
world of official concerns that they are unaware of the massive facts
and the imponderable matrix in which the facts rest.

Likewise, the aid which the press could give to legislators in
following the work of the executive and in forming a picture of the
true state of affairs in the country is not given, and the information
and assessment which the politically interested public needs are not
provided. Legislators are thus rendered further dependent on the
executive and on the central office of the ruling party.

IV

An effectively critical and independent evaluation of economic
policies and practices cannot now be fully carried out by the
newspaper and periodical press. Much of the work of the press in
this regard depends on more basic inquiries, such as should be
conducted, and in some countries are conducted, by the staffs of
independent universities and colleges and research institutes. The
views of these scholars, in the form of journal articles, monographs,
books, lectures and seminars, and newspaper and periodical articles,
can contribute greatly to the guidance and to the critical understanding of governmental action. The formal convocation of university intellectuals as consultants and advisers on governmental
economic activities is no substitute for these other forms of
expression of opinion, however desirable and important it is in itself.
Such occasional drawing-in of the better university economists and
anthropologists can provide, under favorable conditions, a more
detached and broader perspective which the planners and administrators cannot get themselves. Fruitful consultation is possible,
however, only where the consultants can draw upon a rich stock of
knowledge which they have accumulated through their own and
other scholars' research.

Unlike the situation in the West, the academic life in the new
countries has no strong tradition of detached factual research on issues
of importance to the public good. The work of the Oxford Institute
of Statistics, the Cambridge Department of Applied Economics, the
National Bureau of Economic Research, so closely connected with
Columbia University; the continuous stream of individual studies by
qualified university economists, sociologists, and political scientists,
of the problems, policies, and activities of concern to the government; and the research publications of para-academic institutions
like the National Institute of Economic and Social Research in

London, the Acton Society in London, the Brookings Institution in Washington—these have no counterparts in the new countries. The small Gokhale Institute of Economics and Political Science in Poona is almost unique in underdeveloped countries for its intellectual independence from government and for its empirical bent. The Council of Economic and Industrial Research in New Delhi, although formally independent, seems to be largely confined by its terms of reference to problems referred to it by the government of India. Such a framework of problem selection, although it need not damage the probity of the inquiry, certainly deprives the government of the advantages of more detached study of plans for economic development.

There is at present virtually no tradition of impartial social research outside the universities in the new countries, and the Committee on Research Programs of the Planning Commission (in India), UNESCO, and other agencies seem blamelessly to be doing very little to foster it. Nor is the prospect for improvement very bright. Because the universities and the government draw from the same stream, the universities are about as hard put to it as the press to create a tradition of detached factual analysis of governmental economic policy and practice. If a young man is very outstanding in his academic career at home, he either goes abroad to continue his studies or he is taken into the government. When a well-trained young man comes back from a Western university with an advanced degree and with some training in rigorous analysis, a respect and feeling for concrete facts, and an ability to investigate and interpret economic situations, he is usually offered a post in a ministry and also one in a college or university. If he accepts the former, he will probably enjoy—in addition to a higher salary—greater prestige, the feeling of helping his country in the immediate future, and the prospect of company of other persons of outstanding intellectual and cultural qualifications. If he accepts the university or college post, he will have, in addition to a poor salary—sometimes very much lower than the governmental salary—a dreary round of teaching and routine duties and a library very inferior to the library of the ministry; the ministry gets some important books from London and New York as soon after publication as modern transportation allows, while the college or university libraries get them a long time later, if at all. He will, furthermore, have older colleagues who are jealous of his intellectual attainments and ambition and who are unable or unwilling to provide stimulating intellectual companionship. If he teaches in a college he will usually have no research facilities, and if he ever produces manuscripts under such difficult conditions he will usually go out-of-pocket in order to get them typed. And once typed, their publication in book form faces almost insuperable obstacles in the form of the tiny reading public and the disorganized state of the publishing world. So in most cases the government appointment is accepted, and, apart from a small and wholly admirable group of distinguished exceptions, the colleges and universities become the receptacles of the leftovers and the second class. Few indeed are the outstanding young men who leave government service for the university; far more go the opposite way. And so the cycle goes, reinforcing itself with every completion.

Again the result is the same as in the case of the press. The government's planning activities are deprived of a realistic and well-informed scrutiny which, while understanding the difficult problems the government is up against, tries from a wider and more detached point of view to indicate where the plans went wrong and what the planners can do to avoid such errors. Under present conditions, officials do not learn to benefit from criticism emanating from the universities; instead they maintain a secretiveness and touchiness which is injurious to efficiency in economic life and to political democracy. The press, parliament, and the public, which, at several removes, could assimilate the knowledge created by university research, go without the factual sustenance that public opinion needs if it is to keep government from persisting on a faulty course.

V

Frequent and considerable though its shortcomings might be, parliamentary politics generally contribute to the formation of public opinion. They do so, however, only through a continuing scrutiny and criticism of government and the consequent pressure on government to justify its actions in a reasoned manner. The reporting and comment on the ensuing debate in the press and the due notice of it in the more literate sections of the political public enter into the obscure channels through which public opinion is formed. In the underdeveloped countries, parliamentary life suffers either from the overwhelming preponderance of one major party, as in India, or from a plethora of smaller parties, no one of which has a sufficiently large majority to provide stable government and none of which can offer sound opposition. In most underdeveloped countries, legislators of the ruling parties—and this applies, too, to the opposition if any—have demonstrated their merits in the heroism and sacrifice of the campaign for national independence, rather than in particular professions and occupations requiring solid knowledge and responsibility in taking risks and running complex economic organizations. Even where their original educational attainments were high, years of political agitation, imprisonment, and the rough and tumble of oppositional journalism and politics left them standing where they were in their early twenties. Their equally gifted contemporaries who went into administration gained the advantage of elaborate knowledge and political experience. In the conflict which occurs in all governments between the civil servants and the legislators who would control them, and which is aggravated under conditions of underdevelopment and large-scale governmental economic operations, the legislators are at a disadvantage. They need all the help they can get from intellectuals in journalism and in the universities. Unfortunately that help is not forthcoming. For the most part the intellectuals in the press and the universities are unable to give it—for the reasons already examined—and their dispositions toward politicians are so unfriendly and derogatory that they would not give it if they could.

In some respects the back-bench legislator of the ruling and the opposition parties, the party politician, is as much disesteemed by the intellectuals of the underdeveloped countries as is the businessman. In any conflict between, on the one side, the few outstandingly charismatic political leaders who led the national struggle, and the civil service, and, on the other side, the ordinary legislator who was only a local or second-rank figure, the sympathies of the intellectual outside the government are with the former. The press and university intellectuals do little to aid this ordinary legislator. At the same time, because of their lack of curiosity, their lack of routine civil courage, and their "unfactuality," the intellectuals can do little to curb, by the force of exposure to the public eye, the improper pressures on the civil service which the ordinary legislator sometimes exercises on behalf of communal, religious, and even entirely private ends.

Thus, not only does public opinion not receive the benefits that can be conferred by a lively and self-confident parliamentary life, but parliamentary life itself suffers from the insufficient quality of the intellectuals who are left to the press and the institutions of higher education after the civil service has picked them over. The readiness of parliamentarians in single or multiparty regimes to function as rubber stamps, to confirm and acclaim the leadership, is partly a result of their defenselessness, which comes from being uninformed.

VI

In the countries which have undergone a slower and more decentralized development than the underdeveloped countries are contemplating, parliament and press and independent intelligentsia were joined by a mass of voluntary associations which sought to prevent abuses and to further their own aims. Such civic and interest associations are lacking in the underdeveloped societies. The modernization of these societies before independence was only partial and not very autonomous. The civil service and universities, which were the chief elements of modernity, were created and controlled by the foreign ruler; the only autochthonous modern institutions of public life were the oppositional press and agitational political movements. Large-scale native business enterprises, native ecclesiastical and philanthropic organizations, and public activities on behalf of any ends other than national revival and independence were absent. So political leadership in these sectors of society, which in modern Western countries plays an important part in the formation and expression of public opinion, was not called into existence. Local political life either was part of the struggle for national revival and independence or it was entirely traditional. The seedbed of modern civic life was scarcely prepared under colonial conditions.

Where modern interest organizations do exist, as in the case of manufacturers' or merchants' associations, they find it difficult to put their case in public. The atmosphere is unfavorable to their representations, and intellectuals are reluctant to enter their employ because they think that the service of business is a betrayal of the ideal. Communal and political associations express their demands more by personal representation and by public demonstration than by public debate and analysis. Thus although the underdeveloped countries are not free from pressure groups, their pressure groups do not express themselves through organs which would contribute to the improvements of the quality of public opinion.

This immense gap must be filled by intellectuals if it is to be filled at all. Intellectuals in underdeveloped countries must provide the administrative leadership and expertise which the traditions and situations of their countries, and their own prejudices, have thrust upon them. They must also create the public opinion and furnish the external expertise and judgment without which the plans of their governments will go astray.

VII

If the underdeveloped countries are to move in the direction to which they aspire, they must deal economically with their material resources. They will be able to do so only if they husband and cultivate their intellectual resources more effectively.

The task is terribly arduous and the territory is uncharted. Difficult though economic development is, there are precedents which give guidance. Intellectual development, which will pay due attention to the requirements of science, scholarship, and preparation for public service and which will try to do by deliberate arrangement what in the West for better or for worse has taken care of itself, is even more difficult; there are fewer precedents and more indeterminate factors.

In order for public opinion to work effectively, the critics must somehow feel their fundamental parity with those they criticize. The critics must not be rankled by feelings of exclusion and inferiority. Resentment, which comes from a sense of being excluded and dependent, inhibits frankness and darkens the power of reason. Hence central and provincial governments should attempt, insofar as it lies in their powers, to foster a sense of autonomy and self-esteem in the press and in the institutions of higher learning. This can be done in part by the studious avoidance of political pressure or the use of the powers of patronage which intentionally or unintentionally influence the free expression of publicistic or academic opinion. For example, appointments to senior positions should be made by boards which are entirely independent of the government. They should include academic persons from outside the state and, in some cases, even outside the country. More than this, financial and fiscal policies which can make the press and universities more economically self-sufficient should be pursued. For example, tax exemptions for advertising in newspapers and periodicals should be increased, and additional tax allowances should be made for private gifts to universities above specified amounts.

A further requirement in the same direction is the establishment of a greater parity of status between the higher civil service and the universities. The traditional respect for the scholar and teacher in Asia is a valuable asset which has become dilapidated as a result of the reverence in which powerful secular authority is held; it is most desirable that it be renewed in an appropriate modern form. The renewal of a tradition is, however, one of the least manageable of tasks. A rather roundabout approach which would have other favorable consequences would involve an improvement in the intellectual quality and financial rewards of the academic profession, at least on its higher reaches.

One or two first-class universities or colleges should be maintained with salary levels and conditions of service comparable to those which the higher civil service provides for equally qualified persons. This would prevent the government from making off with the best brains in the academic world. It would make the academic career just as attractive financially and intellectually as the higher civil service and would thus provide a base on which the informed assessment and criticism of economic policies and trends could be developed.

The absolute quantity of intellectuals of good quality in any underdeveloped country could conceivably be increased if the students who go to Western countries for advanced degrees could be better prepared before departure and better supervised during their periods of foreign study. At present there are many young people from the underdeveloped countries studying in Britain and the United States, representing a considerable investment of foreign exchange and of capital gifts made available by foreign governments and private institutions. Much of this seems to be poorly employed at present. Many of the students from underdeveloped countries are ill-adjusted in the countries to which they come; they idle away more of their time than seems necessary, and they conduct their studies in a half-hearted way. Would it not be possible for a university grants committee in each of the underdeveloped countries to establish, in cooperation with the major universities to which their students go, a better system of supervision and guidance than exists at present? Deans of students and "foreign-student advisers" who know nothing of the background of their charges and the problems that await them at home are hardly in a position to encourage the student to make more efficient use of his intellectual opportunities during his sojourn abroad.

Another useful measure would be the assimilation of retired senior civil servants into university teaching and research. Senior civil servants are among the most valuable intellectual resources in the underdeveloped countries, and it is wrong to allow them to rusticate when they retire. Many of them are at the height of their powers, and not only their keen intelligence but their general culture and their shrewd and experienced judgment of the current scene would be invaluable additions to university life and, through it, to educated public opinion.

The principle of a permanent higher civil service, which has been adopted by the new countries from the British model, has a great deal to commend it. It builds corporate morale and guarantees integrity and efficiency. Yet, from the point of view of bringing an outside perspective into government and of making outside criticism more concrete and more pertinent, some modification might be in order. Might it not be desirable to assign senior civil servants who have the appropriate desires and aptitudes to research or journalistic work or to teaching for periods of a year or two at a time, and then let them resume their posts at levels and seniorities which they would have enjoyed had they not taken leaves of absence? Such an experience might give economist civil servants a more critical perspective on the economic state of their country, and it would correspondingly instruct those with whom they came in contact during their "outside" period. A system resembling this, under the sponsorship of the Commonwealth Fund, is already in operation, sending civil servants of the administrative class abroad for study and research. The scheme proposed here would send them into the "foreign territory" of industry, journalism, or the university in their own countries, or other underdeveloped countries with problems similar to their own.

A parallel series of measures with respect to the press should be encouraged by the government, since it is desirable that journalists— as well as professors of the social sciences—should improve their understanding of economic life, and that they should be enabled to judge policies and actions in the framework of the real problems facing their country. The chances for this improvement would be enhanced if journalists and professors were given opportunities to participate in governmental and private economic enterprises as regular staff members with appropriate responsibilities, for periods of a year or two at a time, returning afterward to their newspapers or universities at the levels of seniority or rank they would have attained if they had not left.

The quality of journalists in the new countries would be improved if a system like the Niemann Fellowships were devised. This would allow opportunity for advanced academic study and research to those journalists who have shown most independence and intelligent persistence in pursuing some problem in the economic and political life of their countries. Once more advanced university centers are built up in the new countries, then the Fellows should be attached to these institutions rather than to Harvard, the London School of Economics, and the like. The regional and national press institutes founded under the inspiration of the International Press Institute have already shown promising results in this direction.

However excellent the fundamental good sense of inquirers in the fields of government and economics, if they do not have adequate statistical and other descriptive data at their disposal their comments can scarcely rise above the level of generalities and edifying counsel. Governments should therefore develop more adequate reporting practices, making it easier for journalists and research workers to learn, independently of government press officers, just what has been going on in their economies. Civil servants should be allowed to give to journalists or qualified research workers all information which need not be kept secret on grounds of military security. Departmental reports and those of parliamentary commissions of inquiry should be published promptly and should be readily available. Indeed, an overhaul of the government printing department and its system of public distribution is very necessary in most underdeveloped countries.

All these measures and many others which ought to be devised and instituted are intended to unify the different sections of the intellectual classes of the new countries, to make them more realistic in their attitudes, more appreciative of the real problems faced by their countries, more aware of their heavy responsibilities in the titanic undertaking of promoting economic and social development. These proposals might however be no more than advice to the wind. If intellectuals are willing to be time-servers or if, being better than time-servers, they take refuge in professional specialization or empty discontent, their influence will be negligible. Politicians and civil servants, jealous of their power and deaf to criticism, will then stagger on as well as they can in a field strewn with obstacles.

21 Demagogues and Cadres in the Political Development of the New States

The greatest menace to the political development of the new states is demagogy. The first condition of the establishment of a political order is the establishment of effective modern administrations, of stable institutions of public opinion, of modern educational systems, of public liberties, and of representative, deliberative, and legislative institutions. These are the prerequisites of the growth of a polity, of an order to which the inhabitants of the sovereign territory will feel they belong and to whose authorities they will attribute legitimacy. Demagogy, rhetorical charisma, sometimes appears to be a short cut to this. Demagogy, which used to be called "rabble-rousing" and which is now called "mobilization of the masses," by flamboyant oratory and the display of a radiating personality, involves the effort to incorporate the mass of the population into a great national effort. It almost always entails arousing the more responsive among them to demands and expectations which far exceed the possibility of fulfillment. It carries with it the inclination to arouse the "masses" to believe that the occasion of their persistently or momentarily felt grievances results from the deliberate action of the demagogue's opponents. Demagogy causes commotion; it produces changes which are only of the moment; it generates conflicts which impede the growth of a progressive, modern political order.

Of course, demagogy is not the only impediment to the progress of the new states. Poverty of natural resources, insufficient capital to develop what resources they possess, insufficient organizational skill and discipline, etc., are but a few of the deficiencies which stand in the way of the creation of stable modern politics in Africa and Asia. Except for deficient natural resources, none of these obstacles is insuperable—and technological development might modify even that. But none of these obstacles is removable by "crash programs"—and certainly not by "crash programs" which consist largely of the resounding reiteration of irrelevant clichés, reinforced by the coercion of the laggardly and the dissident.

The development of a modern polity calls for a redefinition of the image of the self, a redirection of the cognitive categories, new capacities in relation to time and task. These constitute opinion of a deeper sort. They must first be firmly developed in the minority on

Previously published in a slightly different form in *Communication and Political Development*, edited by Lucien Pye (Princeton, N.J.: Princeton University Press, 1963), pp. 67-77. © 1963 by Princeton University Press.

whose initiative and persistent action national development depends in the first instance. The development of integrity and skill in administrative judgment; the development of cadres of reasonably punctual, reasonably honest, reasonably dutiful persons; and the growth of a standpoint, within a small circle of people, which regards the entire national community as the first object of its public solicitude—all take time. They take time because they depend on the formation of fundamental dispositions; of traditions of institutions; of traditions within families, educational bodies, business enterprises, and government departments. Even though they do not have to be created in the majority of the population, these are not things which can be created quickly. They are formed through study, practice, and personal interaction. What is formed by these processes requires years. They are not formed by oratorical exhortation. They cannot be formed at a distance and they cannot be formed quickly. What is formed quickly—other than religious or quasi-religious attitudes formed by conversion—does not go deeply into the dispositional structure, and it does not last. What is formed quickly is enthusiasm; and it is in the nature of enthusiasm not to last in most people. It is also in the nature of enthusiasm to generate expectations for large and basic transformations in the order which it confronts, and the situation of the new states is not such as to satisfy such expectations.

Persistently sustained exertion is the prerequisite of progress—not just because it might be a moral virtue in itself, but because it is required by the complex undertakings which are on the program of progress. Persistently sustained exertion is a function of attachment to a task, to the norms which govern its performance, and to the roles in which those norms are embodied. Something resembling it can be produced by the zealous hatred of one's opponents and by paranoid beliefs in the incessant efforts of one's opponents to undo one. Obdurate fanaticism, at the peak of the political pyramid, might succeed in giving the impression that it is the ideological orientation which modernizes a political regime. Ideological fanatics can intimidate their immediate subordinates and bring them to obedience; ideological fanaticism can even infect them and cause them to share the beliefs and the affective intensity which characterize its espousal by the elites.

I do not mean that coercion is unable to accomplish something in the way of modernizing a society. People *can* be forced to perform particular roles and even up to a fairly low level of proficiency. If they see their colleagues beaten on the scene or taken away to torment and misery, they are likely to exert themselves and do something like the job that is expected of them. They will not be very adaptive; their efficiency will be low; they will break the tools they are given to do the job; but they will do it—more or less. This will be especially true of routine, manual labor. The more complex the task, the less effective coercion will be. The roles involved in political modernization are not of the order of routine manual labor. Insofar, however, as the creation of a surplus of wealth, the attainment of a higher gross national product, is a contribution to political development, coercion can contribute to political development—but only indirectly.

Hostility toward the West or toward whites and belief in Pan-Africanism do not have an intellectual enough content to constitute ideologies. The impetus and direction that an ideology can give to a passionate, charismatic personality are lacking in the new states. The new states do not yet have their ideologies. Pan-Arabism, Pan-Africanism, the African personality, are often vigorously, even vehemently, expressed; but they are not yet ideologies in the sense of having a more or less differentiated content.

Charisma without an ideology is demagogy, and it is demagogy of which I speak. In all societies, advanced or underveloped, demogogy is an ostensible address to the ordinary people; it is, in fact, an address to the most volatile, most aggressive components in the dispositional system. There are times when it is called for and appropriate, such as in times of national danger from an external enemy; with respect to domestic problems, however, its chief function and its frequent intent are the division of the people by rallying those who respond to it against some presumed internal and external enemies.

The new states are already sufficiently divided by traditionally received identifications which separate rather than unite. The most sensitive and responsive loyalties there are loyalties of division, and the hunger of the demagogue for approbation necessarily leads him to exploit them. Insofar as he attempts to arouse the counter-loyalty to national symbols, he usually does so through the allegations of danger to the national community arising from the machinations of "imperialists" and "colonialists." There are few politicians in the new states who address large audiences of the poor and uneducated and who are able to speak on behalf of the whole society without attempting to arouse hostilities which are irrelevant to the tasks of modernization. (Nehru and Nyerere have, perhaps, been the only ones.)

Demagogy is nearly inescapable in the new states, just as it is a constant presence in the advanced ones. Where political competition for the vote and assent of a society-wide electorate exists, it receives a tremendous impetus, and the impetus is all the stronger where there is a strong populistic element in the culture of the political profession. The availability of the media of mass communication is an invitation to their demagogic use—even more pronouncedly so where the populace is illiterate and scattered in many not easily accessible villages, and where there is the belief that the members of this populace must be "mobilized" for the progress of the country. There is something in the views of the forgotten Le Bon. The mere contemplation of a large audience dilapidates even a rational mind. The structure of political discourse—the length of the communication, the absence of dialogue, and the belief that the audience is on a lower level than oneself—all promote the need to exaggerate and to have recourse to raucous clichés.

Demagogy must be accepted as a fact of life that will be amplified by the use of broadcasting. Its contribution to modernization is not likely to be great except in unusual instances—as, apparently, in Tunisia—where the demagogue is also the kind of charismatic person who impresses by the obvious sincerity of his concern for the public good, and by the amplitude of his executive effectiveness. Max Weber thought that a country with as much particularism as Germany would stand to benefit from a plebiscitary presidential election—he drew some of his inspiration from the consideration of the United States—and Prime Minister Nehru obviously believed that India's centrifugal potentialities could be held in check by his appearance all over India as the symbol of India. It is likely that this proposition was supported by the experience of President Bourguiba in Tunisia. It is also possible that the renowned oratorical capacities of President Sukarno gave Indonesia such unity as it possessed. But the unity which the speeches of Sukarno gave was probably not a very deep one and contributed little to the political modernization of Indonesia as long as practically everything else was neglected; while the reinforcement of the fragile unity of India contributed by Nehru's indefatigable speech-making was only a reinforcement of the much more important factor of the administrative unity of India, embodied in the coherence of the Indian Civil and Administrative Services, the (hitherto) apolitical coherence of the Indian armed forces, and the corps of Indian journalists—mainly in the English-language press—who, whatever their deficiencies, are "all-Indian" in their outlook on most things.

The Indian case is instructive. Unity is a necessity of political modernization. The transcendence of territorial parochiality and of ethnic, tribal, and religious particularism must yield to some measure of consensual acceptance of membership in the larger national community as a basic component in each man's and woman's self-image. But is this sense of membership in the national community as much a product of direct discourse from the center as it is of a belief in the effectiveness of authority, of the good sense of authority, of the fact that it seems "to mean business?" Coherence at the center, strength—not just verbal symbols of strength—will legitimate the elite and the system in which it operates.

The mass of the population is fairly docile in most of the new states, and it is likely to comply with most authority which does not demand fundamental reorientations of its routines—and it will even accept some of these, if those who recommend them seem legitimate. The mass of the population will move slowly into the national society, if the center of the society is sound. It will not move into the national society if it is agitated and divided.

James Mill said that there was no need to worry about the vote of the working classes as long as they had before them the model of a respectable, hard-working middle class. Mutatis mutandis, this principle finds application in the new states. The intellectual centers of the middle class—the intellectuals as the bearers of sober opinion—must be built up to offset the disadvantages and to gather the advantages of such demagogic, charismatic iridescence as exists in the political elite. The building up of these centers will establish standards of technical performance, professional integrity, and genuineness of bearing. From these centers, it will flow—laterally into newcomers, upward into the political elite, downward into the mass of the population.

These qualities are qualities of stable, humdrum dutifulness, of sticking to a task through thick and thin out of conviction as to its imperious necessity. They are the qualities of what we could call *Berufsethos* and *Berufsstolz*. They are part and parcel of a culture in which occupational and professional roles and performances are important things. Such roles and performances are not yet firmly established parts of the cultures of the old societies which are going into the making of the new states of Africa and Asia. They are also not entirely incompatible with these cultures, as numerous individual instances so well demonstrate. Such qualities can be selected from and nurtured in the new states—as testified by the mere existence of so many civil servants and of a no less impressive, though much smaller, number of hard-headed professional journalists, businesslike technologists, and serious and sometimes creative scholarly and scientific intellectuals.

II

The formation of this sober, task-oriented, professionally responsible stratum of the population is perhaps the most important precondition of the political development of the new states. Its formation is a necessity, not just because their technical skills are required to implement the great ambitions of the elite, but rather because their prosaic matter-of-factness is essential as a matrix which can absorb the shocks of demagogy, temper its winds, and perhaps even moderate its resonance.

In nearly all the new countries, the initiative has passed from the notabilities to the demagogues and their "verandah-boy" clientele, and the towns have become the most important theaters of political life. It is imperative that an absorbent counterpoise be constructed in the ambient public opinion, which provides the culture in which the politicians move. They are, after all, urban men—at least, urbanized men—and they are sensitive to what those who are educated, and near at hand, think of them. The counterpoise which can moderate demagogy is matter-of-factness, *Sächlichkeit*.

The carriers of this *Sächlichkeit* come to it through various paths. They come to it largely through the discipline of advanced modern education and the discipline of the practice of professions in which oratory is not a major determinant of success. They are medical doctors, engineers, and technologists, university teachers and research workers, higher civil servants, and some secondary-school teachers and administrators. Overlapping them is a circle of journalists, editors, and broadcasting technicians, producers, and announcers. These are all people with fairly specific jobs to do, jobs about which there are fairly specific expectations and which are the objects of fairly clear standards of performance. Most of their practitioners have acquired their training in the metropolis, in institutions such as universities, hospitals, research institutes, and large business enterprises where it is conventional to expect punctuality, diligence, and reliability, and where most of the professional staff approximate these standards in their performance.

These people are relatively few in number, and they are often isolated from each other by distance, by professional specialization, and by the nature of their cocktail conviviality. The question is, how can they be brought together to form a community sufficiently solidary, sufficiently self-confident, sufficiently well grounded in its opinion, that it can make itself felt among the politicians and even, in the course of time, penetrate into the back country, into the lower ranks of leadership, and into the younger generation?

The establishment of loose communities of professional persons, bound together by a mutual respect for role and proficiency and supported by a parallel conviviality, will help form a body of skilled, businesslike persons, prosaic and hardworking. These are necessary for economic and social development, but their importance for political development is no less great. They will provide the anchor for a matter-of-fact opinion which will be capable of judging policies on their merits and which will be less manipulable into enthusiastic flights of political fantasy.

This culture, which is now beginning to come into existence—it has already done so in India—is not likely to be a technocratic culture. It will not be the "Soviet of technicians," toward which Thorstein Veblen looked for the salvation of Western society. In India there is no sign that these people wish to take over political power as a unitary body. There are various reasons for this. For one thing, although professional persons do interest themselves in their national progress and in the policies which affect it, they are not highly politicized. They render judgments, express opinions, comment on affairs which they feel are their concern; but they do not preoccupy themselves with politics to the exclusion of nearly everything else. Their own jobs are their center of gravity.

III

Is it not likely that the professional matter-of-factness which has begun to emerge in the educated classes of the new states will become a narrow specialization, concentrating exclusively on the technical tasks for which the profession has been trained? Has this not already happened, to some extent, in America? And, if this happens, will this not undermine the incipient formation of a pluralistic system of civil opinion or prevent its emergence? I think not.

My reasons are as follows: Persons in a new state, with foreign training or with advanced modern training acquired in their own country, are set apart into a class which includes all others with similar training. This kind of training, quite apart from its specific substantive content, is characterized by a common uniqueness vis-à-vis the culture of most of the rest of the population. It is *modern* culture, which distinguishes its bearers from all those who do not have it. It confers status on its bearers and enters into their self-consciousness. In each individual, it makes for a certain measure of solidarity with those other individuals who have a no less modern culture, even though its specific and technical content is very different from that of one's own modern culture. The boundaries of technical specialization are transcended, not by an integration of the various spheres of knowledge into a unitary body of knowledge, but by the integration of the individual bearers of the various specialized spheres of modern knowledge into a single class, bound together by their high evaluation of the possession of some segment of modern culture.

This formation of a single class of those with advanced modern education gives rise to a culture of its own. It is a culture which rotates to a considerable extent about convivial things, style and standard of living, eminence of associates, etc. But it has a certain substance, too—namely, professional reputation, respect for accomplishment, diligence, professional integrity.

Despite the attractions of majesty, there is a tendency in this class to be somewhat removed from politics. Disillusionment, an oppositional disposition, the embitterment of frustrated aspirations, snobbery, and dismay, provide some fraction of the motivation for standing at some remove from politics and for taking a detached view of them. These motives alone would lead to an antipolitical attitude if they were not tempered by a number of other factors, such as moderation of affect, relative success in life, a multiplicity of interests, and an acceptance of the new order of life brought about by the first steps of modernization. This new class, without being fanatically nationalistic, has a sense of a "stake in the country." Its members have come to feel that the country is "theirs"—as much as it is the politicians' who declaim about it so volubly. They think that they are its custodians as much as are the politicians, even though they do not clamor and orate about their custodianship.

Not everyone in the educated classes has this attitude. The oppositional mentality dies hard; the fantasies nurtured by the movement for independence leave a residue of sadness when it is seen that reality has not come forward to match them. Poverty and unemployment alienate intellectuals; a belief in their own super-fluousness and ineffectiveness alienates them. The company of other self-designated "failures" aggravates the sense of alienation. These are all phenomena which we notice in India, especially; but there are parallel tendencies in all new states. The tendencies seldom go so far outside India because the rate of development and, more par-ticularly, the capacity of the economy to incorporate the intel-lectuals remuneratively are, for the time being, greater than the capacity of the intellectual institutions of the countries concerned, and that of the overseas institutions which supplement or provide the main supply, to produce aspirants to such incorporation. The simple certainty of employment on the completion of the course of studies, whatever it might do to the intensity of exertion, does much to offset the common inclination toward an antipolitical alienation.

I do not wish to be misunderstood. This class of the educated are not perfect beings. They are not necessarily solidary in their devotion to transcendent values of scientific and scholarly truth, literary and artistic expression, professional proficiency, or civility in matters of public concern. Vanity, sloth, inefficiency will certainly be found among them. There will certainly be unconscionable toadies and place-holders among them, and superior Pococurantés for whom nothing, above all in their own countries, is good enough. And of course there will be many who are simply second- or third-rate, who have allowed their skills to gather dust behind the screen of an indolent complacency.

These tarnished ones of the educated class are the victims of their own personal deficiencies, of the inadequacy of their training, and of their poor environment. They are the victims of the insufficient development of intellectual and professional institutions in their own countries, of the one-sidedness of their ties with the metropolis, or of the rupture of their ties with the metropolis. They are the victims of their scanty numbers, which make for insufficient stimulation in an intellectually impoverished environment.

IV

They are, all this notwithstanding, the executants, and the spirit, too, of any modernization which their countries will undergo. The modernization of their countries cannot proceed without their active and energetic participation. They know they are needed, and this makes possible their self-confidence. Where, in addition to being needed, they actually accomplish something which they regard as significant, their outlook becomes more positive and more stable.

The effective performance of persons in these roles is a function not only of their training but also of the professional culture in which they live. In complete isolation, only the strongest character, only the most powerfully creative individual, can perform up to the level of his capacities. Most persons need the buttressing of other more or less like-minded persons who share their standards, exemplify them, and provide a resonance for their expression and accomplishment. Without this, they relapse into slipshodness and indifference, into a sense of isolation and neglect. They become alienated from their successful contemporaries, more easily tempted by the prospective rewards of judicious subservience to the political elite. And this is a winding path, from which it is difficult to turn back, and from which it is accordingly difficult to return.

The condition of the creation of an independent center of opinion which can withstand, partly counteract, and even moderate the virulent emptiness of demagogy, is a coherent, relatively unified, professional stratum in the capital. This is a condition which is not easily attained. The absolute numbers are quite small in most of the new states. They are often dispersed among different places within the boundaries of their country. Where the university is not in the capital, an important component of educated opinion is withdrawn from frequent intercourse—and there are other pressures among the university teachers which make for an unrealistic and deeply alienated opposition. Journalists, too, are torn between the sensational exposure of scandals and the deferential consideration of the claims of majesty. Those who work for government newspapers are under further constraints, not always moving in a single direction. Civil servants must watch their steps and hold their tongues. Those employed by foreign firms must also be on the lookout lest they lay themselves open to charges of disservice to the national interest— from either journalists or politicians.

Each faces these distracting, disuniting forces and feels them working within himself. Then there are the differences between the American-returned and the English-returned, the Western-returned and the Moscow-returned, the been-to and the never-been-to. There are gradations of status among these, and struggles to modify the balance of status.

There are also the differences of special competence, the differences between the humanistically and juristically educated and the scientifically and technologically educated, and all the other tendencies toward differentiation and segregation imported from the metropolis and also, in some measure, inherent in the various specialities.

It is most necessary for the strength of the educated class, for its contribution to our life as well as to economic and social development, that these patterns of specialized expertise should not be allowed to molder. They must be fostered by strengthening the solidarity of those who possess them: on a local scale, through professional organization; regionally (e.g., on a West African or on a Southeast Asian scale), through congresses, associations, and collaboration; and internationally, by the maintenance of bilateral, recurrent, and more intense communications with the metropolis. In the course of time, as numbers increase, this type of professional development will threaten to dissolve such unity of the educated class as now exists.

Further professional specialization may make for a narrower and even less continuous political concern. In the advanced states, a better civil tradition and a stronger body of institutions of public opinion have enabled their societies to resist the effects of a gratifying and preoccupying specialization in the professions. The weaker civil traditions of the new states may not be able to do so. A critical point may be reached before the moment when independent institutions of opinion are strong enough to dispense with the participation and support of the technologists.

Overspecialization would be especially injurious to the strength of the independent institutions of opinion in most of the new states, because the technologists usually, with the civil service, embody the major practical experiences of the modernized sector of the society. The civil service at its higher reaches can be an important component in the formation of instructed opinion through its participation in convivial circles; but it cannot give any publicly visible manifestation of its outlook. University and high school teachers lack the practical experience and the authority of speaking on the basis of that experience; and their tradition, not diminished by independence, is toward political alienation. Journalists, by their traditions acquired at home or imported from abroad, tend toward an antipolitical attitude; in the new states this is often combined with the necessity of "adjustment" to the regnant authorities and their own factual ignorance and lack of direct reportorial experience of the situations they write about.

Thus the technologists, in which we include educated managers of the larger commercial and industrial enterprises, have a very central position in the promulgation of a practical, level-headed opinion about the course of events in their own society. Specialization and increasing numbers, which will enable them to enjoy more exclusively the conviviality of their professional colleagues, would mean the weakening of a central section of the bearers of public opinion.

What is the protection which exists or can be created in the new states against this withdrawal of the technologists and business managers? The demarcation of the boundaries of those who have received an advanced modern education; their small numbers, which prevent the technologists and managers from being convivially self-sufficient; and the common culture of modernity—these are the present guarantees against this withdrawal. But this bulwark will not survive. Numbers will increase, and the growth of secondary education will erode the sharp demarcation which at present separates those with higher education from those without it. The factors which at present keep the technologist-managers inside the circle of the educated, which make them into intellectuals, will not endure indefinitely; and the centrifugal forces will gain in strength.

V

What kinds of new centripetal forces can be generated in the new states to keep the technologists and, to some extent, the managers from falling away from the "intellectual class?" One solution lies in the syllabus of the course of technological study—and this applies equally to the advanced and to the underdeveloped states. There should be a greater component of a humanistic social science, a component of sociological self-understanding, introduced into the curriculum of the engineering and scientific courses in British, American, and French technological training institutions and in the corresponding institutions in the new states.

The solution which was put forward by Lord Snow seems to me to misstate the problem. It is not a question of a gap between the two cultures—the humanistic and the scientific-technological. It is, rather, a matter of creating and establishing a third culture, a culture of a deeper self-understanding, of a self-understanding which is social self-understanding and not just individual self-understanding. This third culture is already in incipiency in certain parts of the present-day social sciences, and enough exists to become a worthy part of the culture of the new states. (It must be recognized that the prevailing trend in the social sciences is inimical to this third culture.)

It is, therefore—to pursue Lord Snow's formulation a bit further—not an integration of the humanistic and natural science cultures of which the new states stand in need, but a professional and civil culture. The professional culture will root in them the pluralistic orientation necessary for the development of a modern polity; and the civil culture will give them a standpoint to juxtapose alongside the ideological political culture of the demagogic politician.

Naturally, the civil culture might be very feeble in its impact, certainly in its power, in conflict with the demagogic culture. Those at the center of the demagogic culture control the purse strings, and in some ways they have an ascendancy over the conscience of the intellectual class. The intellectual class is reluctant to oppose the demagogic politician, partly for considerations of prudence and concern for their own skins, physical and economic. They are also reluctant to oppose the politicians even where they disagree, because the politicians have arrogated to themselves the symbols of national existence and of anticolonialism, before both of which the intellectuals are cautious to avoid acts or thoughts which might be considered disloyal. Being an intellectual of integrity in an under-developed country is even more difficult than it is in the advanced countries. Many will become time-servers, and others will withdraw.

The withdrawal is by no means an unqualified disadvantage—as long as it is a withdrawal into the professional sphere. It is true that this constitutes an enfeeblement of the civil sphere, but only directly. Indirectly, the building up of the professional sphere, the formation of a professional community or of professional sub-communities, will contribute to the establishment of civility. It will contribute to the subsequent growth of civility by creating alternative modern objects of attachment, and will thus provide an alternative to hyperpoliticization.

22 Scientific Development
in the New States

The leaders of the new states of Africa and Asia are not scientists. Dr. Chaim Weizmann was unique in the association of high scientific distinction with political eminence, but had long ceased his science by the time he became president of Israel. Few of the leaders have ever studied science as a special subject at university. Mr. Nehru was one of the very few; but, although he retained a great appreciation of science and of the "scientific outlook," he never was a practicing scientist.

The situation of most of the other new states is quite different. The professional political elites of the new states have come from a variety of backgrounds: from law, from school teaching, from journalism, from medicine, from the lower levels of civil and private administration, occasionally from small business, but mainly from the peripheries of the intellectual professions.

Yet, although so few of them have a scientific education or experience, most of them speak with great appreciation of science. There are various reasons for this. Science is today part of the regalia of national greatness; it is linked, in popular opinion, with a complex technology and hence ostensibly with economic progress. The image of a great state today includes advanced scientific training and scientific prowess. Sputniks and Nobel prizes have taken the place of battle cruisers, and they rank with the figures on steel and electricity output as measures of greatness. Strong cultural attachments to the metropolises that once ruled these states, and the attraction of socialism, both fortify this belief that science has an important place in the good state. For the few new states that are Marxist in formation and sympathy, a belief in the fertility of science comes readily, because they vaguely equate Marxism and science, and thus envisage science at large as an instrument for the transformation of society.

There are other, better reasons for their concern with science. Sober politicians and civil servants recognize that economic development requires many persons who have had a technological education and some who are capable of doing research which falls somewhere between technology and science. They know that their own natural resources—soil, water, minerals, and plants—will not be improved,

Previously published in a slightly different form in *Science and the New Nations*, edited by Ruth Gruber (New York: Basic Books, 1961), chap. 12, pp. 217-26. © 1961 by Basic Books, Inc., Publishers, New York.

increased, and exploited without technological education and research. In many of the new states the administration has inherited a variety of scientific services from the colonial regime, and in some cases their personnel as well. Such persons, expatriate or indigenous, are a continuing reminder of the necessity of science in the conduct of a modern polity. Moreover, where the new state has inherited or newly established a university or other institution of higher studies, it has simultaneously created a voice, on behalf of science, for scientific education, for technology, and for technological education.

Of the new states, only Israel and India have established science on a large scale. Pakistan has had a commission report on the situation and needs of science, and it has made some sporadic efforts to give reality to some of the recommendations. Nigeria, through the Ashby Report, quickly took a deliberate position on the development of scientific and technological research and training. In most new states, science has still to be seriously considered. Sooner or later the political, educational, and administrative elites will have to pay more than ritual respect to the task of promulgating a policy for the furtherance of research and training in science and technology. I shall attempt to illustrate some of the most general problems with which they will have to deal.

Research Needs

The necessity is pressing. Economic development requires the prospecting of resources, an appraisal of their magnitudes and qualities. This cannot be done without extensive and continuous surveys, applying the best methods of discovery and assessment. Soil, minerals, marine and animal life, vegetation, water resources, rainfall, insects, plant and animal diseases, manpower, public health, etc.—in all these matters a country which aspires to economic development must know where it stands, what it can count on, and what it must reckon with. The instrument for this appraisal is the survey, and it is the first task of almost every new state to organize its survey machinery and to staff it with competent persons.

This does not require original research of a fundamental character. The techniques have already been formed in the advanced states, and most of the colonial powers and their business adjuncts have made some progress in the conduct of geological, zoological, entomological, hydrological, and other types of surveys. The pattern of organization is now well established, the skills required are fairly well defined, and the techniques are available. What is lacking in many of the new states is manpower. Surveys conducted by foreign experts are useful in providing the needed information but they leave no precipitate of qualified indigenous scientists.

They also need another type of research in which the difficulties are similar. This is technological research which goes beyond the enumerative and classificatory inventory, in the sense that it attempts to discover a more analytical truth previously unknown. What it seeks to discover is not some fundamental scientific law but rather a mode of adapting to new circumstances an industrial or agricultural process already known and used in other countries. This type of "adaptive research" is directed toward the application of existing technological knowledge to the climatic, geological, or chemical peculiarities of the local situation and the local product. Such research does not require great genius on the scale that would win a Nobel prize, but it does need a scientific discipline and disposition. It is the promotion of this kind of research that, in the near future, should be one of the main concerns of the ruling bodies of the new states.

Fundamental scientific research on any considerable scale—pure research which has no immediate and evident application to economic problems—need not be placed very high on the immediate agenda of the new states. It is often costly, and to be worth doing it must be very well done, with an aptitude and sensibility which are probably still too rare in the new states. The scarcity of capital in relation to the most insistent needs of economic and social development almost forbids any fundamental research which requires expensive equipment or considerable numbers of expensively trained persons.

Nonetheless, even if this fundamental research is, for the time being, dispensed with, technological research—relatively humdrum as it might seem in comparison with the grandeur of investigations into the nature of life and the universe—requires an elaborate and expensive substructure. For one thing, the conduct of technological research, like any other, needs a corps of trained investigators. These must be trained either in indigenous institutions or abroad. Both these alternatives are very expensive and require imagination and care if they are not to be riddled with wastefulness. However well trained the investigators and however adequate their equipment— usually imported from Europe, Japan, or America at a large expense—they will not be able to progress with their work unless they are supplemented by a corps of skilled technicians or artisans who can maintain or repair complicated machinery and instruments and devise simple ones. Indigenous traditional craftsmanship has reached a high level in many of the new states, but it is not usually mechanical. In Western countries, science developed at first independently of industry, but it benefited from industrial development through the availability of the industrial skills necessary for instrument-making and repair. Such a corps of craftsmen is still lacking in the new states, but technological research cannot progress until this lack has been overcome. The creation of such a corps in the new states cannot wait on an industrial revolution. Some organized effort will be needed, and as in the provision of equipment and facilities for training of research technologists, government action is indispensable.

In a different direction, technological research requires the supplementation of education in science at the elementary and secondary school levels. Apart from technicians who need no more than secondary education, those who will go on to advanced training at the college or university will do so unpreparedly unless they have had a better secondary school education in science than is now available. This is a matter which touches on the training of science teachers for high schools, on the planning of secondary school courses in science, and on the provision of equipment and laboratory facilities. Once more, it is difficult to imagine serious progress in technological research for economic progress without a comprehensive policy for scientific education at the secondary level and vigorous and persistent action on the basis of that policy.

The conduct of research in technology and science in the new states is thus almost inevitably an object in which governmental policy will play a most significant role. Trade associations and private industrial and agricultural enterprises are very unlikely to conduct much technological research in any of the new states. (India, in the ATIRA Institute in Ahmdebad, offers one of the very few exceptions.) Philanthropic foundations and privately endowed laboratories—outside India, where they are scarce enough—are practically nonexistent. If research in science and technology is to be carried on, if research workers are to be trained, if laboratories and training institutions are to be maintained, either government will provide the funds required or there will be no such activities.

The situation in the new states is not what it was in Europe in the seventeenth century, when science was the work of amateurs capable of maintaining themselves or obtaining patronage and of conducting their scientific inquiries with the most meager equipment. The new states do not need extremely expensive nuclear reactors or radio telescopes; they do not need to conduct research into the properties of outer space. Nonetheless, ordinary research in science or technology is beyond the financial resources of any except a tiny number of very exceptionally wealthy scientists in the new states. Privately supported or endowed colleges are unable to provide the facilities for research. The financial means for the conduct of research and for training for research must come, by and large, from governments.

Decisions Facing the New States

The problems before each government in the new states are how to decide how much of its total budget to devote to science and technology; how to allocate this among alternative uses in science and technology; what institutional arrangements it should use to expend the funds so allocated; and, finally, what types of institutions it should attempt to create and promote. More fundamentally, it is a question of how government aid to research and training can best foster creativity, inventiveness, and adaptiveness. These virtues will be necessary regardless of whether the government or the body that acts on its behalf decides to support pure science or applied science and technology, of whether it concentrates all its resources on technological training or divides them with training in pure science, of whether it creates advanced training institutions at home or sends its good young scientists and technologists abroad for advanced training. Each of these alternatives can be justified by reasonable arguments, and they are not in any case mutually exclusive or exhaustive.

Whatever the combination of alternatives chosen, the choice should be made deliberately, with the ends of economic and social development in view. This is not, however, always the situation in many of the new states. Decisions on expenditures in scientific and technological research and training are often impelled by considerations of the enhancement of national prestige (e.g., the atomic energy programs of a number of the new states), by pressure from academic bodies which wish to continue to do research of the sort their members did during their studies overseas, by the accidents of competitive gifts of equipment from the Soviet Union or the United States, and by other factors which should not be given free play.

Of course, it is difficult, if not impossible, for a government—or any central body—to plan scientific and technological research. It is practically impossible to plan fundamental research from a central position. A council of scientific and industrial research can, at best, provide funds and equipment for outstanding, able men and hope for the best. It is, however, possible to plan or to establish a set of priorities for technological research on the basis of an orderly plan of economic development, or at least a sensible survey of the main targets of development and the research requirements appropriate to each of the targets. An approximate assessment of the research required over, for example, a ten-year span—which is bound to be vague and unreliable—may allow a rough estimate of the manpower and equipment required for this research. An adequate register of scientific and technical personnel—which is very difficult to maintain—could then reveal the extent to which the estimated needs for manpower for technological research were unsatisfied and were likely to be left unfulfilled, under stable conditions of supply. The expected discrepancy, in turn, would offer the bases for a scientific and technical manpower policy, for an educational policy for science and technology, etc.

Such policy could be concerned with domestic training of some of the required types of personnel and foreign training of others for whom domestic training would be excessively uneconomical. An enumeration of foreseeable needs for research into technological problems of local agriculture and industry would provide the basis for estimates of costs, of the amount of foreign exchange needed for equipment, of the number of research workers to be trained over the period concerned, of the number of skilled artisans required, of the number of science teachers required if the secondary schools are to produce a reservoir of potential technologists and technological research workers, and so on. The plan could never be precise, but it would be better than random movements impelled by considerations of prestige, momentary enthusiasm, etc.

Another problem is that of the organization of research. How much of it should be carried on in universities, university colleges, and technical colleges; how much in government departments; how much in relatively autonomous laboratories and research stations? What should be the principles governing this division of labor? How can the optimal liaison between agricultural extension and agricultural research be best established—by amalgamating them into unified institutions, or otherwise? How can industry and industrial research best be articulated? One could go on multiplying this list of problems which should be considered in the promulgation of a policy of scientific development. Once again, it should be said that a policy cannot be expected to supply a stable and utterly reliable set of rules. All that can be claimed for it is that it would make decisions more circumspect and more aware of the problems than they otherwise might be.

The Climate of Science

Even if there were a judicious choice of those problems most important for economic progress and most amenable to economic solution; even if the right numbers of qualified scientists were produced by the most economical methods; and even if the right amounts of money were spent on buildings, equipment, and salaries—there would still be no end to the problems of scientific policy. It is not just a matter of equipment, buildings, the right selection of problems, and the right training. It is also a matter of motivation, of tradition, and of a propitious atmosphere within the research establishment.

Scientific and technological research has become so enmeshed in organizational machinery in recent years that the natural protective processes which research workers built up in the earlier centuries of the history of modern science, against the distractions of state and church, might be damaged or prove inadequate in the newly emerging situation. The network of relationships in which scientists work nowadays has become much more dense and intricate than it once was, and the distractions come from other sources. There was a time when scientists, with very little equipment and with no more organization than an assistant or a few students, did the necessary for themselves. Publications were few and could be covered in one's stride. Now the great expense of scientific equipment and, one might say, the higher level of scientific amenities have made scientific work much more dependent than in the past on political and bureaucratic support. The research process itself has become more highly organized, with many more collaborators and a more differentiated hierarchy than in the centuries preceding the present one. The structures of the research community and of the particular research institution have become more complex. Whereas science was once the work of amateurs and university teachers, it now finds cultivation not only in universities but also in independent research institutes, industrial laboratories, and government departments. The relationships of these different modes of conducting research create problems which did not exist before. Above all, they raise questions of scientific policy which were entirely unknown when science was a laissez-faire system.

The relationship between pure and applied science, although still enigmatic, arouses an uneasy attention in a way in which the development of pure science in the past did not. Science has thus come into a forcing house which was inconceivable even to such partisans of organized scientific progress as Francis Bacon and the great figures of the early history of the Royal Society.

These changes have wide ramifications. The acknowledgment of the economic and practical relevance of scientific research integrates science into the economy in an unprecedented way. A certain measure of planning is unavoidable, even while we recognize the impossibility of planning the course of developments of pure science and the many pitfalls in the way of planning the application of technological science.

Thus, in a variety of ways, science has developed an elaborate social system of its own, subtly and intricately connected with the rest of the society in ways which are generally still unknown. Civil servants and politicians, and scientists who have given up their first-hand experience of science to become administrators of science, have now to make decisions which involve the recruitment and induction of new persons into the traditions of the scientific community. They must allocate resources in ways which will affect the balance of various scientific activities, the proportions and relationships of pure and applied science, of universities and independent research institutes, etc. In all these decisions the main consideration must be, and usually is, the growth and elaboration of the stream of scientific knowledge that comes down to us as new problems and new practical tasks.

The extension and elaboration of this scientific tradition are, in the last analysis, a product of the scientific disposition of disciplined curiosity and sensitivity. Organization, equipment, financial support, and large numbers of persons are only instruments for the operations of this scientific disposition. It really does not make any difference whether the new states eschew pure research for the time being and concentrate their efforts on applied research. The successful prosecution of applied research is almost as dependent on the scientific disposition as is pure research. It is, therefore, essential for those who administer and promote scientific research for economic development, for the improvement of human welfare, to remember that the vital center of the disposition is formed by immersion in the tradition of creative scientific work.

Hence in their recruitment policies, in the training of those recruited, and in the employment of those trained, the administrators of science—whether they be politicians, civil servants, or former scientists—must remember that curiosity, sensitivity, and selfless devotion are as important as formally articulated rules and techniques. The decisions to establish new training centers or new departments in existing centers, or to send young men to foreign centers for training, must therefore take into account the fact that their task is the cultivation of the scientific disposition and the provision of an environment which will favor its operation. The organization of laboratories and of teaching departments, and the system of placing graduates returned from foreign training, will have to make provisions to avoid the frustration of this scientific disposition by the dead hand of a desiccated and embittered older generation or by an unsympathetic and insensitive bureaucracy.

The problem of implanting and cultivating the scientific disposition in the new states is more difficult than it is in the more advanced ones, where it has existed for a long time. In the latter, it arose before the introduction of the methods of the forcing house, and in a sense its capacities for self-reproduction through training in research in universities and independent institutions enable it to take care of itself. In the new states there is no such capital of scientific tradition to draw on. It has to be build almost from scratch, from a very few persons. These few persons will have to serve as cadres for training others; for training those who will train others, and above all for maintaining and representing by embodiment a standard of curiosity, inventiveness, and sensitivity which will be a model and a tonic for others. They must not only keep others alive scientifically; they must also keep themselves alive scientifically, lest—under difficult circumstances of overwork, overadministration, and lack of sympathy from administrators and politicians—they relapse into the enjoyment of their importance and lose the scientific touch. To retain this touch and to transmit it to the embryonic scientific community of their own countries, they must retain their active membership in the amorphous, almost boundariless fellowship of the international scientific community. If they lose that membership, by doing nothing considerable, or because of distraction by petty local affairs, or because national pride forbids its cultivation, they will fade away into a dusty provinciality. It will be the end of their scientific fertility, and they will lose the virtues they would otherwise possess for the oncoming generation. The whole scientific enterprise of the state in which this happens will sink into a bog.

To recapitulate the argument: it is regularly said that the new states need far more applied science and technology than pure science. Much of contemporary technology, it is true, is an outgrowth of recent developments in pure science. This in itself does not invalidate the prior claims of technology in the new states. By a temporarily reasonable division of labor, the new states can make use of the scientific achievements of the more developed countries, while concentrating their efforts largely on the adaptation and advancement of technology as it bears on their own practical problems. Even with this division of labor, however, it will not be simply a question of doing exactly what has been done in agriculture or in public health or in animal breeding in the older states. The knowledge gained in the latter will have to be extended and adapted to the particular conditions of each country. This task of extension and adaptation will require ingenuity, curiosity, and imagination—not so great as required for fundamental discoveries but qualitatively of the same family.

The leaders in this process of extension and adaptation will have to be persons of outstanding gifts of intellectual initiative who have assimilated the discipline and sensibility that scientific experience confers. They will have to be members of the scientific community, sharers in its traditions of scientific inquiry. From them, these qualities will have to radiate outward, influencing and enlivening the younger, less highly educated technologists whom they teach or supervise. Their creativity will encourage those who work with them and their fellow nationals, who will be encouraged by their existence to follow in their path. Insofar as a certain amount of provision for fundamental research will be necessary to retain the services of these outstanding scientific personalities in their own countries and to keep them on a fine edge of creativity, qualifications will have to be introduced into that policy which accords priority to technological research.

A Scientific Policy

I have entered upon this lengthy excursion in order to illustrate my contention that the scientific policy of new states will not be merely a matter of deciding priorities and allocating resources. It will also be a matter of creating the appropriate conditions of scientific work in laboratories and universities. These conditions of work will include the organization of research teams, the relationships between administrators and research workers, the relationships between senior and younger research workers, and many other subtle factors which, if not set in the right path, can undo good intentions and large financial provisions.

The problems of scientific policy, of which I have presented only a few general illustrations, cover an extremely wide range. They go beyond the sphere of science proper, beyond technology and economic policy, into subtle questions of interpersonal relations and large-scale administrative organization. A good scientific policy will have to possess a wide horizon and a capacity for balance among many considerations. Once the path of centrally defined policy is entered upon, problems which ordinarily could be left, for better or for worse, to polycentric resolution can no longer be left that way.

Those who make the most general decisions, which will determine the major directions of scientific policy, will usually not be scientists. Certainly they will not be practicing scientists. They will be ministers and civil servants. They will need the counsel of scientists, and they will have to entrust much to scientists, once they have listened to their counsel and made the fundamental financial decisions. These decisions will necessarily be general, but since they will be determinative, and since their ramifications will be intricate, they must be guided by the richest and most responsible scientific sensibilities that each new state can raise from among its own scientists and their foreign colleagues. Unless, therefore, the machinery and spirit of policy formation are of the highest order, the machinery of implementation will be to little avail, and the most worthy and indomitable of scientific spirits will not be able to make good the errors of policy.

23 Color, the Universal Intellectual Community, and the Afro-Asian Intellectual

I

In itself color is meaningless. It is not like religion, which is belief and entails either voluntary or hereditary membership in a community of believers and therewith exposure to an assimilation of a tradition of beliefs. It is not like kinship, which is a tangible structure in which the individual has lived, which has formed him, and to which he is attached. It is not like intellectual culture, which is belief and an attitude toward the world (or particular parts of it). It is not even like nationality, which is a superimposition of beliefs about a community of culture upon a common primordial existence of that community in a given territory. The designation of a person as being of a particular religious community or of a particular school of thought or even of a given nationality is a statement about that person's mind, about the pattern of meaning by which he interprets reality. His participation in the interpretation of reality according to that pattern of meaning might be hypocritical; it is undoubtedly intermittent and vague. All this notwithstanding, the involvement of the mind is a major though not the sole component in the definition of the person in question. It is not this way with color.

Color is just color. It is a physical, a spectroscopic fact. It carries no compellingly deducible conclusions regarding a person's beliefs or his position in any social structure. It is like height or weight—the mind is not involved. Yet it attracts the mind; it is the focus of passionate sentiments and beliefs. The sentiments color evokes are not the sentiments of aesthetic appreciation. Nor does color have any moral significance; color is not acquired or possessed by leading a good or a bad life. No intentions are expressed by color; no interpretations of the world are inherent in it; no attachments are constituted by it. The mind is not at work in it, and it is not a social relationship. It is inherently meaningless.

Why, then, has this inherently meaningless property of man come to assume such great importance in the self-image of many human beings? Has only a historical accident of an unequal distribution of power and wealth between two differently pigmented aggregates of human beings led to this cleavage between those called white and those called colored? Or have sentiments of injury and anger

Reprinted by permission from *Daedalus*, Journal of the American Academy of Arts and Sciences, Boston, Massachusetts, vol. 96, no. 2 (1967).

implicated in the consciousness of being colored developed because those called white have so often used their greater power to injure those called colored in ways beyond what is intrinsic in the exercise of power?

One of the simplest and most obvious reasons why color is a focus of passionate sentiments is that it is an easy way to distinguish between those from the periphery and those from the center of particular societies and of the world society. Differences of pigmentation symbolize or indicate contemporaneous differences between present wealth and power and present poverty and weakness, between present fame and present obscurity, between present eminence in intellectual creativity and present intellectual unproductiveness. It is correlated with past events too—above all, with past events of humiliation, injury, and insult. Military conquest and alien rule, cultural derogation and individual affront, political suppression, military repression, and almost every other kind of coercion form an important part of the history of the colored peoples resident in the once-colonial countries or descended from them, and they are bitterly remembered. Color is the shorthand that evokes all these griefs and grievances. Is it more than that?

Conquest and maltreatment were not first brought to Asia and Africa by the European imperial powers. Long before, Asians had conquered other Asians; Arabs had exploited and enslaved black Africans, often with the aid of other black African rulers. Still, it is the European conquest that is remembered. It is remembered most vividly because it is the most recent, extending well into the memory of all living adults and many young people. It is also remembered because it was experienced more painfully than previous imperial conquests. The greater painfulness stems, in part, from the vividness of freshly remembered events. Moreover, this more recent dominion—imperial and internal—inculcated moral, political, and intellectual standards for its own criticism, a practice previous imperial rulers had not employed. The acquisition of the standards implicit in the religious and political culture that the whites brought to Asia and Africa and that they preached and partly observed in their own countries made the discrepancy between those standards and their own action and presence in Asia and Africa and their conduct toward colored peoples in their own countries uncomfortable to bear.[1] There seem to be some other reasons as well. The European conquerors came from far off, they were not expanding neighbors, and they were of a different color.

Tyranny is always painful, but tyranny exercised by the

---

1. Cf. the dedication of Nirad C. Chaudhuri's great book, *The Autobiography of an Unknown Indian* (New York, 1951).

ethnically alien, whose ethnic alien-ness is underscored by the most easily distinguishable color difference, is especially repugnant. In Asia and Africa, the illegitimacy of an ethnically alien tyranny is almost all gone now. Why does it still rankle so much in the hearts of Afro-Asian intellectuals? They are no longer being exploited, maltreated, or insulted by white men in their own countries. Why do they still feel the slights directed against their fellow-colored in the few parts of the world still under colonial rule or in the United states or in the United Kingdom?[2]

2. In a statement concerning the recent British legislative restrictions on Commonwealth immigration, a great Indian public servant, one of the most rational and modern of men without the slightest trace of xenophobia, demagogy, or revivalism in his mental make-up, wrote: "Sadly it must be recorded that Britain, the mother of parliaments, the originator of democracy and the rule of law, the home of liberty and fair play, the refuge of the persecuted and the oppressed, has fallen far below her high degree. She has now publicly declared herself a country riddled with color consciousness. She needs constant replenishment of her labour force but she will take care to see that most of the new workers have white skins. They need not belong to the Commonwealth. Better by far total strangers politically, Portuguese and Greeks and Spaniards and South Irish than West Indians and Nigerians and Indians. . . .

"The Labour politicians, whatever and however strong their moral convictions in this matter, have discovered, perhaps to the dismay of some of them, that the voter, the ordinary Briton, feels strongly on this subject. He does not like the coloured man, black or brown, and he does not want them near him. They fear the political party which will not keep the coloured out will lose votes, and what after all are principles, moral or other, in comparison with votes? . . . A party led by a statesman and with a few statesmen in it might well have resisted the impact of the alleged general dislike and decided to educate the electorate rather than give way to its prejudice, but the last British statesman was Churchill, and puny are the men of Westminster today.

"So much for the British side. More important for us, our proper attitude to this declaration of national dislike. Not a few of us have come across some instance of colour-prejudice on our visits to England. (The writer can remember experiences on his first visit in 1921 and his last in 1962.) We have however put them down to aberrations on the part of an individual or a small section. No indictment most of us have felt like drawing up was against the British people as a whole. But now proposals in Parliament put forward by Her Majesty's Government in all seriousness and with all solemnity assure us that we were wrong, that the whole British people cannot tolerate us because of the colour of our skins. This is a serious situation and the answer to it from us must be equally serious.

"Since it is obvious that no self-respecting person thrusts himself into company where he is not wanted, all brown and black people should refrain from going to Britain for any purpose whatever. This may entail some loss in the matter of education, but there are many countries now in which quite as good, or even better, training can be obtained than in Britain. Business connections with Britain should be reduced as much as possible, nor should undue friendliness be shown toward British officials and businessmen in black and brown countries. After all, reserve in place of cordiality is the least retort to deadly insult. A special effort must be made to refrain from looking at the world through British eyes, a practice to which educated Indians are in particular addicted. There is no real reason for regarding what happens or is thought in Britain as specially important to us, for keeping up with life there through the *Times*, the *Guardian*, the *New Statesman*, etc. Britain after all

Their feeling of being excluded from the center, of being treated contemptuously as inferiors, of having their weakness "rubbed in" comes to a tormenting focus in their awareness of the differences in color between themselves and the "white" men at the center. The injurious actions explicit in policy and custom, the studied insults implicit in policy, and the random insults of individuals are wounding to those who experience them and to those who identify with the wounded.

II

There is certainly much truth in the explanation of color identification that points to the coincidence of patterns of color distribution and patterns of the distribution of power and wealth. The coincidence of color with inferior positions in the various distributions in colonial societies, in predominantly white societies, and in world society reinforces—some would say, generates—the interpretation of "color identity" as a variant of "class identity." There is truth also in the proposition that color identification arises in part from the assimilation by the colored periphery of the dominant white center's use of the categories "whiteness" and "coloredness." But these hypotheses, valuable though they are, do not provide an exhaustive explanation. Another element should be mentioned not as an exhaustive alternative explanation, but as a complementary one that deals with a vital phenomenon otherwise excluded from consideration. It is this: self-identification by color has its origins in the sense of primordial connection with which human beings find it difficult to dispense.

The prominence and ubiquity of self-identification by kinship connection and territorial location are well known, but they tend to be taken for granted and even neglected in the study of modern society. Because they are taken for granted, they are seldom reduced

---

today is a small island off the West Coast of Europe, not the centre of the world.

"We wish Britain no harm; in the hearts of those of us who knew the best of her people and hold many of her sons and daughters our friends, there will always be a warmth for them and her, but the clear implication of the measures her government proposes we much realize. No special relationship is possible, no special cordiality can be sustained, with those to whom the colour of your skin is anathema. Let the coloured doctors and nurses, so notably welcomed because so emphatically useful, remember this. They are sought as mercenaries. Will they be mercenaries, sell their souls for a mess of pottage to those who scorn the people of their colour, but have no objection to using for their own benefit, as the Roman patrician used the Greek physician slave, the skill they in particular have acquired at the cost of people of that colour?" ("Alas for Britain," *Opinion* (Bombay), vol. 6, no. 15 (August 17, 1965), pp. 3-4.)

analytically to man's need to be in contact with the point and moment of his origin and to experience a sense of affinity with those who share that origin. The need for connections or relationships of a primordial character will be endemic in human existence as long as biological existence has a value to the individual organism. Ethnic identification, of which color identification is a particular variant, is a manifestation of this need. Traces of the sense of affinity and of shared primordial properties occur also in the phenomenon of nationality.

Self-identification by color seems to entail some reference to a common biological origin that is thought to establish ties of affinity, sometimes obligation and solidarity among those who share it, and of separation from those who do not. In its crudest form, it denies the membership of those of other colors in the same species.

There are great interindividual differences in this sense of affinity with those who share a putatively common origin, just as there are great interindividual differences in the need for contact with divinity. The need, where it is weak, is often powerfully reinforced by the cultures and social structures generated by color identification and by those that parallel it. A weak disposition toward color identification can be strengthened by class—or national— identifications that are congruent with color boundaries.

Decrease in the dominance of primordial attachments of kinship and locality has been accompanied by an increase in the importance attributed to ethnicity and color. The latter two represent a broadening of the scope of particularistic primordial identification. Ethnicity in numerous cases—color in very few—has yielded precedence in many respects to nationality, which verges toward civility while retaining much of a primordial, often pseudo-ethnic basis.

In nationality, the primordial element begins to recede. It yields to an "ideal" or "ideational" element—a "spirit," an "essence"—that is recognized as involving the mind. It is not accidental that a common language—the most widely shared of cultural objectivations—has so often been regarded as a crucial element in nationality.

The primordial is one focus of man's disposition to attribute sacredness to particular entities or symbols. It was a great accomplishment of the human race to have relocated the sacred from the primordial to the ideal, from biological and territorial properties of the self and the kinship-local group to entities apprehensible by thought and imagination. But it has done so only very falteringly. Its failure to accomplish it entirely is a source of many of mankind's miseries. The shift occurred in both Judaism and Buddhism, although the Jews retained the primordial ethnic element in a central position. It reached a high development in Christianity and in Islam. Nevertheless, in none of the cultures in which these religions have become established has the sacredness of the primordial been anything more than diminished. Still, it has been displaced to some extent, as the development of religion and politics testifies. The sacred—both primordial and "ideal"—is capable of attenuation and dispersion. The growth of modern society is the history of this attenuation and dispersion—with numerous relapses into intensification and concentration. There is, however, a major primordial property that has been very reluctant to yield its sacredness to attenuation. This is color.

The self-identification by color common among Asians and Africans of wide horizon—and the Afro-Asian intellectuals, in particular—is not attributable exclusively to its primordial quality. Nor is color the sole or always dominant criterion of this self-identification. Color plays a considerable, if indeterminate, part in their self-identification because it symbolizes many other properties of the Africans' and Asians' position in their own societies—both in colonial times and in the world since independence. For intellectuals, additional factors—such as their position in the world-wide intellectual community and their own societies, and the relation of these societies to those of the once-ruling imperial powers and the other advanced countries—coincide with the color self-identification and accentuate its force. When these other factors diminish, the intensity of the total self-identification by color will diminish too. But what of the primordial root of the color-identification? Will color yield some of its power in the formation of the self-image of Asians and Africans? Will it yield some of its power over the intellectual's self-image and its influence on his response to intellectual things?

III

I should now like to turn away for a moment from color as a focus of self-identification and consider possible changes that might enter into the self-identification of intellectuals—literary men, journalists, scientists, and scholars. First of all, their focus on nationality and civility might grow if the new states become consolidated internally as integrated national societies. They might also identify themselves as members of intellectual communities which transcend the boundaries of states and the limits of regions and continents.

The intellectual community, in its territorial scope and its criteria of admission, is the most universal of communities. Its adherents are scattered over the world's surface. To be a member of it, a person must either be engaged in intellectual activities or be in the state of mind that intellectual actions express and engender. In principle, no primordial properties, such as connections of kinship, locality, tribe, or territory, are valid in the assessment of the qualifications for membership in any of its constituent institutions or for advancement in its corporate or honorary hierarchies. (Of course, in practice, primordial properties are sometimes operative in governing admission to membership in particular corporate institutions, but those who apply them know that they are contravening the rules of the intellectual community—unarticulated and amorphous though these are.) The intellectual community is universalistic because it applies criteria of universal validity, criteria generally acknowledged throughout the world as true and relevant by those who have been exposed to them by education and training. Sometimes the intellectual community might seem to have no reality, to be only a figurative name for a class of actions and states of mind, to be, in fact, no community at all. It certainly lacks a corporate structure, although it has many subsidiary corporate structures, such as international scientific and professional associations. It lacks a formal structure of authority, although it has many subsidiary structures of authority, such as universities, research institutions, periodicals, and professional associations. It lacks formal articles of faith, but it has many quite specific actions and beliefs that define membership. Indeed, as a single community, it scarcely exists, and yet it would be excessively and prejudicially tough-minded to deny its existence altogether. Its subsidiary, more specialized spheres certainly have more reality; they are more easily apprehensible.

The world scientific community is one of these. It is the community of those who do scientific research, the real science that is practiced with efficacy in teaching and research in many parts of the world. Its members communicate easily with one another—partly because the subject matter of each substantively specialized subsector is common to all its members wherever and whoever they are, partly because the symbols and notations used are universally uniform, and partly because science, particularly scientific research, uses one or a few common written languages.

The international scientific community has three major lines of internal differentiation. The first, differentiation by substantive spheres of knowledge, is so pronounced that members of some sectors are frequently unable to communicate about their substantive interests and results very efficiently with members of other sectors, even those within the same country or university. The second, differentiation according to the quality of individual and collective performance, results in an approximation of a hierarchy of individuals and institutions (departments, universities, laboratories). The third, which follows from the second, is a territorial differentiation and hierarchy within a larger territory; it is intranational and international. In the international intellectual community, entire countries become the units for assessing the merit of performance on the basis of the average of accomplishment of particular intra-national institutions. (In both, the assessment of the merit of collectivities is a precipitate or average of the assessment of the work of individuals; as a result, the ranks of particular individuals, their institutions, and their countries are only imperfectly correlated with one another.)

Yet despite these vertical and horizontal lines of differentiation and separation, the international scientific community does exist. Specialized scientists, blocked from communicating with one another about what they know best by the specialization of their knowledge, regard one another as "scientists." They consider themselves as having very important, although ordinarily unspecified, things in common. Regardless of their special subjects, they have the same heroes—Galileo, Newton, Darwin, Mendel. They believe that they belong to a common group because they perform and are committed to the performance of certain types of action and to the maintenance of certain states of mind that bring them together and set them apart from other human beings. They accept in common the discipline of scientific procedure, the unconditional value of truth, and the worthwhileness of striving for it. From this mutuality grows an attachment to one another, not as persons but as the bearers of an outlook.

The members of the scientific community are, of course, members of other communities as well, many of them authoritatively elaborated, with specific and specifiable obligations. Citizens of states and municipalities, administrators of laboratories and university departments, they are also members of political parties, churches, clubs, and civic and professional associations. They have different nationalities and religious beliefs. None of these properties or characteristics is, however, allowed in principle to contaminate the obligations scientists acknowledge themselves to have as scientists or to impair the affinity they sense among all scientists. In assessing the results of another scientist's research, a scientist permits none of these other obligations to stand in the way of his over-whelmingly preponderant obligation to observe, to think, and to judge as a scientist. In activities that are more secondary within the scientific community, these other obligations and loyalties sometimes play a greater part, although there, too, it would ordinarily be denied that this is so in particular cases, and it would be emphatically denied in principle.

In the social sciences, with the exception of economics, there is much less common culture among the practitioners. Whereas economic theorists and economists speak to one another out of a knowledge of a common set of problems and a common body of literature, sociologists and political scientists diverge markedly after sharing but a few common elements in their disciplines. They have relatively fewer common symbols and notations. The data of the various social sciences, being largely descriptive of particular situations, are more intimately related to the various territories in which they were gathered and from which the social scientists come. The problems many social scientists study are, moreover, more intimately involved in their own particularistic attachments, even though they seek and often attain a high degree of detachment. Insofar as this detachment becomes more or less articulated in a general theory or in specific techniques, it gives them a common universe of discourse and thereby confers membership in an international community. Nevertheless, the international communities of social scientists are not as unified nor as integrated as those of the natural scientists. The social scientist's self-identification is more affected by his particularistic attachments than is that of the natural scientist.

The humanistic disciplines, except for general linguistics and certain classical subjects, are even more parochial than the social sciences. Much of the work of the humanistic disciplines is concerned with the estabishment, precision, and interpretation of the national or regional (continental or otherwise territorial) cultural inheritance in the form of history, modern languages, literary, religious, philosophical, and artistic works. Much of the work done in these fields is only of interest to nationals of the countries in which it is done, and this not primarily because of linguistic barriers. Some of the scholarship in history and sociology is part of the consensus and dissensus of the various national societies in which it is carried on, and it entails relatively little transnational self-identification.

The practice of the social sciences and the humanistic subjects has nonetheless a considerable internationality. For one thing, the study of the society and the culture of a particular country is not confined to nationals of that country. Oriental and African studies—history, religion, society, literature, and languages—link European and American social scientists and humanistic scholars with scholars indigenous to the countries being studied. These studies, too, have their disciplined techniques, their heroes, and their classics, which are commonly shared by scholars wherever they are. The world communities of scholars in the social sciences and humanities are patchier and less integrated than the world community of natural scientists, but they are international intellectual communities nonetheless.

Literature has not the common institutional (largely academic) foundation, nor the compact, systematically unfolding tradition of the academically cultivated branches of science and scholarship. The diversity and lack of connection among traditions are greater. Nevertheless, the novel in both English-speaking and French-speaking Africa is and must be viewed in the larger context of the English and French literary traditions. Independent oral and written literary traditions enter into the creative work of Asian and African prose writers, but the great European models toward which the novelists outside Europe orient themselves help to form and guide the work of novelists in the Asian and African countries. Poetic creation shows these latter characteristics to an even greater extent. Shakespeare, Hugo, Yeats, T. S. Eliot, and Rimbaud are influences all over the world and create a sense of unity among poets.

IV

The worldwide intellectual community is neither dense, continuous, nor highly organized. Its coverage is very imperfect, and it does not have a complete consensus. Nonetheless, members of the various communities in the major areas of intellectual life evaluate intellectual performance with little or no reference to nationality, religion, race, political party, or class. An African novelist wants to be judged as a novelist, not as an African; a Japanese mathematician would regard it as an affront if an analysis of his accomplishment referred to his pigmentation; a British physicist would find it ridiculous if a judgment of his research referred to his being "white."

Every community has a center in which its highest values are symbolized and represented, from which authority is exercised on behalf of these values, and to which deference is given. Intellectual communities are no different from primordial communities and communities of religious belief in this regard. The centers of the modern intellectual communities are largely in the West—in the United Kingdom, Western Europe, and North America. The Soviet Union has recently become more of a center than Tsarist Russia was—except in literature—and Japan is beginning to become one. These two newer centers are handicapped because their languages are not so widely known outside their borders as those of the Western European and North American centers. They have also come forward more recently, and they have not entered so much into the modern cultures of Asia and Africa as have the older centers. The metropolitan cultures are still the centers for much of the modern intellectual life of the new states for such obvious reasons as the facility offered through the language introduced by the former ruler and the relatively low cultural productivity, in modern works, of the new states. The increased demands for intellectual products in the new states—books, periodicals, services of intellectual institutions, results of research and scientific surveys—have placed a burden on local or indigenous intellectual powers which they cannot yet accommodate.[3] The result is dependence on the most easily available source—which is, in most cases (except Indonesia), the culture of the former ruler. Pride, realism, and the competition of the great powers in seeking the approval of the new states have altered the pattern somewhat, but not fundamentally.

The institutional structure was organized on the assumption—by both parties—that the colonies were, insofar as they had a modern intellectual life, peripheral to the metropolitan centers. Where they had universities, they were formed on the metropolitan pattern. Many who taught in them, indigenous and expatriate, were trained in the metropolitan universities. The books on sale in bookshops came from the publishers in the metropolitan countries, since the publishers were organized to supply the colonial market, such as it was; the same was true for periodicals. The young men who were trained either in the metropolitan universities or in the governmental or missionary institutions acquired the culture of the metropolis. If they became creative and productive, they did so as members of an intellectual community that had its center in the metropolis.

With relatively small differences, these conditions still exist in the new states of Asia and Africa. One of the constitutive differences between the center and the periphery in the intellectual community is that the scholars and the scientists of the center are more widely known. Exceptional individuals at the periphery are accepted as equals at the center because of their accomplishments and regard themselves more or less as equals. They share the standards of the metropolis and judge themselves in that light; they appreciate that their own accomplishments put them in a position equal to that of the leading persons at the center and superior to that of the more mediocre practitioners at the center. The weight of the awareness of peripherality or provinciality persists, however, even among those who have become creative, because their accomplishment has not yet been attended by an intellectual infrastructure of institutions and products. They have not yet succeeded in changing the map that members of the intellectual communities in their own country and abroad carry in their minds.

This might not make much difference within a single country with a common language and culture. When center and periphery are located in different countries, however, it is quite another matter. The intellectual centers are more powerful economically and militarily, more famous, and more populous intellectually. The

---

3. Indeed there is no good reason why local resources or persons should be expected to provide all that is needed when it is available from abroad; to do so would not only be wasteful of scarce resources but also beyond the powers of the underdeveloped countries.

volume of their production is richer and is taken more seriously, not only because it is superior intellectually but also because the countries in which it is produced are more powerful and more famous. Moreover, the metropolitan cultures are the cultures of the former rulers or of those who are somehow associated in the minds of those on the periphery with their former rulers. All this strains the self-esteem of the intellectuals at the periphery. At the same time, the modern culture of the countries at the periphery of the international intellectual community is discontinuous with the indigenous culture of the peripheral areas.

As if to symbolize the whole thing, the inhabitants of the countries at the periphery are of a different color from those at the center.

Within an intranational intellectual community, there are strains of inferiority and superiority. It is not pleasant to adjudge oneself to be mediocre, to be intellectually dependent on others, and to see the world's praise directed toward them. Yet in addition to the usual mechanisms that preserve failures and near-failures from extremes of distress, belonging to a culture with a high position in the intellectual hierarchy also reduces the stress of failure—just as membership in a common nationality alleviates to some extent the distress of inequality.

The situation is more complicated and less favorable for the intellectuals of Asia and Africa. They are not members of this international community of culture of the center. They have their own national and regional cultures in which their own dignity is involved and which they do not share with their intellectual confrères of other nationalities and countries. This cuts them off to some extent from those intellectual confrères and reduces the solidarity of the ties of intellectual affinity. Their own national and regional cultures are, furthermore, like all human creations, subject to assessment. The criteria for the assessment of a complex culture of many strands and a long history are more qualified and more ambivalent than are the criteria of individual accomplishment in the intellectual communities. Given the particularistic attachments that individuals have to their own cultures, bound up with them as they are through kinship ties and early experience, judgments about them are likely to be more "relativistic" than those about accomplishments in the various fields of modern culture, where the criteria are more consensual. Nonetheless, intellectuals in the new states are affected by the order of worth assigned to their culture by those at the centers of the intellectual communities. They feel this way, although the centers' preeminence within any particular field of intellectual work does not qualify them for comprehensive preeminence.

Cultures are assessed, in part, on grounds of their "modernity." Since the criteria of intellectual worth, being so vital to modernity, form such a large ingredient in the criteria of national worth, there is a tendency for national cultures as a whole to be ranked very roughly and approximately in accordance with the level of intellectual eminence.

In the more delimited realms of modern science and scholarship, the present-day nullity of the traditional inheritance of the African and Asian countries seems unchallengeable.[4] This consensus between center and periphery breaks down, however, when attention is shifted to the broader fields of culture, to religion and ethos. There is something substantially contemporaneous in these realms; societies have lived by them over long stretches of time, reaching into the present. They have become incorporated into works of thought and art, some of which have held the attention and aroused the admiration of the center in ways unparalleled by anything else in the social structures and cultures of the African and Asian countries.[5] They are, moreover, objects of genuine primary attachment for many intellectuals in these countries. Even where they are not, they are something to fall back on as evidence of past creativity, of greatness in human accomplishments and quality. They are thereby, worthy of respect before a universal audience; by that token, they enhance the dignity of those who participate in or are otherwise associated with them and who are also part of a worldwide intellectual community and share some of its standards. The indigenous traditional cultures offer the simulacrum of an alternative center to which the intellectuals of Asia and Africa are drawn.

V

The need for a countercenter has a widely ramified origin. The Asian and African intellectuals are more than intellectuals participating in some manner in the universal intellectual community. They are members also of territorially limited but more than local societies, delimited nationalities, and a subspecies of the human race with pigmentation different from that of those in ascendancy.

Their conscious identification of themselves by these classifications is partly a product of their assimilation into the worldwide intellectual community. They came to transcend the narrowly local and ascended to the national, regional, and continental through

4. The situation is quite different as regards the remotely past accomplishments of India, China, and the Islamic Middle East in science and mathematics.

5. It is interesting to speculate on the influence of Max Müller and other Western Indologists on the renewal of Hinduism in the last part of the nineteenth century, and of the European appreciation of African sculpture on African self-esteem in the twentieth century.

participation in the universal intellectual community. Through modern education and training at home, through experience with the metropolis while being educated and trained in metropolitan institutions or in domestic institutions formed on their model, through sojourns in the metropolis, they became aware that they were something different from what they had been and what they were becoming. They became aware that they belonged to the colonial peoples, that they belonged to distinctive continents; they came to perceive themselves as having nationality, which they defined as coterminous with the area over which the authority they rejected ruled. The self-definition was a negative one; it was the product of a process of distinguishing the self from the powerful, oppressively dominating center.

One major primordial property symbolizes through its concentration of all differences their differences from the metropolis. This is skin color. The awareness of differences in skin color heightens awareness of other differences. It does so not just by symbolizing those differences, but by serving as a focus of self-identification as a member of a species with a distinctive biological origin and separateness.

VI

The conflict between the primordial realm and the realm of the mind is especially pronounced in the intellectual, who—by virtue of what he is—is, in a way, the custodian of things of the mind for his society. Intellectual activity is the cultivation of the "ideational" realm. A change in the African or Asian intellectual's relations to the center of the international intellectual community might diminish the intensity of his color identification. The provinciality of his present position in the intellectual community is one of the distractions from which he suffers. This is only aggravated by the structural handicaps, both institutional and social, of his own country and the world.

When many more African and Asian intellectuals become productive and creative in the natural and social sciences, in humanistic scholarship, and in literature, their position will begin to change, and so will their self-identification by color. As individuals in the universities and towns of Africa and Asia begin to produce works that commend themselves to the intellectual appreciation of their colleagues at the centers in other parts of the world, and as they begin to produce some of their own succession, they will emerge from provinciality to centrality. This has already happened in certain fields and in certain places—for example, in statistics and economic theory in Calcutta and Delhi. Once these achievements begin to take deeper root by reproducing themselves and expanding their influence within India, the diminution of Indian intellectual peripherality will be under way. Similar processes are readily imaginable for other parts of Asia and Africa. They are not likely to occur in a very short time, but as they do, the strain of an inferior position in the international intellectual community will be reduced. A sense of genuine equality will then join to the sense of shared standards an awareness of shared accomplishment.

In emerging as new centers in the network of creative centers of the international intellectual community, African and Asian intellectuals will cease to feel so urgently the need for a countercenter, of which color is one of the foci of identification. The argument for a countercenter is only a largely contrived surrogate for the real thing. The countercenter could never be successful in attaining the end these intellectuals seek—the dignity of creative achievement.

The impetus to the "revolt against Western values" will weaken. The values will cease to be Western, except in the sense that in their more recent history they have been most cultivated in the West. They will become more fully what they are already patchily and unevenly—the universalistic values of a worldwide intellectual community.

The enhancement of the quality of civility in their socities will likewise work to diminish the force of the color identification. The closely connected sense of nationality will differentiate the "world of color," and will thereby reinforce the factors shifting the need for "serious" attachments away from color to alternative foci of *la vie sérieuse.*

As these changes occur—and it is reasonable to expect them to occur—the primordial attachment to color will still remain, but it will be deprived of its extraneous supports; it will no longer act so powerfully on the sentiments. Like ethnic, kinship, and local primordial attachments, it will survive but not so strongly as to deflect the intellect and imagination from their appropriate activities. Just as the rule of law and political equality have become established in areas once dominated by primordial attachments and the particularistic standards they dictated, so will the intellectual communities and their universalistic standards constrict the loyalties nurtured by the self-identification of color. This identification will become fainter and fainter, even though it probably will not disappear entirely.